Nepal

Pokhara
p206

The Terai &
Mahabharat Range
p237

Kathmandu to
Pokhara
p196

Kathmandu
★ p62

Kathmandu Valley
& Around
p121

THIS EDITION WRITTEN AND RESEARCHED BY

Bradley Mayhew,
Lindsay Brown, Stuart Butler

Contents

EVEREST BASE CAMP
TREK P292

MONKS, LUMBINI P258

Contents

Nepal and the 2015 Earthquakes

At 11.56am on 25 April 2015, Nepal was hit by a massive earthquake measuring 7.8 on the Richter scale, causing devastation to many parts of the country. This chapter is intended to provide an overview of what happened, how this has affected travel to Nepal, and how we deal with the disaster in this guidebook.

Regions Affected

Nepal's regions were affected to differing levels by the 2015 disaster.

Kathmandu
Severe damage to buildings and monuments, particularly in Kathmandu Durbar Square, but many areas escaped damage.

The Kathmandu Valley
Widespread damage to buildings and monuments, particularly in the historic cities of Patan and Bhaktapur, but many areas escaped damage.

Kathmandu to Pokhara
Gorkha and settlements close to the epicenter suffered severe damage; Bandipur and locations closer to Pokhara suffered only minor damage.

Pokhara & Around
Pokhara town and Annapurna region mostly unaffected but minor damage in rural areas.

The Terai & Mahabharat Range
Buildings destroyed in the foothills closer to Kathmandu, but lowland areas largely escaped damage.

Trekking Regions
Entire villages destroyed in Langtang, Rolwaling, Manaslu, Helambu; less severe damage in the Everest region. The Annapurna region and Eastern and Western Nepal saw only minor damage.

A Dark Day for Nepal

The morning of 25 April 2015 brought destruction to central Nepal. Thousands of buildings collapsed in the initial tremor and in subsequent aftershocks, killing more than 8500 people, and leaving thousands more homeless. Landslides destroyed entire villages and an avalanche at Everest Base Camp killed 18 climbers in Nepal's worst mountaineering disaster. Aftershocks followed for weeks, including a major tremor on 12 May, which killed hundreds more. Around the epicenter in Gorkha district, and across the Kathmandu Valley, communities were devastated and centuries-old monuments were reduced to rubble. Many of Nepal's most famous tourist sights were damaged beyond recognition. The earthquake has been described as the worst disaster to hit Nepal since the deadly Bihar-Nepal earthquake of 1934.

A huge international response has helped Nepal to cope with the immediate aftermath of the crisis but rebuilding lost homes, monuments and livelihoods is likely to be a slow and drawn-out process. Tourism has been severely affected by the disaster, and this comes at a time when Nepal is desperately in need of the revenue from tourism to rebuild. It is our hope at Lonely Planet that this guidebook will inform travellers about the damage caused by the earthquake, and encourage people to return and help the people of Nepal as they rebuild their lives after the crisis.

Counting the Cost of the Disaster

While the earthquake is one of the worst disasters to ever hit the Himalayan region, it is important to note that damage was localised. Kathmandu and other towns in the Kathmandu Valley were badly affected but little damage was recorded in Pokhara and the Annapurna region, and only mild shocks were felt in the Terai and in eastern and western Nepal. Damage to trekking regions was similarly patchy; whole villages were destroyed by landslides and avalanches in Langtang, Helambu, Manaslu, Rolwaling and parts of the Everest region, but other trekking areas were mostly untouched by the disaster.

It's also important to note that the devastation was not total, despite media reports from tourist sites such as Kathmandu's Durbar Square. While dozens of historic temples, palaces and monuments were reduced to piles of bricks and broken timbers, many more escaped undamaged. Much was lost but Nepal is still recognisably Nepal. The historic towns of the Kathmandu Valley still overflow with medieval architecture and the foothills of the Himalaya are still dotted with immaculate stone villages and criss-crossed by carefully maintained walking trails.

Where to Now For Nepal?

The question asked by most travellers in the aftermath of the earthquake was not 'Where can I go instead of Nepal?', but 'When will it be safe to go back to Nepal?' In the days immediately following the disaster, aftershocks were a daily occurrence and millions slept outside under canvas fearing further building collapses. The initial advice was for travellers to stay away, to avoid using valuable resources and impeding the relief effort.

Since then, the aftershocks have largely subsided and the relief effort has moved on to reconstruction and housing people left homeless by the disaster. The authorities in Nepal are now appealling to tourists to return and help Nepal rebuild its economy by spending money with local business and supporting the livelihoods of local people. Nevertheless, the damage is severe and it will be some time before Nepal returns to the position it was in before the disaster.

POST-EARTHQUAKE UPDATE

Lonely Planet's Nepal authors updated the 10th edition of this Nepal guidebook shortly before the first tremor. A subsequent emergency update was carried out by local journalists in the weeks following the disaster. While we do not claim to have captured everything that has changed since the disaster, our writers have visited the affected areas, and where places have been damaged or destroyed, we have noted this in the reviews.

If you discover anything that is incorrect or out of date in this guidebook, please let us know via the following link: http://www.lonelyplanet.com/contact/guidebook_feedback/new.

See p404 for details of those who provided invaluable help in gathering updated information.

Travelling to Nepal After the Disaster

If you travel to Nepal today, you should be ready for some disruption as a result of the earthquake. The impact of the earthquake is plainly visible, particularly in the medieval towns of the Kathmandu Valley. Some buildings are structurally unsound and can no longer be used, and others will need extensive repairs before they are habitable. Many people remain in temporary accommodation and transport links, power supplies and communications may all be disrupted. You should expect to find that some hotels and other businesses are closed for restoration or because of lack of customers.

Despite all this, Nepal remains the same captivating, fascinating and welcoming destination it always was. If you visit today, and spend your money with local businesses, you will be contributing directly to the reconstruction effort, providing valuable revenue that has the potential to change lives. The Nepalis are a resilient people – this is not the first time Nepal has faced this kind of destruction, remember – but now more than ever they need the world to remember Nepal after the headlines have faded.

Welcome to Nepal

Wedged between the high Himalaya and the steamy Indian plains, Nepal is a land of snow peaks and Sherpas, yaks and yetis, monasteries and mantras.

Mountain Highs

The Nepal Himalaya is the ultimate goal for most mountain lovers. Some of the Himalaya's most iconic and accessible hiking is on offer here, with rugged trails to Everest, the Annapurnas and beyond, and most trekking areas escaped with only minor damage in the 2015 earthquake.

Then there's the adrenaline kick of rafting a roaring Nepali river or bungee jumping into a bottomless Himalayan gorge. Canyoning, climbing, kayaking, paragliding and mountain biking all offer a rush against the backdrop of some of the world's most dramatic landscapes.

Medieval Cities & Sacred Sites

Other travellers prefer to see Nepal at a more refined pace, admiring the peaks over a gin and tonic from a Himalayan viewpoint, strolling through the temple-lined medieval city squares of Kathmandu, Patan and Bhaktapur, and joining Tibetan Buddhist pilgrims on a spiritual stroll around centuries-old stupas and monasteries. Even after the 2015 earthquake, Nepal remains the cultural powerhouse of the Himalaya: the Kathmandu Valley offers an unrivalled collection of world-class palaces, hidden backstreet shrines and sublime temple art.

Jungle Adventures

Further south lie Nepal's wild and woolly national parks, where nature buffs scan the treetops for exotic bird species and comb the jungles for rhinos and tigers from the backs of lumbering Indian elephants. Choose from a luxury safari lodge in central Chitwan or go exploring on a wilder trip to remote Bardia or Koshi Tappu. Whether you cross the country by mountain bike, motorbike, raft or tourist bus, Nepal offers an astonishingly diverse array of attractions and landscapes.

Travel Nirvana

There are few countries in the world that are as well set up for independent travel as Nepal. Wandering the trekking shops, bakeries and pizzerias of Thamel and Pokhara, it's easy to feel that you have somehow landed in a kind of backpacker Disneyland. Out in the countryside lies a quite different Nepal, where traditional mountain life continues at a slower pace, and a million potential adventures glimmer on the mountain horizons.

Many people have spent a lifetime exploring the mountain trails of the Himalaya and the atmospheric temple towns of the Middle Hills, and they still keep coming back for more. The biggest problem you might face in Nepal is just how to fit everything in.

Why I Love Nepal

By Bradley Mayhew, Author

If, like me, you get your highs from pristine mountain views and the sense of perspective that a Himalayan journey offers, then you are going to like Nepal. But if, also like me, you've always secretly wished that your mountain wilderness came with a warm slice of apple pie instead of a soggy tent, then you will simply love this place. My favourite thing about Nepal? There's always another adventure. Done Annapurna? Try Manaslu. Done Manaslu? Try a 6000m trekking peak. It's adventure heaven, with an espresso on the side.

For more about our authors, see page 416

Above: View of the Himalaya from Gokyo Ri (p299), Sagarmatha National Park

Nepal

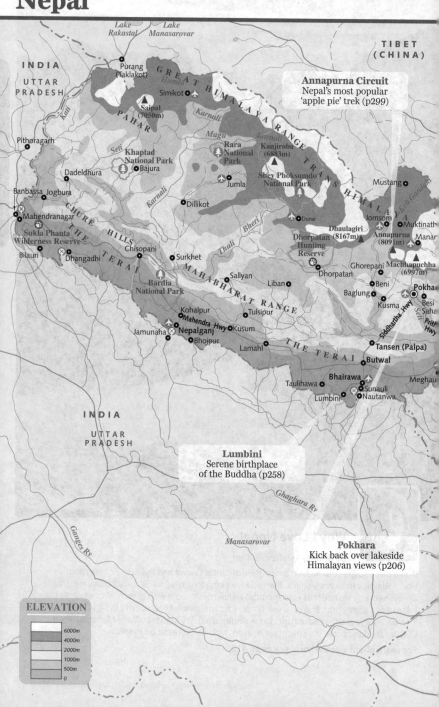

Annapurna Circuit
Nepal's most popular
'apple pie' trek (p299)

Lumbini
Serene birthplace
of the Buddha (p258)

Pokhara
Kick back over lakeside
Himalayan views (p206)

ELEVATION

6000m
4000m
2000m
1000m
500m
0

Swayambhunath
Iconic 'Monkey Temple', with views over Kathmandu (p117)

Bandipur
Medieval Nepal in miniature (p201)

Old Kathmandu
Temples, pagodas and old-town walks (p63)

Bodhnath (Boudha)
Asia's largest stupa and centre of Tibetan culture (p128)

Everest Base Camp
Unrivalled mountain splendour (p292)

Bhaktapur
Temples dot earthquake-damaged backstreets (p152)

Patan
A maze of ancient courtyards (p137)

Chitwan National Park
Rhinos, tigers and elephant treks (p242)

0   100 km
0   60 miles

TIBET (CHINA)

Manaslu (8156m)
Ganesh Himal (7406m)
Himalchuli (7892m)
Langtang Lirung (7246m)
Dorje Lakpa (6966m)
Cho Oyu (8153m)
Gauri Shankar (7145m)
Mt Everest (8848m)
Lhotse (8516m)
Nuptse (7879m)
Makalu (8462m)
Kanchenjunga (8598m)

Gorkha
Mugling
Trisuli Bazaar
Nuwakot
Langtang
Langtang National Park
Dhunche
Kodari
Barabise
ROLWALING
Sagarmatha National Park
Kanchenjunga Conservation Area

KATHMANDU
Shivapuri National Park
Bhaktapur
Charikot
Namche Bazaar
Lukla

Naubise
Patan
Dolalghat
Jiri
Phaplu

Dhulikhel
Panauti
Daman
Ramechhap
Lamidanda
Tumlingtar
Taplejung

Chitwan National Park
Hetauda
Sindhuli
Hile
Dhankuta
Basantapur
Kalimpong

Parsa Wilderness Reserve
Pathlaiya
Simara
Bardibas
Ilam

Birganj
Raxaul Bazaar
Jaleshwar
Janakpur
Jaynagar
Mahanpur
Rajbiraj
Koshi Tappu Wildlife Reserve
Chatara
Dharan
Itahari
Kakarbhitta
Panitanki
Bhadrapur

Birpur
Jogbani
Biratnagar

MAHABHARAT RANGE
CHURE HILLS
THE TERAI
PAHAR
THE HIMALAYA RANGE

Trisuli
Bhote Kosi
Tamba Kosi
Sun Kosi
Dudh Kosi
Arun
Tamur
Kosi
Mahendra Hwy
Tribhuvan Hwy

INDIA
SIKKIM
Darjeeling

INDIA
BIHAR

INDIA
WEST BENGAL

BANGLADESH

Nepal's
Top 15

Old Kathmandu

1 Even after the 2015 earthquake, the historic centre of old Kathmandu (p63) remains an open-air architectural museum of magnificent medieval temples, pagodas, pavilions and shrines. Once occupied by Nepal's cloistered royal family and still home to the Kumari, Kathmandu's very own living goddess, Durbar Square is the gateway to a maze of medieval streets that burst even more vividly to life during spectacular festivals. For an introduction to old Kathmandu, follow our walking tour through the hidden backstreet courtyards and temples of the surrounding warren-like old town. Bottom left: Butter lamps, Durbar Square (p63), Kathmandu

Everest Base Camp Trek

2 Topping many people's travel bucket list is this two-week-long trek (p292) to the base of the world's highest, and most hyped, mountain. Despite some earthquake damage, and only limited views of Mount Everest itself, the surrounding Himalayan peaks are truly awesome, and the half-hour you spend watching the alpenglow ascend beautiful Pumori or Ama Dablam is worth all the altitude headaches you will doubtless suffer. The crowds can be thick in October but the welcome at the Sherpa lodges is as warm as the fresh apple pie that is served.

AMOS CHAPPLE/GETTY IMAGES ©

FOTOVOYAGER/GETTY IMAGES ©

Annapurna Circuit Trek

3 This trek around the 8091m Annapurna massif is Nepal's most popular trek (p299), and it's easy to see why. The lodges are comfortable, there is little earthquake damage, the crossing of the 5416m Thorung La provides a physical challenge and the sense of journey from lowland Nepal to Trans-Himalayan plateau is immensely satisfying. Our best tip is to take your time and explore the spectacular side trips, particularly around Manang. Road construction has eaten away at the western sections but alternative footpaths continue to avoid the road.

Bhaktapur

4 Of the three former city-states – all Unesco sites – that jostled for power over the Kathmandu Valley, medieval Bhaktapur (p152) is the most atmospheric. Despite severe damage in the 2015 quake, its backstreets still burst with temples and pagodas. Winding lanes lead onto squares used by locals for drying corn and making pottery – you'll have to pick your way around earthquake damage to explore but the streets are still fabulously evocative. For the full experience, stay overnight in a guesthouse or attend one of the city's fantastic festivals. Bottom: Woman tending ceramics on Potters' Square (p160)

Bodhnath Stupa

5 The village of Bodhnath is the centre of Nepal's Tibetan community and home to Asia's largest stupa (p128), a spectacular white dome and spire that draws Buddhist pilgrims from hundreds of kilometres away. Equally fascinating are the surrounding streets, bustling with monks with shaved heads and maroon robes, and lined with Tibetan monasteries and shops selling prayer wheels and incense. Come at dusk and join the Tibetan pilgrims as they light butter lamps and walk around the stupa on their daily *kora* (ritual circumambulation).

Elephant Safari, Chitwan National Park

6 In the 'other Nepal', down in the humid plains, Chitwan (p242) is one of Asia's best wildlife-viewing spots and the place to don your safari togs, clamber atop a lumbering elephant and head into the dawn mist in search of rhinos and tigers. There's plenty to keep you busy here, from joining the elephants at bath time to visiting local Tharu villages, and the brave can even take a guided walk through the jungle, surrounded by the hoots and roars of the forest.

Views from Pokhara

7 Nepal's second-biggest tourist town (p207) may lack the historical depth of Kathmandu, but it more than makes up for this with a seductively laid-back vibe and one of the country's most spectacular locations. The dawn views of Machhapuchhare and Annapurna, mirrored in the calm waters of Phewa Tal (p207), or seen from the town's hilltop viewpoints, are simply unforgettable. Take them in on a trek, from the saddle of a mountain bike or, best of all, dangling from a paraglider high above the valley floor. Top: Boats on Phewa Tal, Pokhara

Lumbini – Birthplace of the Buddha

8 A pilgrimage to the Maya Devi Temple (p258), the birthplace of the Buddha, ranks as one of the subcontinent's great spiritual journeys. You can visit the exact spot where Siddhartha Gautama was born 2500 years ago, rediscovered only a century or so ago, and then tour a multi-national collection of temples. But perhaps the most powerful thing to do is simply find a quiet spot and meditate on the nature of existence. Travel experiences don't get much more profound than that. Bottom: Monks meditating, Lumbini

ALEX TREADWAY/GETTY IMAGES ©

RICHARD I'ANSON/GETTY IMAGES ©

Roaming the Valley Fringes

9 There's more to the Kathmandu Valley (p121) than Kathmandu, Patan and Bhaktapur. The rolling hills and steep slopes surrounding Kathmandu are studded with ancient temples, Himalayan viewpoints, biking trails and medieval temple towns such as Panauti (p189) and Kirtipur (p173) where you can step back through the centuries – all within easy striking distance of the capital. Roam around by local bus, or rent a bicycle or motorcycle, and get under the skin of Nepal's heartland. Top left: Reclining Vishnu statue, Budhanilkantha (p135)

White-Water Rafting

10 Nepal is one of the world's best rafting and kayaking destinations. Fuelled by water rushing down from the Himalayan peaks, day runs on the Bhote Kosi (p317) offer thrilling white water that comes straight from Tibet. Even better are the longer multiday adventures – liquid journeys that take you down the Karnali, Tamur and Sun Kosi Rivers through some of Nepal's remotest corners. Sections switch from roller-coaster white water to serene floats through jungle wilderness, with nights spent camping on pristine sand beaches. Top right: Rafters on the Karnali (p319)

Nepal's Fantastic Festivals

11 Nepal has so many spectacular festivals that any visit is almost certain to coincide with at least one. Celebrations range from masked dances designed to exorcise bad demons to epic bouts of tug-of-war between rival sides of a town. For a full-on medieval experience, time your travel with one of the slightly mad chariot processions, such as Rato Machhendranath (p146), when hundreds of enthusiastic devotees drag tottering 20m-tall chariots through the crowded city streets of Kathmandu and Patan. Above: Masked Lakhe dancer at Kathmandu's Indra Jatra festival (p87)

Swayambhunath

12 The iconic whitewashed stupa of Swayambhunath (p117) is both a Unesco World Heritage Site and one of Nepal's most sacred Buddhist shrines. The great stupa – painted with iconic, all-seeing Buddha eyes – survived the 2015 quake with only minor damage and it remains a focal point for Buddhist devotion. Pilgrims wander the shrines, spinning prayer wheels and murmuring mantras, while nearby astrologers read palms, and shopkeepers sell magic amulets and sacred beads. Come at dusk for spectacular views over the city lights of Kathmandu.

Momos

13 These little meat- or vegetable-filled dumplings are Nepal's unofficial national dish. Enjoy them in a grandiose traditional restaurant like Bhojan Griha (p101), at a shared table with monks in a backstreet Tibetan kitchen or in a trekking lodge overlooking the Annapurnas – they are the quintessential taste of the Himalayas. Join a cooking class to learn how to make these deceptively simple morsels that are savoured from China to Central Asia. Kathmandu's restaurants (p100) also fill them with apple and cinnamon. Yum!

RICHARD I'ANSON/GETTY IMAGES ©

Patan

14 Kathmandu's sister city (p137) doesn't get the attention it deserves. This is a city of interconnected Buddhist courtyards and hidden temples, and its greatest treasures escaped the 2015 earthquake. Wander the fascinating backstreets, the magnificent central Durbar Sq and the Patan Museum. Throw in ancient stupas and the valley's best collection of international restaurants and it's clear you need a couple of trips to take it all in. Best of all, spend the night here and you'll have the backstreets all to yourself.
Top: Column on Krishna Mandir temple (p139), Patan

Nepal's People

15 It is often said that while you first come to Nepal for the mountains, you return for the people (p336). From quietly protective Sherpa guides to welcoming Tibetan hotel owners and Newari shopkeepers, all Nepalis receive guests with respect and a *namaste* greeting. They're quick to smile in the most trying circumstances, and you'll rarely hear a raised voice or an angry word anywhere you go. It's one of the great joys of travelling here. Bottom: Fruit sellers in Kathmandu

Need to Know

For more information, see Survival Guide (p367)

Currency
Nepali rupee (Rs)

Language
Nepali

Visas
Tourist visas (15, 30 and 90 days) available on arrival; bring two photos and cash in US dollars

Money
Easy to change cash and access ATMs in Kathmandu, Pokhara and other cities, but almost impossible in rural areas or on treks

Mobile Phones
Buy SIM cards at Kathmandu airport on arrival or at Nepal Telecom (Namaste) or Ncell outlets across the country

Time
Five hours and 45 minutes ahead of GMT

When to Go

Subtropical warm winters, hot wet summers
Cool winters, warm wet summers
High altitude freezing winters, cool summers

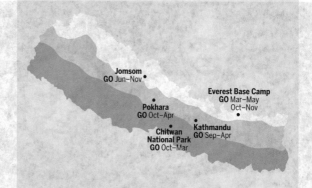

Jomsom
GO Jun–Nov

Everest Base Camp
GO Mar–May
Oct–Nov

Pokhara
GO Oct–Apr

Chitwan
National Park
GO Oct–Mar

Kathmandu
GO Sep–Apr

High Season
(Oct–Nov)

➡ Clear skies and warm days make autumn the peak season. Thousands of people hit the trails in the Everest and Annapurna regions, accommodation in Kathmandu gets booked up and prices peak.

Shoulder
(Mar–Apr)

➡ The second-best time to visit and trek, spring brings warm weather and spectacular rhododendron blooms.

Low Season
(Jun–Sep)

➡ The monsoon rains (mostly at night) bring landslides, and clouds often obscure mountain views. Rain, mud and leeches deter most trekkers, but hefty hotel discounts are common and this is a popular time to travel overland to Tibet.

Useful Websites

Explore Nepal (www.explore nepal.com) Useful Nepal portal; try also www.nepalhomepage. com or www.nepaltourism.info.

Nepal Tourism Board (www. welcomenepal.com) Government site.

Nepal Travel Blogs (http:// nepaltravelblogs.com) Interesting collection of travel tips.

Visit Nepal (www.visitnepal. com) Comprehensive private website with detailed travel tips.

Lonely Planet (www.lonely planet.com/nepal) Hotel bookings, traveller forum and more.

Important Numbers

Country code	☎977
International access code	☎00
Police	☎100
Tourist police	☎01-4247041
Tourism hotline	☎01-4225709

Exchange Rates

Australia	A$1	Rs 83
Canada	C$1	Rs 88
China	Y1	Rs 16
Europe	€1	Rs 124
Japan	¥10	Rs 8
UK	£1	Rs 158
US	US$1	Rs 102
India	₹1	Rs 1.60

For current exchange rates see www.xe.com.

Daily Costs

Budget:
Less than US$50

➡ Budget hotel room in Kathmandu: US$5–US$25

➡ Dinner and breakfast in a trekking lodge: US$10–US$12

➡ Trekking porter/guide: US$15/25 per day

Midrange:
US$50–US$150

➡ Organised camping trek: US$60–US$80 per person per day

➡ Midrange meal in Kathmandu: US$7–US$10

➡ Midrange hotel: US$25–US$80

Top End:
More than US$150

➡ Top-end hotel in Kathmandu or lodge in Chitwan: US$150–US$250

➡ Mountain flight: US$199

➡ Mustang trekking permit: US$500 for 10 days

Opening Hours

Business hours are year-round for banks and most offices. Many places in the mountains keep slightly longer summer hours and shorter winter hours.

Banks 9am–noon and 2–4pm Sunday to Friday, 10am–noon Saturday

Restaurants 7am or 8am–10pm

Bars and Clubs Usually close by midnight, even in Kathmandu

Shops 10am–8pm (varies widely)

Arriving in Nepal

Tribhuvan Airport (Kathmandu; p115) Prepaid taxis are available inside the terminal. Many midrange hotels offer free pick-ups from the airport. Long queues from immigration can slow things up if you are getting your visa on arrival.

Sunauli (Indian border; p257) For Kathmandu and Pokhara take a direct bus from the border. Golden Travels offers the most comfortable service. For other destinations take a jeep or rickshaw to nearby Bhairawa and change there.

Getting Around

Transport in Nepal is reasonably priced and accessible. Roads are often narrow, overcrowded and poorly maintained and delays should be expected. Sadly, air disasters and bus crashes are not uncommon.

Air Flights to/from major centres are efficient, whereas mountain flights to trailheads are highly weather dependent and frequently delayed.

Bus Tourist-class buses are comfortable, usually air-conditioned, and relatively safe and reliable. Micro or minibuses are quick but usually overcrowded, and local buses are, without exception, uncomfortable, crowded and slow.

For much more on **getting around**, see p386

If You Like...

Temples

Nepal's Hindu and Buddhist temples are masterworks in oiled brick, stone and carved wood. Colossal statuary, intricately ornate toranas (lintels) and erotic carvings still inspire the desired amount of wonder.

Kathmandu's Old Town Take a perch on one of the multi-tiered temples to observe the flow of life in this medieval city. (p63)

Bhaktapur Still impressive despite earthquake damage, this medieval town features the country's tallest temple, a royal palace and even some carved elephant erotica. (p152)

Golden Temple, Patan This 15th-century courtyard is centred on a beautiful Buddha statue and displays fine Tibetan frescoes. (p143)

Changu Narayan Temple Earthquake-damaged but still standing, this World Heritage Site is a treasure house of Himalayan art including 1500-year-old Licchavi statues and carvings. (p168)

Swayambhunath Monkeys swarm around this glorious gold-topped stupa, which rises like a beacon over Kathmandu. (p117)

Trekking

In Nepal you can trek for days through the most incredible mountain scenery, safe in the knowledge that you'll find a hot dinner and a place to stay at the end of each day.

Everest Region Still spectacular despite some earthquake damage, with astounding high mountain scenery and cosy Sherpa lodges, but try to visit outside of October. (p292)

Annapurna Circuit Nepal's most popular trek offers lots of variety – subtropical valleys, Tibetan-style villages, glacier views and a challenging 5500m pass. (p299)

Annapurna Sanctuary A direct trek past Gurung villages and bamboo groves straight into the frozen heart of the Himalaya. (p306)

Around Pokhara For treks that take less than a week, but still get you into the hills for spectacular mountain views. (p228)

Villages & Day Hikes

Nepal's mountains and valleys are laced with a network of footpaths travelled for centuries by traders and pilgrims. Pack your daypack for a brief encounter of rural Nepali life in the following hikes.

Tansen Follow ancient trade routes, visit a potters' village and explore the eerie ruins of a riverside palace. (p266)

Jomsom Use this hub as a base to visit fabulous nearby Himalayan villages like Kagbeni and Marpha. (p234)

Bandipur Base yourself in comfortable digs at this charming medieval village and day hike out to temples, viewpoints and caves. (p201)

Pokhara There are loads of options here, including Phewa Tal, Sarangkot and the peace pagoda, all offering superb views. (p206)

Chitwan & Bardia National Parks While visiting these parks, explore a Tharu village and experience a stick dance. (p242)

Wildlife Watching

Nepal's subtropical plains host an array of wildlife worthy of *The Jungle Book*. Tiger enthusiasts should visit between March and June and bring their own binoculars.

Chitwan National Park Spot rhinos, gharial (crocodiles) and maybe one of the park's majes-

tic Bengal tigers from the top of a swaying elephant. (p242)

Bardia National Park Track wildlife on elephant-back, 4WD, raft or foot, well away from the crowds in Nepal's far west. (p272)

Koshi Tappu Wildlife Reserve A birdwatcher's paradise with 450 species, best spotted from guided canoe trips on the Sapt Kosi. (p283)

Sagarmatha National Park Look for Himalayan tahr (wild mountain goats), yaks and maybe even a yeti in this World Heritage Site in the Everest region. (p296)

Sukla Phanta Wildlife Reserve An uncrowded reserve in Nepal's far west that features birdwatching and more. (p275)

An Adrenaline Rush

Nepal is the ultimate outdoor-sports destination. From climbing and mountaineering to mountain biking and ziplining, Nepal does it all – and at a fraction of the cost of other countries.

Paragliding Ride the thermals over Pokhara, relishing the incredible views of Phewa Tal and the Annapurna mountains. (p213)

Rafting Anything from a whitewater rush on the raging Bhote Kosi to a week-long expedition on the Sun Kosi. (p317)

Canyoning Abseil down and through a series of rushing waterfalls and pools near the Tibetan border. (p192)

Bungee jumping Follow Asia's highest bungee jump with a giant Tarzan-style swing. (p192)

Climbing a trekking peak Learn the basics of ropework and crampons before summiting a 6000m Himalayan peak. (p297)

Top: Golden Temple (Kwa Bahal; p143), Patan
Bottom: One-horned Indian rhino, Chitwan National Park (p242)

Ziplining Brave the world's fastest zipline rushing beneath the Annapurna peaks. (p211)

The Sacred & the Spiritual

The fascinating blend of Indian Hinduism and Tibetan Buddhism is one of Nepal's great draws. From holy lakes to marigold-laden crossroad shrines, the sacred imbues every aspect of Nepali life.

Lumbini Explore Buddhist architecture from across Asia and gaze upon the birthplace of the Buddha. (p258)

Bodhnath Light a butter lamp at the subcontinent's largest stupa, the focal point of Nepal's Tibetan community. (p128)

Kopan Monastery One of the best places in Asia to learn about Tibetan Buddhism and meditation, or take a short retreat. (p134)

Kathmandu (p83) **& Pokhara** (p213) Both good places to practise and learn yoga, with classes from an hour to a week.

Pashupatinath Nepal's holiest Hindu shrine, beside the cremation ghats of the sacred Bagmati River, draws holy men from across the subcontinent. (p156)

Devghat Join Hindu pilgrims at the auspicious confluence of two mighty rivers. (p242)

Getting Off the Beaten Track

It's not that hard to find a relatively little visited corner of Nepal. You'll likely have the following towns all to yourself, especially if you visit outside October/November.

Budhanilkantha A monumental Vishnu statue reclines on the valley fringe, close to Kathmandu but far from the madding crowds. (p135)

Panauti Overnight at this sacred confluence to visit the many temples and shrines at dawn and dusk. (p189)

Kirtipur Just beyond the ring-road, with brick-lined back-streets and a Bhairab temple bristling with swords. (p173)

Pharping A miniature Tibet in the southern valley and a magnet for Tibetan pilgrims; continue to Dakshinkali to see Tantric Hinduism at its most visceral and gory. (p175)

Ilam Darjeeling's quiet younger brother offers strolls through cultivated tea estates and some adventurous DIY trips. (p286)

Himalayan Views

Majestic mountain panoramas are not hard to come by in Nepal. That said, the following stand out for their awe-inspiring views. Come at dawn for a spectacular light show.

Nagarkot Despite some earthquake damage, this is still the best place close to Kathmandu from which to get Himalayan views from your hotel bed. (p181)

Sarangkot Machhapuchhare, Dhaulagiri and the Annapurnas dominate this viewpoint that's easily accessed from Pokhara. (p228)

Mountain flight Pray for clear weather on this dawn flight along the spine of the Himalaya, including Everest. (p82)

Kala Pattar Breathless views of Everest and the Khumbu Glacier from 5545m on the Everest Base Camp trek. (p292)

Poon Hill Take a short trek from Pokhara right into the lair of the mountain gods for a stunning sunrise. (p308)

Daman Earthquake-shaken, but still offering Nepal's widest mountain panorama, revealing a 300km-long chain of peaks from the Annapurnas to Everest. (p269)

A Life of Luxury

There's no need to rough it in Nepal. Top-end accommodation includes luxury jungle lodges, converted traditional mansions and wonderful rural retreats, all offering organic food and spa treatments.

Dwarika's Kathmandu's most romantic hotel is all oiled brick and carved wood, linked by lovely traditional pools. (p99)

Chitwan & Bardia National Parks Both parks have lavish jungle tourism lodges run by Tiger Tops, the pioneers of luxury jungle travel. (p253)

Top-end trekking Prefer your hiking days to end with a cosy lodge and cocktails rather than a campsite latrine? Several companies offer luxury lodges in the Everest and Annapurna regions. (p292)

Baithak Get a taste of the royal life in this lush restaurant housed in the converted former palace courtyards of the Baber Mahal. (p101)

Tiger Mountain Pokhara Lodge An ecofriendly tourism pioneer with snowy Himalayan peaks reflected in a luxe swimming pool. (p219)

Dwarika's Resort Dhulikhel A Vedic and Buddhist wellbeing spa on the valley fringe with views to die for. (p189)

Month by Month

February

The end of winter is an especially good time for a low-altitude trek or to visit the national parks of the Terai without the crowds. Pokhara is warmer than chilly Kathmandu.

✯ Losar

Tibetan peoples from Dolpo to the Khumbu celebrate their New Year with parades, pujas (religious offerings or prayers) and prayer flags. Find celebrations in the Kathmandu Valley at Bodhnath, Swayambhunath and Jawalakhel, near Patan.

✯ Maha Shivaratri

Shiva's birthday heralds festivities at all Shiva temples, but particularly at Pashupatinath (p125), and hundreds of sadhus flock here from all over Nepal and India. The crowds bathing in the Bagmati's holy waters are a colourful sight.

March

The trekking season kicks in as the days get warmer. The trails are less crowded in spring than in autumn but cloud is more likely to roll in and obscure the views.

✯ Holi

Known as the Festival of Colours, when coloured powder and water are riotously dispensed as a reminder of the cooling monsoon days to come. Foreigners get special attention, so keep your camera protected and wear old clothes. Can be in February.

✯ Seto Machhendranath

Kicking off in the wake of the sacrificial festival of Chaitra Dasain, crowds drag an image of Seto Machhendranath from its temple at Kel Tole in Kathmandu (p76) on a towering, tottering *rath* (chariot) through the backstreets of the old town for four days.

April

It's getting uncomfortably hot in the lowlands and Terai, but the rhododendrons are in full technicolour bloom at higher elevations, making this the third most popular month for trekking.

✯ Bisket Jatra

Nepalis celebrate their New Year as huge crowds drag tottering chariots through the winding backstreets of Bhaktapur, pausing for a quick tug-of-war. (p161)

✯ Balkumari Jatra

Thimi (p167) celebrates New Year by hosting palanquins from 32 nearby villages at the town's Balkumari Temple for three days of festivities. Nearby Bode holds a grisly tongue-piercing ceremony at the same time.

✯ Balaju Jatra

Thousands of pilgrims keep an all-night vigil at the Swayambhunath temple (p117) during the full moon of Baisakh. The following day they trek to the Baise Dhara (22 waterspouts) at Balaju for a ritual bath.

May

The dusty run-up to the monsoon pushes the mercury over 30°C in the Terai and Kathmandu

Valley, and the coming rains hang over the country like a threat. This is the key month for Everest expeditions and a good time to spot tigers.

✯✯ Rato Machhendranath

Patan's biggest festival (p146) involves the spectacular month-long procession of a temple chariot, culminating in the showing of the sacred vest of the god Machhendranath.

✯✯ Buddha Jayanti

A full-moon fair at Lumbini (p258) marks the Buddha's birth, enlightenment and passing into nirvana, and there are celebrations in Swayambhunath, Bodhnath and Patan. Swayambhunath displays a collection of rare thangkas (Tibetan religious paintings) for one day only.

August

The monsoon rains lash Nepal from mid-June to September, bringing swollen rivers, muddy trails, landslides and leeches. Tourist levels are at a low, though high Trans-Himalayan valleys such as Mustang and upper Dolpo enjoy perfect weather.

✯✯ Ghanta Karna

This festival celebrates the destruction of the demon 'bell ears' when a god, disguised as a frog, lured him into a deep well. Ghanta Karna is burnt in effigy on this night throughout Newari villages to cleanse evil from the land.

Top: Nepali woman dancing at a festival in Pokhara
Bottom: Candles being lit at Deepawali (Festival of Lights; p26), Kathmandu

Naga Panchami

On this day, nagas (serpent deities) are honoured all over the country for their magical powers over the monsoon rains. Protective pictures of the nagas are hung over doorways of houses, and food is put out for snakes in Bhaktapur (p156).

Janai Purnima

On the full moon, high-caste men (Chhetri and Brahmin) change the janai (sacred thread), which they wear looped over their left shoulder. Janai Purnima also brings Hindu pilgrims to sacred Gosainkund lakes and the Kumbeshwar Temple (p143) in Patan.

Gai Jatra

Newars believe that, after death, cows will guide them to Yama, the god of the underworld, and this 'Cow Festival' is dedicated to those who died during the preceding year. Cows are led through towns and small boys dress up as cows (especially in Bhaktapur).

Krishna Jayanta (Krishna's Birthday)

The birthday (also known as Krishnasthami) of the popular Hindu god Krishna is celebrated with an all-night vigil at the Krishna Mandir (p139) in Patan. Oil lamps light the temple and singing continues through the night.

Teej

The Festival of Women starts with a sumptuous meal and party; at midnight, women commence a 24-hour fast. On the second day women dress in their red wedding saris and head

to Shiva temples across the country to pray for a happy marriage.

September

The end of the monsoon brings unpredictable weather but temperatures remain warm, and the land is lush and green. High water levels make for especially exciting rafting.

Indra Jatra

This colourful autumn festival (p87) combines homage to Indra with an annual appearance by Kathmandu's Kumari (living goddess), who parades through the streets of the old town in a palanquin. It also marks the end of the monsoon.

October

Crystal-clear Himalayan views and comfortable temperatures means peak season and competition for airline seats, hotels and trekking lodges, so book ahead. The Dasain festival brings disruptions to some services.

Pachali Bhairab Jatra

The fearsome form of Bhairab, Pachali Bhairab, is honoured on the fourth day of the bright fortnight in early October or September. Bhairab's bloodthirsty nature means that there are numerous animal sacrifices.

Dasain

Nepal's biggest festival lasts for 15 days. It celebrates the victory of the goddess

Durga over the forces of evil (personified by the buffalo demon Mahisa-sura). Across the country hundreds of thousands of animals are sacrificed and bamboo swings are erected at the entrances to villages.

Fulpati (Phulpati)

Fulpati ('Sacred Flowers') is the first really important day of Dasain. A jar of flowers symbolising the goddess Taleju is carried from Gorkha to Kathmandu and presented to the president at the Tundikhel before being transported on a palanquin to Durbar Sq.

Maha Astami

The 'Great Eighth Day' and Kala Ratri, the 'Black Night', mark the start of the sacrifices to Durga. At midnight, in a temple courtyard near Kathmandu's Durbar Sq, eight buffaloes and 108 goats are beheaded, each with a single stroke of a blade.

Navami

The sacrifices continue on Kathmandu's Kot Sq the next day; visitors can witness the bloodshed but you'll need to arrive early to secure a place. Blood is sprinkled on the wheels of cars (and Nepal Airlines' aircraft) and goat is on almost everyone's menu.

Vijaya Dashami

The 10th day of Dasain is a family affair: cards and greetings are exchanged and parents place a *tika* (sandalwood-paste spot) on their children's foreheads, while evening processions and masked dances celebrate the victory of Lord Rama over the demon-king Ravana in the Ramayana.

✿ Kartika Purnima

The full-moon day in September/October marks the end of Dasain. It is celebrated with gambling in many households: you will see even small children avidly putting a few coins down on various local games of chance.

✿ Tihar

Tihar (also called Diwali or Deepawali on the third day of celebrations) is the second most important Hindu festival in Nepal. The festival honours certain animals, starting with offerings of rice to the crows ('messengers of death' sent by the god Yama), followed by dogs (who guide departed souls across the river of the dead), cows and bullocks on consecutive days.

✿ Deepawali (Festival of Lights)

The third day of Tihar is when Lakshmi, the goddess of wealth, comes to visit every home that has been suitably lit for her presence. No one likes to turn down a visit from the goddess of wealth and so homes are brightly lit with candles and lamps.

✿ Newari New Year

The fourth day of Tihar is also the start of the New Year for the Newari people of the Kathmandu Valley. The following day marks Bhai Tika, when brothers and sisters meet to offer gifts of sweets and money and place *tikas* on each other's foreheads.

✿ Haribodhini Ekadashi

On the 11th day after the new moon the god Vishnu awak-ens from his four-month monsoonal slumber. The best place to see the festivities is at the temple of the Sleeping Vishnu in Budhanilkantha (p135).

November

The continued good weather makes this the second most popular month to visit Nepal; conditions are perfect for outdoor activities and trekking, though tourist numbers start to drop off at the end of the month.

✿ Kartik Dances

Patan's Durbar Sq fills with music and dancers for this festival that traces its origins back to human sacrifices during the 17th-century rule of King Siddhinarsingh Malla. Dancers wear masks to represent the god Narsingha and demon Hiranyakashipu. Can fall in late October.

✿ Mani Rimdu

This popular Sherpa festival takes place at Tengboche Monastery in the Solu Khumbu region and features masked dances and dramas. For dates see http://welcomenepal.com. Another Mani Rimdu festival takes place six months later at nearby Thame Gompa.

December

Winter brings chilly nights to Kathmandu, and morning mist sometimes delays flight schedules. Snowfall can close passes on high trekking routes, while visiting Everest Base Camp can be a real feat of endurance.

✿ Bala Chaturdashi

On the new-moon day in late November or early December, pilgrims flock to Pashupatinath (p127), burning oil lamps at night, scattering grain for the dead and bathing in the holy Bagmati River.

✿ Sita Bibaha Panchami

Tens of thousands of pilgrims from all over the subcontinent flock to Janakpur (p279; the birthplace of Sita) to celebrate the marriage of Sita to Rama. The wedding is re-enacted with a procession carrying Rama's image to Sita's temple by elephant.

🏃 World Elephant Polo Championships

Connoisseurs of the absurd flock to this annual five-day elephant polo tournament, hosted by Tiger Tops Karnali Lodge (p274) near Bardia National Park. Referees watch for such pachyderm fouls as laying down in front of the goal or eating the ball.

🍴 Pokhara Street Festival

Around half a million visitors flock to Pokhara to enjoy street food, parades and cultural performances in the run-up to New Year's Day. Book your accommodation well in advance.

Itineraries

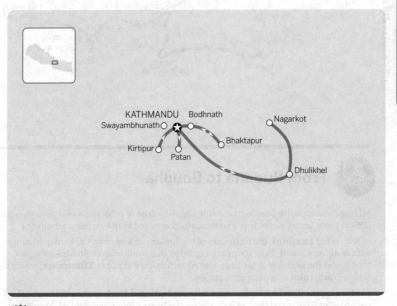

KATHMANDU   Bodhnath
Swayambhunath○   ○   ○ Nagarkot
                  ★
Kirtipur○   ○ Bhaktapur
         Patan
                  Dhulikhel

1 WEEK The Kathmandu Valley

A week gives you time to see the great cultural highlights of the Kathmandu Valley, including no less than six Unesco World Heritage Sites.

Start off in **Kathmandu** with our walking tour south from Thamel to the stunning medieval temples and palaces of Durbar Sq. On day two, walk to the towering stupa of **Swayambhunath** and the quirky National Museum. You can fill the afternoon with a walk around the famous stupa at the Tibetan centre of **Bodhnath**.

Make time for a day trip to **Patan** for its spectacular Durbar Sq and Patan Museum, combined with another great backstreet walking tour and dinner in Jawalakhel. Complete the trilogy of former royal kingdoms with a full-day visit to **Bhaktapur**, ideally with an overnight stay.

Next get your Himalayan kick with dawn mountain views at **Nagarkot** or **Dhulikhel** before returning to Kathmandu on foot via the temple at Changu Narayan. Fill another day by mountain biking to **Kirtipur** and neighbouring towns in the southern valley.

On your last day, take time for some serious shopping in Kathmandu or the fair-trade shops of Patan.

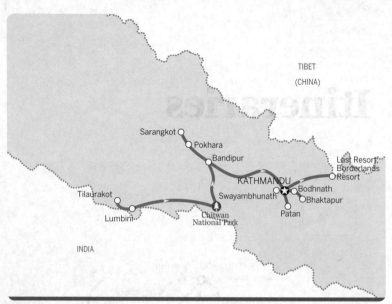

2 WEEKS · From Buddha to Boudha

Mixing contemplative temple tours with a healthy dose of wilderness and adventure, this 500km route across Nepal is one part meditation mixed with two parts adrenaline.

Kick off at **Lumbini**, the birthplace of the Buddha, 20km from the border crossing with India at Sunauli. Take your time exploring this world map of Buddhist temples, then spend the next day at the little-visited archaeological site of **Tilaurakot**, where the Buddha once ruled as a pampered prince.

From Lumbini make a beeline for **Chitwan National Park**, budgeting two or three days to allow dawn and dusk safaris among the tigers, rhinos and gharial. Even if you don't spot a rhino, you can still get up close and personal with some megafauna by helping out at elephant bath time.

From Chitwan take the day-long tourist bus to **Pokhara** for your first proper peek at the mountains. After enjoying the shops and cocktail bars of Lakeside, savour the views of Machhapuchhare from the World Peace Pagoda or lofty **Sarangkot**, or glide past the peaks at eye level on a tandem paraglide.

Another long bus trip will take you to **Kathmandu**, where you can fill up three or four days with the pick of the Kathmandu Valley itinerary. If you want to break the trip, consider a detour to the charming and historic hill town of **Bandipur**.

Once in the valley, make time to explore the backstreets of **Bhaktapur** on our walking tour, gain a deeper understanding of Buddhist art at **Patan Museum** and enjoy the views over the city at dusk from **Swayambhunath**. To escape Kathmandu's traffic and pollution, consider basing yourself in Bodhnath, Bhaktapur or Patan.

There should just be time for a two-day adrenaline rush near the Tibetan border – post-earthquake reconstruction permitting – at the **Last Resort** or **Borderlands Resort**, both a half-day drive from the capital.

On your last day, give thanks for a head-spinning trip at **Bodhnath** (Boudha), where you can buy a Buddha statue or a bundle of prayer flags to take home.

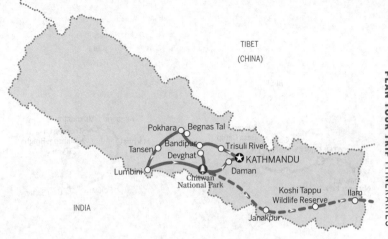

3–4 WEEKS Once Around the Middle

This off-the-beaten-track, 400km-loop route combines the best of Nepal's seldom-visited Middle Hills and offers lots of opportunities for great day hikes.

Start with a few days visiting the temples and stupas of **Kathmandu**, then book a rafting trip or kayak clinic on the **Trisuli River** en route to Pokhara, staying in one of the riverside adventure camps.

Next stop is **Bandipur**, a little-visited gem of a village where you can stroll to eerie caverns and relax among some wonderfully preserved traditional Newari architecture. From here, roll on to **Pokhara** for a row-boat ride around Phewa Tal and a quick jaunt across to **Begnas Tal**.

Take the winding Siddhartha Hwy southwest to charming **Tansen**, the base for some great day hikes. Continue south to peaceful **Lumbini** in the sultry Terai plains to amble around the Buddhist monasteries by bicycle.

Having come this far, it would be a shame to miss **Chitwan National Park**. If your budget allows, stay at one of the lodges deep inside the park for the most atmospheric digs. You might also consider a reflective stroll to the village of **Devghat**, at the sacred confluence of the Trisuli and Kali Gandaki Rivers.

The logical return route to Kathmandu would be to follow the snaking Tribhuvan Hwy north to **Daman**, one of Nepal's most impressive viewpoints, and rise at dawn for a 300km-wide panorama of majestic Himalayan peaks.

Alternatively, if your ultimate destination is India, you could dive off the beaten track, heading east to the temple town of **Janakpur** (aim for the Sita Bibaha Panchami festival in November or December) and then on to **Koshi Tappu Wildlife Reserve** for Nepal's best birdwatching opportunities. Continue east to the tranquil tea fields of **Ilam** for some off-map adventure before continuing to the Indian border and the delights of Darjeeling and Sikkim beyond.

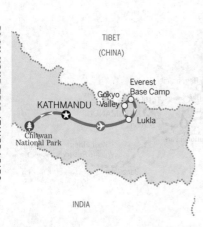

4 WEEKS Kathmandu & Everest

With a month to spare, you can explore the Kathmandu Valley and fit in a trek into the mighty Himalaya.

From Kathmandu, fly east to **Lukla** to start the **Everest Base Camp** trek. Despite some earthquake damage, this is still the definitive Himalayan trek, climbing from teahouse to teahouse among neck-craning peaks to the base of the tallest mountain on earth. The trek takes at least two weeks because of the gain in altitude.

With an extra week to play with, consider doing an Everest loop, detouring to the spectacular glaciers and lakes of the **Gokyo Valley** en route to Base Camp for a total trek of 21 days.

Because of the changeable weather in Nepal, it's wise to leave yourself a buffer at the end of the trip in case flights are cancelled. Finish off by exploring the highlights of the Kathmandu Valley itinerary, but do your sightseeing *after* the trek, not before.

After the thrills and chills of the mountains, finish off with a four-day excursion to steamy **Chitwan National Park**, where you can scan the jungle for rhinos and tigers.

4 WEEKS Annapurna Circuit Trek

The most popular alternative to Everest is the Annapurna region. From **Pokhara** (or Kathmandu) take the morning bus to **Besi Sahar** or Bhulbule to set off on the Annapurna Circuit. The full circuit takes about 20 days but you can shorten it to 12 days by flying or taking public transport back to Pokhara from Jomsom.

The highlights of the trek are around **Manang**, and it's worth tacking on a few extra days to walk the high route between **Pisang** and the lovely village of **Bragha**. The trek's major physical challenge is crossing the 5416m-high pass of **Thorung La**, and it's vital that you acclimatise sufficiently between Manang and the pass.

Muktinath on the other side of the pass is a major Hindu pilgrimage site and there are some fine short walks to the Tibetan-style villages of Jhong and Purang. The medieval village of **Kagbeni** is another highlight, as is the charming village of **Marpha** and nearby Chhairo Gompa.

Back in Pokhara it's worth taking it easy for a couple of days. Get clean clothes, enjoy a hearty yak steak and have a shave and/or head massage at the barbers.

Plan Your Trip

Planning Your Trek

Nepal is one of the easiest places in the world to trek – and one of the most exciting – but it pays to plan ahead. For the lowdown on porters, permits, earthquake damage and ensuring a safe trek, read on. For full information on trekking in Nepal, see Lonely Planet's *Trekking in the Nepal Himalaya*.

When to Trek

In general the best trekking time is the dry season from October to May; the worst time is the monsoon period from June to September. However, this generalisation doesn't allow for the peculiarities of individual treks.

Several festivals enliven the main trekking trails; in particular, the Mani Rimdu festival in October/November brings particularly colourful masked dances at the Everest region's Tengboche Monastery.

October to November The first two months of the dry season offer the best weather for trekking and the main trails are heaving with trekkers at this time, for good reason. The air is crystal clear, the mountain scenery is superb and the weather is still comfortably warm. Freak winter storms are becoming more frequent in October.

December to February Good months for trekking, but the cold can be bitter and dangerous at high altitudes. Getting up to the Everest Base Camp can be a real endurance test, and the Thorung La (Annapurna Circuit) and Laurebina La (Gosainkund trek) are often blocked by snow.

March to April Dry weather and dust means poorer Himalayan views but the compensations are several: fewer crowds, warm weather and spectacular rhododendron blooms. By May it starts to get very hot, dusty and humid in lower altitudes.

Best Mountain Scenery

Everest Base Camp & Gokyo Lakes (p292)
Walk into the heart of the world's highest mountains, following in the footsteps of mountaineers and Sherpas. From 17 days.

Best Overall Trek

Annapurna Circuit (p299) A huge variety of landscapes, charming villages and great lodges make this one of the world's classic walks, despite some road construction. From 12 days.

Best Medium Trek

Annapurna Sanctuary (p306) A relatively short trek with a powerful punch that leads you into a breathtaking amphitheatre of peaks and glaciers. From 11 days.

Best Short Trek

Ghorepani to Ghandruk Loop (p308) Gurung villages, superb Annapurna views and great lodges, all in just six days.

June to September Monsoon rains bring landslides, slippery trails and hordes of *jukha* (leeches). Raging rivers often wash away bridges and stretches of trail. Trekking is difficult but still possible and there are hardly any trekkers on the trails. Good for Trans-Himalayan regions such as Mustang, Dolpo and around Jomsom.

What Kind of Trek?

There are many different styles of trekking to suit your budget, fitness level and available time. Most independent trekkers plan to sleep and eat in lodges every night and forego the complications of camping. You can carry your own pack and rely on your own navigation skills and research; or you might find it makes sense to hire a local porter to carry your heavy backpack so that you can enjoy walking with only a daypack. A good guide will certainly enhance the trekking experience, though a bad one will just make life more complicated. Most popular trails are not hard to follow in good weather, so you don't strictly need a porter or guide for route-finding alone.

To save time, many people organise a trek through a trekking agency, either in Kathmandu or in their home country. Such organised treks can be simple lodge-to-lodge affairs or extravagant expeditions with the full regalia of porters, guides, portable kitchens, dining tents and even toilet tents.

Trekking is physically demanding. Some preparation is recommended, even for shorter treks. You will need stamina and a certain fitness level to tackle the steep ascents and descents that come with trekking in the highest mountain range in the world. It makes sense to start on some kind of fitness program at least a month or two before your trek. That said, Nepal's treks are well within the range of most active people.

On the trail you will begin to realise just how far you are from medical help and the simple comforts that you usually take for granted. For most people this is part of the appeal of trekking, but for some it is a shock to realise just how responsible you are for your own wellbeing. A simple stumble can have catastrophic results. Even a twisted ankle or sore knee can become a serious inconvenience if you are several days away from help and your companions need to keep moving.

In October 2014 over 50 trekkers and guides were killed in the Thorung La region after a blizzard struck. In the wake of the tragedy there were calls to make trekking with a guide compulsory, but this is up in the air following the 2015 earthquake. At the time of writing, the political wind seemed to favour relaxing the permit regulations to encourage more tourists to visit following the disaster, but this could change, so check the current situation when planning your trek.

Independent Trekking

Independent trekking does not mean solo trekking; in fact we advise trekkers never to walk alone. It simply means that you are not part of an organised tour. The main trekking trails have accommodation and food along their entire length, often every hour or two, so there's no need to pack a tent, stove or mat.

There are many factors that will influence how much you spend on an independent trek. Accommodation often costs around Rs 200. A simple, filling meal of daal bhaat (rice, lentils and vegetables) costs around Rs 250 at the start of the trek but can rise to Rs 700 just before a high pass. You can double your bill by having a

---

EARTHQUAKE-DAMAGED TREKKING ROUTES

The 2015 earthquakes caused devastation around the Kathmandu Valley, but many rural areas were even more severely affected. Massive landslides triggered by the tremors destroyed whole villages in Langtang, Helambu, Manaslu, and Rowaling, and buildings collapsed across central Nepal, including on the approach to Everest.

At the time of writing, trekking was possible on all the main trekking routes in the Everest region, the Annapurna region and in eastern and western Nepal. However, routes through Langtang National Park are expected to be off-limits to trekkers until at least mid-2016, and trekking in Helambu and Manaslu is also affected.

cold beer or slice of apple pie at the end of a long hiking day. A reasonable daily budget in the Annapurna and Everest regions is US$15 to US$20 per person per day, which should cover the occasional luxury but not a guide or porter. Add on another US$10 for wi-fi access and the occasional hot shower. You can sometimes negotiate a cheaper room if you promise to eat your meals at your lodge.

The bulk of your expenses will be for food. Menu prices are standardised and fixed across most lodges in a particular region and rates are not unreasonable considering the effort it takes to carry the food up there.

Guides & Porters

If you can't (or don't want to) carry a large pack, if you have children or elderly people in your party, or if you plan to walk in regions where you have to carry in food, fuel and tents, you should consider hiring a porter to carry your baggage.

There is a distinct difference between a guide and a porter. A guide should speak English, know the terrain and the trails, and supervise porters, but probably won't carry a load or do menial tasks such as cooking or putting up tents. Porters are generally only hired for load-carrying, although an increasing number speak some English and know the trails well enough to act as porter-guides.

Professional porters employed by camping groups usually carry their loads in a bamboo basket known as a doko. Porter-guides used to dealing with independent trekkers normally prefer to carry your backpack on their shoulders. They will likely carry a daypack for their own gear, packed on top of your pack or worn on their front.

If you make arrangements with one of the small trekking agencies in Kathmandu, expect to pay around US$25 per day for a guide and US$15 for a porter. These prices generally include your guide/porter's food and lodging.

Finding Guides & Porters

To hire a guide, look on bulletin boards, check out forums, such as www.lonelyplanet.com/thorntree or www.trekinfo.com, hire someone through a trekking agency, or check with the office of the **Kathmandu Environmental Education Project** (KEEP;

www.keepnepal.org). It's not difficult to find guides and porters, but it is hard to be certain of their reliability and ability. Don't hire a porter or guide you meet on the street in Kathmandu or Pokhara.

If during a trek you decide you need help, either because of illness, problems with altitude, blisters or weariness, it will generally be possible to find a porter. Most lodges can arrange a porter, particularly in large villages or near an airstrip or roadhead, where there are often porters who have just finished working for a trekking party and are looking for another load to carry.

Whether you're making the arrangements yourself or dealing with an agency, make sure you clearly establish your itinerary (write it down and go through it day by day), how long you will take, how much you are going to pay and whether that includes your porter's food and accommodation. It's always easier to agree on a fixed daily inclusive rate for your guide and porter's food and accommodation rather than pay their bills as you go. Note that you will have to pay your porter/guide's transportation to and from the trailhead and will have to pay their daily rate for the time spent travelling.

3 Sisters Adventure Trekking (p35) at Lakeside North, Pokhara, organises women porters and guides for women trekkers.

Obligations to Guides & Porters

An important thing to consider when you decide to trek with a guide or porter is that you become an employer. This means that you may have to deal with disagreements over trekking routes and pace, money negotiations and all the other aspects of being a boss. Be as thorough as you can when hiring people and make it clear from the beginning what the requirements and limitations are.

Porters often come from the lowland valleys, are poor and poorly educated, and are sometimes unaware of the potential dangers of the areas they are being employed to work in. Stories abound of porters being left to fend for themselves, wearing thin cotton clothes and sandals when traversing high mountain passes in blizzard conditions.

When hiring a porter you are responsible (morally if not legally) for the welfare of those you employ. Many porters die or are injured each year and it's important that you don't contribute to the problem. If you hire a porter or guide through a trekking agency, the agency will naturally pocket a percentage of the fee but it should provide insurance for the porter (check with the agency).

There are some trekking companies in Nepal, especially at the budget end of the scale, who simply don't look after the porters they hire.

The following are the main points to bear in mind when hiring and trekking with a porter:

➡ Ensure that adequate clothing is provided for any staff you hire. Clothing needs to be suitable for the altitudes you intend to trek to and should protect against bad weather. Equipment should include adequate footwear, headwear, gloves, windproof jacket, trousers and sunglasses.

➡ Ensure that whatever provision you have made for yourself for emergency medical treatment is available to porters working for you.

➡ Ensure that porters who fall ill are not simply paid off and left to fend for themselves (it happens!).

➡ Ensure that porters who fall ill, and are taken down and out in order to access medical treatment, are accompanied by someone who speaks the porter's language and also understands the medical problem.

➡ If you are trekking with an organised group using porters, be sure to ask the company how they ensure the wellbeing of porters hired by them.

In order to prevent the abuse of porters, the **International Porter Protection Group** (IPPG; www.ippg.net) was established in 1997 to improve health and safety for porters at work, to reduce the incidence of avoidable illness, injury and death, and to educate trekkers and travel companies about porter welfare.

You can learn a lot about the hardships of life as a porter by watching the excellent BBC documentary *Carrying the Burden,* shown daily at 2pm at KEEP.

If you're hiring your own porters, contact the porter clothing bank at KEEP, a scheme that allows you to rent protective gear for your porter. A similar clothing bank operates at Lukla, which also accepts donations of gear left over at the end of Everest treks – it is well signposted and just off the main drag in Lukla.

It's common practice to offer your guide and porter a decent tip at the end of the trek for a job well done. Figure on about one day's wages per week, or about 15% to 20% of the total fee. Always give the tip directly to your porters rather than the guide or trekking company.

Organised Trekking

There are more than 300 trekking agencies in Nepal, ranging from those connected to international travel companies down to small agencies that specialise in handling independent trekkers. Organised treks can vary greatly in standards and costs so it's important you understand exactly what you are getting for your money.

Organised treks generally charge solo travellers a supplement if you don't want to share a tent or room.

International Trekking Agencies

At the top of the price range are foreign adventure-travel companies with seductive brochures. The trek cost will probably include accommodation in Kathmandu before and after the trek, tours and other activities, as well as the trek itself. A fully organised trek provides virtually everything: tents, sleeping bags, food, porters, as well as an experienced English-speaking *sirdar* (leader), Sherpa guides and sometimes a Western trek leader. You'll trek in real comfort with tables, chairs, dining tents, toilet tents and other luxuries. All you need worry about is a daypack and camera.

Although the trek leaders may be experienced Western walkers from the international company, the on-the-ground organisation in Nepal will most probably be carried out by a reputable local trekking company.

Foreign-run companies that are based in Nepal include the excellent **Project Himalaya** (www.project-himalaya.com) and **Kamzang Treks** (www.kamzang.com).

Local Trekking Agencies

It's quite possible (and it can save a lot of money) to arrange a fully organised trip when you get to Nepal. Many trekking companies in Nepal can put together a fully equipped trek if you give them a few days' notice. Organised treks normally cost US$50 to US$100 per person per day for a fully equipped camping trek, or US$30 to US$50 for a teahouse trek, depending on the itinerary, group size and level of service.

Smaller agencies are generally happy to fix you up with individual porters or guides. You can either just pay a daily rate for these and then pay your own food and lodging costs or you can pay a package rate that includes your food, accommodation and transport to and from the trailheads. You gain a measure of protection by booking with an agency that is a member of the Trekking Agencies Association of Nepal (TAAN).

Several agencies run specialist treks: **Nature Treks** (☏01-4381214; www.nature-treks.com) focuses on wildlife, birdwatching and community ecolodge treks, while **Purana Yoga & Treks** (☏061-465922; www.nepalyogatrek.com) is one of several agencies that run yoga treks on all the main trails.

3 Sisters Adventure Trekking (☏061-462066; www.3sistersadventure.com)

Adventure Pilgrims Trekking (☏01-4424635; www.trekinnepal.com)

Adventure Treks Nepal (☏9851065354; www.adventurenepaltreks.com)

Alpine Adventure Club Treks (☏01-4260765; www.alpineadventureclub.com)

Ama Dablam Trekking (☏01-4415372; www.amadablamadventures.com)

Asian Trekking (☏01-4424249; www.asian-trekking.com)

Crystal Mountain Treks (☏01-4428013; www.crystalmountaintreks.com)

Earthbound Expeditions (Map p88; ☏01-4701051; www.enepaltrekking.com)

Explore Himalaya (Map p88; ☏01-4418100; www.explorehimalaya.com)

Explore Nepal (☏01-4226130; www.xplorenepal.com)

Firante Treks & Expeditions (☏01-4000043; www.firante.com)

Friends in High Places (☏01-5525656; www.fihp.com)

High Spirit Treks (☏01-4701084; www.allnepaltreks.com)

Himalaya Journey (☏01-4383184; www.himalayajourneys.com)

Himalayan Encounters (p85)

Himalayan Glacier (☏01-4411387; www.himalayanglacier.com)

International Trekkers (☏01-4371397; nepal@intrek.wlink.com.np)

Journeys International (☏01-4414662; journeys@mos.com.np)

Langtang Ri Trekking & Expedition (☏01-4423360, 01-4424268; www.langtang.com)

Mountain Travel Nepal (☏01-4361500; www.mountaintravelnepal.com)

Multi Adventure (☏01-4257791; www.multi-adventure.com.np)

Nepal Social Treks (☏01-4701573; www.nepalsocialtreks.com)

Shangri-la Nepal Trek (☏01-4810373; www.shangrilanepal.com)

Sherpa Society (☏01-4249233; www.sherpasocietytrekking.com)

Sherpa Trekking Service (☏01-4421551; www.sts.com.np)

Sisne Rover Trekking (☏061-462208, 061-461893; www.sisnerover.com; Pokhara)

Thamserku Trekking (☏01-4000701; www.thamserkutrekking.com)

Trek Nepal International (☏01-4701001; www.treknepal.com)

What to Pack

Clothing & Footwear

The clothing you require depends on where and when you are trekking. If you're going to Everest Base Camp in the middle of winter you must take down gear, mittens and thermals. If you're doing a short, low-altitude trek early or late in the season the weather is likely to be fine enough for T-shirts and a fleece to pull on in the evenings.

Apart from ensuring you have adequate clothing to keep you warm, it's essential that your feet are comfortable and will stay dry if it rains or snows. Uncomfortable shoes and blistered feet are the worst possible trekking discomforts. Make sure your shoes are broken in, fit well and are comfortable for long periods. Running shoes are adequate for low-altitude (below 3000m), warm-weather treks where you won't encounter snow, otherwise the minimum standard of footwear is lightweight waterproof trekking boots. Don't even think about buying boots in Kathmandu and then heading on a trek.

If you are going on an organised trek, check what equipment is supplied by the company you sign up with.

Buying or Renting in Nepal

It's always best to have your own equipment since you will be familiar with it and know for certain that it works. That said, you can buy almost anything you need these days from Kathmandu's trekking gear stores. Much of what's for sale is fake; the backpacks won't quite fit comfortably, the seams on the Gore-Tex jackets will leak and stitching will start to fray eventually. Even so, most items are well made and will stand up to the rigours of at least one major trek. The best buys are probably down jackets, fleeces and other jackets. There is also an increasing amount of imported gear, at prices comparable to abroad.

It's possible to rent sleeping bags (four-season) for Rs 80 or a down jacket for Rs 60 in Kathmandu, Pokhara and even Namche Bazaar. Tents are harder to find. Large deposits are often required (never leave your passport). You can purchase sundries, such as sunblock, shampoo and woolly hats on the main trails in places such as Chame and Namche Bazaar.

Butane gas canisters are available in Kathmandu for Rs 450, or for double this in Namche Bazaar.

Equipment Checklist for Teahouse Trekking

Clothing

☐ spare socks (minimum three pairs)
☐ hiking trousers
☐ quick-drying T-shirts (not cotton)
☐ down vest or jacket
☐ fleece
☐ rain shell or poncho
☐ fleece hat
☐ sun hat

Equipment

☐ sleeping bag (three- or four-season)
☐ daypack
☐ head torch and spare batteries
☐ trekking poles
☐ polarised sunglasses
☐ sunscreen (SPF 30+)
☐ water bottle
☐ water purification
☐ camera, batteries and memory cards
☐ phone and charger

MOUNTAIN LITERATURE
••

Trekking offers plenty of time to catch up on your reading. Pack the following titles for those long teahouse evenings:

➡ *Annapurna* by Maurice Herzog – a controversial mountaineering classic from 1950

➡ *Into Thin Air* by Jon Krakauer – the gripping story of the 1996 Everest disaster

➡ *The Ascent of Rum Doodle* by WE Bowman – a highly enjoyable spoof of all those serious mountaineering tomes

➡ *The Snow Leopard* by Peter Matthiessen – profound metaphysical description of a trek through Dolpo in the company of grumpy naturalist George Schaller

➡ *Nepal Himalaya* by WH Tilman – British wit from the 1950s trekking pioneer

➡ *Everest* by Walt Unsworth – the ultimate but hefty Everest reference, if you have a porter to carry it

➡ *Into the Silence* by Wade Davis – similarly encyclopedic history of the earliest attempts to scale Everest, mostly from the Tibet side

➡ *Himalaya* by Michael Palin – tales of travel on Annapurna and Everest by the charming ex-Python

➡ *Chomolungma Sings the Blues* by Ed Douglas – a thought-provoking 'state-of-the-mountain' address detailing the dirtier side of Everest mountaineering

Top: Trekker crossing the Marsyangdi on the Annapurna Circuit trek (p299)

Bottom: Trailside store on the Annapurna Sanctuary Trek (p306)

GRANT DIXON/GETTY IMAGES ©

Miscellaneous

- ☐ pocket knife (optional)
- ☐ lip balm
- ☐ toiletries
- ☐ toilet paper and lighter
- ☐ camp towel (quick-drying)
- ☐ laundry soap (biodegradable)
- ☐ hand sanitiser
- ☐ medical kit
- ☐ blister kit with moleskin, scissors and strong tape
- ☐ book, playing cards
- ☐ stuff sacks and plastic bags
- ☐ padlock
- ☐ emergency whistle

Information

The Himalayan Rescue Association, KEEP and Trekking Agencies' Association of Nepal offer free, up-to-date information on trekking conditions, health risks and minimising your environmental impact. They are also excellent places to visit and advertise for trekking companions.

Himalayan Rescue Association (HRA; Map p88; ☎01-4701223; www.himalayan rescue.org; 1st fl, Mandala St, Thamel; ☺2-5pm Sun-Fri) Runs health posts at Pheriche, Macchermo (with a porters' shelter), Gokyo and Manang and hopes to eventually run a post at Thorung Phedi on the Annapurna Circuit. Free lectures on altitude sickness are held at the Thamel office upstairs at 3pm Monday to Friday, as well as at the various health posts, and you can buy T-shirts and patches to support its work.

Kathmandu Environmental Education Project (KEEP; Map p88; ☎01-44100952; www.keepnepal.org; Thamel; ☺10am-5pm Sun-Fri; ☎) Has a library, some vaguely useful trekkers notebooks, a water refill service, an excellent noticeboard and a small cafe. It also sells iodine tablets (Rs 1000), biodegradable soap, trekking garbage bags and other environmentally friendly equipment. It's a good place to find a trek partner, donate clothes to or rent a set of clothes for your porter from the Porter's Clothing Bank (Rs 500, with a Rs 1500 deposit). It shifts location frequently, so check before heading out.

Trekking Agencies' Association of Nepal (TAAN; ☎01-4427473; www.taan.org.np; Maligaun Ganeshthan, Kathmandu) Details trekking regulations and can mediate in disputes with trekking agencies.

Maps

Most trekkers are content to get one of the trekking route maps produced locally by **Himalayan Map House** (www.himalayanmaphouse.com) or Nepa Maps. They are relatively inexpensive (Rs 400 to Rs 800) and are adequate for the popular trails, though not for off-route travel. They are found everywhere in map and bookshops in Thamel. Be aware that there is a great deal of repackaging going on; don't buy two maps with different covers and names assuming you are getting significantly different maps.

The best series of maps of Nepal is the 1:50,000 series produced by Erwin Schneider and now published by Nelles Verlag. They cover the Kathmandu Valley and the Everest region from Jiri to the Hongu Valley, as well as the Khumbu region. You may also find older 1:100,000 Schneider maps of Annapurna and other regions.

National Geographic produces 1:125,000 trekking maps to the Khumbu, Everest Base Camp, Annapurna and Langtang areas, as part of its Trails Illustrated series.

All of these maps are available at bookshops in Kathmandu and at some speciality map shops overseas.

Melbourne Map Centre (www.melbmap.com.au; Malvern East, Victoria, Australia)

Omni Resources (www.omnimap.com)

Stanfords (www.stanfords.co.uk)

Useful Websites

Lonely Planet Thorn Tree (www.lonelyplanet.com/thorntree) Both the Nepal and Trekking branches of this forum are good places to get the latest trail information and track down trekking partners.

Great Himalaya Trail (www.thegreat himalayatrail.com) Excellent website detailing different sections of the epic trail, with articles, practical advice and a forum board.

Nepal Mountaineering Association (www.nepalmountaineering.org) Everything you need to know about climbing and trekking to the top of Nepal's mountains.

PRACTICALITIES

➡ Rechargeable batteries can be charged at many trekking lodges for a fee of around Rs 300 per hour. To charge batteries or an iPod off the beaten track, consider a battery pack or solar charger.

➡ Tip: batteries lose their juice quickly in cold temperatures so keep them in your sleeping bag overnight at higher elevations.

➡ You can change cash in Namche Bazaar, Chame and at some trailheads, and access ATMs in Jomsom and Namche Bazaar, but you should generally bring all the cash rupees you will need with you, plus a stash of US dollars in case you need to buy an emergency flight home.

➡ Bring something for water purification – either chemical tablets, a filter or a UV steriliser such as a Steripen.

TAAN (www.taan.org.np) The Trekking Agencies' Association of Nepal website details current trekking regulations.

Trek Booking (www.trekbooking.com) Background information, a forum and trekking partner program.

Trekinfo.com (www.trekinfo.com) Some of the information is dated but there's a cracking forum board.

Trekking Partners (www.trekkingpartners. com) Great place to meet a trekking partner or read trip reports.

Yeti Zone (www.yetizone.com) An excellent but dated day-by-day description of the big treks.

Documents & Fees

TIMS Card

All trekkers are required to register their trek by obtaining a **Trekking Information Management System** (TIMS; www. timsnepal.com) card. The card costs the equivalent of US$20 for individual trekkers or US$10 if you are part of a group. South Asian Association for Regional Cooperation (SAARC) trekkers pay US$6 (US$3 for groups). You need to show the TIMS card at the start of the Annapurna and Everest treks (and in Langtang, assuming trekking is possible there post-earthquake).

The easiest place to get a TIMS card in Kathmandu is from the Tourist Service Centre (p379), mainly because you can also get conservation-area and national park tickets in this building. Bring two passport photos (though you can get free digital photos on the spot). The card is issued immediately; green for individuals and blue for group trekkers.

If you just need a TIMS card there's a more central **TIMS Centre** (Map p88; Manang Plaza; ☉7am-6pm Sun-Fri, 10am-noon Sat) office on the eastern side of Thamel, opposite Osho Travels. Bring a copy of your passport, two photos and the equivalent of US$20 in rupees.

National Park & Conservation Fees

If your trek enters a national park such as Sagarmatha (Everest), you will need to pay a national-park fee. You can pay the fee at the entry to the parks, or in advance from the **national parks office** (Map p68; ☏4224406; www.dnpwc.gov. np; ☉9am-2pm Sun-Fri), which is located at the Tourist Service Centre, a 20-minute walk from Thamel in Kathmandu. The fee is Rs 3000 for each park. No photo is required.

If you are trekking in the Annapurna, Manaslu or Gauri Shankar (Rolwaling) regions you must pay a conservation-area fee to the **Annapurna Conservation Area Project** (ACAP; Map p68; ☏4222406; www. ntnc.org.np; ☉9am-4pm), which is also at the Tourist Service Centre. Bring Rs 2000 and two photographs. The permit is issued on the spot.

Conservation fees for the Annapurna area are also payable in Pokhara at ACAP (p225), at Damside inside the Nepal Tourism Board (NTB) office, or in Besi Sahar. Note that if you arrive at another ACAP checkpoint without a permit you will be charged double for the permit.

Trekking Permits

Other than the TIMS card, trekking permits are not required for the main treks in the Everest, Annapurna and Langtang regions.

The following treks require trekking permits, which can only be obtained through registered trekking agencies:

AREA	TREKKING FEE
Humla	US$50 for 1st week, then US$7 per day
Kanchenjunga & Lower Dolpo	US$10 per week
Manaslu	US$70 for 1st week, then US$10 per day Sep-Nov, US$50 for 1st week then US$7 per day Dec-Aug
Nar-Phu	US$90 per week Sep-Nov, US$75 per week Dec-Aug
Tsum Valley	US$35 per week Sep-Nov, US$20 Dec-Aug
Upper Mustang & Upper Dolpo	reduced to US$100 for 1st 10 days (was US$500), then US$50 per day

Responsible Trekking

Nepal faces several environmental problems as a result of, or at least compounded by, tourists' actions and expectations. These include the depletion of forests for firewood; the build-up of nonbiodegradable waste, especially plastic bottles; and the pollution of waterways. You can help by choosing an environmentally and socially responsible company and being responsible with garbage, water and firewood.

KEEP is a good resource for tips on responsible trekking.

Firewood & Forest Depletion

➡ Minimise the use of firewood by staying in lodges that use kerosene or fuel-efficient wood stoves and solar-heated hot water. Avoid using large open fires for warmth – wear additional clothing instead.

➡ Consolidate cooking time by ordering the same items at the same time as other trekkers.

Daal bhaat (rice and lentils) is usually readily available for large numbers of people, does not require lengthy cooking time, and is nutritious.

➡ Those travelling with organised groups should ensure kerosene is used for cooking, including by porters. In alpine areas ensure that all members are outfitted with enough clothing so that fires are not a necessity for warmth.

Garbage & Waste

➡ Purify your own water instead of buying mineral water in nonbiodegradable plastic bottles.

➡ Bring a couple of spare stuff sacks and use them to compact litter that you find on mountain trails to be disposed of down in Kathmandu.

➡ Independent trekkers should always carry their garbage out or dispose of it properly. You can burn it, but you should remember that the fireplace in a Nepali home is sacred and throwing rubbish into it would be a great insult. Don't bury your rubbish. Try to ensure your guide also follows these guidelines.

➡ Carry out all your batteries, as they will eventually leak toxins.

➡ Toilet paper is a particularly unpleasant sight along trails; if you must use it, carry it in a plastic bag until you can burn it. Those travelling with organised camping groups should ensure that toilet tents are properly organised, that everyone uses them (including porters) and that rubbish is carried out. Check on a company's policies before you sign up.

Water

➡ Don't soap up your clothes and wash them in streams. Instead, use a bowl or bucket and discard the dirty water away from watercourses.

➡ On the Annapurna Circuit, the ACAP has introduced the Safe Drinking Water Scheme – a chain of 16 outlets selling purified water to trekkers. Its aim is to minimise the estimated one million plastic bottles that are brought into the Annapurna Conservation Area each year and are creating a serious litter problem. A litre of water here costs a fraction of the cost of bottled water.

Health & Safety

For the majority of trekkers health problems are likely to be minor, such as stomach upsets and blisters, and commonsense precautions are all that are required to avoid illness.

Make sure you and your teeth are in good health before departing, as there is very little medical or dental attention along the trails.

Trekking Safely

Fired up by the gung-ho stories of adventurous travellers, it is easy to forget that mountainous terrain carries an inherent risk. There are posters plastered around Kathmandu with the faces of missing trekkers.

In rural areas of Nepal rescue services are limited and medical facilities are primitive or nonexistent. Helicopter evacuations are possible but the costs run into the thousands of US dollars.

Only a tiny minority of trekkers end up in trouble, but accidents can often be avoided or risks minimised if people have a realistic understanding of trekking requirements. Don't take on a Himalayan trek lightly.

Several basic rules should be followed: don't trek alone, don't make ostentatious displays of valuable possessions and don't leave lodge doors unlocked or valuables unattended.

Embassy Registration

Officials of all embassies in Nepal stress the benefits of registering with them, telling them where you are trekking, and reporting in again when you return. You can register online with embassies of the following countries:

Australia (www.orao.dfat.gov.au)

Canada (www.voyage.gc.ca/register)

New Zealand (https://register.safetravel.govt.nz)

USA (www.step.state.gov)

Choosing Companions

➡ Never trek alone. You'll appreciate having someone around if you're lost, sick or suffering from altitude sickness. It's also useful to have someone to occasionally watch your pack or valuables when you visit the bathroom or take a shower.

➡ Solo women travellers should choose companions and guides carefully, as there have been repeated reports of harassment and isolated instances of assault – ask fellow travellers for recommendations, or contact **3 Sisters Adventure Trekking**

HEALTH ON THE TRAIL

AMS (Altitude Sickness)
Acute Mountain Sickness (AMS), or altitude sickness, is the major concern on all high-altitude treks – be ever-alert to the symptoms.

Diarrhoea
This is a fairly minor problem but it can ruin a trek, so watch what you eat and ensure your medical kit contains antidiarrhoeal medicine such as Lomotil or Imodium (for emergencies only) and a broad-spectrum antibiotic such as Azithromycin or Norfloxacin, available without a prescription at pharmacies in Kathmandu and Pokhara. Always treat your water.

Trekker's Knee
Many people suffer from knee and ankle strains, particularly if they're carrying their own pack. Elastic supports or bandages can help, as can anti-inflammatories such as Ibuprofen tablets and analgesic cream, and using collapsible trekking poles.

Blisters
Always carry moleskin, plasters (Band-Aids) and tape in your daypack in case of blisters. Investigate any hot spot as soon as you feel it. Wear clean socks.

Sunburn & Snowblindness
The high-altitude Himalayan sun is incredibly strong. Bring plenty of high-factor suncreen, a brimmed hat and a good pair of sunglasses for pass crossings.

(www.3sistersadventure.com) in Pokhara, which specialises in providing female guides.

➡ To find a fellow trekking companion, check the bulletin board at KEEP or post a message on www.trekinfo.com, www.trekkingpartners.com, www.yetizone.com or www.lonelyplanet.com/thorntree.

➡ Unless you are an experienced trekker or have a friend to trek with, you should at least take a porter or guide.

Trail Conditions

➡ Walking at high altitudes on rough trails can be dangerous. Watch your footing on narrow, slippery trails and keep your eyes on the trail not the mountains. Never underestimate the changeability of the weather at high altitude – at any time of the year.

➡ If you are crossing high passes where snow is a possibility, never walk with fewer than three people.

➡ Carry a supply of emergency rations, have a map and compass (and know how to use them), and have sufficient clothing and equipment to deal with cold, wet, blizzard conditions.

➡ You will be sharing the trail with porters, mules and yaks, all usually carrying heavy loads, so give them the right of way. If a mule or yak train approaches, always move to the high side of the trail to avoid being knocked over the edge.

Rescue Insurance

➡ Check that your travel insurance policy does not exclude mountaineering or 'alpinism'. Although you will not be engaging in these activities on a trek, you may have trouble convincing the insurance company of this fact. Check what insurance is available through your trekking company, if using one.

➡ Rescue insurance will need to cover an emergency helicopter evacuation or a charter flight from a remote airstrip, as well as international medical evacuation. A helicopter evacuation from 4000m near Mt Everest will cost you US$2500 to US$10,000 and payment must be cleared in advance. Your embassy can help with this if you have registered with it. Bring a credit card as you will likely have to prepay the helicopter company.

➡ Disreputable companies sometimes push fast-paced budget treks that don't allow for adequate acclimitisation in order to earn generous commission from helicopter evacuations. Make sure your itinerary includes acclimitisation days and don't be persuaded to trek higher if you are feeling poorly.

Altitude

Walking the trails of Nepal often entails a great deal of altitude gain and loss; even the base camps of Nepal's great peaks can be very high. Most treks that go through populated areas stick to between 1000m and 3000m, although the Everest Base Camp Trek and the Annapurna Circuit Trek both reach over 5000m. On high treks such as these ensure adequate acclimatisation by limiting altitude gain above 3000m to 500m per day. The maxim of 'walking high, sleeping low' is good advice; your night halt should be at a lower level than the highest point reached in the day.

Make a point to catch the free altitude lectures given by the Himalayan Rescue Association in Kathmandu, or at its Manang and Pheriche/Macchermo aid posts on the Annapurna and Everest treks respectively.

See p394 for more information on AMS (altitude sickness).

Plan Your Trip

Outdoor Activities

Nepal is a playground for lovers of adventure sports and high-adrenaline activities. The country offers some of the best mountain biking and rafting trips in the world as well as canyoning, bungee jumping, zip wires and rock climbing. Getting out on the rivers or cycling the back roads and mountain passes is one of the most satisfying ways of seeing the country.

There's a huge variety of adventures on offer, from short village bike rides in the Kathmandu Valley to challenging mountain trails, and from family friendly warm-water floats to full-on white-water trips through some of the remotest corners of the country. Exploring Nepal's trails and rivers on your own is possible but most people sign up for organised trips, which generally leave every few days in the high season. Kathmandu alone has dozens of adventure companies specialising in both fixed-group departures and customised private trips for rafters and cyclists. For adrenaline sports activities, options are more limited, and adventure packages must be arranged in advance through Kathmandu- or Pokhara-based tour companies.

Mountain Biking

Fat tyres, a soft padded seat and 17 more gears than the average Nepali bike – the mountain bike is an ideal, go anywhere, versatile machine for exploring Nepal. These attributes make it possible to escape sealed roads, and to ride tracks and ancient walking trails to remote, rarely visited areas of the country. Importantly, they allow a liberating freedom of travel – you can stop whenever you like – and they free you from crowded buses and claustrophobic taxis.

Best Wilderness Rafting Trip
Sun Kosi or Tamur (p319) Exciting expedition-style trips that last for a week and traverse a huge range of remote terrain.

Best Place for a Kayak Clinic
Trisuli River (p316) Base yourself at one of several comfortable riverside camps and take a few days to learn about Eskimo rolls and eddies.

Best Place to Get the Adrenaline Pumping
Bhote Kosi (p192) Plunge 160m towards earth on a bungee jump at The Last Resort.

Best Mountain-Biking Trip
Jomsom to Pokhara (p313) Downhill trail that follows jeep tracks down the western half of the spectacular Annapurna Circuit.

Best Place to Get an Unlikely Travel Experience
Parahawking near Pokhara (p214) Hand feed a vulture while paragliding hundreds of metres above the ground.

EARTHQUAKES & LANDSLIDES

In the months following the April 2015 earthquake, landslides blocked a number of popular cycling routes and rafting rivers, including the Kali Gandaki river near Pokhara. Because of the flooding risks posed by blocked rivers, the Nepal authorities usually act quickly to get water flowing again, but further landslides are possible in areas destabilised by the tremors so it pays to check the status of the routes mentioned in this book before booking a trip.

With the nature of off-road travel, most biking routes were not seriously affected by the 2015 earthquake.

While the heart of the Kathmandu Valley is too hectic and traffic-congested nowadays to truly offer a fun biking experience, the fringes of the valley are another story and they quite possibly offer some of the best and most consistent biking in Nepal, with a dense network of tracks, trails and back roads. A mountain bike really allows you to get off the beaten track and discover idyllic Newari villages that have preserved their traditional lifestyle.

Many trails are narrow, century-old walkways that are not shown on maps, so you need a good sense of direction when venturing out without a guide. To go unguided entails some risks, and you should learn a few important words of Nepali to assist in seeking directions.

Nepa Maps and Himalayan Maphouse produce the useful maps *Mountain Biking the Kathmandu Valley* and *Biking around Annapurna,* though they aren't to be relied on completely.

For more information on mountain biking in Nepal, see the Biking, Rafting & Kayaking chapter (p311).

Guided Tours

A booming number of Nepali companies offer guided mountain-bike trips. They provide high-quality bicycles, local and Western guides, helmets and all the necessary equipment. There is usually a minimum of four cyclists per trip, although for shorter tours two is often sufficient. For the shorter tours (two to three days) vehicle support is not required, while for longer tours vehicles are provided at an extra cost.

Local group tours range from US$32 to US$35 for a simple day trip, such as the loop routes north from Kathmandu to Tinpiple, Tokha and Budhanilkantha, or south to the traditional village of Bungamati. Expect to pay around US$22 to US$25 a day if you just want a mountain-bike guide.

A downhill day trip with vehicle support costs around US$55 per person. Options include driving to Nagarkot and riding down to Sankhu and Bodhnath or Bhaktapur, or driving to Kakani and taking the Scar Rd down. Dawn Till Dusk offers exhilarating downhill runs from the top of Phulchowki and Nagarjun peaks.

Multiday trips around the Kathmandu Valley cost around US$45 per day without vehicle backup (US$65 with vehicle support) and range from two to 10 days. Prices include bike hire, a guide, hotel accommodation and meals.

Tour Companies

A number of companies have good-quality imported mountain bikes that can also be hired independently of a tour.

Alternative Nepal (p83)

Annapurna Mountain Bikes (Map p88; ☑9841436811, 01-6912195; www.annapurna biking.com) The young team members behind this new Thamel venture are experienced cyclists and offer trips around the Kathmandu Valley, Annapurna area and Upper Mustang. Charges are around US$75 to US$85 per day for overnight trips. Bike hire (from US$12) and repairs available.

Biking First (Map p88; ☑9851157023; www. bikingfirst.com) Respected Kathmandu operation with everything from day trips in the valley to the full Annapurna Circuit.

Chain 'n' Gear Mountain Bikes (p211)

Dawn Till Dusk (Map p88; ☑01-4700286; www.nepalbiking.com; JP School Rd, Thamel, Kathmandu) Local tours, country-wide tours and rentals at the Kathmandu Guest House office. For bike repairs and servicing, see the workshop a five-minute walk east, near Kilroy's restaurant.

Himalayan Single Track (Map p88; ☑01-4700909; www.himalayansingletrack. com; Saatgumthi) One of the most exciting and comprehensive arrays of bike tours taking in all the favourites, plus Upper Mustang, Manaslu, the Jomsom Muktinath Trail and even overland cycling trips to Tibet. Located in Thamel.

Path Finder Cycling (Map p88; [☎]01-4700468; www.tibetbiking.com; Thamel, Kathmandu) Offers day and multiday tours, Tibet rides, bike rental, repairs and accessories. Located across from La Dolce Vita Restaurant.

Transporting Your Own Bicycle

If you plan to do a mountain-biking trip of more than a day or two, it may be a good idea to bring your own bicycle from home. Your bicycle can be carried as part of your baggage allowance on international flights. You are required to deflate the tyres, turn the handlebars parallel with the frame and remove the pedals. Passage through Nepali customs is quite simple once you reassure airport officers that it is 'your' bicycle and it will also be returning with you, though this requirement is never enforced.

On most domestic flights if you pack your bicycle correctly, removing wheels and pedals, it is possible to load it in the cargo hold. Check with the airline first.

Local buses are useful if you wish to avoid some of the routes that carry heavy traffic. You can place your bicycle on the roof for an additional charge (Rs 50 to Rs 100 depending on the length of the journey and the bus company). Keep in mind that more baggage is likely to be loaded on top once you're inside. A lock and chain is a wise investment.

Equipment

Most of the bicycles for rent in Nepal are low-quality, Indian mountain bikes, not suitable for the rigours of trail riding. The better operators rent high-quality front-shock, 18-gear mountain bikes for around US$12 to US$15 per day, with discounts for a week's hire. The better rental shops can supply helmets and other equipment.

If you bring your own bicycle, it is essential to bring tools and spare parts, as these are largely unavailable outside of Kathmandu. Established mountain-bike tour operators have mechanics, workshops and a full range of bicycle tools at their offices in Kathmandu.

Road Conditions

Nepali roads carry a vast array of vehicles: buses, motorcycles, cars, trucks, tractors, holy cows, wheelbarrows, dogs, wandering children and chickens, all moving at different speeds and in different directions. Traffic generally travels on the left-hand side, though it's not uncommon to find a vehicle approaching you head-on. In practice, smaller vehicles give way to larger ones, and bicycles are definitely at the bottom of the heap.

The centre of Kathmandu is a particularly unpleasant place to ride because of pollution, heavy traffic and the increasingly reckless behaviour of young motorcyclists.

A few intrepid mountain bikers have taken bicycles into trekking areas hoping to find great riding but these areas are generally not suitable for mountain biking and you have to carry your bicycle for at least 80% of the time. In addition, there are always trekkers, porters and local people clogging up the trails. Sagarmatha National Park doesn't allow mountain bikes. Courtesy and care on the trails should be a high priority when cycling.

Note that some routes may have changed as a result of earthquake damage, and landmarks may have been destroyed – now more than ever, it will pay dividends if you learn a few words of Nepali to ask directions.

Trail Etiquette
Clothing
Tight-fitting lycra bicycle clothing might be functional, but it's a shock to locals, who maintain a very modest approach to dressing. Such clothing is embarrassing and also offensive to Nepalis.

A simple way to overcome this is by wearing a pair of comfortable shorts and a T-shirt over your bicycle gear. This is especially applicable to female cyclists, as women in Nepal generally dress conservatively.

Safety
Trails are often filled with locals going about their daily work. A small bell attached to your handlebars and used as a warning of your approach, reducing your speed, and a friendly call or two of '*cycle ioh!*' (cycle coming!) go a long way in keeping everyone on the trails happy and safe. Children love the novelty of the bicycles, the fancy helmets, the colours and the strange clothing, and will come running from all directions to greet you. They also love to grab hold of the back of your bicycle and run with you. You need to maintain a watchful eye so no one gets hurt.

Rafting

Nepal has a reputation for being one of the best places in the world for rafting, with outstanding river journeys ranging from steep, adrenaline-charged mountain streams to classic big-volume wilderness expeditions. Warm water, a subtropical climate (with no bugs!) and huge white sandy beaches that are ideal for camping add further to the appeal.

For more information on rafting in Nepal, see the Biking, Rafting & Kayaking chapter (p316).

When to Go

In general the best times for rafting and kayaking are September to early December, and March to early June.

March to May The summer season has long, hot days and lower water flows, which generally means the rapids are a grade lower than they are from September to November. The rivers rise again in May with the pre-monsoon storms and some snowmelt.

June to August Monsoon rains mean the rivers carry 10 times their low-water flows, and can flood with 60 to 80 times the low-water levels, making most rivers insanely difficult. Only parts of the Seti, Upper Sun Kosi and Trisuli are commercially run during the monsoon.

September to early October and May to June Rivers can be extremely high with monsoon run-off. Any expeditions attempted at this time require a very experienced rafting company with an intimate knowledge of the river and strong teams, as times of high flows are potentially the most dangerous times to be on a river.

Mid-October to November One of the most popular times to raft or kayak, with warm, settled weather and exciting runs.

December Many of the rivers become too cold to enjoy unless you have a wetsuit, and the days are short with the start of winter – the time to consider shorter trips.

What to Bring

If you go on an organised rafting or kayaking trip, all specialised equipment is supplied, as well as tents. Roll-top dry bags keep your gear dry even if the vessel flips.

Usually you will only need light clothing, with a warmer change for cool nights. A swimsuit, a towel, a sunhat, insect repellent, sunscreen and light tennis shoes or sandals (that will stay on your feet) are all necessary. In winter you will need thermal clothing, especially on rivers such as the Bhote Kosi. Check if companies provide paddle jackets and wetsuits.

Waterproof camera containers are useful to take photos along the river – ask your company if they have any for rent or, better, bring your own.

Information

Anyone who is seriously interested in rafting and kayaking should get *White Water Nepal* by Peter Knowles. It has very detailed information on river trips, with 60 maps, river profiles and hydrographs, plus advice on equipment and health. Check out www.riverspublishing.co.uk or get a copy of the book in Kathmandu.

Himalayan Maphouse and Peter Knowles have produced three river maps for kayakers and rafters: *Whitewater Rafting and Kayaking for Western Nepal*, *Central Nepal* and *Eastern Nepal*.

The website of the Nepal Association of Rafting Agencies (www.raftingassociation. org.np) has listings of rafting companies, overviews of river routes and information on the annual Himalayan Whitewater Challenge.

Choosing a River

Before you decide on a river, you need to decide what it is that you want out of your trip. There are trips available from two to 12 days on different rivers, all offering dramatically different experiences.

First, don't believe that just because it's a river it's going to be wet 'n' wild. Some rivers, such as the Sun Kosi, which is a full-on white-water trip in September and October, are basically flat in the low water of early spring. On the flip side, early spring can be a superb time to raft rivers such as the Marsyangdi or Bhote Kosi, which would be suicidal during high flows. The Karnali is probably the only river that offers continually challenging white water at all flows, though during the high-water months of September and May it's significantly more challenging than in the low-water months.

Longer trips such as the Sun Kosi (in the autumn), the Karnali and the Tamur offer some real heart-thumping white water with the sense of journey inherent in a long river trip. With more time on the river,

Top: Traveller carries his mountain bike up a trail in the Tsum Valley

Bottom: Rafters on the Karnali (p319)

ALEX TREADWAY/GETTY IMAGES ©

things are more relaxed, relationships progress at a more natural pace, and memories become entrenched for a lifetime. River trips are much more than gravity-powered roller-coaster rides; they're liquid journeys traversed on very special highways.

For a shorter float combined with some premier wildlife-watching, consider also the two- to three-day raft from Mugling to Chitwan National Park and a day raft on the Geruwa River near Bardia National Park.

Landslides periodically block rivers in Nepal, and these are likely to be more frequent following the 2015 earthquakes. Check locally to make sure that everything is clear before booking a trip.

Organised Trips

There are dozens of companies in Kathmandu claiming to be rafting and kayaking operators. A few are well-established companies with good reputations, and the rest are newer companies, often formed by guides breaking away and starting their own operations. Although these new companies can be enthusiastic and good, they can also be shoestring operations that may not have adequate equipment and staff. Most of the small travel agencies simply sell trips on commission; often they have no real idea about the details of what they are selling and are only interested in getting bums on seats.

If a group has recently returned from a trip, speak to its members. This will give you reliable information about the quality of equipment, the guides, the food and the transportation. Question the company about things such as how groups get to and from the river, the number of hours spent paddling or rowing, where the camps are set up, food provided (rafting promotes a very healthy appetite), who does the cooking and work around the camp, the cooking fuel used (wood isn't convenient or responsible), what happens to rubbish, hygiene precautions and night-time activities. Check how many people have booked

RIVER TRIPS IN NEPAL

Note that in the 'Season/Grade' column, the number in brackets refers to the grade when the high river flows, which is normally at the beginning and end of the season.

RIVER	TRIP DURATION (DAYS)	TRANSPORT	SEASON/GRADE	ADD-ONS
Bhote Kosi	2	3hr from Kathmandu	late Oct–May/4 (5-)	bungee jump, canyoning, kayak clinics, day trips possible
Upper Sun Kosi	2	2hr from Kathmandu	Oct–May/3 (4), Jun–Sep/4 (4+)	
Trisuli	2	2hr from Kathmandu	Oct–May/3 (4), Jun–Sep/4 (4+)	excursions to Bandipur or Pokhara, day trips possible
Seti	2–3	1½hr from Pokhara	Sep–May/2 (3+)	kayak clinics are popular here
Kali Gandaki	3	2hr from Pokhara	late Sep–May/3 (4)	Chitwan National Park
Marsyangdi	4	5hr from Kathmandu	late Oct–Apr/4 (5-)	Annapurna Circuit Trek
Sun Kosi	8–9	3hr from Kathmandu then 16hr bus back to Kathmandu, or fly from Biratnagar	Sep–Nov/3+ (4+), Dec–Apr/3 (4)	Koshi Tappu Wildlife Reserve or continue on to Darjeeling in India
Karnali	10	16hr bus ride, or flight and 4hr bus ride from Kathmandu	late Sep–May/3 (4+)	Bardia National Park
Tamur	12	18hr bus ride, or flight then three-day trek from Kathmandu; flight or 16hr bus back (six days of rafting in total)	Oct–Dec/4 (5-)	trek to Kanchenjunga

WHITE-WATER SAFETY

Safety is the most important part of any river trip. Unfortunately, there are no minimum safety conditions enforced by any official body in Nepal. This makes it very important to choose a professional rafting and kayaking company. Your guide should give you a comprehensive safety talk and paddle training before you launch off downstream. If you don't get this, it is probably cause for concern.

➡ Modern self-bailing rafts, good life jackets and helmets are essential.

➡ There should be a minimum of two rafts per trip. In higher water, three rafts are safer than two.

➡ Good safety kayakers are invaluable on steeper rivers where they can often get to swimmers in places no other craft could manage.

➡ If possible, speak with the guide who will lead the trip to get an impression of the people you will be spending time with and the type of trip they run.

➡ All guides should have a current first-aid certificate and be trained in cardio-pulmonary resuscitation. International accreditation such as the Swiftwater Rescue Technician (SRT) qualification is a bonus.

➡ Always wear your life jacket in rapids. Wear your helmet whenever your guide tells you, and make sure that both the helmet and jacket are properly adjusted and fitted.

➡ Keep your feet and arms inside the raft. If the raft hits a rock or wall and you are in the way, the best you'll escape with is a laceration.

➡ If you do swim in a rapid, get into the 'white-water swimming position'. You should be on your back, with your feet downstream and up where you can see them. Hold on to your paddle as this will make you more visible. Relax and breathe when you aren't going through waves. Then turn over and swim at the end of the rapid when the water becomes calmer. Self-rescue is the best rescue.

and paid for a trip, as well as the maximum number that will be taken.

Shorter trips depart every few days but the longer rafting trips only depart every week or so, so it's worth contacting a company in advance to see when they are planning a trip. The best companies will refer you to a friendly competitor if they don't have any suitable dates.

Generally you'll be rafting or kayaking for around five to six hours a day, and you can expect to be running rapids about 30% of the time depending on the river. The first and last days will most likely be half days. Longer trips of a week or more will probably have one rest day when you can relax or explore the surroundings.

Trips booked in Nepal range in price from US$60 to US$120 a day, depending on the standard of service, number of people on the trip, and the river. Generally you get what you pay for. It is better to pay a bit more and have a good, safe trip than to save US$100 and have a lousy, dangerous trip.

With the constant change in rafting and kayaking companies it's difficult to make individual recommendations; the fact that a company is not recommended here does not necessarily mean it will not deliver an

excellent trip. Nonetheless, a number of companies have been recommended for their professionalism.

Adrenaline Rush (Map p88; ☑01-4701056; www.adrenalinenepal.com; Thamel) Trisuli rafting and kayaking trips, including tubing and 'ducky' (inflatable kayak) trips, from a simple camp at Kuringhat on the Trisuli.

Adventure Aves (Map p88; ☑01-4700230; www.adventureaves.com; Saat Gumti) Thamel-based Nepali-British operation focused on rafting and kayaking.

Drift Nepal (Map p88; ☑01-4700797; www.driftnepal.com) All the major rivers are represented, as well as kayak clinics and treks. Based in Thamel.

Equator Expeditions (Map p88; ☑01-4700854; www.equatorexpeditionsnepal.com; Thamel, Kathmandu) This company specialises in long participatory rafting/kayaking trips and kayak instruction.

GRG Adventure Kayaking (Map p88; ☑01-4266277, 01-4700928; www.grgadventure kayaking.com) Run by Nepal's best kayaker. Operates rafting and kayaking trips and a four-day kayak clinic at a tented camp close to Fishling, near Kuringhat. Also rents kayaks. It's located inside Kathmandu's Hotel Prayer Flag.

Himalayan Encounters (p85)

Paddle Nepal (p212)

Rapidrunner Expeditions (p212)

Ultimate Descents Nepal (Map p88; ☑01-4381214; www.udnepal.com) Near Northfield Cafe in Thamel and part of the Borderlands group; it also has an office in Pokhara. Specialises in long participatory rafting trips as well as kayak instruction and clinics on the Seti River.

Ultimate Rivers (Map p88; www.ultimaterivers.com.np; Mandala St, Thamel, Kathmandu) Associated with the New Zealand company Ultimate Descents International (www.ultimatedescents.com). The Kathmandu office is shared with The Last Resort.

Kayaking

There has been a continuous increase in the number of kayakers coming to Nepal over the last few years, and it is justifiably recognised as a mecca for paddlers. Several companies offer trips that cater specifically to kayakers, where you get to explore the river with rafts carrying all your gear and food, and often camp near choice play spots.

The opportunities for kayak expeditions are exceptional. Also of note at the right flows are the Mardi Khola, Tamba Kosi, Karnali headwaters, Thuli Bheri, Balephi Khola and tributaries of the Tamur.

The upper Modi Khola is also good for experienced kayakers. The side creek of the Bhurungdi Khola, by Birethani village, hides several waterfalls that are runnable by experienced kayakers.

For more information on kayaking in Nepal, see the Biking, Rafting & Kayaking chapter (p316).

Kayak Clinics

Nepal is an ideal place to learn to kayak and several companies offer learner kayak clinics. Due to the high levels of communication required to teach, the best instruction clinics tend to be staffed with both Western and Nepali instructors. Kayak clinics normally take about four days, which gives you time to get a good grounding in the basics of kayaking, safety and river dynamics.

The clinics are a pretty laid-back introduction to kayaking, with around four to six hours of paddling a day. On day one you'll learn self-rescue, T-rescue and Eskimo roll, which will help you to right yourself when you capsize. Day two sees you on the river, learning to ferry glide (cross the river), eddy in and eddy out (entering and leaving currents) and perfecting your paddling strokes. Day three is when you start really having fun on the river, running small (class 2) rapids and journeying down the river, learning how to read the rapids. Expect one instructor for every three people.

Equator Expeditions (p49) and Ultimate Rivers (p50) operate clinics on the upper Sun Kosi. Equator runs the Sukute Beach Resort, just north of Sukute village between kilometre markers 69 and 70. It's fairly comfortable but with squat toilets and cold showers and it has a great spot on the river, with a private beach, a bar area with pool tables and a lovely stretch of river nearby. It also has a pool, which is a real bonus when learning Eskimo rolls.

Ultimate Rivers uses the Ultimate Rivers Bhote Koshi Resort, between kilometre markers 83 and 84, which is a similarly basic camp. Both companies charge around US$250 for a four-day clinic, though you can often negotiate a cheaper price if you take the local bus. For both trips check what kind of transportation is included. You may find yourself flagging down local buses and putting your kayak on the roof for short rides after a trip down the river.

The **Royal Beach Camp** (☑9808413898; www.royalbeachnepal.com) offers two- to seven-day kayak clinics from its fixed camp and swimming pool at Kataudi on the Trisuli River, 85km from Kathmandu. Packages include two- to seven-day kayak clinics, combination kayaking, rafting and canyoning trips and family friendly expeditions. Contact Royal Beach Camp at its office in Kathmandu, just north of the Kathmandu Guest House.

Ultimate Descents Nepal (p50) operates its four-day clinics on the gentle Seti River, for around US$250, from Pokhara to Pokhara. The first day's training takes place on Phewa Tal and the remaining three days are on the Seti, with two nights' riverside camping. The advantage to learning on the Seti is that you get to journey down a wilderness river. Upper Sun Kosi kayak clinics can be structured for instruction from one to four days. Kayaking specialists such as GRG Adventure Kayaking (p49) can often arrange kayaking tuition during the quieter sections of a Sun Kosi rafting run.

Top: Bungee jumping from a bridge at The Last Resort (p192)

Bottom: Climbing near Mera Peak (p297) in the Everest region

DAVID PICKFORD/GETTY IMAGES ©

Pokhara-based operations include Paddle Nepal (p212) and Rapidrunner Expeditions (p212). Paddle Nepal offers white-water rafting, kayak clinics, canyoning and rafting (if it's wet'n'wild these guys do it). Rapidrunner offers hard-core white-water rafting trips, kayak courses and more family-friendly rafting trips.

Nose plugs are useful for those practise Eskimo rolls and you should bring a warm change of clothes as you are going to get wet. The bulk of kayak clinics operate in late October, November, March and April. December to February clinics are still possible, but with shorter days, and there's a lot less sunlight to warm you up at the beginning and end of the day.

Rock Climbing & Caving

Perhaps surprisingly, rock climbing is still in its infancy in Nepal and caving is even less developed. Most of the climbing is around the Kathmandu Valley. Hardcore Nepal (p203) offers a variety of climbing courses. If you prefer to get under rocks, then the same people offer combined climbing, abseiling and caving trips to the Siddha Gufa, a huge cave near Bandipur.

Bungee Jumping

While most visitors to Nepal chose to huff and puff up and down the side of mountains on a trekking trip, a few (slightly deranged) people prefer to just chuck themselves off the side of the mountains with nothing but a giant elastic band between glory and suicide. There are two established bungee jumps. The Last Resort (p193), on the road between Kathmandu and Tibet, offers a 160m plunge (one of the 10 highest bungee jumps in the world) off a bridge spanning a gorge through which the Bhote Kosi rages. It charges from €85 (around US$90) for a bungee package. However, there was some damage to the gorge in the 2015 earthquake, so check that jumps are running before traipsing out there.

Further west more elastic-band 'fun' can be had just outside Pokhara, where Zip-Flyer Nepal (p211) offers a 70m-high tower bungee jump (US$68). The same fiendish minds also offer an 1800m-long zipline ride (US$68) where speeds of 120km/h can be reached.

Canyoning

This wet-and-wild sport is a combination of abseiling, climbing, swimming and, well, falling into rivers. The best known canyoning area is on the turbulent Bhote Kosi north of Kathmandu on the road to Tibet. Canyoning trips are organised by Borderlands Resort (p192) and The Last Resort (p193); both charge around US$150 for a two-day course, which can be combined with other activities. However, both resorts suffered earthquake damage, so check the status of the canyoning trips – and accommodation – before you visit.

Paragliding & Ultralight

Paragliding, where you silently sail on the thermals like a vulture, isn't widely available in Nepal, but just outside Pokhara you really can ride the updrafts like a vulture – or at least with a vulture. Parahawking, as it's called, is a mixture of falconry and paragliding and allows you to hand feed gliding raptors at the same time as flying hundreds of metres above the ground! Blue Sky Paragliding (p214) charges UK£130 for this one-off experience. The same people also offer paragliding, minus the raptors, from Bandipur (p203).

One of the longest established paragliding companies, Sunrise Paragliding (p214) offers flights and courses from its Pokhara base.

Frontiers Paragliding (p214) is also based in Pokhara; if you enjoy its tandem flights you can sign up for a multiday package or take a pilot's course.

An ultralight, which is like a paraglider with a lawnmower strapped to it, is a fabulous way to view the mountain peaks. Flights are available through Avia Club Nepal (p214) and Pokhara Ultralight (p214), both based in Pokhara.

Other Activities

Not all activities in Nepal involve a head for heights, a love of speed or a desire to get soaked in freezing river rapids. The three big national parks of the Terai – Chitwan, Bardia and Koshi Tappu – all offer elephant rides, forest walks and boat/canoe rides. All of these activities are delightfully relaxing and calm. Well, unless a tiger jumps you...

Plan Your Trip

Volunteering & Responsible Travel

Tourism certainly brings revenue and other benefits to the people of Nepal, yet sadly there are also negative impacts, such as begging in city streets and disappearing forests along trekking trails. Read on to see how you can maximise your contribution and minimise your footprint through voluntary work and responsible travel.

Volunteering

Hundreds of travellers volunteer in Nepal every year, working on an incredible range of development and conservation projects, covering everything from volunteering with street children in Kathmandu to counting the tracks of endangered animals in the high Himalaya. The potential for personal growth and the opportunity to forge a deeper connection with a local community can give a profoundly deeper aspect to the notion of travel.

However, it is important to remember the principles of ethical volunteering – good volunteer agencies match a volunteer's skill sets to suitable projects that result in real and lasting benefit to local communities, rather than simply offering travellers the chance to feel better about themselves during a fleeting two-week placement.

As so-called 'voluntourism' has grown in popularity, dozens of organisations have sprung up to take advantage of a new source of revenue, muddying an already murky issue. You'll need to do serious research to ensure that your time and money are genuinely going to help the cause you are trying to advance. Do it right though,

Choosing Where to Volunteer

Consider honestly how your skill set may best benefit an organisation and community, choose a cause that you are passionate about and do some research to ensure your potential organisation is reputable and transparent.

Time is Valuable

Think realistically about how much time you can devote to the project. You are unlikely to be of lasting help if you stay for less than a couple of months.

Paying to Volunteer

It may surprise you to have to pay to volunteer but many companies charge substantial placement fees and ask you to cover your own costs, including accommodation, food and transport.

Resources

www.ethicalvolunteering.org Useful tips on selecting an ethical volunteer agency.

Volunteer: A Traveller's Guide to Making a Difference Around the World Invaluable one-stop information and directory; a Lonely Planet publication.

THE EARTHQUAKE RELIEF EFFORT

Following the April 2015 earthquake, a massive relief effort is underway across affected areas, backed by billions of US dollars in aid from foreign governments. Many local and international organisations are in urgent need of volunteers to help rebuild damaged infrastructure and aid people affected by the disaster, but the usual rules apply: contact organisations in advance to discuss volunteering opportunities and try to find placements where you can use your existing skills to make a practical difference. Above all, please remember: this is not the time for casual voluntourism that leaves no lasting benefits for local people.

and an extended time spent volunteering will bring you much closer to the country. Dare we say it, it may even change your life.

Voluntrekking

A number of trekking and tour agencies use the proceeds from their trips to support charitable projects around Nepal, and many travellers also undertake sponsored treks and climbing expeditions in Nepal to raise money for specific charities and projects.

There are a number of organisations that set up expeditions of this kind, including the following:

➡ **Australian Himalayan Foundation** (www. australianhimalayanfoundation.org.au) Offers fundraising treks to its aid projects.

➡ **Community Action Treks** (www.catreks. com) Offers various treks that contribute to the work of Community Action Nepal.

➡ **Crooked Trails** (www.crookedtrails.com) Runs fundraising treks and volunteer programs.

➡ **Explore Nepal** (www.xplorenepal.com) Trek and tour agency with commendable ethical policies; money from trips helps to fund litter clearing and other environmental projects.

➡ **Restoration Works International** (www. restorationworksinternational.org) Paid volunteer treks to Mustang to help with the restoration of Chairro Gompa.

➡ **Summit Climb** (www.summitclimb.com) Runs an annual service trek providing health care in remote parts of Solu Khumbu.

Volunteer Work

Voluntourism has become a booming business in Nepal, with travel companies co-opting the idea as a branch of their for-profit enterprises. To avoid the bulk of your placement fees going into the pockets of third-party agencies, it's important to do your research on the hundreds of organisations that now offer volunteer work and find a suitable one that supports your skills.

Although you give your time for free, you will be expected to pay for food and lodging, and you may also be asked to pay a placement fee. Volunteers should try to find out exactly how much of their placement fees is going into Nepal, and how much is going towards company profit and administrative costs. Fees paid to local agencies tend to be much lower than those charged by international volunteer agencies.

Nepal's orphanages in particular have come under a critical spotlight in recent years, with several operations linked to child trafficking and adoption scandals. Conor Grennan's book *Little Princes* is an inspiring account of time volunteering in a Nepali orphanage that touches on the corruption and murky moral dilemmas inherent in trying to do the right thing in Nepal. Following a damning UNICEF report in 2014, many foreign governments now advise their citizens against volunteering at orphanages unless they have been verified as legitimate by the Nepali Central Child Welfare Board (CCWB; www.ccwb.gov.np).

When looking for a volunteer placement, it is essential to investigate what your chosen organisation does and, more importantly, how it goes about it. If the focus is not primarily on your skills, and how these can be applied to help local people, that should ring alarm bells. Any organisation that promises to let you do any kind of work, wherever you like, for as long as you like, is unlikely to be putting the needs of local people first.

For any organisation working with children, child protection is a serious concern; places that do not conduct background checks on volunteers should be regarded with extreme caution. For some sobering perspectives on the volunteering industry, see www.nextgenerationnepal.org/

ethical_volunteering and www.just-one.org/your-chance/volunteering.

Following is a list of organisations offering volunteering opportunities in Nepal, but Lonely Planet does not endorse any organisations that we do not work with directly, so it is essential that you do your own thorough research before agreeing to volunteer with anyone.

➡ **Butterfly Foundation** (www.butterflyfoundation.org) Accepts volunteers to help with administration and child care in Pokhara; linked to Butterfly Lodge (p216).

➡ **Child Environment Nepal** (www.cennepal.org.np) Accepts child-care volunteers at its premises at Naya Bazaar in Kathmandu.

➡ **Community Action Nepal** (www.canepal.org.uk) Charity founded by mountaineer Doug Scott, working in porter villages in the Middle Hills.

➡ **Esther Benjamins Trust** (www.ebtrust.org.uk) Can arrange placements working to improve the lives of trafficked and abandoned children.

➡ **Ford Foundation** (www.fordnepal.org) Arranges volunteer work focusing on teaching and child care.

➡ **Global Vision International** (www.gvi.co.uk) Offers both short- and long-term internships and volunteer placements, some combined with trekking.

➡ **Global Volunteer Network** (www.globalvolunteernetwork.org/nepal) A Kiwi

TRAVELLER'S ETIQUETTE

➡ When visiting monasteries or temples, avoid smoking and remove your shoes and hat before you enter.

➡ Always walk clockwise around Buddhist stupas (bell-shaped religious structures), chörtens (Tibetan-style stupas) and mani (stone carved with a Tibetan Buddhist chant) walls.

➡ Some Hindu temples are closed to non-Hindus (this is normally indicated by a sign) and others will not allow you to enter with any leather items (mainly shoes and belts).

➡ Locals always leave a donation in a gompa or temple and you should follow their example.

➡ If you are introduced to a Buddhist lama it is customary to give them a *kata* (white scarf). Place it in the lama's hands, not around their neck.

➡ Short shorts, sleeveless tops and other revealing items of clothing are unsuitable for women or men; nudity is unacceptable anywhere. Women should carry a sarong with them if they will be bathing at local water taps.

➡ Public displays of affection between men and women are frowned upon.

➡ Nepali men often walk around hand in hand, but this does not carry any sexual overtones.

➡ Never point at someone, or beckon them with a single finger. If you do need to beckon someone over to you, use your whole hand instead of one finger, and be careful to keep your palm facing downwards.

➡ Never step over someone's legs – politely ask them to move their legs so you can get past.

➡ Always remove your shoes before you enter a private house.

➡ Food becomes ritually *jhuto* (polluted) if touched by someone else's hand, plate or utensils, so only eat off your own plate and never use your own fork or spoon to serve food off a communal plate.

➡ When using water from a communal jug or cup, pour it straight into your mouth without touching the sides (and without pouring it all over your shirt!).

➡ Don't use your left hand for eating or passing food to others as this hand is used for personal ablutions. Wash your hands and mouth before dining.

➡ When hiring porters and guides for treks, ensure they are properly equipped; as their employer, you are responsible for their wellbeing.

organisation offering placements in health care, education, child care and social development.

➜ **Helping Hands** (www.helpinghandsusa.org) Places medical volunteers at clinics around Nepal.

➜ **Himalayan Children Care Home** (www.hchmustang.org) Accepts volunteers to help with the care and education of kids from remote Mustang who are attending schools in Pokhara.

➜ **Insight Nepal** (www.insightnepal.org) Combines a cultural and education program near Pokhara with a volunteer placement and a trek in the Annapurna region; the package lasts seven weeks or three months.

➜ **Kathmandu Environmental Education Project** (KEEP; www.keepnepal.org) Placements in education and training in and around Kathmandu; minimum two-month placements and a US$50 administration fee.

➜ **Mountain Trust Nepal** (www.mountain-trust.org) British NGO that can arrange volunteer placements in social projects around Pokhara.

➜ **Nepal Trust** (www.nepaltrust.org) A focus on Humla in western Nepal.

➜ **Nepali Children's Trust** (www.nepalichildrenstrust.com) Runs an annual trek for volunteers and disabled Nepali children from the Annapurna region.

➜ **People & Places** (www.travel-peopleandplaces.co.uk) Placements for responsible and ethical volunteering.

➜ **Prisoners Assistance Nepal** (www.panepal.org) Kathmandu-based organisation that needs volunteers to help look after children whose parents are in prison.

➜ **Rokpa** (www.rokpa.org) Swiss-Tibetan organisation that needs volunteers for its soup kitchen and medical tent at Bodhnath for six or more weeks (December to March).

➜ **Rural Assistance Nepal** (www.rannepal.org) UK-based charity that places volunteers in education and health care.

➜ **Sustainable Agriculture Development Program** (www.sadpnepal.org) Arranges placements in sustainable agriculture and social programs near Pokhara.

➜ **Volunteers Initiative Nepal** (www.volunteeringnepal.org) Wide range of opportunities; see also www.friendsofvin.nl.

Responsible Travel

In the 65 years since Nepal opened its borders to outsiders, tourism has brought many benefits, in terms of wealth generation, employment opportunities, infrastructure, health care, education and transport, creating a level of social mobility that would have been unthinkable in the past. Many of the Nepalis who own trekking companies today worked as porters themselves 20 or 30 years ago.

Sadly, the negative effects of tourism are also clear to see. Begging is widespread, litter chokes mountain trails, and forests are diminished as lodge owners collect ever more firewood to keep trekkers supplied with warm showers and hot meals.

There is endless discussion among travellers about the most environmentally and culturally sensitive way to travel. What is certain is that making a positive contribution is as much about the way you behave as the money you spend. Independent travellers may spend less money, but they have a much greater impact on poverty alleviation by contributing directly to the local economy.

Drop into the Kathmandu office of the Kathmandu Environmental Education Project (KEEP; www.keepnepal.org) for more advice. And if you have any clothes, equipment or medications left at the end of your trip, consider donating them to the porter's clothing bank at KEEP.

Economic Choices

Don't underestimate your power as an informed consumer. By choosing local trekking agencies, tour companies and lodges that have a policy of reducing their environmental and cultural impact, you are providing an example to other travellers and an incentive for other companies to adopt the same practices. Hiring guides on treks also helps; as well as improving your cultural understanding, it provides employment, infusing money into the hill economy.

For more on the general issues of responsible travel check out Tourism Concern (www.tourismconcern.org.uk) and World Expedition's *Responsible Travel* guidebook, available at www.worldexpeditions.com.

DONATING IN NEPAL

While travelling in Nepal, many people are struck by the challenges faced by ordinary people. As one of the poorest nations on earth, Nepal has few public services provided by government, and access to even basic essentials such as health care, sanitation and education is limited, particularly in rural areas, leaving many local people in a desperate position. The 2015 earthquake has only worsened the plight of Nepal's poor. Some visitors feel compelled to give money to people they encounter in the hope that this will make a difference, but one-off donations are unlikely to change the lives of those most in need.

Just by visiting Nepal and spending money in businesses owned by local people, you are making a contribution to their future, but should you wish to make a more lasting contribution, consider making a donation to a non-government organisation that is working long-term to improve the lives of people in Nepal. Dozens of Nepali and international organisations are working in areas as diverse as installing water pumps and reuniting trafficked children with their families, and almost all rely on support from donations as well as funding from international governments.

As in any sphere, some organisations are more effective than others, so it is important to investigate the options carefully before you contribute. Seek out organisations that spend the bulk of donations on local projects, rather than on administration costs and salaries for their staff. The website www.ethicalconsumer. org has some useful information on ethical giving – search the site for 'comparing charities'. For listings of charities working in Nepal, visit www.charity-charities.org/ Nepal-charities/Nepal.html.

Ethical Shopping

Many species in Nepal are being driven towards extinction by the trade in animal parts. Although most products made from endangered species are sent to China or Tibet for use in traditional medicine, travellers also contribute to the problem by buying souvenirs made from wild animals.

In particular, avoid anything made from fur, and the metal-inlaid animal skulls and tortoise shells. Another item to avoid is the *shahtoosh* shawl, a form of pashmina that comes from (and results in the death of) the endangered *chiru* (Tibetan antelope). *Shahtoosh* is illegal in Nepal.

Fair Trade

Fair-trade principles can make a genuine difference in Nepal, a nation where 83% of the population live in underdeveloped rural areas. A number of nonprofit organisations support local cooperatives that pay artisans a fair wage to produce traditional crafts in safe working conditions, using sustainable materials, without child labour. Many of these organisations provide work, training and education for workers from neglected economic groups, including women, the disabled and members of the 'untouchable' castes.

Established by the Nepali philanthropist Tulsi Mehar, Mahaguthi (p111) provides employment and rehabilitation for destitute women, funded through the sale of quality handicrafts at its shops in Patan and Lazimpat (in Kathmandu). In Pokhara the Women's Skills Development Organisation (p225) has two outlets in Lakeside selling woven and stitched bags and toys.

The workshops run by Tibetan refugees at Jawalakhel in Patan also contribute directly to the welfare of disadvantaged people (see also the boxed text on p281).

More information on fair trade can be found at www.fairtradegroupnepal.org.

Begging

Hinduism and Buddhism have a long tradition of giving alms to the needy. However, begging in Nepal today is also fuelled by the perception that foreigners will hand out money on demand. In areas frequented by tourists, some groups of beggars work specific street corners using tried-and-tested scams to separate tourists from their money. Among all this, there are also many people who are genuinely in need and there are likely to many more people who fit this description following the 2015 earthquake.

At many religious sites you will see long lines of beggars, and pilgrims customarily give a coin to everyone in the line (there are moneychangers nearby who will change notes for loose change). Sadhus (wandering Hindu holy men) are also dependent on alms, though there are plenty of con artists among their ranks.

In tourist areas, you can expect to be hit with requests for 'one pen, one chocolate, one rupee' by children and even sometimes by adults. Don't encourage this behaviour. Most Nepalis find it offensive and demeaning (as do most visitors), and it encourages a whole range of unhealthy attitudes.

Ways to Help

You only need to look at the standards of dentistry in Nepal to realise that handing out sweets to children is neither appropriate nor responsible. If you want to give something to local people, make the donation to an adult, preferably someone in authority, such as a teacher or a lama at a local monastery. Appropriate gifts include toothbrushes and toothpaste, pens and paper, biodegradable soap, and school books, preferably with lessons in Nepali.

Many international NGOs working in Nepal rely on support from international donors. The late Sir Edmund Hillary's **Himalayan Trust** (📞01-4412168; www. hillaryhimalayantrust.org; Dilli Bazaar, Kathmandu) supports education, health care, cultural projects and afforestation across the Himalaya, and similar work is carried out by the Sir Edmund Hillary Foundation (www.thesiredmundhillaryfoundation. ca) in Canada, the Australian Himalayan Foundation (www.australianhimalayan foundation.org.au) and the American Himalayan Foundation (www. himalayan-foundation.org).

Cultural Considerations

Travellers may find the traditional lifestyle of people in Nepal to be picturesque, but in many places it is a meagre, subsistence-level existence that could be improved in numerous ways. The challenge faced by many charitable organisations working in Nepal is how to bring a modern standard of living without destroying the traditional culture.

You can do your bit by showing respect for local traditions – this will also demonstrate to local people that the relationship between locals and foreigners is one of equals. Many of the problems experienced by travellers in Nepal have been caused by past travellers who have treated locals as second-class citizens.

The behaviour of some photographers at places such as Pashupatinath (the most holy cremation site in Nepal) is shameful – imagine the outrage if a busload of scantily clad, camera-toting tourists invaded a family funeral in the West. Do not intrude with a camera, unless it is clearly OK with the people you are photographing. Ask first, and respect the wishes of local people. Photography is prohibited at many temples and monasteries, and it is plainly inappropriate at cremations or where people are washing in public at riverbanks or cisterns.

Regions at a Glance

Kathmandu

Temples
Food
Shopping

Malla Architecture

Kathmandu's medieval old town is stuffed with ancient stupas, hidden courtyards and millennium-year-old sculptures at every crossroad, while its central Durbar Sq is a masterpiece of medieval Malla architecture.

Global Tastes

The Thamel district is a global mash-up of Tibetan, Japanese, Thai and Italian restaurants, separated only by bakeries offering espresso and lemon cheesecake. For something special, the city's Newari restaurants offer the more refined tastes of the Rana court.

Shopping

Where to start? World-class outdoor gear, Asia's best bookshops, bargain-priced pashminas, Tibetan thangkas (religious paintings) and prayer flags...the list is endless. Bring a spare bag – you'll need it.

p62

Kathmandu Valley & Around

Temples
Outdoor Activities
Traditional Towns

Temple Art

The valley boasts the world's densest collection of World Heritage Sites, with almost every town in the valley blessed with stunning temples and exquisite statuary, even after the 2015 earthquake.

Hiking & Biking

The valley's web of fine hiking and mountain-biking trails offer the best way to explore this area. To up the ante, head for the Tibetan border for some wild rafting and canyoning.

Newari Architecture

Despite earthquake damage, Bhaktapur and Patan still top the list, but there are dozens of other charming villages to explore, from Kirtipur and Bungamati in the south to sleepy Nuwakot in the north. All offer fine traditional architecture and village squares that seem lifted from the 15th century.

p121

Kathmandu to Pokhara

Temples
Outdoor Activities
Traditional Towns

Forts & Sacrifices

Blood sacrifices at the hilltop temple at Manakamana are a macabre draw, especially on Saturdays, while Nepal's first capital at Gorkha boasts a historically important and impressive royal fort palace, with dozens of local temples littering the backstreets.

River Fun

Rafting runs and kayaking clinics on the warm waters of the Trisuli River are the most popular excursions, and there are some exciting canyoning, caving and ziplining add-ons.

Restored Bandipur

Bandipur's Newari-style old town is one of the most atmospheric in Nepal's Middle Hills, with outdoor teahouses, good accommodation options and excellent day hikes.

p196

Pokhara

Relaxing
Mountain Views
Trekking

The Easy Life

With a warm climate, little pollution, and backpacker comforts, Pokhara is the perfect place to take a break, preferably over a leisurely lakeshore breakfast or an ambitious round of yoga and massage.

Mountain Panoramas

It's all about Machhapuchhare and the Annapurnas, with spectacular dawn views from atop Sarangkot ridge, the World Peace Pagoda or while paddling a *dhunga* rowboat around serene Phewa Tal.

Teahouse Trails

A superb range of treks kick off from Pokhara, from short teahouse treks into the foothills around Ghorepani and Ghandruk to the alpine splendour of the Annapurna Sanctuary, Tibet-style Trans-Himalayan deserts around Jomsom or the full monty: the Annapurna Circuit.

p206

The Terai & Mahabharat Range

Temples
Wildlife
Outdoor Activities

Buddha's Birthplace

There are two major religious sites in the Terai. Buddhists celebrate the birthplace of the Buddha at Lumbini, while Hindus flock to the colourful temple complex at Janakpur to commemorate the marriage of Rama to Sita.

Birds, Tigers & Rhinos

Fabulous Chitwan and remote Bardia National Parks both offer big-game wildlife watching in sultry river deltas and grasslands, while Koshi Tappu Wildlife Reserve is ground zero for birdwatchers.

Outdoor Activities

Scanning for wildlife on a lumbering elephant's back or by boat are the major activities in the Terai, though there's also some good off-the-beaten-track walking around Ilam and nontouristy Tansen.

p237

On the Road

Kathmandu

🔊 01 / POP 1 MILLION / ELEV 1337M

Why Go?

For many, stepping off a plane into Kathmandu is a pupil-dilating experience, a riot of sights, sounds and smells that can quickly lead to sensory overload. Whether you're barrelling through the traffic-jammed alleyways of the old town in a rickshaw, marvelling at the medieval temples or dodging trekking touts in the backpacker district of Thamel, Kathmandu can be an intoxicating, amazing and exhausting place.

The 2015 earthquake brought devastation to parts of the city – including Kathmandu's Unesco-listed Durbar Square – but many areas emerged unscathed, and the soul of the city endures. Stroll through the backstreets and Kathmandu's timeless cultural and artistic heritage will reveal itself in hidden temples overflowing with marigolds, courtyards full of drying chillies and rice, and tiny hobbit-sized workshops.

This fascinating, infuriating city has enough sights to keep you busy for a week, but be sure to leave its backpacker comforts and explore the 'real Nepal' before your time runs out.

Best Places to Eat

➡ Gaia (p102)
➡ Third Eye (p104)
➡ Kaiser Cafe (p106)

Best Places to Stay

➡ Hotel Ganesh Himal (p97)
➡ Dwarika's (p99)
➡ Kantipur Temple House (p96)

When to Go
Kathmandu

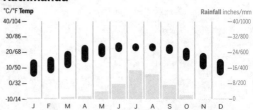

Oct–Dec Fine mountain views and warm days until December, with high-season crowds.

Mar–May March brings the Seto Machhendranath festival. Days can be hot in May.

Jun–Sep Hot days and frequent monsoon showers, but also the spectacular Indra Jatra festival.

History

The history of Kathmandu is really a history of the Newars, the main inhabitants of the Kathmandu Valley. While the documented history of the valley goes back to the Kiratis, around the 7th century BC, the foundation of Kathmandu itself dates from the 12th century AD, during the time of the Malla dynasty.

The original settlements of Yambu and Yangala, at the confluence of the Bagmati and Vishnumati Rivers in what is now the southern half of the old town, grew up around the trade route to Tibet. Traders and pilgrims stayed at rest houses such as the now destroyed Kasthamandap, which lent its name to the city.

Originally known as Kantipur, the city flourished during the Malla era, and the bulk of its superb temples, buildings and other monuments date from this time. Initially, Kathmandu was an independent city within the valley, but in the 14th century the valley was united under the rule of the Malla king of Bhaktapur. The 15th century saw division once more, this time into three independent kingdoms: Kathmandu, Patan and Bhaktapur. Rivalry between the three city-states led to a series of wars that left each state weakened and vulnerable to the 1768 invasion of the valley by Prithvi Narayan Shah.

The ensuing Shah dynasty unified Nepal and made the expanded city of Kathmandu its new capital – a position the city has held ever since. In 1934, a massive earthquake reshaped parts of Kathmandu, and the reconstruction created a network of modern boulevards such as New Rd. Kathmandu escaped the worst of the Maoist uprising in the 1990s, though the city was frequently crippled by demonstrations and strikes. Tens of thousands of Nepalis flooded into the rapidly expanding city to escape the political violence, and the city infrastructure is still struggling to cope even a decade after the end of the conflict.

On 25 April 2015, history repeated itself as another massive earthquake shook the Kathmandu Valley. Thousands were killed and many of Kathmandu's most famous monuments were reduced to rubble. Although life was slowly returning to normal in the Nepali capital in the months following the disaster, many people were homeless and many buildings and monuments required urgent repairs. The repercussions

EARTHQUAKE DAMAGE IN KATHMANDU

Sitting on a bed of vulnerable clay, Kathmandu bore the full force of the earthquake on 25 April 2015, but not all parts of the city were affected equally. Thamel, the most popular district for accommodation, eating and nightlife, saw relatively little damage, and Bodhnath and Pashupatinath also escaped with only minor damage.

The most serious damage was reported in districts with many old buildings, including Kathmandu's famous Durbar Square, but even here, damage was uneven – temples at the south end of the square toppled while those to the north were almost untouched by the disaster. Other badly affected areas include Gongabu, near the main Kathmandu bus station, and Kalanki, at the start of the road to Pokhara.

of the earthquake are likely to be felt for generations.

◉ Sights

Most of the interesting things to see in Kathmandu are clustered in the old part of town, focused on the majestic Durbar Sq and its surrounding backstreets.

◉ Durbar Square

Kathmandu's **Durbar Square** (Map p73; foreigner/SAARC Rs 750/150, no student tickets) was where the city's kings were once crowned and legitimised, and from where they ruled ('durbar' means palace). Tragically, parts of the square were devastated by the 2015 earthquake. As the first tremor hit, palaces crumbled and temples tumbled from their plinths, reducing parts of this Unesco World Heritage Site to a mound of splintered timber and brick dust. Seeing the roll-call of destroyed monuments, it would be easy to imagine that there was nothing left, but much still endures amid the destruction. The area north of Hanuman Dhoka, with its fascinating jumble of statues, shrines and temples, was almost untouched, and even in the worst affected area, key monuments such as the palace of the Kumari – Nepal's living goddess – stand in defiance of the disaster.

Kathmandu Highlights

❶ Follow **walking tours** (p80) through the labyrinthine backstreets of the old town, bursting with hidden courtyards and little-known temples.

❷ Soak up the amazing architectural monuments of **Old Kathmandu** (p63), an artistic and architectural tradition that rivals the great cities of Europe.

❸ Dine on momos (dumplings) and wild boar to the beat of *madal* (drums) and *bansari* (flutes) at one of the city's superb **Newari restaurants** (p101).

❹ Ensure the enduring love of friends and family by snapping up the bargains in the excellent **Thamel shops** (p109).

❺ Chill out in one of the rooftop garden **restaurants** (p100) in Thamel with a good book, a pot of masala tea and a slice of chocolate cake.

❻ Take a day trip to the nearby Unesco World Heritage Site of **Swayambhunath** (p117).

❼ Escape the traffic in the peaceful and beautifully restored Rana-era **Garden of Dreams** (p79).

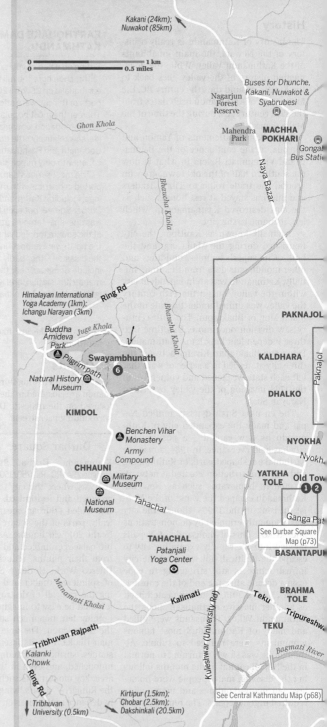

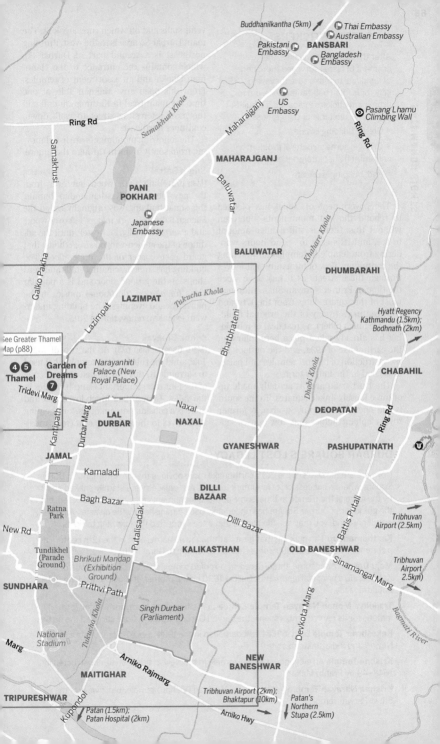

ℹ️ SAFETY STICKERS

After the 2015 earthquakes, the government of Nepal surveyed thousands of buildings to make sure they were safe for human habitation. Look out for prominent stickers indicating if a building is safe, unstable or dangerous:

➡ Green: building is safe

➡ Orange: some structural problems; only enter if absolutely necessary

➡ Red: building is unsafe

The government of Nepal has pledged to rebuild the lost monuments, but even without this, there is still a huge amount to see, and it is easy to spend hours wandering from temple to temple and watching the continuous flow of humanity that moves through these streets as it has done since the time of Prithvi Narayan Shah. Although most of the square dates from the 17th and 18th centuries (many of the original buildings are much older), a great deal of rebuilding has already taken place here following the earthquake of 1934, and the outlook for reconstruction of the lost temples and palaces is good in the longer term.

The Durbar Sq area is actually made up of three loosely linked squares. To the south is the open Basantapur Sq area, a former royal elephant stables that now houses souvenir stalls and off which runs Freak St. The main Durbar Sq area is to the west. Running northeast is a second part of Durbar Sq, which contains the entrance to the Hanuman Dhoka and an assortment of temples. From this open area Makhan Tole, at one time the main road in Kathmandu and still the most interesting street to walk down, continues northeast.

The following monuments are listed moving from south to north through the square.

Singh Sattal   PAVILION

(Map p73) Built with wood left over from the now destroyed Kasthamandap Temple, this squat building was originally called the Silengu Sattal (*silengu* means 'left over wood' and a *sattal* is a pilgrim hostel) until the addition of the golden-winged *singh* (lions) that guard each corner of the upper floor. The building has some fascinating stalls and curd shops on the ground floor and is a popular place for *bhajan* (devotional music) in the mornings and evenings. The building underwent extensive renovation in 2015.

Ashok Binayak   HINDU SHRINE

(Maru Ganesh; Map p73) At the top of Maru Tole, amid the rubble of the temples that used to surround it, this tiny golden shrine is one of the four most important Ganesh shrines in the valley. Ganesh is a much-loved god and there is a constant stream of visitors, helping themselves to the self-serve *tika* (red sandal-

DURBAR SQUARE'S LOST LEGACY

Nowhere are the scars of the 2015 earthquake more obvious than in Kathmandu's Durbar Square, where a succession of landmark temples and palaces were literally shaken apart by the force of the tremor. In time, some of these monuments may be reconstructed, but the grandeur of Durbar Square has undeniably been diminished by the disaster. As you wander around, you may see the plinths that once supported the following temples.

Kasthamandap The building that gave Kathmandu its name, built in the 12th century as a community centre but later converted into a temple to Goraknath.

Maju Deval A handsome, three-tiered step-roofed temple that was formerly one of Kathmandu's principal landmarks, built in 1690 by the mother of Bhaktapur's king Bhupatindra Malla.

Trailokya Mohan Narayan Temple A three-tiered temple to Narayan/Vishnu, formerly famous for its carved timbers; only the carved Garuda statue in front survived the quake.

Kakeshwar Temple Built in 1681, but damaged in the 1934 quake and rebuilt in a hybrid Newari and India shikhara style.

Krishna Temple An elegant octagonal temple in the Newari tiered style, constructed in 1648–49 by Pratap Malla.

Krishna Narayan Temple A three-tiered Narayan (Vishnu) temple to the west of the Shiva-Parvati Temple.

wood) dispenser and then ringing the bells at the back. An offering at this shrine is thought to ensure safety on a forthcoming journey, so come here if you are headed on a trek.

It's uncertain how old the temple is, although its gilded roof was added in the 19th century. Look for the golden shrew (Ganesh's vehicle) opposite the temple.

Maru Tole   STREET
This *tole* (street) leads you away from Durbar Sq down to the Vishnumati River, where a footbridge continues the pathway to Swayambhunath. This was a busy street in the hippie era, but the famous pastry shops that gave it the nickname 'Pie Alley' have long gone. Many buildings were damaged by the earthquake but it's worth strolling down to see Maru Hiti, one of the city's many sunken water conduits.

Shiva-Parvati Temple   HINDU TEMPLE
(Nawa Jogini Temple; Map p73) Looking north from the plinth of the wrecked Maju Deval, a pair of much-photographed white images of Shiva and his consort look out from the upstairs window. The temple was built in the late 1700s by Bahadur Shah, the son of Prithvi Narayan Shah. Although the temple is not very old by Kathmandu standards, it stands on a two-stage platform that may have been an open dancing stage hundreds of years earlier.

Kumari Bahal   COURTYARD
(Map p73) At the junction of Durbar and Basantapur Sqs, this red-brick, three-storey building is home to the Kumari, the girl who is selected to be the town's living goddess until she reaches puberty and reverts to being a normal mortal. The goddess is regarded as a living symbol of *devi* – the Hindu concept of female spiritual energy. Inside the building is Kumari Chowk, a three-storey courtyard. It is enclosed by magnificently carved wooden balconies and windows, making it quite possibly the most beautiful courtyard in Nepal. Amazingly, the bahal escaped with only minor damage despite the devastation all around – a sign perhaps of the Kumari's benign influence.

The Kumari generally shows her face between 9am and 11am. Photographing the goddess is forbidden, but you are quite free to photograph the courtyard when she is not present. The Kumari went on strike in 2005, refusing to appear at her window for tourists, after authorities denied her guardians' request for a 10% cut of Durbar Sq's admission fees!

ℹ️ DURBAR SQUARE TICKETS
The admission ticket to Durbar Sq gives access to all the temples in the square, as well as Hanuman Dhoka and the museums inside it. The ticket is only valid for the date stamped. If you want a longer duration, you need to go to the site office (Map p73; ☏ 01-4268969; www.kathmandu.gov.np; ⊘ 6am-7pm), on the south side of Basantapur Sq, to get a free visitor pass, which allows you access for as long as your visa is valid (if you extend your visa, you can extend your visitor pass). You will need your passport and one photo and the process takes about two minutes. You generally need to show your ticket even if you are just transiting the square to New Rd or Freak St. There is a toilet near the site office.

The building, in the style of the Buddhist *vihara* (monastic abodes) of the valley, was built in 1757 by Jaya Prakash Malla. The courtyard contains a miniature stupa carrying the symbols of Saraswati, the goddess of learning. Non-Hindus are not allowed to go beyond the courtyard.

The large yellow gate to the right of the Kumari Bahal conceals the huge chariot that transports the Kumari around the city during the annual Indra Jatra festival. Look for the huge wooden runners in front of the Kumari Bahal that are used to transport the chariot. The wood is painted at the tips and is considered sacred.

Gaddhi Baithak   PALACE
(Map p73) Dominating the eastern side of Durbar Sq, this white neoclassical building lost parts of its facade during the earthquake and its future is uncertain. For now, it stands as a memorial to the imported European style that became fashionable in Nepal during the Rana period. Built as part of the Hanuman Dhoka palace in 1908, it makes a strange contrast to the traditional Nepali architecture that dominates the square. It is said to have been modelled on London's National Gallery following Prime Minister Jung Bahadur's visit to Europe.

Bhagwati Temple   HINDU TEMPLE
(Map p73) On the northwest corner of the Gaddhi Baithak, this triple-storey, triple-roofed temple is easily missed because it surmounts the building below it. The temple is

Central Kathmandu

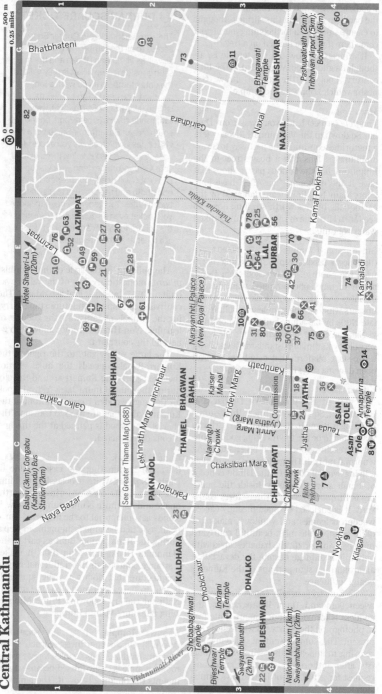

500 m
0.25 miles

A **B** **C** **D** **E** **F** **G**

Bhatbhateni

Balaju (3km); Gongabu
(Kathmandu) Bus
Station (2km)

Naya Bazar

Vishnumati River

National Museum (1km);
Swayambhunath (2km)

Bijeshwari
Temple

Swayambhunath
(2km)

Shobabaghwati
Temple

Indrani
Temple

Dhobichaur

BIJESHWARI

DHALKO

KALDHARA

PAKNAJOL

See Greater Thamel Map (p88)

LAINCHHAUR

THAMEL

Narsingh
Chowk

Chaksibari Marg

Lekhnath Marg Lainchhaur

BHAGWAN
BAHAL

Kaiser
Mahal

Commission

Amrit Marg
(Jyatha Marg)

Tridevi Marg

Kantipath

Narayanhiti Palace
(New Royal Palace)

Tukucha Khola

Galko Pakha

Hotel Shangri-La
(120m)

Lazimpat

LAZIMPAT

Gairidhara

Naxal

NAXAL

GYANESHWAR

Bhagawati
Temple

Pashupatnath (2km);
Tribhuvan Airport (5km);
Bodhnath (6km)

Kamal Pokhari

LAL
DURBAR

Kamaladi

JAMAL

Teuda

Jyatha

JYATHA

ASAN
TOLE

Asan
Tole

Annapurna
Temple

Ikha
Pokhari

CHHETRAPATI

Chhetrapati
Chowk

Nyokha

Kilagal

N

62
69
51
44
57
67
61
10
76
63
52
49
59
21
27
20
28
48
73
11
82
31
80
38
50
37
75
66
41
42
30
70
54
64
43
78
25
56
74
32
14
36
18
24
8
1
9
7
19
23
22
45
60

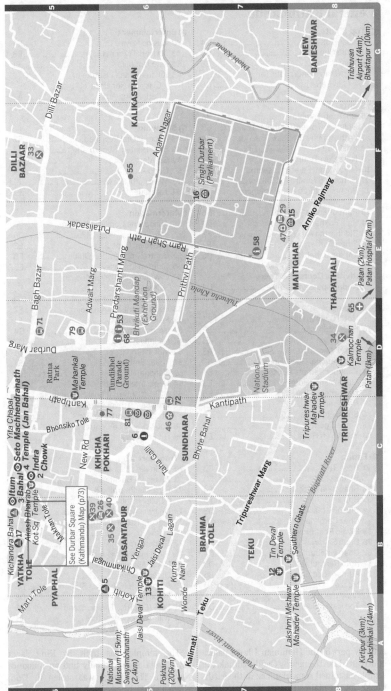

KATHMANDU

KATHMANDU SIGHTS

Central Kathmandu

actually part of the Hanuman Dhoka palace courtyard. Like the nearby Gaddi Baithak, the temple sustained some damage in the earthquake but the main structure is intact.

The temple was built by King Jagat Jaya Malla and originally had an image of Narayan. This image was stolen in 1766; when Prithvi Narayan Shah conquered the valley two years later, he simply substituted it with an image of the goddess Bhagwati. In April each year the image of the goddess is conveyed to the village of Nuwakot, 65km to the north, then returned a few days later.

The building below is lined with shops selling thangkas (Tibetan religious paintings) and their Newari equivalents, called *paubha*.

Great Bell   MONUMENT

(Map p73) On your left as you leave the main square along Makhan Tole is the Great Bell. The bell's ring drives away evil spirits, but it is only rung during puja (worship) at the nearby Degutaleju Temple. Across from the Great Bell is a very ornate corner balcony, decorated in gorgeous copper and ivory, from where members of the royal court could view the festival action taking place in Durbar Sq.

The bell is elevated atop a white building erected by Rana Bahadur Shah (son of Prithvi Narayan Shah) in 1797.

Great Drums & Kot Square   MONUMENT

(Map p73) Once used to warn the city of impending danger, the Great Drums still stand in an earthquake-damaged pavilion to the north of Hanuman Dhoka. Traditionally, a goat and a buffalo must be sacrificed to the drums twice a year. Just behind is the closed-off Kot Sq, where Jung Bahadur Rana perpetrated the famous 1846 massacre that led to a hundred years of Rana rule. Kot means 'armoury' or 'fort'.

During the Dasain festival each year, blood again flows in Kot Sq as hundreds of buffaloes and goats are sacrificed. Young soldiers are supposed to lop off each head with a single blow.

King Pratap Malla's Column   MONUMENT

(Map p73) The northern part of the square is dotted with smaller temples and other structures, all standing on a slightly raised platform in front of the Hanuman Dhoka and the towering Taleju Temple behind. The square stone pillar, known as the Pratap Dhvaja, was previously topped by a famous statue of King Pratap Malla (1641–74), looking towards his private prayer room on the 3rd floor of the Degutaleju Temple, but the statue was topped and crushed in the earthquake. Similar pillars were erected in the Malla era in Patan and Bhaktapur.

This area and its monuments are usually covered in hundreds if not thousands of pigeons; you can buy packets of grain to feed them.

Seto (White) Bhairab   CARVING

(Map p73) Seto (White) Bhairab's horrible face is hidden away behind a grille in an earthquake-damaged pavilion opposite King Pratap Malla's Column. The huge mask dates from 1794, during the reign of Rana Bahadur Shah, the third Shah-dynasty king.

ⓘ ORIENTATION & ADDRESSES IN KATHMANDU

The most interesting part of Kathmandu is the crowded backstreets of the rectangular-shaped old town. This is bordered to the east by the sprawling modern new town and to the north by the main tourist and backpacker district of Thamel (pronounced tha-*mel*). With over 2500 tourist-related companies jammed into half a dozen narrow streets, Thamel boasts a collection of hotels, restaurants, trekking agencies, bakeries and shops that is rivalled only by Bangkok's Khao San Rd. Thamel is 15 to 20 minutes' walk north from Durbar Sq.

East of Thamel is Durbar Marg, a wide street flanked by airline offices, restaurants and expensive hotels. Further north are the embassy and NGO districts of Lazimpat and Maharajganj. To the south of town is Patan, a historically distinct city, which has now partially merged with Kathmandu's southern sprawl. Both Kathmandu and Patan are encircled by the Ring Rd.

In old Kathmandu, streets are only named after their *tole* (district). The names of these districts, squares and other landmarks (perhaps a monastery or temple) form the closest thing to an address. For example, the address for everyone living within a 100m radius of Thahiti Tole is Thahiti Tole. 'Thamel' is now used to describe a sprawling area with at least a dozen roads and several hundred hotels and restaurants.

Given this anarchic approach it is amazing that any mail gets delivered – it does, but slowly. If you're trying to find a particular house, shop or business, make sure you get detailed directions.

Each September during the Indra Jatra festival the gates are opened to reveal the mask for a few days. At other times of the year you can peek through the lattice to see the mask, which is used as the symbol of Nepal Airlines.

During Indra Jatra, Bhairab's face is covered in flowers and rice; at the start of the festivities beer is poured through the horrific mouth as crowds of men fight to get a drink of the blessed brew.

Jagannath Temple
HINDU TEMPLE

(Map p73) This temple, noted for the erotic carvings on its roof struts, is the oldest structure in this part of Durbar Sq. Pratap Malla claimed to have constructed the temple during his reign, but it may actually date back to 1563, during the rule of Mahendra Malla. The temple has a three-tiered platform and two storeys. There are three doors on each side of the temple, but only the centre door opens.

Degutaleju Temple
HINDU TEMPLE

(Map p73) This triple-roofed temple is actually part of the darker, red-brick Hanuman Dhoka, surmounting the buildings below it, but it is most easily seen from outside the palace walls. Despite some earthquake damage, the painted roof struts are particularly fine. Degutaleju is another manifestation of the Malla's personal goddess Taleju.

Kala (Black) Bhairab
HINDU MONUMENT

(Map p73) North of the Jagannath Temple is the figure of Kala (Black) Bhairab. Bhairab is Shiva in his most fearsome aspect, and this huge stone image of the terrifying Kala Bhairab has six arms, wears a garland of skulls and tramples a corpse, which is symbolic of human ignorance. It is said that telling a lie while standing before Kala Bhairab will bring instant death and it was once used as a form of trial by ordeal.

The figure is said to have been brought here by Pratap Malla, having been found in a field to the north of the city. The image was originally cut from a single stone but the upper left-hand corner has since been repaired.

Indrapur Temple
HINDU TEMPLE

(Map p73) Little is known about this mysterious temple. Even the god to which it is dedicated is controversial – the lingam inside indicates that it is a Shiva temple but the Garuda image half-buried on the southern side indicates that it is dedicated

to Vishnu. To compound the puzzle, however, the temple's name clearly indicates it is dedicated to Indra! The temple's unadorned design and plain roof struts, together with the lack of an identifying *torana* (pediment above the temple doors), offer no further clues.

Stone Inscription
CARVING

(Map p73) On the outside of the white palace wall, opposite the Vishnu Temple, is a long, low stone inscription to the goddess Kalika written in 15 languages, including one word of French. King Pratap Malla, renowned for his linguistic abilities, set up this inscription in 1664 and a Nepali legend tells that milk will flow from the spout in the middle if somebody is able to decipher all 15 languages!

Kotilingeshwar Mahadev Temple
HINDU TEMPLE

(Map p73) This distinctive early stone Malla temple dates from the reign of Mahendra Malla in the 16th century. The three-stage plinth is topped by a temple in the *gumbhaj* style, which basically means a square structure topped by a bell-shaped dome. The bull facing the temple on the west side indicates that it is dedicated to Shiva.

Mahendreshwar Temple
HINDU TEMPLE

(Map p73) At the extreme northern end of Durbar Sq, this popular temple dates from 1561, during the reign of Mahendra Malla, and is always bustling with pilgrims. The temple was clumsily restored with marble in 1963 and is dedicated to Shiva. At the northeastern corner there is an image of Kama Deva. The temple has a wide, two-level plinth and a spire topped by a golden umbrella.

Taleju Temple
HINDU TEMPLE

(Map p73) Durbar Sq's most magnificent temple stands at its northeastern extremity but is not open to the public. Even for Hindus admission is restricted; they can only visit it briefly during the annual Dasain festival. The 35m-high temple was built in 1564 by Mahendra Malla. Taleju Bhawani was originally a goddess from the south of India, but she became the titular deity, or royal goddess, of the Malla kings in the 14th century. Perhaps because of the influence of the royal goddess, the temple escaped with only minor damage in the 2015 earthquake.

The temple stands on a 12-stage plinth, dominating the Durbar Sq area. The eighth stage of the plinth forms a wall around the

Durbar Square (Kathmandu)

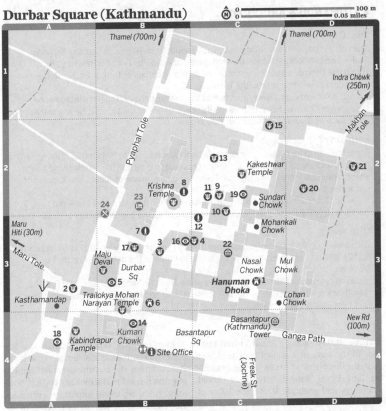

Durbar Square (Kathmandu)

temple, in front of which are 12 miniature temples. Four more miniature temples stand inside the wall, which has four beautifully carved wide gates.

Tana Deval Temple & Makhan Tole HINDU TEMPLE, STREET
(Map p73) Directly north of the Taleju Temple is a 10th-century kneeling

KATHMANDU & AROUND IN...

Two Days

Start off the day with a **walking tour** (p80) south from Thamel to **Durbar Square**. Grab lunch overlooking **Basantapur Square** or in nearby **Freak Street** and then spend the afternoon soaking up the architectural grandeur of Durbar Sq. Finish the day with a cold beer and dinner in the Thamel area.

Next day head out to **Swayambhunath** in the morning and spend the afternoon shopping in **Thamel**. For your final meal splurge at one of the blowout Newari restaurants such as **Bhojan Griha** or **Thamel House**.

Four Days

If you have an extra couple of days, take a short taxi ride out to **Patan** (p137) for a full day exploring its Durbar Sq and Patan Museum (the best in the country) and taking a fascinating backstreet walking tour. Take your dinner in one of Jhamsikhel's excellent restaurants.

On day four take a taxi to **Pashupatinath** and then make the short walk out to **Bodhnath** (p128) to soak up some Tibetan culture as the pilgrims gather at dusk.

One Week

With a week up your sleeve you can spend a day (and preferably a night) at **Bhaktapur** (p152). When stress levels build, fit in some quiet time at the delightful **Garden of Dreams**.

Seven days gives you the chance to gorge on Thai (Yin Yang), Indian (Third Eye), Korean (Hankook Sarang), steak (K-Too), felafel (Or2k) and maybe even some Nepali food! Don't get us started on lunch...

Garuda statue facing a small Vishnu temple. To the east, in a walled courtyard just past the long row of stalls, is the neglected Tana Deval Temple, with three carved doorways and multiple struts, the latter of which show the multi-armed Ashta Matrikas (Mother Goddesses). It's possible to enter the temple. Crowded and fascinating Makhan Tole (*makhan* is the Nepali word for butter, *tole* means street) starts from here.

Makhan Tole runs towards the busy marketplace of Indra Chowk; it was at one time the main street in Kathmandu and the start of the main caravan route to Tibet.

★**Hanuman Dhoka**   PALACE, MUSEUM
(Map p73; admission free with Durbar Sq ticket; ⏱10.30am-4pm Tue-Sat Feb-Oct, to 3pm Tue-Sat Nov-Jan, to 2pm Sun) Kathmandu's royal palace, known as the Hanuman Dhoka, was originally founded during the Licchavi period (4th to 8th centuries AD) but the compound was expanded considerably by King Pratap Malla in the 17th century. Sadly, the sprawling palace was hit hard by the 2015 earthquake and damage was extensive. At the time of research, the palace was closed for reconstruction, but once this work is complete, visitors should again be able to access the beautiful royal courtyards and royal museum.

Even from the outside, the palace is impressive. Hanuman's assistance to the noble Rama during the exciting events of the Ramayana has led to the monkey god's appearance guarding many important entrances. Here, cloaked in red and sheltered by an umbrella, a **Hanuman statue** marks the *dhoka* (entrance) to the Hanuman Dhoka and has even given the palace its name. The statue dates from 1672; the god's face has long disappeared under a coating of orange vermillion paste applied by generations of devotees.

Standards bearing the double-triangle flag of Nepal flank the statue, while on each side of the palace gate are gaudy stone lions, one ridden by Shiva, the other by his wife Parvati. Above the gate a brightly painted niche is illustrated with a central figure of a ferocious Tantric version of Krishna. On the left side is the gentler Hindu Krishna in his traditional blue colour accompanied by two of his comely gopi (milkmaids). On the other side are King Pratap Malla and his queen.

The Hanuman Dhoka originally housed 35 courtyards, but the 1934 earthquake reduced the palace to today's 10 chowks (courtyards).

➡ Nasal Chowk

Assuming that the palace reopens, your first taste of the royal palace will be this handsome courtyard inside the main entrance. Nasal Chowk was constructed in the Malla period, but many of the buildings around the square are later Rana constructions. During the Rana period, Nasal Chowk was used for coronations, a practice that continued until as recently as 2001 with the crowning of King Gyanendra here. The former coronation platform stands in the centre of the courtyard, while the damaged Basantapur (Kathmandu) Tower looms over the southern end of the courtyard.

Beyond the door is the large Narsingha Statue, Vishnu in his man-lion incarnation, in the act of disembowelling a demon. The stone image was erected by Pratap Malla in 1673 and the inscription on the pedestal explains that he placed it here for fear that he had offended Vishnu by dancing in a Narsingha costume. The Kabindrapur Temple in Durbar Sq was built for the same reason.

Next is the Audience Chamber (Sisha Baithak), of the Malla kings. The open verandah houses the Malla throne and contains portraits of the Shah kings.

At the northeastern corner of Nasal Chowk stands the damaged Panch Mukhi Hanuman Temple, with its five circular roofs. Each of the valley towns has a five-storey temple, although it is the great Nyatapola Temple of Bhaktapur that is by far the best known. Hanuman is worshipped in the temple in Kathmandu, but only the priests may enter.

In Nepali, *nasal* means 'dancing one', and Nasal Chowk takes its name from the Dancing Shiva statue hidden in the whitewashed chamber on the northeastern side of the square.

On display along the east side of the courtyard are the palanquins used to carry Queen Aishwarya at her wedding to Birendra in 1970 and later to transport her body to her cremation in 2001. Also displayed here is the royal throne.

➡ Tribhuvan Museum

The palace wing to the west of Nasal Chowk, overlooking the main Durbar Sq area, was constructed by the Ranas in the middle to late part of the 19th century after they wrested power from the royal Shah dynasty. Ironically, it later became a museum celebrating King Tribhuvan (r 1911–55) and his successful revolt against their regime, along with memorials to Kings Mahendra (1955–72) and Birendra (1972–2001). Sadly, this wing of the palace bore the brunt of the damage in the 2015 earthquake. Many exhibits were destroyed and the Department of Archaeology has estimated that reconstruction may take up to five years. It is unclear at this stage whether such unusual treasures as the king's favourite stuffed bird and his Landrover, with the scars of an attempted assassination, survived the disaster.

Rising above the museum is the nine-storey Basantapur (Kathmandu) Tower (1770), which once stood like a beacon at the end of Freak St. Unfortunately, the upper tiers collapsed during the earthquake and the tower is closed to visitors. The struts supporting the tower are notable for their erotic carvings.

➡ Lohan Chowk & Mul Chowk

Assuming the palace reopens, the next square you will discover after the Tribhuvan Museum is Lohan Chowk. This courtyard was formerly ringed by four red-coloured towers constructed by King Prithvi Narayan Shah, representing the four ancient cities of the valley. The upper parts of the Basantapur (Kathmandu) Tower and Bhaktapur Tower (Lakshmi Bilas) collapsed, but the Kirtipur Tower and Patan (Lalitpur) Tower (known more evocatively as the Bilas Mandir, or House of Pleasure) are still standing.

North of Lohan Chowk, Mul Chowk was completely dedicated to religious functions within the palace and is configured like a *vihara*, with a two-storey building surrounding the courtyard. Mul Chowk is dedicated to Taleju Bhawani, the royal goddess of the Mallas, and sacrifices are made to her in the centre of the courtyard during the Dasain festival. Non-Hindus are not allowed in the square, but you can get views from the doorway in the northeastern corner of Nasal Chowk.

➡ Mohankali Chowk & Sundari Chowk

On the northern side of Nasal Chowk, a beautifully carved doorway leads to the Malla kings' private quarters, which rank as the oldest parts of Hanuman Dhoka. This area was also damaged and reconstruction may take some time.

The first courtyard is Mohankali (Mohan) Chowk, which dates from 1649. At one time, a Malla king had to be born here to be eligible to wear the crown. (The last Malla king, Jaya Prakash Malla, had great difficulties during his reign, even though he was the legitimate heir, because he was born elsewhere.) Impressive wood carvings line the wall alcoves, many of them depicting the exploits of young Krishna, and the central hiti (water reservoir) is the palace's finest.

Pride of place in the intimate black and white Sundari Chowk behind is the ritual bathing pool with its Lichhavi-era carving of Krishna subduing the coils of the Kaliya serpent, hewn from a single block of stone in the 6th century. The Malla kings would ritually bathe each morning at the golden waterspout, whose waters allegedly flow from Budhanilkantha in the north of the valley.

North of Durbar Square

Hidden in the fascinating backstreets north of Durbar Sq is a dense sprinkling of colourful temples, courtyards and shrines. The best way to get a feel for this area is on a walking tour (p80).

Kathesimbhu Stupa
BUDDHIST STUPA
(Map p68) The most popular Tibetan pilgrimage site in the old town is this lovely stupa, a small copy dating from around 1650 of the great Swayambhunath complex. The stupa is set in a hidden courtyard that saw only minor damage in the 2015 earthquake. Just as at Swayambhunath, there is a two-storey pagoda to Hariti, the goddess of smallpox, in the northwestern corner of the square. In the northeast corner is the

SETO MACHHENDRANATH FESTIVAL

Kathmandu's Seto (White) Machhendranath festival kicks off a month prior to the larger Rato (Red) Machhendranath festival in Patan. The festival starts with removing the white-faced image of Seto Machhendranath from the temple at Kel Tole and placing it on a towering and creaky wooden temple chariot known as a *rath*. For the next four evenings, the chariot totters slowly from one historic location to another, eventually arriving at Lagan in the south of Kathmandu's old town, where the chariot is hauled three times around the square. The image is taken down from the chariot and carried back to its starting point in a palanquin while the chariot is disassembled and put away until next year.

Drubgon Jangchup Choeling Monastery. It's just a couple of minutes' walk south of Thamel.

★ Asan Tole ✓
SQUARE
(Map p68) From dawn until dusk the junction of Asan Tole is jammed with vegetable and spice vendors selling everything from yak tails to coconuts. It's the busiest square in the city and a fascinating place to linger, if you can stand the crowds. Cat Stevens wrote his hippie-era song 'Katmandu' in a smoky teahouse in Asan Tole.

Every day, produce is carried to this popular marketplace from all over the valley, so it is fitting that the three-storey Annapurna Temple in the southeast corner is dedicated to the goddess of abundance; Annapurna is represented by a *purana* (bowl) full of grain. At most times, but especially Sundays, you'll see locals walk around the shrine, touch a coin to their heads, throw it into the temple and ring the bell above them.

Nearby the two-storey Ganesh shrine is coated in bathroom tiles. The historic Yita Chapal (Southern Pavilion), which was once used for festival dances, was sadly destroyed in the 2015 earthquake.

On the western side of the square are spice shops. Near the centre of the square, between two potted trees, is a small Narayan shrine (Narayan is a form of Vishnu).

Krishna Temple
HINDU TEMPLE
(Map p68) This old building, jammed between gleaming brass shops just southwest of Asan Tole, looks decrepit at first glance. Look closer and you'll notice some fabulously elaborate woodcarvings, depicting beaked monsters and a tiny Tibetan protector, holding a tiger on a chain like he's taking the dog for a walk. Look also for the turn-of-the-century plaques depicting marching troops, on the building to the left, and the ornately carved entryway just below it.

★ Seto Machhendranath Temple (Jan Bahal)
TEMPLE
(Map p68) Southwest of Asan Tole at the junction known as Kel Tole, this temple attracts both Buddhists and Hindus – Buddhists consider Seto (White) Machhendranath to be a form of Avalokiteshvara, while to Hindus he is a rain-bringing incarnation of Shiva. The temple's white-faced god is taken out during the Seto Machhendranath festival in March/April each year and paraded around the city in a chariot.

WALKING KATHMANDU'S OLD TOWN

Kathmandu's backstreets are dense with beautiful temples, shrines and sculptures, especially in the crowded maze of streets and courtyards in the area north of Durbar Sq, and exploring these half-hidden sights is a real highlight.

The old town is bursting with traditional markets, temples, *tole* (streets), bahal (Buddhist monastery courtyards), *bahil* (residential courtyards) and chowk (intersections), which remain the focus of traditional Nepali life. You only really appreciate Kathmandu's museum-like quality when you come across a 1000-year-old statue – something that would be a prized possession in many Western museums – being used as a plaything or a washing line in some communal courtyard.

For the best markets and most important temples explore the backstreets between Thamel and Durbar Sq. For fewer spectacular sights but where the everyday life of city dwellers goes on and tourists are few and far between, follow a walking tour (p84) south of Durbar Sq.

If walking tours leave you wanting more, pick up Annick Holle's book *Kathmandu the Hidden City* or John Child's *Streets of Silver, Streets of Gold,* both of which detail dozens of backstreet courtyards across town.

The temple's age is not known but it was restored during the 17th century.

The arched entrance to the temple is marked by a small Buddha figure on a high stone pillar in front of two metal lions.

In the courtyard there are lots of small shrines, chaitya (small stupas) and statues, including a mysteriously European-looking female figure who is surrounded by candles and faces the temple. It may well have been an import from Europe that has simply been accepted into the pantheon of gods. Facing the other way, just in front of the temple, are two graceful bronze figures of the Taras seated atop pillars. Buy some grain to feed the pigeons and boost your karma.

Inside the temple you can see the white-faced image of the god covered in flowers. You can follow the interior path that circles the central building.

In the courtyard you may see men standing around holding what looks like a bizarre string instrument. This tool is used to separate and fluff up the downlike cotton padding that is sold in bulk nearby. The string is plucked with a twang by a wooden double-headed implement that looks like a cross between a dumb-bell and a rolling pin.

As you leave the temple, to the left you'll see the small, triple-roofed **Lunchun Lunbun Ajima**, a Tantric temple that's red-tiled around the lower level and has some erotic carvings at the base of the struts at the back.

Just to the north of the temple on the side street known as Bhedasingh is a collection of shops selling *topi* (cloth hats) and the Nepali traditional dress known as a *daura suruwal* (a long shirt over tapered drainpipe trousers), including adorable miniature versions for children.

★**Indra Chowk**   SQUARE

(Map p68) The busy street of Makhan Tole spills into Indra Chowk, the courtyard named after the ancient Vedic deity, Indra. Locals crowd around the square's newspaper sellers, scanning the day's news. Indra Chowk is traditionally a centre for the sale of blankets and cloth, and merchants cover the platforms of the **Mahadev Temple** to the north. The next-door stone **Shiva Temple** to the northeast is a smaller and simplified version of Patan's Krishna Temple.

On the west side of the square is the facade of the **Akash Bhairab Temple** (Bhairab of the Sky Temple). From the balcony four metal lions rear out over the street. The temple's entrance is at the right-hand side of the building, guarded by two more brass lions, but non-Hindus cannot enter. The silver image inside is visible through the open windows from out in the street, and during important festivals the image is displayed in the square. In a small niche just to the left of the Akash Bhairab Temple is a very small but much-visited brass Ganesh shrine.

Before you leave the chowk, look for the market hidden in the alleyways to the east, crowded with stalls selling the lurid beads and bangles that are so popular with married Nepali women.

EROTIC ART (OR HOW THEY DID IT IN ANCIENT TIMES)

The most eye-catching decorations on Nepali temples are the erotic scenes, often quite explicit, that decorate the *tunala* (roof struts). These scenes are rarely the central carving on the strut; they're usually the smaller carving at the bottom of the strut, like a footnote to the larger image and in a crude, even cartoon-like style.

The purpose of the images is unclear. Are they simply a celebration of an important part of the life cycle? Are they a more explicit reference to Shiva's and Parvati's creative roles than the enigmatic lingams (phallic symbols) and yonis (female sexual symbols) scattered around so many temples? Or are they supposed to play some sort of protective role for the temple? It's rumoured that the goddess of lightning is a shy virgin who wouldn't dream of striking a temple with such goings-on, although that's probably more a tour-guide tale than anything else.

Whatever the reason for their existence, these Tantric elements can be found on temples throughout the valley. Some temples reveal just the odd sly image, while others are plastered with the 16th-century equivalent of hard-core pornography, ranging from impressively athletic acts of intercourse to medieval *ménages à trois*, scenes of oral or anal intercourse or couplings with demons or animals.

The temples you may want to avoid showing your kids include Kathmandu's Jagannath Temple, Basantapur (Kathmandu) Tower and Ram Chandra Temple; Patan's Jagannarayan Temple; and Bhaktapur's Erotic Elephants and Pashupatinath Temples.

★ **Itum Bahal**   COURTYARD
(Map p68; www.itumbaha.org) The long, rectangular courtyard of the Itum Bahal is the largest bahal (Buddhist monastery courtyard) in the old town and remains a haven of tranquillity in the chaotic surroundings. On the western side of the courtyard is the Kichandra Bahal, one of the oldest bahals in the city, dating from 1381. A chaitya in front of the entrance has been completely shattered by a Bodhi tree, which has grown right up through its centre.

Inside the Kichandra Bahal (also called Keshchandra Paravarta Mahar Bihar) is a central pagoda-like sanctuary, and to the south is a small chaitya decorated with graceful standing bodhisattvas.

On the northern side of the courtyard are four brass plaques mounted on the upper-storey wall. The one on the extreme left shows a demon known as Guru Mapa taking a misbehaving child from a woman and stuffing it greedily into his mouth. Eventually the demon was bought off with the promise of an annual feast of buffalo meat, and the plaque to the right shows him sitting down and dipping into a pot of food. With such a clear message on juvenile misbehaviour, it is fitting that the courtyard for many years housed a primary school – right under the Guru Mapa plaques!

To this day, every year during the festival of Holi the inhabitants of Itum Bahal sacrifice a buffalo to Guru Mapa on the banks of the Vishnumati River, cook it in the afternoon in the courtyard and in the middle of the night carry it in huge cauldrons to a tree in the Tundikhel parade ground where the demon is said to live.

In autumn and winter the main square is decorated in ornate swirling patterns of drying grain.

Nara Devi Temple   HINDU TEMPLE
(Map p68) Halfway between Chhetrapati and Durbar Sq, the Nara Devi Temple is dedicated to Kali, Shiva's destructive consort. It's also known as the Seto (White) Kali Temple. It is said that Kali's powers protected the temple from the 1934 earthquake, which destroyed so many other temples in the valley. A Malla king once stipulated that a dancing ceremony should be held for the goddess every 12 years, and dances are still performed on the small dance platform that is across the road from the temple.

Yatkha Bahal   BUDDHIST TEMPLE
(Map p68) Hidden off the main road just north of Durbar Sq is this large open courtyard set around a central stupa that resembles a mini-Swayambhunath. Directly behind it is an old building, the Yatkha Bahal, whose upper storey is supported by four superb carved-wood struts. Dating from the 12th to 13th century, they are carved in the form of *yaksha* (attendant deities or nymphs), one of them gracefully balancing a baby on her hip.

East of Thamel

★ **Garden of Dreams**   GARDENS
(Swapna Bagaicha; Map p88; ☑01-4425340;
www.gardenofdreams.org.np;   adult/child   Rs
200/100; ⊙9am-10pm, last entry 9pm) Despite
some damage from the 2015 earthquake,
the beautifully restored Swapna Bagaicha
remains one of the most serene and beautiful enclaves in Kathmandu. It's two minutes'
walk and one million miles from central
Thamel.

Field marshal Kaiser Shamser (1892–
1964), whose palace the gardens comple-
ment, built the Garden of Dreams in the
1920s after a visit to several Edwardian
estates in England, using funds won from
his father (the prime minister) in an epic
Rs 100,000 game of cowrie shells. The gardens and its pavilions suffered neglect to the
point of collapse before they were lovingly
brought back to life over a six-year period by
the same Austrian-financed team that created the Patan Museum.

There are dozens of gorgeous details in
the small garden, including the original gate,
a marble inscription from Omar Khayam's
Rubaiyat, the new fountains and ponds,
and a quirky 'hidden garden' to the south.
Of the original 1.6 hectares and six pavilions
(named after the six Nepali seasons), only
half a hectare and three pavilions remain. To
truly savour the serenity, come armed with a
book or picnic to distract you from the amo-
rous Nepali couples and relax on one of the
supplied lawn mats. Wi-fi is available (Rs 50
per hour). Dwarika's hotel operates the serene Kaiser Cafe (p106) here, and there are
occasional cultural events and exhibitions.

Three Goddesses Temples   TEMPLE
(Map p88) Next to the modern Sanchaya
Kosh Bhawan Shopping Centre in Thamel
are the often ignored Three Goddesses Temples. The street on which the temples are
located is Tridevi Marg – *tri* means 'three'
and *devi* means 'goddesses'. The goddesses
are Dakshinkali, Manakamana and Jawala-
mai, and the roof struts have some creative
erotic carvings.

Narayanhiti Palace Museum   MUSEUM
(Map p68; ☑01-4227844; foreigner/SAARC
Rs 500/250; ⊙11am-4pm Thu-Mon, closes 3pm
Nov-Jan) Few things speak clearer to the political changes that have transformed Nepal
over the last decade than this walled palace
at the northern end of Durbar Marg. King

KATHMANDU'S CITY MUSEUM

When it opened in 2014, Kathmandu's
City Museum (☑9808563570; www.
thecitymuseum.org) was a breath of
fresh air for art enthusiasts. The sleek
modern gallery provided a much-needed space for contemporary art, which
had struggled to find its place in a city
preoccupied with historic artworks and
traditional crafts. Since the 2015 earthquake, museum staff have continued to
advocate for local artists, even supporting a local painter who was blamed for
triggering the earthquake by creating a
'disrespectful' image of the Kumari! At
the time of research, the museum was
closed while organisers looked for a new
location, following earthquake damage
to the original site – check its website
for more information.

Gyanendra was given 15 days to vacate the
property in 2007 and within two years the
building was reopened as a people's museum by then prime minister Prachandra, the
very Maoist guerrilla leader who had been
largely responsible for the king's spectacular
fall from grace.

Full of chintzy meeting rooms and faded
1970s glamour, the palace interior is more
gaudy than opulent. The highlights are
the impressive throne and banquet halls
and the modest royal bedrooms (check out
the great armchair with built-in speakers).
Stuffed gharial, tigers and rhino heads line
the halls next to towering portraits of earlier
Shahs and photos of the royal family taken
with other doomed leaders – Yugoslavia's
Tito, Romania's Ceaușescu and Pakistan's
Zia ul-Haq.

The locations where Prince Dipendra
massacred his family in 2001 are rather
morbidly marked, though the actual building was rather suspiciously levelled after the
crime. Bullet holes are still visible on some of
the walls. Just as interesting are the building
are the locals' reactions to it, as they peek at
a regal lifestyle that for centuries they could
only have dreamed about. Cameras and bags
are not allowed inside the complex.

Rani Pokhari   POND
(Map p68) This large fenced tank just off
Kantipath is said to have been built by King
Pratap Malla in 1667 to console his queen

over the death of their son (who was trampled by an elephant). The pool (*pokhari* means pool or small lake) was apparently used during the Malla era for trials by ordeal and later became a favourite suicide spot. During the earthquake, which damaged the flanking pavilions, the area around tank became a refuge for people sleeping outside because of fears of further building collapses.

The tank and its central Shiva Temple is unlocked only once a year, on the fifth day of the Tihar festival. At other times you can get the best views from the footbridge over the nearby chowk (the chowk has rather optimistically been declared a no-horn zone!).

Siddhartha Art Gallery
GALLERY
(Map p68; ☏01-4218048; www.siddharthaart-gallery.com; Baber Mahal Revisited; ⏱11am-5pm Sun-Fri, noon-5pm Sat) FREE This is the city's best gallery for contemporary Nepali art, with a wide range of top-notch exhibitions, and worth a visit if you're shopping at Baber Mahal Revisited.

National Birendra Art Gallery
GALLERY
(Map p68; ☏01-4411729; admission Rs 75; ⏱9am-5pm Sun-Fri) The offbeat location of this gallery in a crumbling old Rana palace at the Nepal Academy of Fine Arts is probably more interesting than the dusty collection of Nepali oils and watercolours. The building was undergoing much-needed restoration in 2015.

⊙ South of Durbar Square
The southern part of Kathmandu's old city was the heart of the ancient city in the Licchavi period (4th to 8th centuries). Unfortunately, more monuments were lost here in the 2015 earthquake, including the historic Jaisi Deval Temple, a triple-tiered Shiva temple that played an important part in the city's ceremonial life. Further south, the **Bhimsen Tower** (Dharahara; Map p68) became the unfortunate symbol of the earthquake in the international media when it collapsed to its foundations, showering rubble onto crowded shopping streets and killing 180 people, many of whom were sightseers who had climbed the tower to admire the views. Today, just the base remains as an unofficial memorial to the disaster.

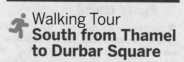

🏃 Walking Tour
South from Thamel to Durbar Square

START THAHITI TOLE
END DURBAR SQ
LENGTH 2KM; TWO HOURS

This walk is best made en route from Thamel to Durbar Sq, or vice versa. To get to Thahiti Tole, walk south from Thamel on the road from the main Thamel Chowk; the first square you come to is Thahiti.

Thahiti Tole wraps around a 15th-century ➊ **stupa**. The ➋ **Nateshwar Temple**, on the northern side of the square, is dedicated to a form of Shiva that doubles as the local Newari god of music; the brass doorway depicts creatures busily playing a variety of musical instruments, as well as a yeti in the top right plaque.

Take the road heading south past shops selling prayer flags, khata (ritual scarves) and Buddhist brocade, then bear west to the impressive ➌ **Kathesimbhu Stupa** (p76), radiating colourful prayer flags.

About 30m down on the left, past a Ganesh statue, is a small recessed area and a dark grilled doorway marking a small but intricate central ➍ **stone relief** dating from the 9th century. It shows Shiva sitting with Parvati on Mt Kailash, her hand resting proprietarily on his knee in the pose known as Uma Maheshwar. To the right of the door is an almost unrecognisable orange-coloured Ganesh head. Incidentally, the impressive wooden balcony across the road is said to have had the first glass windows in Kathmandu (it looks like it's the same glass!).

Continue south past a string of dentists' shops (the reason will soon become clear), advertised by signs showing a grinning mouthful of teeth, until you get to ➎ **Bangemudha Square**. Don't miss the wooden shrine to the ➏ **toothache god** (shaken but not destroyed by the earthquake) that gives the square its name.

Head 50m east to the triple-roofed ➐ **Ugratara Temple** by a small square known as Nhhakantalla; a prayer at the half-sunken shrine is said to work wonders for the eyes. Just further on your right you will pass the Krishna Music Emporium (maker and repairer of harmoniums),

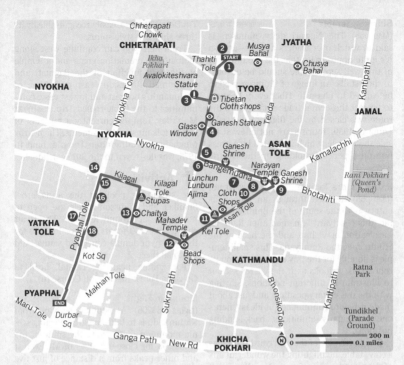

before spotting a gated entrance on the right that leads into **⑧ Haku Bahal**. Look for the sign that advertises 'Opera Eye Wear'. Despite earthquake damage, this tiny bahal has some fine carvings, including an ornate wooden window overlooking the courtyard, which doubles as motorbike parking.

You'll soon come to the bustling chowk of **⑨ Asan Tole** (p76), old Kathmandu's busiest junction and an utterly fascinating place to linger. The diagonal southwest-to-northeast main road was for centuries the start of the caravan route to Tibet.

The street continues southwest past the ornate and octagonal **⑩ Krishna Temple** (p76), which survived the quake, into Kel Tole, where you'll find one of the most important and ornate temples in Kathmandu, the **⑪ Seto Machhendranath Temple** (p76)

The busy shopping street spills into **⑫ Indra Chowk** (p77), with its stepped Mahadev Temple and Akash Bhairab Temple.

Take the quiet alleyway west from Indra Chowk, past *bindi* (forehead decoration) shops and bangle stalls, and after 200m or so, by a small square, look for a tiny entryway to the right, by a triple shrine and under the sign for 'Jenisha Beauty Parlour'. The

entryway leads into the long, rectangular courtyard of **⑬ Itum Bahal** (p78), one of the oldest and largest bahals in the city, with some lovely architecture and stupas.

Exit the courtyard at the north end and turn left (west). On your right at the next junction is the **⑭ Nara Devi Temple** (p78). On the south side of the **⑮ dance platform** is a small shop occupied by one of Kathmandu's many marching bands, mainly used for weddings – look for gleaming tubas, red uniforms and tuneless trumpeting.

At the Nara Devi corner, turn left (south); after 30m or so you come to a corner photocopy-magazine shop on your left with a magnificent **⑯ wooden window** above it. It has been called *deshay madu* in Nepali, which means 'there is not another one like it'.

Further south, on the right is the entrance to the **⑰ Yatkha Bahal** (p78), one of the old town's many Buddhist squares.

Back on the road you'll see the deep red-brick **⑱ temple** to Newari mother goddess, Chaumanda, which features a six-pointed star in the upper window frame. Head south again, past the drum and marching-band shops on the right, to Durbar Sq, your final destination for this walk.

Bhimsen Temple
BUDDHIST TEMPLE

(Map p68) The Newari deity Bhimsen is said to watch over traders and artisans, so it's quite appropriate that the ground floor of this well-kept temple should be devoted to shop stalls. An image of Bhimsen used to be carried to Lhasa in Tibet every 12 years to protect those vital trade routes, until the route was closed by the flight of the Dalai Lama in 1959. Tourists are not allowed inside the temple, which is fronted by a brass lion on a pedestal holding up the electric wires.

Ram Chandra Temple
HINDU TEMPLE

(Map p68) Reached through an innocuous entryway to the south of the Bhimsen Temple, this courtyard is named after Ram, an incarnation of Vishnu and the hero of the Hindu epic, the Ramayana. This small temple is notable for the tiny erotic scenes on its roof struts; it looks as if the carver set out to illustrate 16 different positions, starting with the missionary position, and just about made it before running out of ideas (there's one particularly ambitious, back-bending position).

The north side of the courtyard is used as a cow stable, highlighting the wonderful mix of the sacred and profane in Nepal!

Pachali Bhairab & the Southern Ghats
HINDU TEMPLE

(Map p68) The northern banks of the Bagmati River south of the old town are home to several little-visited temples and shrines, as well as the worst urban poverty in Kathmandu; rarely do such splendour and squalor sit so close. The banks are worth a stroll, especially as an extension of a walking tour (p84). There are plans to redevelop the ghats with new pedestrian walkways.

Between Tripureshwar Marg and the Bagmati River at Pachali Bhairab a huge, ancient pipal tree forms a natural sanctuary for an image of Bhairab Pachali, surrounded by tridents (Pachali is a form of Shiva). To the side lies the brass body of Baital, one of Shiva's manifestations. Worshippers gather here on Tuesday and Saturday. It is particularly busy here during the festival of Pachali Bhairab Jatra, held during the time of Dasain.

From the temple head south towards the ghats (riverside steps) on the holy riverbank. To the right is the Newari-style pagoda of the Lakshmi Mishwar Mahadev; to the left (southeast) is the damaged but striking Tin Deval Temple, easily recognisable by its three shikhara-style spires.

From here you can continue west along footpaths to cremation ghats and a temple at the holy junction of the Bagmati and Vishnumati Rivers; or east past some of Kathmandu's poorest and lowest-caste communities to the triple-roofed Tripureshwar Mahadev Temple, currently a museum of Nepali folk musical instruments. The nearby Mughal-style Kalmochan Temple, built in 1873, was destroyed in the 2015 earthquake.

🏃 Activities

The swimming pools at the Annapurna, Shanker and Radisson hotels are open to nonguests for around Rs 1000. The Hyatt charges Rs 1250 for its pool, or Rs 1700 for its pool, gym, tennis court and sauna. Add tax to all these.

For golfing near the capital, head to Gokarna Forest Resort Golf Course (p171).

Mountain Flight
SCENIC FLIGHTS

(flights US$206) A popular activity from Kathmandu is to take an early morning scenic mountain flight along the spine of the Himalaya for close-up views of Mt Everest and other peaks from a distance of just five nautical miles. Major airlines like Buddha Air and Yeti Airlines offer the hour-long flights and each passenger on the six- to 30-seat turbo props is guaranteed a window seat.

The quality of the views depends on weather conditions. If the flight is cancelled due to bad weather, airlines offer a full refund or a seat on a later flight. In 2011 a Buddha Air mountain flight crashed outside Kathmandu, killing 19 people.

Seeing Hands
MASSAGE

(Map p88; 01-4253513; www.seeinghands-nepal.org; massage 60/90min Rs 1800/2800; ⊙10am-6pm) A branch of the Pokhara-based organisation that offers massage from blind masseurs, providing employment to some of Nepal's 600,000 blind people. Choose between a relaxing post-trek Swedish massage or remedial sports therapy for specific issues.

Himalayan Healers
MASSAGE

(Map p88; 01-4437183; www.himalayanheal-ers.org; Tilicho Bldg, Tridevi Marg; ⊙9am-8pm summer, 10am-7pm winter) This impressive operation trains 'untouchables', war widows and victims of human trafficking or domes-

KATHMANDU'S ROYAL PALACES

Kathmandu is littered with hidden Rana-era palaces, some still in use, others crumbling in neglect. The most impressive is the royal palace of the **Singh Durbar** (Singha Durbar; Map p68) at the end of Prithvi Path, built in 1907 and now home to Nepal's government. With over 1700 rooms, it was once the largest private residence in Asia, until fire destroyed 90% of the complex in 1973. The compound was further damaged in the 2015 earthquake and it is not open to visitors.

Near Tridevi Marg, the **Keshar (Kaiser) Mahal Palace** (Map p88), built in 1895, still retains some atmosphere thanks to its creaky Kaiser Library, though its western wing was long ago sold off and developed as part of Thamel. The palace grounds were restored as the **Garden of Dreams** (p79). Another notable former palace is the **Electoral Commission Building** (Map p88), visible from Kantipath. At one point the building housed Kathmandu's first hotel, the Royal, established by Boris Lissanevitch (p96). Other notable palace conversions include the restaurant **Bhojan Griha** (p101) and the shopping arcade of **Baber Mahal Revisited** (p111).

Kathmandu's most impressive palace is the huge **Narayanhiti Palace** (p79), home to the royal family until 2008 and currently a museum.

tic violence in 500 hours of massage therapy and then organises a placement.

Treatments are a flat rate of Rs 2200/2750 for 60/90 minutes of massage (Swedish, Nepali), reflexology, body wraps or scrubs. Hot stone treatments and *shirodhara* (a treatment involving a stream of warm oil on your forehead) are pricier. You can get a discount of up to 30% for morning treatments.

Pranamaya Yoga　　　　　　　　　YOGA
(Map p88; ☑ 9802045484; www.pranamaya -yoga.com; Tridevi Marg) Faced with one too many hairy male yoga teachers displaying contortive poses in their underpants, the owners of this centre decided to set up a modern, comfortable environment for drop-in practitioners. Classes take place in the studio on Tridevi Marg above Himalayan Java, as well as in Patan and Bodhnath. See the website for a schedule. They also run a three-day retreat at Pharping in the southern Kathmandu Valley.

**Himalayan Buddhist
Meditation Centre**　　　　　MEDITATION
(Map p88; ☑ 9849909986; hbmc.programs@ gmail.com) The Thamel branch of this Buddhist organisation offers free hour-long introductory meditation classes at 6pm on Monday, Wednesday and Friday. If that whets your appetite, try the half-day program on Saturdays (Rs 600). It's on the top floor of the Hotel Himalaya Yoga, down a side alley from Thamel's central chowk.

Astrek Climbing Wall　　　CLIMBING WALL
(Map p88; ☑ 01-4419265; www.astrekclimbing-wall.com; 8am-4pm Sun-Fri Rs 200, 4-8pm & all day Sat Rs 400) If you need to polish your climbing skills before heading to the big peaks or if you just want to learn some free-climbing techniques, you can do so at Nepal's tallest artificial climbing wall, here in the compound of the Asian Trekking office. Add Rs 250 for shoes (limited sizes) and a harness. There's a pleasant cafe here.

Hash House Harriers　　　　　　RUNNING
(www.aponarch.com/hhhh) The Nepal branch of these 'drinkers with a running problem' meets for a run every Saturday afternoon. Check the website for details.

Adventure Sports

A number of adventure operators offer mountain biking, rafting and kayaking trips from Kathmandu.

Alternative Nepal　　　CYCLING, KAYAKING
(Map p88; ☑ 01-4700170; www.alternativenepal. com) Mountain-bike hire in Thamel with guided day/overnight trips throughout the country, plus kayak clinics and rafting.

Borderlands　　　　　ADVENTURE SPORTS
(Map p88; ☑ 01-4701295; www.borderlandre-sorts.com; by Northfield Cafe, Thamel) Rafting, canyoning and trekking based at the resort (p192) near the Tibetan border, together with Ultimate Descents Nepal. Call ahead to check the status of rooms and activities following the earthquake.

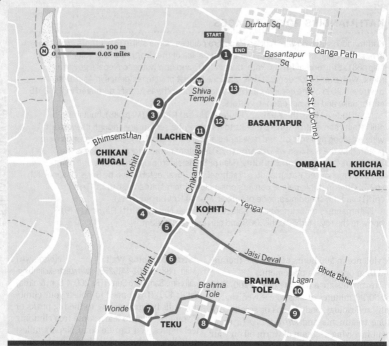

🏃 Walking Tour
South from Durbar Square

START DURBAR SQ
END DURBAR SQ
LENGTH 2KM; ONE HOUR

Starting from the damaged southwestern corner of Durbar Sq, fork right at the ❶ **Singh Sattal**, and follow the road for 50m past a stone Shiva temple with a finely carved pilgrim shelter. Soon you come to a large sunken ❷ **hiti** (water tank), beside the highly decorated ❸ **Bhimsen Temple** (p137).

Continue south beyond the Bhimsen Temple, then continue straight (ie left) at the junction, instantly losing the traffic. Swing left and pass the deep and ornate ❹ **Kohiti water tank**. Earthquake damage was extensive in this area. At the top of the hill you'll come out by the ruined base of the 17th-century Jaisi Deval Temple, destroyed in the 2014 earthquake; just southwest is the damaged ❺ **Ram Chandra Temple** (p82).

Heading southwest you pass through the small and lived-in courtyard of ❻ **Tukan Bahal**. Despite some earthquake damage, the Swayambhunath-style 14th-century stupa in the centre is still rather impressive.

The road continues with a few bends, then turns sharply left (east) at Wonde junction, which is marked by temples, including a tall, white ❼ **shikhara temple**.

Our walk continues past Brahma Tole to the ❽ **Musum Bahal**, with its phallic-shaped Licchavi-style chaityas, an enclosed well and surrounding interconnecting bahals. Take a right back at the main road and then a sharp left (north) at the next main junction. After 25m look out for ❾ **Ta Bahal**, with its garishly repainted chaityas, hidden down an alley on the right.

The road turns into an open square, known as Lagan, featuring the white, 5m-high ❿ **Machhendranath Temple**, as well as the occasional neighbourhood cricket match.

Continue straight out of Lagan, swinging left back to the ruins of Jaisi Deval Temple, then turn right (northeast) back towards Durbar Sq. Pass the slender, red-brick ⓫ **Hari Shankar Temple** (1637) and continue north past a ⓬ **Vishnu (Narayan) Temple** to a second, larger Vishnu temple, the ⓭ **Adko Narayan Temple**, one of the four most important Vishnu temples in Kathmandu.

Chhango
CANYONING

(Map p88; ☑01-4701251; www.canyoninginne-pal.com; Thamel) Canyoning day trips to Sundarijal for US$110, including transportation and equipment.

Hardcore Nepal
ROCK CLIMBING

(Map p88; ☑9803010011, 9813901983; www.hardcorenepal.com; Chaksibari Marg, Thamel) Hardcore Nepal offers a four-day climbing clinic (US$250), which teaches you the basics about knots, anchors and safety to give you the confidence to climb solo. The course is based in Nagarjun Hill, before moving onto more technical climbs in Hattiban and Bimalnagar.

Himalayan Encounters
RAFTING

(Map p88; ☑01-4700426; www.himalayanen-counters.com; Kathmandu Guest House courtyard, Thamel) This company has a solid reputation. Its overnight Trisuli trips stay at the Trisuli Center camp, near Big Fig beach, while its Seti trips hike in from Bandipur. It also arranges treks.

The Last Resort
ADVENTURE SPORTS

(Map p88; ☑01-4700525; www.thelastresort.com.np; Mandala St, Thamel) Rafting, canyoning, bungee jumping and accommodation near Borderlands, together with Ultimate Rivers. Call ahead to check the status of activities following the earthquake.

Nepal Mountain Bike Tours
CYCLING

(Map p88; ☑01-4701701; www.nepalmountain-biketours.com) Mountain bike hire from Rs 500 to Rs 1500 per day, including helmet, lock and repair kits. Also runs day trips and multiday bike tours around the valley. It's in the same compound as Equator Expeditions. Contact Ranjan Rajbhandari.

☙ Courses

Nepal is a particularly popular place for people to take up spiritual pursuits. Check the noticeboards in Thamel for up-to-date information about yoga and Buddhism courses and shop around before you commit yourself.

Backstreet Academy
COURSE

(☑9818421646; www.backstreetacademy.com; half day Rs 1200-1500) This organisation uses English-speaking facilitators to link travellers with local craftspeople, many of whom are from disadvantaged backgrounds. Crash courses include mask carving, pottery making, stone carving, silk weaving, sari wearing and momo making. Facilitators meet you at your hotel.

Himalayan International Yoga Academy
YOGA

(HiYA; ☑01-2021259; www.yogainnepal.com; 2-day tent s/d US$50/90, bungalow US$65/110, house US$85/150) In a peaceful location between Swayambhunath and Nagarjun hill, HiYA offers residential yoga and meditation courses to help you decompress. Rates include tent or bungalow accommodation, vegetarian meals, a morning yoga and evening guided meditation lesson and one massage or alternative medicine treatment.

Nepal Vipassana Centre
MEDITATION

(Map p68; ☑01-4250581; www.dhamma.org.np; Jyoti Bhawan Bldg, Kantipath; ⊙10am-6pm Sun-Fri) This office is the place to sign up for the 10-day retreats held twice a month (starting on the 1st and 14th of the month) at the centre just north of Budhanilkantha outside Kathmandu. There are also occasional shorter courses for intermediate students. These are serious meditation courses that involve rising at 4am every morning, not talking or making eye contact with anyone over 10 days, and not eating after midday. The fee is donation only.

Kathmandu Inside Out
COURSE

(www.kathmanduinsideout.com) Budding bloggers, photojournalists and citizen journalists might be interested in this annual eight-day photography course, which focuses on storytelling through photos. The course fee of US$1500 includes the course, B&B accommodation and funding for two aspiring Nepali journalists. The course takes place in December.

Gandharba Culture & Art Organisation
COURSE

(Map p88; ☑01-4700292; Thamel) This organisation represents the city's musician caste and members offer lessons in the *sarangi* (four-stringed instrument played with a bow), *madal* and *jambey* (drums), *bansari* (flute) and *arbaj* (four-string guitar). Expect to pay around Rs 500 per hour. The office is located in central Thamel (on the 3rd floor) and musicians play nightly in the nearby Northfield Cafe.

☞ Tours

Social Tours
COOKING COURSE

(Map p88; ☑01-4412508; www.socialtours.com) This innovative company runs a half-day Nepali cookery course that involves a trip to a local market to get ingredients for momos, spinach curry, *alu gobi* (potato and cauliflower), tomato pickle and *alu paratha* (fried *chapati* with potato). Pay what you think the experience is worth and then eat your homework.

The company also runs a pottery tour to Bhaktapur to learn how to throw pots (pick up your pot a week later), in addition to mountain bike trips, a Newari culture and snack tour in Kirtipur, a local market walk to Asan Tole and a 'lunch with nuns' hike to Nagi Gompa in Shivapuri Nagarjun National Park.

Hidden Journeys TOUR
(☑ 9818039645; www.hiddenjourneysnepal.com) If you are looking for a different perspective on Nepal, this innovative company specialises in connecting visitors to Nepal's new generation of social entrepreneurs, artists and activists aiming to bring change to their country. To book, contact the company well in advance.

★ Festivals & Events

Kathmandu has many religious festivals, of which the most outrageous is probably Indra Jatra in September, closely followed by the Seto Machhendranath chariot festival in March/April, Dasain in October, and the Pachali Bhairab Jatra, also in October.

Kathmandu
International Marathon SPORTS
(www.kathmandumarathon.com) This annual road race attracts over 6000 runners in September/October, with courses ranging from 5km to 42km. Registration costs US$40 for foreigners. Amazingly, the police hold back Kathmandu's revving traffic for a full five hours to let the race take place.

Jazzmandu Festival MUSIC
(www.jazzmandu.org; tickets around Rs 900) This annual music event is a week-long program of local and international jazz, fusion and world music acts that is staged in venues across town in late October/early November. See the website for details.

KUMARI DEVI

Not only does Nepal have hundreds of gods, goddesses, deities, bodhisattvas, Buddhas, avatars (incarnations of deities) and manifestations – which are worshipped and revered as statues, images, paintings and symbols – it also has a real, living goddess. The Kumari Devi is a young girl who lives in the building known as the Kumari Bahal, right beside Kathmandu's Durbar Sq.

The practice of having a living goddess probably came about during the reign of the last of the Malla kings of Kathmandu, and although there are actually a number of living goddesses around the Kathmandu Valley, the Kumari Devi of Kathmandu is the most important. The Kumari is selected from a particular caste of Newari gold- and silversmiths. Customarily, she is somewhere between four years old and puberty, and must meet 32 strict physical requirements ranging from the colour of her eyes and shape of her teeth to the sound of her voice. Her horoscope must also be appropriate, of course.

Once suitable candidates have been found they are gathered together in a darkened room where terrifying noises are made, while men dance by in horrific masks and 108 gruesome buffalo heads are on display. These goings-on are presumed unlikely to frighten an incarnation of Durga, so the young girl who remains calm and collected throughout this ordeal is clearly the new Kumari. In a process similar to the selection of the Dalai Lama, as a final test the Kumari then chooses items of clothing and decoration worn by her predecessor.

Once chosen as the Kumari Devi, the young girl moves into the Kumari Bahal with her family and makes only a half-dozen ceremonial forays into the outside world each year, mainly during the September Indra Jatra festival, when she travels through the city on a huge temple chariot.

The Kumari's reign ends with her first period, or any serious accidental loss of blood. Once this first sign of puberty is reached she reverts to the status of a normal mortal, and the search must start for a new Kumari. On retirement the old Kumari is paid a handsome dowry but readjusting to normal life can be hard. It is said that marrying an ex-Kumari is unlucky, perhaps because taking on a spoilt ex-goddess is likely to be too much hard work!

KATHMANDU'S INDRA JATRA FESTIVAL

Indra, the ancient Aryan god of rain, was once captured in the Kathmandu Valley while stealing a flower for his mother, Dagini. He was imprisoned until Dagini revealed his identity and his captors gladly released him. The festival celebrates this remarkable achievement (villagers don't capture a real god every day of the week). In return for his release Dagini promised to spread dew over the crops for the coming months and to take back with her to heaven all those who had died in the past year.

The Indra Jatra festival thus honours the recently deceased and pays homage to Indra and Dagini for the coming harvests. It begins when a huge wooden pole, carried via the Tundikhel, is erected outside the Hanuman Dhoka. At the same time images and representations of Indra, usually as a captive, are displayed and sacrifices of goats and roosters are made; the screened doors obscuring the horrific face of Seto (White) Bhairab are also opened and for the next three days his gruesome visage will stare out at the proceedings.

The day before all this activity, three golden temple chariots are assembled in Basantapur Sq, outside the home of the Kumari living goddess. In the afternoon the Kumari appears to a packed crowd, either walking on a rolled-out carpet or carried by attendants so that her feet do not touch the ground. The Kumari mounts the central chariot, flanked by two boys also in chariots, playing the roles of Ganesh and Bhairab.

The chariots move off and the Kumari is greeted from the balcony of the old palace by the president, before continuing to the huge Seto (White) Bhairab mask. The Kumari greets the image of Bhairab and then, with loud musical accompaniment, beer starts to pour from Bhairab's mouth! Getting a sip of this beer is guaranteed to bring good fortune, but one lucky individual will also get the small fish that has been put to swim in the beer – this brings especially good luck (though probably not for the fish).

Numerous other processions also take place around the town until the final day, when the great pole is lowered and carried down to the river. A similar pole is erected in Bhaktapur as part of the Bisket Jatra festival, celebrating the Nepali New Year.

Kathmandu International Art Festival ART (www.artmandu.org) Every three years (most recently in 2015) artists from three dozen countries exhibit works at venues across the city. It's normally held during November/December.

Kathmandu International Film Festival FILM (www.kimff.org) An interesting weeklong festival of international and Nepali documentary and short films, held in December.

🛏 Sleeping

Kathmandu has a huge range of places to stay, from luxurious international-style hotels to cheap and cheerful lodges, and only a few hotels and guesthouses were severely affected by the 2015 earthquake, though many places closed briefly for safety checks following the disaster. The hotels listed in this chapter were open for business at the time of research, but repairs may be ongoing, so ask to see the room before you commit to staying.

It's difficult to recommend budget and midrange hotels, as rooms in each hotel can vary widely. Many of these hotels have multiple wings and, while some rooms may be very gloomy and run-down, others (generally the upper floors) might be bright and pleasant. In general, roadside rooms are brighter but noisier than interior rooms, and top-floor rooms are the best because you stand a chance of getting a view and have easy access to the roof garden.

Budget places generally don't have heating so in winter you'll want the warmer south-facing rooms and garden access, as it's always pleasant to sit outside during the cool, but sunny, autumn and winter days.

Quite a few hotels bridge the budget and midrange categories by having a range of room standards – these places have been grouped according to their lowest price.

It's always worth asking for a discount, particularly during low season when most places offer discounts of between 20% and 40%. At the time of writing, many hotels were discounting their prices even in high season to tempt tourists back after the 2015

KATHMANDU

Greater Thamel

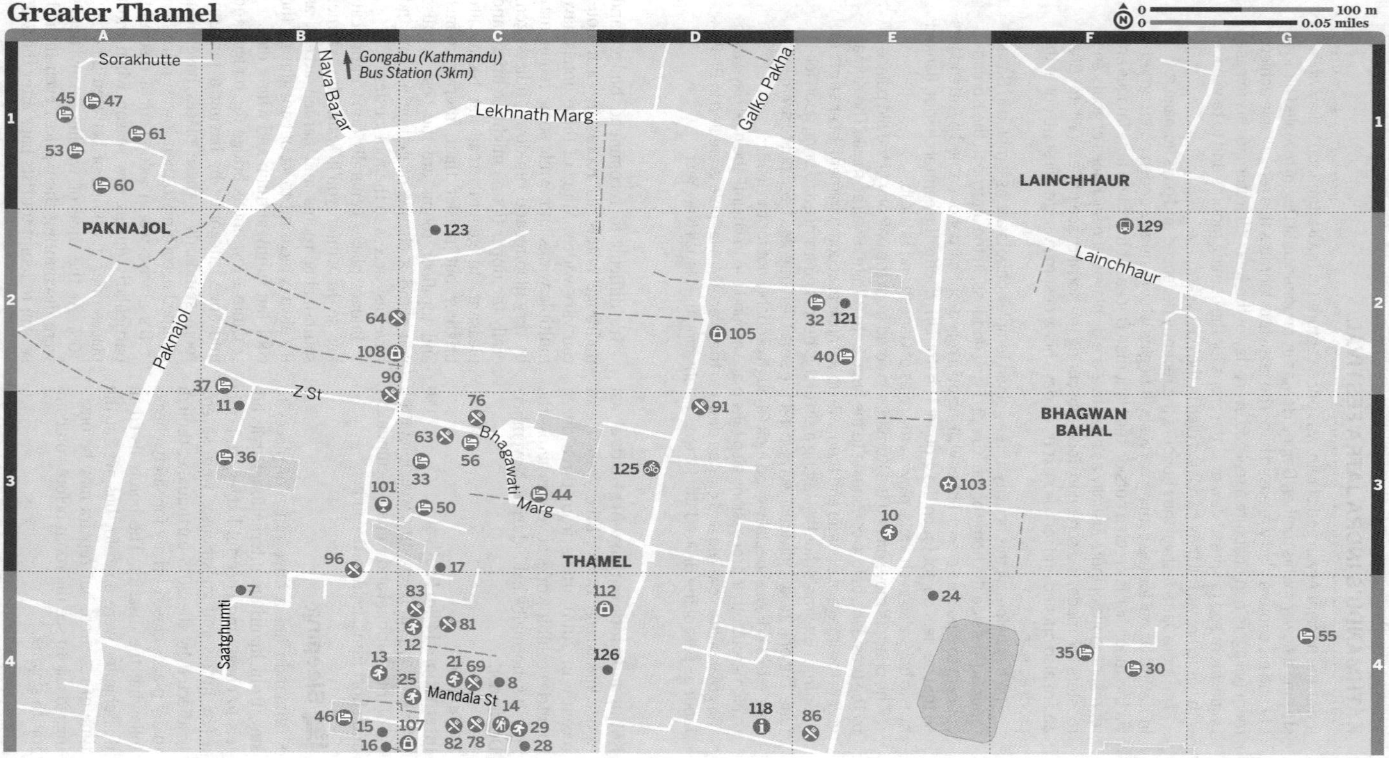

Sorakhutte

45
47
61
53
60

PAKNAJOL

37
11
36

Paknajol

Z St

Naya Bazar

Gongabu (Kathmandu)
Bus Station (3km)

123

Lekhnath Marg

64
108
90

101
76
63
33
50
56
Bhagawati

17

7
Saatghumti

96
13
25
83
12
46
15
16
107

81
21 69
82 78
Mandala St 14
29
28
8

THAMEL

112
126

44
Marg

125

105
91

Galko Pakha

32 121
40

10

103
24

LAINCHHAUR

Lainchhaur

129

BHAGWAN
BAHAL

35
30

55

86
118

100 m
0.05 miles

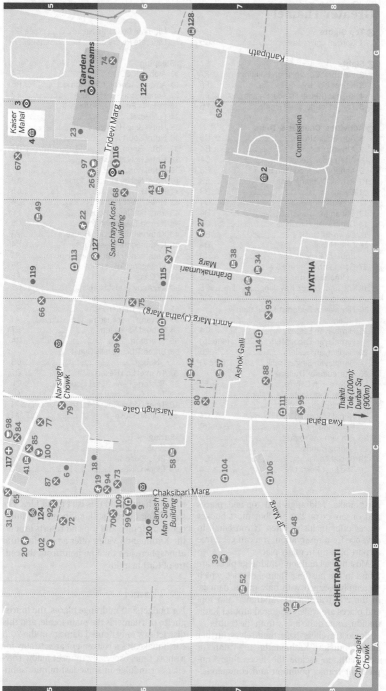

Greater Thamel

earthquake. Midrange and top-end places add on an extra 23% tax but most budget places offer inclusive rates. If you email in advance for a reservation, you can get a free airport pick-up in many places.

Most budget and some midrange places are found in the bustling Thamel district, which mercifully escaped with only minor damage in the 2015 earthquake. Midrange and top-end places are widely scattered around Kathmandu, some quite a way from the centre.

Some travellers base themselves further afield, outside Kathmandu in Patan or Bodhnath, to escape the increasingly unpleasant traffic, pollution and commercialism of Thamel, and this isn't a bad idea. For something quieter still, an increasing number of midrange and top-end resorts around the Kathmandu Valley offer a peaceful rural atmosphere less than an hour from the centre of Kathmandu.

Thamel

For budget and midrange places, the tourist ghetto of Thamel is the main locale, and this district saw only limited damage in the 2015 earthquake. It's a convenient area to stay for a short time, especially to meet fellow travellers or indulge in some last-minute shopping, but you are likely to tire of the noise and congestion in a couple of days.

In an attempt to establish some order in this sprawling chaos, we have somewhat arbitrarily divided the Greater Thamel area as follows: central Thamel, around the two central intersections; Paknajol, to the north; Bhagwan Bahal, to the northeast; Jyatha, to the southeast; and Chhetrapati, to the southwest.

Central Thamel

Hotel Potala　　　　　　　GUESTHOUSE **$**
(Map p88; ☑01-4700159; www.potalahotel.com; s/d US$12/18, without bathroom US$8/13, deluxe US$15/20; @🛜) Bang in the beating

heart of Thamel, this small backpacker place is a good option, and has free internet, a nice rooftop area and a convenient momo restaurant overlooking Thamel's main drag. Rooms are simple but clean and decent, with sunny corner deluxe rooms the best. It's down an alleyway near the Maya Cocktail Bar. Don't confuse it with Potala Guest House.

Karma Travellers Home　　　　GUESTHOUSE **$**
(Map p88; ☑01-4417897; www.karmatravellershome.com; Bhagawati Marg; s/d US$14/18, deluxe US$20/25; 🎍🛜) This popular central place has decent rooms, several nice terrace sitting areas and helpful owners. The air-con

deluxe rooms are more spacious and some rooms come with a balcony. You can get a 20% discount online and a free airport pick-up.

Hotel Silver Home
GUESTHOUSE $

(Map p88; ☑01-4262986; www.hotelsilverhome.com; dm Rs 300, s/d Rs 700/1100, deluxe r Rs 1200-1500; @🛜) Plus points here include a quiet but central location on the main drags, friendly helpful management and one free airport pick-up. The rooms are simple but come with proper mattresses and hot water in the bathroom, and the hotel shares a little garden with two other good budget places, including the Pokhara Peace Hotel (which has good corner deluxe rooms). Sunny south-facing rooms are best.

Mustang Guest House
GUESTHOUSE $

(Map p88; ☑01-4700053; www.mustangguesthouse.com.np; s/d US$8/10, without bathroom US$5/7; 🛜) An acceptable cheapie, popular with Japanese people, this place is tucked away down a dingy alleyway. It has neat, carpeted rooms and clean bathrooms but a dearth of natural light, no TVs, hard mattresses and no real sitting areas. At the time of research deluxe rooms (US$15) were under construction on the upper floors.

Hotel Florid
GUESTHOUSE $

(Map p88; ☑01-4701055; www.hotelflorid.com.np; Z St; s/d US$18/20, without bathroom US$10/12, deluxe r US$25; @) This is one of several small guesthouses just north of central Thamel down Z St. There is a pleasant garden restaurant at the rear and no buildings behind, so there's a feeling of space that is often lacking in Thamel. The suitelike deluxe rooms overlooking the garden are sunny and spacious. Doubles overlooking the road are noisier but come with a shared balcony. You'll need to negotiate a discount to get good value here. Rates include breakfast and tax.

★ Kathmandu Guest House
HOTEL $$

(Map p88; ☑01-4700800; www.ktmgh.com; r US$60-100, without bathroom US$2-16, deluxe US$120-180; ✳@🛜) The KGH is an institution. A former Rana palace, it was the first hotel to open in Thamel in the late 1960s and still serves as the central landmark. Everyone from Jeremy Irons to Ricky Martin has stayed here. In strictly dollar terms you can get better rooms elsewhere, but most people enjoy the atmosphere here and it's often booked out weeks in advance. Note

that the atmospheric heritage wing of the hotel was damaged in the 2015 earthquake, so check to see which parts of the hotel are open when you book.

The particularly pleasant rear garden and its shady pomelo tree acts as a much-needed haven from the Thamel mayhem and the front courtyard is a good place to meet up or for dinner.

A vast range of rooms is available. The cheapest rooms without bathroom form part of the original 13-room guesthouse and are very basic. These rooms cannot be reserved. In the new north Siddhi wing, the best-value rooms are the superior garden-facing rooms (US$80). Rooms come with breakfast and discounts of 40% are standard.

Ask the owners about their new property, the **Maya Manor Hotel** (Map p68; opening in Naxal in 2016.

Hotel Horizon
HOTEL $$

(Map p88; ☑01-4220904; www.hotelhorizon.com; Chaksibari Marg; s/d US$20/25, deluxe US$25/30; ✳@🛜) The Horizon is a good upper budget choice down an alley off the main street in southern Thamel, making it a quiet and central option. All rooms have a bathroom and most are bright and spacious, if a little old fashioned, plus there are some nice terrace seating areas, including around the newly designed courtyard. The recent jump in room rates means you can get better value elsewhere if you dig around.

Ambassador Garden Home
BOUTIQUE HOTEL $$

(Map p88; ☑01-4700724; www.aghhotel.com; s/d US$51/63, deluxe US$63/72, super deluxe US$87/105; ✳@🛜) Right in the eye of the Thamel storm but surprisingly peaceful, this place has splashes of style and a nice garden and lobby reading area. Back-facing rooms are quietest, away from the noisy pub. Standard rooms are a bit small; deluxe rooms come with air-con and minibar and are more spacious. What you are paying for is the location.

The hotel is named after the owner's great grandfather, once the Nepali ambassador to China.

Hotel Courtyard
BOUTIQUE HOTEL $$

(Map p88; ☑01-4700648; www.hotelcourtyard.com; s/d US$50/56, deluxe US$75/81, ste US$113/118; 🛜) This hotel is built in a traditional style with oil bricks, Newari-style carved wooden lintels and stone waterspouts, brought up to date with dramatic orange walls and black trim. The rooms are big enough to tango in and there are pleasant seating areas far removed from the Thamel madness. That said, the scuffed and peeling rooms are starting to need some serious renovation.

A small massage room, cosy library and bar create a sociable environment. Rates include breakfast and taxes.

Thamel Eco Resort HOTEL $$
(Map p88; ☑01-4263810; www.thamelecoresort.com; Chibahal; s/d without bathroom US$35/40, with bathroom US$50/55, deluxe US$60/65; ☏) A new complex set back off the road, it has fresh modern rooms of varying size set around a pleasant central stupa courtyard decorated with carved wood and traditional touches. Good breakfast buffet, central location and rooftop yoga classes are a bonus. This place is popular with trekking groups and so can feel crowded when it's full. Discounts of 20% are possible.

Thorong Peak Guest House GUESTHOUSE $$
(Map p88; ☑01-4253458; www.thorongpeak.com; s/d US$23/33, superior US$33/41; @☏) A clean and well-tended place, off the main street in a small cul-de-sac that is popular with Chinese travellers. Most rooms are spacious, light and airy, if a little bland, and have super-clean bathrooms. Plus points include nice communal balconies and a decent courtyard restaurant, though without the standard discount of 20% it's a bit overpriced.

Paknajol (Northern Thamel)
This area lies to the northwest of central Thamel and can be reached by continuing north from the Kathmandu Guest House, or by approaching from Lekhnath Marg to the north.

Not far from the steep Paknajol intersection with Lekhnath Marg (northwest of Thamel) are half a dozen pleasant guesthouses grouped together in a district known as Sorakhutte. They're away from traffic, a short walk from Thamel (but it could be a million miles), with fine views across the valley towards Balaju and Swayambhunath.

Nirvana Peace Home GUESTHOUSE $
(Map p88; ☑01-4383053; www.nirvanapeacehome.net; Sorakhutte; s Rs 800, d Rs 1000-1300, r with shared bathroom Rs 700; ☏) New management has revitalised this superior place in budget-friendly Paknajol. Simple but clean

KATHMANDU FOR CHILDREN

➡ Pilgrims Book House (p109) has a fine collection of kids' books, including colouring books.

➡ Away from the tourist areas highchairs are virtually nonexistent, but finding nonspicy food that children will eat isn't a problem.

➡ Kids will probably enjoy the zoo in nearby Patan and older kids will get a thrill from spotting the monkeys at Swayambhunath.

rooms, a nice garden and upstairs lounge hang-out make it one of the best options in this area.

Kathmandu Garden House GUESTHOUSE $
(Map p88; ☑01-4381239; www.hotel-in-nepal.com; Sorakhutte; s/d Rs 1000/1200, annex r Rs 1000-2000; ☏) This small and intimate guesthouse is cosy and deservedly popular. The views from the roof are excellent and there are nice sitting areas and a lovely garden where you can sit back and marvel at the staff cutting the grass by hand (literally!). The new annex 100m away has modern rooms with balconies and great views from the rooftop.

Yellow House GUESTHOUSE $
(Map p88; ☑01-4381186; theyellowhouse2007@gmail.com; Sorakhutte; r Rs 700-2000; ☏) This friendly Swiss-run place across the road from Tibet Peace Guest House is an excellent addition to the expanding budget Paknajol scene. The 20 rooms are bright, there's a concrete terrace and the house restaurant dishes up decent Thai food.

Kathmandu Peace Guest House GUESTHOUSE $
(Map p88; ☑01-4380369; www.peaceguesthouse.com; Sorakhutte; s US$16-20, d US$20-26, s/d without bathroom US$8/12; @☏) Rooms here come with satellite TV in either the slightly ramshackle old wing or the fresher pine-clad new block. The ground floor and rooftop garden are pleasant. Rates include taxes.

Tibet Peace Guest House GUESTHOUSE $
(Map p88; ☑01-4381026; www.tibetpeace.com; Sorakhutte; s/d Rs 1300/1600; ☏) This is a quiet and mellow hang-out with a small garden and restaurant. There's a wide range of

rooms, some ramshackle and others with private balconies, so have a dig around before committing. Friendliness isn't their forte.

Shree Tibet Family Guest House
GUESTHOUSE $

(Map p88; ☑ 01-4700902; www.hotelshreetibet.com; Bhagawati Marg; s/d from US$11/15, deluxe US$14/18; @ 🕲) It's easy to miss this budget place and most people do (it's often deserted). It's a clean, quiet and friendly place with cosy rooms, although most are dark and smallish due to the buildings being very close together. As always, the back rooms on the higher floors are best. Prayer wheels mark the entrance.

International Guest House
HOTEL $$

(Map p68; ☑ 01-4252299; www.ighouse.com; s/d US$29/31, deluxe US$38/43, superior deluxe US$49/54, ste US$60; 🕲) This is a solid and quietly stylish place that boasts century-old carved woodwork, terraced sitting areas, a spacious garden and one of the best rooftop views in the city, which you can enjoy in the sun loungers. Some rooms were damaged by the 2015 earthquake so ask to see a few before deciding.

Though not exactly luxurious, the superior rooms in the renovated wing are generally bright, spacious and well decorated, while the best deluxe rooms in the old building come with a garden view. The plainer standard rooms vary.

The hotel is west from the Saatghumti (Seven Bends St) in an area known as Kaldhara. This area is quieter and much less of a scene than Thamel but still close to plenty of restaurants. Rates include tax, breakfast, wi-fi and airport pick-up.

Dalai-la Boutique Hotel
BOUTIQUE HOTEL $$$

(Map p88; ☑ 01-4701436; www.dalaiboutique-hotel.com; deluxe r US$80-100, super deluxe US$120; ❋🕲) New Tibetan-run place set around a charming prayer-flag-strewn courtyard that offers romantic alfresco dining. Rooms in the new wing are best, and come with a small balcony. There are some stylish Tibetan touches with crafts collected from across the valley, and ecofriendly efforts such as plastic-free shampoo containers are commendable.

Bhagwan Bahal (Northeastern Thamel)

Alobar 1000
HOSTEL $

(Map p88; ☑ 01-4410114; www.alobar1000; dm Rs 350-550, r Rs 1700-2700) If you are looking to hook up with other young backpackers, this well-run and oddly named place (taken from a Tom Robbins novel) is the most popular hostel in the city. The travel desk offers treks, language classes and city walks, and there's fair-priced laundry and airport transfers. The sociable rooftop hang-out and restaurant is the place to meet a trekking buddy.

Dorm rooms have between three and 12 beds, all of which come with a locker.

For a private room you can get better value elsewhere.

Annapurna Guest House
GUESTHOUSE $

(Map p88; ☑ 01-4420159; www.annapurna-guesthouse.com; s/d US$12/15, without bathroom US$7/9, deluxe US$15/20; 🕲) The rooms at this somewhat dour family guesthouse are smallish but clean and most come with a private bathroom, though some are dark. Down a side alley near the Hotel Norbu Linka, this area is quieter than Thamel proper and has not yet been completely taken over by restaurants, souvenir shops and travel agencies. The rooftop restaurant is pleasant. Rates include tax.

Hotel Blue Horizon
HOTEL $$

(Map p88; ☑ 01-4421971; www.hotelblue horizon.com; Keshar Mahal; s/d US$18/23, deluxe US$28/33, super deluxe US$37/42, ste US$42/46; ❋@🕲) Renovations have revitalised this old favourite, adding a spacious garden and a new block of midrange rooms. The deluxe and new block rooms are mostly bright and fresh and offer the best value (suites are great for families). Best of all is the secluded location down an alleyway off Tridevi Marg, which makes it super easy for transport around the city.

Mi Casa
BOUTIQUE HOTEL $$

(Map p88; ☑ 01-4415149; www.micasanepal.com; r US$50-70; ❋🕲) For a stylish, cosy option this place has just nine rooms with splashes of colour from Nepali fabrics and potted plants. The pricier rooms come with kitchenette and terrace; others are smallish. There are a couple of small terraces and a courtyard cafe serving breakfast. The location is useful for both Thamel and the new town. Prices include tax.

Hotel Norbu Linka HOTEL $$

(Map p88; ☏ 01-4410630; www.hotelnorbulinka.
com; deluxe s/d US$60/80, ste US$80-100; ✳🖥) This modern, secluded place is central and quiet. The spacious modern rooms aren't as Tibetan as you'd think from the name but they are clean and comfortable, and there are a couple of rooms on the rooftop garden area. The deluxe rooms are great for families and the restaurant is open 24 hours, so if you are jet-lagged and with kids, look no further.

The hotel is down an alley opposite the colourful Thamel Gaa Hiti (water tank). Rates include taxes, and discounts of 20% to 30% are standard.

Sheraton LUXURY HOTEL $$$

(Map p88) One of several big hotels currently under construction on the fringes of Thamel, this will be the closest luxury hotel to central Kathmandu when it opens in 2018. Other hotels currently under construction include a Marriott Fairfield hotel in Jyatha (Thamel) and a five-star Marriott in Naga Pokhara, Naxal.

Jyatha (Southeastern Thamel)

The neighbourhood southeast of Thamel is traditionally known as Jyatha. The southern section has evolved into a popular area with Chinese tourists.

Turn east a short way down Jyatha Rd, and a couple of twists and turns will bring you to a neat little cluster of modern guesthouses, whose central but quiet location feels a million miles from the Thamel hustle.

THE PROBLEM WITH GIVING

We chatted with Dhan Saru, the director of an NGO working with disadvantaged children in Nepal, about the problem of street children in Kathmandu and how, or even if, travellers should help.

What drives children onto the streets of Kathmandu? Many children on the streets of Kathmandu are there because of poverty and domestic violence. Although illegal, child labour is commonly accepted in Nepal and is often seen as a good escape from poverty – both for the children themselves and for the families that send them away. Kids often come to the streets of Kathmandu in search of better fortune, either of their own accord or under the influence of friends or family. Perhaps a more important question is what 'keeps' these children on the street? Bizarrely, kindness is often the answer. Consider the following scenario: a child is sent by poor and uneducated parents to Kathmandu to work and discovers that the 'boss' is unkind, uncaring and often quite cruel. Seeing how other children seem able to survive on the street, the child decides to try their luck and falls under the influence of older street kids – kids who've learnt that begging can be a lucrative game, who know the escape of solvent abuse, who no longer have the tension of living with impoverished and overstressed parents, and who are prepared to put up with various hardships in return for what they see as a life of total freedom.

What can travellers do to help? More often than not, doing nothing probably won't make the traveller feel better about a particular situation, but that should never be their reason for wanting to help. Often the best thing travellers can do to help is to do nothing. There are many organisations working to help Nepal's street children lead a 'normal' life of school, learning, family, routine, structure and rules. Handing out food, money and other gifts in the street will not provide a lasting solution to the child's problems. What it will do is give the child a reason to stay on the street – at home, parents rarely give them any of the gifts that travellers bestow on them.

What is your advice for travellers who are interested in donating or volunteering in Nepal? While there are thousands of organisations in Nepal, and many welcome volunteers and donations, travellers on tourist visas are prohibited from working in Nepal. Also, the volunteering industry is unregulated – travellers should look very carefully at any organisation that they donate time or money to. When volunteering, think about your own skills and experience and look for an organisation that can use those skills in its work.

Imperial Guest House GUESTHOUSE $
(Map p88; ☑01-4249339; http://imperial.idia.ru; s/d US$12/15; ☎) Across from the Mustang Holiday Inn, this cheap and plain guesthouse has a boarding-school feel, with threadbare but functional and clean rooms and narrow beds with elephant-grey blankets. There's a pleasant garden rooftop that overlooks a small shrine.

Mustang Holiday Inn HOTEL $
(Map p88; ☑01-4249041; www.mustangholiday.com; s/d US$20/25, deluxe US$45/40, super deluxe US$50/60; ☎) Once owned by the king of Mustang, the dimly lit rooms here are looking a bit neglected these days, with old mattresses and bedside speakers that date from around 1962, but rooms are spacious and some come with a balcony. It's quiet and has sunny terrace seating. Rates include tax and breakfast; discounts of 25% are standard (without them it's overpriced).

Sacred Valley Inn HOTEL $$
(Map p88; ☑01-4251063; www.sacredvalley-inn.com; r US$30, deluxe r US$40; @☎) This branch of the popular Pokhara hotel is a good upper-budget choice. The carpeted rooms are clean, modern and fresh and some have sunny balconies, though there are no single rates for solo travellers. The excellent rooftop garden and the ground-floor lounge and library are a bonus, as is the quiet but central location, tucked away in a lane behind Hotel Utse. Rates include tax.

Hotel Holy Himalaya HOTEL $$
(Map p88; ☑01-4263172; www.holyhimalaya.com; 117 Brahmakumari Marg; s/d US$35/40, deluxe US$45/55, ste US$75-85; ❄@☎) This is a good midrange find frequented by small in-the-know tour groups. The rooms are simple but reassuring and some come with

a balcony. Perks include organic coffee, a nice rooftop garden and free guided meditation in the mornings. The spacious deluxe rooms in the new building across the road offer the best value. Rates include tax and breakfast.

Fuji Hotel HOTEL $$
(Map p88; ☑01-4250435; www.fujiguesthouse.com; s/d from US$22/32, deluxe US$40/50, super deluxe US$50/60; ❄❄@☎) The well-run Fuji is popular with Japanese travellers and rooms are neat, quiet and spotlessly clean. Some rooms have a balcony and the sunny rooms on the rooftop are particularly spacious. Rooms with a bathtub cost an extra US$8. Aim for a 25% discount.

★ **Kantipur Temple House** BOUTIQUE HOTEL $$$
(Map p68; ☑01-4250131; www.kantipurtemplehouse.com; s/d US$70/80, deluxe US$110/140) ✆
Hidden down an alley on the southern edge of Thamel, this Newari-temple-style hotel has been built with meticulous attention to detail. The spacious rooms are tastefully decorated, with traditional carved wood, terracotta floor tiles, window seats and fairtrade dhaka (hand-woven) cloth bedspreads. Due to the traditional nature of the building, rooms tend to be a little dark.

This place is also doing its best to be ecofriendly – guests are given cloth bags to use when shopping and bulk mineral water is available free of charge in traditional bronze pitchers (in fact, there's no plastic anywhere in the hotel). The rooms encircle a traditional brick courtyard and there's free yoga in the garden at 8am. Don't expect TVs, AC or heating. The old-town location is close to almost anywhere in town, but taxi drivers might have a hard time finding it.

BORIS LISSANEVITCH

Boris Lissanevitch is known as the godfather of tourism in Nepal. He was a fascinating figure, a white Russian émigré who fled the Bolshevik Revolution, and also a one-time ballet dancer, chef, tiger hunter, fighter pilot, Shanghai club owner and trapeze artist. A friend of Ingrid Bergman, he acted in a film with Jean-Paul Belmondo.

Boris was running the Club 300 in Calcutta when he first met King Tribhuvan in 1944 (some even whisper that Boris helped pass secret messages between the king and Nehru, helping overthrow the Rana regime). Tribhuvan later invited him to Nepal to open Nepal's first hotel, the Royal, in a former royal palace (now the Electoral Commission Building). He brought the first tour group to the kingdom, setting up its first souvenir stand, and hosted early mountaineering groups who would camp on the front lawn. The hotel and its famous Chimney Restaurant closed in the 1970s but would later morph into the Yak & Yeti Hotel, where to this day you can sip on Russian borscht at the Chimney Restaurant.

Chhetrapati (Southwest Thamel)

This area is named after the important five-way intersection (notable by its distinctive bandstand) to the southwest of Thamel. The further you get from Thamel, the more traditional the surroundings become.

Khangsar Guest House
HOTEL $

(Map p88; 01-4260788; www.khangsarguesthouse.com; s/d US$12/14;) This is a friendly and central option, though there are few bells and whistles. The threadbare rooms come with a very thin but clean bathroom with (generally) hot water, plus there's a pleasant garden rooftop bar for cold beers under the stars. The upper-floor rooms are best, especially the sunny corner rooms away from the road. Rates include tax.

★ Hotel Ganesh Himal
HOTEL $$

(Map p68; 01-4263598; www.ganeshhimal.com; s/d US$20/25, deluxe US$30/35, super deluxe r US$40-45;) Our pick for comfort on a budget is this well-run and friendly place. The rooms are among the best value in Kathmandu, with endless hot water and lots of balcony and garden seating. Throw in free airport pick-up and this place is hard to beat, even if the booking system gets a bit overwhelmed at times.

The best standard rooms are in the new block (and are the sunniest in winter). The deluxe rooms are more spacious and a little quieter and the spacious super-deluxe rooms have brick floors. It's located a 10-minute walk southwest of Thamel – far enough to be out of range of the tiger-balm salesmen but close enough to restaurants for dinner. Here's a tip: bring earplugs, as the residential neighbourhood can be noisy.

Tibet Guest House
HOTEL $$

(Map p88; 01-4251763; www.tibetguesthouse.com; s/d US$16/20, standard US$40/45, deluxe US$50/60, superior US$70/80, ste US$90-100;) This busy, efficient and popular hotel gets heavy use and things are looking a bit worn in places but it's a solid choice, so book in advance. There's a lovely breakfast patio, a lobby espresso bar and the superb views of Swayambhunath from the rooftop just cry out to be appreciated at sunset with a cold beer.

All but the cheapest rooms here are comfortable, though lower floors can be dark; the superior rooms have a lot more space. Some of the simple standard rooms are located in a separate block across the street

ℹ️ LOAD SHEDDING

Electricity cuts ('load shedding') are a fact of life in Kathmandu; they last for up to 16 hours a day in winter when hydro power levels are at their lowest. Electricity is currently rationed across the city, shifting from district to district every eight hours or so. Most hotels post a schedule of planned electricity cuts. Try to choose a hotel with a generator and make sure your room is far away from it.

and come with a balcony. Discounts of 20% are standard.

Nirvana Garden Hotel
HOTEL $$

(Map p88; 01-4256200; www.nirvanagarden.com; s/d US$40/50, deluxe US$50/60;) The relaxing garden here isn't quite nirvana but it is a real oasis, making this hotel a decent choice close to the centre. The deluxe rooms with sunny balcony and garden view are the ones to opt for, though all are getting a bit tired and overpriced these days. Add US$15 for air-con and expect a 20% discount.

📖 Freak Street (Jochne) & Durbar Square

Although Freak St's glory days have passed, a few determined budget restaurants and lodges have clung on. Staying here offers three pluses – you won't find much cheaper, there are fewer crowds and you're right in the heart of the fascinating old city. On the downside, the pickings are slimmer and the lodges are generally grungier than in Thamel.

Monumental Paradise
HOTEL $

(Map p68; 01-4240876; mparadise52@hotmail.com; s/d from US$6/12, ste US$30;) Most places in Freak St are old and grungy but this newish place has clean, fresh and spacious rooms with a tiled bathroom, and the upper-floor back rooms come with a private balcony and lots of natural light. There's an excellent rooftop bar-restaurant and one suite in the crow's nest has its own private balcony with views towards Durbar Sq.

World Heritage Hotel
BOUTIQUE HOTEL $$

(Map p73; 01-4261862; www.dwarikaschhen.com; Hanuman Dhoka; s US$30-55, d US$40-75 s/d without bathroom US$10/15,) Well away from the Thamel bustle, this traditional-style

FREAK STREET – THE END OF THE ROAD

Running south from Basantapur Sq, Freak St dates from the overland days of the late 1960s and early 1970s, when it was one of the great gathering places on 'the road east'. In its hippie prime, this was the place for cheap hotels (Rs 3 a room!), colourful restaurants, hash and 'pie' (pastry) shops, the sounds of Jimi and Janis blasting from eight-track players and, of course, the weird and wonderful foreign 'freaks' who gave the street its name. Along with Bodhnath and Swayambhunath, Freak St was a magnet for those in search of spiritual enlightenment, cheap dope and a place where the normal boundaries no longer applied.

Times change and Freak St (better known these days by its real name, Jochne) is today only a pale shadow of its former funky self. While there are still cheap hotels and restaurants, it's the Thamel area in the north of the city that is the main gathering place for a new generation of travellers. However, for those people who find Thamel too slick and commercialised, Freak St retains a faint echo of those mellower days.

hotel is just a stone's throw north of the splendours of Durbar Sq. The handful of rooms are decked out in stone and carved wood and come with ikat bedspreads and window seats. The location is great and the building is handsome but it's not brilliantly run, so don't expect everything to work.

The deluxe rooms are much larger than the pokey standard rooms but all suffer from a lack of natural light. The three budget rooms in the back courtyard share a single bathroom. A good range of Newari snacks is available from the restaurant. Note that this hotel is sometimes called Dwarika's Chhen.

Central Kathmandu

These hotels are within walking distance of Durbar Marg and the Thamel area, and fall into the top-end price range.

Yak & Yeti Hotel HOTEL $$$
(Map p68; ☎ 01-4248999; www.yakandyeti.com; d US$240-280; ❄❒☎) This hotel is probably the best known in Nepal, due to its connections with the near-legendary Boris Lissanevitch (see boxed text, p96), who ran the original restaurant. The hotel is centred on a Rana-era palace that was slightly damaged in the 2015 earthquake, but the actual rooms are in two modern wings that were not affected. The recently renovated Newari wing incorporates woodcarvings, oil brick walls and local textiles, while the deluxe rooms in the Durbar wing are fresh, modern and stylish.

The oldest section of the hotel is part of the Lal Durbar, a former Rana palace that is worth a look for traces of an overblown but spectacular baroque decor and some ex-

cellent old black-and-white photos of Rana royalty. The borscht at the famous Chimney Restaurant here retains a tenuous link with its Russian past. There's also a spacious garde (ask for a garden-facing room), two pools, tennis courts and a fitness centre. Discounts of 20% are standard.

Shanker Hotel HISTORIC HOTEL $$$
(Map p68; ☎ 01-4410151; www.shankerhotel.com.np; s/d US$105/121; ❄☎❒) There's nowhere in town quite like this creaky 19th-century former Rana residence – the kind of place where you expect to bump into some whiskered old Rana prince shuffling around one of the wooden corridors. The entry columns of neoclassical whipped cream overlook a palatial manicured garden and one of the city's nicest swimming pools. The historic lobby area was damaged in the 2015 earthquake, but repairs are ongoing and rooms were unaffected.

The palace conversion means that rooms are idiosyncratic, with some rooms split over two floors and featuring hobbit-sized half-windows, and others comfortable but disappointingly modern. The rooms in what they call the 'Fourth Line' offer the most historical touches. For real grandeur you'll have to track down the dining halls and Durbar Hall conference space. Rates include tax and breakfast.

Three Rooms BOUTIQUE HOTEL $$$
(Map p68; ☎ 9808517245; www.thepaulines.com/3rooms; Baber Mahal Revisited; r €80-95; ☎) No prizes for guessing how many rooms are available in this intimate French-run secret in the Baber Mahal complex. What

is surprising is how spacious and charming the rooms are, with traditional dark slate and brass sinks given a cool modern twist by some well-chosen B&W photographs. One room even has its own fabulous private patio.

Staff are only around between 10am and 5pm so start the day right by arranging to have breakfast delivered to your room from nearby Chez Caroline (p107).

Lazimpat

North of central Kathmandu is the Lazimpat embassy area, popular with NGO staff, repeat visitors and business people.

Hotel Manaslu HOTEL $$
(Map p68; 01-4410071; www.hotelmanaslu.com; s/d US$60/65;) Just beyond Hotel Tibet, the big draw at this nice modern hotel is the lovely terrace garden and its pool fed by Newari-style fountains. The glorious carved windows in the restaurant were brought in from Bhaktapur. Rooms have been freshened up in recent years, making this a good choice, especially if you get a room in the back block overlooking the garden.

⭐ **Hotel Tibet** HOTEL $$$
(Map p68; 01-4429085; www.hotel-tibet.com.np; s/d US$80/90, ste US$110-120;) Tibetophiles and tour groups headed to or from Tibet like the Tibetan vibe of this recommended place. The 56 quiet and comfortable rooms are plain compared to the opulent lobby, but several of the larger front-facing rooms have a balcony. There's also a great rooftop terrace bar and a side garden cafe.

The hotel is just in front of the Radisson. The attached **Shambhala Spa** (www.donald-spa.com) offers a 'trekkers' recovery massage' alongside hot-stone therapy.

Hotel Shangri-La HOTEL $$$
(01-4412999; www.hotelshangrila.com; r incl breakfast from US$140;) The real draw at this five-star place is the large relaxing garden, with its terrace restaurant and small but nice pool. Come for the Friday barbecue or Saturday champagne brunch, or try a High Lama cocktail during happy hour (4pm to 6pm) at the cosy Lost Horizon Bar. The rooms have been renovated in recent years; request a garden-view room.

Surprisingly, it's not connected to the Shangri-La chain.

Radisson HOTEL $$$
(Map p68; 01-4423888; www.radisson.com/kathmandune; r US$185-250;) A favourite of embassy staff and business travellers, the Radisson is a modern if somewhat soulless five-star choice, with a 5th-floor pool and a good gym. Rooms are looking a bit faded and the instant coffee supplied with the kettle doesn't exactly scream five stars, but several good cafes and bars loiter outside the main gates.

Elsewhere

Benchen Vihar Guest House GUESTHOUSE $
(01-4284204; www.benchen.org; Chhauni; r Rs 500-700;) If you've ever fancied staying in a Tibetan monastery, try this guesthouse attached to the Benchen Phuntsok Dargyeling Monastery, 10 minutes' walk from Swayambhunath. It's surprisingly comfortable, with en suite bathrooms, a garden cafe and fine views from the upper floors, and there are plenty of opportunities for meditation (prayers at 6am and 4pm) or learning some Tibetan from the local monks. Note that some repairs are ongoing at the monastery following the 2015 earthquake.

Hotel Vajra BOUTIQUE HOTEL $$
(Map p68; 01-4271545; www.hotelvajra.com; Bijeshwari; s/d from US$33/38, without bathroom US$16/18, ste US$85-90) Across the Vishnumati River on the way to Swayambhunath, this is one of Kathmandu's most interesting hotels in any price category. The brick complex feels more like an artists' retreat than a hotel, with lush gardens, a library, a rooftop bar and an ayurvedic massage room. The only catch is the location, which, though peaceful, makes it tricky for getting a taxi.

All the rooms in the old wing are unique (the cheapest share bathrooms), so take a look at more than one. If you are in the new wing (single/double US$60/70), try to score a balcony. Some rooms are looking a bit tired and the service is somewhat begrudging but it's still a good option.

⭐ **Dwarika's** BOUTIQUE HOTEL $$$
(01-4479488; www.dwarikas.com; Battis Putali; s/d US$275/295, ste from US$400;) For stylish design and sheer romance, this outstanding hotel is unbeatable; if you're on your honeymoon, look no further. Over 40 years the owners have rescued thousands of woodcarvings from around the valley and incorporated them into the hotel design.

The end result is a beautiful hybrid – a cross between a museum and a boutique hotel, with a lush, pampering ambience.

The hotel consists of clusters of traditional Newari buildings separated by brick-paved courtyards. All rooms are unique and some have sensuous open-plan black-slate bathrooms. Highlights include a lovely library lounge, a back pool, a spa where they make their own in-house soaps, a good Japanese restaurant and a bar in the hotel's original building. The location on a busy street east of town, a short walk southwest of Pashupatinath, is a horror, but finding a taxi is never a problem.

★ Hyatt Regency Kathmandu
LUXURY HOTEL $$$

(☎01-4491234; www.kathmandu.regency.hyatt. com; d from US$235; ☜☒) No expense has been spared on this superb palace-style building, from the dramatic entrance of Newari water pools to the modern Malla-style architecture. It's worth popping in just to admire the gorgeous Patan-style chaitya in the foyer. As you'd expect, the spacious rooms are furnished tastefully, with huge bathrooms, and many have views over nearby Bodhnath stupa.

The large swimming pool, good restaurants and Sunday brunch make this the perfect spot for a splurge: after a tough day's sightseeing unwind with a *shirodhara* ayurvedic treatment at the spa. Extra touches like a 24-hour gym and good room security make this the best hotel in Kathmandu. The Hyatt is a couple of kilometres outside Kathmandu, on the road to Bodhnath. The club rooms can be great value for couples; for US$55 extra you get breakfast for two, airport transfers, cocktails and wi-fi.

Soaltee Crowne Plaza
LUXURY HOTEL $$$

(☎01-4273999; s/d US$190/200, club r US$240; ☒) Space and tranquillity are precious commodities in Kathmandu but the Soaltee has acres of both: 11 acres, to be precise. Spread around the palatial grounds are excellent restaurants, a lovely poolside area and even a bowling alley. The price you pay is a crummy location on the western edge of town, a 15-minute taxi ride from the centre.

✕ Eating

Kathmandu has an astounding array of restaurants. Indeed, with the possible exception of the canteen at the UN building, there are few places where you can have the choice of Indian, Chinese, Japanese, Mexican, Korean, Middle Eastern, Italian or Irish cuisines, all within a five-minute walk. After weeks trekking in the mountains, Kathmandu feels like a culinary paradise.

Many restaurants in Kathmandu try to serve something from everywhere – pizzas, momos, Indian curries, a bit of Thai here, some Mexican tacos there. Predictably, the ones that specialise generally serve the finest food.

Thamel's restaurant scene has been sliding upmarket for a few years now, with most places charging US$5 per main course, plus 24% tax. A bottle of beer will double your bill in most places. Finding a budget meal is still possible but it involves some hunting.

Thamel remains the focus for most diners, and most restaurants here came through the 2015 earthquake with little damage.

✕ Thamel

The junction outside the Kathmandu Guest House is the epicentre of Thamel dining and you'll find dozens of excellent restaurants within a minute's walk in either direction. At most of these places you need to make reservations in October's high season.

Utse Restaurant
TIBETAN $

(Map p88; ☎01-4257614; Jyatha Rd; mains Rs 180-400; ☺8am-10pm) In the hotel of the same name, this is one of the longest-running restaurants in Thamel (since 1971!) and still turns out excellent Tibetan dishes, including unusual Tibetan desserts such as *dhayshi* (sweet rice, curd and raisins) and *mendha* (rice pudding with fruits). The mellow, old-school decor feels lifted straight from an old Lhasa backstreet.

For a group blowout, *gacok* (also spelt *gyakok*) is a form of hotpot named after the brass tureen that is heated at the table (Rs 1100 for two). The set meals are also a worthy extravagance.

Yangling Tibetan Restaurant
MOMOS $

(Map p88; Saatghumti Chowk; momos Rs 150-190; ☺noon-9pm Sun-Fri) Both locals and tourists flock to this unpretentious family-run place for possibly the best momos in town (try the chicken ones). The kitchen here is a nonstop momo production line. You can also get soupy Tibetan butter tea and tasty *thenthuk* (noodle soup).

NEPALI & NEWARI RESTAURANTS

A growing number of restaurants around town specialise in Nepali (mostly Newari) food. Most are in converted Rana-era palaces that offer a set meal, either veg or nonveg, and you dine on cushions at low tables. All offer a cultural show that consists of musicians and dancers performing 'traditional' song and dance routines. The whole thing is a bit touristy but it's a classy night out nonetheless. At most places it's a good idea to make a reservation during the high season.

The food stretches to half a dozen courses that generally include a starter of momos and such main dishes as *alu tareko* (fried potato with cumin and tumeric), *bandhel* (boar), *kukhura ko ledo* (chicken in gravy), *chicken sekuwa* (barbecued or smoked meat), *alu tama kho jhol* (bamboo shoot stew) and *gundruk* (sour soup with dried greens), finished off with *shikarni* (sweet yoghurt with dried fruit and cinnamon) and a masala tea. Look out also for *kwati*, a soup consisting of a dozen types of sprouted beans, prepared during Newari festivals.

Thamel House (Map p88; ☑ 01-4410388; Paknajol; dishes Rs 225-650, veg/nonveg set meals Rs 990/1090; ☺ 11am-10pm) This place is set in a traditional old Newari building and has bags of atmosphere, as well as a dance show at 7pm. Choose between the downstairs courtyard or upper-floor balcony seating. The food is traditional Nepali and Newari, and there are à la carte options. It's particularly convenient for Thamel.

Baithak (Map p68; ☑ 01-4267346; www.baithak.com.np; snacks Rs 200, 12-course veg/nonveg set menus Rs 1200/1500; ☺ 10am-10pm) Briefly closed following the 2015 earthquake, but now open for business, this restaurant in the Baber Mahal Revisited complex has a dramatic and regal, almost Victorian, setting, with crystal and threadbare linens. The menu features 'Rana cuisine', a courtly cuisine created by Nepali Brahmin chefs and heavily influenced by north Indian Mughal cuisine. A *baithak* is a royal suite or state room, and diners are attended by waiters dressed in royal costume and watched over by looming portraits of various disapproving Ranas. The setting is probably the most memorable part of the restaurant. The attached K2 Bar has a delightful terrace for a predinner drink.

Bhojan Griha (Map p68; ☑ 01-4416423; www.bhojangriha.com; Dilli Bazaar; set menus Rs 997; ☺ 11am-2pm & 5-10pm) The most ambitious of the city's traditional Newari restaurants, Bhojan Griha is located in a restored 150-year-old mansion in Dilli Bazaar, just east of the city centre. It's worth eating here just to see the imaginative renovation of this beautiful old building, once the residence of the caste of royal priests. There's a cultural show at 7pm. Most of the seating is traditional (ie on cushions on the floor), although these are actually legless chairs, which saves your back and knees. In an effort to reduce waste, plastic is not used in the restaurant and mineral water is bought in bulk and sold by the glass. A shop in the coutyard sells organic produce.

Bhanchha Ghar (Map p68; ☑ 01-4225172; set menu & show per person Rs 1100; ☺ 10am-10pm) Bhanchha Ghar is a traditional three-storey Newari house in Kamaladi, just east of Durbar Marg, next to a Ganesh temple. Stretch out on handmade carpets and cushions for a drink, snacks and cultural show in the upstairs loft bar, before moving downstairs to an excellent set menu of traditional Nepali dishes, as musicians stroll between the tables playing Nepali folk songs.

Krishnarpan Restaurant (☑ 01-4470770; www.dwarikas.com; set meals from US$38; ☺ dinner only) One of the best places for traditional Nepali food is this impressive place at Dwarika's hotel. The atmosphere is superb and the organic food gets consistent praise from diners. Set meals range from six to 22 courses. If you are coming on Friday, arrive in time for the 6pm dance show in the hotel courtyard and take advantage of happy hour. Reservations required.

Nargila Restaurant   MIDDLE EASTERN $

(Map p88; ☑ 01-4700712; mains Rs 160-300; ☺ noon-10pm; ☜) Across from the Northfield Cafe, on the 1st floor, this somewhat dour budget favourite is a quiet place to just take a break from the bustle outside. Try a *lafa shwarma* (grilled meat, salad and fries in a pitta) or hummus, washed down by fresh *nana* mint tea. The hot waffle with fruit and yoghurt is probably the best in Kathmandu.

Momo Hut   MOMOS $

(Map p88; momos Rs 160-220; ☺ 11am-10pm) Buff (water buffalo) momos, mushroom momos, cheese and spinach momos, fish momos, chocolate momos – sweet or savoury, steamed or fried... Honestly, you'd be silly not to order the momos but they do have other dishes, including curry with Bhutanese pink rice. It's bright, buzzing and very popular with Chinese travellers. Be warned; the cryptic 'C' on the menu means 'with chilli'.

BK's Place   FAST FOOD $

(Map p88; chips Rs 180-240; ☺ 10am-10pm) This place has a well-deserved reputation for good old-fashioned chips (French fries), with a variety of sauces (try the house sauce of mayo, ketchup and onions), as well as good momos and samosas.

Yak Restaurant   TIBETAN $

(Map p88; mains Rs 150-400; ☺ 7am-10pm) We always find ourselves returning to this unpretentious and reliable local place at the southern end of Thamel. The booths give it a 'Tibetan diner' vibe and the clientele is a mix of trekkers, Sherpa guides and local Tibetans who come to shoot the breeze over a tube of *tongba* (hot millet beer).

The menu includes Tibetan dishes, with good *kothey* (fried momos), and some Indian dishes, all at unbeatable prices. It feels just like a trekking lodge, down to that familiar electronic sound of a chicken being strangled every time a dish leaves the kitchen.

Mustang Thakali   NEPALI $

(Map p88; veg/nonveg daal bhaat Rs 180/240; ☺ 10am-3.30pm & 5.30-10pm) Located on the 2nd floor, this is a good option for local Thakali daal bhaat (rice, curry and lentil soup) or a curry with rice, and is popular with local Manangis. It's quiet, intimate and, best of all, authentic.

Pumpernickel Bakery   BAKERY $

(Map p88; mains Rs 80-250; ☺ 7am-7pm) Bleary-eyed tourists crowd in here every morning for fresh croissants, yak-cheese sandwiches, cakes, pastries and filter coffee in the pleasant garden area at the back. The cafeteria-style restaurant is self-service.

Dahua Restaurant   CHINESE $

(Map p88; ☑ 01-4410247; dishes Rs 200-300; ☺ 11am-9pm) Mainland Chinese travellers won't recognise many of the dishes at this Nepali restaurant – sticky sweet-and-sours and greasy egg foo yong are the rule here – but it's quiet, cosy and tasty. It's on the eastern edge of Thamel.

Thakali Bhanchha   NEPALI $

(Map p88; ☑ 01-4701910; veg/nonveg daal bhaat Rs 136/250; ☺ 9am-10pm) If, after having travelled all the way to Nepal, you actually fancy some Nepali food (!), this upstairs restaurant is a good bet and popular with local Thamel workers on their lunch break. Most opt for the spicy but flavourful daal bhaat, but there's also a range of Thakali snacks such as *bandel* (boar).

For the full-on local experience, swap the rice for *dhido*, the doughy buckwheat paste eaten daily by millions of Nepalis.

★ Gaia Restaurant   INTERNATIONAL $$

(Map p88; mains Rs 350-480; ☺ 7am-9pm; ☜) This popular and dependable place combines good breakfasts, salads, sandwiches and organic coffee in a pleasant garden courtyard with global music, reasonable prices (tax included) and good service. The Thai red curry is surprisingly good and the chicken *choiyla* (spicy barbecued meat) packs a punch; you're bound to find something good in a menu that ranges from daal bhaat to carrot cake.

★**Friends Restaurant** INTERNATIONAL **$$**
(Map p88; ☑01-4700063; Mandala St; mains Rs 200-500; ⊙10am-10pm; 🖥) Run by the same people as Or2k, but a less grungy, more grown-up option, Friends shows its Israeli roots through its hummus, *shawarma* and *borek* (filo pastry pies), but the menu also stretches to burgers, pizza, steaks and a particularly fine Thai beef salad. The decor is warm and relaxed, with exposed brick and farmhouse tables and the service is normally good.

Or2k MIDDLE EASTERN **$$**
(Map p88; www.or2k.net; mains Rs 180-400; ⊙8am-10pm; 🍴) This bright, buzzy and popular Israeli-run vegetarian restaurant is a favourite for fresh and light Middle Eastern dishes. The menu spreads to crêpes, zucchini pie and *ziva* (pastry fingers filled with cheese), as well as a great meze sampler of hummus, felafel and *labane* (sour cream cheese) served in neat little brass bowls.

All seating is on cushions on the floor and you have to take your shoes off, so make sure you're wearing your clean pair of socks. A small stand at street level serves takeaway felafel wraps.

Black Olives INTERNATIONAL **$$**
(Map p88; ☑01-4700956; www.bolivescafe. com; mains Rs 200-500; ⊙7am-10pm) Maybe it's because of happy hour's free *papad* (pappadam) with salsa or perhaps it's the super friendly staff – either way, we like this good-value courtyard restaurant. The menu offers something for everyone, with good burgers and salads, and there are seasonal dishes, wines by the glass, pleasant courtyard seating and live music on Sunday.

Rosemary Kitchen INTERNATIONAL **$$**
(Map p88; ☑01-4267554; www.rosemary-kitchen.net; mains Rs 250-375; ⊙7am-10pm; 🖥) There's a little bit of everything here, from Indian thalis and tasty Thai curries to fresh salads, homemade bread and wine by the glass. Choose from the classy interior or little garden; either way, book in high season. Prices include tax, making it particularly good value.

Roadhouse Cafe PIZZERIA **$$**
(Map p88; ☑01-4262768; Arcadia Bldg; pizzas Rs 350-475; ⊙11am-10pm) The big attractions at this well-run place are the pizzas from the wood-fired oven and the warm and intimate decor, with an open-air courtyard located out the back. The salads, soups, sandwiches,

desserts (sizzling brownie with ice cream) and espresso coffees are all top-notch and there are some good Newari snacks, including smoked chicken *sandekho* (marinated with spices).

Hankook Sarang KOREAN **$$**
(Map p88; ☑01-4256615; www.hankooksarang. com; mains incl tax Rs 300-650; ⊙10am-10pm) The Hankook is that rare combination of authentic taste and good value. The spicy Korean main dishes come with crunchy kimchi, salad, soup, dried fish, sweet beans and green tea. Alternatively, fire up the barbecue for some *bulgogi* (barbecued beef), cooked at your table and eaten with lettuce, or try the good-value *kimbap* (vegetarian rice rolls).

If you are new to Korean food, try the *bibimbap* – rice and vegetables in a stone pot, to which you add egg and sweet chilli sauce and mix it all together. The service is friendly and there's a choice of floor seating or pleasant alfresco garden dining. It's down an alley near Tamas Spa Lounge.

Furusato JAPANESE **$$**
(Map p88; ☑01-4265647; set meals Rs 400-600; ⊙11am-9pm) Bright and calming, Furusato is perfect for a light dinner. Dishes include udon or cold soba noodles, *donburi* (rice bowls), bento boxes and *gyoza* dumplings (the Japanese version of a momo), but most people opt for one of the set meals, which come with sesame-flavoured salad, miso soup and pickles. It's hidden down an alley opposite Weizen Bakery.

New Orleans Cafe INTERNATIONAL **$$**
(Map p88; ☑01-4700736; mains Rs 450; ⊙8am-10pm; 🍴) Hidden down an alley near the Kathmandu Guest House, New Orleans boasts an intimate candlelit vibe and live music on Wednesdays and Saturdays. It's a popular spot for a drink but the menu also ranges far and wide, from Thai curries and good burgers to Creole jambalaya and oven-roasted vegies. You need to book a table in the high season.

Revolution Cafe INTERNATIONAL **$$**
(Map p88; www.revocafenp.com; mains Rs 200-450; ⊙7am-10pm) Revolution is a decent option if you need a break in northern Thamel. It's a pretty cool place, with courtyard, indoors or traditional seating, all grooving to a solid blues soundtrack. The coffee and fruit juices are good and the menu offers a taste of everything, from *thukpa* (Tibetan noodle soup) to chicken tikka masala.

Krua Thai
THAI $$

(Map p88; ✆01-4701291; www.kruathainepal. com; curries Rs 380; ⊙10am-10pm) Reopened following post-earthquake repairs, this respectable Thai place has food that's reasonably authentic (ie spicy), with decent curries (our favourite is the chicken Penang), *tom yam* soup and *som tam thai* (green papaya salad), although some dishes taste more Chinese than Thai. The garden rooftop has a nicer atmosphere than the glum dining room.

Dechenling
TIBETAN, BHUTANESE $$

(Map p88; ✆01-4412158; mains Rs 250-500, set meals Rs 800; ⊙11am-9pm) Quality Himalayan food and one of the most relaxing courtyards are the draws of this charming garden restaurant-bar. It's also one of the few places in town to offer interesting Bhutanese dishes such as *kewa dhatsi* (potato and cheese curry). If you can't decide, opt for one of the grand Tibetan or Bhutanese set meals.

Northfield Cafe
INTERNATIONAL $$

(Map p88; breakfast Rs 185-285, mains Rs 360-500; ⊙8am-10pm) This pleasant open-air spot is the place for serious breakfast devotees (think waffles and *huevos rancheros*), with the option of half or full portions. The Mexican and Indian tandoori dishes (dinner only) are also excellent (though other Indian dishes can be bland) and the American comfort food spreads to burgers, nachos and even chilli fries.

The sunny garden and outdoor firepit is a real plus in winter and there's traditional Nepali music in the evenings. It's also one of the few places to offer kids' meals.

Helena's
INTERNATIONAL $$

(Map p88; ✆01-4266979; mains Rs 200-450; ⊙7am-10pm; 🛜) Helena's is deservedly popular for its cosy interior, super-friendly service and one of the highest rooftops in Thamel (amazingly, unshaken by the 2015 earthquake). It has a wide range of kebabs, good cakes, tandoori dishes, steaks and even Bengali-style *kathi* rolls (meat and vegetables rolled up in Indian-style flat bread). If you are heading off trekking, consider breakfast on the 8th floor as a form of high-altitude training.

★Fire & Ice Pizzeria
PIZZERIA $$$

(Map p88; ✆01-4250210; www.fireandicepizzeria.com; 219 Sanchaya Kosh Bhawan, Tridevi Marg; pizzas Rs 480; ⊙8am-11pm) This excellent and informal Italian place serves the best pizzas in Kathmandu (wholewheat crusts available, as well as combo pizzas), alongside breakfasts, smoothies, crêpes and good espresso, to a cool soundtrack of Cuban son or Italian opera. The ingredients are top-notch, from the imported anchovies to the house-made tomato sauce.

It's very popular so make a reservation and expect to share one of the tavern-style wooden tables.

★Third Eye
INDIAN $$$

(Map p88; ✆01-4260289, 4260160; www. thirdeyerestaurant.com; JP School Rd; mains Rs 475-650; ⊙11am-10pm) This long-running favourite is popular with well-heeled tourists. Indian food is the speciality and the tandoori dishes are especially good, even if the portions are a bit small. Spice levels are set at 'tourist' so let the efficient (if not friendly) suited waiters know if you'd like extra heat.

Reserve a window seat at the sit-down section at the front or try the more informal section with low tables and cushions at the back; both are candlelit to create an intimate vibe.

Yin Yang Restaurant
THAI $$$

(Map p88; ✆01-4425510; www.yinyangrestaurantbar.com; curries Rs 580; ⊙11am-10pm) Yin Yang is one of Thamel's most highly regarded restaurants, serving authentic Thai food that is a definite cut above the imitation Thai food found elsewhere. The green curry is authentically spicy; for something sweeter try the massaman curry (with onion, peanut and potato). There's also a good range of vegetable choices, as well as some Continental alternatives.

La Dolce Vita
ITALIAN $$$

(Map p88; ✆01-4700612; pastas Rs 310-385, mains Rs 500-850, house wine per glass Rs 375; ⊙11am-10pm) Life is indeed sweet at Thamel's best Italian bistro, offering up such delights as parmesan gnocchi; goat's cheese, spinach and walnut ravioli; and sinfully rich chocolate torte. Choose between the rustic red-and-white tablecloths and terracotta tiles of the main restaurant, the rooftop terrace, the yummy-smelling espresso bar or sunny lounge space; either way the atmosphere and food are excellent.

K-Too Steakhouse
STEAKHOUSE $$$

(Map p88; ✆01-4700043; www.kilroygroup. com; mains Rs 450-615; ⊙10am-10pm) The food and warm and buzzy atmosphere here are excellent. Dishes range from chip butties (sandwiches) to healthy salads, but it's really all about the steaks. The pepper steak sizzler followed by fried apple momos and an Everest Beer is a post-trekking classic. For a quieter vibe, head for the garden.

Kilroy's
INTERNATIONAL **$$$**

(Map p88; ☏01-4250440; www.kilroygroup.com; mains Rs 550-900; ☺10am-10pm) It may not be quite as good as it thinks it is (the eponymous founding chef left Nepal years ago), but this place is still a definite cut above the average Thamel restaurant. The menu ranges from Balti chicken to Irish stew, with some seasonal specials, and the desserts are worth leaving space for, especially the bread-and-butter pudding.

Rum Doodle
INTERNATIONAL **$$$**

(Map p88; ☏01-424915; www.rumdoodlebar.com; mains Rs 500-800; ☺10am-10pm) The original Rum Doodle was a favourite meeting place for mountaineering expeditions – Edmund Hillary, Reinhold Messner, Ang Rita Sherpa and Rob Hall all left their marks on the wall. The cavernous new location doesn't have the history, but it's a pleasant group-oriented place with a fine rooftop terrace. The steaks, pasta and pizzas are all decent.

The restaurant is named after the world's highest mountain, the 40,000½ft Mt Rum Doodle (as depicted by WE Bowman, author of *The Ascent of Rum Doodle*, a spoof of serious mountaineering books). Fans of the book should try 'Pong's Revenge', a bacon cheeseburger with egg. Modern trekking groups can add their own yeti footprint to the walls.

✖ Freak Street (Jochne) & Durbar Square

Freak St has a number of budget restaurants where you can find good food at lower prices than Thamel. Even if you're staying in other areas of the city, it's nice to know there are some good places for lunch if you're sightseeing around Durbar Sq.

Snowman Restaurant
BAKERY **$**

(Map p68; Freak St; cakes Rs 80-100) A long-running and mellow place, perhaps too dingy for some, this is one of those rare Kathmandu hang-outs that attracts both locals and nostalgic former hippies. The chocolate cake has been drawing overland travellers for close to 40 years now. When Lennon starts singing 'I am the Walrus' on the eight-track, it suddenly feels like 1967 all over again...

Diyalo Restaurant
INTERNATIONAL **$**

(Map p68; Freak St; mains Rs 150-300; ☺8am-10pm) At the Annapurna Lodge, this is a cosy little garden restaurant with a large menu, including tasty crêpes, burgers, sizzlers and a few Chinese and Indian dishes.

Kumari Restaurant
INTERNATIONAL **$**

(Map p68; Freak St; mains Rs 150-300; ☺9am-9pm) Next to the Century Lodge, this friendly hang-out is one of few places that seems to have hung onto some of the mellowness of times past. Grab a seat outside if the interior is too glum. All the travellers' favourites are here at basement prices.

Cosmo de Café Restaurant
INTERNATIONAL **$$**

(Map p73; Durbar Sq; mains Rs 250-400; ☺10am-8pm) This is the best value of the several rooftop tourist restaurants that overlook Durbar Sq. The views over the tiered Maju Deval temple are nice, the range of food is good and prices are reasonable.

✖ Central Kathmandu

The restaurants in the Kantipath and Durbar Marg areas are generally more expensive than around Thamel, but there are several worthwhile splurges.

Dudh Sagar
INDIAN **$**

(Map p68; ☏01-4232263; Kantipath; dosas Rs 100-200; ☺8am-8pm) This bustling local sweet house is the place to reacquaint yourself with South Indian vegetarian snacks such as dosas, *idly* (pounded rice cakes) and *uthapam* (pizza-like rice-and-daal pancake), topped off by a vast range of milk-based Indian sweets. A *masala* dosa followed by *dudh malai* (cream-cheese balls in chilled pistachio milk) makes a great meal for less than Rs 150.

Baan Thai
THAI **$$**

(Map p68; ☏01-4231931; Durbar Marg; mains Rs 350-500; ☺11am-10pm) This unpretentious place overlooking Durbar Marg is a good choice for authentic Thai food. Starters include squid salad and *som tam thai* (young papaya and dried shrimp salad), the curries are creamy and the soups come served in a hotpot big enough for two. Be prepared for the hike up to the 4th floor.

★ **Kaiser Cafe** INTERNATIONAL, AUSTRIAN $$$
(Map p88; ✆01-4425341; Garden of Dreams, Tridevi Marg; mains Rs 600-1650; ⊙9am-10pm) This cafe-restaurant in the Garden of Dreams is run by Dwarika's so quality is high. It's a fine place for a light meal (such as savoury crêpes or build-your-own sandwiches), a quiet breakfast or to linger over a pot of tea or something stiffer. More than anything else, it's one of the city's most romantic locations, especially at dusk.

Austrian-inspired dishes such as Wiener schnitzel and Sachertorte are a nod to the country that financed and oversaw the garden's restoration. The house meatballs are described modestly (by themselves) as 'one of the greatest bar snacks in the world'... You'll have to pay the garden's admission fee to eat here.

Koto Restaurant JAPANESE $$$
(Map p68; ✆01-4226025; Durbar Marg; dishes Rs 360-530, set menus Rs 880; ⊙11.30am-3pm & 6-9.30pm) There are now two branches of long-running Koto next to each other on Durbar Marg; the southern one has the larger selection of sushi and nigiri rolls. Both branches have a wide range of Japanese dishes, from cold soba noodles and mackerel dishes to sukiyaki and bento boxes, plus several set menus.

The Old House FRENCH $$$
(Map p68; ✆01-4250931; www.theoldhouse. com.np; mains Rs 350-1150; ⊙11am-10pm) This easily missed but charming 200-year-old residence features French-Nepali food. Dishes range from light lunch sandwiches and salads to set five-course tasting menus, with standout dishes including the lime trout, chicken leg with olives, bacon and wine sauce and fine desserts such as lime curd on almond cream. It's also a good place for a coffee in the peaceful garden and patio bar area.

Mezze INTERNATIONAL $$$
(Map p68; ✆01-4223087; Mercantile Plaza, Durbar Marg; mains Rs 350-650; ⊙11am-10pm) The folks behind Roadhouse recently opened this hip rooftop bar-restaurant on Durbar Marg. The urban warehouse vibe, open kitchen and striking rooftop location provides a splash of glamour. There are good salads, mezze, paninis and pizza, but it's also a great place for a summer sangria or cocktail under the stars.

1905 INTERNATIONAL $$$
(Map p88; ✆01-4215068; www.1905restaurant. com; Kantipath; lunch mains Rs 350-600, dinner Rs 700-900; ⊙9am-10pm) This classy restaurant is set in a charming former Rana summer palace whose bridge and lily pond add a vaguely colonial-era Burmese air. Lunch is light and casual, with wraps, paninis and salads. Dinner is a more serious affair, with dishes such as hoisin chicken and oyster mushrooms. If nothing else, it's a romantic place for drinks, though the decor and service are a bit faded these days.

Ghar-e-Kebab INDIAN $$$
(Map p68; Durbar Marg; dishes Rs 700-1000; ⊙6.30-11pm) Located inside the Hotel de l'Annapurna on Durbar Marg, this has some of the best north Indian and tandoori food in the city. Indian miniatures hang on the walls underneath an ornate carved-wood ceiling and in the evenings classical Indian music is played and traditional Urdu *ghazals* (love songs) are sung. Try the pistachio sherbet for dessert.

✖ Elsewhere

Dwarika's has a candlelit Friday-night poolside barbecue and dance show that makes for a great splurge.

There are also several excellent midrange and top-end dining options in Patan, a short taxi ride away.

Saigon Pho VIETNAMESE $$
(✆01-4443330; mains Rs 320-500; ⊙10am-10pm) This authentic Vietnamese-run place in Lazimpat is bursting with the flavours of cilantro, lemongrass and fish sauce. The light and tasty dishes include shrimp rice wraps, spring rolls, green papaya salad, *pho* noodles and *ca kho* (fish stew with ginger and onion). Grab a seat in the house's upper balcony.

Kotetsu JAPANESE $$$
(✆01-6218513; Panipokhari; teppanyaki Rs 300-600, sushi Rs 400-1000; ⊙noon-3pm & 5-10pm) It takes a brave person to order sushi in the Himalaya but raw-fish experts (afishionados?) generally rate Kotetsu as the best Japanese place in town. The seafood is flown in fresh from Thailand. The focal point of the restaurant is definitely the central teppanyaki grill. It's at the northern end of Lazimpat, right across from the Japanese embassy, which is no coincidence.

Chez Caroline
FRENCH $$$

(Map p68; ☑01-4263070; mains Rs 500-1500; ⊙9.30am-10pm) In the Baber Mahal Revisited complex, Caroline's is a sophisticated outdoor bistro popular with expat foodies. It offers French-influenced main courses such as wild-mushroom tart with walnut sauce, Roquefort salad, and crêpes Suzette with passionfruit sorbet, plus fine quiches and pastries, daily specials and a lazy weekend brunch (Rs 995), all with a wide range of desserts, teas and wines.

Try a swift glass of pastis (liquorice-flavoured liqueur) with mint syrup: it's the perfect aperitif to an afternoon's shopping.

Self-Catering
For trekking food such as noodles, nuts, dried fruit and cheese, there are several extensive supermarkets grouped around central Thamel Chowk. For more supermarkets try the various branches of **Bluebird Mart** (Map p68; www.bluebirdmart.com.np; ⊙9am-9pm), notably the one by the main bridge across the Bagmati River to Patan; **Big Mart** (Map p68; ⊙7am-9pm) in Lazimpat, near the Radisson Hotel; and **Bhat Bhateni Supermarket** (Map p68; ☑01-4419181; www.bbsm.com.np; ⊙7.30am-8.30pm), south of the Chinese embassy.

Weizen Bakery
BAKERY $

(Map p88; www.weizenrestaurant.com; pastries Rs 65-120, mains Rs 150-280) This bakery-restaurant has decent cakes, breads and pastries, with bakery goods (but not cakes) discounted by 50% after 7pm. The pleasant attached garden is a nice quiet place for breakfast.

Curry Kitchen/Hot Bread
BAKERY $

(Map p88; pastries Rs 60-110) This bakery on the main Thamel junction does a roaring trade in sandwiches, bread rolls, pizza slices and pastries. Add an espresso and head upstairs to the sunny terrace for a leisurely breakfast or pack a ham-and-veg roll for lunch on the run. Bakery items are discounted by 50% after 9.30pm.

Organic Farmer's Market
MARKET $

(Map p88; 1905 Restaurant, Kantipath; ⊙9am-noon Sat) On Saturday mornings local expats and foodies head to 1905 restaurant to stock up on local cheeses, organic produce, jams and other freshly made goodies.

🍷 Drinking & Nightlife

There are bars scattered around Thamel, all within a short walk of each other, and few were affected by the 2015 earthquake. Just poke your nose in to see which has the crowd and style that appeals. Most places have a happy hour between 5pm and 8pm, with two-for-one cocktails, and many have live music, though the playlists can get monotonously familiar. Most bars in Thamel close by 11pm, though there are moves to extend hours. A beer costs between Rs 350 and Rs 450 in most places.

Be wary of Thamel's sleazy 'dance bars' or 'shower dance' bars. At first glance many seem quite tame, but most are simply fronts for prostitution.

Himalayan Java
CAFE

(Map p88; ☑01-4422519; www.himalayanjava.com; Tridevi Marg; coffee Rs 110, snacks Rs 300; ⊙7am-9pm) The various branches of this modern and buzzing coffeehouse are the place to lose yourself in a sofa, a laptop and a pulse-reviving Americano. There are also breakfasts, paninis, salads and cakes. The main Tridevi Marg branch has a balcony, lots of sofas and a big-screen TV for the football, but feels a bit like a hotel foyer; the smaller Mandala St branch (Map p88) in Thamel is quiet and popular.

New Maya Cocktail Bar
COCKTAIL BAR

(Map p88; cocktails Rs 390-475; ⊙4-11pm) A long-running favourite; the two-for-one cocktails between 4pm and 10pm are a guaranteed jump-start to a good evening and there are decent Mexican burritos and chimichangas if you get peckish. Weekends bring free snacks.

Tom & Jerry Pub
BAR

(Map p88; ☑01-4700264; beer from Rs 350; ⊙10am-11pm) This is a long-running, rowdy upstairs place that has pool tables and a dance floor. Thursday is ladies' night.

Jatra
LOUNGE

(Map p88; ☑01-4211010; cocktails Rs 310; 🛜) A quiet, intimate and pretty cool venue for a beer or dinner (mains Rs 400 to Rs 500), with spacious indoor and outdoor seating, global music and candlelight. Happy hour brings modest drink discounts between 5pm and 7pm; on Wednesdays ladies get a free cocktail.

Tamas Spa Lounge
LOUNGE

(Map p88; ☑01-4275658; drinks Rs 300; ⊙10am-midnight) You need to dress up to enjoy this glam lounge bar, decked out in sofas and satin in a lush palette of cool creams. Take a seat in the courtyard or the old Rana house and indulge your inner princess with a sparkling Bellini or espresso martini. A basement club pumps out the bass on Friday and Saturday after 10pm.

Sam's Bar
BAR

(Map p88; ⊙4-11pm) A long-time favourite with trek leaders, mountain guides and other Kathmandu regulars. There's reggae every Saturday.

☆ Entertainment

Nepal is an early-to-bed country and even in Kathmandu you'll find few people on the streets after 10pm, especially when the capital's political situation is tense.

Duelling cover bands compete for aural supremacy at various Thamel restaurants on Friday and Saturday nights in the high season – just follow the sound of Bryan Adams and Coldplay covers.

Beyond this, you could take in a Bollywood blockbuster or try to earn back your flight money at one of half a dozen casinos. Major sporting events such as Premier League football and the Formula 1 Grand Prix are televised in all the major bars.

There are also several cultural performances, which generally involve local youths wearing a variety of dress over their jeans and performing traditional dances from Nepal's various ethnic groups, accompanied by a live band that includes a tabla, harmonium and singer.

Casinos

Kathmandu's casinos are attached to most of the five-star hotels and are open 24 hours, though they are frequently closed by the government due to disputes over unpaid taxes. You can play in either Indian rupees or US dollars, and winnings (in the same currency) can be taken out of the country when you leave. The main games offered are roulette and blackjack. Most clients are Indian; Nepalis are officially forbidden from entering.

Casino Royale
CASINO

(Map p68; ☑01-4271244; ⊙24hr) Pull your tuxedo out of your backpack, polish up your best Sean Connery impersonation ('Aaah, Mish Moneypenny...') and make a beeline for this former Rana palace at the Yak & Yeti Hotel. Hang around the tables (not the slots)

long enough and staff may ply you with a dinner buffet, though sadly the Russian dancing girls have gone back to Moscow.

Music & Dance

As well as the bands blasting out covers of 'Rockin' in the Free World' in the bars of Thamel, there are a few performances of Nepali music and dancing in the restaurants of the top-end hotels, but you'll find little in the way of more cultured music and dance.

Jazz Upstairs
LIVE MUSIC

(Map p68; ☑01-4410436; cover Rs 200; ⊙noon-11pm Sun-Fri, 7-11pm Sat) It's worth schlepping out to Lazimpat on a Wednesday and Saturday night (from 8pm) to catch the live jazz in this tiny upstairs bar, recently relocated to new top-floor digs. The stage is intimate, the vibe is friendly and the clientele is an interesting mix of locals and expats. Monday brings live blues.

House of Music
LIVE MUSIC

(Map p88; ☑9851075172; cover Rs 200-400; ⊙11am-11pm Tue-Sun) This beery bar is the best place in Kathmandu to listen to original Nepali rock, reggae and R'n'B music, mostly on Friday and Wednesday. It's in northern Thamel but miles away from the cover bands of the centre. Upcoming concerts are posted on the venue's Facebook page. It's part-owned by the drummer of 1974AD, one of Nepal's biggest bands.

Kalamandapa Institute of Classical Nepalese Performing Arts
DANCE

(Map p68; ☑01-4271545; admission Rs 600) Nepali classical dance (and occasional theatre) is performed at Hotel Vajra most Tuesdays at 7pm. Phone ahead to check schedules.

Cinemas

Sadly, the video cafes made famous by the title of Pico Iyer's book *Video Night in Kathmandu* have disappeared, replaced by fake DVD stores.

Jai Nepal Cinema
CINEMA

(Map p68; ☑01-4442220; www.jainepal.com; Narayanhiti Marg; stalls/balcony Rs 210/250) This is the most convenient place to catch the latest Bollywood-style Hindi or Nepali hit. Not understanding the dialogue is really only a minor hindrance to enjoying these comedy-musical 'masala movies'.

QUIRKY KATHMANDU

Kathmandu has more than its fair share of quirk and, as with most places in the subcontinent, a 10-minute walk in any direction will throw up numerous curiosities.

The corridors of the **Natural History Museum** (p120) are full of bizarre moth-eaten animals and jars that lie somewhere between a school science experiment and *The Texas Chainsaw Massacre*. The 20ft python skin and nine-month-old baby rhino in a jar are guaranteed to give you nightmares. The other exhibits are a bit slapdash, including the line of stuffed birds nailed carelessly to a bit of wood to indicate their distribution, or the big pile of elephant dung deposited randomly in the front corner.

The nearby **National Museum** (p120) also houses more than its fair share of weirdness, including the skin of a two-headed calf and a portrait of King Prithvi Narayan Shah giving everyone the finger (apparently symbolising the unity of the nation...).

Once it reopens following earthquake repairs, the **Tribhuvan Museum** (Map p73; ⊘10.30am-4pm Tue-Sat Feb-Oct, to 3pm Tue-Sat Nov-Jan, to 2pm Sun) in Hanuman Dhoka will be the place to see such quirky gems of royal paraphernalia as the king's personal parachuting uniform, his film projector and his walking stick with a spring-loaded sword inside – very '007'.

Kathmandu's **Kaiser Library** (Map p88; ☑01-4411318; Ministry of Education & Sports compound, cnr Kantipath & Tridevi Marg; ⊘10.30am-4.30pm Sun-Thu, to 2.30pm Fri) is definitely worth a visit, partly for its remarkable collection of antique travel books but also for the main reading room, which has antique globes, a stuffed tiger and suits of armour that you expect to spring to life at any moment.

Compared to all this funkiness, Kathmandu's old town is pretty docile. Look for the antique **fire engines** hidden behind a grille just west of the junction of New Rd and Sukra Path.

If you get a toothache during your trip, be sure to visit the old town's **toothache god** across from Sikha Narayan Temple – the god is represented by a tiny image in a raggedy old stump of wood covered with hundreds of nails and coins.

QFX Civil Mall   CINEMA
(Map p68; ☑01-4442220; www.qfxcinemas.com; 7th fl, Civil Mall, Sundhara; tickets Rs 210-340) The main cinema for English-language Hollywood blockbusters, with morning and matinee discounts.

🔒 Shopping

Kathmandu offers the best shopping in the country. Everything that is turned out in the various centres around the valley can be found here, although you can often find a better choice, or more unusual items, in the centres that produce the items – Jawalakhel (southern Patan) for Tibetan carpets, Patan for cast-metal statues, Bhaktapur for woodcarvings, and Thimi for masks. Head over to Patan to fnd well-stocked fair-trade shops.

Thamel has some excellent trekking gear for sale, but don't think that you are necessarily getting the genuine article. Most of the 'Columbia' fleeces and 'North Face' jackets are Chinese knock-offs or made locally but with imported fleece and Gore-Tex.

Kathmandu has dozens of excellent bookshops with a great selection of Himalaya titles, including books that are not usually available outside the country. Most dealers will buy back books for 50% of what you paid.

An endless supply of curios, art pieces and plain old junk is churned out for the tourist trade. Most does not come from Tibet but from the local Tamang community. Prayer flags and prayer wheels are a popular buy in Durbar Sq, Bodhnath and Swayambhunath, but be prepared to bargain.

Remember that antiques (over 100 years old) cannot be taken out of the country. Get a receipt and a description of any major purchase from the shop where you bought it.

Thamel in particular can be a stressful place to shop, what with all the tiger-balm sellers, rickshaw drivers and high-speed motorbikers. Dive into a side street or garden haven when stress levels start to rise.

Pilgrims Book House   BOOKS
(Map p88; ☑01-4221546; www.pilgrimsonline-shop.com) Kathmandu's best bookstore tragically burned down in 2013. Hopefully it will be reincarnated phoenix-like; however in

the meantime its branch location contains as many of the saved books as possible.

Amrita Craft Collection HANDICRAFTS
(Map p88; ☑01-4240757; www.amritacraft.com) This broad collection of crafts and clothing is a good place to start your Thamel shopping. Quality isn't top-notch but subtract 20% from its fixed prices and you get a good benchmark for what you should aim to pay on the street if you don't mind haggling.

Aroma Garden INCENSE
(Map p88; ☑01-4420724; www.aromagarden.biz) As the name suggests, this is Thamel's sweetest-smelling shop. It's a good one-stop shop for *dhoop* (incense), essential oils, Himalayan soaps and almost anything else that smells great.

Paper Park PAPER PRODUCTS
(Map p88; ☑01-4700475; www.handmadepaperpark.com) One of the best of several shops in Thamel that sell handmade paper products, from photo albums to paper lamps. The paper comes from the *lokta* (daphne) plant, whose bark is boiled and beaten with wooden mallets into a pulp and spread over a frame to dry. The finished product folds

THE ESSENTIAL THAMEL SHOPPING GUIDE

From Kashmiri carpets and fake CDs to trekking poles and yak-milk soap, Thamel offers the best collection of shops in the country. Bring an extra bag and stock up on next year's Christmas presents.

Spices Plenty of shops and supermarkets in Thamel sell small packets of spices, from momo mixes to chai spices, or head to Asan Tole, where the locals buy their freshly ground masalas.

Embroidery Sewing machines around Thamel whir away late into the night adding logos and Tibetan symbols to jackets, hats and T-shirts. Trekkers can commission badges and T-shirts commemorating their successful trek or even get a business logo made.

Jewellery Kathmandu is a great place for jewellery, particularly silver. Buy it ready-made, ask the jeweller to create a design for you or bring in something you would like copied. The price of silver is quoted per *tola* (11.7g) in the daily newspaper.

Puppets Puppets make good gifts for children and are made in Bhaktapur as well as other centres. They're often of multiarmed deities clutching little wooden weapons in each hand. The puppet heads may be made of easily broken clay or more durable papier mâché.

Pashminas A shawl or scarf made from fine pashmina (the underhair of a mountain goat) is a popular buy. The cost of a shawl depends on the percentage of pashmina in the mix and from which part of the goat's body the hair originated, starting from the cheapest back wool and rising through the belly and chest to neck hair, which is about five times more expensive than back hair. The cheapest shawls are a 70/30% cotton/pashmina blend, silk-pashmina blends cost around 30% more and pure pashmina shawls range from around US$50 to US$275 for a top-end ring shawl (named because they are fine enough to be pulled through a finger ring; also known as a water shawl).

Tea Ilam, Ontu, Kanyan and Mai Valley teas are the best Nepali teas, from the east of the country near Darjeeling. Expect to pay anything from Rs 600 (in Ilam) to Rs 3000 (in Thamel) per kilogram for good Ilam tea. The excellently named 'super fine tipi golden flower orange pekoe' tea is about as good as it gets. Connoisseurs choose the first (March) or second (May) flush, rather than the substandard monsoon flush. Lemon tea flavoured with lemongrass is another favourite, as is pre-spiced masala tea (Rs 100 to Rs 150 per 100g).

Clothes There are lots of funky wool hats, felt bags, embroidered T-shirts (our favourite has 'Same Same...' on the front and '...But Different' on the back!), jumpers etc, particularly on the twisting road known as Saatghumti. Always try clothes on before handing over the cash. Impossibly cute baby-sized North Face fleeces and down jackets are hard to pass by.

Prayer flags The best place to buy is the street in front of the Kathesimbhu Stupa south of Thamel. Choose between cheaper polyester and better-quality cotton flags and remember, this is your karma that we are talking about.

Baber Mahal Revisited — ARTS & CRAFTS
(Map p68) Originally built in 1919 by the then prime minister for his son, this unique complex of neoclassical Rana palace outbuildings has been redeveloped to house a warren of chic clothing shops, designer galleries and handicraft shops, as well as a couple of top-end restaurants and bars. Neatly touched up after the 2015 earthquake, it's aimed squarely at expats and wealthy locals so prices are as high as the quality.

Curio Arts — ARTS & CRAFTS
(Map p68; ☑01-4224871; www.devasarts.com) Durbar Marg has several top-end showrooms concentrating on statues, Tibetan furniture and other crafts. Curio Arts is a good place to start.

Mahaguthi — FAIR TRADE, HOMEWARES
(Map p68; ☑01-4438760; www.mahaguthi.org; ⊙10am-6.30pm Sun-Fri, to 5pm Sat) Good range of crafts and home furnishings, much of it made by disadvantaged or minority groups, with nice batiks made by paralysed women. There's a larger outlet (p151) and collection of other fair-trade stores in Kopundol in Patan.

Shona's Alpine Rental — OUTDOOR EQUIPMENT
(Map p88; ☑01-4265120) Reliable rentals and gear shop that makes its own sleeping bags and offers advice on the best trek gear for your trip. Get a season warmer than they recommend. Sleeping bags and down jackets cost Rs 80 to Rs 100 each per day to rent. You can make a deposit in any combination of currencies.

Sports Wear International — OUTDOOR EQUIPMENT
(Map p88; www.hi-himal.com) Several trekkers have recommended this friendly gear shop for equipment rental.

Holyland Hiking Shop — OUTDOOR EQUIPMENT
(Map p88; ☑01-4248104) The better trekking gear shops are at the southern end of Thamel. Both this and the nearby **Sonam Gear** (Map p88; ☑01-4259191) have been recommended.

North Face — OUTDOOR EQUIPMENT
One of several *pukka* (not fake) gear shops on Tridevi Marg, offering imported gear at foreign prices. These shops sell everything from Black Diamond climbing gear to US Thermarests. Other brands such as Mountain Hard Wear, Marmot, and locally made Sherpa, are nearby.

Tibet Book Store — BOOKS
(Map p88; ☑01-4415788; Tridevi Marg) The best collection of Tibet-related titles, once owned by the Tibetan government-in-exile.

Vajra Books — BOOKS
(Map p88; ☑01-4220562; www.vajrabooks.com.np; Jyatha) This knowledgeable local publisher offers an excellent selection of academic books and is a magnet for local writers and researchers. Ask to see the expanded section upstairs.

Nepal Book Depot — BOOKS
(Map p88; ⊙9am-9pm) Good prices, a central location and a huge selection of new and secondhand titles.

Tara Oriental — WOMEN'S CLOTHING
(Map p68; ☑01-4436315; www.taraoriental.com; Lazimpat) This designer's studio is the best place for top-end designer pashmina throws, scarves and sweaters, retailing at around US$160. Yes, it's expensive but it's top-end stuff.

ℹ Information

EMERGENCY
Ambulance Service (☑102, 01-4521048) Provided by Patan Hospital.
Fire Brigade (☑101, 01-4221177)
Police (☑100, 01-4223011; www.nepalpolice.gov.np)
Red Cross Ambulance (☑01-4228094)
Tourist Police (☑in Bhrikuti 01-4247041, in Thamel 01-4700750)

INTERNET ACCESS
There are a few cybercafes in Thamel, though almost all cafes, restaurants and hotels offer free wi-fi.

LAUNDRY
Several laundries across Thamel will machine-wash laundry for Rs 50 per kilo. Get it back the next day or pay double for a three-hour service. Amazingly, it all comes back relatively clean, even after a three-week trek. Power cuts can delay wash times so don't cut it too fine by handing in your laundry the day before your flight.

MEDICAL SERVICES
Dozens of pharmacies on the fringes of Thamel offer all the cheap antibiotics you can pronounce.
CIWEC Clinic Travel Medicine Center (Map p68; ☑01-4424111, 01-4435232; www.ciwec-clinic.com; ⊙emergency 24hr, clinic

ⓘ DANGERS & ANNOYANCES

The combination of ancient vehicles, low-quality fuel and lack of emission controls makes the streets of Kathmandu particularly dirty, noisy and unpleasant. Bear in mind the following:

➡ Traffic rules exist, but are rarely enforced; be especially careful when crossing streets or riding a bicycle.

➡ Traffic is supposed to travel on the left side of the road, but many drivers simply choose the most convenient side, which can make walking in Kathmandu a deeply stressful experience.

➡ Remember that pedestrians account for over 40% of all traffic fatalities in Nepal.

➡ Consider bringing a face mask to filter out dust and emission particles, especially if you plan to ride a bicycle or motorcycle in Kathmandu. After a few days in the city you will likely feel the onset of a throat infection.

➡ Post-earthquake repairs are ongoing and there is lots of rubble piled up in the streets; some of Kathmandu's historic bahals (courtyards) are inaccessible because of debris.

Other annoyances in Thamel are the crazy motorcyclists, and the barrage of irritating flute sellers, tiger-balm hawkers, chess-set sellers, musical-instrument vendors, travel-agency touts, hashish suppliers, freelance trekking guides and rickshaw drivers.

Note that the colourful sadhus (itinerant holy men) who frequent Durbar Sq and Pashupatinath will expect *baksheesh* (a tip) if you take a photo, as will the Thamel 'holy men' who anoint you with a *tika* on your forehead.

Kathmandu is occasionally the focus of political demonstrations and bandhs (strikes), which close shops and shut down transport.

9am–noon & 1-4pm Mon–Fri) In operation since 1982 and has an international reputation for research into travellers' medical problems. Staff are mostly foreigners and a doctor is on call around the clock. A consultation costs around US$65. Credit cards are accepted and the centre is used to dealing with insurance claims.

CIWEC Dental Clinic (Map p68; ☎01-4440100, emergency 4424111; www.ciwec-clinic.com; Lazimpat) US dentist on the top floor of CIWEC Clinic.

Healthy Smiles (Map p68; ☎01-4420800; www.smilenepal.com; Lazimpat) UK-trained dentist, opposite the Hotel Ambassador.

Nepal International Clinic (Map p68; ☎01-4435357, 4434642; www.nepalinternational clinic.com; Lal Durbar; ☺9am-1pm & 2-5pm) Just south of the New Royal Palace, east of Thamel. It has an excellent reputation and is slightly cheaper than the CIWEC Clinic. Credit cards accepted.

NORVIC International Hospital (Map p68; ☎01-4258554; www.norvichospital.com; Thapathali) Private Nepali hospital with a good reputation for cardiology.

Patan Hospital (p151)

MONEY

There are dozens of licensed moneychangers in Thamel. Their hours are longer than those of the banks (generally until 8pm or so) and rates are similar, perhaps even slightly higher if you don't need a receipt.

Useful ATMs in the Thamel area are located beside Yin Yang Restaurant, Ganesh Man Singh Building and Roadhouse Cafe.

Himalayan Bank (Map p88; ☎01-4250208; www.himalayanbank.com; Tridevi Marg; ☺10am-3pm Sun-Fri, 10am-1pm Sat) The most convenient bank for travellers in Thamel, this kiosk on Tridevi Marg changes cash and travellers cheques until 3pm; after this, head to the main branch in the basement of the nearby Sanchaya Kosh Bhawan shopping centre. Cash advances on a Visa card are possible and there's a prominent ATM next to the kiosk. It's in front of the Three Goddesses Temples. There is no commission for changing cash but travellers cheques incur a charge of 0.75% (minimum Rs 250).

Standard Chartered Bank (Map p68; ☎01-4418456; Lazimpat; ☺9.45am-7pm Sun-Thu, 9.45am-4.30pm Fri, 9.30am-12.30pm Sat & holidays) Well-located ATMs include opposite the Third Eye restaurant and in the compound of the Kathmandu Guest House. The main branch in Lazimpat charges 1.5% (minimum Rs 300) to change travellers cheques and Rs 200 per transaction for cash. There's no charge for a rupee cash advance on a credit card, but you pay 2% to get the cash in US dollars.

POST

Most bookshops in Thamel sell stamps and deliver postcards to the post office, which is much easier than making a special trip to the post office yourself.

Main Post Office (Map p68; Sundhara; ⊙7am-6pm Sun-Thu, to 3pm Fri) Facing the Tundikhel near the ruins of the Bhimsen Tower. Stalls in the courtyard sell airmail and padded envelopes. You can post packages up to 2kg at counter 16; beyond that you need to go to the foreign post office, which is a bit of an ordeal so, if you're short of time, use a cargo agency such as **Diki Continental Exports** (Map p88; ☑01-4256919; www.dikiexports.com; JP School, Thamel).

Foreign Post Office (Map p68; Sundhara; ⊙10am-5pm Sun-Thu, 10am-3pm Fri) Parcels can be sent from here, in a separate building just north of the main post office. Parcels have to be examined and sealed by a customs officer. Start the process before 2pm.

DHL (Map p88; ☑01-2298124; www.dhl.com.np; ⊙10.30am-6.30pm Mon-Fri) The Thamel service centre has the most convenient location.

FedEx (Map p68; ☑01-4269249; www.fedex.com/np; Kantipath; ⊙9am-6pm Sun-Fri, to 1pm Sat) As a guide, 1kg of documents costs around Rs 4500 to the USA and takes three days.

TELEPHONE

If for some reason you don't have a mobile phone or access to Skype or Viber, you can make international telephone calls from internet cafes for around Rs 20 per minute.

There are dozens of Ncell offices around town where you can buy or top up a SIM card.

TOURIST INFORMATION

There are a number of good noticeboards in Thamel that are worth checking for information on apartments, travel and trekking partners, courses and cultural events. The Kathmandu Guest House (p92) has a good noticeboard, as do the Pumpernickel Bakery (p102) and Fire & Ice Pizzeria (p104).

For more on trekking permits and related organisations, see the Planning Your Trek chapter.

Tourist Service Centre (Map p68; ☑01-4256909 ext 223, 24hr tourism hotline ☑01-4225709; www.welcomenepal.com; Bhrikuti Mandap; ⊙10am-1pm & 2-5pm Sun-Fri, TIMS card 7am-7pm daily, national parks tickets 9am-2pm Sun-Fri) On the eastern side of the Tundikhel parade ground; has an inconvenient location but is the place to get trekking permits and a TIMS card, and pay national park fees.

TRAVEL AGENCIES

Flight Connection International (Map p88; ☑01-4258282, international flights 4233111; www.flightconnectionintl.com; Jyatha, Thamel) Good for flight tickets. The international department is in Gaia Restaurant (p102).

President Travel & Tours (Map p68; ☑01-4220245; www.pttnepal.com; Durbar Marg) Professional agency favoured by expats and wealthy Nepalis; particularly good at getting seats on heavily booked flights.

Wayfarers (Map p88; ☑01-4266010; www.wayfarers.com.np; JP School Rd, Thamel; ⊙9am-6pm Mon-Fri, to 5pm Sat & Sun) For straight-talking ticketing, bespoke tours and Kathmandu Valley walking trips.

VISA EXTENSIONS

Visa extensions of 30 to 60 days are fairly painless at the Central Immigration Office (p381). You need to make your application online and upload a photo up to 15 days before arriving at the office, though there is currently a computer in the hall in case you forget. The process generally takes less than one hour. Extensions cost US$30 for a minimum 15 days, plus US$2 per additional day

ⓘ Getting There & Away

AIR

Kathmandu's international and domestic airports reopened quickly after the 2015 earthquake and flights are operating as normal. However, it's a good idea to double-check the departure time of your return flight before flying. This goes double for the notoriously unreliable Nepal Airlines, with whom you should reconfirm at least once.

Domestic Airlines

Kathmandu is the main hub for domestic flights, including to Pokhara (US$119), Lukla (US$165), Bharatpur (US$108; for Chitwan) and Bhairawa (US$142). The most reliable airlines are Buddha and Yeti/Tara airlines; others seem to change with the weather. It's far less hassle to buy tickets through a travel agency, and you'll probably get a better deal this way.

Nepal Airlines domestic office (Map p68; ☑01-4227133; ⊙9.30am-1pm & 2-5pm) has flights to remoter airstrips but only has computerised booking on some of its flights. The other domestic carriers are much more reliable if you have a choice. Book at a travel agent or direct with the office to the side of the main Nepal Airlines international booking centre.

Be aware that Nepali airlines don't have the best safety record (p387).

BUS
Long-Distance Buses

The **Gongabu bus station** (Ring Rd, Balaju) is north of the city centre; the surrounding area saw some earthquake damage, but the bus stand is fully operational. It is also called the Kathmandu

Bus Terminal, or simply 'new bus park'. This bus station is basically for all long-distance buses, including to Pokhara and destinations in the Terai. It's a huge and confusing place and there are very few signs in English, but most of the ticket sellers are very helpful. There's often more than one reservation counter for each destination. Bookings for long trips should be made a day in advance – Thamel travel agents will do this for a fee and this will save you both time and the taxi fare. Note that travel to some destinations may be disrupted by landslides following the 2015 earthquakes – check before you travel.

Bus 23 (Rs 15) runs to Gongabu bus station from Lekhnath Marg on the northern edge of Thamel but takes an age. A taxi from Thamel costs around Rs 200.

Buses serving the Langtang region leave from the **Pasang Lhamo Transport** (☎ 01-4356342) stand at Machha Pokhari (Fish Pond), diagonally across the Ring Rd from Gongabu bus station. However, this region was devastated by the 2015 earthquakes and the area is unlikely to be fully open to trekkers for some time. Before the disaster, there were daily tourist buses (Rs 500, 7am) and local services (Rs 340, 6.20am, 6.50am and 7.30am) to Syabrubesi via Dhunche, and daily buses to Nuwakot (Rs 190, 9.20am and 1pm) and Kakani (Rs 50, every 30 minutes); however, all these routes may be disrupted, so check that buses are running and trails are open before you travel.

Popular tourist buses to Pokhara (Rs 800, seven hours) and Sauraha for Chitwan National Park (Rs 600, six hours) depart daily at 7am from a far more convenient location at the Thamel end

BUSES FROM GONGABU BUS STATION

DESTINATION	DISTANCE (KM)	DEPARTURES	DURATION (HR)	COST (RS)	TICKET WINDOW
Besi Sahar	150	tourist bus 7am, 8am & 10am	6	450	25, 32
Bhairawa/ Sunauli	282	ordinary bus every 15min, tourist bus 8am	8	550 (tourist bus 960)	23, 24, 29
Bharatpur	150	hourly	5	330	17, 16
Biratnagar	540	5am, 3.30pm	14	1250	10, 11
Birganj	300	7am, 8am, 7.15pm	8	550	16
Butwal	237	ordinary bus every 15min, tourist bus 8am	7-9	510	28, 29
Gorkha	140	6am-noon	5	300	27, 43
Hile (via Dharan)	635	3pm	14	1250	39
Kakarbhitta	610	4.30am, 4-5pm	14	1150-1380	26, 39
Lumbini	260	7am (AC), 7.15am, 7.30pm	9-10	600-700 (AC 1035)	28, 29
Nepalganj	530	deluxe 6am & 6pm; ordinary 4pm, 5pm & 7pm	12	1180-1230	24, 20, 36
Pokhara	200	tourist bus 8.30am, 10am, 11am; others every 15min to 1pm	6-8	425 (tourist bus 500)	27, 28
Tansen (Palpa)	300	7.20am, 5.30pm	10	620	28, 29

of Kantipath. Buses are comfortable and you get a fixed seat number with your ticket.

Greenline (Map p88; ☑ 01-4253885; www.greenline.com.np; Tridevi Marg; ⊘7am-5.30pm) offers air-con deluxe services that are considerably more expensive than the tourist buses (but include lunch). There are daily morning buses at 7.30am to Pokhara (US$23, six hours) and Chitwan (US$20, six hours), with a lunch break and bus change in Kurintar. You should book a day or two in advance.

Golden Travels (Map p68; ☑ 01-4220036; Woodlands Complex, Durbar Marg) runs similar services, departing at 7am from Kantipath to Pokhara (US$15 with lunch). Golden and affiliated transport companies Baba Bhairav and Buddha Darshhan run daily services at 7am to Sunauli (US$15) and Lumbini (US$15, nine hours). The latter two depart from Kalanki on the southwestern corner of the Ring Rd; all three companies offer a free transfer to Kalanki from Kantipath at 7am. On the return you will be dropped at Sundhara on the eastern edge of Kathmandu's old town. Buy tickets at any travel agency.

To/From the Kathmandu Valley

Buses for most destinations within the Kathmandu Valley, and for those on or accessed from the Arniko Hwy (for Jiri, Barabise and Kodari on the Tibetan border), operate from the **Ratna Park bus station** (Map p68), also known as the old/new city bus stand, in the centre of the city on the eastern edge of Tundikhel parade ground. The station is a bit of a horror, drenched in diesel fumes, with no English signs and not much English spoken. Keep shouting out your destination and someone will eventually direct you to the right bus. Again, be aware that some routes may be disrupted by earthquake damage.

Some services leave from other stops around Kathmandu. Buses to Bhaktapur (Rs 30, one hour) run from a stand on Bagh Bazar. Drivers often try to charge foreigners double on this route.

Buses to Pharping and Dakshinkali leave from Shahid Gate (Martyrs' Memorial) at the southern end of the Tundikhel parade ground, as well as the Ratna Park station.

Buses heading to Bungamati, Godavari and Chapagaon in the southern valley leave from Patan.

A daily direct tourist bus to Nagarkot (Rs 400, two hours) departs at 1pm from a lot in front of the Hotel Malla in Lainchhaur, though it's not the most reliable service and you may have to ask around to find it.

CAR

Although you cannot rent cars on a drive-yourself basis, they can be readily rented with a driver from a number of travel agencies. The rental cost is relatively high, both in terms of the initial hiring charge and fuel. Charges are as high as US$50 per day, although they can be lower, especially if you are not covering a huge distance.

TAXI

A better option than hiring a car is to hire a taxi for the day. Between several people, longer taxi trips around the valley, or even outside it, are affordable. A half-/full-day sightseeing trip within the valley starts at around Rs 1000/1800.

For longer journeys outside the valley count on about Rs 3000 per day plus fuel, which is generally cheaper than hiring a car through a travel agency.

ℹ Getting Around

Most of the sights in Kathmandu itself can easily be covered on foot, and this is by far the best way to appreciate the city, even if the traffic is atrocious. If and when you run out of steam, there are plenty of reasonably priced taxis available.

TO/FROM THE AIRPORT

Kathmandu's international airport is called **Tribhuvan Airport** (☑ 01-4472256; www.tiairport.com.np) after the late king; the area's former name of Gaucher (literally 'cow pasture') speaks volumes about Kathmandu's rapid urban expansion.

Getting into town is quite straightforward. Both the international and domestic terminals

BUSES FROM RATNA PARK BUS STATION

DESTINATION	DEPARTURES	DURATION	COST (RS)
Banepa		2hr	45
Barabise	every 30min, 5am-4pm	4hr	207
Dhulikhel		2hr	55
Kodari	7am express, 8am, 11.30am, 2pm	4½hr	270-320
Panauti		1½-2hr	60
Patan		20min	15

Unless otherwise noted, buses depart when full.

DAY TRIPS FROM KATHMANDU

The great thing about Kathmandu is that there are so many fantastic sights just a couple of kilometres outside the city centre. You can check out any of the following sites and still be back in Thamel for the start of happy hour:

Bhaktapur (p152)

Patan (p137)

Bodhnath (p128)

Budhanilkantha (p135)

offer a fixed-price prepaid taxi service, currently Rs 700 to Thamel.

Once outside the international terminal you will be confronted by hotel touts, who are often taxi drivers making commission on taking you to a particular hotel. Many hold up a signboard of the particular hotel they are connected with and, if the one you want is there, you can get a free lift. The drawback with the taxis is that the hotel is then much less likely to offer you a discount, as it will be paying a hefty commission to the taxi driver. During strikes, the government often arranges a special airport bus that operates with a military guard!

If you book a room in advance for more than one night, many hotels will pick you up for free.

Public buses leave from the main road – about 300m from the terminal – but they're only really practical if you have very little luggage and know exactly how to get to where you want to go.

From Kathmandu to the airport you should be able to get a taxi for Rs 500, a bit more for a late or early flight.

BICYCLE

Cycling is a great way to explore parts of the Kathmandu Valley and many companies offer bike rentals and tours. You need to be selective about your routes to avoid the heavy traffic and ask around to make sure routes are clear following the 2015 earthquake.

Mountain bikes cost from around Rs 500 per day for simple models. For longer trips around the valley, the major mountain-bike companies such as Dawn Till Dusk (p44) and Path Finder Cycling (p45) hire out high-quality bikes with front suspension and disc brakes for around US$10 to US$15 per day. See p44 for more information.

If you want to make an early start, most places are happy to give you the bike the evening before. For all bikes, negotiate discounts for rentals of more than a day. You should get a helmet,

lock and repair kit. Check the brakes before committing and be certain to lock the bike whenever you leave it.

For cycling routes outside Kathmandu city, see p311.

CYCLE-RICKSHAW

Cycle-rickshaws cost around Rs 60 for short rides around Thamel or the old town, but you can expect to have to haggle hard. It's essential to agree on a price before you start.

MOTORCYCLE

There are a number of motorcycle rental operators in Thamel. You will have to leave your passport as deposit. For Rs 600 per day you'll get a 150cc Indian-made Hero Honda or Pulsar road bike, which is generally fine for road trips in the Kathmandu Valley.

Reputable rental companies will require you to have an international driving licence to ride a motorbike in Nepal. On the road this regulation hasn't been enforced for years, but recent reports suggest traffic police are targeting foreigners on this and other hitherto disregarded traffic violations in an attempt to raise funds. A traffic fine will set you back around Rs 1000.

Motorcycles can be great fun outside the town, once you master the traffic. The main problem is getting out of Kathmandu, which can be a stressful, choking and dangerous experience. You will need a pair of goggles and some kind of face mask (available in most pharmacies).

Fuel currently costs Rs 135 per litre; you'll only need a couple of litres for a day trip. Beyond the Ring Road petrol stations are few and far between.

Singh Motorbike Centre (Map p88; 🔊 01-4418594; pyare4059@gmail.com; Bhagawatisthan, Thamel; ☻8am-7pm) is a reliable place for bike hire. New Indian-made Pulsar 200cc (Rs 1500) motorbikes are most commonly available, though you might find a cheaper Hero Honda (Rs 700) or an Enfield Bullet (Rs 3000).

Pheasant Transportation Service (Map p88; 🔊 01-4701090; www.biketournepal. com; Thamel Chowk), in a side street off the central Thamel junction, has somewhat more elastic prices, ranging from Rs 600 for an older 150cc Hero Honda to Rs 1200 for a 220cc Pulsar.

TAXI

Taxis are quite reasonably priced, though few drivers use the meters in these days of rising fuel prices. Shorter rides around town (including to the bus station) cost around Rs 200. Night-time rates (between 10pm and 6am) cost 50% more.

Most taxis are tiny Suzuki Marutis, which can just about fit two backpackers and their luggage.

The closest taxi stand to Thamel is on Tridevi Marg, close to the junction with Jyatha Rd. Taxis can be booked in advance on ☎ 01-4420987; at night call ☎ 01-4224374.

Other approximate taxi fares from Thamel:

Bhaktapur Rs 700
Bodhnath Rs 400
Budhanilkantha Rs 700
Changu Narayan Rs 1600
Nagarkot Rs 3000
Pashupatinath Rs 400
Patan Rs 350
Swayambhunath Rs 250

AROUND KATHMANDU

There are several outlying attractions inside the Ring Road that surrounds Kathmandu. All can be reached by taxi or rickshaw, by rented bicycle or motorcycle, or on foot.

Swayambhunath

A journey up to the Buddhist temple and Unesco World Heritage Site of Swayambhunath is one of the definitive experiences of Kathmandu. Mobbed by monkeys and soaring above the city on a lofty hilltop, the 'Monkey Temple' is a fascinating, chaotic jumble of Buddhist and Hindu iconography. Even the 2015 earthquake failed to topple Kathmandu's best loved temple, though outlying buildings crumbled in the tremor.

Coming to Swayambhunath is an intoxicating experience, with ancient carvings jammed into every spare inch of space and the smell of incense and butter lamps hanging heavy in the air. The mystical atmosphere is heightened in the morning and evening by local devotees who make a ritual circumnavigation of the stupa, spinning the prayer wheels set into its base. It is a great place to watch the sun set over Kathmandu.

According to legend, the Kathmandu Valley was once a lake – geological evidence supports this – and the hill now topped by Swayambhunath rose spontaneously from the waters, hence the name *swayambhu*, meaning 'self-arisen'. The compound is centred on a gleaming white stupa, topped by a gilded spire painted with the eyes of the Buddha. Depictions of these eyes appear all over the Kathmandu Valley.

The emperor Ashoka allegedly visited 2000 years ago, but the earliest confirmed activity here was in AD 460. During the 14th century, Mughal invaders from Bengal broke open the stupa in the search for gold, but the stupa was restored and expanded over the following centuries.

◉ Sights

Eastern Stairway BUDDHIST MONUMENT

There are two ways to approach Swayambhunath temple, but by far the most atmospheric is the stone pilgrim stairway that climbs the eastern end of the hill. The 2015 earthquake caused some damage – and certainly gave the resident monkeys one hell of a fright – but the stairway is once again open to pilgrims and sightseers. Constructed by King Pratap Malla in the 17th century, this steep stone staircase is mobbed by troops of rhesus macaques, who have made an artform of sliding down the steep handrails. A word of advice: keep foodstuffs out of sight of these simian hoodlums!

From a collection of brightly painted Buddha statues at the bottom of the hill, the steps climb past a series of chaitya and bas-reliefs, including a stone showing the birth of the Buddha, with his mother Maya Devi grasping a tree branch. You can often see Tibetan astrologers reading fortunes here. At the top, the steps are lined with pairs of Garudas, lions, elephants, horses and peacocks, the 'vehicles' of the Dhyani Buddhas. Near the end of the climb is the ticket office (there's another one at the western entrance, near the tourist bus park). When you reach the top, remember to walk around the stupa in a clockwise direction.

Great Thunderbolt BUDDHIST MONUMENT

At the top of the eastern stairway is an enormous, brass-plated dorje (thunderbolt), one of the core symbols of Tibetan Buddhism. Known as the vajra in Sanskrit, the thunderbolt is a symbol of the power of enlightenment, which destroys ignorance, but is itself indestructible. In rituals the dorje is used to indicate male power, while female power is represented by a ceremonial bell.

Around the pedestal supporting the symbol are the animals of the Tibetan calendar. The plinth was formerly flanked by the **Anantapura** and **Pratapura** temples, two slender, Indian-style shikhara towers built by King Pratap Malla in the 17th century, but sadly the Anantapura temple collapsed in the 2015 earthquake. Nearby is a viewpoint and a raised area with telescopes for hire.

Swayambhunath Stupa BUDDHIST STUPA

(foreigner/SAARC Rs 200/50) The Swayambhunath stupa is one of the crowning glories of Kathmandu Valley architecture. This perfectly proportioned monument rises through a whitewashed dome to a gilded spire, from

Swayambhunath

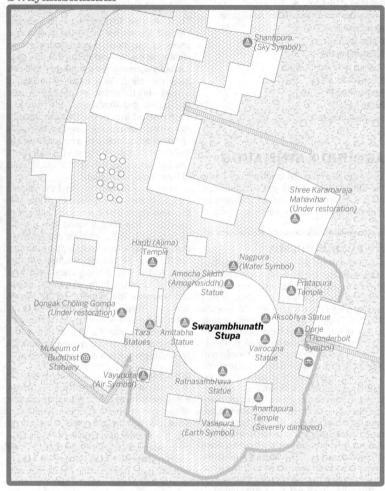

Shantipura
(Sky Symbol)

Shree Karamaraja
Mahavihar
(Under restoration)

Hariti (Ajima)
Temple

Nagpura
(Water Symbol)

Amocha Siddhi
(Amoghasiddhi)
Statue

Pratapura
Temple

Dongak Chöling Gompa
(Under restoration)

Aksobhya Statue

**Swayambhunath
Stupa**

Dorje
(Thunderbolt
Symbol)

Tara
Statues

Amitabha
Statue

Vairocana
Statue

Museum of
Buddhist
Statuary

Vayupura
(Air Symbol)

Ratnasambhava
Statue

Anantapura
Temple
(Severely damaged)

Vasapura
(Earth Symbol)

where four faces of the Buddha stare out across the valley in the cardinal directions. The noselike squiggle below the piercing eyes is actually the Nepali number *ek* (one), signifying unity, and above is a third eye signifying the all-seeing insight of the Buddha. The site was shaken severely by the 2015 earthquake but the main stupa sustained only superficial damage.

The entire structure of the stupa is symbolic – the white dome represents the earth, while the 13-tiered, beehivelike structure at the top symbolises the 13 stages that humans must pass through to achieve nirvana.

The base of the central stupa is ringed by prayer wheels embossed with the sacred mantra *om mani padme hum* ('hail to the jewel in the lotus'). Pilgrims circuiting the stupa spin each one as they pass by. Fluttering above the stupa are thousands of prayer flags, with similar mantras, which are said to be carried to heaven by the winds. Set in ornate plinths around the base of the stupa are statues representing the Dhyani Buddhas – Vairocana, Ratnasambhava, Amitabha, Amocha Siddhi (Amoghasiddhi) and Aksobhya – and their shakti (consorts). These deities represent the five qualities of Buddhist wisdom.

Stupa Platform
BUDDHIST MONUMENT

The great stupa is surrounded on all sides by a veritable sculpture garden of religious monuments. At the rear of the stupa is a small, poorly lit **museum** of Buddhist statuary, but the adjacent Kagyud-school **Dongak Chöling gompa** was badly damaged by the 2015 earthquake.

North of the pilgrim shelter is the golden pagoda-style **Hariti (Ajima) Temple**, with a beautiful image of Hariti, the goddess of smallpox. This Hindu goddess, who is also responsible for fertility, illustrates the seamless interweaving of Hindu and Buddhist beliefs in Nepal.

On the west side of the stupa are two figures of the goddess Tara, attached to stone columns. The **White and Green Tara** are said to symbolise the Chinese and Nepali wives of King Songtsen Gampo, the first royal patron of Buddhism in Tibet, and are also female consorts to two of the Dhyani Buddhas. The upper part of one of the columns tumbled in the earthquake, but may be restored.

Nearby is an eternal flame in a cage; it used to be guarded by bronze images of the river goddesses Jamuna and Ganga but these were lost in the quake. Northwest of these statues is a garden of ancient chaityas, and at the back of this group is a slick **black statue of Dipankara**, carved in the 7th century. Also known as the 'Buddha of Light', Dipankara is one of the 'past Buddhas' who achieved enlightenment before the time of Siddhartha Gautama, the historical Buddha. Also note the black chaityas set atop a yoni – a clear demonstration of the mingling of Hindu and Buddhist symbology.

Back at the northeast corner of the complex, the Buddhist temple known as **Shree Karmaraja Mahavihar** became structurally unsound after the earthquake and was carefully taken down following a ritual prayer ceremony, but devotees hope to eventually raise a new temple on the site.

Symbols of the five elements – earth, air, water, fire and ether – can be found around the hilltop, though several were damaged by the earthquake. Behind the ruins of the Anantapura temple are shrines dedicated to **Vasupura**, the earth symbol, and **Vayupura**, the air symbol, beside the ruins of a whitewashed stupa. **Nagpura**, the symbol for water, is a stone set in a muddy pool just north of the stupa, while **Agnipura**, the symbol for fire, is the red-faced god on a polished boulder on the northwestern side

of the platform. **Shantipura**, the symbol for the sky, is north of the platform, in front of the damaged Shantipura building.

Western Stupa
BUDDHIST STUPA

If you follow either path leading west from the main stupa, you will reach a smaller stupa near the car park for tourist buses. Just behind is a **gompa** surrounded by rest houses for pilgrims and an important **shrine** to Saraswati, the goddess of learning. At exam time, many scholars come here to improve their chances, and school children fill the place during Basanta Panchami, the Festival of Knowledge.

❶ Getting There & Away

You can approach Swayambhunath by taxi (Rs 250), by bicycle or as part of an easy stroll from Kathmandu. Taxis can drop you at the tourist bus park at the western end of the hill or the steep pilgrim stairway at the eastern end of the hill.

Safa (electric) tempo 20 (Rs 20) shuttles between Swayambhunath's eastern stairway and Kathmandu's Sundhara district (near the main post office), via the National Museum.

WALKING & CYCLING

There are two possible walking or bicycle routes to Swayambhunath – using both offers a useful circuit, either in the direction described or in reverse, though traffic can make walking hard work.

Starting at the Chhetrapati Tole junction near Thamel, the road runs west to the Vishnumati River (with Swayambhunath clearly visible in the distance), passing the pagoda-style Indrani Temple, which is surrounded by ghats used for cremations.

Cross the river and detour right to the Shobabaghwati Temple, with its gaudy painted statues of Shiva and other Hindu deities. Return to the bridge and follow the steps uphill past the courtyard-style Bijeshwari Temple, following an arcade of shops selling *malas* (prayer beads) and *gau* (Tibetan-style amulets) that lead to the statue-lined stairway at the east end of Swayambhunath hill.

You can return to the centre of old Kathmandu via the National Museum. From the bottom of the eastern stairway, go west around the base of the hill and turn left at the first major junction, past the Benchen monastery and cafe, then left again at the large T-junction to reach the museum. Continue southeast along this road to reach Tankeshwor, then turn left again and cross the Vishnumati River. On the other side, it's a short walk north to the bottom of Durbar Sq.

Around Swayambhunath

There are several other sights scattered around Swayambhunath. Before moving on, get a taste of Tibet by joining the old pilgrims on a clockwise kora (pilgrim circuit) around the base of the hill, passing a series of gigantic chörtens (reliquary shrines), *mani dungkhor* (giant prayer wheels) and Buddhist chapels.

Starting from the eastern gateway to Swayambhunath, walk around the southwest side of the hill, passing the turn-off to the tourist bus park and the Natural History Museum. The path meets the Ring Rd at **Buddha Amideva Park**, a compound containing three enormous shining golden statues of Sakyamuni Buddha, four-armed Chenresig and Guru Rinpoche, constructed in 2003. Return past the string of chörtens and chapels along the north side of the hill.

◉ Sights

Natural History Museum   MUSEUM
(foreigner/SAARC Rs 50/20, camera Rs 50; ⊙10am-5pm Sun-Fri) Below Swayambhunath, on the road to the tourist bus park, this neglected museum offers a faded but quirky collection of exhibits, including varnished crocodiles, model dinosaurs and mounted animal heads that look suspiciously like hunting trophies.

National Museum   MUSEUM
(⏍01-4271504; www.nationalmuseum.gov.np; Tahachal; foreigner/SAARC Rs 150/50, camera/video Rs 10/200; ⊙10.30am-4.30pm Wed-Sun, to 2.30pm Mon Feb-Oct, to 3.30pm Wed-Sun, to 2pm Mon Nov-Jan) Around 800m south of Swayambhunath at Chhauni, this sprawling museum set in a walled compound looks a little moth-eaten and overgrown, but there are some interesting treasures on display and it never gets crowded. It's worth a visit.

As you enter the compound, turn left to reach the **Judda Art Gallery**, which contains some exquisite stone, metal and terracotta statues of Nepali deities and fabulous *paubha* cloth paintings. Look out for the 1800-year-old life-sized statue of standing Jayavarma, only discovered in 1992, as well as the bronze statue of buffalo-headed Sukhavara Samvara with 34 arms, 16 feet and 10 faces!

At the back of the compound is the temple-style **Buddhist Art Gallery**. As well as Buddhist statues, votive objects, thangkas and manuscripts as big as coffee tables, there are some informative displays on mandalas (geometric Buddhist diagrams). A highlight here is the 8th-century stone depiction of the birth of Buddha, showing Queen Maya holding onto the branch of a tree.

Don't miss the antique Hudson car just around the corner, which was imported from Detroit.

To the north of the main compound, housed in a handsome Rana-era palace, is the **Historical Gallery**, which displays a bloodthirsty collection of weapons, including the personal *kukri* (daggers), *katar* (punch-daggers), *tulwar* (curved swords) and *khanda* (hatchet swords) of such national heroes as Prithvi Narayan Shah, the founder of Nepal. Note the leather cannon seized in the 1792 Nepal-Tibet War.

The same building formerly housed the **Natural History Gallery**, with arthritic-looking stuffed animals and old bones, but the building and collection were damaged in the 2015 earthquake. The upstairs **Numismatic** and **Philatelic Galleries** were also damaged beyond repair.

Ticket sales stop an hour before closing time; bags must be left in the free lockers at the gate.

Military Museum   MUSEUM
(⏍01-4271504; Tahachal; foreigner/SAARC Rs 100/40, camera/video Rs 50/200; ⊙10am-4.30pm Wed-Sun, to 2pm Mon Apr-Oct, to 3.30pm Wed-Sun, to 2pm Mon Nov-Mar) Opposite the National Museum in an army compound, this will likely appeal only to fans of military history. It's open despite earthquake damage and lined up on parade outside the museum are a two-person tank, Nepal's first ever Rolls-Royce, gifted by Queen Elizabeth II in 1961, and a Skyvan transport plane.

The interior displays lead past endless paintings of death and mayhem depicting Nepali battles over the centuries, including several against British and Tibetans, as well as an armoury, including a fine bazooka and circular weapon rack. Look for the portrait of the intriguing 18th-century queen Rajendra Laxmi Devi Shah, who trained as a soldier and led her army on three campaigns.

Kathmandu Valley & Around

Best Hikes

➡ Nagarkot to Dhulikhel (p184)

➡ Dhulikhel to Panauti via Namobuddha (p186)

➡ Gokarna Mahadev Temple to Bodhnath, via Kopan (p172)

Best Places to Stay

➡ Shivapuri Heights (p135)

➡ Famous Farm (p194)

➡ Neydo Tashi Choeling Monastery Guest House (p178)

Why Go?

In many ways the Kathmandu Valley *is* Nepal. Created from the bed of a sacred lake by the deity Manjushri, according to Buddhist legend, the basin is a patchwork of terraced fields and sacred temple towns that showcase the glory of the architects and artisans of Nepal. Sadly, the area also bore the brunt of the 2015 earthquake. This took its toll on the valley's medieval villages and sacred sites, but there is still a huge amount to see, from centuries-old temples to Himalayan viewpoints and two adventurous roads to Tibet.

Aside from the great Unesco World Heritage Sites of Patan, Bodhnath and Bhaktapur, try to visit one or two of the smaller Newari villages off the mainstream tourist circuit. Many attractions can be explored by minibus, taxi, mountain bike, motorcycle, even on foot, following a web of ancient trails. You'll likely see fewer tourists just 10km outside Kathmandu than you will if you trek for days through the Himalaya.

When to Go
Nagarkot

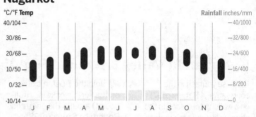

Mar–Apr Warm weather, green farmland and spectacular chariot festivals.

Oct–Jan Clear views and sunny days but chilly nights at Nagarkot and Dhulikhel.

May–Sep Hot and humid, regular rainfall and temperatures peaking over 30°C.

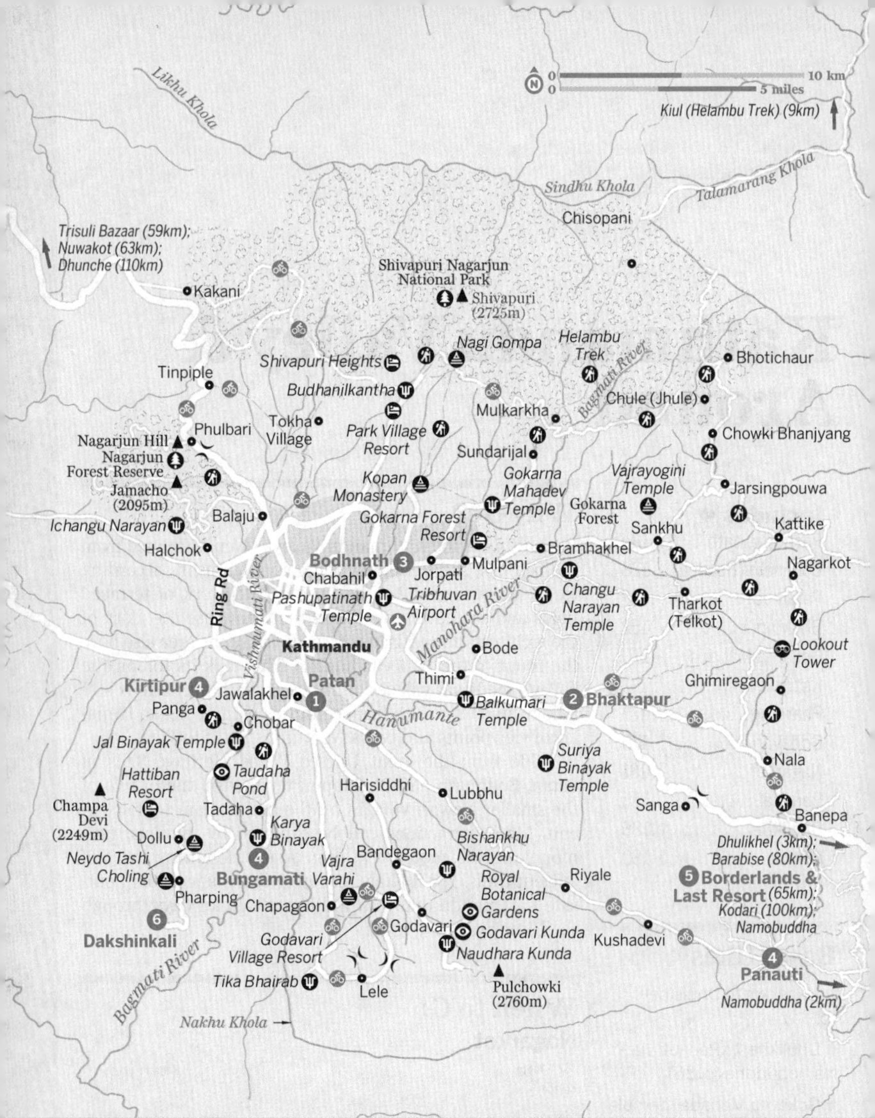

Map labels (geographic features and locations):

Likhu Khola

Kiul (Helambu Trek) (9km)

Sindhu Khola

Talamarang Khola

Chisopani

Trisuli Bazaar (59km);
Nuwakot (63km);
Dhunche (110km)

Shivapuri Nagarjun
National Park

Kakani

Shivapuri
(2725m)

Helambu
Trek

Bhotichaur

Nagi Gompa

Shivapuri Heights

Chule (Jhule)

Tinpiple

Budhanilkantha

Chowki Bhanjyang

Phulbari

Tokha
Village

Park Village
Resort

Mulkarkha

Sundarijal

Vajrayogini
Temple

Jarsingpouwa

Nagarjun Hill
Nagarjun
Forest Reserve
Jamacho
(2095m)

Kopan
Monastery

Gokarna
Mahadev
Temple

Gokarna
Forest

Sankhu

Kattike

Ichangu Narayan

Balaju

Gokarna Forest
Resort

Bramhakhel

Nagarkot

Halchok

Bodhnath 3

Mulpani

Chabahil
Pashupatinath
Temple

Jorpati
Tribhuvan
Airport

Changu
Narayan
Temple

Tharkot
(Telkot)

Ring Rd

Kathmandu

Bode

Lookout
Tower

Kirtipur 4

Patan 1

Thimi

Balkumari
Temple

Bhaktapur 2

Ghimiregaon

Jawalakhel

Panga

Chobar

Hanumante

Suriya
Binayak
Temple

Nala

Jal Binayak Temple

Taudaha
Pond

Harisiddhi

Lubbhu

Sanga

Banepa

Hattiban
Resort

Tadaha

Karya
Binayak

Bishankhu
Narayan

Dhulikhel (3km);
Barabise (80km);

Champa
Devi
(2249m)

Dollu

Bandegaon

Royal
Botanical
Gardens

Riyale

Borderlands &
Last Resort (65km);
Kodari (100km);
Namobuddha

Neydo Tashi
Choling

Bungamati 4

Vajra
Varahi

Pharping

Chapagaon

Godavari

Godavari Kunda

Kushadevi

Dakshinkali 6

Godavari
Village Resort

Naudhara Kunda

Panauti 4

Tika Bhairab

Lele

Pulchowki
(2760m)

Namobuddha (2km)

Nakhu Khola

Kathmandu Valley & Around Highlights

1 Lose yourself in the courtyards of **Patan** (p137) on a walking tour, soak in the glorious Newari architecture of its Durbar Sq and visit Patan Museum, the best in the country.

2 Explore the fascinating backstreets of **Bhaktapur** (p152), where grand Newari temples still stand despite the 2015 quake.

3 Join the Tibetan exiles on the kora (clockwise ritual circuit) around the enormous **Bodhnath Stupa** (p128).

4 Have a medieval mini-adventure in the historic city of **Panauti** (p189), which escaped the earthquake's destruction.

5 Get the pulse racing on a bungee, canyoning or rafting trip at the adventure resorts of **Borderlands** (p192) or **The Last Resort** (p193), just a stone's throw from the Tibet border.

6 Find Nepal's spiritual side on the monastery-strewn road to **Dakshinkali** (p177), where Tibetan Buddhism jostles for space with Tantric Hinduism.

History

The legend that the Kathmandu Valley was formed when the Buddhist deity Manjushri drained a sacred lake with his flaming sword is in fact rooted in reality. The uprising of the Himalaya trapped rivers draining south from Tibet, creating a vast lake that eventually burst its banks and drained away around 10,000 years ago.

As people settled from the north and south, the valley became the biggest clearinghouse on the trade route from India to Tibet. Himalayan missionaries and saints transferred Buddhism across the Himalaya into Tibet and centuries later migrating Tibeto-Burman tribes carried Buddhism back into Nepal, fusing Tantric Indian beliefs with the ancient Bön religion of Tibet. This has resulted in a fascinating hybrid culture, where Hindu and Buddhist beliefs jointly infuse Nepali life.

Historically, the Kathmandu Valley has been the homeland of the Newars, great traders and craftspeople, of mixed Indian and Tibeto-Burman origin. Much of the iconography, architecture and culture associated with Nepal today is actually based on Newari culture.

The first formal records of Newari history come from the Licchavi era (AD 400 to 750), but the golden age of the Newars came in the 17th century when the valley was dominated by three rival city-states – Kantipur (Kathmandu), Lalitpur (Patan) and Bhadgaon (Bhaktapur) – all of which competed to outshine each other with architectural brilliance. The reign of the Malla kings saw the construction of many of Nepal's most iconic palaces, temples and monuments.

The unification of Nepal in 1768–69 by Prithvi Narayan Shah signalled the end of this three-way scramble for supremacy. Nepali, an Indo-European language spoken by the Khas of western Nepal, replaced Newari as the country's language of administration and Kathmandu became the undisputed capital of the nation.

Tragically, many of the historic towns in the Kathmandu Valley were devastated by the 2015 earthquake, with huge loss of life. Reconstruction is underway and local people are rebuilding their lives and livelihoods, but the scars of the earthquake will be visible on the landscape for many years to come.

Dangers & Annoyances

If you explore the Kathmandu Valley on a rented motorcycle, be wary of the traffic police, particularly after dark. Locals are routinely stung with fines for trumped-up traffic offences and foreigners are being increasingly targeted.

Women in particular should avoid hiking alone in remote corners of the valley. Nagarjun Hill near Kathmandu and Pulchowki Mountain south of Godavari have historically seen robberies and worse.

Be aware of the risk of landslides on the roads to Langtang and Kodari – these were a problem even before the 2015 earthquake.

ℹ Getting Around

If you intend to do any biking, hiking or motorcycling, it's worth investing in Nepa Maps' useful 1:50,000 *Around the Kathmandu Valley* or 1:60,000 *Biking Around Kathmandu Valley*. Both are available from bookstores in Kathmandu.

BICYCLE & MOTORBIKE

By far the most efficient and economical way of getting around the valley is by rented bicycle or motorbike. Once you get beyond the Kathmandu Ring Rd, there is surprisingly little traffic and the valley offers some charming riding country, as long as you choose your routes wisely.

It's not all plain sailing though. Traffic and road conditions can be terrible, especially on the main roads, so it's worth getting advice on the best routes from Kathmandu's many bike rental and tour companies. Take corners slowly as buses and trucks will not give way. Be sure to securely lock your bike or motorcycle when you stop, and carry plenty of petrol from Kathmandu as rural petrol stations regularly run dry. On day trips, give yourself time to get back to Kathmandu by nightfall – you really don't want to ride these roads after dark.

BUS & TAXI

From Kathmandu's Ratna Park bus station, inexpensive public buses run to every town in the valley, though you may need to change in Patan or Bhaktapur. However, the buses can be incredibly crowded, and they are glacially slow. As a more comfortable alternative, consider hiring a car or taxi – as a guide, a day hire to Bodhnath, Pashupatinath and Bhaktapur or to Dakshinkali, Chobar and Kirtipur costs around Rs 3000.

HIKING

A web of footpaths around the valley links its villages and towns and there are many interesting day hikes and overnight treks around the valley, allowing you to take shortcuts that are not accessible by bicycle or motorcycle. You can easily

DON'T MISS

TOP FIVE TEMPLES IN THE KATHMANDU VALLEY

The following are our five favourite temples in the valley:

Changu Narayan (p168) A treasure house of sculpture at this Unesco World Heritage Site, damaged but not destroyed in the 2015 quake.

Gokarna Mahadev Temple (p170) A visual A to Z of Hindu iconography.

Indreshwar Mahadev Temple (p190) A perfect temple by a mystical river confluence south of the highway to Tibet.

Budhanilkantha (p135) Impressive monolithic stone carving of a sleeping Vishnu.

Dakshinkali (p177) Spooky place of blood sacrifices and wrathful goddesses.

link several towns on foot and could even put together a five- or six-day hike linking Kakani to Budhanilkantha, Chisopani, Nagarkot, Dhulikhel, Balthali, Namobuddha and Panauti.

See the website of the **Nepal Environment Tourism Initiative Foundation** (Netif; www. netif-nepal.org) for full details of multiday hikes around the valley.

ORGANISED TOURS

Many of the travel agents in Thamel, in Kathmandu, can arrange day trips around the valley, but standards vary.

If you prefer a guided walk, Wayfarers (p113) offers guided day hikes through Kirtipur, Khokana, Bungamati and Chapagaon (US$35 per person), which include lunch and local transport. Three-day minitreks to Panauti, Namobuddha, Dhulikhel (overnight), Nagarkot (overnight), Changu Narayan and Sankhu (US$175 per person with accommodation) operate with a minimum of two people. However, check that these itineraries are still operating after the earthquake.

AROUND THE RING ROAD

There are several interesting sights just outside the Kathmandu Ring Rd, all accessible by public transport or by rented bike or motorcycle, and all easy day trips from

the capital. Pashupatinath and Bodhnath rank among Nepal's most famous religious sites and both escaped the worst of the earthquake's destructive force.

Pashupatinath

Nepal's most important Hindu temple stands on the banks of the holy Bagmati River, surrounded by a bustling market of religious stalls selling marigolds, prasad (offerings), incense, rudraksha beads, conch shells, pictures of Hindu deities and temples, *tika* powder in rainbow colours, glass lingams, models of Mt Meru and other essential religious paraphernalia. Some shrines were damaged in the sprawling complex surrounding the temple during the 2015 earthquake, but the main mandir (temple) was unscathed. In the weeks after the earthquake, cremation fires burning continuously on the funeral ghats alongside the Bagmati River became a defining image of the disaster.

At first glance, Pashupatinath might not look that sacred – the temple is just a few hundred metres from the end of the runway at Tribhuvan Airport, overlooking a particularly polluted stretch of the Bagmati. However, in religious terms, this is a powerhouse of Hindu spiritual energy. Elsewhere in Nepal, Shiva is worshipped in his wrathful form as the destructive Bhairab, but at Pashupatinath he is celebrated as Pashupati, Lord of the Beasts.

Sadhus and devotees of Shiva flock to Pashupatinath from across the subcontinent and many Nepalis choose to be cremated on the banks of the holy river. Even the kings of Nepal used to come here to ask for a blessing from Pashupati before commencing any important journey. Nepal's Dalit (untouchable) community was only allowed access to the shrine in 2001.

Non-Hindus cannot enter the main temple, but the surrounding complex of Shaivite shrines, lingams and ghats (stone steps) is fascinating and highly photogenic. Groups of 'photo me' sadhus loiter around in outlandish paraphernalia hoping to make a little money posing for tourist photos. Be respectful with your camera at the funeral ghats – you wouldn't take snaps of bereaved relatives at a funeral back home, so don't do it here.

You can visit Pashupatinath as a half-day trip from central Kathmandu and walk on easily to Bodhnath. The entry fee for foreigners is surprisingly high, considering non-Hindus are not allowed into the main temple, and some travellers consider it overpriced. Guides can be hired from the office of the **Guide Association of Pashupatinath** (1½hr tours Rs 500; ⊙9am-5pm) close to the main temple.

The best times to visit are early in the morning or around 6pm during evening prayers. The following sights are all covered by the Pashupatinath entry ticket.

⊙ Sights

Pashupatinath Temple   HINDU TEMPLE
(admission foreigner/Chinese Rs 1000/500, child under 10yr free; ⊙24hr) Undiminished by the earthquake, the pagoda-style Pashupatinath temple was constructed in 1696 but this has been a site of Hindu and Buddhist worship for far longer. Only Hindus are allowed to enter the compound of the famous main temple, but you can catch tantalising glimpses of what is going on inside from several points around the perimeter wall.

From the main gate on the west side of the compound, you can view the mighty golden behind of an enormous brass **statue of Nandi**, Shiva's bull. Inside the shrine, hidden from view, is a black, four-headed image of Pashupati. If you climb the terraces to the west of the temple, you can look down on the gilded rooftop. There are more views from the top of the terraces on the east side of the Bagmati, inside the temple complex.

If you follow the road running south from the side entrance to the temple, you will pass the **Panch Deval** (Five Temples), a former temple complex that survived the quake and acts as a social welfare centre for destitute elderly Nepalis.

Cremation Ghats   HINDU SITE
Despite being clogged with garbage and black with pollution, the fetid Bagmati River is actually an extremely sacred river; Pashupatinath is the Nepali equivalent of Varanasi on the sacred Ganges River. The cremation ghats along the Bagmati are used for openair cremations, but only members of the royal family can be cremated immediately in front of Pashupatinath Temple. The funerals of 10 members of the Nepali royal family took place here after the massacre in 2001.

Funerals of ordinary Nepalis still take place daily on the ghats to the south of the temple. Fires burned day and night after the 2015 earthquake as hundreds of families dealt with the human cost of the disaster.

LOST MONUMENTS AT PASHUPATINATH

While the most sacred monuments at Pashupatinath survived the 2015 earthquake, many structures were damaged and some were destroyed completely, including the Vishwarup Temple, and a number of the small Shiva shrines used as shelters by pilgrims. However, overall, the complex got off lightly compared with other World Heritage sites around the valley.

Bodies are wrapped in shrouds and laid out along the riverbank, then cremated on a wooden pyre in a surprisingly businesslike way. It's a powerful place to contemplate notions of death and mortality. Needless to say, this is a private time for relatives to grieve and tourists intruding with cameras is not appropriate.

At the north end of the ghats, best viewed from across the river, are a series of **yogis' caves** used as shelters in medieval times.

If you walk south along the west bank, you will pass a huge uprooted lingam and a small 7th-century **standing Buddha image**, next to the damaged **Raj Rajeshwari Temple**, with its rounded stucco outbuildings.

Bachhareshwari Temple   HINDU TEMPLE
Between the two groups of ghats on the west bank of the Bagmati is this small, 6th-century temple, decorated with Tantric figures, skeletons and erotic scenes. It is said that human sacrifices were once made at this temple as part of the Maha Shivaratri Festival.

Eastern Ghats   HINDU SITE
Pashupatinath's ghats are often full of life and it's worth taking a few minutes to absorb it all. Devotees ritually bathe in the dubious-looking waters of the Bagmati, holy men perform rituals on the stone steps and children fish for coins from the murky river using a magnet on the end of a string. You may also see families preparing the funeral pyres across the river.

Two footbridges cross the Bagmati in front of the Pashupatinath Temple, entering a garden of stone terraces covered in dozens of small **Shiva shrines**, most of which survived the earthquake. These one-room temples are often used as lodgings by wandering sadhus and each contains a central Shiva lingam. Although the shrines are built

Pashupatinath

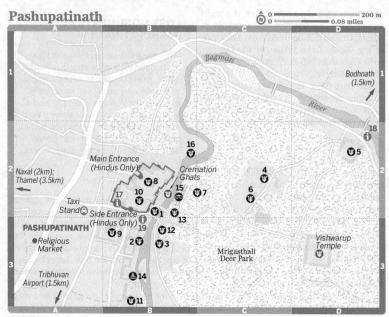

Pashupatinath

in many styles, all share certain design features – note the mask of Bhairab, Shiva's fearsome incarnation, on the south wall, and the Nandi statue and animal-head water spout to the north. Look for the interesting **lingam with the Shiva face** at the northern end of the group.

Two flights of steps lead up the hillside between the shrines, passing the damaged but still elaborately frescoed **Ram Temple**, which is often thronged by visiting sadhus, especially during the Maha Shivaratri Festival. At the top, where the path enters the forest, a side track leads north along the top of the terraces to an excellent viewpoint over the Pashupatinath Temple. Look for the

enormous golden trident on the northern side of the temple and the golden figure of the king kneeling in prayer under a protective hood of *naga* (serpent deities) to the south.

Lingam Shrines　　HINDU SITE

The steps from the Pashupatinath ghats lead uphill to a huge complex of lingam shrines on the edge of the forest that is well worth exploring. There are more than 50 shrines here and the variety of architectural forms is quite stunning.

Gorakhnath Temple　　HINDU TEMPLE

Turning left at the top of the hill will take you to the towering red-and-white shikhara (temple with tall corn-cob-like spire) of the Gorakhnath Temple, which survived the quake with minor damage, dedicated to the 11th-century yogi who founded the Shaivite monastic tradition and invented Hatha yoga. Past the Gorakhnath Temple, the path drops down through the forest, passing the Mrigasthali Deer Park, a fitting blend of nature and religion, as Shiva is said to have frolicked here once in the shape of a golden deer.

Guhyeshwari Temple   HINDU TEMPLE
The path drops out of the forest to the large, courtyard-style Guhyeshwari Temple, built by King Pratap Malla in 1653 and dedicated to Parvati (the wife of Shiva) in her terrible manifestation as Kali. The temple sustained some damage in the earthquake and entry is banned to non-Hindus, but you can peek into the compound from the path to see the four huge gilded snakes that support the roof finial. The riverbank in front of the temple is lined with Shiva shrines and octagonal plinths for ritual bathing.

The temple's curious name comes from the Nepali words *guhya* (vagina) and *ishwari* (goddess) – literally, it's the temple of the goddess's vagina! According to legend, the father of Parvati insulted Shiva and the goddess became so incensed that she burst into flames, providing the inspiration for the practice of *sati*, where widows were burned alive on the funeral pyres of their husbands. The grieving Shiva wandered the earth with the disintegrating corpse of Parvati and her genitals fell at Guhyeshwari. However, Indian Hindus make the same claim for the Kamakhya Temple at Guwahati in Assam.

🎎 Festivals & Events
Pashupatinath is generally busiest (with genuine pilgrims rather than tourists) from 6am to 10am and again from 6pm to 7.30pm, especially on *ekadashi,* which falls 11 days after the full and new moon each month. As night falls, pilgrims release butter lamps on boats made of leaves onto the Bagmati as part of the *arati* (light) ceremony.

Maha Shivaratri Festival   RELIGIOUS
In the Nepali month of Falgun (in February or March), thousands of pilgrims throng to Pashupatinath from all over Nepal and India to celebrate Shiva's birthday. It's an incredible spectacle, and a chance to see members of some of the more austere Shaivite sects performing rituals through the night.

Bala Chaturdashi   RELIGIOUS
During the new moon of November/ December, pilgrims hold a lamplit vigil and bathe in the holy Bagmati the following morning. Pilgrims then scatter sweets and seeds around the compound for their deceased relatives to enjoy in the afterlife.

ℹ️ Getting There & Away
From Kathmandu, the most convenient way to Pashupatinath is by taxi (Rs 400 from Thamel) – taxis often drop you off by the police station at Gaushala, but you can ask to be dropped off closer to the temples.

If you are walking or cycling, head east from the Narayanhiti Palace through Naxal, meeting the Ring Rd near the Jayabageshwari Temple, with its fine painting of Bhairab. To reach Pashupatinath Temple, cross the Ring Rd and follow the winding lanes lined with religious stalls towards the Bagmati.

If you want to walk on from Pashupatinath to Bodhnath, it's a pleasant 20-minute walk through villages and farmland, offering a window onto ordinary life in the Kathmandu 'burbs. Take the footbridge across the river in front of the Guhyeshwari Temple and head north for five minutes, then turn right by a temple surrounding a large pipal tree. At the next junction follow the Buddha's example and take the middle (straight) path, which eventually emerges on the main Bodhnath road, right across from the stupa.

Chabahil
Northeast of the centre of Kathmandu, on the way to Bodhnath, the suburb of Chabahil has a number of historic temples and shrines. Right on the Ring Rd is the imposing **Chabahil Stupa** `FREE`, the fourth largest stupa in the Kathmandu area after Bodhnath, Swayambhunath and the Kathesimbhu Stupa near Thahiti Chowk. According to legend, the stupa was constructed by Charumati, the daughter of Ashoka, but it has been patched up numerous times, most recently in 2015, after damage from the Gorkha earthquake.

If you take the lane just north of the Chabahil Stupa, and turn left at a smaller white stupa, you will reach the slightly damaged **Charumati Vihar**, a medieval Buddhist monastery that used to house the monks who tended the Chabahil stupa. Continuing past this turning (back at the white stupa) will take you to the white arch of the revered **Chandra Binayak Ganesh Temple**, which is now being rebuilt after sustaining severe damage in the 2015 quake. The surrounding courtyard is full of *tika*-powder-covered statues – note the Budhanilkantha-style statue of Narayan reclining on his serpent bed, next to a human figure made of beaten brass panels.

Bodhnath (Boudha)

🎧 01

There is nowhere quite like Bodhnath. Asia's largest stupa pulses with life as thousands of pilgrims gather daily to make a kora (ritual circumnavigation) of the dome, beneath the watchful eyes of the Buddha, which gaze out from the gilded central tower. Tibetan monks in maroon robes and with shaved heads wander the prayer-flag-decked streets while pilgrims spin prayer wheels and stock up on yak butter and *tsampa* (roasted barley flour). This is one of the few places in the world where Tibetan Buddhist culture is accessible and unfettered, and the lanes around the stupa are crammed with monasteries and workshops producing butter lamps, ceremonial horns, Tibetan drums, monks' headgear and the other paraphernalia essential for Tibetan Buddhist life. The stupa shook ominously in the 2015 earthquake, but only sustained some minor damage; at the time of writing, the tower was covered in scaffolding but it is expected to be fully restored.

Historically, the stupa was an important staging post on the trade route between Lhasa and Kathmandu, and Tibetan traders would pray here for a safe journey before driving their yaks on to the high passes of the Himalaya. Originally a Tamang settlement, today most of the people living in the village of Boudha (pronounced *boe*-da) are Tibetan refugees who fled China after 1959. The stupa also attracts many Sherpas, descendants of eastern Tibetans who migrated to the Everest region of Nepal in the 16th century. Many of the monasteries around the stupa have opened their doors to foreign students, so you'll see plenty of Western dharma students in maroon robes as you stroll around the backstreets.

The best time to visit Bodhnath is late afternoon, when the group tours head home and elderly exiles stroll down to the stupa to light butter lamps, spin prayer wheels, chant mantras, socialise and stroll clockwise around the monument as part of their daily spiritual workout. Try to visit on the evening of the full moon, when the plaza surrounding the stupa is lit up by thousands of butter lamps.

◉ Sights

★ **Bodhnath Stupa**   BUDDHIST STUPA
(foreigner/SAARC Rs 200/50) The first stupa at Bodhnath was built sometime after AD 600, when the Tibetan king, Songtsen Gampo, converted to Buddhism. In terms of grace and purity of line, no other stupa in Nepal comes close to Bodhnath. From its whitewashed dome to its gilded tower painted with the all-seeing eyes of the Buddha, the

---

STUPAS

The Kathmandu Valley is dotted with impressive stupas ('chörten' in Tibetan). The most impressive are at Bodhnath and Swayambhunath, but there are also substantial examples at little-visited Chabahil and Kathesimbhu in Kathmandu. The oldest stupas are the four in Patan that were allegedly built by Indian emperor Ashoka. You'll pass smaller chörtens and chörten-shaped *kani* (arch-like gateways) on almost every trek in Nepal.

The very first stupas were built to house the ashes and relics of Siddhartha Gautama (the Historical Buddha) and became a powerful early symbol of the new faith at a time when images of the Buddha had not yet become popular. Many Tibetan-style chörtens still house religious relics or the ashes of lamas. The range of styles is immense, from the huge platforms of Bodhnath to the fragile stone chörtens atop a mountain pass.

Each of the elements of a stupa has a symbolic meaning, from the square base (earth) and the hemispherical dome (water) to the tapering spire (fire), whose 13 step-like segments can symbolise the steps leading to Buddhahood. On top of the 13 steps is an ornament shaped like a crescent moon (air), and a vertical spike, which represent ether or the sacred light of Buddha.

In Nepal the central rectangular tower is painted with the all-seeing eyes of Buddha. What appears to be a nose is actually the Sanskrit character for the number one, symbolising the absoluteness of Buddha.

Bodhnath (Boudha)

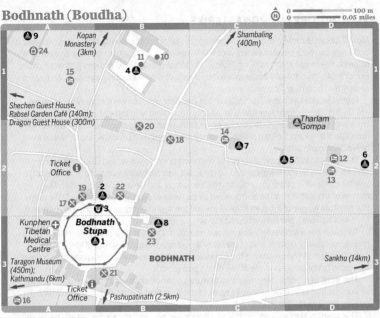

Bodhnath (Boudha)

⊙ **Top Sights**
  1 Bodhnath Stupa B3

◎ **Sights**
  2 Guru Lhakhang Gompa B2
  3 Harati (Ajima) Shrine B2
  4 Ka-Nying Sheldrup Ling Gompa B1
  5 Pal Dilyak Gompa D2
  6 Pal Nye Gompa D2
  7 Sakya Tharig Gompa C2
  8 Samtenling Gompa B3
  9 Shechen Gompa A1

⊕ **Activities, Courses & Tours**
  10 Centre for Buddhist Studies B1
  11 Rangjung Yeshe Institute B1

⊜ **Sleeping**
  12 Lotus Guest House D2

  13 Pema Guest House D2
  14 PRK Guest House C2
  15 Rokpa Guest House A1
  16 Tibet International Hotel A3

⊗ **Eating**
  17 Café du Temple A2
  18 Double Dorjee Restaurant B2
  19 Flavors Café A2
  20 Garden Kitchen B2
  21 La Casita de Boudhanath B3
  22 Stupa View Restaurant B2
  23 White Dzambala Tibetan
     Restaurant B3

⊜ **Shopping**
  24 Tsering Art School Shop A1

monument is perfectly proportioned. The stupa had a lucky escape in the 2015 earthquake, with repairs to the tower expected to take only a few months.

According to legend, the king constructed the stupa as an act of penance after unwittingly killing his father. The first stupa was wrecked by Mughal invaders in the 14th century, so the current stupa is a more recent construction.

The highly symbolic construction serves in essence as a three-dimensional reminder of the Buddha's path towards enlightenment. The plinth represents earth, the *kumbha* (dome) is water, the harmika (square tower) is fire, the spire is air and the umbrella at the top is the void or ether beyond space. The 13 levels of the spire represent the stages that a human being must pass through to achieve nirvana.

VISITING TIBETAN MONASTERIES

Most Tibetan Buddhist monasteries welcome visitors and entering these atmospheric buildings can be a powerful and evocative experience. During the morning and evening prayers, the lamas (high-ranking Tibetan Buddhist monks) and novices gather to chant Buddhist texts, normally accompanied by a cacophony of crashing cymbals, thumping drums and booming Tibetan horns.

From Ladakh to Lhasa, Tibetan gompas (monasteries) follow a remarkably consistent layout. The main prayer hall is invariably decorated with intricate murals depicting the life of Buddha, alongside various bodhisattvas and protectors, who also appear on dangling thangkas (Tibetan religious paintings) edged with brocade and in statue form behind the main altar.

Many gompas also have a library of cloth-wrapped, loose-leafed Buddhist manuscripts, known as the Kangyur and Tengyur, set into alcoves around the altar. The altar itself is covered in offerings, including butter lamps and seven bowls of water. The throne of the abbot is often surrounded by pictures of past abbots and the Dalai Lama, the spiritual leader of Tibetan Buddhism and the representation on earth of Chenresig (Avalokiteshvara), the deity of compassion.

As you enter a monastery you will see murals of the four guardian protectors – fearsome-looking deities who scare away ignorance – and the wheel of life, a highly complex diagram representing the Buddha's insights into the way humans are chained by desire to the endless cycle of life, death and rebirth.

The front of a monastery may also feature enormous *mani dungkhor* – giant prayer wheels stuffed with thousands of copies of the Buddhist mantra *om mani padme hum* (hail to the jewel in the lotus).

This mantra also appears on the smaller prayer wheels around the outer wall and on the fluttering prayer flags outside. On the monastery roof you may see a statue of two deer on either side of the wheel of law, symbolising the Buddha's first sermon at the deer park of Sarnath.

Cultural Considerations

Visitors are welcome in most monasteries, but stick to the following guidelines:

➡ Remove your shoes and hat before you enter a gompa.

➡ Ask before taking photos and avoid taking photos (especially flash) during prayers.

➡ Do not smoke anywhere in the main compounds.

➡ Do not step over or sit on the monks' cushions, even if no one is sitting on them.

➡ During ceremonies, enter quietly and stand by the wall near the main entrance; do not walk around while monks are engaged in rituals.

➡ Always walk around stupas and chörten (Tibetan-style stupas) in a clockwise direction and, likewise, spin prayer wheels clockwise.

➡ It is appropriate to make an offering – a khata (Tibetan prayer scarf) is traditional, or cash donations help fund the monastery and its charitable works in the community.

Stupas were originally built to house holy relics and some claim that Bodhnath contains the relics of the past Buddha, Kashyapa, while others say it contains a piece of bone from the skeleton of Siddhartha Gautama, the historical Buddha. Around the base of the stupa are 108 small images of the Dhyani Buddha Amitabha (108 is an auspicious number in Tibetan culture) and a ring of prayer wheels, set in groups of four or five into 147 niches.

To reach the upper level of the plinth, look for the gateway at the north end of the stupa, beside a small shrine dedicated to Hariti (Ajima), the goddess of smallpox. The plinth is open from 5am to 6pm (to 7pm in summer), offering a raised viewpoint over the tide of pilgrims surging around the stupa. Note the committed devotees prostrating themselves full-length on the ground in the courtyard on the east side of the stupa.

Shechen Gompa
BUDDHIST MONASTERY

(Shechen Tengyi Dargyeling Gompa; www.shechen. org) This huge complex was established by the famous Nyingmapa lama Dilgo Khyentse Rinpoche to replace the destroyed Shechen Gompa in eastern Tibet. Today, the monastery has a thriving community of over 300 monks and the main prayer hall features fabulous murals by artists from Bhutan. The main prayer hall was damaged by the earthquake but repairs were underway at the time of writing. Find it west of the stupa, behind a metal gate down the alley leading to the Dragon Guest House.

Ka-Nying
Sheldrup Ling Gompa
BUDDHIST MONASTERY

Down a side alley, the handsome 'white gompa' is home to 225 monks and features ornamental gardens and a richly decorated interior with some exquisite paintings and thangkas (Tibetan religious paintings). Unfortunately the main prayer hall became unstable in the 2015 earthquake and was being rebuilt at the time of research. Classes in Tibetan, Sanskrit, Nepali and Buddhist studies are run by the attached Rangjung Yeshe Institute but check that these are still operating during the reconstruction.

Taragaon Museum
MUSEUM

(☑01-4497505; www.taragaonmuseum.com; ☺10am-5pm Mon-Sat) FREE This small museum houses a collection of maps, photos and archaeological plans drawn by the first foreign architectural advisers to arrive in Kathmandu in the 1970s. Highlights include the museum building itself, originally built in 1974 as a hostel for foreign experts, and the wall-sized reproduction of Erwin Schneider's first map of the Kathmandu Valley.

There are also temporary exhibits of contemporary art, occasional cultural events, a cafe and some top-end galleries. It's in the grounds of the Hyatt Regency, accessible from Bodhnath.

Other Gompas

Since the Chinese sent thousands of troops to enforce their claim on Tibet in the 1950s, dozens of new monasteries have been constructed at Bodhnath by refugees. All welcome visitors but many close their doors in the middle of the day. Most places have prayer sessions around 4am and 3pm.

The main monasteries worth visiting are the **Guru Lhakhang Gompa**, **Samtenling Gompa** (damaged but under restoration), **Sakya Tharig Gompa** (www.sakyatharig.org. np), **Pal Dilyak Gompa** and **Pal Nye Gompa**.

There's little to choose between them, so follow the sounds of booming trumpets and crashing cymbals to see which are open.

Look also for the plaque beside the Guru Lhakhang Gompa that commemorates Ekai Kawaguchi, the Japanese monk and traveller who stayed here in 1899 before heading off on a remarkable journey to Mustang and Tibet.

⚡ Courses

Rangjung Yeshe Institute
BUDDHISM COURSE

(☑01-4483575; www.ryi.org) Located at Ka-Nying Sheldrup Ling Gompa, this Buddhist institute offers an advanced 10-day course on Tibetan Buddhist teachings, practice and meditation, led by the monastery's abbot Chokyi Nyima Rinpoche. The popular course is held in mid-November and costs US$130. A follow-up retreat is held at Nagi Gompa. Courses were temporarily suspended while the monastery compound was restored after the 2015 earthquake, so contact the institute for the latest schedule.

The institute also offers a university-accredited summer course in Buddhist theory and meditation in June/July, as well as eight-week summer Tibetan and Nepali language courses, staying with local families. The noticeboard here is a good place to find a language tutor or room for rent.

✪ Festivals & Events

Losar
RELIGIOUS

Bodhnath goes into spiritual overdrive every year in February or March for the Tibetan New Year. Long copper horns are blown, a portrait of the Dalai Lama is paraded around, thousands of pilgrims throng the stupa, and monks from the surrounding monasteries perform masked *chaam* (religious dances).

Buddha Jayanti (Saga Dawa)
RELIGIOUS

April/May is another good time to visit, as Buddhists everywhere commemorate the birth, enlightenment and death of the Buddha. Thousands of butter lamps are lit by devotees and an image of the Buddha is paraded around the stupa. Tibetans know the festival as Saga Dawa.

🛏 Sleeping

The guesthouses in the tangle of lanes north and east of the stupa offer an interesting and much more peaceful alternative to basing yourself in Kathmandu. Most guesthouses here are modern constructions and earthquake damage was limited. It's a good idea to book ahead if visiting in October.

Lotus Guest House GUESTHOUSE $

(📞01-4472320; s/d/tr Rs 400/700/750, without bathroom s/d Rs 350/600; 🛜) This calm, contemplative budget guesthouse is located close to Pal Dilyak Gompa. Rooms are spread over two floors around a marigold-fringed garden lawn, and the shared bathrooms are clean.

Shechen Guest House GUESTHOUSE $

(📞01-4479009; www.shechenguesthouse.com.np; s/d/tr Rs 1035/1420/1970; 🛜) Located in the back of the Shechen Gompa compound, this agreeable guesthouse caters to a mix of long-term dharma students, shaven-scalped Buddhist groups and ordinary travellers. Nepali bedspreads add colour to the otherwise plain rooms and the attached Rabsel Garden Café (mains Rs 380-525; 🍴) cooks up excellent vegetarian food in a peaceful garden.

Rooms on the south side have the more reliable hot water. To get here, enter the monastery compound and turn left, then right beside a line of giant chörten (Tibetan-style stupas). Profits go to the monastery.

Dragon Guest House GUESTHOUSE $

(📞01-4479562; dragon@ntc.net.np; Mahankal; s/d without bathroom Rs 600/850; 🛜) This friendly, family-run place is set in a peaceful location north of Shechen Gompa. Staff keep the rooms spick and span and there's a vegetarian restaurant in the pleasant garden. To get here, walk north through the gate beside the Shechen Guest House.

PRK Guest House GUESTHOUSE $

(Pal Rabten Khansar; 📞01-4914911; www.sakyatharig.org.np; s/d Rs 1000/1250, deluxe r Rs 1500; @🛜) This simple guesthouse is run by the next-door Sakya Tharig Gompa. The carpeted deluxe rooms are comfortable and offer the best value; other rooms are smaller with thin mattresses. Out back is a small ornamental garden with a large stupa, plus there's a nice rooftop and a library with computers.

Pema Guest House GUESTHOUSE $

(📞01-4915862; pemagurung@gmail.com; r from Rs 1100, without bathroom from Rs 800, deluxe r Rs 1400; 🛜) This tidy house is set in a neat courtyard garden. The spacious rooms on the upper levels get lots of natural light and there are terraces on each level where you can sit and enjoy some sun. Ground-floor rooms are darker.

★ Rokpa Guest House HOTEL $$

(📞01-4479705; www.rokpaguesthouse.org; s/d US$25/30, deluxe US$35/40, ste US$45; 🛜) Even if guests here didn't get a warm glow from knowing that their money was funding a nearby children's home (see http://rokpa.org), it would still be a great place to stay in its own right. The rooms are modern and spacious, staff are helpful and there's a relaxing garden with a reasonably priced restaurant. Prices include breakfast and there are good monthly rates for long-term visitors.

Ask about its second property at the nearby Bodhi Guest House.

★ Shambaling BOUTIQUE HOTEL $$$

(📞01-4916868; www.shambaling.com; standard s/d US$70/80, deluxe US$125/135, ste US$220/230; @🛜) This former pilgrim resthouse has recently been reincarnated by its Tibetan owners into Bodhnath's most stylish boutique option. Each floor is designed in a different colour scheme to reflect the colours of Tibetan prayer flags. The more spacious deluxe rooms are the best bet, especially those that overlook the quiet and spacious garden centred around a pipal tree.

Rates include breakfast in the excellent garden restaurant, where you can relax with an Illy coffee or a shot of house-made spiced rum infused with cardamom and ginger.

Tibet International Hotel LUXURY HOTEL $$$

(📞01-4488188; www.hoteltibetintl.com.np; r US$225; ❄@🛜) A lot of thought has gone into this top-of-the-line Tibetan hotel, from the stylish Tibetan decor, including carpets from its own factory (check out the on-site showroom and courtyard working display of hand-knotted carpets) to the choice of room pillows and free hour-long guided meditation offered each morning. The views of the Bodhnath Stupa from the 6th-floor buffet are fabulous. Request a room away from the busy main road.

✖ Eating

Buddhist Bodhnath is nirvana for vegetarians. Traveller-oriented rooftop restaurants ring the stupa and offer superlative views, or for cheaper eats, head to the back lanes radiating out from the stupa, where any building with a curtain across an open door is a local cafe serving Tibetan momos (dumplings) and *thukpa* (noodle soup). Few eating places were affected by the earthquake and most restaurants open from 8am to 9pm.

Double Dorjee Restaurant TIBETAN $

(📞01-4488947; dishes Rs 150-250) On the lane north of the stupa, this borderline dingy

CHINA'S LONG REACH

China's influence is on the rise globally, and Nepal is no exception. China has become an increasingly vital investor and aid donor in the country, funding everything from roads to hydroelectric plants. In the last decade China built five new roads from Tibet into Nepal and even the Tibet train line is tentatively scheduled to arrive near the Nepal border in 2020.

One group eyeing this growing economic and political clout with apprehension is Nepal's 20,000-strong community of Tibetan refugees. Organisations such as Human Rights Watch claim that China's growing influence has led to increased pressure on Tibetans in Nepal amid increasingly violent crackdowns on pro-Tibetan demonstrations. Since 2008 over 100 Tibetans have set themselves on fire in Tibet protesting China's policies in Tibet. In 2013 two Tibetan protestors set themselves alight in front of the Bodhnath stupa. Chinese advisors have allegedly played a role in suppressing anti-Chinese demonstrations in Bodhnath and training Nepali border guards to catch and send back Tibetan refugees crossing the border into Nepal.

Tibetan-run old-timer caters to backpackers and the dharma crowd with rock-bottom prices, tasty Tibetan and Western food, and soft sofas that you'll have to prise yourself out of.

Garden Kitchen　INTERNATIONAL $
(☏01-4470760; mains Rs 200-330) A partly open-air place serving the usual globetrotting menu in quiet and pleasant surroundings. Reasonable prices (including tax) attract many long-term dharma students.

Flavors Café　INTERNATIONAL $$
(☏01-4495484; www.flavorscafe.org; meals Rs 325-540; ⏱7.30am-9.30pm; 🖥🍴) There's something for everyone here, from stuffed eggplant to Thai curries, pizzas and steak. There are no views from the pleasant interior courtyard just off the stupa, but it's a quiet, secluded place and the service is good.

La Casita de Boudhanath　SPANISH $$
(mains Rs 400-800; ⏱10am-9.30pm Sun-Fri) For something a bit different, climb the narrow stairs at this tiny place and grab a romantic perch for wine and tapas overlooking the stupa. The authentic gazpacho, Spanish omelette and toast with chorizo are best washed down with a rioja wine or hot chocolate with churros.

Café du Temple　INTERNATIONAL $$
(☏01-2143256; www.cafedutemple.com.np; mains Rs 300-450; set meals Rs 500-600; ⏱9am-8.30pm) Run by the same people as the Café du Temple in Patan, this smart and efficient place targets tour groups with a variety of Indian, Chinese and Tibetan dishes, plus unbeatable rooftop views that shine in afternoon light.

White Dzambala Tibetan Restaurant　CHINESE $$
(mains Rs 250-400) It's hard not to feel a twinge of guilt eating Chinese food in Tibetan Bodhnath, but this doesn't seem to deter the local Tibetan businessmen and monks who come here to tuck into authentic Sichuanese *gongbao jiding* (spicy chicken with peanuts) or to nurse a *wanzi* fruit tea in the garden pavilions. It's just 40m from the stupa and sees almost no tourists.

Stupa View Restaurant　INTERNATIONAL $$$
(☏01-4914962; mains Rs 500-600, set meals Rs 800; ⏱8.30am-8.30pm; 🍴) The views are as good as they claim at this superior traveller-oriented vegetarian place overlooking the stupa, so come early to nab one of the coveted top-floor seats. The mezze and sampler platters are excellent, with fresh and tasty dishes such as chickpea balls in peanut sauce, and the pizzas are cooked in clay ovens.

🛍 Shopping

The stupa is ringed by shops selling Tibetan crafts, thangkas, votive objects and Tibetan cowboy hats, but you'll get better prices by exploring the winding side streets. For tea bowls, butter lamps, prayer flags and juniper incense, try the shops on the alleyway leading north from the stupa.

Several shops sell Tibetan 'singing bowls', beloved by New Age Tibetophiles, which have an alloy of seven metals that creates a ringing sound when you rotate a dowel around the rim, said to be conducive to meditative thought.

Tsering Art School Shop HANDICRAFTS
(Shechen Gompa; ⊙ 8-11.30am & 1.30-5pm Mon-Sat) The shop at Shechen Gompa has an on-site tailor and a workshop that produces thangkas, incense and sculptures. The shop also sells Buddhist reference books and CDs.

ⓘ Information

Kunphen Tibetan Medical Centre (☑ 01-4251920; consultation free; ⊙ 9am-noon & 2-5pm Sun-Fri) If you fancy trying out Tibetan traditional medicine, pay a visit to this clinic on the west side of the stupa square, near Tsamchen Gompa. Diagnosis is based on the speed and regularity of the pulse and the condition of the tongue, and illnesses are treated with pills of Himalayan herbs available for purchase at the attached pharmacy.

ⓘ Getting There & Away

From Kathmandu, the easiest way to reach Bodhnath is by taxi (Rs 400 one way), but you can also come by bicycle (watch the heavy traffic), by bus from Ratna Park bus station (Rs 15, 30 minutes) or by tempo from Kantipath (Rs 15, routes 2 and 28).

There's also an interesting short walk (p127) between Bodhnath and Pashupatinath, or you could combine Bodhnath with a visit to Kopan Monastery and Gokarna Mahadev Temple (p172).

Kopan Monastery

On a hilltop north of Bodhnath, **Kopan Monastery** (☑ 01-4821268; www.kopan-monastery.com) was founded by Lama Thubten Yeshe, who died in 1984, leading to a worldwide search for his reincarnation. A young Spanish boy, Osel Torres, was declared to be the reincarnated lama, providing the inspiration for Bernardo Bertolucci's film *Little Buddha*. Lama Tenzin Osel Rinpoche no longer resides at Kopan (he recently renounced his vows to become a cinematographer in Ibiza!), but visitors are welcome to explore the monastery and many people come here to study Buddhist psychology and philosophy. The complex was damaged in the 2015 earthquake but repairs were underway at the time of research.

You can visit Kopan on the pleasant walk between Bodhnath and the Gokarna Mahadev Temple (p172) or even from Nagi Gompa in Shivapuri Nagarjun National Park. A taxi here from Kathmandu costs around Rs 600.

Courses

Kopan Monastery MEDITATION
(☑ 01-4821268; www.kopan-monastery.com) Kopan is probably the best place in the Himalaya to learn the basics of meditation and Tibetan Buddhism. The reasonably priced and popular seven-day (US$95) or 10-day (US$120, with a two-day retreat) courses are generally given six or seven times a year by foreign teachers. There's also a popular annual one-month course (US$460) held in November, followed by an optional seven-day retreat. The schedule may be affected by the restoration work, so contact the monastery for the latest information.

Visitors can also attend the daily dharma talks at 10am, except between 11 November and 20 December, when the monastery is closed to visitors.

THE NORTHERN & NORTHWESTERN VALLEY

There are several interesting detours to the north and northwest of the capital, which can easily be visited by bus, tempo, taxi, rented bicycle or motorcycle, or even on foot.

Ichangu Narayan

About 3km northwest of Swayambhunath, **Ichangu Narayan** (admission free; ⊙ dawn-dusk) is one of several important temples dedicated to Vishnu in his incarnation as Narayan, the 'eternal man'. Built in the two-tiered pagoda style, the temple was founded in around AD 1200 and its courtyard is dotted with ancient Garuda statues and other Vaishnavite symbols. The complex was shaken by the 2015 earthquake, but most structures have been stabilised and repaired.

Microvans (route 23) go to Ichangu Narayan (Rs 25) about every half-hour from Ratna Park or New Road Gate (near the Nepal Airlines office). They stop at the Aadeswor Temple, from where you have to walk about 2km to Ichangu Narayan. A taxi from Thamel to Ichangu Narayan costs Rs 500.

Nagarjun Hill (Shivapuri Nagarjun National Park)

If you continue uphill from Balaju on the road towards Trisuli Bazaar, you'll reach **Nagarjun**

Hill (Rani Ban, Queen's Forest; admission Rs 500; ⊙ entry 7am-2pm, latest exit 5pm), also known as the Rani Ban (Queen's Forest), now formally part of Shivapuri Nagarjun National Park. This protected forest is one of the last undamaged areas of woodland in the valley, providing a home for pheasants, deer and monkeys. It's a peaceful spot but safety is a consideration. Female visitors are discouraged from walking here alone after two foreign tourists were murdered in the reserve in 2005.

The 2095m summit – accessible by the winding unpaved road or a two-hour hike on the footpath leading directly up the hill – is a popular Buddhist pilgrimage site and there's a small shrine to Padmasambhava which survived the 2015 earthquake with minor damage. The viewing tower offers one of the valley's widest mountain panoramas, stretching all the way from the Annapurnas to Langtang Lirung (a plaque identifies the peaks).

Several Kathmandu-based adventure companies run introductory rock-climbing courses here. Hardcore Nepal (p85) offers a one-day beginners rock-climbing course (US$75) and an expert four-day climbing clinic (US$250), which teaches you the basics about knots, anchors and safety to give you the confidence to climb solo. The course is based in Nagarjun Hill, before moving on to more technical climbs in Hattiban and Bimalnagar.

❶ Getting There & Away

The main entrance to the reserve is at Phulbari, about 2km north of Balaju. A ride up to the summit makes for a fine motorbike excursion.

Budhanilkantha

The Kathmandu Valley is awash with ancient temples and sacred sites, but Budhanilkantha is a little bit special. For one thing, it lies off the main traveller circuit, so most visitors are local devotees. This gives Budhanilkantha a uniquely mystical air – come on a busier day and you'll discover butter lamps flickering in the breeze, incense curling through the air, and devotees tossing around *tika* powder like confetti. The village saw only minor damage in the 2015 earthquake.

The focal point of the devotions at Budhanilkantha is a large reclining statue (admission free; ⊙ dawn-dusk) of Vishnu as Narayan, the creator of all life, who floats on the cosmic sea. From his navel grew a lotus and from the lotus came Brahma, who in turn created the world. The 5m-long Licchavi-style image was created in the 7th or 8th century from one monolithic piece of black stone and hauled here from outside the valley by devotees. It's one of the most impressive pieces of sculpture in Nepal, and that's saying something!

Only Hindus can approach the statue to leave offerings of fruit and flower garlands, but visitors can view the statue through the fence that surrounds the sacred tank. Narayan slumbers peacefully on the knotted coils of Ananta (or Shesha), the 11-headed snake god who symbolises eternity. In each hand, Narayan holds one of the four symbols of Vishnu: a chakra disc (representing the mind), a conch shell (the four elements), a mace (primeval knowledge) and a lotus seed (the moving universe).

Vaishnavism (the worship of Vishnu) was the main sect of Hinduism in Nepal until the early Malla period, when Shiva became the most popular deity. The Malla king Jayasthithi is credited with reviving the Vishnu cult by claiming to be the latest incarnation of this oft-incarnated god. Every subsequent king of Nepal has made the same claim, and because of this they are forbidden, on pain of death, from seeing the image at Budhanilkantha.

Vishnu is supposed to sleep through the four monsoon months and a great festival takes place at Budhanilkantha for Haribodhini Ekadashi – the 11th day of the Hindu month of Kartik (October–November) – when Vishnu is said to awaken from his annual slumber.

🛏 Sleeping & Eating

There are no budget sleeping options in the area, but seeing as it's only a very short taxi ride from central Kathmandu that's no great disaster. The road to the sacred pavilion is lined with *bhojanalayas* (stalls) serving *sel roti* (rice-flour doughnuts), *channa puri* (fried bread with chickpeas), pakora (battered vegetables) and outsized pappadams.

★ **Shivapuri Heights**   COTTAGE $$$
(🖂 9851012245, 9851088928; www.shivapuri-cottage.com; half-board r per person US$50-85; 🛜) Perched on the hillside above Budhanilkantha, Shivapuri Heights offers a peaceful, private bolthole far away from the chaos of Kathmandu. There are three cottages for hire, all decked out with charming living rooms and flower-fringed terraces that offer great views over the Kathmandu Valley. The buildings were damaged in the earthquake

but are expected to reopen before the end of 2015. The compound is a 15-minute uphill walk from Budhanilkantha; staff can arrange transport on request.

You can rent a whole cottage (each housing four to six guests, so great for families) or just a room if you don't mind sharing the living room. The Jasmine House cottage offers the most luxury. The location makes it a great base for guided forest hikes to Nagi Gompa, or just relax with an open-air massage beside the plunge pool. It's worth staying for two or three nights.

Park Village Resort RESORT $$$
(☏01-4375280; www.ktmgh.com; fan only s/d from US$75/85, s/d with air-con from US$100/110; ❇❈❄) This delightful hotel feels like a country retreat, despite being smack in the middle of Budhanilkantha. The tidy but really rather plain standard rooms and the much smarter pricier rooms are surrounded by leafy gardens and there's a lovely pool. The hotel also offers various spa treatments and activities, including bird-spotting tours to Shivapuri Nagarjun National Park.

❶ Getting There & Away

From Kathmandu, minibus 5 runs from the northern end of Kantipath to the main junction in Budhanilkantha (Rs 30, 35 minutes). There are also tempos (from Sundhara) and buses (from both Gongabu and Ratna Park bus stations). The shrine is about 100m uphill from the junction. From Thamel, a taxi costs around Rs 600 one way or Rs 1000 return.

Shivapuri Nagarjun National Park

The northern part of the Kathmandu Valley rises to the sprawling forests of Shivapuri Nagarjun National Park (☏01-4370355; admission Rs 500, mountain bike Rs 1000), upgraded to national park status in 2002 to protect the valley's main water source, as well as 177 species of bird and numerous rare orchids. This is one of the last areas of woodland left in the valley, and the forest is alive with monkeys, and maybe even leopards and bears.

In the past the park was mainly visited by trekkers en route to Helambu, but today the reserve is a popular destination for birdwatching tours from Kathmandu. Several trekking and mountain-bike routes crisscross the park, including the challenging Scar Rd cycle path.

You can combine a nature-spotting tour with a trip to the Tibetan nunnery of Nagi Gompa, about 3km uphill from the main gate above Budhanilkantha. Some buildings were badly damaged in the earthquake, but the main prayer hall survived. Around 100 nuns are resident and there are soaring valley views – you can walk here from Budhanilkantha in 1½ hours or drive in 20 minutes by motorcycle or hired 4WD.

From the gompa it's possible to climb steeply for about three hours to reach Shivapuri Peak (2725m), via Baghdwar (where the source of the holy Bagmati River pours out of two stone tiger mouths), returning to the park entrance via the Pani Muhan water tank (reservoir), for a very long day of around seven hours. This is a serious hike that you shouldn't do alone. Take a map, plenty of water and preferably a guide.

There are several easier walks from Nagi Gompa. Consider the relaxing downhill stroll to Budhanilkantha, or continue south along the ridgeline for three hours to reach Kopan Monastery and Bodhnath. Another good option on foot or by mountain bike is to follow the dirt track east to Mulkarkha and then descend to Sundarijal – a mostly level 11km trip.

The only accommodation option here was destroyed in the 2015 earthquake.

ASHOKA STUPAS

Legend claims that the four ancient stupas marking the boundaries of Patan were built when the great Buddhist emperor Ashoka visited the valley 2500 years ago. All are worth a quick visit, especially during the auspicious full moon of August when Buddhist and Tibetan pilgrims walk around all four stupas in a single day.

Northern Stupa (Map p138) Just beyond the Kumbeshwar Temple, on the way to the Sankhamul ghats.

Lagan (Southern) Stupa Just south of the Lagankhel bus stand, crowning a hilltop and offering good views over southern Patan.

Western Stupa (p119) Covered in grass beside the main road at Pulchowk. A set of steps leads uphill to the Akshesh-wor Mahavihar, a courtyard-style Buddhist monastery on the hilltop.

Eastern Stupa Well to the east of the centre, across Kathmandu's Ring Rd.

PATAN ✓

📓 01 / POP 200,000

Once a fiercely independent city-state, Patan (pronounced '*pah*-tan') is now almost a suburb of Kathmandu, separated only by the murky Bagmati River. Many locals still call the city by its original Sanskrit name of Lalitpur (City of Beauty) or by its Newari name, Yala. Almost everyone who comes to Kathmandu also visits Patan's spectacular Durbar Sq – even after the 2015 earthquake, this remains the finest collection of temples and palaces in the whole of Nepal.

Another good reason to come here is to take advantage of the shops and restaurants set up to cater to the NGO workers and diplomats who live in the surrounding suburbs. Then there are Patan's fair-trade shops, selling superior handicrafts at fair prices and channelling tourist dollars to some of the most needy people in Nepal.

Most people visit Patan on a day trip from Kathmandu but there is some charming traditional accommodation here. Patan becomes a different place once the crowds of day-trippers retreat across the Bagmati. Stay overnight and you'll be able to explore the myriad *tole* (squares) and bahal (courtyards) at your leisure.

History

Patan has a long Buddhist history, which has even had an influence on the town's Hindu temples. The four corners of the city are marked by stupas said to have been erected by the great Buddhist emperor Ashoka in around 250 BC. Today there are still around 1200 Buddhist monuments scattered around the city.

The town was ruled by local noblemen until King Shiva Malla of Kathmandu conquered the city in 1597, temporarily unifying the valley. Patan's major building boom took place under the Mallas in the 16th, 17th and 18th centuries.

The 2015 earthquake did not spare Patan. Many temples were damaged and several collapsed completely in Patan's Durbar Sq, but as in previous quakes, the city fared better than Kathmandu and Bhaktapur.

☉ Sights

Most of the famous sights are centred on Durbar Sq. We describe the temples in the square as one visits them from north to south.

Ticket offices at the main entrances to the old town charge a combined Durbar Sq and old town entry fee. If you don't pay it here,

EARTHQUAKE DAMAGE IN PATAN

Although Patan weathered the 2015 earthquake better than Kathmandu and Bhaktapur – as was the case in the 1934 quake – several iconic temples were completely destroyed. The government has promised to restore the damaged monuments, but the Jagannarayan Temple, Hari Shankar Temple, Mani Mandap pavilions and statue of King Yoganarendra Malla were reduced to rubble. The latter is particularly poignant as a local legend stated that the king of Patan would always be able to return to his palace so long as the small brass bird remained atop his statue. While enough buildings remain to ensure that Patan's Durbar Sq is still spectacular, and a world-class repository of medieval art and architecture, a little of its grandeur has been lost forever.

you'll have to pay it at ticket offices at either end of Durbar Sq. For repeat visits ensure that your visa validity date is written on the back of your ticket.

☉ Durbar Square

As in Kathmandu, the ancient Royal Palace of Patan faces on to a magnificent **Durbar Square** (Royal Sq; Map p142; foreigner/Chinese/SAARC Rs 500/250/100; ☉ ticket office 7am-7pm). Temple construction in the square went into overdrive during the Malla period (from the 14th to 18th centuries), particularly during the reign of King Siddhinarsingh Malla (1619–60).

This concentrated mass of temples is perhaps the most visually stunning display of Newari architecture to be seen in Nepal, even after the 2105 earthquake. Nevertheless, the tremor caused a number of revered temples to collapse into rubble, including the iconic Jagannarayan Temple (formerly the oldest temple in the square), Hari Shankar Temple and statue of King Yoganarendra Malla.

Bhimsen Temple   HINDU TEMPLE

(Map p142) At the northern end of Durbar Sq, the Bhimsen Temple is dedicated to the god of trade and business, which may explain its prosperous appearance. One of the five Pandavas from the Mahabharata, Bhimsen is credited with superhuman strength – he is often depicted as a red muscleman, lifting a horse or crushing an elephant under his knee.

The three-storey pagoda has an unusual rectangular plan that sets it apart from other temples in Patan. The current temple was completely rebuilt in 1682 after a fire and was later restored after the 1934 earthquake, and again in 1967; further repairs are underway after the 2015 quake. Once repairs are complete, non-Hindus should once again be able to climb to the upper level (the inner sanctum is usually upstairs in Bhimsen temples) to view the wild-eyed statue of Bhimsen.

Patan

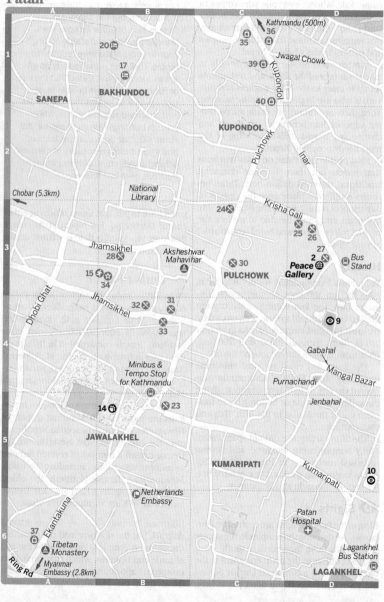

Manga Hiti
WATER TANK

(Map p142) Immediately across from Bhimsen Temple is the sunken Manga Hiti, one of the water conduits with which Patan is liberally endowed. The tank contains a cruciform-shaped pool and three wonderfully carved *dhara* (water spouts) in the shape of makara (mythical crocodile-elephants). The two wooden ceremonial pavilions that used to overlook the tank – known as the Mani Mandap – collapsed completely in the 2015 earthquake.

Vishwanath Temple
HINDU TEMPLE

(Map p142) South of the Bhimsen Temple stands the Vishwanath Temple, dedicated to Shiva. Damaged but not destroyed in the earthquake, this elaborately decorated two-tiered pagoda was built in 1627 and it features some particularly ornate woodcarving, especially on the torana (pediment) above the colonnade.

On the west side is a statue of Shiva's loyal mount, Nandi the bull, while the east side features two stone elephants with mahouts, one crushing a man beneath its foot. When the doors are open, you can view the enormous lingam inside.

★ Krishna Mandir
HINDU TEMPLE

(Map p142) Continuing into the square, you can't miss the splendid Krishna Mandir built by King Siddhinarsingh Malla in 1637. Constructed from carved stone – in place of the usual brick and timber – this fabulous architectural confection shows the clear influence of Indian temple design and is the earliest stone temple of its type in Nepal. The distinctive temple is often depicted on the ornate brass butter lamps hung in Nepali homes. The temple was severely shaken but stayed intact through the 2015 earthquake.

The temple consists of three tiers, fronted by columns and supporting a North Indian–style shikhara. Non-Hindus cannot enter to view the statue of Krishna, the goatherd, but you'll often hear temple musicians playing upstairs. Vishnu's mount, the man-bird Garuda, kneels with folded arms on top of a column facing the temple. The delicate stone carvings along the beam on the 1st floor recount events from the Mahabharata, while the hard-to-see beam on the 2nd floor features scenes from the Ramayana.

A major festival, **Krishna Jayanta**, also known as Krishnasthami, is held here in the Nepali month of Bhadra (August to September) for Krishna's birthday.

Vishnu Temples
HINDU TEMPLES

(Map p142) West of the palace, near the site of the ruined Jagannarayan Temple and statue of King Yoganendra Malla are three smaller Vishnu temples, including a brick-and-plaster shikhara temple, built in 1590

0 ——— 500 m
0 ——— 0.25 miles

Bagmati River

Sankhamul Ghats

Arniko Hwy (1.2km)

8
38
4

Golden Temple (Kwa Bahal)
1 13
16 19
6 12 22
29 21

Durbar Square

Sundari Chowk
See Durbar Square (Patan) Map (p142)

Ekhalakhu
Safa Tempos to Kathmandu

3
Hakha Tole

HAUGAL Saugal Tole
7
Sundhara Tole

5
18

11

Lagan (Southern) Stupa (250m);
Patan Industrial Estate (500m);
Godavari (19km)

KATHMANDU VALLEY & AROUND PATAN

Patan

to enshrine an image of Narsingha, Vishnu's man-lion incarnation.

Taleju Bell   MONUMENT
(Map p142) Facing the palace is a huge, ancient bell, hanging between two stout pillars, erected by King Vishnu Malla in 1736. Petitioners could ring the bell to alert the king to their grievances. The bell tolled ominously during the 2015 disaster, but the pavilion stayed intact. Behind the bell pavilion is a fountain crossed by an ornamental bridge.

Krishna Temple   HINDU TEMPLE
(Chyasim Deval; Map p142) This attractive, octagonal stone temple completes the 'front line' of temples in the square. It has strong architectural similarities to the Krishna Mandir at the north end of the square, and also survived the earthquake with only minor damage. The tiered structure was built in 1723 in a style clearly influenced by the stone temples of northern India.

Royal Palace   PALACE
(Map p142) Forming the whole eastern side of Durbar Sq, the Royal Palace of Patan was originally built in the 14th century, but was expanded massively during the 17th and 18th centuries by Siddhinarsingh Malla, Sriniva-

sa Malla and Vishnu Malla. The Patan palace predates the palaces in Kathmandu and Bhaktapur and remains one of the architectural highlights of Nepal. Despite some damage during the earthquake, the palace and museum have been stabilised and restoration works were underway when we visited.

Behind the extravagant facade, with its overhanging eaves, carved windows and delicate wooden screens, are a series of connecting courtyards and a trip of temples dedicated to the valley's main deity, the goddess Taleju. The closed external **Bhairab gateway** leading to the central Mul Chowk courtyard is flanked by two stone lions and colourful murals of Shiva in his wrathful incarnation as Bhairab. Strings of buffalo guts are hung above the door in his honour.

The northern courtyard is reached through the **Golden Gate** (Sun Dhoka; Map p142). Installed in 1734, this finely engraved and gilded gateway is topped by a golden torana showing Shiva, Parvati, Ganesh and Kumar (an incarnation of Skanda, the god of war). Directly above the gateway is a window made from gold foil wrapped around a timber frame, where the king once made public appearances. The gateway now forms the entrance to the Patan Museum.

The current restoration works are not the first to take place at the palace – parts of the building had to be reconstructed after the conquest of the valley by Prithvi Narayan Shah in 1768, and again after the great earthquake of 1934.

★ **Patan Museum** MUSEUM
(Map p142; ☑01-5521492; www.patanmuseum. gov.np; foreigner/SAARC & Chinese Rs 400/250; ⌚10.30am-5.30pm, last admission 4pm) Formerly the residence of the Malla kings, the section of the palace surrounding Keshav Narayan Chowk now houses one of the finest collections of religious art in Asia. The museum is a national treasure and an invaluable introduction to the art, symbolism and architecture of the valley. You need at least an hour, preferably two, to do this place justice, and it's worth taking a break at the Museum Café before diving in for another round. Some rooms and exhibits were damaged in the 2015 earthquake, but the building was stabilised and has reopened to the public.

The collection is displayed in a series of brick and timber rooms, linked by steep and narrow stairways. There are informative labels on each of the hundreds of statues, carvings and votive objects, allowing you to put a name to many of the deities depicted at temples around the valley.

There are also some interesting displays on the techniques used to create these wonderful objects, including the art of repoussé and the 'lost wax' method of casting. The top floor houses some fascinating photos of Patan at the end of the 19th century.

The museum has a shop selling reproductions of some of the works displayed inside. For a sneak preview of the museum's highlights and the story of its renovation, go to www.asianart.com/patan-museum. Photography is allowed.

★ **Mul Chowk** COURTYARD
(Map p142; entry with Patan Museum ticket) South of the Patan Museum, a gateway opens onto the stately Mul Chowk, the largest and oldest of the palace's three main chowk (squares). The original buildings were destroyed by fire in 1662 but rebuilt just three years later by Srinivasa Malla. The temples in the courtyard were restored in 2014 but Mul Chowk took a fair bit of damage in the 2015 earthquake. Its buildings have been stablilised pending repairs.

In the centre of the square is the small, gilded, central **Bidyapith Temple** (Map p142), beside a wooden post used to secure animals for sacrifices. The central deity is Yantaju, a form of Durga, and a personal deity to the Malla kings.

On the south side of the squre is the **Taleju Bhawani Temple** (Map p142), flanked by statues of the river goddesses Ganga, on a tortoise, and Jamuna, on a makara. The upper galleries now form part of the museum's architectural displays, with fine examples of carved wooden struts.

At the northeastern corner of the square is the tall **Degutalle Temple**, topped by an octagonal triple-roofed tower. The larger, triple-roofed **Taleju Temple** is directly north, looking out over Durbar Sq, and dedicated to Taleju, another protective deity of the Malla kings.

★ **Sundari Chowk** COURTYARD
(Map p142) South of Mul Chowk is the smaller Sundari Chowk, arranged around a superbly carved sunken water tank known as the **Tusha Hiti** (Map p142). The chowk was restored in 2014 but several structures were damaged in the 2015 earthquake and the rear wall collapsed, but the site had been stabilised pending repairs when we visited. Built in 1647, the renovated water tank has 72 carved stone plaques depicting Tantric deities and was used by the king for ritual ablutions. The spout is new; the original

> ### NARSINGHA
>
> The image of Vishnu in his man-lion incarnation as Narsingha (or Narsimha) can be seen all over the Kathmandu Valley. The deity is normally depicted gleefully disembowelling the demon Hiranyakashipu with his bare hands, recalling a famous legend from the Bhagavata Purana. Because of a deal made with Brahma, the demon was granted special powers – he could not be killed by man or beast, either inside or outside, on the ground or in the air, by day or by night, nor by any weapon. Vishnu neatly got around these protections by adopting the form of a man-lion and killing the demon with his fingernails, at dusk, on his lap, on the threshold of the house. You can see statues of Narsingha at his grisly work at the Gokarna Mahadev Temple, in front of the palace in Patan and just inside the Hanuman Dhoka entrance in Kathmandu.

KATHMANDU VALLEY & AROUND PATAN

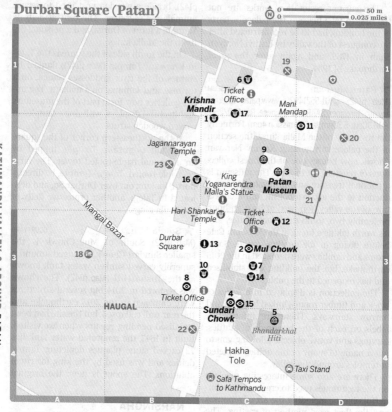

Durbar Square (Patan)

◉ Top Sights
1 Krishna Mandir	C2
2 Mul Chowk	C3
3 Patan Museum	C2
4 Sundari Chowk	C3

◎ Sights
5 Bhandarkhal Water Tank	C4
6 Bhimsen Temple	C1
7 Bidyapith Temple	C3
8 Durbar Square	B3
9 Golden Gate	C2
10 Krishna Temple	C3
11 Manga Hiti	D2
12 Royal Palace	C3
13 Taleju Bell	C3

14 Taleju Bhawani Temple	C3
15 Tusha Hiti	C3
16 Vishnu Temples	B2
17 Vishwanath Temple	C1

⌂ Sleeping
18 Café de Patan	A3

✕ Eating
Café de Patan	(see 18)
19 Café du Temple	C1
20 Casa Pagoda	D2
21 Patan Museum Café	D2
22 Si Taleju Restaurant & Bar	B4
23 Third World Restaurant	B2

was stolen in 2010 but recently recovered. Ancient carved wooden struts lie scattered in the corners like kindling wood.

On the way out look at the recently restored **Bhandarkhal water tank** (Map p142), once the main water supply for the palace, featuring a charming meditation pavillion.

Back in Durbar Sq, the traditional gateway to Sundari Chowk features three magnificent statues of **Hanuman** (barely recognisable beneath layers of orange paint), **Ganesh** and Vishnu as **Narsingha**, the man-lion, tearing out the entrails of a demon.

◉ North of Durbar Square

★ Golden Temple
(Kwa Bahal)
BUDDHIST TEMPLE

(Hiranya Varna Mahavihara; Map p138; foreigner/SAARC Rs 50/10; ⊙5am-6pm) Untouched by the earthquake, this unique Buddhist monastery is just north of Durbar Sq. It was allegedly founded in the 12th century, and it has existed in its current form since 1409. The temple gets its name from the gilded metal plates that cover most of its frontage and it is one of the most beautiful in Patan. Outside of winter, look for the tortoises pottering around the compound – these are the temple guardians.

Entry is via an ornate narrow stone doorway to the east, or a wooden doorway to the west from one of the interlinked courtyards on the north side of Nakabhil.

Entering from the east, note the gaudy lions and the 1886 signature of Krishnabir, the master stonemason who sculpted the fine doorway with its frieze of Buddhist deities. This second doorway leads to the main courtyard of the Golden Temple; shoes and leather articles must be removed to enter the lower courtyard. The main priest of the temple is a young boy under the age of 12, who serves for 30 days before handing the job over to another young boy.

The temple itself is a magnificent example of courtyard temple architecture. Two elephant statues guard the doorway and the facade is covered by a host of gleaming Buddhist figures. Inside the main shrine is a beautiful statue of Sakyamuni (no photos allowed). To the left of the courtyard is a statue of Green Tara and in the right corner is a statue of the Bodhisattva Vajrasattva wearing an impressive silver-and-gold cape. Both are inside inner shrines.

Facing the main temple is a smaller shrine containing a 'self-arisen' (*swayambhu*) chaitya (small stupa). The four corners of the courtyard have statues of four Lokeshvaras (incarnations of Avalokiteshvara) and four monkeys, which hold out jackfruits as an offering. A stairway leads to an upper-floor chapel dedicated to a white eight-armed Avalokiteshvara, lined with Tibetan-style frescoes including a wheel of life. Finally, as you leave the temple at the eastern exit, look up to see an embossed mandala mounted on the ceiling.

IMAGES OF WAR

As with so many conflicts, the decade-long civil war in Nepal is marked by a public photo exhibition that brings the conflict poignantly to life, based on the book *A People War* by Nepali Times editor Kunda Dixit. Before the 2015 earthquake, the exhibition was on display at the **Peace Gallery** (Map p138; ☎school office 01-5522614; www.apeoplewar.com.np; ⊙10am-4pm) inside the Rato Bangla School, but the collection may move to a new home. Contact the **Bhaktapur Tourism Development Committee** (p167) for an update.

It's worth ducking south towards Durbar Sq to see the small, two-tiered **Uma Maheshwar Temple** (Map p138) and the handsome stone **Gauri Shankar Temple** (Map p138), in the Indian shikhara style; both were shaken by the 2015 earthquake but not destroyed. Across the road, the Buddhist **Maru Mandapa Mahavihar** (Map p138) is set in a small courtyard.

Kumbeshwar Temple
HINDU TEMPLE

(Map p138) Due north of Durbar Sq is the eye-catching Kumbeshwar Temple, one of the valley's three five-storey temples. This tall, thin mandir (temple) features some particularly artistic woodcarving, and it seems to defy gravity as it towers above the surrounding houses. Amazingly, this precarious structure survived the earthquake, though the top tier toppled in May 2015 and the tower is now leaning slightly. A large Nandi statue and central lingam indicate that the shrine is sacred to Shiva.

The temple platform has two ponds whose water is said to come straight from the holy lake at Gosainkund, a weeklong trek north of the valley. Bathing in the tank at Kumbeshwar Temple is said to be as meritorious as making the arduous walk to Gosainkund.

The surrounding square is dotted with temples sacred to Bhairab and Baglamukhi (Parvati). Local women gather at the tank known as **Konti Hiti** to socialise, wash clothes and fill up their water jugs. Down an alley to the north of the temple is the Kumbeshwar Technical School (p151).

From here you can detour north to see the **Northern Stupa**, one of four marker shrines showing the old city limits of Patan.

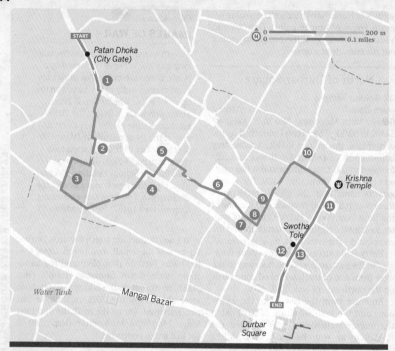

Town Walk
Patan: North of Durbar Square

START PATAN DHOKA
END DURBAR SQ
LENGTH 1.5KM; TWO HOURS

From Patan Dhoka, stroll southeast to a handsome two-storey **1 Ganesh shrine**, then swing right past **2 Sulima Square** to the **3 Pim Bahal Pokhari** pond.

At the road junction on the southeast corner of the pond, walk northeast past fine wooden windows to a large square at Nakabhil. On the south side is the courtyard-style **4 Lokakirti Mahavihar**, a former Buddhist monastery that is now used to store parts of the chariot used during the Rato Machhendranath Festival (you can see the runners by the front door); it has some minor earthquake damage. An alley leads north off the square, signposted 'Bhaskar Varna Mahavihar', to the Buddhist courtyard of **5 Nyakhuchowk Bahal**.

Head past a row of stupas to the eastern wall and go through the covered entrance (signed 'please mind your head'), straight across an alley, into another chaitya-filled courtyard, the **6 Naga Bahal**. Walk past the Hindu statue of a bull surrounded by Buddhist prayer wheels to

a painting of a naga (snake spirit) on the wall, repainted every five years.

Go through the eastern passageway to the Ilanani Courtyard with the red-walled Harayana Library in the southwestern corner. Follow a diagonal path to the southeastern corner and walk beneath a wooden torana (entry pediment) to enter the **7 Golden Temple** (p143).

After visiting the temple, exit east onto the main street, then turn left. You'll soon see a small blue sign for the courtyard-style **8 Manjushri Temple**. From here, continue north past a group of ancient **9 megaliths**, possibly the oldest objects of worship in the Kathmandu Valley, and continue to the earthquake-scarred but still impressive **10 Kumbeshwar Temple** (p143).

From this temple, head east and take a right (south) back to Durbar Sq. This road is lined with shrines to different incarnations of Vishnu, including a North Indian–style Krishna temple and the two-tiered **11 Uma Maheshwar Temple**.

Further south, at Swotha Tole, are the pagoda-style **12 Rada Krishna Temple** and the Garuda-fronted **13 Narayan Temple**, both showing some earthquake damage. A few more steps will take you to Durbar Sq.

Uma Maheshwar Temple   HINDU TEMPLE

(Map p138) Peer inside this temple (it's the back of the two temples) to see a very beautiful black-stone relief of Shiva and Parvati in the pose known as Uma Maheshwar – the god sitting cross-legged with his consort leaning against him rather seductively. The exterior was slightly damaged in the 2015 quake.

Pim Bahal Pokhari   POND

(Map p138) This large pond is a hidden gem centred around a charming lakeshore pavilion. On the north side is three-tiered Chandeswari Temple built in 1663. Walk around the pond clockwise and you'll pass a 600-year-old whitewashed stupa that was damaged by Muslim invaders in 1357. The compound took some damage in the 2015 earthquake, but repairs were underway at the time of research.

Northeast of the pond is Sulima Square, a crumbling brick-lined space with a 17th-century Mahadev (Shiva) shrine – it's crumbling a little more now after the earthquake, but can still be visited. On the east side of the square is the derelict house of a famous 16th-century Tantric master.

◉ South of Durbar Square

Most sights south of Durbar Sq are in the backstreets south of Mangal Bazar, the main shopping street. If you continue south, you will reach the busy marketplace surrounding the Lagankhel bus stand. Most structures here were not damaged by the earthquake.

I Baha Bahi   BUDDHIST MONASTERY

(Map p138) Just a one-minute walk south of Durbar Sq, a large new-looking doorway flanked by black lions with Cheshire-cat grins leads to a quiet bahal containing the I Baha Bahi. This handsome Buddhist monastery was founded in 1427 and the structure was restored in the 1990s by a team of architects from Japan.

Minnath Temple   BUDDHIST TEMPLE

(Map p138) Just 200m south of I Baha Bahi, a large water tank marks the entrance to a courtyard strewn with wooden beams. In the centre is the brightly painted, two-tiered Minnath Temple, dedicated to the Bodhisattva Jatadhari Lokesvara, who is considered to be the little brother of Rato Machhendranath. The temple was founded in the Licchavi period (3rd to 9th centuries) but the multiarmed goddesses on the roof struts were added much later.

Note the metal pots and pans nailed to the temple rafters by devotees. The timbers surrounding the temple are assembled into a chariot every year to haul the statue of Minnath around town as part of the Rato Machhendranath Festival.

Rato Machhendranath Temple   TEMPLE

(Map p138) Almost directly across the road from the Minnath Temple, down an alley, a white-columned gateway leads to the wide, open square containing the revered Rato Machhendranath Temple. Dedicated to the god of rain and plenty, the temple, like so many in Nepal, blurs the line between Buddhism and Hinduism. Buddhists regard Rato (Red) Machhendranath as an incarnation of Avalokiteshvara, while Hindus see him as an incarnation of Shiva.

Set inside a protective metal fence, the towering three-storey temple dates from 1673, but there has been some kind of temple on this site since at least 1408. The temple's four ornate doorways are guarded by stone snow lions and at ground level on the four corners of the temple plinth are curious yeti-like demons known as *kyah*.

Mounted on freestanding pillars at the front of the temple is a curious collection of metal animals, including a peacock, Garuda, horse, buffalo, lion, elephant, fish and snake. Look up to see the richly painted roof struts of the temple, which show Avalokiteshvara standing above figures being tortured in hell.

The main image of Machhendranath resides here for six months a year, before moving to Bungamati during the spectacular Rato Machhendranath Festival in April–May.

Mahabouddha Temple   BUDDHIST TEMPLE

(Map p138; foreigner/SAARC Rs 50/30; ☺9am-5.30pm) As you step through the entryway of this hard-to-find courtyard in the southeast of Patan, the temple suddenly looms above you, crammed into a tiny courtyard like a plant straining to get some sunlight. Built in the Indian shikhara style, the shrine takes its name from the hundreds of terracotta tiles that cover it, each bearing an image of the Buddha. Apart from some cracks, the sikhara is undamaged, unlike many similar brick-built structures in the Kathmandu Valley.

The temple dates from 1585, but was totally rebuilt after the 1934 earthquake. Unfortunately, without plans to work from, the builders ended up with a different-looking temple, and had enough bricks and tiles left over to construct a smaller shrine to Maya

RATO MACHHENDRANATH FESTIVAL

The image in the Rato Machhendranath Temple may look like a crudely carved piece of painted wood, but each year it forms the centrepiece for the Rato Machhendranath Festival in the Nepali month of Baisakh (April–May). Machhendranath is considered to have powers over rain and, since the monsoon is approaching at this time, this festival is essentially a plea for generous rains.

Immediately prior to the festival, the scattered timbers of Rato Machhendranath's chariot are gathered and assembled and the statue is installed on his awesome coach. It takes a full month to move the chariot across Patan to Jawalakhel, where the chariot is finally dismantled. The main chariot is so large and the route is so long that the Nepali army is often called in to help transport it.

The towering main chariot is accompanied for much of its journey by a smaller chariot, which contains the image of Rato Machhendranath's companion, Jatadhari Lokesvara, which normally resides in the Minnath Temple. The highlight of the festival is the Bhoto Jatra, or showing of the sacred vest. According to the legend, the jewelled vest was given to the god for safe keeping after a dispute between two potential owners. Every year, the vest is displayed three times in order to give the owner the chance to claim it.

From Jawalakhel, Rato Machhendranath is conveyed on a khat (palanquin – portable covered bed) to his second home in the village of Bungamati, 6km to the south, where he spends the next six months of the year, before returning to Patan. However, the future of this arrangement is in doubt after the destruction of the Rato Machhendranath Temple in Bungamati in the 2015 earthquake. Check locally to see if there have been any developments before planning a trip around the festival.

Devi, the Buddha's mother, in the corner of the courtyard. The temple is loosely modelled on the Mahabouddha Temple at Bodhgaya in India, where the Buddha gained enlightenment.

The surrounding lanes are full of shops selling high-quality Patan-style metal statues. The roof terrace of the shop at the back of the courtyard has a good view of the temple.

To reach the Mahabouddha Temple, you must walk southeast from Durbar Sq along Hakha Tole, passing a series of small Vaishnavite and Shaivite temples. When you reach Sundhara Tole, with its temple and sunken hiti (water tank) with three brass water spouts, turn right and look for the tiny doorway leading to the temple.

Uku Bahal　　　　BUDDHIST MONASTERY
(Rudra Varna Mahavihar; Map p138; foreigner/SAARC Rs 50/30; ⊙9am-5.30pm) South of the Mahabouddha Temple, this ancient Buddhist monastery is one of the best known in Patan. The main courtyard is jam-packed with statuary and metalwork – dorje (thunderbolt symbols), bells, peacocks, elephants, Garudas, rampant goats, kneeling devotees, a regal-looking statue of a Rana general and, rather incongruously, a pair of Victorian-style British lions that look like they could have been lifted straight from London's Trafalgar Sq.

The monastery has been used for centuries, and the wooden roof struts are some of the oldest in the valley, but much of what you can see today dates back to the 19th century. Behind the monastery is a Swayambhunath-style stupa accessed by a side door.

◉ West Of Durbar Square

Zoo　　　　　　　　　ZOO
(Map p138; ☎01-5528323; adult/child Rs 500/250; ⊙10am-5pm, to 4pm Dec-Mar) Nepal's only zoo is in southwestern Patan by the Jawalakhel roundabout and it was not affected by the earthquake. The animals live in better conditions than you might expect and there are always crowds of local kids being wowed by such exotic creatures as elephants, tigers, leopards, hyenas, gaur, blue bulls, gharial, langur monkeys and some very noisy hippos. People routinely get freaked out by the giant 60cm-long squirrels. Kids can take an elephant ride between 1pm and 4pm (Rs 500).

🏃 Activities

Pranamaya Yoga　　　　　YOGA
(Map p138; ☎9851002920; www.pranamaya-yoga.com; classes Rs 600) Branch of the well-run chain of yoga centres, inside a courtyard. See the website for a schedule.

⚜ Festivals & Events

Rato Machhendranath Festival   RELIGIOUS
Patan's most dramatic festival takes place in April–May.

Janai Purnima Festival   RELIGIOUS
Thousands of pilgrims visit the Kumbeshwar Temple in July–August, as members of the Brahmin and Chhetri castes replace the sacred thread they wear looped over their left shoulder. A silver-and-gold lingam is set up in the tank and devotees take a ritual bath while jhankri (faith healers) in colourful headdresses dance around the temple beating drums.

🛏 Sleeping

Not many tourists overnight in Patan, which is a shame because there's a small but stylish spread of accommodation, especially in the upper midrange category. Few of the accommodation options were affected by the 2015 earthquake.

Mahabuddha Guest House   GUESTHOUSE $
(Map p138; ☎01-5540575; mhg@mos.com.np; s/d Rs 500/700, ste Rs 1000; @) Southeast of Durbar Sq, across the road from the Mahabouddha Temple, this is a simple, somewhat grim budget choice. The location is a bit inconvenient and there are no common sitting areas but the tidy rooms are acceptable and there's an internet cafe. Rooms are named after Nepal's highest peaks with the better ones higher up. Rates include tax.

Café de Patan   HOTEL $
(Map p142; ☎01-5537599; www.cafede-patan.com; s/d Rs 900/1200, without bathroom Rs 600/900) This courtyard hotel is almost on Durbar Sq and there's a rooftop garden and a pleasant downstairs cafe. The rooms are simple, with thin mattresses but there's plenty of common seating. Only two rooms have attached bathrooms.

Cosy Nepal   BOUTIQUE HOTEL $$
(Map p138; ☎9860111757; www.cosynepal.com; Swotha Sq 18; r US$25-70; 🛈) This French-Nepali agency manages several traditional houses in the old town, all renovated with modern touches. The website details the different options, from simple single crashpads to family suites with kitchenettes. All strike a great balance between traditional architecture and modern style. Good discounts are available for long-term stays.

The office is in a hidden courtyard next to the main Yala Chhen address at Swotha Sq, behind the Swotha Tea & Coffee Shop. Book in advance.

Newa Chén   BOUTIQUE HOTEL $$
(Map p138; ☎01-5533532; www.newachen.com; s/d US$25/40, without bathroom US$20/30, deluxe US$35/50; @🛈) Housed inside the Unesco-restored Shestha House mansion, this place is more traditional than most and offers a window onto what it must have been like to be a well-to-do resident of Patan in centuries past. Rooms are all different but are decked out in traditional style, with divan seating areas and coir matting, and there's a nice communal living room. As with many older buildings, there was some earthquake damage but repairs were underway when we visited.

On a practical level the roadside rooms are noisy during the day, while anyone over 168cm (5ft 6in) will feel a bit cramped. Rates include breakfast.

Hotel Greenwich Village   HOTEL $$
(Map p138; ☎01-5521780; www.greenwichnepal.com; s/d from US$75/85, deluxe r US$95; ❄🛈⊞) The oddly named Greenwich Village is peaceful and secluded, though less luxurious than the rates might suggest. The modern rooms are smart and comfortable but you'll probably spend most of your time at the lovely poolside patio and cafe. Foreign exchange and free airport pick-up are useful perks, as is free breakfast.

The Inn   BOUTIQUE HOTEL $$$
(Map p138; ☎01-5547834; www.theinnpatan.com; s/d US$70/80, ste US$80/90; 🛈) This century-old residence has been converted by a local architect into a stylish and well-run option. The harmonious use of cream tones and natural fibres gives a sense of calm, while designer touches, such as niche lighting and walk-in showers bring touches of luxury. The suite room is worth it for the extra space and private balcony.

Traditional Homes Swotha   BOUTIQUE HOTEL $$$
(Map p138; ☎01-5551184; www.traditional-homes.com.np; s/d/ste US$80/90/120; 🛈) Just 50m from Durbar Sq, this 70-year-old traditional house is another that has been revamped into stylish accommodation. Unlike most traditional homes, the six rooms here are actually bright and spacious, with pressed-concrete floors, reclaimed wood, and gas heaters to provide winter heat. Bathrooms are small due to the nature of

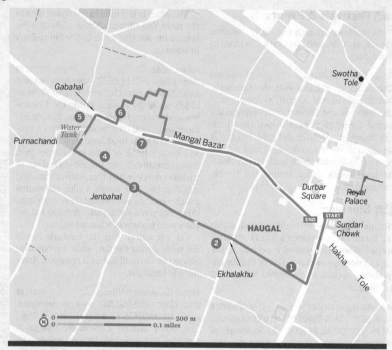

Gabahal

Swotha
Tole

Water
Tank

Purnachandi

Mangal Bazar

Jenbahal

Durbar
Square

Royal
Palace

END   START

HAUGAL

Sundari
Chowk

Ekhalakhu

Hakha
Tole

0   200 m
0   0.1 miles

🏃 Town Walk
Patan: South of Durbar Square

START DURBAR SQ
END DURBAR SQ
LENGTH 1.25 KM; ONE HOUR

Start this walk by heading south from Durbar Sq, then take the lane leading west to the **1 Bishwakarma (Bishokarma) Temple**, whose entire facade is covered in sheets of embossed copper. The temple is dedicated to the patron deity of carpenters and craftspeople.

Continuing northwest past Ekhalakhu junction with its Nepali-style **2 Vishnu shrines**, you pass a Ganesh shrine, a Shiva shrine, another three-tiered **3 Ganesh Temple** at Jenbahal junction and then a stone shikhara-style **4 Narayan Temple**.

At Purnachandi junction, turn right past a pagoda-shaped **5 Vaishnavite Temple** to the junction at Gabahal. Turn right and look for a small gateway on the left leading to **6 Bubahal**, a courtyard full of Buddhist statues and chaityas in front of the ornate but slightly damaged Yasodhar Mahabihar Temple.

Here's where things get fun! It's possible to continue east along the main road to reach the Haka Bahal but it's more interesting to detour there through the maze of interconnecting courtyards. Follow our instructions, leave a popcorn trail and if in doubt turn right.

From the Bubahal courtyard take the far right (northeastern) entryway through a courtyard into a second hidden brick courtyard with ornate wooden carvings. Continue through the far (northeastern) corner into a third small courtyard with a black chaitya and exit through a door in the eastern side, through a dark alleyway to another courtyard. Take the southeastern exit and swing right into another courtyard that has a small printing press, then continue south through a small courtyard to a larger courtyard (the seventh!) with a Vishnu Temple. From here you can rejoin the main road to the south and take a right to see the Haka Bahal.

Assuming you aren't hopelessly lost (well done!), pop into **7 Haka Bahal**, the restored courtyard of the Ratnakar Mahavihar, linked to Patan's Kumari (living goddess) cult. The red sign pointing to the 'Living Goddess' is something you don't see every day! Continue east through Mangal Bazar to finish at the south end of Durbar Sq for a well-deserved cup of tea.

the house but most rooms enjoy a private terrace. The attached restaurant is one of the best in town.

Summit Hotel RESORT $$$
(Map p138; ☑01-5521810; www.summit-nepal. com; budget s/d €30/35, s/d from €95/105; ✳@☀) Expats and NGOs like to keep the Summit secret so that there is room when relatives and friends come to visit. The Dutch-founded resort-style hotel is built in mock-Newari style, with lots of red brick and carved timber, and the atmosphere is superbly romantic and relaxed. The Garden Wing and larger and pricier Himalayan View rooms are delightful.

The swimming pool comes into its own in summer, while multiple fireplaces keep things snug in winter, especially in the cosy bar. Budget rooms with shared bathrooms in Holland House are aimed at students. The hotel is tucked away in the quiet lanes west of Kupondol, offering fine views over Kathmandu. Weekend barbecues are a highlight.

✗ Eating

Several restaurants overlook Durbar Sq, offering bland food but magical views, and are aimed squarely at day-tripping tour groups. In general, the further you get from Durbar Sq the better the food becomes. Few of Patan's restaurants were affected by the earthquake. Most places open from 8am to 8pm.

For a classy dinner for two while in Patan, consider the expat-oriented restaurants around Pulchowk (p150).

✗ Durbar Square

Third World Restaurant INTERNATIONAL $
(Map p142; ☑01-5543206; mains Rs 150-300) Located on the quiet western side of the square, with budget prices, Newari set meals and good rooftop views of the Krishna Mandir.

Patan Museum Café INTERNATIONAL $$
(Map p142; ☑01-5526271; mains Rs 400-700; ⊙10am-5pm) In the rear courtyard of the Patan Museum, this pleasant open-air place is run by the team behind the Summit Hotel. It survived the earthquake with minor damage. It's a good place to take a break from museum- and temple-gazing, and the garden terrace setting feels elegant and refined, though both the service and food suffer during the lunchtime group rush. You don't

need to buy a museum ticket to eat at the cafe. Reserve a table at lunchtime.

Si Taleju Restaurant & Bar INTERNATIONAL $$
(Map p142; ☑01-5538358; mains Rs 300-500) A narrow, towering place with four floors, each with a different feel. Best is the top-floor dining room with magical views north across Durbar Sq to the mountains beyond. You'll find all your favourites on the menu.

Kwalakhu Café INTERNATIONAL $$
(Map p138; ☑01-5522395; mains Rs 280-575; ⊙10am-8.30pm) An island of calm in the courtyard of the Unesco-restored Rajbhandari House, this simple local cafe has a peaceful back terrace and a menu of Nepali, Tibetan, Chinese and Continental food.

Café de Patan INTERNATIONAL $$
(Map p142; ☑01-5537599; www.cafedepatan. com; dishes Rs 200-300) Southwest of Durbar Sq behind a small Uma Maheshwar Temple, this quiet place is a long-running travellers' favourite, with an open-air courtyard and a rooftop garden (though no views). The menu runs to momos, pizza and Newari set meals.

Café du Temple INTERNATIONAL $$
(Map p142; ☑01-5527127; www.cafedutemple. com.np; mains Rs 250-400, set meals Rs 500-600) There was some minor earthquake damage at this tour-group favourite at the north end of Durbar Sq but it's open for business. The airy rooftop tables are covered by red-and-white sun umbrellas and the menu runs from Chinese fried rice to daal bhaat (traditional Nepali dish of rice and vegetables), via chicken stroganoff. The nearby **Casa Pagoda** (Map p142; mains Rs 300-700) is slightly pricier but has nicer decor.

✗ Elsewhere

Bakery Café CAFE $
(Map p138; ☑01-5522949; www.nanglo.com.np; mains Rs 135-385; ⊙10.30am-9.30pm; ☎) All the branches of this excellent chain provide work for deaf Nepalis. Patan has two restaurants – one by the main roundabout at Jawalakhel and a **branch** (Map p138; mains Rs 135-385) opposite UN House at Pulchowk. Both offer good-value coffee, momos, *dosas* (South Indian crêpes), sizzlers and sandwiches.

Namaste Supermarket SUPERMARKET $
(Map p138; ☑01-5520026; Pulchowk; ⊙8.30am-8pm) Sharing a building with the Hotel Narayani, this is where expats come

EXPAT EATS

The area around Pulchowk and Jhamsikhel is a favourite hang-out of diplomats, NGO staff and other expats, and it feels a long way from the tourist crowds of Thamel or Patan's Durbar Sq. This area also escaped damage in the 2015 earthquake. There are now so many restaurants here that locals have dubbed the area 'Jhamel'.

For when you can't face battling traffic, **Foodmandu** (☑01-4444177; www.foodmandu.com) offers delivery to Patan or Kathmandu from over 100 local restaurants with no fee for a minimum purchase of Rs 650.

Sing Ma Food Court (Map p138; ☑01-5509092; mains Rs 320-465; ⊗8.30am-9pm Sun-Fri) For the authentic tastes of Malaysia, head to this busy food court south of Pulchowk. The noodle soups, *nasi lemak* (coconut rice with anchovies) and beef rendang (dry coconut curry with lime leaves) are the real *mamak* (Malay Tamil) deal. It also does a surprisingly good cheesecake!

New Orleans (Map p138; ☑01-5522708; mains Rs 270-380; ⊗8am-10pm; 🛜) Set around a pleasant courtyard that is often full of expats with laptops, this branch of the popular Thamel restaurant serves everything from Goan-style fish to Mongolian beef, plus there's on-site shiatsu massage (Rs 1000 per hour).

Roadhouse Cafe (Map p138; ☑01-5521755; pizzas Rs 525-600; ⊗11am-10pm) A chintzy branch of the ever-popular Thamel pizza parlour, with a relaxed, family vibe.

El Mediterraneo (Map p138; ☑01-5527059; www.elmediterraneo.com.np; Jhamsikhel; mains Rs 400-600; ⊗12.30-9pm) This local tapas bar feels surprisingly authentic thanks to the attentive owner, a Spanish-speaking Nepali who lived in Spain for several years. Dishes range from paella and risotto to chicken with *pisto* (tomato, peppers, onion and garlic sauce) and a particularly delicious gazpacho (available until the end of October). Perhaps the best bet is to order a sangria and linger over the 13-course tapas menu (Rs 1000), featuring imported jamón and chorizo.

to stock up on quality local produce and the tastes of home.

Bhat Bhateni Super Store SUPERMARKET $ (Map p138; www.bhatbhatenionline.com; Krishna Gali; ⊗7.30am-8.30pm) The largest supermarket in town.

Dhokaima Café INTERNATIONAL $$ (Map p138; ☑01-5522113; mains Rs 250-540; ⊗8am-10pm; 🛜) A sophisticated cafe set inside a Rana-era storehouse by the Patan Dhoka gateway. Shaded by a sprawling walnut tree, the courtyard garden is a peaceful place to enjoy a good range of light and healthy dishes, such as the arugula salad with apple, pear and cheese, or a sandwich and soup combo, plus good coffee and cakes.

Café Cheeno INTERNATIONAL $$ (Map p138; www.cafecheeno.com; mains Rs 300-600; ⊗7.30am-8pm) A great place just outside Patan Dhoka with a charming garden (sadly next door to the noisy bus stand), good salads and soups, tasty breakfast crêpes and an upper floor 'Wellness Sanctuary' for beauty treatments and massage (Rs 1200 per hour).

☆ Entertainment

Moksh Live LIVE MUSIC (Map p138; ☑01-5528362; Gyanmandala, Jhamsikhel; ⊗11am-11pm Tue-Sun) Moksh has some of the best live rock, funk and folk music in town (not just the standard cover bands), most frequently on Friday from 7.30pm but also some acoustic bands on Tuesday. Other nights there are pizzas from the outdoor oven.

🔒 Shopping

Patan is a famous centre for bronze casting, repoussé work and other metal arts. Most of the statues that you see on sale in Kathmandu are actually made in Patan, and you can save money by buying them at their source.

There are dozens of metalwork shops north and west of Durbar Sq, and more around the Mahabouddha Temple. The price of a bronze statue of a Buddhist or Hindu deity can range from Rs 3000 to more than Rs 100,000, depending on the size, the complexity of the casting, the level of detail and the amount of gilding and enamelling on the finished statue.

Patan is also the best place in the valley for interior design and fair-trade products, specifically along Kupondol road, which is lined with shops that support the work of Nepali craft cooperatives, channelling money directly from travellers to disadvantaged and neglected communities.

The Jawalakhel area around the zoo has the best selection of carpet shops.

Jawalakhel Handicraft Centre   CARPETS
(Map p138; ☎01-5521305; ⊗9am-noon & 1-5pm Sun-Fri) Anyone who appreciates carpets should visit this Tibetan refugee cooperative, where Nepal's enormous carpet industry was essentially born in 1960. You can watch the carpet-makers at work (the centre employs 1000 refugees) before shopping upstairs for the finished article. The quality is high, there is a good selection, the prices are transparent and staff can arrange shipping.

Carpet quality depends on knots per inch and the price is worked out per sq metre. A 60-/100-knot carpet made with Tibetan wool costs around US$120/260 per sq metre. The size of a traditional Tibetan carpet is 1.8m by 90cm, so around US$420. It also sells fixed-price cashmere and yak-hair shawls. Credit cards are accepted for a 4% fee.

Image Ark   ART GALLERY
(Map p138; ☎01-5006665; www.image-ark. com; Kulima; ⊗10am-5pm Sun-Fri, 11am-4pm Sat) This bright and colourful modern gallery in Patan's old town casts a light on Nepali multimedia and pop art, selling both limited-edition prints and cheaper cards. It's next to the Uma Maheshwar Temple and is a nice break, physically and visually, from the surrounding temple gazing.

Mahaguthi   FAIR TRADE
(Map p138; ☎01-5521607; www.mahaguthi.org; ⊗10am-6pm) Mahaguthi was founded by a Nepali disciple of Mahatma Gandhi and its Kupondol showroom is a treasure house of dhaka weavings, handmade paper, ceramics, block prints, pashminas, woodcrafts, jewellery, knitwear, statues, leather bags, embroidery and Mithila paintings. There's a smaller branch in Kathmandu's Lazimpat district. Credit cards are accepted.

Dhukuti   FAIR TRADE
(Map p138; ☎01-5535107; www.acp.org.np; ⊗9am-7pm) Dhukuti packs in three floors of home furnishings, textiles, shawls, scarves, bags and rugs from the Nupri region of Manaslu, and even has Christmas decora-

tions, created by over 1200 low-income producers. It's probably the single best shop on Kupondol. Credit cards are accepted.

Sana Hastakala   FAIR TRADE
(Map p138; ☎01-5522628; www.sanahastakala. org; ⊗9.30am-6pm Sun-Fri, 10am-5pm Sat) A recommended place for paper, batiks, Mithila crafts, felt products and clothing woven from natural fibres. Credit cards acccepted.

Dhankuta Sisters   FAIR TRADE
(Map p138; ☎9841555990; ⊗11am-6.30pm Sun-Fri) Come here for tablecloths, cushion covers and clothing made from dhaka-style cloth from eastern Nepal . The fabric is made mostly from cotton but also silk, banana and nettle fibres.

Kumbeshwar Technical School   FAIR TRADE
(Map p138; ☎01-5537484; www.kumbeshwar. com; ⊗9am-1pm & 2-5pm Sun-Thu, 9am-1pm Fri) Near the Kumbeshwar Temple in the backstreets of Patan, this small workshop provides disadvantaged low-caste families (primarily the Pode or streetsweepers' caste) with training, education and a livelihood, producing carpets, knitwear and furniture. There was some damage from the 2015 earthquake but their work continues and sales from the showroom help fund the attached primary school.

Patan Industrial Estate   HANDICRAFTS
(☎01-5521367; www.patan.com.np; ⊗10am-5pm Sun-Fri) Despite the unpromising name, this tourist-oriented crafts complex boasts a number of workshop showrooms selling high-quality carpets, woodcarvings and metalwork, if you have a special interest. It's around 500m south of Lagankhel bus stand.

ⓘ Information

There are banks with ATMs at Mangal Bazar, at the south end of Durbar Sq, and at Pulchowk and the restaurant street of Jawalakhel.

Patan Hospital (Map p138; ☎01-5522278; www.patanhospital.org.np) Probably the best hospital in the Kathmandu Valley, in the Lagankhel district of Patan. Partly staffed by Western missionaries. Some reconstruction work was underway when we visited.

ⓘ Getting There & Away

You can get to Patan from Kathmandu by bicycle, taxi, bus or tempo. The trip costs around Rs 350 by taxi.

Safa (electric) tempos (Rs 20, route 14A) leave for Patan from Kantipath's Sundhara stop, near the Kathmandu main post office. In Nepali script the number 14 looks like '98'. Double-check the destination when getting in, as some run to Mangal Bazar/Durbar Sq while others to Lagankhel bus station, in the south of the city. In the reverse direction, ask for Kantipath or RNAC. Local buses and minibuses run frequently between Kathmandu's Ratna Park bus station and Patan Dhoka or the chaotic Lagankhel bus stand (Rs 15, 30 minutes).

Buses and faster minibuses to the southern valley towns leave when full from **Lagankhel Bus Station** (Map p138). There are regular services till nightfall to Godavari (Rs 28, 45 minutes), Bungamati (Rs 20, 40 minutes) and Chapagaon (Rs 23, 45 minutes). Buses run until around 6.30pm. There are also frequent buses to Bhaktapur (Rs 25, 30 minutes).

An interesting route back to Kathmandu on foot or bike is to continue northeast from the Northern Stupa down to the riverside ghats at Sankhamul, across the footbridge over the Bagmati River and then up to the Arniko Hwy near the big convention centre, from where you can take a taxi or minibus back to Thamel.

BHAKTAPUR

♩ 01 / POP 65,000

The third of the medieval city-states in the Kathmandu Valley, Bhaktapur was always described as the best preserved. Tragically, the 2015 earthquake caused terrible devastation, with whole streets of traditional houses lost to the disaster. Only a few temples were destroyed but many traditional buildings that survived the earthquake have since been declared uninhabitable and are now being torn down. The scars of the disaster are still clearly visible and it will take years for the city to fully recover.

Nevertheless, there is still much to see here, though visitors will have to pick their way through damaged streets and rubble in many areas. Many Nepalis still use the old name of Bhadgaon (pronounced '*bud*-gown') or the Newari name Khwopa, which means City of Devotees. The name fits – Bhaktapur has not one but three major squares full of towering temples that comprise some of the finest religious architecture in the entire country.

When it comes to sightseeing post-disaster, the attractions remain the same as they ever were: temple-studded medieval squares, narrow streets winding between red-brick houses and hidden courtyards peppered with temples, statues, cisterns and wells. And Bhaktapur remains refreshingly devoid of the traffic and pollution of Kathmandu and Patan, though more and more motorbikes and cars are beginning to threaten Bhaktapur's pedestrian charms.

The town's cultural life also remains proudly on display. Artisans weave cloth and chisel timber by the roadside, squares are filled with drying pots and open kilns, and locals gather in communal courtyards to bathe, collect water and socialise – often over intense card games. To view this tapestry of Nepali life visitors must pay a town entry fee (p166), which goes into protecting and maintaining the temples.

History

As with many other towns in the valley, Bhaktapur grew up to service the old trade route from India to Tibet, but the city became a formal entity under King Ananda Malla in the 12th century. The oldest part of town, around Tachupal Tole, was laid out at this time.

From the 14th to the 16th century, Bhaktapur became the most powerful of the valley's three Malla kingdoms, and a new civic square was constructed at Durbar Sq in the west of the city.

Many of the city's most iconic buildings date from the rule of King Yaksha Malla (1428–82), but there was another explosion of temple-building during the reign of King Bhupatindra Malla in the 18th century. At its peak the city boasted 172 temples and monasteries, 77 water tanks, 172 pilgrim shelters and 152 wells.

The 15th-century Royal Palace in Durbar Sq was the principal seat of power in the valley until the city was conquered by Prithvi Narayan Shah in 1768 and relegated to the status of a secondary market town. An earthquake that hit in 1934 caused major damage to the city but locals were able to restore most of the buildings, though you can still see the occasional unoccupied temple plinth.

Bhaktapur's streets were paved and extensively restored in the 1970s by the German-funded Bhaktapur Development Project, which also established proper sewerage and waste-water management facilities. Reconstruction after the 2015 earthquake is likely to alter the appearance of Bhaktapur significantly as families tear down damaged houses and rebuild in 'earthquake proof' steel and concrete.

◉ Sights

◎ Durbar Square

Bhaktapur's Durbar Sq was once much more crowded than it is today. Victorian-era illustrations show the square packed with temples and buildings, but the disastrous earthquake of 1934 reduced many of the temples to empty brick plinths, with lion-guarded stairways leading to nowhere. More structures were destroyed in the deadly earthquake of 2015, including the iconic Vatsala Durga Temple, the reconstructed Chyasilin Mandap and the Fasidega Temple, and many village houses collapsed at the entrance to the square. However, the square was less damaged than suggested by media reports at the time of the disaster and there is still plenty of stunning medieval architecture on display.

Expect to be approached by a string of freelance guides as you walk around.

Erotic Elephants Temple   HINDU TEMPLE
(Map p158) Outside the main Durbar Sq entrance gate is this little piece of architectural whimsy on the roof of the small Shiva Parvati Temple. Giving graphic representation to the lyric 'birds do it, bees do it...', the temple roof struts feature camels, cows, armadillos and even elephants engaged in the act of making sweet love!

Shiva Parvati Temple   HINDU TEMPLE
(Map p158) Similar to Nyatapola Temple (p157), this much smaller version also features pairs of statues of elephants, lions, bulls and the wrestlers Jayamel and Phattu leading up the stairs.

Indrayani Temple   HINDU TEMPLE
(Map p154) Just outside the square, head down the path near the hiti that leads down the stairs to this atmospheric Kali temple that was built around a gnarled pipal tree. Blood flows on Saturdays with animal sacrifices.

Ugrachandi & Bhairab Statues   MONUMENT
(Map p158) As you enter Durbar Sq through the western gate, look left to a gateway flanked by two stocky stone lions, erected by King Bhupatindra Malla in 1701. On either side are statues of the terrible Bhairab (right), the rending, sundering incarnation of Shiva, and his consort on the left side, the equally terrible Ugrachandi (Durga). It is said that the unfortunate sculptor had his hands cut off afterwards, to prevent him from duplicating his masterpieces.

EARTHQUAKE DAMAGE IN BHAKTAPUR

The medieval city of Bhaktapur, long feted as the best preserved of the Kathmandu Valley's medieval cities, felt the full destructive force of the 2015 earthquakes. Dozens of buildings collapsed, hundreds of people were killed and many more were left homeless by the disaster. With its winding streets of traditional brick buildings, Bhaktapur was particularly vulnerable to the earthquake, and reconstruction is a process that will take years, perhaps even decades.

Ugrachandi has 18 arms holding various Tantric weapons symbolising the multiple aspects of her character. She is depicted casually killing a demon with a trident to symbolise the victory of wisdom over ignorance. Bhairab gets by with just 12 arms, one holding two heads impaled on a trident and another holding a cup made from a human skull. The statues originally guarded a courtyard that was destroyed in the 1934 quake.

Char Dham Temples   HINDU TEMPLE
(Map p158) Standing at the western end of Durbar Sq, the four Char Dham temples were constructed to provide spiritual merit for pilgrims who were unable to make the journey to the Indian state of Uttaranchal to visit its famed Char Dham temples. After the 2015 earthquake, only three remain – the shikhara-style Kedarnath Temple, dedicated to Shiva, was shaken apart by the tremor.

Although damaged, the three remaining temples are worth visiting. The two-roofed Gopi Nath Temple (Map p158), also called Jagharnath, features different incarnations of Vishnu on the ceiling struts and a statue of Garuda on the pillar at the entrance.

The small Rameshwar Temple (Map p158), topped by an ornate white dome, is still standing but its four pillars are lying on the ground awaiting restoration. The Badrinath Temple (Map p158) is sacred to Vishnu in his incarnation as Narayan.

National Art Gallery   GALLERY
(Map p158; foreigner/SAARC Rs 150/50, camera/video Rs 100/200; ◎10am-5pm Wed-Sun, to 3pm Mon, to 4pm mid-Oct–mid-Jan) The western end of Bhaktapur's Royal Palace contains the best of the three museums in Bhaktapur,

Bhaktapur

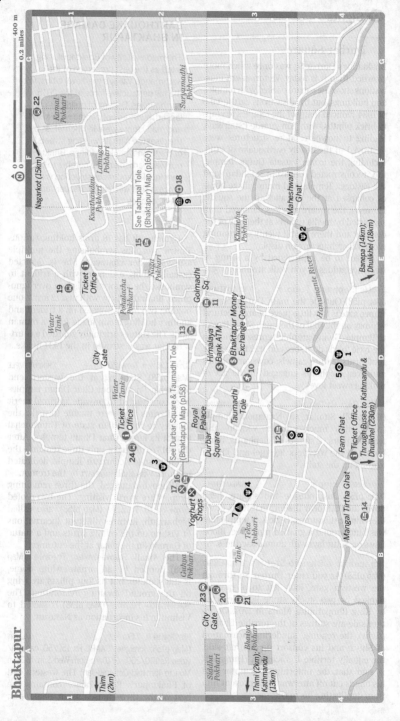

N

0   0.2 miles
0   400 m

Thimi (2km)

Nagarkot (15km)

Kamal Pokhari

Kwathandau Pokhari

Lemuga Pokhari

See Tachupal Tole (Bhaktapur) Map (p160)

Suryamadhi Pokhari

Maheshwari Ghat

Hanumante River

Banepa (14km); Dhulikhel (18km)

Khalena Pokhari

Golmadhi Sq

Himalaya Bank ATM

Bhaktapur Money Exchange Centre

Nagu Pokhari

Pokhalacha Pokhari

Water Tank

City Gate

Ticket Office

Water Tank

Ticket Office

Royal Palace

Durbar Square

Taumadhi Tole

See Durbar Square & Taumadhi Tole (Bhaktapur) Map (p158)

Yoghurt Shops

Teka Pokhari

Guhya Pokhari

Tank

City Gate

Siddha Pokhari

Bhaiya Pokhari

Thimi (2km); Kathmandu (13km)

Mangal Tirtha Ghat

Ram Ghat

Ticket Office

Through Buses to Kathmandu & Dhulikhel (230m)

Bhaktapur

despite minor damage to the building and some exhibits. Inside, you can view an extensive collection of Tantric cloth paintings – the Hindu version of Buddhist thangkas – as well as palm-leaf manuscripts and metal, stone and wooden votive objects, some of which date to the 12th century. Keep hold of your ticket as this also covers the Woodcarving Museum and Brass & Bronze Museum in Tachupal Tole.

The entrance to the gallery is flanked by two huge guardian lions, one male and one female. Beside the lions are some imposing 17th-century statues of Hanuman the monkey god, in his four-armed Tantric form, and Vishnu, as the gut-ripping Narsingha.

Inside the gallery are portraits of all the Shah kings, except Gyanendra (the last of the Nepali kings), who was excised from the gallery following the abolition of the monarchy in 2008. Look out for depictions of the nightmarish Maha Sambhara, with 21 faces and an unbelievable number of arms, as well as scenes from the Kama Sutra.

★ **Golden Gate**   HISTORIC BUILDING

(Sun Dhoka; Map p158) The magnificent Golden Gate is a visual highlight of Durbar Sq. Set into a bright red gatehouse surrounded by white palace walls, the fabulous golden portal boasts some of Nepal's finest repoussé metalwork. The gilded torana features a fabulous Garuda wrestling with a number of supernatural serpents, while below is a four-headed and 10-armed figure of the goddess Taleju Bhawani, the family deity of the Malla kings.

Construction of the gate began during the reign of King Bhupatindra Malla (r 1696–1722), and the project was completed by his successor, Jaya Ranjit Malla, in 1754. The death of Jaya Ranjit Malla marked the end of the Malla dynasty and the end of the golden age of Newari architecture in Nepal.

The gate opens to the inner courtyards of the Royal Palace, a once vast compound until the 1934 earthquake levelled all but a handful of its 99 courtyards. More walls toppled during the 2015 earthquake. To the right of the Golden Gate is the 55 Window Palace (Map p158), which, you guessed it, has 55 intricate wooden windows stretching along its upper level.

As you enter the palace complex, hidden behind grills in the darkness on either side of the inner gate is a pair of enormous war drums (Map p158), which were used to rouse the city in the event of attack. From here you'll pass the two statues of traditionally dressed guards standing either side of an ornate door, brought here from Rajasthan.

Continuing on you'll reach the main entrance to Mul Chowk, the oldest part of the palace and the site of Taleju Temple (Map p158), built in 1553. Damaged in the quake but not destroyed, it is one of the most sacred temples in Bhaktapur, only Hindus can enter, but you can peer in and admire its entrance, which is fronted by magnificent woodcarvings. Photography is prohibited.

Continuing on around the corner from Mul Chowk is the Naga Pokhari (Map p158), a 17th-century water tank used for the ritual immersion of the idol of Taleju. The pool is encircled by a writhing stone cobra and more serpents rise up in the middle and at the end of the tank, where water pours from a magnificent *dhara* (spout) in the form of a goat being eaten by a makara.

King Bhupindra Malla's Column   MONUMENT

(Map p158) With hands folded in a prayer position, the bronze statue of King Bhupindra Malla sits atop a column in front of the ruined Vatsala Durga Temple. The statue was created in 1699 and it is now the only surviving royal pillar in the valley; similar statues in the Durbar Sqs of Kathmandu and Patan collapsed in the disaster. Bhupatindra was the best known of the Malla kings of Bhaktapur, and contributed to much of the architecture in town.

Taleju Bell   MONUMENT

(Map p158) In front of what was the Vatsala Durga Temple is a large bell, which was erected by King Jaya Ranjit Malla in 1737 to mark morning and evening prayers at the Taleju Temple.

A smaller bell on the plinth of the Taleju Temple is known as the 'barking bell'. According to legend, it was erected by King Bhupatindra Malla in 1721 to counteract a vision he had in a dream, and to this day dogs are said to bark and whine if the bell is rung – which could have a physical explanation in terms of resonance frequencies.

Behind the bell pavilion is an ornate sunken hiti containing a fine stone *dhara* in the form of a makara, topped by a crocodile and a frog – the only part of the famous Vatsala Durga Temple to survive the 2015 earthquake.

Pashupatinath Temple   HINDU TEMPLE

(Map p158) Behind the Vatsala Durga Temple site, the Pashupatinath Temple is dedicated to Shiva as Pashupati and is a replica of the main shrine at Pashupatinath. Originally built by King Yaksha Malla in 1475 (or 1482), it is the oldest temple in the square. Like many temples, the roof struts feature erotic images, but what exactly the dwarf is doing with that bowl takes things to a new level.

Siddhi Lakshmi Temple   HINDU TEMPLE

(Map p158) By the southeastern corner of the palace stands the attractive 17th-century stone Siddhi Lakshmi Temple. There was minor earthquake damage here but the temple is still standing. The steps up to the temple are flanked by male and female attendants, each leading a child and a rather eager-looking dog. On successive levels the stairs are flanked by horses, garlanded rhinos, human-faced lions and camels. The temple itself is built in the classic shikhara style, commonly seen in the north of India.

Behind the temple is a neglected corner of the square that contains a pair of lost-looking curly-haired stone lions who, de-

BHAKTAPUR'S PONDS

Around the outskirts of Bhaktapur are a series of enormous tanks, constructed in the medieval period to store water for drinking, bathing and religious rituals. The tanks still play an important role in the social life of Bhaktapur – in the mornings and afternoons, locals gather by the ponds to bathe, socialise, take romantic walks and feed the giant carp and turtles that keep the water free from detritus.

The most impressive tank is the ghat-lined **Siddha Pokhari** near the main bus park. This rectangular reservoir is set inside an enormous wall that is broken by rest houses and towers that have been consumed by the roots of giant fig trees. You can buy bags of corn and rice to feed the fish for a few rupees.

During the annual festival of **Naga Panchami** in the Nepali month of Saaun (July–August), residents of Bhaktapur offer a bowl of rice to the nagas (serpent spirits who control the rain) who live in the Siddha Pokhari. According to legend, a holy man once attempted to kill an evil naga who lived in the lake by transforming himself into a snake. An attendant waited by with a bowl of magical rice to transform the yogi back into human form, but when the victorious holy man slithered from the water, his terrified assistant fled, taking the holy rice with him and leaving the yogi trapped for eternity in his scaly form. To this day, locals leave a bowl of rice out at Naga Panchami in case the snake-yogi decides to return.

Other significant tanks include the nearby **Bhaiya Pokhari** (across the road to the south), the **Guhya Pokhari** (across the road to the east) and the **Kamal Pokhari** (at the northeast end of Bhaktapur on the road to Nagarkot).

pending on what theory you subscribe to, are either guarding the palace or the site of a lost temple that crumbled to dust in the 1934 earthquake. The small red-brick Vatsala Temple collapsed in the 2015 earthquake.

Tadhunchen Bahal BUDDHIST TEMPLE
(Chatur Varna Mahavihara; Map p158) Walking east from Durbar Sq, you'll pass the gateway to the restored Tadhunchen Bahal monastery, tucked between souvenir shops, now in need of further restoration after the 2015 earthquake! This Buddhist temple is linked to the cult of the Kumari, Bhaktapur's living goddess. Bhaktapur actually has three Kumaris, but they lack the political importance of Kathmandu's.

In the inner courtyard the roof struts on the eastern side have unusual carvings that show the tortures of the damned. In one, a snake is wrapped around a man, another shows two rams butting an unfortunate's head, while a third strut shows a nasty tooth extraction being performed with a large pair of pliers!

◎ Taumadhi Tole

★ Nyatapola Temple HINDU TEMPLE
(Map p158) You will be able to see the sky-high rooftop of the Nyatapola Temple long before you reach the square. With five storeys towering 30m above Taumadhi Tole, this is the tallest temple in all of Nepal and one of the tallest buildings in the Kathmandu Valley. This perfectly proportioned temple was built in 1702 during the reign of King Bhupatindra Malla, and the construction was so sturdy that the 1934 earthquake caused only minor damage (the upper storey was rebuilt), and the 2015 earthquake just damaged the very tip of the spire.

The temple is reached by a stairway flanked by stone figures of the temple guardians. At the bottom are the legendary Rajput wrestlers Jayamel and Phattu, depicted kneeling with hefty maces. Subsequent levels are guarded by elephants with floral saddles, lions adorned with bells, beaked griffons with rams' horns and finally two goddesses – Baghini and Singhini. Each figure is said to be 10 times as strong as the figure on the level below.

The temple is dedicated to Siddhi Lakshmi, a bloodthirsty incarnation of the goddess Durga (Parvati). The idol of the goddess is so fearsome that only the temple's priests are allowed to enter the inner sanctum, but less brutal incarnations of the goddess ap-

WORTH A TRIP

RIVERSIDE GEMS

Hanuman Ghat (Map p154), in the southeast of town, has an impressive collection of chaitya, Shiva statues, Shaivite shrines and lingam, and includes what could well be the two largest Shiva lingam in Nepal. The site was damaged in the 2015 quake, but most structures are still standing. Through the archway is another splendid collection of statues beside the stinking confluence of rivers at the ghat. Note the exquisitely carved images of Ganesh, Sakyamuni, Ram and Sita, Hanuman and Vishnu/Narayan, reclining on a bed of snakes. Hindu yogis often come here to meditate.

pear on the torana above the door, beneath a canopy of braided snakes, and also on the temple's 180 carved roof struts. In a classic piece of religious crossover, the Buddhist eight lucky signs are carved beside the temple doorways.

Look for the chariot runners piled up on the north side of the temple.

Bhairabnath Temple HINDU TEMPLE
(Kasi Vishwanath, Akash Bhairab; Map p158) The broad-fronted, triple-roofed Bhairabnath Temple is dedicated to Bhairab, the fearsome incarnation of Shiva, whose consort occupies the Nyatapola Temple across the square. The temple was damaged but not destroyed in the 2015 earthquake but several adjacent buildings collapsed. Despite Bhairab's fearsome powers and his massive temple, the deity is depicted here as a disembodied head just 15cm high! Casually stacked against the north wall of the temple are the enormous wheels and runners from the chariot used to haul the image of Bhairab around town during the Bisket Jatra Festival in mid-April.

The first temple on this site was a modest structure built in the early 17th century, but King Bhupatindra Malla added an extra storey in 1717 and a third level was added when the temple was rebuilt after the 1934 earthquake. The final version of the temple has a similar rectangular plan to the Bhimsen Temple in Patan's Durbar Sq.

A small hole in the temple's central door (below a row of carved boar snouts) is used to push offerings into the temple's interior; prior to the 2015 earthquake, priests accessed

Durbar Square & Taumadhi Tole (Bhaktapur)

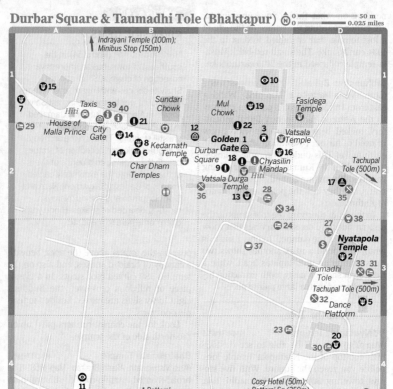

the interior through the small **Betal Temple**, on the south side of the main pagoda, but this collapsed entirely, and restoration work was underway when we visited.

The temple's facade is guarded by two brass lions holding the Nepali flag, the only national flag that is not rectangular or square. To the right of the door is an image of Bhairab painted on rattan, decorated with a gruesome garland of buffalo guts. Head here at dusk to hear traditional devotional music.

Next to the temple is a sunken **hiti** with a particularly fine spout in the form of a makara.

Til Mahadev Narayan Temple   HINDU TEMPLE
(Map p158) The third interesting temple at Taumadhi Tole is hidden away behind the buildings at the south end of the square. The Til Mahadev Narayan Temple is set in an untidy courtyard, but this is actually an important place of pilgrimage and one of the oldest temples in the city. An inscription

states that the site has been in use since 1080 and that the image of Til Mahadev was installed here in 1170.

The double-tiered temple is fronted by an elegant kneeling Garuda statue on a pillar and two columns bearing the sacred sankha and chakra symbols of Vishnu. In case Shiva was feeling left out, a lingam symbol on a yoni base (the Shaivite symbol for the male and female genitals) stands behind a grill in front and to one side of the temple. A plaque to the right of the door depicts the Buddhist deity Vajrayogini in a characteristic pose with her left leg high in the air.

Tachupal Tole

Tachupal Tole was the original central square of Bhaktapur and it formed the official seat of Bhaktapur royalty until the late 16th century. There was some damage to the square in the 2015 earthquake, but the key sights survived intact.

Durbar Square & Taumadhi Tole (Bhaktapur)

Dattatreya Temple   HINDU TEMPLE
(Map p160) At the east end of the square, the eye-catching Dattatreya Temple was originally built in 1427, supposedly using the timber from a single tree. The slightly mismatched front porch was added later. Undamaged by the 2015 earthquake, the temple is dedicated to Dattatreya, a curious hybrid deity, blending elements of Brahma, Vishnu and Shiva. Judging from the Garuda statue and the conch and chakra disc mounted on pillars supported by stone turtles in front of the temple, Vishnu seems to have come out on top.

The three-storey temple is raised above the ground on a brick and terracotta base, which is carved with erotic scenes, including unexpected humour where one bored-looking woman multitasks by washing her hair while being pleasured by her husband. The main steps to the temple are guarded by statues of the same two Malla wrestlers who watch over the first plinth of the Nyatapola Temple.

Bhimsen Temple   HINDU TEMPLE
(Map p160) At the western end of Tachupal Tole, this two-storey, 17th-century temple is sacred to Bhimsen, the god of commerce. The squat rectangular structure has an open ground floor and an inner sanctum on the second level. In front and to the side is a pillar topped by a brass lion with his right paw raised (covered by a bucket when we saw it). Steps lead down behind it to the deeply sunken **Bhimsen Pokhari tank**.

Pujari Math   HISTORIC BUILDING
(Map p154) Tachupal Tole is flanked by a series of ornate brick-and-timber buildings that were originally used as math (Hindu priests' houses). The best known is the Pujari Math, which now serves as the Woodcarving Museum. The building took some damage in the 2015 earthquake, but its most famous feature – the superb 15th-century **Peacock Window** (Map p154), widely regarded as the finest carved window in the valley – is still intact, despite damage to the adjacent wall.

The building was first constructed in the 15th century during the reign of King Yaksha Malla, but rebuilt in 1763. German experts renovated the building in 1979 as a wedding gift for the then King Birendra. Many surrounding shops sell miniature wooden copies of the Peacock Window as souvenirs.

Woodcarving Museum   MUSEUM
(Map p160; foreigner/SAARC Rs 150/50, camera/video Rs 100/200; ◎10am-4pm Wed-Sun, to 3pm Mon, to 5pm mid-Jan–mid-Oct) This museum has

Tachupal Tole (Bhaktapur)

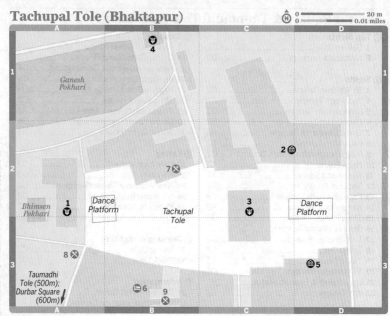

some fine examples of Bhaktapur woodcarving displayed in dark, creaky rooms. There isn't enough light to justify paying the camera fee, but it's worth a visit, not least for the extravagantly carved windows in the inner courtyard, which survived the earthquake with only minor damage. The same ticket covers entry to the nearby Brass & Bronze Museum and the National Art Gallery.

Brass & Bronze Museum   MUSEUM
(Map p160; foreigner/SAARC Rs 150/50, camera/video Rs 100/200; ⊙10am-4pm Wed-Sun, to 3pm Mon, to 5pm mid-Jan–mid-Oct) Directly across from the Woodcarving Museum, in another old math with similar lighting problems and similar damage from the 2015 earthquake, this museum has some excellent examples of traditional metalwork, including ceremonial lamps and ritual vessels from around the valley. Hold on to your ticket to avoid paying entry at the Woodcarving Museum and National Art Gallery.

Salan Ganesh Temple   HINDU TEMPLE
(Map p160) On the north side of Tachupal Tole is an open area with a small temple dating from 1654. Backed by a large tank, the open temple is ornately decorated, but the image is a natural rock with only the vaguest elephant-head shape.

◎ Potters' Square & Around

Potters' Square   SQUARE
(Map p154) Hidden by the alleyways leading south from the curving road to Taumadhi Tole, Potters' Sq is exactly what you would expect – a public square full of treadle-power wheels and rows of clay pots drying in the sun. Several buildings were damaged by the 2015 earthquake, but life – and pottery – in the square continues as normal. This is the centre of Bhaktapur's ceramic industry, and it's a fascinating place to wander around. Several shops

sell the finished article, and you can see the firing process at the back of the square, which is lined with mud-covered straw kilns.

On the northern side of the square a small hillock is topped by a shady pipal tree and a **Ganesh shrine**, surrounded by piles of straw for the pottery kilns. In the square itself is a solid-brick **Vishnu Temple**, which was constructed from remnants of temples destroyed in the 1934 quake, and the double-roofed **Jeth Ganesh Temple**, whose priest is chosen from the Kumal (potters) caste. During the harvest in October, every square inch that is not covered by pots is covered by drying rice.

Khalna Tole   SQUARE
(Map p154) Southeast of Potters' Sq and above the river is the wide open square of Khalna Tole, the setting for the spectacular Bisket Jatra Festival. Many flanking houses were damaged in the 2015 earthquake but restoration work was underway at the time of writing. In the middle of the square, note the huge stone yoni where the giant lingam is erected during the festival. You may have to pick your way through mountains of drying rice and grain to get here.

Just south of the bridge, past an orange Hanuman statue on the riverbank is the campus of the **Kathmandu University Department of Music** (Map p154), where the sound of traditional music wafts over the peaceful ornamental gardens. It's closed on Saturday.

Across the river are the modern **cremation plinths** (Map p154) at Chuping Ghat.

Nasamana Square   SQUARE
(Map p158) This square just northwest of Potters' Sq lost its temples in the 1934 quake, but it still has a large **Garuda statue** praying to a vanished Vishnu shrine. Also here is a tall shikhara housing an important lingam, and two small **Shiva shrines** by a tank filled with alarmingly green algae.

Jaya Varahi Temple   HINDU TEMPLE
(Map p154) About 200m west of Potters' Sq, the red-brick Jaya Varahi is dedicated to Parvati as the boar-headed Varahi. Look for two very different depictions of the goddess on the torana above the central doorway and the torana over the window above. The main entrance is actually at the eastern end of the facade, flanked by stone lions and banners.

Ni Bahal   BUDDHIST TEMPLE
(Jetbarna Maha Bihar; Map p154) Signposted next to a hairdresser, look for the tiny, tunnel-like entrance to this small Buddhist temple dedicated to Maitreya Buddha, the future Buddha. The courtyard contains a very old whitewashed chaitya and several Buddhist shrines. Just to the east is a pilgrims' rest house with finely carved timbers, now home to a simple chai shop.

🏃 Activities

Green Valley Mountain Bike BICYCLE RENTAL
(Map p154; ☎01-6617752; www.tourpackages-nepal.com) Rents imported Trek mountain bikes for Rs 1500 per day, or local bikes for Rs 1000, and runs local biking tours (try the single track between Nagarkot and Nala).

BISKET JATRA AT KHALNA TOLE

Held annually in the Nepali month of Baisakh (typically in the middle of April), the dramatic Bisket Jatra Festival heralds the start of the Nepali New Year. The focal point of the celebrations is the mighty chariot of Bhairab, which is assembled from the timbers scattered beside the Bhairabnath Temple and Nyatapola Temple in Taumadhi Tole. As the festival gets under way, the ponderous chariot is hauled through the streets by dozens of devotees to Khalna Tole, with Betal, Bhairab's sidekick, riding out in front like a ship's figurehead. Bhadrakali, the consort of Bhairab, follows behind in her own chariot. Khalna Tole was damaged by the earthquake but this should still be the focal point for future festivals.

The creaking and swaying chariots lumber around the town, pausing for a huge tug of war between the eastern and western sides of town. The winning side is charged with looking after the images of the gods during their week-long sojourn in Khalna Tole. The chariots then skid down the steep road leading to Khalna Tole, where a huge 25m-high lingam is erected in a stone base shaped like a yoni.

As night falls the following day (New Year's Day), the pole is pulled down in another violent tug of war, and as the pole crashes to the ground, the new year officially commences. Bhairab and Betal return to Taumadhi Tole, while Bhadrakali goes back to her shrine by the river. It certainly beats 'Auld Lang Syne'...

✦ Festivals & Events

Bisket Jatra
RELIGIOUS

Bhaktapur celebrates Bisket Jatra (Nepal's New Year's Day) in mid-April with a stupendous chariot festival (p161).

Gai Jatra
RELIGIOUS

Bhaktapur is the best place to witness the antics of Gai Jatra, where cows and boys dressed as cows are paraded through the streets. It's not quite the running of the bulls at Pamplona, but it's all good fun.

🛌 Sleeping

Ganesh Guest House
GUESTHOUSE $

(Map p154; ☎01-6611550; www.ganeshguesthouse.com; Sakudhoka; r with/without bathroom Rs 600/500, dm Rs 200; @🛜) A magnet for shoestring travellers, this laid-back guesthouse gets rave reviews from backpackers for its cheap rates, friendly staff and piping-hot showers. Beds are just a mattress on the floor and the bathrooms are tiny. Its terrace restaurant has the cheapest prices in town and is a good hang-out spot. Repairs to earthquake damage were underway when we stopped by.

Shiva Guest House
GUESTHOUSE $

(Map p158; ☎01-6613912; www.bhaktapurhotel.com; Durbar Sq; s/d US$20/25, without bathroom US$6/10; 🛜) A well-maintained place on Durbar Sq with comfy rooms (though tiny bathrooms) and a good ground-floor restaurant and coffee shop. Ask for one of the larger corner rooms if you want a view. Otherwise enquire about the larger and quieter rooms for the same price in the annex (Map p158) on the western side of Durbar Sq.

Golden Gate Guest House
GUESTHOUSE $

(Map p158; ☎01-6610534; www.goldengateguesthouse.com; s/d US$15/20, deluxe US$25/35, without bathroom Rs 600/900; 🛜) A quiet courtyard and attentive staff are the drawcards at this brick-built guesthouse between Durbar Sq and Taumadhi Tole. Rooms won't win any design awards, but they're clean and some have balconies. Look for the 400-year-old carved window separating the restaurant from the kitchen. Top-floor deluxe rooms are bright and spacious. The rooftop offers views over both Taumadhi and Durbar squares. Rates include tax.

Siddhi Laxmi Guest House
GUESTHOUSE $

(Map p158; ☎01-6612500; siddhilaxmi.guesthouse@gmail.com; s/d from Rs 1000/1500, deluxe US$45; 🛜) Sharing a courtyard with the

🏃 Town Walk
Bhaktapur

START DURBAR SQ
END TAUMADHI TOLE
LENGTH 3KM; TWO HOURS

Starting from the northeastern corner of Durbar Sq, walk to the east of the ruined Fasidega Temple, passing a multicoloured **1 Ganesh shrine**, where the god is worshipped in the form of a rock that naturally resembles an elephant's head. Turn right to reach a square with disused palace buildings and a ruined temple plinth. Walk around the north side of the square and exit at the northeast corner past the hiti, by the strut-roofed **2 Tripurasundari Temple**, sacred to one of the Navadurgas. Continue east passing several Indian sweet shops, where the road bends right at a brick Narayan shrine. Past the next alley, a doorway leads into a cramped bahal containing a small **3 Bhimsen Temple**, which was created from remains of the Lun Bahal, a 16th-century Buddhist monastery. Note the pots and pans nailed to the roof struts by devotees.

Head back to the Narayan shrine, take a right and head 200m to the unassuming brick facade of the **4 Ganesh Temple**, with fine figures of the elephant-headed deity on its torana and an unusual terracotta Ganesh window above the door.

At the next junction take a right, past some lovely carved windows, and then swing left past a small **5 Mahakali shrine** with caged windows and buffalo horns, and the Pohalacha Pokhari tank. Continue past a city ticket office to the Bhaktapur–Nagarkot road, where you take a left and cross the road to climb the small hillock to a large, slightly damaged **6 Mahakali Temple**, which has an eccentric collection of statues inside a gated pavilion. Note the buffalo entrails draped over the guardian statues inside the temple.

Return to the ticket office, turn left and continue until you reach a brick square containing the tiny, yellow-roofed **7 Mahalakshmi Temple**, sacred to the goddess of wealth. Turn right (south) and continue straight to a large tank, the **8 Naga Pokhari** (p155), where skeins of dyed yarn hang drying on large racks beside the lurid green waters. In the middle of the tank is a statue of a rearing cobra.

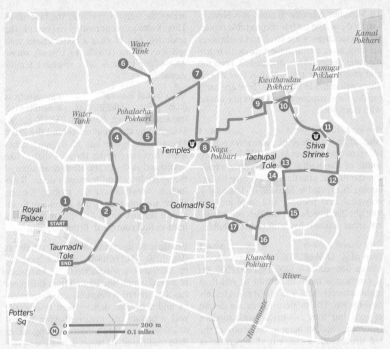

Pass along the north side of the tank, turn left and enter the second courtyard entrance on the right (signed the Dipankar & Prsaannasila Mahavihar), now scarred by earthquake damage. Continue out the far end past another charming courtyard. On the left you'll see the white stucco pillars that mark the entrance to the ⑨ **Mul Dipankar Bihar**, enshrining an image of Dipankar, the Past Buddha.

Continue east to the road junction; look left to see a white lotus-roofed Vishnu shrine, behind which is the large Kwathandau Pokhari. Head south at the far end of the tank and you'll pass the ⑩ **Nava Durga Temple**, a Tantric Shaivite temple with a fine gilded torana. Only Hindus are allowed to enter.

Swing southeast through a square, past the gallery occuping the ⑪ **Toni Hagen house**, restored in honour of the famous Swiss geologist. Continue to the junction by a stupa and a dance platform, on the main east–west road. Turn right and immediately on your left you'll see the elaborate entrance to the ⑫ **Wakupati Narayan Temple**, built in 1667. Despite some damage to neighbouring buildings, the ornate, golden mandir survived the 2015 quake; note the entourage of five Garudas supported on pillars on the backs of turtles.

Continue from here past the centuries-old wooden frontage of the ⑬ **Brahmayani Temple**, fronted by two lions and sacred to the patron goddess of Panauti, and then on to ⑭ **Tachupal Tole** (p158), passing several collapsed houses.

From Tachupal Tole turn left down the side of the Pujari Math, passing the famous Peacock Window. Follow the road around south and turn right at the small square with a ⑮ **Vishnu Temple** on an octagonal plinth.

Go straight down an atmospheric alley lined with brick houses and follow it around to the left, then to the right into a large square. Detour south from this square down a wide cobbled road to reach a large statue of ⑯ **Sakyamuni**, the historical Buddha, overlooking the river from the east end of the Khancha Pokhari tank.

Return to the square and take a left and walk west towards the main road linking Taumadhi Tole and Tachupal Tole. Just before the junction turn to the left to enter the unassuming gateway to the ornate Inacho Bahal, containing the narrow ⑰ **Sri Indravarta Mahavihar**, a 17th-century Buddhist temple topped by a lopsided miniature pagoda roof.

From here, head back to Taumadhi Tole or visit the Hanuman Ghat (p157) at the bottom of the hill.

Til Mahadev Narayan Temple, this Newari-inspired guesthouse has comfortable rooms, though mattresses are hard and bathrooms are tiny. Most rooms have TVs, small balconies and decent views, and there's a rooftop and ground-floor restaurant. A pair of earplugs will come in handy, as there are barking dogs and ringing temple bells to contend with from 4am.

Khwopa Guest House   GUESTHOUSE $
(Map p158; ☑01-6614661; www.khwopa-guesthouse.com.np; s/d from Rs 800/1200; ☏) Just south of Taumadhi Tole, this tiny, creaking family-run guesthouse is a rare budget choice in expensive Bhaktapur. The vibe is easygoing and friendly, and there are nice touches like towels, but the lack of communal areas makes it feel a bit claustrophobic.

City Guest House   HOTEL $
(Map p154; ☑01-6613038; www.cityguesthouse.com.np; Godmadhi; s Rs 1500, d Rs 2200-2500; ☏) If function is more important to you than architectural charm, you might consider this new option. The modern rooms are devoid of style but they are bright with modern bathrooms and sit bang in the centre of the old town, with a convenient supermarket next door. Rates include tax.

Peacock Guesthouse   BOUTIQUE HOTEL $$
(Map p160; ☑01-6611829; www.peacockguesthousenepal.com; s/d US$35/55, deluxe US$50/75; ☏) Right on Tachupal Tole, this wonderful 15th-century building ticks many boxes. It has eight comfortable, traditional rooms and historic character – though anyone over 183cm (6ft) might struggle with its low ceilings and tiny bathrooms. There's also an attractive front courtyard in which woodworkers beaver away, and a fine courtyard bakery-cafe serving pulse-raising Illy coffee. There was minor earthquake damage but the guesthouse quickly reopened.

The spacious deluxe room overlooking the square has the best views but also the most street noise. Cheaper back rooms are darker but quieter. Rates include tax and breakfast, and credit cards are accepted.

Pagoda Guest House   GUESTHOUSE $$
(Map p158; ☑01-6613248; www.pagodaguesthouse.com; s/d from US$20/25, without bathroom US$10/12; ☏) A family-run place in the northwest corner of Taumadhi Tole, set back from the hubbub and piled high with pot plants. The six rooms in the old building are clean, if a little small; rooms with bathroom

across the hall are probably the best value. There's also a decent rooftop restaurant. The midrange new block is a better choice with spacious rooms (US$35 to US$45) whose upper-floor terraces offer splendid temple views.

Milla Guest House   BOUTIQUE HOTEL $$
(Map p154; ☑9851024137; www.millaguesthousebhaktapur.com; Devli Sq 4; d US$70-80; ☏) Designed by the architect behind the Patan Museum there are lots of stylish touches here, from the circular showers shaped like traditional baths to the sleek clean lines of the warm brick and terracotta decor. Rates include breakfast on the rooftop terrace. There are only four rooms so reserve in advance. It's just north of Dattatraya Sq in a hard-to-find courtyard. Bring earplugs.

Bhadgaon Guest House   GUESTHOUSE $$
(Map p158; ☑01-6610488; www.bhadgaon.com.np; Taumadhi Tole; s/d US$50/60; ☏) An update of a traditional Newari building, this place has a courtyard restaurant, a rooftop balcony and a coveted deluxe room (room 505) with a private balcony overlooking Taumadhi Tole. Rooms are modern-looking rather than traditional. Its annex across the square is less appealing.

Heart of Bhaktapur
Guest House   GUESTHOUSE $$
(Map p158; ☑01-6612034; www.heartofbhaktapur.com; Kulmanani; s/d Rs 1725/3100, ste Rs 5200) This modern 13-room guesthouse supports the Suvadra Foundation (www.sf-nepal.org), a local NGO helping children with disabilities. Guests are drawn more by the cause than the rooms, which have hard mattresses and tiny bathrooms, but it's a friendly place with a fine rooftop terrace and the hallways are enlivened by artwork and photos of the children. Some earthquake damage was under repair at research time. Rates include tax, breakfast and coffee.

Sunny Guest House   GUESTHOUSE $$
(Map p158; ☑01-6616094; www.sunnyguesthousenepal.com; s/d from US$28/39; ☏) This long-established place scores points mainly for its atmospheric location at the north end of Taumadhi Tole. The front building has some Newari touches but the modern back building is quieter, and there's a rooftop restaurant. Rooms are decorated with screen-printed bedspreads and carved wooden lattice windows. Rates include tax and breakfast.

Cosy Hotel
HOTEL **$$**

(Map p154; ☎01-6616333; www.cosyhotel.com. np; standard/superior/deluxe r incl breakfast from US$30/40/55; ❀@☎) Tucked away on a narrow road to Potters' Sq, you might not get views here, but this business-chic hotel definitely lives up to its name, with decent rooms, big beds, bath-tubs and double-glazed windows. Free laundry, mineral water and heaters in winter are thoughtful gestures. Rates include tax but are still over-priced without a discount. Rooms overlooking the internal courtyard are much quieter. There was some earthquake damage to the modern, Newari-style building.

Thagu Chhen
BOUTIQUE HOTEL **$$$**

(Map p154; ☎01-6613043; www.thaguchhen. com; Itachhen; ste US$75-95; ❀@☎) If you need more space and mod cons than the average Bhaktapur house allows, Thagu Chhen offers apartments with sitting areas and kitchenettes livened up with a dash of style through reclaimed brick and carved woods. Each of the rooms takes up an entire floor and all except one have balconies offering views north over the Kathmandu Valley. It's perfect for families. Rates include breakfast and tax.

Hotel Heritage
BOUTIQUE HOTEL **$$$**

(Map p154; ☎01-6611628; www.hotelherit-age.com.np; Barahipith; s/d from US$130/140; ❀@☎) Outside the southern boundaries of the old town, this multistorey red-brick Newari building is an eclectic blend of old and new – incorporating reclaimed windows and bricks into its design. While it's well overpriced, it remains the plushest option in Bhaktapur with all of the mod cons and nice seating in the garden and rooftop terrace.

✖ Eating

No-Name Restaurant
NEPALI **$**

(Map p158; Tadhunchen Bahal; pancakes Rs 25-50) This nameless hole-in-the-wall consists of little more than a hot plate and a bucket of pancake mix, but it serves up what might be the best street food in the Kathmandu Valley. The only thing on the menu is *wo* (called *bara* in Nepali), a savoury lentil pancake served with a delicious paneer and peas gravy.

Look for the sign advertising 'Nepal bara-wo available here' and squeeze yourself into the two-table cubby hole adjoining Tad-hunchen Bahal.

Namaste Cafe
CAFE **$$**

(Map p158; Taumadhi Tole; mains Rs 250-300; ☎) This tiny upstairs cafe is decked out in attractive decor and offers great views of Taumadhi Tole. The Nepali curries with rice are particularly good, breakfasts are good value and there's a ground-floor coffee bar.

Peaceful Garden Café
NEPALI, INTERNATIONAL **$$**

(Map p160; Tachupal Tole; dishes Rs 200-400; ☺8am-8pm) This sleepy outdoor eatery, in a quiet courtyard behind the souvenir shops on the south side of the square, does the usual menu, but at good prices.

Newa Chhen Restaurant
NEPALI **$$**

(Map p160; Tachupal Tole; mains Rs 200-375; ☺9am-7pm) Slightly rundown and dingy, however, the food here is cheap and tasty. It gets points for excellent Newari snacks and a corner table with killer views over the square. The owners run a dirt-cheap homestay (double room Rs 600).

Cafe Beyond
KOREAN **$$**

(Map p154; www.beyondnepal.org; mains Rs 350-400; ☺9am-8pm; ☎) 🍴 In a town with little variation between menus, this Korean restaurant offers something a little different. Established to support an NGO that promotes local organic farming, the funkily decorated restaurant serves a good range of fresh-tasting Korean food, most of which is grown in the cafe's own vegie garden. It also serves *soju* (rice liquor from Korea) and has a coffee machine.

New Watshala Garden Restaurant
NEPALI, INTERNATIONAL **$$**

(Map p158; ☎01-6610957; Durbar Sq; mains Rs 400, set meals Rs 700; ☎) Set in a pot-plant-filled courtyard behind the Shiva Guest House, this place came through the 2015 earthquake with only minor damage and it offers a genuine retreat from the Durbar Sq crowds, even if the food is tour-group bland. Sit back with a cold Belgium beer and gently exhale...

Palace Restaurant
NEPALI, INTERNATIONAL **$$**

(Map p158; Durbar Sq; mains Rs 230-375, set meals Rs 650) Opposite the Royal Palace in a long, historic building, this regal place with one long balcony offers the chance to dine with a view that used to be reserved for the Malla kings.

New Cafe de Peacock
NEPALI, INTERNATIONAL **$$**

(Map p160; Tachupal Tole; mains Rs 350-500) Tachupal Tole's answer to Café Nyatapola

KING OF CURDS

While in Bhaktapur, be sure to try the town's great contribution to the world of desserts – *juju dhau*, 'the king of curds'. Just how special can yoghurt be, you might ask? Well, this could just be the richest, creamiest yoghurt in the world! You'll find this delicacy in many tourist restaurants, but the best places to try it are the hole-in-the-wall restaurants between Durbar Sq and the public bus stand (look for the pictures of bowls of curd outside). King curd comes set in an earthenware bowl for Rs 35.

in a wood-fronted former priest's house on the north side of the square is certainly atmospheric, with great views over the square. Earthquake damage was minor and the food is decent enough.

Café Nyatapola   NEPALI, INTERNATIONAL $$$
(Map p158; ☑01-6610346; Taumadhi Tole; mains Rs 300-600, set meals Rs 800; ☺8am-7pm) Occupying prime real estate in Taumadhi Tole, this landmark cafe has tables set out on the balconies of a historic pagoda temple – there are even erotic carvings on the roof struts. Unfortunately, the building sustained some structural damage in the quake and it may be some time before they reopen. Assuming they do, expect a familiar menu of the usual Nepali, Chinese and Continental standards. A portion of the profits supports a local hospital.

🍷 Drinking

Beans Cafe   CAFE
(Map p158; coffee Rs 100; ☺7am-9pm; 🛜) Good-value, excellent Nepali organic espresso, free wi-fi and baked treats off Durbar Sq make this our favourite java stop.

Shiva's Café Corner   CAFE
(Map p158; Shiva Guest House, Durbar Sq; espresso Rs 160, mains Rs 300-650; 🛜) With an espresso machine and free wi-fi, this inviting cafe with a bistro feel is a good spot for breakfast and a break.

Black Olive   BAR
(Map p158; cocktails Rs 450-550, mains Rs 250-350; ☺until 9.30pm; 🛜) This is a good place to head for a rooftop beer or cocktail in the shadow of the towering Nyatapola Temple. It also does decent food and has an espresso bar.

🛍 Shopping

Bhaktapur is famed for its pottery, which is sold in a staggering number of souvenir shops around the main squares, particularly at Tachupal Tole and Taumadhi Tole. There's also some good metalwork on sale – look out for beaten metal dishes embossed with Buddhist symbols and ornate brass butter lamps in the shape of the Krishna Temple in Patan's Durbar Sq.

Many small factories in Bhaktapur produce handmade paper from the pulp of the *lokta* (daphne) bush, which is sold all over town as cards, notepads, photo albums, envelopes and other stationery items.

Bhaktapur has long been renowned for its woodcarving, and this craft is now used to make objects that fit well into Western homes. Some of the best work is sold from the stalls around Tachupal Tole and the alley beside the Pujari Math. Miniature models of the famous Peacock Window are always popular souvenirs.

Peacock Shop   HANDICRAFTS
(Map p154; ☑01-6610820; ☺10am-5pm, workshop closed Sat) This paper emporium is near the Peacock Window, down the side of Pujari Math. The on-site paper workshop was badly damaged by the 2015 earthquake but the owners are repairing the attached shop and this should still be a good place to buy quality Nepali paper products.

ℹ Information

To enter Bhaktapur you must pay a hefty fee of US$15. SAARC nationalities and Chinese pay Rs 500 and children under 10 are free. This fee is collected at over a dozen entrances to the city and your ticket will be checked whenever you pass one of the checkpoints. If you are staying here for up to a week, you need only pay the entrance fee once, but you must ask the ticket desk to write your passport number on the back of the ticket.

For longer stays (up to one year or the validity of your visa), a Bhaktapur Visitor Pass is available within a week of purchasing your entry ticket. You need to bring two passport photos and a photocopy of your visa and passport details to the **tourist information centre** (Map p158; Durbar Sq; ☺6am-7.30pm) next to the ticket office, which also offers maps and free internet for 30 minutes.

The **Bhaktapur Money Exchange Centre** (Map p154; ☺9am-6pm) is one of several places that change cash, and the nearby Himalaya Bank has an ATM.

Guides touting their services around Durbar Sq charge Rs 300 per hour. Look out for the booklet *Bhaktapur: A Guide Book*, published by the **Bhaktapur Tourism Development Committee** (www.btdc.org.np) and sold in local shops.

❶ Getting There & Away

Taxis from Kathmandu cost Rs 800 one way. Buses run very frequently from Kathmandu's Bagh Bazar bus stand (Rs 25 to Rs 30, one hour) until around 6pm but stop endlessly, dropping off next to the Guhya Pokhari, a short walk west of Durbar Sq. For Thimi (Rs 15, 20 minutes), take a local bus along the old road to Kathmandu rather than an express bus along the main highway.

Buses for Kathmandu's Gongabu bus station also leave from a stand at the northeastern edge of Bhaktapur by the Lamuga Pokhari, but the Bagh Bazar buses are much more convenient.

The stand for buses to Nagarkot (Rs 45, 1½ hours, from 7am to 5.30pm) is nearby, beside the Kamal Pokhari tank. A taxi from here takes 45 minutes and costs around Rs 1000.

Buses to Changu Narayan (Rs 15, 30 minutes) leave every 30 minutes or so from the junction with the Changu Narayan road, or take a taxi for Rs 500.

For Dhulikhel (Rs 35, one hour) or anywhere further east, you'll have to walk 20 minutes south across the river to the Arniko Hwy to catch a (probably packed) through bus from Kathmandu. Count on around Rs 1000 for a taxi to Dhulikhel.

AROUND BHAKTAPUR

Suriya Binayak Temple

South of Bhaktapur, on the south side of the Arniko Hwy, Suriya Binayak is an important Ganesh temple dating back to the 17th century and it came through the 2015 earthquake unscathed. The white shikhara-style temple contains some interesting statuary, but the main attraction is the peaceful setting and the walk uphill above the temple to a hillside with sweeping views over Bhaktapur. The temple is flanked by statues of Malla kings and a large statue of Ganesh's vehicle, the rat.

To get here, take the road south from Potters' Sq to Ram Ghat (where there are areas for ritual bathing and cremations) and cross the river to the Arniko Hwy. On the other side, it's a 1km walk along the road to the

---

NAVADURGA DANCERS

The colourful masks sold around Bhaktapur and Thimi are not just souvenirs. Every year, as part of the Dasain celebrations in September or October, local residents perform frenetic dances in Bhaktapur's public squares, during which they are said to be possessed by the spirits of the Navadurga, the nine incarnations of the fearsome consort of Shiva. The masks worn by dancers are cremated every year and new masks are made from the ashes, mixed with black clay from the fields around Bhaktapur. Although most of the masks for sale in Bhaktapur are made for the tourist market, they are full of Tantric symbolism. Popular figures include Ganesh, Kali, Bhairab, boar-headed Varahi, red-faced Kumari and roaring Sima and Duma, the eerie harbingers of death.

---

start of the steps to the temple. Bank on around 30 minutes from Taumadhi Tole.

Thimi

Thimi, known historically as Madhyapur, was once the fourth-largest town in the valley. Today, it's a sleepy backwater but its winding, brick-paved streets are lined with medieval temples. The town takes its modern name from the Newari phrase for 'capable people', which is fitting as the town is a major centre for the production of pottery and papier-mâché masks. You'll pass a string of mask shops on the road that cuts across the north end of town towards Bhaktapur.

Its most well-known temple is 16th-century Balkumari Temple, dedicated to one of Bhairab's shaktis. The goddess's peacock vehicle is depicted on a column in front of the temple, as well as each corner of the temple. It's the focus for the Balkumari Jatra, a festival where Thimi welcomes the new year (around mid-April) with riotous scenes as the 32 khats (palanquins) whirl around the temple while red powder is hurled at them.

A passage on the south side of the square leads to Thimi's potters' square, which is full of kilns made from straw covered with ash. However, pottery-making here has been affected by the 2015 earthquake, which destroyed several homes around the square.

One kilometre north of Thimi is the village of **Bode**, with its 17th-century **Mahalakshmi Temple**, with a small image of Narayan reclining on his snake bed just behind. The village is famous for its annual tongue-piercing festival, during which one lucky volunteer pierces his tongue with a 13-inch spike. The festival is believed to protect the village from natural disasters and takes place just after Bisket Jatra in mid-April; it doesn't seem to have been effective seeing the many houses that collapsed here in the 2015 earthquake.

❶ Getting There & Away

Any of the Bhaktapur-bound minibuses from Kathmandu will be able to drop you at Thimi (Rs 20, 40 minutes), either at the southern gateway on the Arniko Hwy, or on the back road at the north end of Thimi.

If you are biking to Bhaktapur, the northern (old) road offers a far more pleasant ride. The road branches off the Arniko Hwy to the east of the runway at Tribhuvan Airport.

Changu Narayan Temple

Perched atop a narrow ridge due north of Bhaktapur, the beautiful and historic temple of Changu Narayan is a living museum of carvings from the Licchavi period. The temple is a Unesco World Heritage Site and rightly so, because the statues, and the temple itself, are genuine works of art. However, the site was shaken badly by the 2015 earthquake; several buildings in the temple compound were badly damaged and houses collapsed in the adjacent village. At the time of writing, the temple was closed for restoration, which is expected to take some time.

❍ Sights

Changu Narayan Temple   HINDU TEMPLE
(foreigner/SAARC Rs 100/25; ⊘ dawn-dusk) This historic temple is said to be the oldest Hindu temple still in use in the Kathmandu Valley, but Changu Narayan was badly hit by the 2015 earthquake and the temple is closed to visitors while restoration is underway. A full description of the site is included here for when the temple reopens.

Built in the two-tiered pagoda style, the main shrine here is guarded on all sides by pairs of mythical beasts – lions, elephants and ram-horned griffons – and its roof struts feature some amazingly intricate carvings of Tantric deities. The statue inside shows Vishnu as Narayan, the creator of all life, but the beautifully decorated metal-plate doors are only opened for rituals and only Hindus may enter. The temple came very close to collapsing in the earthquake, and

Changu Narayan Temple

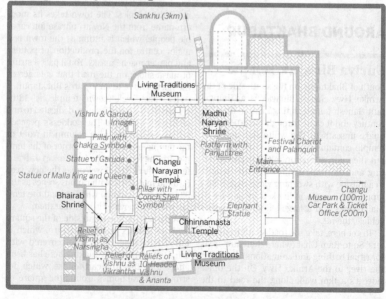

HIKING THE SHORTCUT BETWEEN CHANGU NARAYAN & SANKHU

From Changu Narayan there's an interesting shortcut north to the Bodhnath–Sankhu road, allowing a detour to Sankhu and Bodhnath on your way to Kathmandu. From the northern entrance of the Changu Narayan Temple, follow the obvious path that drops to Manohara River, where you cross over the bridge. This brings you out to the Sankhu road at Bramhakhel, about 4km southeast of Gokarna. Frequent minibuses head east and west from here.

Coming from the other direction, you'll see a small sign for Changu Narayan on a building wall on the south side of the road as you enter Bramhakhel. It's a five-minute walk across fields to the river and temporary bridge, then a steep and tiring 45-minute scramble up the hill to the temple – look for the golden rooftop on the final bump of the spur running down from the eastern edge of the valley.

Note that some features of this walk may have changed since the earthquake; seek local advice on the route before you set off.

much work will be required to stabilise the structure.

The surrounding compound was badly damaged and the status of all monuments here cannot be verified until collapsed walls are removed. Before the earthquake, the following were the highlights.

The Garuda figure facing the west door is said to date from the 5th century, and in front of this statue is the oldest stone inscription in the valley, dating from AD 464, which recalls how the king persuaded his mother not to commit *sati* (ritual suicide) after his father's death. Two large pillars carrying a conch and chakra disc, the traditional symbols of Vishnu, were damaged and are awaiting restoration.

Dotted around the courtyard are a series of extraordinary carvings dating from the Licchavi era, showing Vishnu in his various avatars (incarnations), but it is not clear if all survived the earthquake. Prior to the disaster, Vishnu appeared in the southwest corner of the compound as Narsingha (his man-lion incarnation), disembowelling a demon with his fingers, and as Vikrantha (Vamana), the six-armed dwarf who transformed himself into a giant capable of crossing the universe in three steps to defeat King Bali (look for his outstretched leg).

To the side of these images stood a broken slab showing a 10-headed and 10-armed Vishnu, with Ananta reclining on a serpent below (the plaque was divided into three sections – the underworld, the world of man and the heavens). In the northwest corner of the compound stood an exquisite 7th-century image of Vishnu astride Garuda, which is illustrated on the Rs 10 banknote.

The squat temple in the southeast corner of the complex is dedicated to the Tantric goddess Chhinnamasta, who beheaded herself to feed the bloodthirsty deities Dakini and Varnini. The temple was damaged and restoration is underway.

Down the steps leading east from the temple complex are the one-storey Bhimsen Pati, with its stone guardians, and the remains of a Malla-era royal palace.

Living Traditions Museum
MUSEUM

(www.livingtraditionsmuseum.org; foreigner/SAARC/Nepali Rs 250/100/60; ⊙8am-5pm) This well-curated museum, housed in a restored building south of Changu Narayan Temple, features over 400 exhibits covering artefacts and displays on ethnic groups from the Kathmandu Valley, the Terai, Middle Hills and Himalayan Highlands. However, the site was badly damaged in the earthquake and it was closed for restoration at the time of writing.

Changu Museum
MUSEUM

(foreigner/SAARC/Nepali Rs 200/100/50; ⊙9am-5pm) The single brick-paved street in Changu village climbs from the car park and bus stand past the privately owned Changu Museum, which offers a quirky introduction to traditional village life and which escaped the earthquake without serious damage. The owner will give you a whistle-stop tour of such oddities as a rhino-skin shield, a raincoat made of leaves, a 500-year-old dishwashing rack and some 225-year-old rice. Not to mention a cow's gallstone and the navel of a musk deer.

There's also a fascinating coin collection, including the world's smallest coin, leather coins from the 2nd century and one that equates to one-eighth of a paise – meaning 800 pieces are needed to make one rupee!

🛏 Sleeping & Eating

There are several tourist-oriented restaurants at the start of the village, but damage was extensive from the quake and it may take time to rebuild.

Changu Guest House　　GUESTHOUSE **$**
(📞01-5141052; www.changuguesthouse.com; r US$10-15; 🖥) Just outside the temple entrance, this family-owned brick guesthouse has sunny rooms with hard mattresses and simple attached bathrooms, plus a good restaurant and an espresso stand with free wi-fi. The owners, whose family have been temple priests for 400 years, are passionate about promoting their home town and offer some interesting local tours, including hiking tours and thangka painting classes. Unfortunately, some buildings were damaged in the 2015 disaster and the guesthouse was closed for restoration at the time of writing.

ℹ Getting There & Away

Regular public buses run the 6km between Changu Narayan and Bhaktapur (Rs 20, 30 minutes), with the last bus around sunset. A taxi from Kathmandu costs around Rs 1500 return, or Rs 800 from Bhaktapur.

By bike or on foot, it's a steep climb uphill from Bhaktapur (one hour), but an easy downhill trip on the way back. If you're headed to Nagarkot you can take the footpath east to Tharkot (Telkot) and catch a bus for the final uphill stretch. You can also hike west to Bodhnath in about 90 minutes.

THE NORTHEASTERN VALLEY

Most travellers miss this corner of the valley, which means things are blissfully peaceful and quiet. It's a great destination for mountain biking, motorbiking and hiking excursions. The 2015 earthquake caused some damage in this area.

Gokarna Mahadev

Set beside the Bagmati River, which at this stage is a comparatively clear mountain stream, the Gokarna Mahadev (Gokarneshwar, or Lord of Gokarna) Temple is an easy 5km trip from Bodhnath on the road to Sundarijal. You can make a day of it by combining a visit to the temple with the interesting hike to Kopan Monastery and back to Bodhnath.

◉ Sights

Gokarna Mahadev Temple　　HINDU TEMPLE
(foreigner/SAARC Rs 100/50) Dedicated to Shiva as Mahadev (Great God), this handsome three-tiered temple is a fine example of Newari pagoda style. The main reason to come is to see the exquisite stone carvings dotted around the compound, some dating back more than a thousand years. Gokarna Mahadev sustained some damage in the 2015 earthquake but most of its treasures were not affected.

The sculptures provide an A to Z of Hindu deities, from Aditya (the sun god), Brahma and Chandra (the moon god) to Indra (the elephant-borne god of war and weather) and Ganga (with four arms and a pot on her head from which pours the Ganges). Vishnu is depicted as Narsingha, making a particularly thorough job of disembowelling the demon Hiranyakashipu, while Shiva makes several appearances, including as Kamadeva, the god of love, complete with one suitably erect celestial body part.

The god Gauri Shankar is interesting since it contains elements of both Shiva and Parvati. The goddess appears on her own, wearing a dress and standing on a snow lion, in a particularly elegant **statue** in the northwest corner of the compound. The **Brahma figure** in the southwest corner appears to have only three heads (he should have four) until you peer around the back and discover the hidden head. Many of the deities have one foot on their *vahana* (spiritual vehicle). Shiva's vehicle **Nandi** appears as a large statue made of brass laid over a stone base, in front of the main temple, and Shiva is venerated in the form of an enormous lingam inside the main chamber. There's some fine woodcarving on the temple struts.

Behind the temple, just above the river, is the **Vishnu Paduka**, a low pavilion enshrining a metal plate with a footprint of Vishnu. Just in front is an image of **Narayan** reclining on a bed of snakes, just like the images at Budhanilkantha and Balaju. To the north of the pavilion is an earthquake-damaged **shrine** that has almost been consumed by a fig tree that must have started as a seed on its roof.

Nepalis who have recently lost a father often visit the temple, particularly during

Gokarna Mahadev Temple

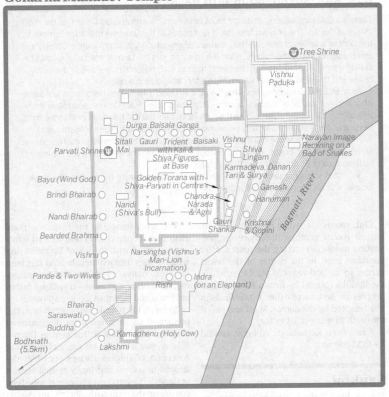

Map labels:
Tree Shrine · Vishnu Paduka · Durga · Baisala Ganga · Sitali Mai · Gauri · Trident · Baisaki · Vishnu · Shiva Lingam · Narayan Image Reclining on a Bed of Snakes · Parvati Shrine · with Kali & Shiva Figures at Base · Karmadeva, Danan Tari & Surya · Bayu (Wind God) · Golden Torana with Shiva-Parvati in Centre · Ganesh · Brindi Bhairab · Chandra, Narada & Agni · Hanuman · Nandi Bhairab · Nandi (Shiva's Bull) · Gauri Shankar · Krishna & Gopini · Bearded Brahma · Vishnu · Narsingha (Vishnu's Man-Lion Incarnation) · Pande & Two Wives · Rishi · Indra (on an Elephant) · Bhairab · Saraswati · Buddha · Bodhnath (5.5km) · Kamadhenu (Holy Cow) · Lakshmi · Bagmati River

Gokarna Aunsi, the Nepali equivalent of Father's Day, which falls in September.

ℹ Getting There & Away

You can walk, take a minibus from Kathmandu's Ratna Park station (Rs 25, 45 minutes) or Bodhnath (or Jorpati), or hire a taxi (Rs 700 one way from Kathmandu or Rs 400 from Bodhnath). The temple is 4km from the Jorpati junction.

Gokarna Forest

The 188-hectare forest at Gokarna was formerly set aside as a hunting reserve for the Nepali royal family, which saved it from the woodcutters. Today, the sound of gunshots has been replaced by the thwack of flying golf balls.

The forest forms part of the **Gokarna Forest Resort Golf Course** (☑ 01-4451212; www.gokarna.com), which was designed by the team behind the famous Gleneagles course

in Scotland. It's the best course in the country. Green fees for 18 holes are Rs 5000/7000 on weekdays/weekends for nonguests, and you can rent clubs, shoes and caddies for an extra Rs 2200. Note that the course was providing space for refugees from the 2015 earthquake at the time of research.

🛏 Sleeping

Gokarna Forest Resort RESORT $$$
(☑ 01-4451212; www.gokarna.com; s/d incl breakfast from US$140/160) For a top-of-the-line rural retreat this sublimely peaceful former Le Meridien property is hard to beat. Wicker furniture on the garden terrace lends a colonial feel, and the surrounding forest is alive with deer and monkeys. If golf is not your thing you can pamper yourself with all sorts of luxury spa treatments, and the resort can arrange guided forest walks, mountain-bike hire and horse riding.

GOKARNA–KOPAN–BODHNATH WALK

There's a pleasant walking or biking route between Gokarna and Bodhnath via the monastery at Kopan. The obvious trail starts just opposite the Gokarna Mahadev Temple, to the right of a series of four roadside statues (signposted 'Sahayogi Multiple College'), and branches left at the college. After five minutes, join the tarmac road as it follows the side of a pine-clad hill. Stay on the paved road as it climbs, offering views of the valley below and the yellow walls of Kopan Monastery ahead atop a hill.

After another 10 minutes, branch left onto a dirt road, which soon becomes a footpath. After another couple of minutes, branch left, passing below Rato Gompa, and follow the hillside to a saddle on the ridge. Where the path forks, take the trail heading uphill to the right, passing another small monastery before reaching the entrance to Kopan (45 minutes).

From Kopan, follow the main road south for 40 minutes to Bodhnath, or jump on one of the frequent minibuses. Travelling on foot, branch off to the left before you hit the built-up area of Bodhnath to reach the stupa.

Note that some features of this walk may have changed since the earthquake; seek local advice on the route before you set off.

Club rooms are worth the extra US$40, but all rooms come with 'advice for preventing monkeys entering the rooms'. After breakfast head to the corner of the resort garden to the 200-year-old pipal tree, where the Buddha (played by Keanu Reeves, of all people) in Bertolucci's film *Little Buddha* was tempted by the demon Mara and called the earth to witness his victory.

A taxi from Kathmandu will cost around Rs 1500 one way.

Sankhu

The red-brick town of Sankhu was once an important stop on the old trade route from Kathmandu to Lhasa (Tibet), but this historic settlement was severely damaged by the 2015 earthquake. The imposing Vajrayogini Temple still stands on the hillside north of the village, but the winding brick backstreets and traditional squares of the old town were devastated.

⊙ Sights

Vajrayogini Temple　　HINDU BUDDHIST TEMPLE
The main reason for visiting the Vajrayogini Temple is not the temple itself but rather the hike up through Sankhu and the sense of getting off the beaten track. The stately, three-tiered temple was damaged in the 2015 earthquake, but not destroyed – note the fine gilded doorway flanked by images of Bhairab, Garuda and other celestial beings. The image of the revered female yogi is only visible when the priest opens the doors for devotees (no photos).

The other temple in the main courtyard enshrines a huge chaitya and its roof struts are decorated with images of Buddhist protector deities. Immediately behind this temple is a chaitya with four Buddha images mounted on a yoni base – a striking fusion of Hindu and Buddhist iconography.

To reach the temple, walk north from the bus stand under a colourful deity-covered archway, jogging left at the central Dhunla Tole. As you leave the village, an interesting collection of lingam shrines (one-half destroyed by a tree) and finely crafted statues of Ganesh, Vishnu and Hanuman will show you are on the right path. Shortly afterwards the road forks at a bend; turn left and head downhill to reach the pedestrian steps to the temple or right by bike or car to reach the parking area about halfway up.

The 40-minute climb from the bus station up the stone steps to the temples is steep and hot for the second half, but water spouts along the route offer a chance to cool off. About halfway up is a shelter with carvings of a very thin Kali and an overweight orange Ganesh. A natural stone lingam represents Bhairab, and sacrifices are made at its foot. If you climb the stairway above the Vajrayogini Temple, you will reach a rest house for pilgrims and several small tea stands.

🛏 Sleeping

Backspace　　COTTAGE $$
(☑ 9751003265; www.backspacenepal.com; s/d incl breakfast Rs 1750/2500) With just one room available in the only accommodation in town, you are guaranteed solitude at this rural retreat by the entrance to Sankhu. The simple

but cosy suite comes with a minikitchen and a bathroom with hot water, as well as a fire pit. Breakfast comes delivered in an outdoor iron box, maximising privacy. There was some earthquake damage, so contact Suraj to check that the room is available.

❶ Getting There & Away

Minibuses run to Sankhu from Kathmandu's Ratna Park bus station (Rs 35 to Rs 40, one hour). The last bus back to Kathmandu leaves Sankhu around 6pm. Some minibuses run to Patan. A one-way taxi from Kathmandu costs Rs 1500.

It's an easy 20km cycle to Sankhu from Kathmandu, or an even easier motorcycle ride. Head to Bodhnath and turn right at Jorpati, then skirt around the Gokarna Forest. If you are walking, you can continue from Sankhu to Changu Narayan by crossing the Manohara River near Bramhakhel (see the boxed text on p169).

THE SOUTHERN VALLEY

There are some fascinating temples and Buddhist monasteries in the southern part of the Kathmandu Valley, but it's hard to see too many together in a single day trip, as the villages are strung out on four different roads branching south from the Kathmandu Ring Rd. There's a useful dirt-road shortcut that links the roads to Godavari and Chapagaon, and a walking-only route linking the road to Bungamati and Chobar on the way to Dakshinkali.

Kirtipur

Just 5km southwest of Kathmandu, the sleepy town of Kirtipur has a wonderful sense of faded grandeur thanks to the impressive medieval temples dotted around its backstreets. When Prithvi Narayan Shah stormed into the valley in 1768, he made a priority of capturing Kirtipur to provide a base for his crushing attacks on the Malla kingdoms. Kirtipur's resistance was strong, but eventually, after a bitter siege, the town was taken. The inhabitants paid a terrible price for their brave resistance – the king ordered that the nose and lips be cut off every male inhabitant in the town, sparing only those who could play wind instruments for his entertainment.

The town was shaken by the 2015 earthquake, but most of its historic treasures survived the disaster. As you approach Kirtipur from the Ring Rd, the old town is up the hill straight ahead, best approached by follow-

EXPLORING THE SOUTHERN VALLEY

The towns and villages of the southern valley can be explored by using local buses – which are cheap, frequent, overcrowded and slow – or by hiring a taxi for the day from Kathmandu. While most settlements saw some damage in the 2015 earthquake, only a few temples were completely destroyed and there is still much to see amid the ongoing reconstruction work.

If you do hire a taxi, set off early and you can probably whiz through Kirtipur, Chobar, Pharping and Dakshinkali in a long day. Expect to pay around Rs 3500 from Kathmandu. In the past, the most enjoyable way of getting from Kathmandu to any towns in the southern valley was by rented bicycle. Today, however, ever increasing traffic and a quickly expanding city make this a far less enjoyable prospect, though the stretch between Pharping and Dakshinkali is still a pleasant ride.

ing the main road to the right and climbing the hillside on a wide flight of steps.

◉ Sights

Everything of interest in Kirtipur is at the top of the hill above the road into town.

Bagh Bhairab Temple   HINDU TEMPLE
In a courtyard off the north side of the main square, the imposing Bhairab Temple features an incredible armoury of *tulwars* (swords) and shields belonging to the soldiers defeated by Prithvi Narayan Shah. Despite some earthquake damage this is still a striking temple and befitting the militaristic mood, animal sacrifices are made here early on Tuesday and Saturday mornings.

Main Square   SQUARE
Ringed by the former residences of the royal family of Kirtipur, this square is now a popular hang-out for locals. In the middle is a large tank and a whitewashed Narayan Temple with some minor earthquake damage, guarded by lions and griffons.

Uma Maheshwar Temple   HINDU TEMPLE
From the main square, go right heading west through the village to a Ganesh shrine and a stone stairway that climbs to the

triple-roofed Uma Maheshwar Temple. It's flanked by two stone elephants, decked out in spiked saddles to discourage children from sitting on them! The temple was originally built in 1673 with four roofs, but one was lost in the earthquake of 1934. This was the spot where Kirtipur's residents made their last stand during the 1768 siege.

Nagar Mandap
Sri Kirti Vihar
BUDDHIST TEMPLE

At the bottom of the hill, follow the left fork of the main road around the base of the hill to this classic Thai-style *wat* (Buddhist monastery) inaugurated by the Supreme Patriarch of Thailand in 1995. There is some minor earthquake damage.

Lohan Dehar
HINDU TEMPLE

From the main square, take a turn right, exiting at the southeast corner of the square to reach the 16th-century stone shikhara-style Lohan Dehar. There's some earthquake damage but the temple is still in use for religious ceremonies.

Chilanchu Vihara
BUDDHIST TEMPLE

Built in 1515, this stately stupa crowns the hilltop and the harmika above the dome is painted a rich blue. Another earthquake survivor, the main stupa is surrounded by a garden of chaitya and fronted by a giant dorje symbol. To get here, go behind the Lohan Dehar temple, take a left down the narrow passageway and follow the alleyway down to the stupa.

⛺ Courses

Kagyu Institute of
Buddhist Studies
MEDITATION

(KIBS; ☑01-4331679; www.kirtipur.org) Offers various courses for aspiring scholars of Buddhism, from three-day dharma studies to three-year certificates, at this peaceful hilltop gompa. Personal retreats and thangka painting courses are also offered. Application forms are available online. Some buildings were badly damaged in the 2015 earthquake so call to check the status of courses.

🛏 Sleeping & Eating

The Kirtipur Guide Association can organise local homestays (half-board single/double Rs 1500/2500), which have been getting great feedback from travellers after a deeper immersion into Newari town life.

Kirtipur Hillside Hotel
HOTEL $$

(☑01-4334010; www.kirtipurhillside.com.np; s/d without view US$15/25, with view US$20/30; 🛜) A great option for those wanting to escape Kathmandu's fumes, with large and clean rooms – the best of which look out to the valley, with the Himalaya looming in the distance. Some rooms have balconies. There's some nice artwork (painted by the manager) and a pleasant rooftop restaurant. It can be a little cold in the rooms though.

Kirtipur View Point
Restaurant
NEPALI, INTERNATIONAL $

(mains Rs 150-250; ⊙11am-9pm) Tasty Newari food, cheap beer and fantastic views make this a great stopover. Its rooftop is the prime viewing area, looking out to mountains ahead or Uma Maheshwar Temple to the side, and its set lunch plates, which come with several different curries, are a crash course in Newari cuisine.

❶ Information

There's a Rs 100 entry charge to the village payable at the Kirtipur Guide Association office.

Kirtipur Guide Association (☑01-4334817; Chlthu 3; ⊙9am-5pm) The community-run guide association maintains a very useful tourist office on the old town's main street. It can arrange two-hour guided tours of the town for Rs 500, as well as homestays. Staff happily hand out information pamphlets about the town in English.

❶ Getting There & Away

Minibuses leave regularly for Kirtipur from Kathmandu's Ratna Park bus station (Rs 20, 30 minutes); the last is at 7pm. Taxis charge around Rs 600.

Chobar

The tiny village of Chobar, 6km from Kathmandu, tops a hill overlooking the Bagmati River where it flows through the Chobar Gorge, allegedly chopped out by the sacred sword of Manjushri. The village itself is lovely, with a tangle of old streets surrounding a famous temple, but the gorge has been ravaged by mining to supply cement for construction in Kathmandu, and the 2015 earthquake has added further scars.

⊙ Sights & Activities

Adinath Lokeshwar Temple
TEMPLE

In the village of Chobar is the curious Adinath Lokeshwar Temple, originally built in the 15th century. It's a handsome three-tiered Newari temple and its roof struts, walls and courtyard are adorned with hundreds of metal plates, cups, dishes, knives, ladles and ceremonial vessels, nailed there by newlyweds to ensure a happy married life. The temple is sacred to both Hindus and Buddhists, and in front is an octagonal stone shikhara temple fronted by a gilded dorje symbol. The compound suffered some damage in the 2015 earthquake.

A tangle of lanes leads off the square in front of the temple to the main part of the village and a small Tibetan Buddhist monastery.

Jal Binayak Temple   HINDU TEMPLE
Built in 1602, Jal Binayak Temple is one of the valley's most important Ganesh shrines. The temple's three-tiered roof struts depict eight Bhairabs and the eight Ashta Matrikas (Mother Goddesses) with whom Ganesh often appears. There is some damage from the 2015 earthquake but the mandir offers scenic views from the base of the gorge, with plenty of birdlife about. The temple is accessed from a car park off the main road and is a 10-minute walk downhill from the village itself. You can cut down through the Manjushree Park.

Manjushree Park & Cave   CAVING
(park entry Rs 100, short/medium/long caving Rs 500/1000/1500) Looking over Chobar Gorge, Manjushree Park is popular with romancing teenagers, but is of more interest to foreigners for its caves. At 3250m, it's said to be the longest in South Asia. Only 350m of the cave is open to visitors and it's accessed from five different entry points – the largest of which is Bagh Gohpha, which involves clambering through a series of warren-like tunnel (headlamps and guides are included in the price). Note that the cave was closed to visitors at the time of research pending surveys to declare the caverns safe after the 2015 earthquake.

✖ Eating

While there's no accommodation in Chobar, there are a couple of simple places to eat.

Hira's Coffee Shop   CAFE $
(snacks from Rs 80; ⊙7am-5pm) On the wide lane south of the Adinath Lokeshwar Temple in Chobar village, this intimate and quaint cafe in a village house came through the quake with only minor damage.

❶ Getting There & Away

To reach Chobar, follow the road that turns south off the Kathmandu Ring Rd at Balkhu and follow the Bagmati River. There are no direct buses here, but any bus to Pharping or Dakshinkali can drop you at the turn-off, a 10-minute walk below the village, for Rs 20. A taxi from Kathmandu will cost Rs 600 to Rs 700 one way. You can also walk here from Kirtipur in around an hour, via the village of Panga, which has several old temples, including the revered Vishnu Devi Mandir.

Pharping

About 19km south of Kathmandu, Pharping is a thriving Newari town whose ancient Buddhist pilgrimage sites have been taken over by large numbers of Tibetans. A circuit of its religious sites makes for a compelling day out from Kathmandu. Pharping lies on the road to Dakshinkali and it's easy to visit both villages in a day by bus or bicycle. En route you'll pass the pond at Taudaha, allegedly home to the nagas released from the Kathmandu lake. More Buddhist monasteries are opening up around here every year, some of which accept foreign dharma students. The town saw only minor damage in the 2015 earthquake.

⦿ Sights

Shesh Narayan Temple   HINDU TEMPLE
About 600m downhill from the main junction at Pharping, in the direction of Kathmandu, the Shesh (or Sekh) Narayan Temple is a highly revered Vishnu shrine surrounded by ponds and statues, tucked beneath a rocky cliff wall and a **Tibetan monastery**. The main temple was built in the 17th century, but it's believed that the cave to the right (now dedicated to Padmasambhava, or Guru Rinpoche) has been a place of pilgrimage for far longer.

There are some artfully carved Licchavi-era statues in the courtyard, including lively depictions of Ganesh and Hanuman. The surrounding ponds are full of koi carp and semisubmerged carvings, including an image of Aditya, framed by a stone arch. If you are lucky you might catch devotional religious music being played in the pavilion by the pools. Temple priests might try and bless you – for a donation.

◉ The Pilgrimage Route

The best way to visit the sights of Pharping is to join the other pilgrims on an easy, clockwise pilgrimage circuit (a *parikrama* in Nepali, or kora in Tibetan) around the centre of the town taking one to two hours. Every year more and more monasteries seem to open in the hills around town.

Auspicious Pinnacle Dharma
Centre of Dzongsar   BUDDHIST MONASTERY

As you enter the town from the main road, take the first right and head uphill, passing a **Guru Rinpoche statue** in a glass case. Next to the statue is a giant chörten that contains 16 enormous prayer wheels; cracks from the earthquake are under repair.

Ralo Gompa   BUDDHIST MONASTERY

The large white Ralo Gompa has a brightly painted chörten. It's located up the hill past the line of Tibetan restaurants.

Sakya Tharig Gompa   BUDDHIST MONASTERY

This is an enormous and brightly painted chörten – step inside to see hundreds of miniature chörten and statues of Guru Rinpoche set into alcoves in the walls. If you're lucky dozens of monks will be chanting inside; at such times a visit is utterly magical.

Drölma Lhakhang   BUDDHIST MONASTERY

The shrine is sacred to both Hindus and Buddhists, who identify Saraswati as Tara. It's accessed via a set of steps to the right of Sakya Tharig Gompa. To the right of this chapel is the **Rigzu Phodrang Gompa**, slightly damaged in the earthquake but still worth visiting for its impressive frieze of statues, with Guru Rinpoche surrounded by his fearsome incarnations as Dorje Drolo (riding a tiger) and Dorje Phurba (with three faces, Garuda-like wings and a coupling consort).

Guru Rinpoche Cave   BUDDHIST SHRINE

Climb the steps behind the Drölma Lhakhang, passing a rocky fissure jammed full of *tsha tsha* (stupa-shaped clay offerings) and cracks stuffed with little bags of wishes and human hair. Eventually you'll come to the walls of a large white monastery, inside which is a small cave (also known as the Gorakhnath Cave). Take off your shoes and duck between the monastery buildings to reach the soot-darkened cavern, which is illuminated by butter lamps and a Liza Minnelli–style row of coloured light bulbs.

Vajra Yogini Temple   BUDDHIST MONASTERY

This sacred 17th-century Newari-style temple is devoted to the Tantric goddess Vajrayogini. One of the few female deities in Buddhist mythology, Vajrayogini was a wandering ascetic who achieved a level of enlightenment almost equivalent to the male Buddhas. Sadly, many of the historic Rana-style buildings that used to flank the courtyard collapsed in the 2015 earthquake. Architecturally, Vajra Yogini is quite different to any of the other temples in town and is more of a classic Newari design. The temple is accessed down a flight of stairs leading from the Guru Rinpoche Cave.

🛏 Sleeping & Eating

Along the main road uphill from Pharping bazaar are numerous Tibetan restaurants serving momos, *thukpa* and butter tea to hungry pilgrims.

Family Guest House   GUESTHOUSE $

(☑ 01-4710412; r with/without bathroom Rs 700/500) The only choice in the middle of Pharping, opposite the Guru Rinpoche Statue, this well-run guesthouse is right on the pilgrim circuit and has a good rooftop restaurant.

Hotel Ashoka   GUESTHOUSE $

(☑ 01-4710057; bungalow r Rs 700, r Rs 1000; 🛜) On the road that passes around Pharping to Dakshinkali, Ashoka has a peaceful location, with sublime views from the rooms in the main building. Unfortunately, said rooms are a little tatty and the garden-side bungalows without views are probably a better deal. Some buildings here were damaged in the earthquake so call ahead to see which rooms are open.

Dakchhinkali Village Resort   HOTEL $$

(☑ 9801112525, 9801112323; www.dakchhinkali-villageresort.com; r Rs 2000-2500; 🛜) Just outside the town centre, this somewhat dated resort, set beside an impressive modern monastery, has good-sized rooms in spacious and very peaceful grounds.

Hattiban Resort   RESORT $$$

(☑ 01-4370714; www.haatiban-resort.com; s/d US$100/125; 📶🛜) Perched on a ridge high above the valley in a pine forest, this small resort has 30 good-quality rooms, most with balconies that make the most of the stunning Himalayan views. The rooms are huge, with big comfy beds, heaters and modern bathrooms.

From the resort you can make an excellent three-hour (return) hike up to the peak of Champa Devi (2249m). The resort's main drawback is that it's very inaccessible; to get here you'll need a car to travel 2km on a steep, rutted dirt road that branches off about 3km north of Pharping. The condition of the road varies so ask the hotel about arranging transfers.

❶ Getting There & Away

Buses on route 22 leave throughout the day for Pharping from Kathmandu's Ratna Park bus station (Rs 31, 1½ hours), continuing to Dakshinkali. The last bus back to Kathmandu leaves around 5.30pm.

Around Pharping

Dakshinkali

The road from Pharping continues a few kilometres south to the blood-soaked temple of Dakshinkali, a favourite Hindu pilgrimage destination. Set at the confluence of two sacred streams in a rocky cleft in the forest, and undamaged in the 2015 earthquake, the temple is dedicated to the goddess Kali, the most bloodthirsty incarnation of Parvati. To satisfy the blood-lust of the goddess, pilgrims drag a menagerie of chickens, ducks, goats, sheep, pigs and even the occasional buffalo up the path to the temple to be beheaded and transformed into cuts of meat by the temple priests, who are also skilled butchers.

Once the sacrifice is made, the meat goes in the pot – pilgrims bring all the ingredients for a forest barbecue and spend the rest of the day feasting in the shade of the trees. Saturday is the big sacrificial day, and the blood also flows freely on Tuesday. For the rest of the week Dakshinkali is very quiet. During the annual celebrations of Dasain in October the temple is washed by a crimson tide and the image of Kali is bathed in the gore.

The approach to the temple from the bus stand winds through a religious bazaar, which is often hazy with smoke from barbecue fires. Local farmers sell their produce here to go into the postsacrifice feasts, along with piles of marigolds, coconuts and other offerings for the goddess. Only Hindus can enter the temple courtyard where the image of Kali resides, but visitors can watch from the surrounding terraces. However, remember that the sacrifices are a religious event, with profound spiritual significance for local people, and not just an excuse to snap gruesome photos.

A pathway leads off from behind the main temple uphill to the small Mata Temple on the hilltop, which offers good views over the forest. Several snack stalls at the Dakshinkali bus park serve reviving tea and pappadams.

❶ Getting There & Away

Buses on route 22 run to Dakshinkali regularly from Kathmandu's Shahid Gate (Martyrs' Memorial) and Ratna Park bus station (Rs 45, 2½ hours). There are extra buses on Tuesday and Saturday to accommodate the pilgrimage crowds. From Pharping it's an easy 1km downhill walk or ride, but a steep uphill slog in the other direction.

Dollu

Located 3km before Pharping on the road from Kathmandu, a side road turns north along a small valley to the village of Dollu, passing several huge Tibetan Buddhist monasteries, including the Rigon Tashi Choeling, which took some earthquake damage but still contains some fine murals and statuary, including a fearsome image of Guru Dorje Drolo and his tiger.

If you walk a few hundred metres towards Kathmandu from the Dollu junction, you will reach a cluster of houses tucked into a hairpin bend, where a track leads uphill to the enormous Neydo Tashi Choeling monastery. This modern gompa looms over the surrounding landscape and the main prayer hall contains some stunning mural work

---

PLEASING KALI

The consort of Shiva, Kali, one of the most bloodthirsty of all Hindu gods and goddesses, is the goddess of power and change, time and destruction. Her most famous pose is that of Dakshinkali, where she appears dancing in a destructive frenzy, with her tongue sticking out and drunk on the blood of her victims. The Dakshinkali temple is dedicated to her in this form and animal sacrifices are a common occurrence at this and other Kali temples.

The sacrifices are made in order to placate the goddess's desire for blood, and there are strict rules specifying the ritual for how the animals should be sacrificed. While sacrifices occur frequently in certain Nepali Hindu temples, it's nowadays somewhat rarer in much of India (it's still common in parts of the south and Bengal though). If you think sacrificing an animal is gruesome, then just be glad you weren't visiting the major Kali temple in Kolkata (India) around 200 years ago, when it's said that a human male child was sacrificed every day...

and a 15m-high statue of Sakyamuni. There are nearly 200 monks here, so the morning and evening prayer ceremonies are quite an experience. Some minor earthquake damage was under repair at the time of writing.

🛏 Sleeping

★Neydo Tashi Choeling Monastery Guest House
GUESTHOUSE $$

(☑ 01-6924606; www.neydohotel.com; s/d incl breakfast US$60/70; 🛜) This guesthouse, attached to the Neydo Tashi Choeling monastery, is something a bit different – and quite wonderful. It offers subtly coloured, calming and highly comfortable rooms, but the best part of a stay is the opportunity to get to know the 200 resident monks: you can eat with them and participate in daily monastic life.

It's a few kilometres out of Pharping on the road to Kathmandu.

Bungamati

Formerly one of the prettiest villages in the valley, Bungamati faced the full force of the 2015 earthquake. Many buildings and temples collapsed as the valley shook and the scars of the disaster will be a long time healing. Nevertheless, some monuments survived the disaster and are still worth visiting.

This historic village is the birthplace of Rato Machhendranath, the patron god of Patan, but the enormous shikhara temple that used to house the deity in the main square in Bungamati was shaken to rubble in the earthquake. The sacred idol of Rato Machhendranath was recovered from the wreckage, but it is unclear what effect the loss of the temple will have on the Rato Macchendranath festival, which features a famous chariot parade between Bungamati and Patan. The historic Bhairab temple that shared the same square was also destroyed.

Many local people make a living as woodcarvers and there are several workshops and showrooms around the main square. To reach the centre from the bus stand, follow the wide road south, then turn right, and then right again at an obvious junction by a Ganesh shrine.

◎ Sights

With the destruction of the Rato Machhendranath Temple and Bhairab Temple in the 2015 quake, Bungamati lost part of its soul. These shrines played a hugely important role in the religious life of the valley and their loss is keenly felt by local people. With their spiritual significance, the temples may one day be reconstructed, but for the time being, visitors must make do with the the rubble-filled square where they once stood and a handful of smaller temples in the backstreets.

Bungamati Culture Museum MUSEUM
(admission Rs 25; ⊙10am-4pm Sat-Thu) On the narrow lane towards the main square is this low-key, dusty museum displaying cultural objects from the area, and some cracks from the earthquake.

Dey Pukha WATER TANK
(Central Pond) If you leave the main square by the northern gate, you'll pass a crumbling Buddhist courtyard monastery and an assortment of chaityas and shrines, then the brick-lined water tank of the Dey Pukha.

Karya Binayak Temple HINDU TEMPLE
Halfway between Bungamati and Khokana, this historic Ganesh temple survived the earthquake with minor damage. Local pilgrims flock here on Saturdays for a *bhoj* (feast) and some *bhajan* (devotional music) – the Newari version of a barbecue and sing along. To reach the temple, turn left when the path from Bungamati meets a larger track by a school.

ℹ Getting There & Away

Buses to Bungamati leave frequently from Patan's Lagankhel station (Rs 20, 40 minutes). There are also a few buses direct to Kathmandu's Ratna Park bus station (Rs 30). You can also get here easily by motorcycle (or bike if you're not scared of the crazy traffic), turning off the Kathmandu Ring Rd at Nakhu.

Khokana

Another medieval Newari town, Khokana is smaller and sleepier than Bungamati, but it's still worth a quick look, despite much damage to older buildings in the 2015 earthquake. The main road leads through the village, which offers a window back in time, with mattress-makers stuffing cases with cotton, farmers baling straw, tailors stitching and women spinning wool and winnowing rice. In the main village square is the triple-tiered **Shekala Mai Temple** (also known as Rudrayani), damaged but still standing after the disaster, with carved balconies covered by fretwork screens. The five-day **Khokana Jatra festival**, with its masked dancers, is usually held in October and is a good time to visit.

You'll need to pay Rs 100 to visit the town, collected at the tourist office. The fee goes to general upkeep of the village's streets.

Chapagaon

Another victim of the 2015 earthquake, Chapagaon saw widespread damage to its tall brick Newari houses, but its temples were still standing when the dust settled. Beside the main road, which cuts through the central square en route to Tika Bhairab, are a number of shrines, including temples to Bhairab, Krishna and Narayan, but the main attraction here is the **Vajra Varahi Temple** (parking Rs 20), about 500m east of the main road on the back route to Godavari (turn left by the Narayan Temple).

Set in a peaceful wood, this important Tantric temple was built in 1665 and it came through the earthquake mostly intact. The temple attracts lots of wedding parties, pilgrims and picnickers who descend en masse on Saturdays. Visitors pour milk and offerings over the statue of a bull in front of the temple and make similar offerings to the image of Vajra Varahi, an incarnation of the 'female Buddha' Vajrayogini. There are lots of birds in the forest – check the sign by the car park for a list of species.

For a bit of exploring further afield, you can head towards the **Lele Valley**, which runs east off the valley of the Nakhu Khola, about 5km south of Chapagaon. Few tourists make it out here and the valley offers a window into a way of life that is fast vanishing in other parts of the Kathmandu Valley.

To get to Lele, follow the trucking road south from Chapagaon to the **Tika Bhairab**, a large rock shrine with a multicoloured painting of Bhairab, set at the confluence of two rivers. Buses run here from Chapagaon, sharing the road with noisy lorries hauling gravel back to Kathmandu for construction projects.

⬤ Getting There & Away

Local minibuses leave from Lagankhel in Patan to Chapagaon (Rs 20, 45 minutes) or direct to the Vajra Varahi Temple (Rs 20).

The road to the Vajra Varahi Temple continues through peaceful countryside to meet the Godavari road just south of Bandegaon. You can walk it in about an hour or cycle it in 20 minutes.

Godavari

Godavari is best known for the green fingers of its inhabitants. The village is home to Nepal's National Botanical Gardens and the approach road is lined with the nurseries that supply Kathmandu with flowers and potted plants. Earthquake damage here was minor.

The 10km road from the Kathmandu Ring Rd forks in the middle of Godavari – the left fork goes to the botanical gardens while the right fork climbs past the Naudhara Kunda temple and turns into a dirt track running up to Pulchowki Mountain.

⦿ Sights

If you plan on walking the remote trails in the forests surrounding Godavari, it's a good idea to get a guide, with locals warning of robberies. Hotels or restaurants should be able to help with a guide.

National Botanical Gardens GARDENS (foreigner/SAARC Rs 226/57, camera/video Rs 20/150, child under 10yr 50% discount; ⦿ 10am-5pm, to 4pm Nov-Jan) The verdant botanical gardens are a quiet and peaceful spot for a walk or picnic, except on Friday and Saturday when the place is overrun with school kids. The visitor centre has some good exhibits on Nepal's flora and in the middle is the decorative **Coronation Pond** with its 7m commemorative pillar. The cactus house, orchid house and tropical house took some damage in the earthquake and repairs are ongoing.

Godavari Kunda HINDU If you turn to the right at the junction before the Royal Botanical Gardens, you'll reach a cluster of local restaurants, the Godavari Kunda – a sacred spring on the right-hand side of the road – and, on the left, a tank bordered by a neat line of Shaivite shrines. Every 12 years (there was one in 2015 and the next is in 2027) thousands of pilgrims come to the spring to bathe and gain spiritual merit. Next door is the large ⦿ **Sal Choling Godavari** Tibetan monastery, carrying some scars from the earthquake.

Godavari Kunda Community Forest FOREST Across the road from Godavari Kunda is a tiny scenic lake that leads to the entrance of a 30-hectare woodland, which is managed by local people and provides a haven for 300 species of bird and loads of picnickers.

Naudhara Kunda HINDU TEMPLE
(Pulchowki Mai Temple) Damaged but not destroyed in the quake, the three-tiered pagoda is dedicated to one of the Tantric mother goddesses and the two large pools before the temple compound are fed by nine spouts (known as the Naudhara Kunda) that represent the nine streams that flow from Pulchowki Mountain. It's located along the road at the junction by St Xavier's School, which veers off to the right.

Although entrance to the temple is free there's a pretty good chance you'll be asked to pay Rs 100 by the Naudhara Community Forest Group, as the temple sits on the edge of the forest.

Naudhara Community Forest FOREST
(admission Rs 100, parking Rs 20; ⊗7am-4pm) The Naudhara Community Forest is 147 hectares of locally managed woodland, established with support from Bird Conservation Nepal (www.birdlifenepal.org). Guides (who almost certainly won't speak English) can be arranged through the ticket office for Rs 500 for a two- to three-hour tour. Note that some trails were affected by landslides – check locally to see if tours are currently possible.

Shanti Ban Buddha BUDDHIST SHRINE
On the hillside above Godavari is an enormous golden Buddha image, created by local Buddhists who were inspired by the Japanese Peace Pagoda movement.

You'll probably need to ask directions to get here, but it's just west of the village proper and quite high above the main road. From the turn-off it's a 20-minute walk along a dirt road. As you get to the very end of the village, look for the green gate with a sign that says 'Shanti'; push through here and clamber up the steps to the statue.

🍴 Sleeping & Eating

There's nothing in the way of budget hotels here, but there are a few cheap restaurants in front of the Godavari Kunda where day trippers can grab a bite for lunch for not too many rupees. The **Godavari Village Resort** (📋01-5560675; www.godavariresort.com.np; s/d incl breakfast US$150/165; 🛜🗮) was badly damaged in the 2015 earthquake and was closed at the time of writing pending major restoration works; contact the office for updates.

Hotel View Bhrikuti HOTEL **$$**
(📋01-5560542; www.hotelviewbhrikuti.com; incl breakfast US$65/75; 🛜) A slightly tacky, but nice enough businesslike hotel. Rooms here are large and surprisingly plush, with mod cons such as minibars, modern bathrooms and cable TV. It has an appealing rooftop garden too, with postcard mountain views on a clear day. There was some earthquake damage to the newer building and operations are centred on the older building while repairs are underway.

❶ Getting There & Away

Local minibuses (No 5) and buses (No 14) run between Lagankhel in Patan and Godavari (Rs 8, 45 minutes). The road is in good condition for cycling or motorcycling, but watch for trucks headed for the mines near Tika Bhairab.

Around Godavari

Harisiddhi

About 7km northwest of Godavari, on the main road, Harisiddhi is notable for the towering, four-tiered **Harisiddhi Bhagwan Temple** on its brick-paved market square. Dedicated to one of the fearsome incarnations of Durga, the temple has been painted in bright colours by local devotees and is still imposing, despite some earthquake damage. Any bus bound for Godavari can drop you here.

Bishankhu Narayan

If you're looking for an excuse to get off the beaten track, the shrine of Bishankhu Narayan may do nicely. Dedicated to Vishnu, this chain-mail-covered shrine is reached by a steep stairway that climbs to the temple and then drops into a narrow fissure in the rock, where pilgrims test their sin levels by trying to squeeze through the tiny gap. If you get stuck, the sin in question is either gluttony or pride...

The unsealed 3km road to Bishankhu Narayan starts at Bandegaon on the Godavari road, and runs southeast over a small stream. At Godamchowr village, take the left fork at the football ground and climb for about 2km to reach the shrine.

Pulchowki Mountain

This 2760m-high mountain is the highest point around the valley and there are magnificent views from the summit, also home to the sacred **Pulchowki Mai Temple**. Here you'll find over 570 species of flowering plant and it's a popular spot for birdwatching, home to one-third of all the bird species in Nepal. There have been rumours for years that the government will turn this into a national park. The mountain is famous for its springtime (March–April) flowers, in particular its magnificent red and white rhododendrons.

To get here, the only options are a full-day hike along dirt tracks from Naudhara Kunda, or a very rough unsealed road that is only suitable for 4WDs, mountain bikes or trail motorcycles. There are no facilities so bring water, food, a compass and fellow travellers for company (trekkers have been robbed here in the past). It's about a six-hour return hike, but check the status of the trails before you head off as landslides may have blocked sections.

THE VALLEY FRINGE

Beyond Bhaktapur the landscape starts to rise, revealing views north to the rugged mountain wall of the Himalaya, which is rarely visible from the bottom of the valley. Technically, most towns are outside the valley, on the roads to Langtang or the Tibetan border, but it is easy to visit these places on day trips or overnight stays from Kathmandu. Many towns on the valley wall suffered earthquake damage – check ahead to make sure hotels are operating normally before planning an overnight trip.

Nagarkot ✓

📍 01 / ELEV 2175M

Nagarkot has a reputation as the top spot for enjoying Himalayan views from the comfort of your hotel balcony. Just 32km from Kathmandu, the village is packed with hotels, stacked up on a ridge facing one of the broadest possible views of the Himalaya. However, many hotels were damaged in the 2015 earthquake and it will be some time before the village is fully back on its feet. In terms of views, a visit to Nagarkot between October and March will nearly always be rewarded with a view, but be warned the mountains are notorious for disappearing behind cloudy skies on any given day (or hour). It can get very cold at Nagarkot, so bring warm clothing.

◉ Sights & Activities

Other than taking it easy and admiring mountain views, day hikes in the area are the main activities to keep you busy.

YOGA, MASSAGE & MORE

Nepal Yoga Retreat (☎9851092635, 9851037083; www.yogaretreatnepal.com; s/d all-inclusive 3-day/2-night US$127/174; 🛜), located between Bhaktapur and Nagarkot 1km from the village of Tharkot (Telkot), is one of the best-regarded yoga retreats in Nepal. This place offers a full complement of expertly guided yoga courses, ayurveda massage, steam baths and more. Accommodation is in fairly simple bamboo cottages. It's more suitable for serious yoga students.

Views   VIEWPOINT
Nagarkot only exists because of the views, as there is not much else to the village. But what views! From any clear point on the ridge, you can take in a panorama, from Dhaulagiri in the west to Mt Everest and Kanchenjunga in the east, via Ganesh Himal (7406m), Langtang Lirung (7246m), Shisha Pangma (8012m), Dorje Lakpa (6975m) and Gauri Shankar (7146m).

The most popular place to soak in the splendour is the **Lookout Tower**, perched at 2164m on a ridge and still standing after the earthquake, with killer 360-degree views at sunrise. It's around an hour's walk (4km) south from the village, otherwise taxis and private cars (return Rs 1200) are easily arranged through any hotel or the tourist offices if you're not up for the dark, chilly morning walk. Another good vantage point is from the damaged **Mahakali Temple** on the small hilltop near several of the hotels.

Nature Trail   WALKING
A popular trail is the easy two- to three-hour trekking loop around Nagarkot known as the Nature Trail, which passes through scenery of terraced hills, forests, fields of mustard flowers and rustic mudbrick farmhouses belonging to Tamang and Gurung people.

Rock Climbing   ROCK CLIMBING
(☎9851115014; www.himalayantrailfinder.com; incl homestay, basic meals & transport from Kathmandu US$65) It's an activity that's very much in its infancy, but climbers keen for some action can tackle a 30m rock here, where climbing routes are graded from four to eight. It's arranged through Himalayan Trailfinder in Kathmandu.

🛏 Sleeping

Nagarkot has numerous guesthouses and hotels that take advantage of the views on

Nagarkot

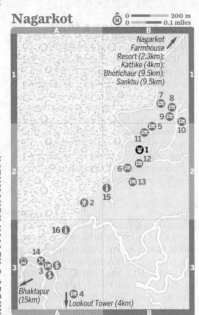

⌖ N   0 ——— 200 m
       0 ——— 0.1 miles

Nagarkot
Farmhouse
Resort (2.3km);
Kattike (4km);
Bhotichaur (9.5km);
Sankhu (9.5km)

Bhaktapur
(15km)

↓ Lookout Tower (4km)

the north side of the ridge, and charge a premium for the privilege. However, earth-quake damage was extensive and a number of hotels were closed at the time of research, including the **Hotel Green Valley** (☏01-6680078; www.hotelgreenvalley.com.np; s/d from Rs 2000/2500; ☏) and **Hotel Himalayan Villa** (☏01-6680119; www.hotelhimalayanvilla.com; s/d incl breakfast Rs 3000/3500; ❄☏) – check locally for updates.

The town is more popular with domestic and Indian tourists than foreigners and can get very busy (and noisy with parties of young Nepalis playing loud music until late into the night – or until the power cuts out!), and hotel prices are much higher, and standards lower, than in areas more popular with foreign tourists. However, most of the hotels offer significant discounts so always ask when you book or check in.

Sherpa Alpine Cottage   GUESTHOUSE $
(☏9841265231; sherpacottage@gmail.com; r with/without hot water Rs 1200/800; ☏) Basic cottages that are about as cheap as you'll find in Nagarkot. Most have memorable views. There's also a pleasant alfresco restaurant, with tables in huts around a terraced garden overlooking the valley.

Berg House Café   GUESTHOUSE $
(☏9841914242; r Rs 1500; ☏) Large and bright rooms looking down into the Kathmandu Valley (which probably isn't the view you came here for) are found above this popular cafe, still operating while earthquake repairs are underway.

★ Nagarkot Farmhouse Resort   RESORT $$
(☏01-6202022; www.nagarkotfarmhouse.com; s/d incl half-board & taxes Rs 5000/7500; ❄☏) Away from the main hotel sprawl, this cosy, character-laden place has an attractive Tibetan Buddhist motif throughout and even its own stupa and meditation room. The best rooms are in the Newari-inspired brick complex on the edge of the garden, with spotless bathrooms and deckchairs on the balconies, which face a sensational sweep of peaks. The restaurant saw some damage in the earthquake, but guest rooms were not badly affected. It's about 2km past the Hotel Country Villa down the dirt track to Sankhu.

★ Resort Eco-Home Nagarkot   GUESTHOUSE $$
(☏01-6680180; www.ecohomenagarkot.com; s/d incl taxes US$25/35; ☏) ⬥ This German–Nepali–run guesthouse has very small

rooms with low-slung beds and is slathered in prayer flags, masks and ethnic, hippy-chic flavours. There was some earthquake damage but not enough to close the resort. The upstairs dining room with partial views centres on a huge circular open fire. Meals contain lots of organic vegies but can take a long time to prepare – order well in advance. A great almost-budget base.

A portion of profits goes towards local community projects – a rarity in Nepal and something the guesthouse should be commended for.

Hotel at the End of the Universe
GUESTHOUSE **$$**

(☑ 01-6680011; www.endoftheuniverse.com.np; r with bathroom US$24-40, without bathroom US$12, ste US$60; ☎) 🏄 As well as a great name, this eclectic resort offers an intriguing selection of cottages, bamboo cabins and gingerbread-style cottages, set in a verdant garden. There's an atmospheric stone-walled restaurant with big windows looking out to mountains. The hotel saw a fair bit of earthquake damage but repairs are ongoing so check ahead to see which rooms are open.

There's also free water to refill your bottle. A portion of profits goes to local education projects.

Peaceful Cottage
HOTEL **$$**

(☑ 01-6680077; www.peaceful-cottage.com; r with/ without view US$60/35; ☎) One of Nagarkot's better deals, this architectural hotchpotch has rooms to suit most budgets and suffered only minor earthquake damage. Each room differs in style, with some having carved wooden beds and others pebbles for walls, but the unifying factor is that they are all unusually good value for Nagarkot.

There's also an intriguing octagonal tower housing what might be one of the town's better restaurants, Café du Mont; earthquake repairs to this building are ongoing.

Nagarkot Sunshine Hotel
HOTEL **$$**

(☑ 01-6680105; r US$35-45; ❄☎) An attractive red-brick hotel with room rates that correspond to the quality of the view. The best rooms (numbers 206 and 306) on the upper levels have windows on three sides, facing directly onto the panorama. Earthquake damage was minor.

Club Himalaya Resort
RESORT **$$$**

(☑ 01-6680046; www.clubhimalaya.com.np; s/d incl breakfast from US$85/110, economy s/d excl breakfast US$50/80; ☎❄) The swankiest place in town, this resort has large, modern rooms with all the mod cons that make it terrific value. The views from the terraces and rooms are probably the best in town. It has the bonus of a heated pool, jacuzzi and massage services. Some areas were closed for postearthquake repairs at the time of writing – check before visiting.

If you want to stay in one of the 'economy' rooms (which are only a little less impressive than the standard rooms but don't have mountain views), you'll have to specifically ask staff about them. It's just uphill from the bus stand on the main road.

Fort Resort
RESORT **$$$**

(☑ 01-6680069; www.mountain-retreats.com; s/d/ ste US$90/110/160; @☎) Built in the Newari red-brick style, and with an impeccably trimmed garden terrace looking out over a natural amphitheatre of peaks, the Fort Resort makes for a memorable place to stay. The dignified rooms and suites are set in stylish cottages or in the main building, some with rustic wood-fire furnaces, and there's a good restaurant serving food made with home-grown ingredients. Unfortunately, part of hotel collapsed in the earthquake and repairs may take some time – check the status of rooms before visiting.

Hotel Country Villa
RESORT **$$$**

(☑ 01-6680128; www.hotelcountryvilla.com; s/d incl breakfast & taxes from US$75/95; ❄☎) This very popular resort tumbles down the side of the mountain and all rooms have mountain views that can be admired from your bed. Talking of the bedrooms, they're all livened up by prints of Robert Powell's paintings of Nepal and have blond-wood details and modernist carpets that were handwoven in the Kathmandu Valley. The hotel escaped serious damage in the quake.

The only real drawback is the resort's restaurant. It's best to eat elsewhere.

🍴 Eating

Most people eat at the lodges, but there are a few independent restaurants that survived the 2015 disaster.

Café du Mont
INTERNATIONAL **$$**

(☑ 01-6680077; Peaceful Cottage; mains Rs 200-300) Open to nonguests, the restaurant at the Peaceful Cottage hotel is housed inside a bizarre octagonal tower and has an eclectic menu of local, Chinese, Indian and Continental dishes served with a big dollop of

HIKING & CYCLING TO/FROM NAGARKOT

There are a number of hiking and cycling routes in this area, best walked downhill from Nagarkot. Nepa Maps' 1:25,000 *Nagarkot – Short Trekking on the Kathmandu Valley Rim* is useful, though its 1:50,000 *Around the Kathmandu Valley* is probably good enough.

Mountain bikes can be hired from the Nagarkot Naldum Tourism Development Committee for Rs 300 per hour.

Bottled water is mostly unavailable on these routes, so be sure to pack plenty of water. Note that some features on these routes may have changed since the earthquake; seek local advice before you set off.

To Dhulikhel (Six to Seven Hours from Nagarkot)

The Kathmandu Valley Cultural Trekking Trail, established by NETIF (www.netif-nepal.org), is a direct 20km trail to Dhulikhel. While for the most part it's well signed, there remain some confusing sections, so you'll probably need to ask passing villagers for directions along the way. The trail starts past Club Himalaya Resort, following the road past the army barracks. Keep an eye out for the sign to Dhulikhel, which leads you to the village of Rohini Bhanjyang. From here follow the road straight (don't take the left or right paths) and take the hill up, where you'll need to turn left at the intersection.

After 1km take the small trail on the right that's a steep downhill into the valley, leading you to the villages of Kankre and Tanchok. At Tanchok take the main jeep track and follow it uphill to Tusal. Head right to Opi where you cross the main jeep track and on to the final 5km stretch to Dhulikhel, crossing over the Arniko Hwy to Himalayan Horizon Hotel – 500m from the bus park.

To Changu Narayan (4½ Hours from Nagarkot, 1½ Hours from Telkot)

From Nagarkot, it's an easy stroll along the spur to Changu Narayan. The trail runs parallel to the road to Bhaktapur along the ridge, branching off at the sharp hairpin bend at Telkot (marked on some maps as Deurali Bhanjhang). Catching a bus to here from Nagarkot will save you the tedious first half of the walk.

From the bend, follow the middle dirt road up into the Telkot Forest and keep to the left. The track climbs uphill through a pine forest for about 20 minutes to the top of the ridge and then follows the ridge line, dropping gently down to Changu Narayan. On clear days there are good views of the Himalaya. You can follow this track on foot or on a mountain bike or motorcycle.

---

mountain-view love. Temporarily closed for repairs at the time of research.

Berg House Café INTERNATIONAL $$
(dishes Rs 180-350) By the main junction on the highway, this colourful cafe is packed with fossils, gnarled tree roots and other found bits of bric-a-brac, and the traveller-oriented menu runs to pizzas, sandwiches and steaks. It can take an age for food to arrive though.

❶ Information

There are several ATMs near the bus park, while internet is available at Nagarkot Guide.com.

Nagarkot Naldum Tourism Development Committee (NNTDC; ☏ 01-6680122; ◷ 10am-5.30pm Sun-Fri) The Nagarkot Naldum Tourism Development Committee is very helpful, with good information on walks in the area. It can arrange hiking guides for around Rs 3000 per day.

Nagarkot Guide.com (☏ 9841412762; www.nagarkotguide.com) Privately run, Nagarkot Guide.com is a tourist information service that also sells local tours and organises transport to Kathmandu. It's a brilliant resource for information on Nagarkot and its environs.

❶ Getting There & Away

There's a direct tourist minibus that runs daily to Kathmandu (Rs 400, two hours), departing Nagarkot at 10am from the bus park (it will also collect from hotels in advance if you organise this through your hotel or the tourist office). From Kathmandu it departs at 1pm from a lot in front of the Hotel Malla in Lainchhaur. However the service isn't that reliable and in Kathmandu you may have to ask around to find the actual bus!

To get here by public bus you'll need to transfer at Bhaktapur and jump on another bus to Nagarkot (Rs 45, one hour); these leave every

In the reverse direction, pick up the track near the Changu Narayan Hill Resort, and take the middle road where the track splits. You can also take an onward hike to Bodhnath or Sankhu.

To Sankhu (2½ to Four Hours from Nagarkot)

The quickest route from Nagarkot is via a dirt road that leads all the way to Sankhu. Take the northwest road down to the Nagarkot Farmhouse Resort and follow switchbacks down to the village of Kattike, which has a teahouse for refreshments. Go left at the junction at the edge of town. You can continue all the way down this track, or take a minor road that turns off sharply to the right after 15 minutes. Follow this track for 20 minutes as it shrinks to a trail and then take a sharp left downhill past several houses to rejoin the main track. From here it's an hour's slog to Sankhu village.

A more scenic route along village trails starts from just past the Nagarkot bus park, where you take a right downhill and continue on to the village of Bakhrigaun. From here you keep following trails that take you through to the main track joining at Bisambhar.

To Sundarijal (One to Two Days from Nagarkot)

It takes two easy days – or one very long day – to skirt around the valley rim to Sundarijal, from where you can travel by road to Gokarna, Bodhnath and Kathmandu, trek for another day along the valley rim to Budhanilkantha, or start the treks to Helambu or Gosainkund. Accommodation is available at Bhotichaur and Sundarijal in local guesthouses, but the trails can be confusing so ask for directions frequently.

Start by following the Sankhu trail as far as Kattike (about one hour), then turn right (north) to Jorsim Pauwa. Walk further down through Bagdhara to Chowki Bhanjyang (about one hour) and on for one more hour through Nagle to Bhotichaur, a good place to stop overnight in a village inn.

On day two, walk back up the trail towards Chowki Bhanjyang and take the fork leading uphill by a chautara (porters' resting place). This path climbs uphill to cross a ridge line before dropping down on the middle of three trails to Chule (or Jhule). Here the path enters the Shivapuri Nagarjun National Park and contours around the edge of the valley for several hours, before dropping down to Mulkarkha, on the first stage of the Helambu trek. From Mulkarkha, it's an easy descent beside the water pipeline to Sundarijal.

An alternative route runs northwest from Bhotichaur to Chisopani, the first overnight stop on the Helambu trek, which has several trekking lodges. The next day, you can hike southwest over the ridge through Shivapuri Nagarjun National Park to Sundarijal.

30 minutes. There are also buses from here to Sankhu and Bodhnath.

A one-way taxi to Nagarkot costs around Rs 5000 from Kathmandu.

Banepa

POP 24,000

The first major town you reach heading east out of the valley, Banepa is a lot more attractive once you get off its hellish highway and into the brick-paved backstreets snaking north from the highway. It's worth spending an hour or so exploring, with a number of Hindu and Buddhist temples. Most were built in the 14th and 16th centuries, when Banepa was an important stop on the trade route to Tibet, boasting trade links as far afield as the Ming dynasty on the east coast of China. The 2015 earthquake damaged some buildings in town, and the local hospital became a major centre for treating earthquake victims from around the valley, but most of the temples were spared.

Legend has it that the people of this valley were once terrorised by a demon known as Chand, who was defeated by one of the fearsome incarnations of Parvati, earning the goddess a new title – Chandeshwari, 'Slayer of Chand'. The Chandeshwari Temple has an enormous mural of Bhairab on its wall, and is a popular pilgrimage spot where animals are sacrificed on feast days. The main mandir, built in the stepped Newari style is intact, but the brick shikhara temple in the courtyard collapsed in the 2015 earthquake.

Located in front of the temple is a row of columns supporting statues of a menagerie,

WORTH A TRIP

SHIVA THE GIANT

Kailashnath Mahadev (admission Rs 100), a 43.5m-high Shiva statue said to be the tallest in the world, lords it over the small village of Sanga, on the main road between Bhaktapur and Banepa. Completed in 2010, you wouldn't describe the statue as beautiful but it's certainly memorable. Entry is via the Hilltake Health Spa & Resort.

and the struts supporting the triple-tiered roof show the eight Ashta Matrikas and eight Bhairabs.

On the north side of the approach road is a smaller temple dedicated to the 'Mother of Chandeshwari'.

ⓘ Getting There & Away

Regular buses leave from Kathmandu's Ratna Park bus station (Rs 35 to Rs 45, two hours) and continue on to Dhulikhel and beyond.

Buses going to Panauti (Rs 15, 20 minutes) turn off the Arniko Hwy at the main Banepa junction.

Dhulikhel

📞 011 / POP 9800 / ELEV 1550M

Dhulikhel is one of the more popular places from which to observe the high Himalaya. From the edge of the ridge, a stunning panorama of peaks unfolds, from Langtang Lirung in the east, through Dorje Lakpa to the huge bulk of Gauri Shankar and nearby Melungtse (7181m) and as far as Numbur (5945m) in the east. The old town escaped the 2015 earthquake with little damage, but almost all of the resorts on the ridge sustained some damage to their buildings and repair works are ongoing.

There's more to Dhulikhel than breathtaking views though. This is a real Newari town, with a temple-lined village square and a life outside of exposing tourists to the views.

⊙ Sights

The old part of Dhulikhel had a lucky escape in the 2015 quake and there are several interesting temples dotted around the brick backstreets.

Shiva Temple   HINDU TEMPLE

If you take the road leading southeast from the bottom of the town square for 2km, you'll

pass a playing field and the turn-off of the road to the Kali Temple. Just beyond this junction, a Ganesh shrine marks the path down to a picturesque little temple at the bottom of a gorge. The temple enshrines a four-faced lingam topped by a metal dome with four nagas arching down from the pinnacle.

Note the statues of a Malla royal family in the courtyard. The trickling stream flowing through the site gives it added atmosphere.

Old Town   NEIGHBOURHOOD

The old part of the town is an interesting area to wander around. The main square contains a triple-roofed **Hari Siddhi Temple** and a three-tiered **Vishnu Temple** fronted by two worshipful Garudas in quite different styles and heights. Northwest of the square are the modern **Gita Temple** and the three-tiered, Newari-style **Bhagwati Shiva Temple**.

Kali Temple   HINDU TEMPLE

If you don't mind a steep 30-minute uphill climb, you can head up a series of shortcuts on concrete steps to reach this modern hilltop temple for excellent mountain views. The site is occupied by the army, but there's a viewing tower that attracts hordes of local sightseers at weekends and villagers sell *suntala* (small oranges) beside the path in autumn. On the way you'll pass **Shanti Ban**, a massive golden statue of Buddha.

It's also the way to Namobuddha, so if you plan on heading there, it makes sense to save the walk up here till then.

🏃 Activities

Dhulikhel to Namobuddha
& Panauti Hiking Trail   HIKING

The hike or mountain-bike trip from Dhulikhel to Namobuddha is a fine leg-stretcher, and one of the most popular activities for visitors here. It takes about three hours each way, or you can continue to Panauti in around two more hours.

From Dhulikhel the trail first climbs up to the Kali Temple lookout then drops down to the left after the Deurali Restaurant for half an hour to the village of **Kavre**, by the new road to Sindhuli. Cross the road and walk down beside prayer flags for around an hour to the village of **Phulbari**. As you crest the ridge, you'll see a Tibetan monastery on a hilltop, with Namobuddha just below it. To reach the stupa, take the right branch where the path forks. The trail is well signed, so you shouldn't need a guide to get here.

NAMOBUDDHA

Along with Bodhnath and Swayambhunath, the stupa at Namobuddha is one of the three most important Buddhist pilgrimage sites in Nepal, attracting large numbers of Tibetans from Nepal, India and Tibet itself.

The site is sacred due to the inspiring legend about the Buddha, who, when in a previous life as a prince, encountered a tigress that was close to death from starvation and unable to feed her cubs. In an act of compassion he allowed the hungry tigress to consume him, a deed that transported him to the higher realms of existence. A marble tablet depicts the event in a small cave up the forested path to the left of the stupa. At the top of the hill is also the magnificent **Thrangu Tashi Yangtse Monastery**, a sprawling monastic complex of Tibetan Buddhist temples and monasteries with gleaming golden arched roofs. It was officially opened in December 2008 and survived the 2015 earthquake with only minor damage.

Namobuddha Resort (☑9851106802; www.namobuddharesort.com; s €45-60, d €60-70; @☏) is a delightful eco-retreat that's a 20-minute walk from Namobuddha stupa. Its tasteful cottages are spread throughout its garden and feature charming Nepali-inspired decor and Himalayan views. A few buildings were damaged in the quake, but repairs were underway when we visited. It's all organic here, and they bake their own sourdough bread, grow their own vegetables and even make their own paneer cheese for the entirely vegetarian menu. If its peaceful setting and mountain views don't relax you, there's also a sauna, flotation tank and yoga-meditation hall. Reservations are highly recommended.

Most people arrive at Namobuddha via the walking trail from Dhulikhel. However, there's a road here, too, and buses (Rs 55, 20 minutes) heading to/from Banepa and Dhulikhel leave at the bottom of the hill near the stupa.

From Namobuddha, a trail also descends from the right side of the stupa through forest to the small village of **Sankhu** (distinct from the other village called Sankhu in the Northeastern Valley), with temples and riverside ghats. Shortly after, the track splits – the right fork leads to Batase and Dhulikhel, while the left fork winds past terraced fields to **Sunthan** and **Panauti**, about 2½ hours from Namobuddha. As you approach Panauti, cross the stream over a suspension bridge to the ghats and then follow the road as it curves round to the Indreshwar Mahadev Temple.

Note that some features of this walk may have changed since the earthquake; seek local advice on the route before you set off.

🛏 Sleeping

Most of the expensive places with good views are strung out on dirt roads leading off the highway. The cheapies are down the winding back road that leads southeast from the main square. Note that most resorts took some damage in the earthquake and repairs are likely to take some time.

Shiva Guest House GUESTHOUSE $
(☑9841254988; d with/without bathroom Rs 700/600) This family-run farmhouse has five clean, but very basic rooms, and great views from the upper floors and rooftop. Earthquake damage was minor and food comes fresh from the organic garden and you can pick mandarins and other fruit right off the trees. It's reached by stairs leading up from the Shiva Temple, a 15-minute walk from the bus station.

Snow View Guest House GUESTHOUSE $
(☑9841482487; r Rs 800) This homestay is probably the cheapest place with a proper mountain view, and is set beside a pleasant garden restaurant. There's some minor earthquake damage and only two rooms look directly onto the mountains, but the rooftop has enough views for everybody.

★ Dhulikhel Lodge Resort HOTEL $$
(☑011-490114, Kathmandu 01-4991353; www.dhulikhellodgeresort.com; s/d from US$55/70; ✳☏) Modern but built in a vaguely traditional style, this place, with its cracking views (particularly from the top-floor rooms), has supremely comfortable rooms that combine business slick with local Newari style. The highlight of the bar-restaurant is the great circular fireplace, which makes for an après-ski atmosphere, while the coffee bar is

Dhulikhel & Around

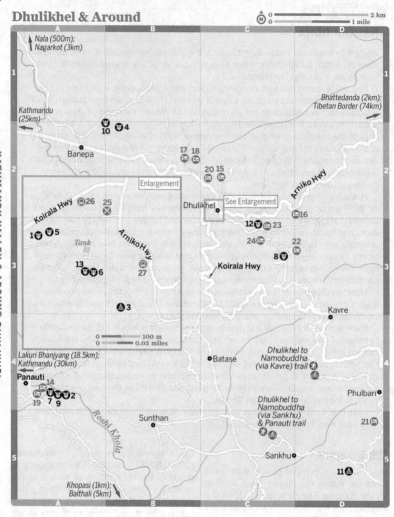

equally inviting. Some buildings here were badly damaged so check which rooms are currently available before you visit.

Mirabel Resort
HOTEL **$$**

(☏ 011-490972; www.mirabelresorthotel.com; s/d incl breakfast US$50/70; ☏) This large but somewhat aged resort would look more at home on a Balearic island, with its tiled white villas and hacienda vibe. Rooms have balconies facing the Himalayan vista, and you can also admire the peaks from the rooftop and gardens. Hot water is only available during certain hours of the morning and evening.

Panorama View Lodge
HOTEL **$$**

(☏ 011-490887; www.panoramaviewlodge.com.np; r Rs 2500; ☀☏) An option for those who really want to get away from it all, this place offers the full 'panorama view' plus good food served in an unexpectedly elegant dining room, and it escaped damage in the earthquake. The bedrooms have new mattresses and a recent makeover. Just don't expect crowds of people for company.

The hotel is 2km above town on the dirt track to the Kali Temple and is a pain to get to and from without your own transport. The price is very good though.

Dhulikhel & Around

Sights

Sleeping

Eating

Transport

High View Resort HOTEL $$
(☎011-490966; www.highviewresort.com; deluxe s/d US$60/65; 📶) A 1980s atmosphere pervades this secluded place, but the huge deluxe rooms come with a private balcony and the views are superb. Earthquake damage was minor. Discounts can bring rates down by as much as 50%.

★**Dwarika's Resort Dhulikhel** LUXURY HOTEL $$$
(☎011-490612; www.dwarikas-dhulikhel.com; s/d all-inclusive from US$410/440; ❄📶🏊) One of the finest and most exclusive places to stay in Nepal, this beautifully conceived boutique resort built of red Newari brick sprawls over 9 lush hectares. It takes in infinity pools with mountain vistas, meditation suites, massage rooms, a couple of restaurants and bars, and huge but understated terracotta-style rooms. The complex saw some earthquake damage and reconstruction was underway when we visited, so check which facilities are available.

Rates include all meals and a host of activities ranging from pottery workshops to cooking classes, yoga and meditation. Advance bookings essential.

Himalayan Horizon Hotel HOTEL $$$
(☎011-490296; www.himalayanhorizon.com; s/d incl breakfast from US$81/103; 📶) Also known as the Hotel Sun-n-Snow, this huge place uses traditional brickwork and woodcarving to create a Newari ambience. It's not quite 'old Dhulikhel' but the restaurant and garden terrace are great and the rooms have sublime views of the snow peaks. However, some were damaged in the earthquake so check which rooms are in use before you visit.

Eating

There's a very limited choice of places to eat, and most travellers opt to dine at their hotels.

Newa Kitchen INTERNATIONAL, NEPALI $
(dishes Rs 100-250) Cheap and cheerful upstairs eatery by the bus stand with a full menu of Nepali, Indian, Chinese and European standards.

Information

There's a Nabil ATM at the junction of the main and BP roads and a couple of internet places in town.

Getting There & Away

Frequent buses to Dhulikhel leave from Kathmandu's Ratna Park bus station (Rs 55, two hours), passing Bhaktapur (Rs 35, 45 minutes) en route. The last bus goes back to Kathmandu at around 6.30pm.

The walk to Dhulikhel from Nagarkot is an interesting alternative.

Panauti

Tucked away in a side valley off the Arniko Hwy, about 7km south of Banepa, Panauti sits at the sacred confluence of the Roshi Khola and Pungamati Khola. A third 'invisible river' called the Padmabati is said to join the other two rivers at Panauti, making this a particularly sacred spot. Accordingly, there are some fabulously ancient temples that have stood the test of time partly because of Panauti's legendary resistance to earthquakes. This certainly held true during the 2015 earthquake, when the town escaped with minor cuts and bruises, though less so in the smaller tremor in 1988, which damaged several monuments.

Panauti was once a major trading centre with its own royal palace but today the small town has a bustling new quarter and a serene old quarter. Most of the town's few visitors come on day trips, but we recommend staying over and exploring the streets at dawn and dusk, when they are at their most magical. As well as its ornate temples, the village has some striking Rana-era mansions, which have been restored with assistance from the French government.

◉ Sights

Most sights are located in Panauti's old town and none of the temples here were damaged in the 2015 earthquake.

Indreshwar Mahadev Temple   HINDU TEMPLE

(foreigner/SAARC incl guide & entry to museum Rs 300/100; ⊙7.30am-5pm Oct-Mar, to 5.30pm Apr-Sep) Panauti's most famous temple is set in a vast courtyard full of statuary in the middle of the isthmus between the two rivers. Topped by a three-storey pagoda roof, the temple is a magnificent piece of Newari architecture. The first temple here was founded in 1294 but the shrine was rebuilt in its present form in the 15th century. The lingam enshrined here is said to have been created personally by Shiva.

The woodcarvings on the temple's windows, doorways and roof struts are particularly fine, and the erotic carvings here are subtle and romantic rather than pornographic.

To the south of the main temple is the rectangular **Unamanta Bhairab Temple**, with three faces peering out of the upstairs windows. Located within is a statue of Bhairab, accompanied by goddesses. A small, double-roofed Shiva temple stands in one corner of the courtyard, and a second shrine containing a huge black image of Vishnu as Narayan faces the temple from the west.

Inside the temple compound is also the **Panauti Museum**, an interesting collection of artefacts from the region, and original sections from the Indreshwar Mahadev Temple.

Brahmayani Temple   HINDU TEMPLE

Dating from the 17th century, the three-tiered Brahmayani Temple was built to honour Brahmayani, the chief goddess of the village. The image from the temple is hauled around town during the lively annual chariot festival, marking the end of the monsoon. To get here, cross a small suspension bridge to the north bank of the Pungamati Khola.

Krishna Narayan Temple   HINDU TEMPLE

Cross to the south bank over the weir, then take another bridge back to the end of the spur, which is covered by the shrines and statues of the Krishna Narayan Temple.

There are also temples to various incarnations of Vishnu here – the largest temple has roof struts depicting Vishnu as the carefree, flute-playing Krishna. Many of the shrines are embellished with Rana-era stucco-work.

Civic Square   SQUARE

There are some interesting buildings in the middle of the village. Walk west along the northern brick lane and turn right just before you reach the main road. You'll soon come to a large square with a music platform, a large white stupa, a Brahmayani Temple and classic Newari-style architecture.

Panauti Peace Gallery   MUSEUM

(⊙10.30am-4pm Sun-Fri) FREE Next to the tourist office in a rickety building that needed some repair work after the 2015 earthquake, this museum has a rambling collection, including an antique walking-

---

TRICKERY & REPENTANCE AT PANAUTI

Legend has it that Ahilya, the beautiful wife of a Vedic sage, was seduced by the god Indra, who tricked her by assuming the shape of her husband. When the sage returned and discovered what had happened he took his revenge by causing Indra's body to become covered in yonis – female sexual organs! Naturally, Indra was somewhat put out by this and for many years he and his wife Indrayani repented at the auspicious *sangam* (river confluence) at Panauti.

Parvati, Shiva's consort, took pity upon Indrayani and turned her into the invisible river, Padmabati, but it was some years before Shiva decided to release Indra from his strange affliction. The god appeared in Panauti in the form of a giant lingam and when Indra bathed in the river, his yonis disappeared. Locals maintain that this miraculous Shiva lingam is the one enshrined in the Indreshwar Mahadev Temple.

stick sword, straw-brush comb and the gall bladder of an elephant!

Festivals & Events

Chariot Festival
RELIGIOUS

Held at the end of the monsoon each year (usually in September), when images of the gods from the town's various temples are drawn around the streets in wooden chariots, starting from the main square.

Magh Sankranti
RELIGIOUS

Every year during the Nepali month of Magh (usually January), pilgrims come to Panauti to bathe at the confluence of the two rivers to celebrate the end of the month of Poush, a dark time when religious ceremonies are forbidden. Every 12 years – next in 2022 – this is accompanied by a huge *mela* (country fair) attracting devotees and sadhus from all over Nepal.

Sleeping & Eating

There are options for homestays in the area, arranged through the tourist office or Ananda Café.

Ananda Café & Guest House
GUESTHOUSE $

(☑011-6211924; s/d Rs 300/500) Set in an authentic village house, with drying corn cobs in the windows, rooms here are creaky and very basic, but the building survived the quake with minor cracks. There's a fantastic outdoor garden with a table and chairs, surrounded by sprouting vegetables used for meals. It's opposite the Indreshwar Mahadev Temple.

Hotel Panauti
HOTEL $

(☑011-440055; r Rs 1000, without bathroom Rs 500; ☎) An above-average cheap hotel with a superior rooftop restaurant, set under a thatched canopy. It's close to the old town and saw only minor damage in the earthquake.

Information

Panauti Tourism Development Center

(☑9841360750, 011-440093; www.welcome-panauti.com; ⊙10.30am-4pm Sun-Fri) The tourist office at the start of the old town has brochures and very helpful staff, and can arrange homestays (half-board Rs 1200).

Getting There & Away

Buses run frequently between Panauti and Kathmandu's Ratna Park bus station (Rs 70, 1½ to two hours); the last bus leaves Panauti at 5.30pm. For Dhulikhel you'll have to change in Banepa (Rs 15, 20 minutes). It's also possible to walk to Panauti from Dhulikhel.

Around Panauti

Many of the small villages dotted around the valley have Newari-style temples and traditional brick architecture. Get hold of Nepa Maps' 1:50,000 *Around Kathmandu Valley* map and explore. One place to check out is the village of **Shrikandapur**, just off the Banepa–Panauti road. On the hilltop is a three-tiered Bhairab Temple with good views over the valley.

Sleeping

Balthali Resort
RESORT $$

(☑01-4108210; www.balthalivillageresort.com; s/d incl breakfast from US$57/64; ☎) At Balthali, 7km southeast of Panauti, the Balthali Resort can arrange all sorts of volunteering and cultural immersion activities and superb short (three- to six-day) lowland treks to the surrounding villages that are good for all the family. The resort, which has rather plain but sufficient rooms, is perched on the hilltop above Balthali village, with sweeping Himalayan views. One building here was badly damaged in the 2015 earthquake so check which rooms are operational before you visit.

BEYOND THE VALLEY

The following destinations lie outside the Kathmandu Valley on the roads north to Syabrubesi and Kodari, on the Tibetan border, but both routes saw severe damage in the 2015 earthquake. The roads were open at the time of research, but further landslides are a possibility so check that things are open before travelling on these routes. You can only cross into Tibet on an organised tour, but a tiny trickle of independent travellers come up this way on overnight trips to peer wistfully at the Tibetan border. This is also the birthplace of Nepal's adventure-sports industry.

Arniko Highway to Tibet

The Arniko Hwy provides Nepal's overland link with Tibet and China, but the road has a long history of being blocked by landslides, particularly during the monsoon months

ADVENTURE SPORTS ON THE ROAD TO TIBET

The Ultimate Bungee

The bungee at the Last Resort straddles a mighty 160m drop into the gorge of the Bhote Kosi and ranks as one of the world's 10 longest bungee jumps (higher than the highest bungee in New Zealand). The roars and squeals of free-falling tourists echo up and down the valley for miles.

As if the tallest bungee in South Asia wasn't enough, the fiendish minds at the resort have devised the 'swing', a stomach-loosening eight-second free fall, followed by a Tarzan-like swing and then three or four pendulum swings back up and then down the length of the gorge. We feel ill just writing about it.

At the time of writing, jumps were not operating because of landslides in the valley, but the bridge was undamaged by the 2015 earthquake and operations are expected to resume. Before the quake, the fee for a swing or bungee jump was €82 from Kathmandu (including return transport). The price includes whatever lunch your stomach can handle, wisely served up *after* the jump.

Canyoning

This exciting sport is a wild combination of rappelling/abseiling, climbing, sliding and swimming that has been pioneered in the canyons and waterfalls near the Last Resort and Borderlands.

Before the quake, both operators were offering two-day canyoning trips for about US$150, or two days of canyoning combined with a two-day Bhote Kosi rafting trip for US$355 (half this for one day's canyoning and one day's rafting). This involved a drive up from Kathmandu, lunch, and some basic abseiling training and practise on nearby cascades on day one. Day two involved a trip out to more exciting falls, with a maximum abseil of up to 45m.

At the time of writing, trips were suspended because of landslide damage but these are expected to resume once the terrain has stablised. Assuming this is the case, the key bits of kit required are a pair of closed-toe shoes that can get wet (these are better than sandals), hiking shoes for reaching the cascades, a water bottle and a bathing suit. A waterproof camera is a real bonus. Note that canyoning is not possible during the monsoon, and after November wetsuits are a must and are provided.

from May to August. A major landslide in 2014 created a large lake that blocked the highway north of the town of Khadu Chaur for more than a month, and repairs were still underway when the 2015 earthquake brought more devastation. At the time of writing, it was possible to travel as far as the Nepal–China border crossing, but some places along the route were only accessible by 4WD or walking part of the way. Assuming the route is open, this is a popular roadride for mountain bikers, though bus and truck traffic can be heavy.

Sunkoshi Beach Camp

There are several resorts and camps to stay at along the Arniko Hwy. Most are geared to daredevil travellers doing adrenaline sports their mothers would rather not know about. **Sunkoshi Beach Camp** (☑01-400023, Kathmandu 01-4381214; http://sunkoshibeach.com; full board per person camping/r US$35/45) is different and offers family-friendly rafting and kayaking. Accommodation is in simple tents and rooms, but some buildings were damaged in the 2015 earthquake, so check ahead to see what is available.

Borderlands Resort

Tucked away in a bend of the Bhote Kosi River, 97km from Kathmandu and 15km from Tibet, the superb **Borderlands Resort** (☑Kathmandu 01-4700894; www.borderland-resorts.com; full board s/d camping US$49/72, r s/d US$74/110, 2-day/1-night adventure packages per person from US$150) is one of Nepal's top adventure resorts. Adrenaline-charged activities include rafting, trekking and canyoning but you can also just kick back and enjoy the peace and quiet. The riverside resort is centred on an attractive bar and dining area, surrounded by thatch-roofed safari tents dotted around a lush tropical garden, but a number of buildings were damaged or destroyed in the earthquake so check ahead to see what is available.

Most people visit on a package that includes activities, accommodation, meals and transport from Kathmandu – drop in to the resort's Kathmandu office next to the Northfield Cafe in Thamel to discuss the options. Two days of canyoning/rafting cost US$150/100, including transportation, food and accommodation, and there are plenty of combo options. The resort supports several local schools.

The Last Resort

Thrill-seekers also drop off the Kodari road – quite literally – at **The Last Resort** (📞01-470124; www.thelastresort.com.np; accommodation with transport & meals €47, overnight stay with activities €102-180; 📶). Set in a gorgeous spot on a ridge above the raging Bhote Kosi River, 12km from the Tibetan border, the resort is reached by a vertiginous suspension bridge that acts as a launch pad for Nepal's only bungee jump.

Accommodation at the resort is in comfortable and private two- or four-person safari tents, set around a soaring stone-and-slate dining hall and bar, but earthquake damage was extensive and it will take some time for everything to be restored – check what is available before you visit. The resort took an active role in distributing aid to rural communities following the disaster.

Most people come on all-inclusive adventure packages – as well as swinging from a giant elastic band, you can combine rafting, trekking, mountain biking and canyoning. For less endorphin-motivated travellers, there are gas-heated showers, a plunge pool and a sauna and spa, making it slightly more luxurious than Borderlands and a great place to escape the city or relax en route to or from Tibet. Package rates include accommodation, meals and transport to and from Kathmandu – drop into the Kathmandu office near the Kathmandu Guest House for more information and to book.

Kodari

The road linking Kathmandu and Lhasa was constructed in the 1960s, but political wrangles and the ever-present risk of landslides prevented the Arniko Hwy from ever

BORDER CROSSING SURVIVAL

If you're part of a tour group (which you will have to be to enter Tibet), then crossing the border at Kodari in either direction is straightforward. Entering Nepal as an independent traveller is also a breeze. Entering Tibet as an independent traveller, however, is impossible.

The Nepali immigration post, open from 8am to 5pm, is just before the Friendship Bridge. Tourist visas are available on arrival for the standard rates. Payment is in US dollars or euros (cash only) and you need one passport photo.

There are official and unofficial money changers on both sides of the border who will change cash. There are also a couple of banks who will change US dollars and euros.

becoming a mainstream route between the two countries. Even today, traffic on the road from Barabise to Kodari is mainly limited to freight trucks and the occasional overland jeep tour. Kodari sustained damage in both the 25 April and 12 May 2015 earthquakes, and cross-border traffic was severely affected, though the border was open for business at the time of writing.

It is not possible for foreigners to enter Tibet here except as part of an organised tour with a group Chinese visa and Tibetan travel permit. However, a few people traipse up to the border to pose for photos on the **Friendship Bridge** that separates the two countries. From here, everything to the north is Tibet, though at this elevation there is no real difference in the landscape. The nearest Tibetan town is Khasa (Zhangmu), about 8km uphill from the border.

It's worth taking a 15-minute walk up the steps opposite the Friendship Restaurant to the damaged hilltop **Liping Gompa** for views over the Chinese side of the border, with its long lines of trucks snaking up the hill towards Khasa. The small main gompa is left at the trail junction; a charming meditation retreat and stupa are a 10-minute walk uphill to the right. Liping is the local name for Kodari.

🛏 Sleeping & Eating

There are several rough and ready places to stay, but unless you are stuck for transport,

WORTH A TRIP

NUWAKOT

Before the 2015 earthquake, the small village of Nuwakot (Nine Forts), just southeast of Trisuli Bazaar, had a deserved reputation as a miniature Shangri La, floating somewhere between the 17th and 21st centuries. Unfortunately, the town was hit badly by the earthquake. Many village houses collapsed and several historic temples and palaces were badly damaged. The owners of the Famous Farm, who played a major role in rescuing the town of Bandipur from dereliction, are spearheading the restoration effort, but it will take some time before this charming village is fully back on its feet.

The centrepiece of Nuwakot is its historic Durbar Sq, currently occupied by the army. The most striking monument is the **Saat Tale Durbar** (foreigner/SAARC & Chinese Rs 150/100; ⊙10.30am-4pm Tue-Sat, to 3pm Sun Feb-Oct, 10.30am-3pm daily Nov-Jan), a seven-storey fortress built in 1762 by Prithvi Narayan Shah as his family palace after taking the town. The town served as Nepal's capital until Shah conquered the Kathmandu Valley six years later, and this was also where the great king died in 1775. However, the building was badly damaged in the earthquake and was off-limits to visitors at the time of writing.

In the same courtyard, the **Ranga Mahal** (a Malla entertainment hall) came through the disaster intact, but the adjacent **Garad Ghar** (Tilganga Ghar) was so badly damaged that it may need to be rebuilt from the ground up. The **Taleju Temple** (p72) is Durbar Sq's most magnificent temple, but is not open to the public. Even for Hindus admission is restricted; they can only visit it briefly during the annual Dasain festival. The 35m-high temple was built in 1564 by Mahendra Malla. Taleju Bhawani was originally a goddess from the south of India, but she became the titular deity, or royal goddess, of the Malla kings in the 14th century.

Nearby is the golden-roofed **Bhairab Temple**, said to be one of Nepal's oldest, and used for animal sacrifices during the annual Sinduri Jatra festival. The temple is flanked by two pilgrim rest houses but the structure was badly damaged and reconstruction will take some time to complete.

There are several possible walks around Nuwakot, including to the new **viewpoint** tower at the Kalika Temple. Another popular destination is the nearby hilltop **Malika Temple**, but earthquake damage was extensive and repairs are ongoing.

It would be hard to imagine a more idyllic après-trek recovery spot than the wonderful **Famous Farm** (☑ Kathmandu 01-4700426; www.rural-heritage.com; s/d full board US$105/140; ☎), a charming lodge in a pair of artfully converted old village houses. Some rooms were damaged in the earthquake, but repairs are ongoing and owners were hoping to have all rooms restored before the end of 2015. The comfortable rooms are surrounded by a peaceful garden, with views over the Trisuli Valley, and the open kitchen serves up superb organic food (cookery lessons are possible). It's one of Nepal's most serene getaways and it's worth staying at least two nights.

There are three direct buses a day from Kathmandu (Rs 190, four hours) at 9am, 11am and 1pm, or you can get here via a steep 7km (1½-hour) uphill hike from Bidur, on the bus route to Trisuli Bazaar.

you are better off heading to either the Last Resort or Borderlands.

ⓘ Getting There & Away

The Arniko Hwy between Nepal and Tibet was declared fully open after earthquake repairs in August 2015. There are four daily buses to Kathmandu (Rs 400, 4½ hours), but the route is vulnerable to landslides and the trip can take much longer if road crews are doing repairs.

The Road to Langtang

A tarmac road heads northwest out of Kathmandu towards Dhunche, offering fantastic views of the Ganesh Himalaya as it gains the ridge at Kakani. Beyond Trisuli Bazaar, the road deteriorates and is travelled mainly by mountain bikers and trekkers headed for the Langtang region. However, Langtang was one of the areas hardest hit by the 2015 earthquake, with whole villages destroyed on the trekking route from Syabrubesi to Kyanjin Gompa. The village of Langtang, where just a handful of houses are still standing, has been described as Nepal's Ground Zero. Hundreds of people are still dependent on emergency aid and it will be some time before trekking can resume. Travellers should seek local advice before travelling beyond Syabrubesi.

At Trisuli Bazaar a reasonable road branches southwest to Dhading and Malekhu, on the Kathmandu–Pokhara (Prithvi) Hwy, offering a shortcut route to Bandipur and Pokhara and a possible bicycle ride taking in Kakani, Trisuli Bazaar, Dhading and Malekhu.

Kakani

Most of the towns around Kathmandu sit at the bottom of the valley – you have to travel to the valley rim to get decent views of the Himalaya. Set atop a ridge at 2073m, just off the road to Trisuli Bazaar, Kakani is the quieter, more peaceful cousin of Dhulikhel and Nagarkot. From a series of high points along the ridge, there are magnificent views of the Himalayan skyline stretching all the way from Annapurna to Everest, via Manaslu, Ganesh Himal, Gauri Shankar, Dorje Lekpa and Shishapangma. Part of the fun is getting here – the 24km road that winds uphill from Balaju makes for a challenging cycle ride and an even better motorcycle trip (but be careful of crazy truck and bus drivers). There was some earthquake damage here, but the hotels are open for business.

⊙ Sights

Apart from staring open-mouthed at the view, there's not much to do. The handsome colonial-era mansion at the start of the village was built as a summer villa for the British embassy, but it's closed to visitors.

🛏 Sleeping & Eating

View Himalaya Resort　　　　　HOTEL **$**
(☏ 01-6915706; viewhimalayaresort@gmail.com; s Rs 1500-2500, d Rs 2000-3000, s/d without bathroom & breakfast Rs 1200/1500) Easily the best option in town, this place has rooms for all tastes, is well-managed and the delightful restaurants and garden come with views to remember. Further rooms, with views over nothing very much at all, were under construction at the time of research, but this may be held back by postearthquake repairs.

Tara Gaon Resort Hotel　　　　HOTEL **$**
(☏ 01-6227750; s/d US$12/16) This old-school government hotel came through the quake with only minor damage and it offers good food and sublime views from its lawns. Although clean, the old-fashioned rooms are very tired, but some have mountain views from the bed. Come for lunch or a sunset beer.

❶ Getting There & Away

Kakani is 1½ hours from Kathmandu by bus or motorcycle but you'll burn plenty of calories powering up here by bicycle. It's uphill all the way, but there are numerous trout restaurants where you can stop for a break. It's a thrilling freewheel back to Kathmandu but watch for trucks or buses on the corners.

The road to Kakani turns off the Kathmandu–Trisuli Bazaar road just before the Kaulithana police checkpoint, at the crest of the hill. Frequent buses bound for Trisuli Bazaar can drop you at the junction (Rs 70, 1½ hours) and you can walk the 4km to Kakani in 45 minutes. There is also one direct bus a day to Kathmandu (Rs 70) at 8am from Kakani village centre.

Kathmandu to Pokhara

Best in Culture

➔ Gorkha Durbar (p199)

➔ Bandipur's Newari architecture (p201)

➔ Manakamana Temple (p199)

➔ Gorkha Museum (p201)

Best in Adventure

➔ Rafting on the Trisuli River (p198)

➔ Paragliding in Bandipur (p203)

➔ Rock climbing at Bimalnagar (p203)

➔ Caving in Siddha Gufa (p202)

➔ Canyoning near Mugling (p198)

Why Go?

Before you sprint from Kathmandu to Pokhara, consider the 206km of classic Middle Hills countryside that you will pass through en route. Despite widespread damage from the 2015 earthquake, the precipitous yet fertile countryside that flanks the Prithvi Hwy is still dotted with historic villages and temples, but many travellers see nothing of this area apart from the views flashing by the bus windows.

Better yet, forget the bus altogether and grab a paddle to join a white-water rafting trip that tumbles along the Trisuli River. With resorts, camping grounds and white, sandy beaches along the way, this is a good opportunity to wind down and laze in a hammock.

In addition to the river and the resorts there are some exceptional detours into the surrounding countryside. Historic and atmospheric towns such as Gorkha and Bandipur are bases for exploring the heartland of the country. Bandipur, in particular, is a picture-postcard village, lovingly restored and offering Europe-style ambience in the middle of gorgeous Nepali vistas, with no traffic, restaurant tables set up on flagstone streets and old-world Newari architecture.

When to Go

The best time to travel between Kathmandu and Pokhara is during the winter months of November to January, which will maximise your chances of catching sweeping Himalayan views during glorious mild sunny days. For those planning to tackle the Trisuli River on a rafting expedition, you should aim to visit from October to December or March to May for rollicking rapids and camping on sandy river beaches. Even more adventurous souls wanting to head up into the skies can arrange tandem paraglide flights in Bandipur between September and June.

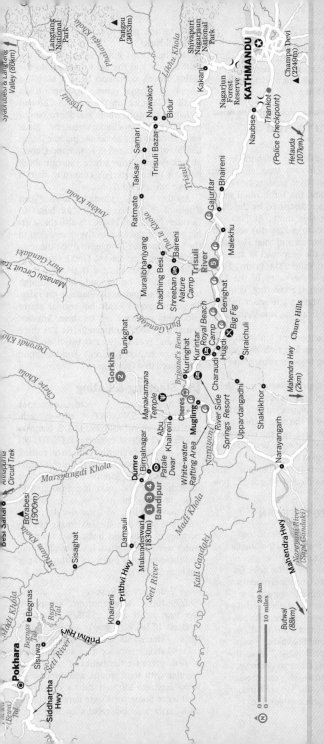

Kathmandu to Pokhara Highlights

1 Step back in time among the Newari houses of **Bandipur** (p201), on the ancient trade route to India.

2 Find moments of majesty among the earthquake damage in the former royal capital at **Gorkha** (p199).

3 Scramble into the gloom to see spectacular stalactites and stalagmites at **Siddha Gufa** (p202), Nepal's largest cave.

4 Trek to caves, viewpoints, villages and mountain shrines in the **Bandipur hills** (p202).

5 Raft down Nepal's most accessible white-water rafting trip, before chilling out at one of its beach camps.

ⓘ Getting There & Away

Several dozen tourist buses and countless public buses and microbuses run daily between Kathmandu and Pokhara, linking most of the important towns en route. The winding journey takes at least seven hours.

Kathmandu to Abu Khaireni

The main thoroughfare to Pokhara is the Prithvi Hwy, which runs west along the gorge of the Trisuli River, passing two turn-offs to the south and the Terai. You'll see a lot of village houses destroyed by the 2015 earthquake along this route. At Naubise, the Tribhuvan Hwy (aka Rajpath) veers off south and up to Daman and then Hetauda; for years this was the only road in and out of the Kathmandu Valley. The Prithvi Hwy continues to follow the valley of the Mahesh Khola to meet the twisting, contorting Trisuli River. Many white-water rafting companies set off from the small village of **Bhaireni**.

At the next big settlement, **Malekhu**, look out for its famous smoked river fish, which are sold from long wooden rakes along the roadside.

Following the highway west from Malekhu, you reach **Benighat**, where the roaring Buri Gandaki River merges with the Trisuli. The increased bore of the river creates some impressive rapids and rafting companies break for the night between Benighat and Charaudi, about 20km downstream.

About halfway between Benighat and Mugling, the tiny village of **Hugdi** is a pos-

sible starting point for treks to Chitwan National Park.

Marking the junction between the Prithvi Hwy and the main highway to the plains, there's no reason to visit **Mugling** except to change buses. However, 10km south of Mugling on the road to Chitwan is Jalbire Canyon, where **Hardcore Nepal** (☎9803010011; www.hardcorenepal.com; Bhagwati St, Thamel; 1-day, all-inclusive trip from Thamel US$75), which is based in Kathmandu, operates **canyoning** trips where you can abseil down a 100m waterfall, climaxing with a plunge into a natural pool.

Another dusty junction town, **Abu Khaireni** is the access point for buses to Gorkha (Rs 65, one hour). It's also the starting point for the four- to five-hour climb to the Manakamana Temple. To reach the temple, turn onto the road to Gorkha and turn right by the Manakamana Hotel, then cross the suspension bridge and climb through terraced fields and small villages to the ridge. There are several ATMs, but regular power cuts mean you can't rely on them. Any bus running between Kathmandu (Rs 350, three hours) and Pokhara (Rs 250, two hours) can drop you at Abu Khaireni. For Bandipur, you'll need to go via Dumre.

🛏 Sleeping & Eating

Royal Beach Camp   HOTEL, CAMPGROUND **$$**
(☎01-4700531, 9741010866; www.royalbeachnepal.com; tent incl full board US$25, bungalow US$35, r with/without bathroom US$75/60; ☒) While it caters primarily to those on rafting or kayaking packages, Royal Beach Camp's soft sandy beach, hammocks and outdoor restaurant-bar also make it a great spot to chill out along the river for a day or two. The new building with hotel-style rooms sustained some earthquake damage but the permanent tents and bungalows near the water were not affected. It's near Charaudi, and three hours by bus from Kathmandu or Pokhara (Rs 300).

River Side Springs Resort   LODGE **$$**
(☎056-540129; www.rsr.com.np; s/d permanent tents incl breakfast US$38/51, cabins incl breakfast US$68/86; ❉☒) Around 10km before Manakamana, this sophisticated, colonial-style resort occupies a prime piece of real estate on the banks of the Trisuli. Popular with tour groups, accommodation is in Japanese-inspired cabins or permanent tents. Some areas were damaged in the 2015 earthquake but repairs are underway.

TREKKING TO CHITWAN

From tiny Hugdi, it is possible to trek south into the homeland of the Chepang tribe, reaching Sauraha on the edge of Chitwan National Park in five days. En route, you can visit forts and mountain viewpoints, go birdwatching and get involved in a variety of cultural activities en route to Chitwan. However, the overnight stops along this route – Hattibang, Jyandala, Gadi and Shaktikhor – were all severely affected by the 2015 earthquake, with many buildings destroyed. Seek advice from trekking operators in Kathmandu or Pokhara to see if trekking is currently possible on this route.

WORTH A TRIP

MANAKAMANA

From the tiny hamlet of Cheres (6km before Mugling), an Austrian-engineered cable car soars up an almost impossibly steep hillside to the ancient **Manakamana Temple** (⊙ dawn-dusk), one of the most important temples in the Middle Hills. Hindus believe that the goddess Bhagwati, an incarnation of Parvati, has the power to grant wishes, and newlyweds flock here to pray for male children.

Built in the tiered pagoda style and basking in front of Himalayan views, the temple dates back to the 17th century, but the 2015 earthquake caused massive structural damage and a major reconstruction project is now underway. Despite the scaffolding, pilgrims still come here in hope of good fortune, sealing the deal by sacrificing a goat, chicken or pigeon in a gory pavilion behind the temple – there's even a dedicated carriage on the cable car for sacrificial goats! On Saturdays and other feast days, the peak days for ritual sacrifice, the paving stones run red with blood.

Part of the highlight of a visit here is getting to the temple in the awesome **Manakamana cable car** (adult/child return US$20/15, luggage per 1kg Rs 15; ⊙ 9am-noon & 1.30-5pm, from 8am Sat), which rises more than 1000m as it covers the 2.8km from the Prithvi Hwy to the Manakamana ridge; services were suspended at the time of writing but are expected to resume once the temple resumes full operations. Note that goats pay a reduced ticket price of Rs 220 but they only get a one-way ticket...

There are dozens of pilgrim hotels in the village surrounding the temple but many sustained earthquake damage. Repairs are underway at the popular **Sunrise Home** (☏ 064-460055; r from Rs 600), where spacious rooms come with fans and TVs. Prices double on Saturdays and religious holidays.

All buses that run between Kathmandu (Rs 230, three hours) and Pokhara (Rs 260, four hours) or Chitwan (Rs 180, 1½ hours) pass the turn-off to the Manakamana cable car (look for the red-brick archway). Otherwise if you want to walk to Manakamana, the trail starts at the village of Abu Khaireni, and takes around five hours.

The restaurant, beside an extravagant ring-shaped swimming pool (nonguests Rs 300) and a sandy beach, is a popular stop for day trippers.

Shreeban Nature Camp　　　LODGE $$
(☏ 01-4258427; www.shreeban.com.np; outside Dhading; 2-day/1-night package per person €40) This is a low-key operation, but with a program of trekking, birdwatching and cultural activities, lovers of the outdoors should consider stopping by. You'll need to make a reservation before visiting. Note that some buildings took some damage in the 2015 earthquake.

Big Fig　　　CAFE $
(www.himalayanencounters.com; mains Rs 100-450) Part of an attractive little roadside village, Big Fig is a good stopover for a bite and to stretch your legs. Its outside tables look over the Trisuli River, and a magnificent suspension bridge leads to a sandy beach at Himalayan Encounter's rafting camp, the Trisuli Centre. The village took some damage in the earthquake, but the cafe and camp are operating as normal.

Gorkha

☏ 064 / ELEV 1135M

About 24km north of Abu Khaireni, Gorkha is famous as the birthplace of Prithvi Narayan Shah, who unified the rival kingdoms of Nepal into a single cohesive nation in 1769, but the Shah dynasty ended with the ignominious 'retirement' of Gyanendra Shah in 2008. In 2015, Gorkha became notorious as the epicenter of the worst earthquake to hit Nepal in almost a century, but many buildings avoided damage and the town remains an important pilgrimage destination for Newars, who regard the Shahs as living incarnations of Vishnu.

The main attraction is the Gorkha Durbar, the former palace of the Shahs, which looks over Gorkha from a lofty ridge. There are also historic temples dotted around the old part of Gorkha.

◉ Sights

Gorkha Durbar　　　PALACE
(admission Rs 50, camera Rs 200; ⊙ 6am-6pm Feb-Oct, 7am-5pm Nov-Jan) Regarded by many as

Gorkha

Gorkha

◎ Sights

⊜ Sleeping

⊕ Transport

the crowning glory of Newari architecture, Gorkha Durbar is a fort, palace and temple all in one. Miraculously, the main structure survived the 2015 earthquake but damage was extensive. Repairs are underway and the site will remain closed until this work is complete. The temple-palace perches high above Gorkha on a knife-edge ridge, with superb views over the Trisuli Valley and magnificent panoramas of the soaring peaks of the Annapurna, Manaslu and Ganesh Himalaya.

As the birthplace of Prithvi Narayan Shah, the Durbar has huge significance for Nepalis. The great Shah was born here around 1723, when Gorkha was a minor feudal kingdom. Upon gaining the throne, Prithvi Narayan worked his way around the Kathmandu Valley, subduing rival kingdoms and creating an empire that extended far into India and Tibet.

The Durbar is an important religious site, so leather shoes and belts etc should be removed. Most pilgrims enter through the western gate, emerging on an open terrace in front of the exquisite **Kalika Temple**, a psychedelic 17th-century fantasy of peacocks, demons and serpents, carved into every available inch of timber. Only Brahmin priests and the king can enter the temple, but non-Hindus are permitted to observe from the terrace.

The east wing of the palace complex contains the former palace of Prithvi Narayan Shah, the **Dhuni Pati**, covered in elaborate woodcarvings, but this structure was severely damaged in the earthquake, as was the nearby **mausoleum of Guru Gorakhnath**, the reclusive saint who acted as a spiritual guide for the young Prithvi Narayan.

If you leave via the northern gate, you'll pass the former **Royal Guest House** – note the erotic roof struts and the crocodile carvings on the window frames.

Down from here is a vividly painted **Hanuman statue**, and a path leading to a large **chautara** (stone resting platform) on an exposed rocky bluff with awesome views and a set of carved stone footprints, attributed variously to Sita, Rama, Gorakhnath and Guru Padmasambhava.

To reach the Durbar, you can climb an exhausting stairway of 1500 stone steps, snaking up the hillside, or take a taxi (Rs 500 including waiting time) along the road winding up to a car park just below the northern gate.

Old Town   NEIGHBOURHOOD

There are more temples dotted around the Old Town, but all sustained earthquake damage. Immediately above the bus stand is the fortified **Ratna Temple**, the former Gorkha residence of King Gyanendra, which is now unoccupied. If you follow the road uphill, you'll reach the two-tiered temple dedicated to **Vishnu**; a squat white temple with the Nandi statue that's dedicated to **Mahadev** (Shiva); and a small, white shikhara (Indian-style temple with tall corn-cob-like spire) by the tank, which is sacred to **Ganesh**.

A little further along, the road opens onto a small square with a **miniature pagoda temple** dedicated to Bhimsen, the Newari god of commerce. Stone steps leading up to the Gorkha Durbar start next to the temple.

Gorkha Museum
MUSEUM

(foreigner/SAARC Rs 50/20, camera Rs 200/100; ☉10.30am-4.30pm, to 3.30pm Wed-Mon winter) Housed inside the grand Tallo Durbar, a Newari-style palace built in 1835, the museum's exhibits are limited, but it's interesting to see the finely carved woodwork up close. It's set in 3.5 hectares of garden, which are nice for a stroll. There was some earthquake damage to the complex.

🛏 Sleeping & Eating

Gorkha is off most travellers' itineraries and most of the accommodation is unexceptional, particularly the hotels immediately northwest of the bus stand.

Cafe Dé Gorkha Chautari
HOTEL $

(☑9841328431, 064-420399; dipeshjoshee@gmail.com; Satipipal; dm Rs 300, r with/without bathroom Rs 1500/800; @🛜) The earthquake caused some damage to this wonderful, clean budget hotel and restaurant, and it was closed for repairs at the time of writing, but the owners plan to reopen. The hotel is on the road to the Durbar, with stunning views towards Manaslu, and it is too far and steep to walk from the bus with a heavy pack. Host Flo suggests you make contact with him and he can advise on how much to pay a taxi from the bus stand (usually less than Rs 100).

Hotel Gorkha Bisauni
HOTEL $

(☑064-420107; gh_bisauni@hotmail.com; r Rs 800-1500, r without bathroom from Rs 500; 🛜) Set in landscaped grounds about 500m downhill from the bus stand, this acceptable lodge has a promising facade and lobby, but the neglected rooms are a let down. Some rooms have no windows, while others have bright balconies, so it's important to check a few. The restaurant serves a little bit of everything. The outdoor terrace is a wonderful spot at sunset. The old building was damaged in the earthquake and at the time of writing, rooms were only available in the new building.

New Hotel Gorkha Prince
GUESTHOUSE $

(Prince Hotel; ☑064-420030; r without bathroom Rs 500) There's no hot water and it's bare bones and glum, just like all the others near the bus stand. We single out New Hotel Gorkha Prince because it has a snooker table!

Gurkha Inn
HOTEL $$

(☑064-420206; bishnurg@yahoo.com; r US$30; @🛜) It's overpriced and could do with a few renovations (and new towels!), but we like the Gurkha Inn. This probably has something to do with the lovely, stepped garden facing the valley, the patio restaurant and the bright, airy (though well-worn) rooms. At the time of writing, the hotel was booked out by relief workers and some guests were staying in tents because of damage to the buildings.

❶ Getting There & Away

The noisy bus stand is right in the middle of town and there are ticket offices at either end of the stand.

There are daily microbuses to Pokhara (Rs 240, five hours) and numerous buses (Rs 300, five hours) and microbuses (Rs 380, four hours) to Kathmandu from 6.15am until 2.20pm. A single microbus leaves Gorkha at 7am for Bhairawa (Rs 430, six hours) or there are regular buses to Narayangarh (Rs 155, two hours) until noon.

Bandipur
☑065 / ELEV 1030M

Bandipur is a living museum of Newari culture, a beautifully preserved village crowning a lofty ridge above the highway stop of Dumre. Its winding lanes are lined with traditional Newari houses. Time seems to have stood still here, although it has taken a lot of effort to preserve the magic while developing the town as a destination. Despite its proximity to the epicenter of the 2015 earthquake, Bandipur escaped with only minor damage, though a number of village houses collapsed.

With impetus and substantial help from the owners of the adventure company Himalayan Encounters, the Bandipur Social Development Committee has put Bandipur firmly on the map. Derelict buildings have been reborn as cafes and lodges, and temples and civic buildings have been pulled back from the edge of ruin. With its glorious 18th-century architecture, absence of motorised vehicles and restaurant tables set out on the bazaar, it has a distinct European feel. Yet Bandipur remains very much a living community, bustling with farmers and traders going about their business alongside the tourists.

Bandipur was originally part of the Magar kingdom of Tanahun, ruled from nearby Palpa (Tansen), but Newari traders flooded in after the conquest of the valley by Prithvi Narayan Shah.

The town was an important stop on the India–Tibet trade route until it was bypassed by the Prithvi Hwy in the 1960s.

◉ Sights

Thani Mai Temple HINDU TEMPLE, VIEWPOINT

Perched atop Gurungche Hill, the main reason to climb up to Thani Mai is for its spectacular sunrise views. On a clear morning it has some of the most memorable 360-degree vistas in the country, with the Himalaya stretching out along the horizon, while the valley beneath is cloaked in a thick fog that resembles a white lake. The trail starts near the school at the southwest end of the bazaar, and is a steep 30-minute walk.

Siddha Gufa CAVE

(adult Rs 200) Making for a popular half-day trip, at 437m deep and 50m high, Siddha Gufa is said to be the largest cave in Nepal. Its cathedral-like chasm is full of twisted stalactites and stalagmites and hundreds of bats chirp and whistle overhead. Guides (Rs 400) are compulsory and await you at the cave's entrance. Flashlights are also available for hire.

Getting here is definitely a trek, taking 1½ hours one way (consider hiring a guide from Bandipur's tourist office). Follow the signs starting from the north end of the village, taking you along a dirt path running north over the edge of the ridge, turning right at the obvious junction. The stone path is slippery so mind your step. From here it's a 25-minute walk downhill to Bimalnagar for buses to Pokhara or Kathmandu.

Tundikhel VIEWPOINT

In centuries past, traders would gather on this man-made plateau to haggle for goods from India and Tibet before starting the long trek to Lhasa or the Indian plains. It was also a former parade ground for Gurkhas serving with the British Army. These days it's all about the views. At dawn and sunset, the clouds peel back to reveal a stunning panorama of Himalayan peaks that include Dhaulagiri (8167m), Machhapuchhare (6997m), Langtang Lirung (7246m), Manaslu (8162m) and Ganesh Himal (7406m).

Things can get rowdy here on weekends during the picnic season from October to November.

At the start of the Tundikhel are five enormous fig trees. In Nepali mythology, the different types of fig are symbols for different Hindu gods, and Vishnu, Brahma and Hanuman are all represented here.

Silkworm Farm FARM

(☑ 065-520104; admission by donation; ⊙ 10am-4pm Sun-Fri) An offbeat choice, a visit to Silkworm Farm takes you through the fascinating process of how silk is produced. The farm comprises orchards of mulberry plants, which are grown for worm food – the worms themselves are reared indoors, usually from August to December and March to May. But you can visit any time, with someone on hand to explain the process using jars of preserved displays. To get here follow the road past Green Hills View Lodge downhill for around 2km.

Bindebasini Temple HINDU TEMPLE

At the northeast end of the bazaar (which is the main shopping strip) this ornate, two-tiered temple is dedicated to Durga. Its ancient walls are covered in carvings and a priest opens the doors each evening. Facing the temple across the square is the **Padma library**, a striking 18th-century building with carved windows and beams.

Nearby, a set of stone steps runs off east to the small **Mahalaxmi Temple**, another centuries-old Newari-style temple.

Khadga Devi Temple HINDU TEMPLE

A wide flight of stone steps leads up the hillside to this barnlike temple, which enshrines the sword of Mukunda Sen, the 16th-century king of Palpa (Tansen). Allegedly a gift from Shiva, the blade is revered as a symbol of shakti (consort or female energy) and once a year during Dasain it gets a taste of sacrificial blood.

🏃 Activities

It's easy to pass several peaceful days exploring the countryside around Bandipur. There are dramatic Himalayan backdrops to a gorgeous patchwork of terraced rice and mustard fields and small orchards. Most guesthouses can arrange walking guides for Rs 500 to Rs 1000 a day.

Along with Siddha Gufa, one of the most popular walks is to the Magar village of **Ramkot**. The scenic four-hour walk takes you to this charming and friendly little village where there are some traditional round houses. There's nowhere to buy food or wa-

Bandipur

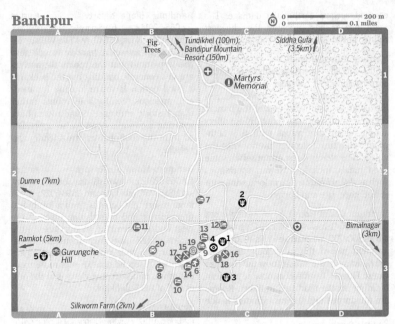

ter here, so pack a lunch, which you can enjoy under the two banyan trees atop the hill, with a great Himalayan panorama. Enquire at the Old Inn Bandipur about homestays in this village.

Blue Sky Paragliding PARAGLIDING
(☑ 065-520091; www.blue-sky-paragliding.com; 30min/1hr Rs 8000/13,000) Blue Sky (based in Pokhara) is the pioneer of paragliding at Bandipur. Make enquiries directly with the company or at the small general store in Bandipur with the Blue Sky paragliding sign. It launches from just above the village and the views are stunning.

Hardcore Nepal ROCK CLIMBING, CAVING
(☑ 9803010011; www.hardcorenepal.com; 2-day all-inclusive rock climbing & caving US$140, 3-day packages from US$200) Keen climbers can tackle the 40m limestone wall along the highway in Bimalnagar, a couple of kilometres east of Dumre. Hardcore Nepal can also arrange caving in Siddha Gufa, involving abseiling 70m through the ceiling entrance. Departures from Thamel, Pokhara and Bandipur.

🛌 Sleeping

There's no shortage of accommodation in Bandipur to suit all budgets and the hotels escaped serious earthquake damage. The main bazaar has probably the cheapest rooms, but most come with rock-hard beds.

Heritage Guest House GUESTHOUSE $

(☑065-520015; heritageguesthouse60@gmail. com; r with/without bathroom Rs 700/500; 🛜) Housed in a majestic, crumbling old residence at the southwest end of the bazaar, the welcoming Heritage Guest House offers simple, clean, airy rooms with tiny bathrooms and tiny balconies overlooking the village. The attached restaurant serves some good meals, including Newari specialities such as *jhwai khattee* (warm local wine with millet, ghee, rice and honey).

Bandipur Guest House GUESTHOUSE $

(☑065-520041; asutoshpradhan2047@gmail.com; s/d Rs 500/700, mountain-view r Rs 1000) Management moved this guesthouse from the old building in the bazaar (now the Heritage Guest House) to this comfortable modern building on the road to Tundikhel. Rooms are unadorned and the gas cylinders inside the bathrooms may provide hot water but do little for the ambience.

Pradhan Family Guest House GUESTHOUSE $

(☑065-520106; s/d Rs 300/400) A cheapie right on the main bazaar with an atmospheric street-side cafe. The rooms in this traditional building are tiny and basic and the hot water comes in a bucket.

Khadagmai Hillway Cafe GUESTHOUSE $

(☑065-520120; r Rs 1000, mains Rs 190-320) This old building is just around the corner from the main square. There are six rooms of various shapes and sizes, all with attached hot-water bathrooms. Much of the character of the building has been retained, including low door lintels, and the cafe downstairs has good Newari food, but lacks the sunny disposition of the cafes in the main street.

Hotel Depche LODGE $$

(☑9841226971; www.hoteldepche.com.np; s/d incl breakfast US$30/60) A gem on the edge of Bandipur, this attractive mudbrick cottage is tucked away among the fields a 300m walk from the bazaar. While the rooms themselves lack character (they're typical modern rooms with good bathrooms), the location, candle-lit courtyard and rooftop are the real appeal of this place.

Bandipur Village Resort HOTEL $$

(☑065-520143; bandipurvillageresort@gmail. com; r incl breakfast US$40; 🛜) The Village Resort has an attractive historic facade near the jeep stand, but the rooms themselves are in a concrete building out the back. It's a good option if you're looking for modern, spacious, comfortable rooms rather than historic ambience. Some rooms have amazing mountain views – also appreciated from the rooftop. Staff are friendly and helpful.

Bandipur Mountain Resort HOTEL $$

(☑065-520125; www.islandjungleresort.com.np; s/d US$50/54, with full board US$84/122; 🛜) A large resort that benefits from a lovely setting, surrounded by swishing pines at the west end of Tundikhel. Rooms are a little dated but all have great mountain views. Popular with tour groups; reservations are essential. A second annexe with more modern rooms and sweeping views is at the other end of the Tundikhel.

★Old Inn Bandipur LODGE $$$

(☑065-520110; www.theoldinnbandipur.com; s/d/tr US$105/140/180, without bathroom US$80/110/145; 🛜) Operated by Himalayan Encounters, this beautifully restored mansion offers atmospheric rooms decorated with Buddhist and Newari art, set around a terracotta terrace facing the mountains. Take your pick from rooms with views of mountains or those looking out to captivating streetscapes. Some rooms are on the cosy side (and watch your head!), but newer rooms are spacious with private bathrooms and balconies. Breakfast included.

Look out for the new enterprise by the Old Inn team, Panche Baja, a lovingly restored building at the northeast end of the square. When finished it will provide more exceptional heritage accommodation.

Gaun Ghar HOTEL $$$

(☑065-520129; www.gaunghar.com; s/d full board US$225/300) A renovated historic home, Gaun Ghar is almost a carbon copy of the Old Inn Bandipur (its next-door neighbour) but it's more expensive. The building is very atmospheric and beds are fitted with electric blankets for chilly winter nights. It's also one of the best places to try classic Newari food, with many of its ingredients being organic.

Eating

Ke Garne Café
NEPALI, INTERNATIONAL $

(snacks Rs 50-300) The name of this cosy cafe (part of the Old Inn enterprise) means 'What to do?', so here are some suggestions for you: sip tea, munch on Nepali snacks, play giant chess on the cafe's terrace, or head upstairs to the cosy Monkey's Flunky bar.

Old House Cafe
INTERNATIONAL $

(☏ 9846082371; oldhousecafe01@gmail.com; thali Rs 120-250, r Rs 400-500; 🛜) A delightful eatery on the bazaar with good momos, pizza and delicious Newari *khaja* (*thali* or set meals). It also has a few basic, clean rooms upstairs with separate cold showers.

Hill's Heaven
NEPALI $

(meals Rs 100-380; 🛜) On the main strip, Hill's Heaven is popular for its cheap beer and free wi-fi.

ⓘ Information

The **Bandipur Tourist Information Counter** (www.bandipurtourism.com; ⊙10am-5pm Sun-Fri) has brochures and basic information on the area. Guides can be arranged for around Rs 1000 for a half day.

There's no ATM in Bandipur; the closest is at Dumre, a 30-minute drive away. You can get online at **Cyber Café** (per hour Rs 40) in the bazaar.

ⓘ Getting There & Away

The road to Bandipur branches off the Prithvi Hwy about 2km west of Dumre; buses (Rs 30) and taxis/jeeps (Rs 100) depart by the highway junction. The first jeep is at 7am and the last at 4pm, departing every 45 minutes or when full. Hotels can organise a car and driver to Pokhara for Rs 3500.

Dumre

About 17km west of Abu Khaireni, Dumre is yet another dusty highway town, and is visited solely as a connecting place for Bandipur (bus Rs 30, taxi or jeep Rs 100 per person, Rs 500 for the whole taxi, one hour). It's also a handy spot from which to head to Besi Sahar, the starting point for the Annapurna Circuit Trek. There are several ATMs here.

There are regular buses and microbuses to Kathmandu (Rs 300) and Pokhara (Rs 150). From the main junction, local buses and minivans also run regularly to Besi Sahar (Rs 150 by bus, Rs 200 by microbus, three hours).

Pokhara

☎ 061 / POP 265,000 / ELEV 884M

Best Places to Eat

➜ Moondance Restaurant (p222)

➜ Potala Tibetan Restaurant (p222)

➜ Caffe Concerto (p222)

➜ Krishna's Kitchen (p223)

➜ Metro (p219)

Best Places to Stay

➜ Temple Tree Resort & Spa (p217)

➜ Nanohana Lodge (p216)

➜ Hotel Nirvana (p216)

➜ Dhaulagiri Lodge (p232)

➜ Begnas Coffee House (p230)

Why Go?

Far from the earthquake epicenter and almost unaffected by the disaster, Pokhara ticks all the right boxes, with spectacular scenery, adventure activities, and accommodation and food choices galore. Whether you've returned from a three-week trek or endured a bus trip from hell, Lakeside Pokhara is the perfect place to recharge your batteries. The scene is a chilled-out version of Thamel, stretching along the shore of a tranquil lake with bobbing paddle boats. From the lake, and possibly even from your hotel bed, you can enjoy a clear view of the snowcapped mountains, just 20 or so kilometres away.

There's much more to Pokhara than its laid-back charm. It also boasts a booming adventure sports industry; it is arguably the best paragliding venue on the globe and is surrounded by white-water rivers. There's a fascinating museum dedicated to the world-famous Gurkha soldier. And last but not least, it's the gateway to the world-famous treks in and around the Annapurna Range and beyond.

When to Go
Pokhara

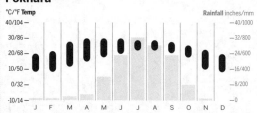

Oct–Mar Ideal time for clear mountain views and fewer rainy days.	28 Dec–1 Jan Enjoy food and cultural shows at the Pokhara Street festival.	Apr Tourists and locals alike celebrate the Nepali New Year.

Climate

Pokhara sits about 400m lower than Kathmandu, so the autumn and winter temperatures are generally much more comfortable. Even in winter you can get away with a T-shirt during the daytime and you'll only need a sweater or jacket for evenings and early mornings. From June to September the skies open and the mountains spend a lot of time behind blankets of cloud.

Dangers & Annoyances

There have been infrequent reports of solo walkers being mugged trekking up to the World Peace Pagoda and around Sarangkot, as well as reports of attacks on solo women near trance parties. Clearly there's a safety-in-numbers message for both activities.

POKHARA

◉ Sights

Forming a spectacular backdrop to Pokhara is the dramatic Annapurna Massif. Most prominent is the emblematic Mt Machhapuchhare, whose triangular mass looms large over the town, and remains the only virgin mountain in Nepal set aside as forbidden to be climbed.

From west to east, the peaks are Annapurna South (7219m), Hiunchuli (6441m), Annapurna I (8091m), Machhapuchhare (6997m), Annapurna III (7555m), Annapurna IV (7525m) and Annapurna II (7937m).

A word of warning: the mountains can occasionally disappear behind cloud for several days, particularly during the monsoon season.

Phewa Tal   LAKE

Phewa Tal is the travellers' focal point in Pokhara, and is the second-largest lake in Nepal. In contrast to the gaudy tourist development of Lakeside, the steep southwestern shore is densely forested and alive with birdlife. The lush Rani Ban, or Queen's Forest, bestows an emerald hue to the lake, and on a clear day, the Annapurna mountains are perfectly reflected on its mirror surface.

You can take to the lake in one of the brightly painted *doongas* (boats) available for rent at Lakeside. Many people walk or cycle around the lakeshore – the trek up to the World Peace Pagoda affords breathtaking views over the tal (lake) to the mountains beyond.

POKHARA & THE 2015 EARTHQUAKE

Despite being just 73km from the epicenter of the earthquake on 25 April 2015, Pokhara escaped with just a few cracked walls, while Kathmandu, actually 4km further from the epicenter, was devastated. Seismologists credit Pokhara's good fortune to the ground beneath its feet – specifically, a bed of solid rock, rather than seismically vulnerable clay.

The Annapurna range also escaped serious earthquake damage and all of the trekking routes around Pokhara are fully open to trekkers, but the area is suffering a significant drop in visitor numbers because of the disaster. Local people are desperate to get the message out that Pokhara – along with its trekking routes, mountain viewpoints and rafting rivers – is open for business.

Varahi Mandir   HINDU TEMPLE

(Map p220) Pokhara's most famous Hindu temple, the two-tiered pagoda-style Varahi Mandir stands on a small island in Phewa Tal, near the Ratna Mandir (Royal Palace). Founded in the 18th century, the temple is dedicated to Vishnu in his boar incarnation. It's been extensively renovated over the years and is inhabited by a loft of cooing pigeons. Rowboats to the temple (per person return Rs 50) leave from near the city bus stand in Lakeside.

Old Pokhara   HISTORIC BUILDINGS

For a glimpse of what Pokhara was like before the traffic, chaos and tourist restaurants besieged the erstwhile village, head out to the old town, north of the bustling Mahendra Pul. The best way to explore is on foot.

From the Nepal Telecom building at Mahendra Pul, head north along Tersapati, passing a number of religious shops selling Hindu and Buddhist paraphernalia. At the intersection with Nala Mukh, check out the Newari houses with decorative brickwork and ornately carved wooden windows.

Continue north on Bhairab Tole to reach the small two-tiered Bhimsen Temple (Map p210), a 200-year-old shrine to the Newari god of trade and commerce, decorated with

Pokhara Highlights

1 Wake up to a spectacular mountain panorama at **Sarangkot** (p228) as the rising sun illuminates the Himalaya.

2 Paddle a colourful boat out to the middle of **Phewa Tal** (p207) to reveal a magical reflection of Machhapuchhare and its surrounding peaks.

3 Climb a forest trail to the dazzling white **World Peace Pagoda** (p213) for a bird's-eye view of Pokhara.

4 Celebrate your trekking triumph with a delicious meal and a cold beer at one of Lakeside's **restaurants** (p219).

5 Take to the sky and ride

the thermals like an eagle while **paragliding** (p213).

6 Learn the survival story of Tibetan refugees and listen to chanting monks at **Jangchub Choeling Gompa** (p212).

7 Escape the Lakeside crowds and explore the coffee farms and quiet shores of **Begnas Tal** (p230).

POKHARA IN...

Two Days

Start your day browsing through the **handicraft shops** and **cafes** of Lakeside before renting a colourful boat for a leisurely paddle on **Phewa Tal** (p207). After lunch on the strip climb up to the sublime **World Peace Pagoda** (p213) for more incredible views. On day two get up early to watch the sunrise light up the Himalaya at **Sarangkot** (p228). On the return to Lakeside stop off in **Old Pokhara** (p207) and visit the **Gurkha Museum** (p209).

Four Days

Hire a bike and ride north around the lake, before visiting a **Tibetan refugee settlement**. Drop in on **Devi's Falls** (p209) and muster the courage to have a go at **tandem paragliding** or on an ultralight flight with a Himalayan backdrop. Get some background research on your trek at the **International Mountain Museum** (p209) and vary it up by wriggling through the **Bat Cave** (p230).

One Week

Consider a short trek to **Poon Hill**, **Ghandruk** or **Panchase Danda**. Head out to **Begnas Tal** to spend a peaceful night and explore the villages on the northern shore of **Phewa Tal** (p207).

erotic carvings. The surrounding square is full of shops selling baskets and ceramics.

About 200m further north is a small hill, topped by the ancient **Bindhya Basini Temple** (Map p210). Founded in the 17th century, the temple is sacred to Durga, the warlike incarnation of Parvati, worshipped here in the form of a saligram (see p268).

International Mountain Museum MUSEUM
(Map p210; ☑ 061-460742; www.international-mountainmuseum.org; foreigner/SAARC Rs 400/200; ☻ 9am-5pm) This expansive museum is devoted to the mountains of Nepal, the mountaineers who climbed them and the people who call them home. Inside, you can see original gear from many of the first Himalayan ascents, as well as displays on the history, culture, geology, and flora and fauna of the Himalaya.

Once you've been inspired by the climbers of the past, head outside where there's a 21m climbing wall and a 9.5m-high climbable model of Mt Manaslu. A taxi here from Lakeside will cost you around Rs 700 return.

Gurkha Museum MUSEUM
(Map p210; ☑ 061-441762; foreigner/SAARC Rs 200/100, camera Rs 20; ☻ 8am-4.30pm) Located just north of Mahendra Pul, near the KI Singh Bridge, the Gurkha Museum celebrates the achievements of the renowned Gurkha regiments. Accompanied by sound

effects, it covers Gurkha history from the 19th-century Indian Uprising, through two World Wars to current-day disputes and peace-keeping missions, with a fascinating display on Gurkhas who have been awarded the Victoria Cross medal.

Pokhara Regional Museum MUSEUM
(Map p210; ☑ 061-520413; foreigner/SAARC Rs 100/50, camera Rs 50/30; ☻ 10am-5pm, closed Tue) North of the bus station on the road to Mahendra Pul, this little museum is devoted to the history and culture of the Pokhara Valley, including the mystical shamanic beliefs of the original inhabitants of the valley.

Seti River Gorge PARK
(Map p210; park adult Rs 25; ☻ park 7am-6pm) The roaring Seti River passes right through Pokhara, but you won't see it unless you go looking. The river has carved a deep, narrow chasm through the middle of town, turning the water milky white in the process. The best place to catch a glimpse of the Seti River is the **park** just north of Old Pokhara near the Gurkha Museum.

Devi's Falls WATERFALL
(Map p210; adult Rs 30; ☻ 6am-6pm) Also known as Patale Chhango, this waterfall marks the point where the Pardi Khola stream vanishes underground. When the stream is at full bore after monsoon rains,

Greater Pokhara

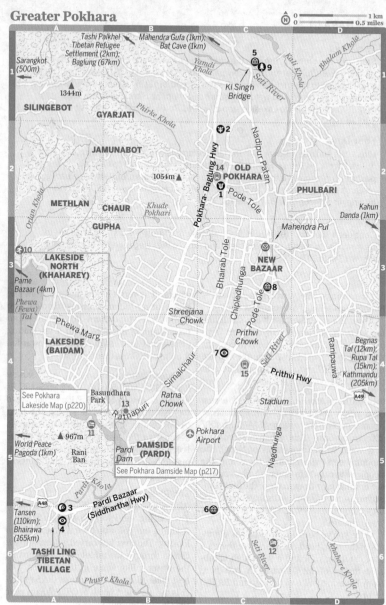

See Pokhara Lakeside Map (p220)

See Pokhara Damside Map (p217)

the sound of the water plunging over the falls is deafening.

According to one of the many local legends, the name is a corruption of David's Falls, a reference to a Swiss visitor who tumbled into the sinkhole and drowned, taking his girlfriend with him. The falls are about 2km southwest of the airport on the road to Butwal, just before the Tashi Ling Tibetan camp.

POKHARA SIGHTS

Gupteshwor Mahadev Cave CAVE
(Map p210; foreigner/SAARC Rs 100/50; ☺6am-7pm) Across the road from Devi's Falls, this venerated cave contains a huge stalagmite worshipped as a Shiva lingam. The ticket allows you to clamber through a tunnel behind the shrine, emerging in a damp cavern adjacent to the thundering waters of Devi's Falls.

🏃 Activities

There are some fascinating short treks in the lower foothills around Pokhara (see p290) with epic views of the Annapurna Himalaya.

Stand Up Paddle Nepal WATER SPORTS
(Map p217; ☎9813066656; Damside; per hour/day Rs 700/3500) It had to happen – stand-up paddle-boarding on Phewa Tal. Prices include all equipment, including bouyancy vest, and even some personal instructions to get you going. Put in at Damside park, a short stroll from the shop.

Zip-Flyer Nepal ADVENTURE SPORTS
(Map p220; ☎061-466399; www.highgroundnepal.com; per ride US$68) This awesome zipline launches from Sarangkot and drops 600m over 1.8km achieving a speed of 120km/h. It is claimed to be the highest, longest and fastest zipline in the world. You can also bungee jump from a 70m tower for the same

price, which includes pick-up and drop-off from Lakeside. Weight and age restrictions apply.

Boating
Heading out onto the calm waters of Phewa Tal is the perfect way to unwind and gain a spectacular reflective mountain view. Colourful wooden *doongas* are available for rent at several boat stations, including near the city bus stand and next to the Fewa Hotel. Rates start at Rs 400 per hour with a boatman, or Rs 350/800 per hour/day if you paddle yourself. You can also rent aluminium pedalos (Rs 410 per hour) and sailboats (Rs 510 per hour, or Rs 710 per hour for lessons). Weak swimmers should rent a lifejacket at Rs 20. Another popular way to explore Phewa Tal is by kayak; see Kayaking & Rafting for details.

Cycling & Mountain Biking
Cycling is a great way to get around Pokhara, whether you are visiting the museums, braving the bazaar or just cruising Lakeside. Indian mountain bikes are available from dozens of places on the strip in Lakeside and cost around Rs 100/300 per hour/day.

Contact any of the Lakeside travel agents for details of mountain-biking trips in the hills around Pokhara (see p311 for more information).

Chain 'n' Gear Mountain Bikes CYCLING
(Map p220; ☎061-463696; Gaurighat Marg; per day from US$10) To hire quality Trek and Giant mountain bikes, and/or to organise short or extended mountain-bike rides, drop in to see the experts at Chain 'n' Gear in Pokhara's Lakeside.

Horse Riding
Travel agents in Pokhara offer pony treks to various viewpoints around town, including Sarangkot, Kahun Danda and the World Peace Pagoda. Half-day trips (Rs 3000) stick to the lakeshore; you'll need a full day (Rs 5000) to reach the viewpoints.

Kayaking & Rafting
Pokhara is a great place to organise rafting trips, particularly trips down the Kali Gandaki and Seti Rivers (see p318 for more information). Half-day rafting/kayak trips start at US$50/65 per person. All-inclusive overnight rafting trips start at US$80 per person and trips can be as long as 10 days.

Kayak clinics (US$65 per day) are held on the Seti River, and scenic drifts down the

POKHARA ACTIVITIES

TIBETAN REFUGEE SETTLEMENTS

Many of the Tibetan refugees who hawk souvenirs in Lakeside live in the Tibetan refugee settlements within and around Pokhara.

The largest settlement close to Pokhara is **Tashi Palkhel**, about 5km northwest of town at Hyangia, on the road to Baglung. With prayer flags flapping in the breeze in the rocky valley, it genuinely feels like you're in Tibet. The colourful **Jangchub Choeling Gompa** in the middle of the village is home to around 200 monks. Try to time your visit in the afternoon to experience the rumbling of monks chanting and horns blowing during the prayer session (held 3.30pm to 5pm).

Masked dances are held here in January/February as part of the annual Losar (Tibetan New Year) celebrations. To reach the gompa you have to run the gauntlet past an arcade of very persistent handicraft vendors. A 'tashi delek' (a greeting in Tibetan) will win many smiles here. Nearby is a chörten (Tibetan Buddhist stupa) piled with carved mani stones bearing Buddhist mantras, and a carpet-weaving centre, where you can see all stages of the process and buy the finished article. If you'd like to spend the night, **Friend's Garden** (☏ 9806535582; r without bathroom Rs 250) has spartan rooms and a restaurant serving Tibetan food. A few other hole-in-the-wall restaurants, such as **Rita's** (no English sign), serve excellent *thukpa* (Tibetan noodle soup) and momos (dumplings). You can reach Tashi Palkhel by bike, bus, taxi or foot.

The folks from Tashi Palkhel have recently opened a Tibetan Mini Market (p224) in Lakeside with craft shops and restaurants.

About 3km south of Lakeside, on the road to Butwal and near Devi's Falls, is the smaller settlement of **Tashi Ling**. Near the entrance of the camp is a small open space where handicraft purveyors set up stalls and entice visitors to part with cash. There's also a small carpet factory and showroom. A smaller settlement, **Paljorling** (Map p210), resides in the city centre near Prithvi Chowk.

Narayani River to Chitwan National Park can be arranged.

Paddle Nepal
RAFTING

(Map p220; ☏ 061-465730; www.paddlenepal.com) As well as several white-water rafting options, there are beginner kayak clinics and combined canyoning/rafting expeditions at this Pokhara-based operation.

Rapidrunner Expeditions
RAFTING

(Map p220; ☏ 061-462024; www.rapidrunnerexpeditions.com; 2-day family rafting adult/child from US$95/70) Offers kayak clinics and 'ducky trips' (gentle paddles in small rafts), in addition to serious white-water rafting trips. Pokhara based.

Kayak Shack
KAYAKING

(Map p220; 1/3/6 hours Rs 200/500/1000; ⊙ 7am-6pm) The Kayak Shack is a lakeshore branch of Rapidrunner where you can hire a kayak for one, three or six hours. The price includes a life vest.

Adrenaline Rush Nepal
RAFTING

(Map p220; ☏ 061-466663; www.adrenalinenepal.com) Big white-water rafting trips are sup-

plemented by river 'tubing' and canyoning; add-on treks can also be organised.

Ganesh Kayak Shop
KAYAKING

(Map p220; ☏ 061-462657; www.ganeshkayak.com; kayaks per hour/half-day/day Rs 200/500/650, 4-day kayaking & camping safaris US$225) Ganesh Kayak Shop, beside the Moondance Restaurant, rents out kayaks for paddling in Phewa Tal. Fishing safaris (best from March to April and October to November) can also be arranged here.

Massage

Trekkers with aching muscles can get relief from experienced masseurs, including the barbers, in Lakeside.

Seeing Hands Nepal
MASSAGE

(Map p220; ☏ 061-464478; www.seeinghandsnepal.org; 45 min/1hr massage Rs 1500/1800; ⊙ 10am-5.30pm) Seeing Hands Nepal has professionally trained blind Nepali therapists who, with a heightened sense of perception and touch, provide excellent Swedish-style massages. Run by volunteers, Seeing Hands does excellent work in supporting Nepali blind people in a society where they're often marginalised.

Jiva Cafe & Spa   MASSAGE
(Map p220; ☑061-465379; massage Rs 2000-3000) Jiva does excellent massages, from feet to head, and including a special trekker's massage. You can also get a facial or a body scrub, and the cafe serves snacks and healthy smoothies.

Meditation & Yoga
Pokhara is an ideal setting to contemplate the nature of the universe, and there are several centres offering to help you on your way.

Himalayan Yogini   YOGA
(Map p220; ☑061-463710; www.himalayanyogini.com; 1½hr Rs 500; ⊙7.30-9.30am & 4.30-6pm) Program includes daily meditation and Hatha yoga classes. One- to five-day courses also available.

Ganden Yiga Chopen
Meditation Centre   MEDITATION
(Pokhara Buddhist Meditation Centre; Map p220; ☑061-462923; www.pokharabuddhistcentre.com;

3-day course incl room & meals Rs 6500) This serene retreat holds three-day meditation and yoga courses that start every Friday at 2.45pm. There are also daily sessions; enquire at the centre.

Sadhana Yoga   YOGA
(Map p210; ☑061-694041; www.sadhana-asanga-yoga.com; from US$22) This retreat is secluded in the village of Sedi Bagar, 2.5km northwest of Lakeside. One- to 21-day courses in Hatha yoga include tuition, steam and mud baths, accommodation and meals. Enquire about yoga treks.

Paragliding
Soaring silently on the thermals among gliding Himalayan raptors against a backdrop of the snowcapped Annapurna is a once-in-a-lifetime experience. Operators usually offer both 20-minute (Rs 8500) and 45-minute (Rs 11,500) flights.

Paragliding operates during suitable weather year-round, including during the monsoon. Numerous operators have started up in recent years; the ones recommended

TREK TO THE WORLD PEACE PAGODA

Balanced on a narrow ridge high above Phewa Tal, the brilliant-white **World Peace Pagoda** was constructed by Buddhist monks from the Japanese Nipponzan Myohoji organisation to promote world peace. In addition to the access road, there are three walking paths up to the pagoda and several small cafes for snacks and drinks once you arrive.

The Direct Route (One Hour)
The most obvious route up to the pagoda begins on the south bank of Phewa Tal, behind the Lychee Garden Resort at Anadu. Boatmen charge around Rs 500/900 one-way/return to the trailhead from Lakeside and the path leads straight up the hillside on cut stone steps. Ignore the right-hand fork by the small temple and continue uphill through woodland to reach the pagoda. You can either continue on to Pokhara via the scenic route (described below), catch a bus or taxi, or walk/boat back the way you came.

The Scenic Route (Two Hours)
A more interesting route to the pagoda begins near the footbridge over the Pardi Khola, just south of the Phewa Dam. After crossing the bridge, the trail skirts the edge of paddy fields before turning uphill into the forest near a small brick temple. From here the trail climbs for about 2km through gorgeous forest and follows the ridge west. When you reach a clearing with several ruined stone houses, turn left and climb straight uphill to reach the flat, open area in front of the pagoda. An alternative starting point for this route is Devi's Falls – a small but obvious trail crosses the paddy fields behind the falls and runs up to meet the main path at the bottom of the forest.

The Easy Route (20 Minutes)
For views without the fuss, take a taxi (Rs 500) or local bus (Rs 20) from the public bus stand to the car park south of the pagoda. The rough access road to the Pagoda leaves the Siddhartha highway just south of town. A steep trail of stairs leads up from the car park to the entrance to the pagoda. Instead of returning by car, you can walk down to the lake and catch a boat to Lakeside.

POKHARA ACTIVITIES

PHEWA TAL CIRCUIT

If you get an early start, it's possible to walk right around the shore of Phewa Tal, beginning on the path to the World Peace Pagoda. Starting from the pagoda, continue along the ridge to the village of Lukunswara and take the right fork where the path divides. Once you reach Pumdi, ask around for the path down to Margi on the edge of the lake. From Margi, you can either cut across the marshes over a series of log bridges or continue around the edge of the valley to the suspension bridge at Pame Bazaar, where a dirt road continues along the northern shore to Pokhara. If you run out of energy, local buses pass by every hour or so.

here are experienced companies that have stood the test of time.

Blue Sky Paragliding   GLIDING
(Map p220; ☑ 061-464737; www.blue-sky -paragliding.com) With many years of paragliding experience in Nepal, Blue Sky offers tandem flights, as well as pilot courses, multiday paratrekking, and parahawking. It also operates from Bandipur (p203).

Frontiers Paragliding   ADVENTURE SPORTS
(Map p220; ☑ 061-466044; www.himalayan-paragliding.com) One of the pioneering companies, Frontiers offers pilot courses and multi-day tours in addition to the popular tandem flights.

Sunrise Paragliding   ADVENTURE SPORTS
(Mapp220;☑061-463174;www.sunrise-paragliding. com) Sunrise offers courses and tours, and has stood the test of time.

Swimming

The cool waters of Phewa Tal may beckon on a hot day, but there's a fair bit of pollution, so if you do swim it's advisable that you hire a boatman to take you out to the centre of the lake. Keep a watch for currents and don't get too close to the dam in Damside.

A few upmarket hotels let nonguests swim in their pool for a fee, including Hotel Barahi (Rs 625), Fish Tail Lodge (Rs 650) and Temple Tree Resort & Spa (Rs 650).

Walking

Even if you don't have the energy or perhaps the inclination to attempt the Annapurna Circuit, there are plenty of short treks in the hills around Pokhara. If you just want to stretch your legs and escape the crowds, stroll along the north shore of Phewa Tal. A paved walkway runs west along the shoreline to the village of Pame Bazaar, where you can pick up a bus back to Pokhara or continue on a circuit of Phewa Tal.

Another hike is the three-hour trip to the viewpoint at **Kahun Danda** (1560m) on the east side of the Seti River. There's a viewing tower on the crest of the hill, built over the ruins of an 18th-century fort. The easiest trail to follow begins near the Manipal Teaching Hospital in Phulbari – ask for directions at the base of the hill.

One of the most popular walks around Pokhara is the trip to the World Peace Pagoda (p213).

Ultralight Flights

On a clear day you can't miss the buzzing ultralights flying above Pokhara, providing their customers with unrivalled mountain views.

Avia Club Nepal   SCENIC FLIGHTS
(Map p220; ☑ 061-463338; www.aviaclubnepal. com; ultralight flights 15/30/60/90 minutes €70/125/198/290, paragliding 25 minutes Rs 8500) Avia Club offers exhilarating ultralight flights around the Pokhara Valley. In 15 minutes you can buzz around the World Peace Pagoda and lakeshore, but you'll need more time to get up above Sarangkot for the full Himalayan panorama. Avia also offers paragliding and ultralight plus paragliding packages.

Pokhara Ultralight   SCENIC FLIGHTS
(Map p220; ☑061-466880; www.flypokhara. com; ultralight flights 15/30/60/90 minutes €70/125/198/285) Pokhara Ultralight offers a range of flights from a quick buzz above Pokhara to more exhilarating flights towards the mountains.

☞ Tours

Travel agents in Pokhara can arrange local tours and activities, and it's easy to rent a bike and do things under your own steam.

Tibetan Encounter   GUIDED TOUR
(Mapp220;☑061-466486;www.tibetan-encounter. com; half-/full-day tour US$60/80) This is a great way to experience Pokhara's refugee

settlements and learn about Tibetan culture, traditional foods and medicine, and the contemporary life of Tibetan refugees in Nepal. Tibetan Encounter can also arrange long-term homestays and overnight tours to Jampaling Tibetan Settlement.

🎎 Festivals & Events

Pokhara Street Festival STREET FESTIVAL
Lakeside comes alive with a festive spirit during this annual event (28 December to 1 January), when the main strip closes to traffic as restaurants set up tables on the road. Visitors cram the street to enjoy food, parades, performances and carnival rides.

Phewa Festival NEW YEAR
Celebrations for the Nepali New Year, in April, organised by the Pokhara hotel association to promote tourism.

Bagh Jatra NEWARI
Every August, Pokhara's Newari community celebrates this three-day festival that recalls the slaying of a deadly marauding tiger.

Losar BUDDHIST
(Tibetan New Year) Tibetan Buddhists hold celebrations and masked dances at gompas around Pokhara in January/February.

🛏 Sleeping

Most people stay in Lakeside, a strip of hotels, travel and trekking agents, restaurants and souvenir shops. As the main traveller centre, Lakeside is packed with hotels, ranging from dirt cheap to three-star luxury.

People looking for more peace and quiet tend to head to the north end of the strip or go south to Damside. All hotels will hold your luggage if you plan on trekking.

Most will add a 10% service charge, while midrange and top-end hotels load the bill with 13% VAT (value-added tax) on top of the combined tariff and service charge. It's always worth asking for a discount (the VAT can magically disappear). During the summer low season most places offer discounts of between 20% and 30%.

Central Lakeside

Hotel Travel Inn HOTEL $
(Map p220; ☎061-462631; www.hoteltravelin. com; s/d incl breakfast & taxes US$10/22, r with aircon US$35-50; ✳️📶) Although catering for all budgets, even the cheapest rooms are spotless here. It's worth the step up to deluxe for the comfy beds and bathtubs. The owner here claims tourists want three things: cleanliness, friendliness and quietness, and this modern hotel delivers on all fronts. It's the UN's choice of hotel when it's in town.

Lake City Hotel HOTEL $
(Map p220; ☎061-464240; www.lakecityhotel. com; dm Rs 250, s/d Rs 700/900, without bathroom Rs 440/550, ste Rs 2500; ✳️📶) Rooms at Lake City are arranged around a courtyard – much like a motel – and are surprisingly comfortable. Some rooms sport well-appointed, stone-tiled bathrooms. There's also a rooftop restaurant with a fireplace and lake views. Its recycling bins and refillable water supply (Rs 10 per bottle) set an excellent example.

Hotel Peace Plaza HOTEL $
(Map p220; ☎061-461505; www.hotelpeaceplaza. com; r standard/deluxe/ste US$15/40/50; ✳️📶) This centrally located, modern four-storey building comfortably straddles budget and midrange. Rooms, many with balconies and lake views, boast soft beds, a desk, a bar

---

PARAHAWKING

Created by British falconer Scott Mason, **parahawking** (www.parahawking.com; tandem flights £130) is unique to Pokhara and is a must for thrill seekers and bird-of-prey lovers. Parahawking involves a combination of falconry and paragliding where raptors are trained to lead gliders to the best thermal currents. As a reward for their guidance, a whistle is blown to call in the bird to land on your outstretched gloved arm for you to feed it in mid air! The parahawking birds (Egyptian vultures) and other raptors are taken in as injured or orphaned birds unable to survive in the wild, and you can see them at their roost at the **Himalayan Raptor Centre** at Maya Devi Village (p218), where falconry lessons are available. Tandem parahawking trips, which include falconry lessons and background information are organised through Blue Sky Paragliding (p214). A portion of the price helps fund vulture conservation projects in Nepal.

fridge and satellite LED TV. Some also have a bathtub. Downstairs is a bright lake-view restaurant plus a street-front cafe.

Little Tibetan Guest House   GUESTHOUSE $

(Map p220; ☑461898; littletibgh@yahoo.com; s/d from US$9/18; ☎) This Tibetan-run lodge east of Camping (Hallan) Chowk is rightly popular for its calm and relaxed atmosphere. Rooms are elegantly decorated with Tibetan wall hangings and bedspreads. Balconies overlook a serene garden and while there's no restaurant, bed and breakfast packages are available.

Mountain Villa   HOTEL $

(Map p220; ☑461954; prabindwa@gmail.com; 183 Fewa Marg; s/d Rs 880/1100, r with AC Rs 2500; ✴☎) Mountain Villa's 22 rooms stretch back from busy Fewa Marg on a long block of land with a narrow garden running the length of the property. The rooms at the back are quiet and private. Rooms vary but most have cool and clean stone-tiled floors and Western bathrooms. The recommended Japanese restaurant AoZoRa (p222) is downstairs.

Butterfly Lodge   HOTEL $$

(Map p220; ☑061-461892; www.butterfly-lodge.org; s/d standard US$20/30, deluxe US$30/40, ste US$50/60; ✴☎) Even the standard rooms at Butterfly Lodge are big and super clean, and all rooms are designated nonsmoking. Outside there's a lovely lawn with banana lounges. Staff are very helpful and some of the profits go to the Butterfly Foundation supporting local children. Breakfast is only an extra Rs 350.

Kotee Home Hotel   HOTEL $$

(Map p220; ☑061-464008; www.koteehomehotel.com; s/d incl breakfast US$25/30) Centrally located on the Lakeside strip, Kotee is a comfortable midrange choice with a range of different-sized rooms. All boast air con, LED TVs and quality bathrooms; you should be able to get a discount on one of the smaller rooms when the hotel isn't busy. The in-house Red Tomato restaurant has a bar and international menu.

Hotel Fewa   HOTEL $$

(Map p220; ☑061-463151; www.hotelfewa.com; s/d US$15/25, s/d cottages US$35/45; ☎) Hotel Fewa gets marks for its rustic stone cottages set right on the lake and its pleasant lakeshore restaurant. A long-time favourite, the cottages with lofts make for a memorable stay, and include a fireplace and Buddhist motifs. The rooms in the back building, however, lack the same charm.

Hotel Barahi   HOTEL $$$

(Map p220; ☑061-460617; www.barahi.com; s/d standard US$57/79, deluxe US$115/145; ✴@☎✉) The stone-clad Hotel Barahi features very smart, well-appointed rooms with small balconies. It has 24-hour room service, a sparkling pool and an excellent restaurant. There's also a nightly cultural show. Many rooms boast incredible mountain vistas, but the standard rooms are quite tiny.

🛏 Lakeside East

Lakeside East (Multhok) is separated from Central Lakeside by the Royal Palace, but it doesn't take long to walk between the two.

★ Nanohana Lodge   HOTEL $

(Map p220; ☑061-464478; www.nanohanalodge.com; r US$10-20, with AC US$30-35; ☎) This recently renovated hotel is spotless and well managed. Each level has a balcony with table and chairs and many of the rooms have wonderful Annapurna views. The aircon rooms feature plush mattresses, but all rooms are comfortable. It's in a quiet location yet still convenient to the Lakeside restaurants and is associated with the nearby Seeing Hands blind massage clinic.

Sacred Valley Inn   HOTEL $

(Map p220; ☑061-461792; www.sacredvalleyinn.com; r with/without bathroom US$15/10, upstairs US$25-30; ☎) Set in a shady garden across from the Royal Palace, Sacred Valley is a long-established traveller favourite (book early!). All the rooms are well maintained and those upstairs have gleaming marble floors and windows on two sides, allowing in plenty of light. Attached is the pleasant Monsoon Café.

★ Hotel Nirvana   HOTEL $

(Map p220; ☑061-463332; hotelnirvana@hotmail.com; r ground/1st/2nd fl Rs 1000/1500/2000; ✴) Almost invisible behind a giant bougainvillea hedge, Hotel Nirvana is a much-loved, fastidiously clean place with a prim garden and spacious rooms with colourful bedspreads and curtains. Hotel management are welcoming and helpful. Rooms get pricier as you climb the stairs.

Peace Eye Guest House   HOTEL $

(Map p220; ☑061-461699; www.peaceeye-guesthouse.com; s/d Rs 600/800, without bathroom Rs 450/600, deluxe r Rs 1200; ☎) Established in 1977, the chilled-out Peace Eye retains all

Pokhara Damside

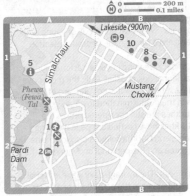

POKHARA SLEEPING

the qualities that attracted the original visitors to Pokhara 30 years ago. Inexpensive, laid-back and friendly, its brightly decorated rooms are well-kept and clean. Budget rooms are smallish but the others are spacious. It also has a vegetarian restaurant and small German bakery.

Gauri Shankar Guest House HOTEL $
(Map p220; 061-462422; www.gaurishankar.com; dm Rs 200, s Rs 600-800, d Rs 750-1500;) Calm, quiet and reasonably priced, Gauri Shankar has cosy, bright rooms set in a secluded garden of pebbles and plants. The better and pricier rooms are upstairs. It has a garden cafe for breakfasts, a rooftop terrace, a TV common room and library; its atmosphere is social and friendly.

Hotel Yeti HOTEL $
(Map p220; 061-462768; www.hotelyeti.com.np; r US$13-30;) Draped in vines that flower bright red or yellow (depending on the time of year), Hotel Yeti's striking facade makes an excellent first impression. Rooms vary in size and price but all are clean and bright. The manager here is very helpful with onward travel arrangements.

Lake View Resort HOTEL $$
(Map p220; 061-461477; www.pokharahotels.com; s/d standard US$25/30, deluxe US$55/65, huts US$90/100;) Lake View Resort is one of Lakeside's oldest resorts, and as such it offers old-fashioned spacious rooms set in a neat garden. The air-con deluxe rooms and huts are great value considering the quality of the beds and other furnishings. The respected restaurant with lake views and a

nightly culture show are a bonus. Big discounts available in summer.

Blue Planet Lodge HOTEL $$
(Map p220; 061-465706; www.blueplanetlodge.com; r incl breakfast €25-50;) Blue Planet Lodge has a range of rooms including seven 'chakra' rooms energised with the colours of the rainbow, special stones and singing bowls. There is also a meditation and yoga hall with a Nepali yoga master. The peaceful garden sports a colourful Ganesh. The rates shown here include all taxes and there are discounts for long stays and singles.

**★ Temple Tree
Resort & Spa** LUXURY HOTEL $$$
(Map p220; 061-465819; www.templetreenepal.com; s/d from US$160/180;) Tricked-out Temple Tree raises the bar in Lakeside. Plenty of timber and slate and straw-coloured render add delightful earthy tones. The standard rooms aren't huge but are exceptionally comfortable and most sport a bathtub and private balcony. There are two restaurants, a health spa, and a bar beside the lovely pool.

Fish Tail Lodge LUXURY HOTEL $$$
(Map p210; 061-465201; www.fishtail-lodge.com.np; r from US$170;) Reached by a rope-drawn pontoon from Basundhara Park, Fish Tail is charmingly understated, with heritage rooms housed in low

BRAVEST OF THE BRAVE

It might seem like an odd leftover from the days of empire, but the British army maintains a recruiting centre on the outskirts of Pokhara. Every year hundreds of young men from across Nepal come to Pokhara to put themselves through the rigorous selection process to become a Gurkha soldier.

Prospective recruits must perform a series of backbreaking physical tasks, including a 5km uphill run carrying 25kg of rocks in a traditional doko basket. Only the most physically fit and mentally dedicated individuals make it through – it is not unheard of for recruits to keep on running with broken bones in their determination to get selected.

Identified by their curved khukuri knives, Gurkhas are still considered one of the toughest fighting forces in the world. British Gurkhas have carried out peacekeeping missions in Afghanistan, Bosnia and Sierra Leone, and Gurkha soldiers also form elite units of the Indian Army, the Singapore Police Force and the personal bodyguard of the sultan of Brunei.

The primary motivation for most recruits is money. The average daily wage in Nepal is little more than one British pound, but Gurkha soldiers earn the equivalent of a Western wage, with a commission lasting up to 16 years and a British Army pension for life, plus the option of settling in Britain on retirement.

slate-roofed bungalows in a lush garden. Rooms 16, 17 and 18 have excellent lake and mountain views but you'll need to book well in advance. Discounts are usually available. Profits here are donated to a trust that helps cardiac patients in Nepal.

Lakeside North

As you head north from Camping (Hallan) Chowk towards Khaharey and beyond, it's clear that this is where Lakeside's main expansion is occurring. New hotels and restaurants are appearing where once there were rice paddies.

Banana Garden Lodge GUESTHOUSE $

(Map p220; ☑061-464901; www.bananagardenlodge.com; s/d without bathroom Rs 300/400) Banana Garden Lodge is one of a cluster of super friendly, budget guesthouses that are owned and managed by the same genial family. The clean guestrooms at Banana Garden share four solar-heated showers. Adjacent to Banana Garden among the terraced fields are the similar Palm Garden and Lemon Tree, as well as the slightly more upmarket Green Peace Hotel.

Hotel Tropicana HOTEL $

(Map p220; ☑061-462118; www.hoteltropicana.com.np; r US$11-22; ☎) This time-honoured hotel of more than 20 years has large, spotless rooms with great lake and mountain views from the upper floors. Rooms on the 3rd floor (US$17) are the best value. The

swing chair upstairs is a lovely spot to read a book, looking out to the lake.

Freedom Café & Bar HUT $

(Map p220; ☑061-464135; freedomcafe@hotmail.com; r without bathroom front/back Rs 600/800; ☎) The huts here are very basic and tiny – one bed, one window, one desk – with no attached bathrooms. The lake-front huts sport a hammock; however, here it's all about the communal areas, chilled-out alcoves where folks strum a guitar, curl up with a book and cool down with a drink. There's a pool table and live music most evenings.

Chhetri Sisters Guest House HOTEL $$

(Map p220; ☑061-462912, 061-462066; www.3sistersadventuretrek.com; s/d incl breakfast US$20/30, without bathroom US$15/25; ☎) Much smarter than the surrounding hotels, this tidy pink-brick lodge is owned by the same folk as 3 Sisters Adventure Trekking (p381). Rooms are tastefully decorated and the location is peaceful, but the hotel is very popular so booking well ahead is advised. Pick-up from the airport or bus station is offered with prior notice.

Maya Devi Village HUT $$

(Map p228; ☑9806647917; www.mayadevivillage.com; Khapaudi; r US$65) Run by the friendly folks from Blue Sky and Frontiers Paragliding, this ultrarelaxed spot at the north end of the lake is on the road to Pame village. Accommodation is in tricked-out, thatched, round huts with a balcony, bathroom and second storey. Also here is a recommended restaurant-bar (p223) and several well-trained raptors (p215).

Damside & Elsewhere

You don't have to stay in Lakeside. There are budget hotels and luxury lodges outside the centre, across the lake, by the Seti River and high in the hills east of town. The area around Phewa Dam is officially known as Pardi, but most people call it Damside. It was one of the first areas to be developed for tourists, but it feels very quiet these days, with loads of local flavour.

Park Anadu Restaurant & Lodge   HOTEL $
(Map p228; ☎9846025557; parkanandu@gmail.com; Anandu; r with/without bathroom Rs 500/1500; ☏) Perched high on Phewa Tal's western shore, the secluded Park Anadu has unbeatable views with rooms opening up to a perfect lake vista framed by a Himalayan backdrop. Situated a 20-minute boat trip from Lakeside (free transit back and forth), the simple rooms share a common bathroom and an inexpensive restaurant.

Hotel Mona Lisa   HOTEL $$
(Map p217; ☎061-463863; www.hotelmonalisa.com.np; Damside; s/d US$20/30, with air-con US$40/50; ❄) The best and brightest of several similar places in this area, Hotel Mona Lisa tempts Japanese visitors with brightly coloured rooms and lounges with low *kotatsu* tables and cushions. Rooms are spotless and the best have balconies with mountain and lake views.

Tiger Mountain Pokhara Lodge   HOTEL $$$
(Map p228; ☎061-691887, in Kathmandu 01-4426427; www.tigermountainpokhara.com; cottages per person US$250; ❄@☏❄) ✈ This lodge is set on a lofty ridge about 10km east of Pokhara, and the owners have made a real effort to make it blend into the surroundings. Rooms are contained in stylish stone bungalows and there's an amazing mountain-view swimming pool. Rates include meals and transfers to/from Pokhara. Tiger Mountain prides itself on its independently audited sustainable-tourism initiatives.

Fulbari Resort   LUXURY HOTEL $$$
(Map p210; ☎061-523451; www.fulbari.com; r from US$200, ste from US$500; ❄@☏❄) Dramatically sited on the bank of the Seti River Gorge south of Pokhara, the Fulbari is a vast, five-star resort hotel. It's far enough from town for uninterrupted mountain views, and beyond the stunning lobby you'll find every conceivable luxury, including a huge pool, health spa, tennis courts and golf club.

Eating

Lakeside has numerous restaurants, bars and cafes serving up Western, Nepali, Indian and Chinese food to hungry travellers and trekkers. Restaurants are generally open from 7am to 10pm.

Central Lakeside

★ Metro   CREPES $
(Map p220; crepes Rs 150-350; ☺7am-9pm; ☏) Metro is teeny tiny creperie secreted down a sidestreet. The crêpes are deliriously delicious: lemon sugar, cinnamon sugar, apple and caramel cream etc. Also on the menu are savoury crêpes, espresso coffee, ice cream and slushies.

Pokhara Thakali Kitchen   NEPALI $
(Map p220; thali veg Rs 250-290, non-veg Rs290-420; ☺11am-9pm) This cosy, atmospheric restaurant specialises in regional Thakali cuisine presented as *thalis*, each with three curries – choose veg or non-veg, standard or special. Snacks include exotic offerings such as Mustang potatoes, buckwheat finger chips, and fried strips of goat meat.

China Town   CHINESE $
(Map p220; mains Rs 170-470; ☺11am-10pm; ☏) With red-tassled lanterns and paintings of rotund children riding goldfish, this is a bona fide Chinatown experience. The Chinese chef creates authentic Cantonese and spicy Sichuan dishes with a delicious selection of duck and pork dishes. We recommend the spicy *mapo dofu* and *gong bao* chicken.

Boomerang Restaurant & German Bakery   INTERNATIONAL $
(Map p220; mains Rs 170-400; ☺7am-10pm; ☏) The best of the 'garden and dinner show' places, Boomerang has a large, shady garden with fresh flowers on each table. The food is very good, as is its Lakeside setting. There's a cultural show nightly from 7pm. The roadside German bakery is also recommended.

POKHARA EATING

Pokhara Lakeside

POKHARA

0 _____ 200 m
0 _____ 0.06 miles

LAKESIDE NORTH (KHAHAREY)

Sadhana Yoga (500m);
Maya Devi Village (2.5km);
Krishna's Kitchen (3km);
Pame Bazaar (4km)

Khahare Baidan

7

1

24

21

9

5

31

Phewa Tal

29

46

Camping Chowk

53

3

14 8

Phewa Marg

36

34

61

70

37

11

LAKESIDE (BAIDAM)

Sailing Boat Ghat

50

18

23

27 13

67

62

45

16

72

57 75

12

58

65

49

42

CENTRAL LAKESIDE (PALLO PATAN)

30

33

59

69

43

20

68

64

15

47

Phewa Ghat

10

51

26

63

22

2

39

LAKESIDE EAST (MULTHOK)

25

71

40 19

60

28

55

6

48 73 44

54

56

41

Ratnapuri

32

38

35

66 4

52

17 74

Rani Ban

Pokhara Lakeside

Maya Pub & Restaurant INTERNATIONAL $
(Map p220; mains Rs 140-430; ⊙7am-10pm)
Serving up travellers' fare since 1989, the atmospheric Maya is still going strong, with an almost identical sister restaurant nearby. The walls are decorated with colourful images of Hindu deities, and the comfortable wicker furniture makes this a great spot to people-watch with a pizza, pasta, momos, or Nepali thali and a cold beer.

POKHARA EATING

Byanjan
INTERNATIONAL $

(Map p220; mains Rs 325-495) This eatery, associated with the upmarket Hotel Barahi, uses chilled white-and-blue decor, raw rocks and subtle lighting to achieve a modern-global air of sophistication. The menu is wide-ranging with Chinese, Thai, Indian and Nepali dishes. If the low tables look uncomfortable, head upstairs or out the back into the garden.

★Moondance Restaurant
INTERNATIONAL $$

(Map p220; www.moondancepokhara.com; mains Rs 240-1400; ☺7am-10.30pm; ☎) The much-loved Moondance is a Lakeside institution and deservedly so. Quality food, good service and a roaring open fire all contribute to the popularity of this tastefully decorated restaurant. Its menu features salads, pizzas, imported steaks and excellent Indian and Thai curries. For dessert, the lemon meringue pie is legendary.

AoZoRa
JAPANESE $$

(Map p220; ☑061-461707; Phewa Marg; mains Rs 280-450; ☺8am-9pm; ☎) AoZoRa is a bamboo-lined 'hole-in-the-wall' with a classic Japanese menu featuring *donburi*, ramen, sushi and several set menus, such as chicken teriyaki served with rice, miso and pickle. The Japanese-speaking staff welcome you with a glass of *mugi* (roasted barley tea), and point out the seasonal specials board. There's seating out the back if the front tables are full.

Mike's Restaurant
INTERNATIONAL $

(Map p220; mains Rs 250-450; ☺7am-9pm; ☎) With a lakeside setting under the spreading boughs of a pipal tree, Mike's makes a delightful spot for a hearty breakfast, lunch or dinner. Among the wide range of dishes are several Mexican options, such as quesadillas and tostadas. The lakeside tables are a great place to settle in with an evening drink.

Koto
JAPANESE $$

(Map p220; ☑061-463414; set meals Rs 430-880; ☺11.30am-3pm & 6-9pm) Though it never seems busy, Koto is the real deal, and its authentic Japanese food is prepared and presented with great care. The set meals that include miso soup and rice are the way to go. The barbecued teriyaki beef is highly recommended.

New Everest Steak House
STEAK $$

(Map p220; ☑061-466828; Phewa Marg; mains Rs 400-1400; ☺9am-10pm) Carnivores flock to this old-fashioned steakhouse for 5cm-thick hunks of freshly grilled beef flown in from West Bengal. Take your pick from an impressive selection of 34 versions of steak sauces, including the popular 'Trekkers steak with veges and chips' and the 'Really red wine sauce'. Other meats such as fish and chicken are available.

Lakeside East

★Potala Tibetan Restaurant
TIBETAN $

(Map p220; Tibetan Mini Market; mains Rs 130-205, momos Rs 95-270; ☺8am-9pm) The family-run Potala Tibetan has some of the best momos in town (veg, buffalo, chicken, cheese) and is located upstairs at the front of the Tibetan Mini Market. You can also slurp your way through *thukpa, tingmo* and *sha bak ley* and other noodley offerings along with *tungba* (Tibetan millet beer).

Marwadi Restaurant
INDIAN $

(Map p220; ☑9856027322; mains Rs 150-280; ☺7.30am-10pm; ☎☑) Marwadi is a skinny, technicolour, pure-veg restaurant with inexpensive North and South Indian cuisine, including *dosa*, uttapam and *idli*. The food here is a bit more authentic (ie with spices and chilli) than the multicuisine eateries that dominate Lakeside. We like the chequered tablecloths and attentive staff, and the *tawa* and tandoori breads to mop up the curries.

★Caffe Concerto
ITALIAN $$

(Map p220; ☑061-463529; mains Rs 350-800; ☺7am-10.30pm; ☎) Rustic ambience, an open fireplace and jazz on the stereo add to the bistro atmosphere of this cosy Italian pizzeria. The breakfasts are big and tasty, while the thin-crust pizzas come in two sizes and 30 varieties and are the best in town. The pasta dishes and salads are authentic, wine is available by the glass or bottle, and the espresso and gelato are superb. *Bellissimo*!

Natssul
KOREAN $$

(Map p220; mains Rs 420-700; ☺noon-10pm; ☎) After a welcoming drink of *bonicha* (tea), Natssul serves up lip-smacking Korean barbecue, *kimchi*, and plenty of pork and chicken dishes. Try the *Samgyeopsal* – sliced pork belly, pan-fried at the table to be dipped sesame or red soy paste and wrapped in fresh lettuce. Vegetarians can feast on *bibimbap* (rice coated in sesame oil with mixed vegetables and fried egg).

Lakeside North

Things get decidedly simpler as you go north of Camping (Hallan) Chowk, but there are plenty of cosy and rustic restaurants with a sleepy charm, and an unexpected gem of a Thai restaurant.

Godfather's Pizzeria
ITALIAN $

(Map p220; 061-466501; pizzas Rs 200-450; 8am-11pm;) The aromas from the open kitchen and wood-fired oven entice many passers by to drop in for delicious veg and non-veg pizzas. Many locals vote this lively establishment as the best pizza in town – and there's a lot of competition these days, so that's saying something. Pastas and salads also grace the menu.

★ Krishna's Kitchen
THAI $$

(Map p228; 9846232501; www.krishnaskitchen. com; Kapaudi; mains Rs 305-555; 10am-11pm;) Krishna's is a superb Thai garden restaurant nestling at the north end of Phewa Tal. Homemade tofu, organic herbs and vegetables, and professional presentation mean this would be a great Thai restaurant anywhere. To match the excellence of the food there are gourmet teas and a quality wine list. Walk, cycle or taxi the 3km from Lakeside. The restaurant can organise a taxi back to your hotel.

Maya Devi Village
CAFE $$

(Map p228; 9806647917; www.mayadevivillage. com; Kapaudi; sandwiches Rs 300, Sun BBQ Rs 850; 7am-6pm;) Out along the road to Pame Bazaar, and beside the paragliding landing zone, this small resort is known for its collection of rescued birds of prey and its parahawking owners. It is also a great place to relax with a meal and a drink and learn about the birds. Try the BLT sandwiches or join the social Sunday-afternoon all-you-can-eat barbecues.

Damside

In Damside there are a cluster of *sekuwa* or *jhir* restaurants where succulent morsels of chicken, pork or buffalo are barbecued before your eyes and served up with a fiery sauce. The dish goes down a treat with a cold beer on a warm afternoon. Look for the smoky barbecues and the throng of locals' motorbikes parked out front (afternoons only).

German Bakery
BAKERY $

(Map p217; cakes Rs 40-210; 7am-9pm) This is one of the original 'German bakeries', which supplies cafes from Pokhara to Jomsom. Come here for breakfasts, decent coffee plus sweet cheesecake, Danish pastries, and apple pie or crumble.

Don't Pass Me By
INTERNATIONAL $

(Map p217; mains Rs 110-290) The pick of the Damside eateries is this cosy restaurant that sits smack on the edge of the lake. It has decent if not exciting travellers' fare of Italian, Indian and Continental dishes, but the outdoor seating among colourful flowers by the lake is peaceful and delightful.

Drinking & Nightlife

Olive Café
CAFE

(Map p220; espressos from Rs 150;) This sophisticated yet relaxing cafe is brought to you by the folks from Moondance Restaurant. With Italian or local espresso, Baskin Robbins ice cream and its very own mischievously sweet Machhapuchhare ice-cream cake, it makes a great place to break a shopping spree. At night it becomes a romantic restaurant (mains Rs 380-1820).

Himalayan Joe Espresso Bar
CAFE

(Map p220; espressos Rs 120-150; 7am-10pm;) Himalayan Joe's is a funky cafe-shack where you can get a caffeine fix in any number of ways, including coffee cocktails. There are also sundaes, banana splits and fruit smoothies, but we think the oversized, sticky chocolate donuts could become legendary.

Am/Pm Organic Café
CAFE

(Map p220; espressos from Rs 100; 6am-9.30pm;) This cosy cafe, up a side street, is run by a Nepali who trained as a barista in London and boasts organic Himalayan coffee from Palpa (Tansen) plus tasty pastries from its German bakery. It's also recommended for breakfasts and light lunches.

Busy Bee Café
BAR

(Map p220; 9am-late) The Busy Bee has live bands rocking every night, though Friday and Saturday are usually the best nights when locals and travellers converge en masse. There's a restaurant and bar plus a courtyard with a fire pit, which is a great spot to meet other travellers, and there's also a smoky pool room down in the den.

Club Amsterdam
BAR

(Map p220; ☺9am-late) The boisterous and loud Club Amsterdam is an old favourite on the Lakeside strip. With live music, pool tables, cocktails and mocktails, and football on the TV, it's got it all covered. Head for the fire pit out back if you want a conversation.

Bullet Basecamp
BAR

(Map p220; Jarebar; ☺4-11.30pm; ☜) Away from the Lakeside glitz and adjacent to a motorcycle repair workshop, Bullet Basecamp has an unmistakable storyline. Sprockets, driveshafts and Tata truck grills have been turned into light fittings and bar furniture. If you are travelling on an Enfield, this place is a must-do pit stop. It's located about a kilometre east of Camping (Hallan) Chowk on Phewa Marg.

Old Blues Bar
BAR

(Map p220; ☺4-11.30pm) A super-relaxed option, the Blues Bar is popular with stoners, and large banners of Jimi Hendrix and John Lennon add to its appeal. Most nights there's a local covers band.

☆ Entertainment

Several restaurants located along the strip have nightly Nepali cultural song-and-dance shows that are enthusiastic, if not entirely authentic, and there is no additional charge.

Pokhara nightlife (see previous section) generally winds down around 11pm, but a handful of bars flaunt the rules and rock till around midnight. Local bands move from bar to bar on a nightly rotation, playing covers of Western rock hits.

Hotel Barahi
DANCE

(Map p220; ☺show 6.30pm) Bookings are required for the buffet dinner and cultural show from 6.30pm (Rs 1240). If you reserve a table early, you can use the pool for free during the day.

Boomerang Restaurant & German Bakery
DANCE

(Map p220; ☺show 7pm) A long-standing and popular restaurant with an evening cultural show.

Fewa Paradise Restaurant
DANCE

(Map p220; ☺show 6.30pm) An all-day restaurant with a traveller menu and an evening song-and-dance show.

Hungry Eye Restaurant
DANCE

(Map p220; ☺show 6.30pm) One of many long-standing dinner-and-show venues. This one is indoors.

🔒 Shopping

Boutiques in Lakeside sell Hindu and Buddhist paraphrenalia, prayer flags, counterfeit trekking gear, wall hangings, khukuri (traditional curved knifes of the Ghurkas) and antiques of dubious antiquity. Pokhara is also a good place to pick up saligram fossils.

As well as the shops in Lakeside, Tibetan refugee women set out their wares under the shade of trees offering Tibetan jewellery for sale. For an even greater selection of Tibetan arts and crafts, including handmade carpets, head either to the Tashi Palkhel and Tashi Ling Tibetan communities, respectively north and south of Pokhara, or to the Tibetan Mini Market in Lakeside East.

There are numerous supermarkets in Lakeside where you can stock up on chocolate, biscuits, toiletries and other goods before heading out on your trek.

Helping Hands
HANDICRAFTS

(Map p220; www.yeshelpinghands.com; ☺8am-8pm) Over 80% of the woven products on sale here have been made locally by deaf and blind men and women in an initiative to empower local people with disabilities.

Nepal Mandala Bookshop
BOOKS

(Map p220; ☺8am-8pm) There is no dearth of bookshops in Lakeside but Nepal Mandala probably has the best selection of books and maps in town.

Sherpa Adventure
OUTDOOR EQUIPMENT

(Map p220; ☺9am-8pm) Upstairs and above Ganesh Kayak Shop, Sherpa Adventure is the place to find outdoor gear that is of a better quality than most of the counterfeit stuff that dominates the bazaar.

The North Face
OUTDOOR EQUIPMENT

(Map p220; ☺9am-8pm) The only outlet selling the real thing at prices similar to home.

Tibetan Mini Market
HANDICRAFTS

(Map p220; ☺8am-8pm) The people's cooperative society of Tashi Palkhel have opened this arcade in Lakeside East where you can shop for Tibetan crafts, organise a tour of the

ℹ TREKKING PERMITS

If you plan to trek anywhere inside the Annapurna Conservation Area, you'll need a permit from the **Annapurna Conservation Area Project** (ACAP; Map p217; ☎061-463376; ⊙10am-5pm Sun-Fri, to 4pm Sat, to 4pm winter) in Damside.

The admission fee to the conservation area is Rs 2000/200 (foreigner/SAARC) and permits are issued on the spot (bring two passport-sized photos). There are ACAP checkpoints throughout the reserve and if you get caught without a permit, the fee rises to Rs 4000/400 (foreigner/SAARC). Independent trekkers without a guide will need to register their trek by obtaining a **Trekkers' Information Management System** (TIMS; www. timsnepal.com) card which can be purchased from the **Nepal Tourism Board** (Map p217; ⊙10am-5pm Sun-Fri) or the office of the **Trekking Agencies Association of Nepal** (TAAN; Map p220; ☎01-4427473; ⊙10am-5pm). Another two passport-sized photos are necessary for TIMS, which costs the equivalent of US$10 in Nepali currency, if booking through a local registered travel agent, or US$20 for totally independent trekkers.

refugee camps and grab a plate of steaming-hot momos.

Women's Skills Development Organisation HANDICRAFTS

(Map p220; www.womensskilldevelopment.org; ⊙8am-8pm) The woven and stitched bags, belts and toys display real skill and care and make a great souvenir. Sales help generate income for disadvantaged women across rural Nepal. There's a branch in Lakeside Central (above Salt n Pepper) and one in Lakeside East.

ℹ Information

EMERGENCY

The direct phone number for the police is ☎100. The **tourist police** (Map p217; ☎462761) are located in Damside at the same site as the tourist office and they operate a small booth opposite Moondance Restaurant.

IMMIGRATION OFFICE

The **immigration office** (Map p210; ☎465167; Sahid Chowk; ⊙10am-4pm Sun-Thu, 10am-3pm Fri) is in Damside. Visa extensions need to be applied for online at www.nepal immigration.gov.np. Click 'Online Application' and 'Tourist Visa', upload a photo (by clicking on the photo box) and note down your Submission ID number. You have 15 days to take this number to the Immigration Office. Fees are US$30 for 15 days, and US$2 per extra day (up to 15 extra days). There's an additional US$20 for multiple-entry visas. Bring your passport and the visa fee in Nepali rupees.

INTERNET ACCESS

Free wi-fi can be accessed just about anywhere – most hotels, restaurants and cafes. Internet cafes charge Rs 50 per hour, usually with a minimum 15-minute charge.

LAUNDRY

Hotels can arrange same-day laundry services if you drop your clothes off first thing in the morning, or there are plenty of small laundry shops along the strip in Lakeside. They charge Rs 50 to Rs 100 per kilogram.

MEDICAL SERVICES

There are several pharmacies in Lakeside selling everyday medicines, antibiotics and first-aid supplies. For anything serious, head to CIWEC Clinic.

CIWEC Clinic (Map p220; ☎061-463082; www. ciwec-clinic.com; Mansarovar Path; ⊙24hr) CIWEC Clinic provides emergency treatment and travel medicine advice and should be your first choice for medical treatment in Pokhara. Payments can be made by credit card and the clinic is used to liaising with insurance companies.

MONEY

There are plenty of foreign-exchange offices in Lakeside that change cash and travellers cheques in major currencies. All are open daily but rates are better at the **Standard Chartered Bank** (Map p220; ☎462102; ⊙9.45am-3.30pm Sun-Thu, to 1pm Fri), near Camping (Hallan) Chowk. There are several ATMs along the main strip in Lakeside, including Nabil Bank and Standard Chartered Bank, that accept foreign cards.

POST

The main **post office** (Map p210; ⊙10am-5pm Sun-Thu, to 3pm Fri) is a hike from Lakeside at Mahendra Pul. There's a much smaller branch in Lakeside East, though alternatively most bookstores in Lakeside sell stamps and have a post box for letters and postcards.

If you want to send anything valuable, **UPS** (Map p220; ☎463209) in Lakeside is reliable.

TELEPHONE

Mobile-phone reception is good and there are numerous outlets selling recharge vouchers for the major companies. Internet cafes in Lakeside offer phone calls to Europe and most other places for around Rs 50 per minute.

TOURIST INFORMATION

Nepal Tourism runs a helpful **tourist office** (Map p217; ☎ 465292; ☺ 10am-1pm & 2-5pm Sun-Fri) in Damside, sharing a building with the Annapurna Conservation Area Project. Here you can get your TIMS card. (p225)

TRAVEL AGENCIES

Most of the travel agents in Lakeside can book tours, flights and bus tickets. The businesses listed below are all reputable travel agents.

Adam Tours & Travels (Map p220; ☎ 061-461806; www.adamnepal.com) IATA accredited agency for international flights.

Blue Sky Travel & Tours (Map p220; ☎ 061-462199; www.blue-sky-tours.com) In addition to ticketing, Blue Sky runs its own Kathmandu–Pokhara coach service.

Wayfarers (Map p220; ☎ 061-463774; www.wayfarers.com.np) For all ticketing and trekking.

ℹ Getting There & Away

AIR

There are numerous flights to Kathmandu (US$120, 25 minutes) all day, weather permitting, with **Buddha Air** (Map p217; ☎ 061-465998; www.buddhaair.com; ☺ 8am-5.30pm), **Yeti Airlines** (Map p217; ☎ 061-464888, airport 061-465888; www.yetiairlines.com), **Nepal Airlines** (Map p217; ☎ 061-465021, airport 061-465040; www.nepalairlines.com.np) and **Simrik Airlines** (Map p217; ☎ 061-465887; www.simrikairlines.com; ☺ 8.30am-5pm) sharing the load. There are great Himalayan views if you sit on the right-hand side of the plane heading into Pokhara (or the left on the way to Kathmandu).

Simrik Airlines, Nepal Airlines and a division of Yeti Airlines called **Tara Air** (☎ 061-464888, airport 061-465888; www.taraair.com) have daily flights to Jomsom (US$111, 20 minutes). Nepal Airlines also flies to Manang (US$113, 25 minutes) on Friday.

All the airlines have offices near the **airport** (Map p210) and Mustang Chowk, but it's often easier to use the services of one of the travel agents in Lakeside.

BUS

There are three bus stations in Pokhara. Tourist buses to Kathmandu and Royal Chitwan National Park leave from the **tourist bus park** (Map p217) near Mustang Chowk. The dusty and chaotic **main Pokhara bus park** (Map p210) at the northeast end of the Pokhara airstrip has buses to Kathmandu and towns in the Terai. You will find the main ticket office at the back and the night buses office at the top of the steps near the main highway. Buses going to the trailheads for the Annapurna Conservation Area leave from the **Baglung bus park** (Map p210), about 2km north of the centre on the main highway.

To/From Kathmandu

The bus trip between Kathmandu and Pokhara takes six to eight hours, depending on the condition of the road. Tourist buses (Rs 800 non air-con, from Rs 1000 air-con) are the most hassle-free option and leave from the tourist bus park at 7.30am. Taxis meet the tourist buses on arrival but brace yourself for Pokhara's notorious hotel touts.

Greenline (Map p220; ☎ 061-464472; www.greenline.com.np) has a daily air-con bus to Thamel (US$23 with lunch, six to seven hours) departing at 8am from its Lakeside East office. **Golden Travels** (☎ 061-460120) has a similar service to Durbar Marg (US$15 with lunch) in central Kathmandu, leaving from the tourist bus park. Other reputable tourist buses include Mountain Overland and Blue Sky Travel.

Public buses to Kathmandu (day/night Rs 500/550) leave from the main public bus

POKHARA TO BENI BUS STOPS

STOP	FARE (RS)	DURATION (HR)	TREK
Hyangja	50	1	Ghachok trek
Phedi	70	1½	Annapurna Sanctuary Trek
Naya Pul	180	2	Ghorepani (Poon Hill) to Ghandruk trek, Annapurna Sanctuary Trek, Annapurna Circuit Trek
Baglung	200	3	Annapurna Circuit Trek
Beni	250	4	Annapurna Circuit Trek

station. Faster microbuses run to Kathmandu (Kalanki) for Rs 550, leaving from the highway in front of the public bus stand.

Stops along the road to Kathmandu include Dumre (for Bandipur, Rs 150, two hours), Abu Khaireni (Rs 250, three hours) and Mugling/Manakamana (Rs 300, four hours).

There are also four daily direct buses going to Gorkha (Rs 350, five hours) leaving from the main bus park.

To/From Chitwan National Park

The best way to get to Chitwan is by tourist bus (seven hours). Buses leave the tourist bus park daily at 7.30am for Sauraha (Rs 600 non air-con, from Rs 8000 air-con), arriving at Bachhauli, a 15-minute walk from town, or there are taxis waiting to transfer travellers to their hotel.

Greenline has a daily air-con bus to Sauraha (US$20 including lunch, 5½ hours) departing at 7.30am from its Lakeside East office (the return journey drops off at the tourist bus park). Mountain Overland charges US$17 and leaves from the tourist bus park at 7.30am.

To/From the Indian Border

The closest border crossing to Pokhara is Belahiya/Sunauli, which is just south of the town of Bhairawa.

Travel agents might try to tempt you with the offer of direct buses to towns in India. Don't be fooled – there are no through-buses to India; without exception, you must change at the border.

There are two (sometimes three) buses to Bhaiwara (Rs 800, seven to nine hours), via Narayangarh (departing 7.15am) or the Siddhartha Hwy (the speedier option, departing at 6.30am), from the tourist bus park. From the main Pokhara bus park there are nearly 20 day and night buses daily for Bhairawa (day/night Rs 450/500, eight hours), where you can pick up a local bus to the border post at Sunauli.

There are buses heading to Birganj (Rs 550, nine hours), Nepalganj (Rs 1100, 12 hours), Mahendranagar (Rs 1420, 16 hours) and Kakarbhitta (Rs 1500, 17 hours).

To/From the Terai

As well as the buses to the Indian border, there are regular day/night services to Narayangarh (Rs 400, five hours), where you can change to buses heading east and west along the Mahendra Hwy. All buses leave from the main Pokhara bus park.

Most buses go via Mugling, but there are also buses along the dramatic Siddhartha Hwy to Butwal (Rs 600, six hours) via Tansen (Rs 500, five hours).

To/From Trekking Routes

Buses to the trailheads for most treks in the Annapurna Conservation Area leave from the Baglung bus park. One important exception is the Annapurna Circuit Trek, which normally starts at Besi Sahar.

Buses leave Baglung about every half-hour from 5.30am to 3.30pm (see table opposite).

For Besi Sahar (Rs 450, five hours), there is a tourist bus leaving at 6.30am from the tourist bus park, or you can take any bus bound for Kathmandu and change at Dumre.

TAXI

Getting a group together and taking a taxi to the trailheads is worth considering. Costs from Lakeside are roughly: Hyangia (Rs 800), Phedi (Rs 1200), Nayapul/Birenthanti (Rs 2000), Baglung (Rs 3000), Beni (Rs 4000).

ⓘ Getting Around

BICYCLE

There are lots of bicycle-rental places at Lakeside charging Rs 100/300 per hour/day. Pay more (up to Rs 900 per day) for better-quality bikes. See also p211.

BUS

Local buses shuttle between Lakeside, the airport, the public bus stand and Mahendra Pul but routes (like the driving) are erratic and there isn't much space for baggage. Fares start at Rs 20.

Local buses to Pame Bazaar (Rs 20) and other places on the north shore of Phewa Tal leave Camping (Hallan) Chowk every hour or so until mid-afternoon. Buses to Begnas Tal (Rs 60) leave from the main bus stand.

MOTORCYCLE

Several places in Lakeside rent out bikes (scooters/motorcycles/Royal Enfields Rs 1000/1200/3500 per day, not including fuel). A helmet will be provided, and if you don't wear it the police are likely to fine you and impound the bike. Check the bikes out first to make sure they start easily, brake smoothly and the lights work.

Hearts & Tears (Map p220; ☏ 9846020293; www.heartsandtears.com) is tucked away in the entrance to Busy Bee Café. It's a great place to learn to ride (it rents bikes from Rs 5000 per day) or join a motorcycle tour around Nepal. **Raju Bullet Surgery** (Map p220; ☏ 9806511845) is, as the name implies, a motorcycle workshop specialising in Royal Enfield Bullets. It's adjacent to the Bullet Basecamp bar.

Around Pokhara

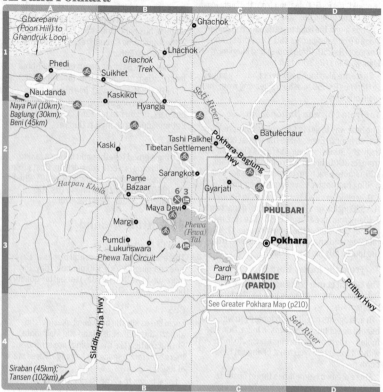

Around Pokhara

🛏 **Sleeping**
1 Begnas Coffee House............................F4
2 Begnas Lake Resort & Villas F4
3 Maya Devi Village.................................B3
4 Park Anadu Restaurant & Lodge........B3
5 Tiger Mountain Pokhara Lodge D3

🍴 **Eating**
6 Krishna's Kitchen...................................B3
  Maya Devi Village........................(see 3)

TAXI

Taxis meet tourist buses at the tourist bus park (Mustang Chowk), but you can expect a hotel tout to come along for the ride. The fare to Lakeside is Rs 200 whether you take the tout's advice or not, so insist on being taken where you want to go. Heading out from Lakeside, you'll pay Rs 300 to the main Pokhara bus park and the airport, and Rs 400 to the Baglung bus park. Taxis from the airport charge at least Rs 300 to Lakeside.

AROUND POKHARA

Trekking in the Annapurna Conservation Area Project (ACAP) is easily the biggest attraction around Pokhara, but you don't have to be a seasoned trekker to appreciate the glory of the peaks. There are several dramatic viewpoints on the rim of the Pokhara Valley that can be reached by foot, taxi, mountain bike or rented motorcycle from Pokhara.

Sarangkot

The view of the Annapurna Himalaya from Sarangkot (adult Rs 30) is almost a religious experience. From here, you can see a panoramic sweep of Himalayan peaks, from Dhaulagiri (8167m) in the west to the perfect pyramid of Machhapuchhare (6997m), the tentlike peak of Annapurna II (7937m) to Lamjung (6983m) in the east. Most people come here at dawn or dusk, when the

N 0 ——————— 5 km
0 ——————— 2.5 miles

Madi Khola

●Chitepani

Kalikathan ● ●Thulokot

Skyline ●Naudanda
●Lipini

Annapurna Shaklung ● *Trek*

Dipang Tal Chisopani ●

Sisuwa ● *Begnas Tal*

Begnas Bazaar ● Pachabhaiya

Rupa Tal

View Top Lodge
(☏ 9746064324; bikithapa@gmail.com; r with/without bathroom Rs 1500/800; ☎) Just below the viewing tower, this inviting hotel has a bright lobby and cosy, freshly carpeted rooms. The sunny verandah, with mountain and lake views, is a wonderful spot for breakfast.

Sherpa Resort
(☏ 061-691171, in Kathmandu 01-4259769; www.sherparesort.com; r with/without view Rs 1500/1000; ☎) A few hundred metres west of the viewing tower is this venerable, light-filled hotel with wide corridors and old-fashioned, comfortable rooms. Rooms vary in size as do bathrooms, and some beds are on the hard side, though its a small sacrifice to wake up with the Himalaya outside your window. Rooms 201 and 202 are good picks.

Hotel Mountain Garden
(☏ 9806748684; www.mountaingarden.com; Bhumare Gaira; s/d Rs 800/1500; ☎) Just west of the viewing tower, this friendly hotel has a garden with exceptional views. Rooms are clean and bright, some with their own balcony, and you can dine on the roof for more of the great views.

❶ Getting There & Away

Taxi drivers in Lakeside offer dawn rides up to the ridge to catch the sunrise for around Rs 2000. The taxi fare is the same whether the driver waits to drive you back or you walk down. Be prepared for a guide to jump in your taxi and do his best to convince you of his services, though a guide is unnecessary as it is easy to get to the top via the path.

By motorcycle or mountain bike, follow the road that branches off the Baglung Hwy near the Bindhya Basini Temple. When the road levels out below the ridge, look for the Sarangkot turn-off on the right, opposite a large group of tin-roofed school buildings.

A more challenging option is the three- to four-hour walk from Pokhara. The most popular path begins on the highway opposite the Baglung bus park. The obvious trail runs west across the fields and up the side of Gyarjati Hill, meeting the dirt road at Silangabot, about 1km east of the Sarangkot turn-off.

There's also a scenic route from Phewa Tal but the trail is hard to follow and there have been muggings along this path. The trail begins near the village of Kapaudi on the road to Pame Bazaar (look for the signpost about 50m after the Green Peace Lodge), meeting the road just west of the turn-off to Sarangkot. It's easier to follow this trail on the way down.

sun picks out the peaks, transforming them from a purple-pink to a celestial gold. If you feel noisy teenagers are ruining the peace at the viewing tower, try walking further along to the secluded grassy helicopter pad.

The main village is just below the ridge, but a set of steps leads uphill to a dramatic viewpoint, the site of an ancient kot (fort).

There's a ruined fort at Kaskikot (1788m), a one-hour walk west of Sarangkot along the ridge road, with similarly jaw-dropping views.

🛏 Sleeping & Eating

There are several places to stay and eat in Sarangkot. The cheapest options are along the concrete steps to the viewpoint, the better places are beyond the viewpoint. The massive construction site is a new Japanese-funded hotel that will boast a cable car!

Bat Cave & Mahendra Gufa

You won't find Adam West or Christian Bale lurking in the dark and spooky **Bat Cave** (Chameri Gufa; adult Rs 100; ☺6am-6pm), but rather thousands of horseshoe bats clinging to the ceiling of a damp, smelly and slippery chamber and occasionally chirruping into the darkness – claustrophobics beware. Daredevils can continue to the back of the vault and wriggle out through a tiny chute to the surface.

Torches are supplied, and guides (Rs 300) can show you the narrow exit tunnel. Ask about tours to other caves in the vicinity. It's easily visited from Pokhara on foot, by bike or by taxi (Rs 1200).

Nearby is the underwhelming **Mahendra Gufa** (Chameri Gufa; adult Rs 50; ☺6am-6pm), the first large cave to be discovered in Pokhara. The first 125m of the cave is lit only to reveal dusty vandalised limestone formations, some revered as Shiva lingams. Beyond the electric lights there are bats.

Begnas Tal & Rupa Tal

About 10km southeast of Pokhara, a road leaves the Prithvi Hwy for Begnas Tal and Rupa Tal, two gloriously serene lakes that receive few foreign visitors, despite their proximity to Pokhara.

After leaving the highway, a narrow road runs through a dead-flat terrain of rice fields towards the hills that nestle the lakes. Begnas is the larger of the twin lakes. As well as the scruffy Begnas Bazaar there is a large fish farm and paddle boats are available for a leisurely paddle. The village of Begnas lies across the waters to the north among the terraced fields.

There are hotels near Begnas Bazaar, but if you are after tranquillity you are are much better off heading up along the narrow ridge that separates the lakes. Here you will find a top-end lodge and a village that specialises in budget guesthouse accommodation. Pachabhaiya village is spread out along the ridge and the guesthouses look down on the either lake depending upon their orientation. There are also views across the lakes to the snowy Himalaya peaks. The village is reached via a 3km hike or drive along a road that winds uphill directly from the bus stand in Begnas Bazaar. It's more isolated than staying near the bazaar, but the surrounding countryside, friendly guesthouses and stunning views make it all worthwhile.

🛏 Sleeping & Eating

★**Begnas Coffee House**   GUESTHOUSE $
(Map p228; ☑9856037082, 692775; www.nepali organiccoffee.com; Pachbhaiya; r with/without bath Rs 600/300; ☎) Delightful family home in an idyllic setting with seven guestrooms – all spotless and comfortable. Wonderful views, wonderful food – and this is the home of Machhapuchhare Flying Bird coffee. Coffee beans from the surrounding hills are processed and roasted on-site. The family also have honey bees and make several flavours of honey, depending on the blossoms in season, including coffee honey! There are discounts for long-term stays.

Rupa View Point   GUESTHOUSE $
(☑061-622098; rupaview@hotmail.com; Pachbhaiya; r old/new bldg Rs 500/750) This family-run place, situated on a ridge overlooking Rupa Tal, has a brick building with decent rooms and solar hot water. There's another two, more basic, rooms in a separate building. In the evening home-cooked meals are prepared using vegetables from the garden.

Begnas Lake Resort & Villas   HOTEL $$$
(Map p228; ☑061-560030; www.begnaslakeresort.com; Sundari Danda; s/d incl breakfast from US$120/130, ste US$220; ❊☎) A delightful, luxury resort on the sloping shores of Begnas Tal. All rooms – set in stone and wood cottages and surrounded by gardens – have lake and mountain views. The balconied restaurant, BBQ area and bar are the focal point at mealtimes and in between you can relax at the pool and Ayurvedic spa. Pick-up and drop-off services to the airport (US$20) are provided.

❶ Getting There & Away

Buses to Begnas Tal (Rs 50, one hour) stop on the highway opposite the main public bus stand in Pokhara.

By bike or motorcycle, take the Prithvi Hwy towards Mugling and turn left at the obvious junction in Tal Chowk. A taxi will cost Rs 1000 to Begnas Bazaar and Rs1500 to Pachbhaiya one way.

THE ROAD TO JOMSOM

With the upgrading of the path to Jomsom (Dzongsam) into a road, growing numbers of travellers are heading north into the mountains to savour the views and clean mountain air. As well as offering a shortcut to explore mountain villages such as Tatopani and Muktinath, which used to take days of trekking to reach, the road opens up opportunities to several trailheads. There was some damage along this road from small landslides during the 2015 earthquake but transport was operating on this route at the time of research.

To journey beyond Tatopani, you must be able to present an Annapurna Conservation Area Project (ACAP) permit (Rs 2000) and and a TIMS card (p225) at the respective ACAP and TIMS checkpoints. If you don't have an ACAP permit when you reach the checkpoint at Ghasa you will have to pay Rs 4000.

While the Annapurna region escaped serious earthquake damage, landslides are a risk because of the destablising effect of the tremors. The Kali Gandaki river was briefly blocked by a landslide in May 2015, triggering widespread evacuations downstream, and further landslides are a possibility, so check the situation before you travel.

Pokhara to Beni

Although the road is mostly blacktop, the 80km drive to Beni will take three to four hours by taxi and longer by bus. It's a scenic mountain drive that weaves you past the Annapurna trailheads of **Phedi**, **Kande** and **Naya Pul**. The valley of the Kali Gandaki is reached at Kusum, and the next major town is **Baglung**, where you may have to change vehicles to continue north. **Beni** (830m) is a short drive from Baglung along the Kali Gandaki valley. It's a scruffy settlement, from which trails and roads from Dolpo, Mustang and Pokhara converge. If you must spend a night, there are several hotels opposite the bus park or a short stroll away. Beni has three ATMs that accept foreign cards and banks for foreign exchange.

🛏 Sleeping

Hotel Yeti   HOTEL **$**
(☎ 069-520142; www.hotelyeti.com; Beni; r with/ without bathroom Rs 800/500; 🖳) The best of

Beni's hotels, the Yeti has clean and tolerably comfortable rooms, a welcoming host and good food in its Thakali Restaurant. It's a short stroll from the bus park and close to the Machhapuchhare Bank.

ℹ Getting There & Away

There are buses (Rs 250, several daily) to/from Pokhara (Baglung bus park), as well as taxis (Rs 4000). Less frequent buses run north from Beni to Ghasa (Rs 780) via Tatopani (Rs 600). It's a similar fare in a share 4WD. (These are fares for foreigners, as opposed to the much lower local fares.) If you are going straight through to Jomsom you still need to change buses in Ghasa (a district border); the fare from Ghasa to Jomsom is Rs 830. The entire journey from Beni to Jomsom will take six to eight hours – if all goes well!

Beni to Tatopani

From Beni the road deteriorates, and, depending on recent rainfall, it can be quite a challenging and exciting drive – when it's raining, it can be downright scary. Often the 'road' is just a bulldozer scrape into the side of a mountain, and you get the feeling that mother nature would like to heal the scar at every opportunity. During the monsoon season, landslides, rivers and waterfalls periodically cut the road, delaying rather than preventing your journey. Onward travel requires relay teams of vehicles on either side of the blockage. Nonplussed passengers simply hoist their luggage on to their shoulders and walk through the stream or across a hastily constructed foot bridge to the waiting vehicles on the other side. It's not unheard of to do this several times during the rainy season.

The 25km drive from Beni to Tatopani (1190m) could take two to three hours depending on the conditions. The views of the river and the steep gorge are spectacular as the forested valley walls close in and the terraced hills disappear.

Tatopani means 'hot water' in Nepali and the village gets its name from the hot springs that emanate from the rocks beside the Kali Gandaki river. Tatopani has long been a favourite stop with weary trekkers, and while the road has lured away some of these visitors, it now also brings folks up from Pokhara on short overnight trips. After crossing the river at Tatopani, the **Annapurna Circuit trail** heads up to Ghorepani (2750m) on the greatest ascent of the entire trail. In the other direction, the road and the trail – often the latter is on the opposite bank of the river to the former – continue north towards Jomsom. Tatopani is a great place to break the journey no matter which direction you are headed. There is a TIMS checkpoint at the southern end of town beside the road.

At the **hot springs** (Rs 100) there are two stone-lined pools that are used on alternate days, so that each can be cleaned regularly. There is a snack bar (happy hour in the afternoon brings beer and popcorn for Rs 400) on-site. Don't forget your bathing costume, and be prepared to take some time acclimatising to the astonishingly hot water. Thirty-seven degrees Celsius may not

sound hot, but you'll get a good idea of what it feels like to be a lobster in a cooking pot!

🛏 Sleeping

⭐ Dhaulagiri Lodge HOTEL $
(☑ 9741194872; Tatopani; r with/without bathroom from Rs 500/250) The delightful Dhaulagiri Lodge sits just above the hot springs, which are a short walk from its back gate. The comfortable rooms are arranged around a sunny garden of orange and banana trees. The restaurant here deservedly gets rave reviews for its travellers' fare, including Mexican, Italian, Continental, Indian and Nepali dishes.

Hotel Himalaya HOTEL $
(☑ 993695006; Tatopani; r with/without bathroom Rs 800/300) Hotel Himalaya is in the old bazaar above the new road and the hot springs, which are only a short walk away. Along with its clean and comfortable rooms, it has a bakery, a restaurant, laundry services and moneychanging – a one-stop shop.

Hotel Annapurna HOTEL $
(☑ 9847611928; Tatopani; r with/without bathroom Rs 600/300) This new hotel has been built beside the road on the north edge of the village. It is a concrete tower and lacks the charm of the hotels in the old bazaar, but it is a comfortable, if predictable option. There is a decent restaurant, and of course it is convenient to the road for parking.

Tatopani to Marpha

From Tatopani the road enters the 'deepest valley in the world'. The rationale for this claim is that between the top of Annapurna I and the top of Dhaulagiri I (both above

---

TRADE ALONG THE KALI GANDAKI

The Kali Gandaki/Thak Khola valley was a major trade route fo centuries. Until 1959 traders exchanged salt, collected from the salt lakes of Tibet, for rice and barley from the Middle Hills of Nepal. The Tibetans also traded wool, livestock and butter for sugar, tea, spices, tobacco and manufactured goods from India, but the salt-for-grain trade dominated the economy. This trade diminished, not only because of the political changes in Tibet, but also because Indian salt is available throughout Nepal at a much lower price than Tibetan salt.

In addition, Indian salt comes from the sea and contains iodine. Many people in Nepal once suffered from goitres because of the absence of iodine from their diet. Indian aid programs distributed sea salt in a successful effort to prevent goitres, but the Tibetan salt trade suffered. The Thakali people of the Kali Gandaki valley had a monopoly on the salt trade in this region and grew conspicuously wealthy. They have now turned to agriculture, tourism and other forms of trade for their livelihood.

8000m and only 38km apart) the terrain drops to below 2200m. The road sticks to the west bank of the Kali Gandaki, passing the villages of Guithe and Dana before reaching the spectacular and notorious **Rupse Chhahara** (Beautiful Waterfall).

Man's attempts at traversing this natural wonder apparently get swept away each monsoon season. So if you are here any time before October, don't be surprised if you have to alight from your bus, cross the footbridge below the thunderous falls, and find a bus on the other side. There is a colourful little teahouse below the road right by the Rupse Khola (stream). The next stretch of road is through the steepest and narrowest part of the Kali Gandaki valley; much of the road is cut through solid rock and subject to frequent landslides.

Here, in its upper reaches, people call the Kali Gandaki the Thak Khola, thus the name Thakali for those who live in this region. **Ghasa** (2010m) is the first Thakali village on the road north and the southernmost limit of Tibetan Buddhism in the valley. At Ghasa there is an ACAP checkpost where you will need to show your permit. Also, because you are moving from one jurisdiction to another, currently the bus companies make you change vehicles here.

There is no dearth of accommodation options in the spread-out village of Ghasa, or further on at Lete, Kalopani, Larjung, Kobang, Tukuche or Marpha – all erstwhile halts on the great trading route of the Kali Gandaki, and subsequently teahouse stops on the Annapurna Circuit.

The best of the overnight options can be found at the towns of Tukuche and Marpha, just south of Jomsom. **Tukuche** (2580m) was the main meeting point along the trade route, where traders coming with salt and wool from Tibet and the upper Thak valley bartered with traders carrying grain from the south. The hotels of Tukuche are in beautiful old Thakali homes with carved wooden windows, doorways and balconies. It's worth spending some time here to visit the **Tukuche Distillery** or the village's four Buddhist gompas.

From Tukuche you'll notice a dramatic change in the scenery: gone are the verdant conifer forests – instead you'll travel through dry, wind-swept desertlike country. A feature of the dramatic topography is the fierce anabatic wind that howls up

CHHAIRO GOMPA

Between Tukuche and Marpha a footbridge leads across the Kali Gandaki to the Tibetan refugee settlement of Chhairo. The 300-year-old **Chhairo Gompa** here is currently under restoration under the auspices of Restoration Works International (www.retorationworksinternational.org). See the website for how you can be part of this. The Guru Rinpoche Lhakhang in particular has some fine old statues, thangkas and murals.

the valley throughout the late morning and afternoon. From here to Jomsom (and beyond into Mustang), this daily strong wind will be blowing dust and sand into every crack and crevice of your vehicle if not your body.

As the road proceeds north, it passes the apple orchards of a successful agricultural project that started in 1966. As well as the fruit, most shops around here stock bottles of apple, apricot and peach brandy from the distillery.

🛏 Sleeping

High Plains Inn HOTEL $

(☑ 9756703091; www.highplainsinn.com; Tukuche; r with/without bathroom Rs 500/200) This Nepali-Dutch enterprise at the northern end of the village is a delight. It has super-clean rooms and bathrooms, a fireplace, a Dutch bakery and a fine restaurant with great food featuring multicuisine dishes.

Tukuche Guest House GUESTHOUSE $

(☑ 9741170035; Tukuche; r with/without bathroom Rs 500/400) Within the stone-walled and flagstoned village is this charming whitewashed building that features spotless, comfortable rooms surrounding a central courtyard and a cosy Tibetan-style dining room. There's a fascinating explanation of local history on the wall of the entranceway.

Eagle Nest Guest House HOTEL $

(☑ 9857650101; Ghasa; dm Rs 100, r with/without bathroom Rs 700/300) At the southern end of the village, Eagle Nest has the best location in Ghasa. The hotel has clean and comfortable rooms and there is a pleasant garden and a good restaurant and bakery. Ask the owner about birdwatching opprtunities in the region.

Kalopani Guest House   HOTEL $

(☎019-446518; Kalopani; r Rs 500-1000; ☎) The large and conspicuous Kalopani Guest House provides comfortable rooms in a modern building that features a cavernous lobby with plush couches and a good restaurant.

Lodge Thasang Village   HOTEL $$$

(☎019-446514; www.lodgethasangvillage.com; Larjung; s/d US$215/250) High on a ridge above Larjung, with exceptional views of Dhaulagiri, Nilgiri and the Thak Khola, is this luxury lodge. This is not your average teahouse – as you no doubt guessed from the tariff. As well as the luxurious beds and the fire-warmed lobby, you can organise short walks and jeep rides to surrounding villages and viewpoints.

Marpha

Fortunately the dusty road bypasses the old flagstoned main street of Marpha (2680m), and so has not destroyed the town's historic atmosphere. Marpha huddles behind a ridge for protection from the up-valley wind, and exhibits typical Thak Khola architecture of flat roofs and narrow paved alleys. The low rainfall in this region makes these flat roofs practical; they also serve as a drying place for grains and vegetables.

You can easily go on to Jomsom, but it is not as interesting or pleasant as Marpha. There are lots of things to do here, including climbing the ridge to the west of town to the original settlement of Old Marpha. Marpha's large **Samtenling Gompa** (Tashi Lhakang) was renovated in 1996. This is a Nyingma Buddhist gompa, and the Mani Rimdu festival is celebrated here in autumn. Like all the buildings in Marpha, the gompa is painted in whitewash produced from a local stone. If you have time, take in the views of the town from the ochre-painted, natural stone chörten on the mountainside north of town.

Jomsom

Straddling the Kali Gandaki, Jomsom (2760m), or more correctly Dzongsam (New Fort), is the region's administrative headquarters and the main travel hub for onward travel to Upper Mustang and Muktinath. At the southwestern end of town is the airport, where you'll also find the bus station and ticket office, tourist hotels, restaurants, shops and airline offices. Many buildings here were damaged in the 2015 earthquake, including the historic wooden bridge across the Kali Gandaki, which warped dramatically, but restoration work is underway and the town is open to trekkers.

Also at this end of town, a concrete stairway leads to the **Mustang Eco Museum** (admission Rs 100; ☉10am-5pm Tue-Sun, to 3pm Fri, to 4pm in winter), which is worth a visit for its displays on *amchi* (Tibetan herbal medicine) and its re-created Buddhist chapel.

Taking the bus or flying here brings you very close to the peaks. With a few days to spare, you could walk south to Marpha or go northeast to Kagbeni and Muktinath. Hotels can arrange porters for around Rs 1000 per day.

🛏 Sleeping

There many hotels in the southwestern part of Jomsom alongside the airfield. Alternatively you could cross the river to old Jomsom and stay in one of the smaller hotels there. Keeping warm at night can be a real issue in the cheaper places during winter, so consider bringing a sleeping bag.

Alka Marco Polo Hotel   HOTEL $

(☎069-440007; r with/without bathroom from Rs 700/300; @☎) The Alka Marco Polo has a range of comfortable rooms. The hotel boasts a sauna (Rs 500) and an internet cafe in the lobby – which is faster than the free wi-fi on offer.

Xanadu Guesthouse   HOTEL $

(☎069-440060; chandramohangauchan@yahoo. com; r from Rs 700, r without bathroom Rs 300; ☎) This friendly guesthouse is popular for its clean rooms, excellent restaurant (yak steaks and hot chocolate apple pie!) and laundry service. The downstairs shop and cafe sells books, espresso coffee, cake and good nak cheese. It also has a 4WD for hire.

Hotel Majesty   HOTEL $

(☎9843509222; r Rs 800-1200) The Majesty is a sprawling complex of 32 rooms spread over two buildings. The cheaper rooms are in the old wing, the better rooms and restaurant in the new wing. It's not majestic or palatial, but is a good choice with clean rooms and friendly staff.

Thak Khola Lodge
HOTEL **$**

(📞 069-440003; r without bathroom Rs 300) The very basic Thak Khola is found over the bridge towards the northeastern end of town. Rooms are drab and share a shower. This lodge's claim to fame is the graffiti message – behind the TV in the dining room and almost obscured by overzealous splashes of whitewash – left behind by Jimi Hendrix in 1967: 'If I don't see you in this world I'll see you in the next one; don't be late.'

Om's Home
HOTEL **$$**

(📞 069-440042; info@omshomejomsom.com; s/d Rs 1750/2200, incl breakfast Rs 2100/2900; 🛜) The extensive Om's Home comprises 26 comfortable rooms all with TVs and tiled hot-water bathrooms. There's also a sunny courtyard with an espresso cafe, a decent restaurant, bike hire and a table tennis table.

ℹ Information

The **Machhapuchhare Bank** (🕐 9am-2.30pm Sun-Thu, 9am-12.30pm Fri) changes cash and travellers cheques and has an ATM (Visa only). The **Nepal Bank** also changes cash.

Internet access is available at the Alka Marco Polo hotel.

The **ACAP Tourist Information Centre & Checkpost** (🕐 6am-6pm, winter 7am-5pm) is across the road from Om's Home hotel and a **TIMS Check Post**. You will need to have both your ACAP and TIMS cards recorded and stamped. You can buy water from the **Safe Drinking Water station** beside the ACAP office (Rs 40/L).

ℹ Getting There & Away

Tara Air (p226), **Simrik Airlines** (📞 069-440167; www.simrikairlines.com; Jomsom) and **Nepal Airlines** (www.nepalairlines.com.np) operate flights between Pokhara and Jomsom (US$90, 20 minutes) and have offices where you can book and confirm tickets. All flights depart between 7am and 10am.

Buses and share-4WDs head south to Marpha (Rs 180), Tukuche (Rs 305), Larjung (Rs 415), Kalopani (Rs 630) and Ghasa (Rs 830). Buses depart at 7am, 8am, noon and 4pm from outside the ticket office beside the Alka Marco Polo Hotel. At Ghasa you need to change buses to continue on to Beni (Rs 780). Beni is about 80km by road west of Pokhara, and where you can board a bus to Pokhara (Rs 250, four hours). Road blockages (where you may need to carry your gear over a landslide to find waiting vehicles) are fairly common, especially after heavy rain.

Around Jomsom

Thini

The small village of Thini, or Thinigaon (2860m), is visible across the valley from Jomsom and makes for an excellent short hike; if you are still feeling energetic, there is a small lake and a wonderful gompa to explore. From the bridge dividing old and new Jomsom, take the signed trail southwest, a 30-minute walk through terraced fields.

Thini is the oldest village in the valley and features an old **Gompa** (once Bön now Buddhist). From the village an obvious trail leads uphill to **Tilicho Tal**, but this is certainly not for day-trippers. Instead, if you want to continue exploring, turn south and drop down to cross the Lungpuhyun Khola, climb the other side and pass by the hilltop ruins of **Gharab Dzong**, a fortress built by king Thing Migchen. Beyond is the pretty, prayer-flag-festooned **Dhumba Tal** (2830m).

From the ridge above the lake you can head towards the Katsapterenga Gompa (2920m) for its spectacular 360-degree views of Nilgiri peak, Tilicho Pass, Syang village and Thini and Jomsom below you.

Muktinath

The pilgrimage centre of Muktinath (3800m) is a feasible overnight excursion from Jomsom. Vehicles heading up to Muktinath leave from Old Jomsom, near the large monastery at the north of town. When the road is open, 4WDs depart from 7am to 6pm when full (12 passengers). The bumpy journey takes 1½ hours and costs Rs 710. The temple and religious shrines of Muktinath are the most important pilgrimage sites for Hindus and Buddhists in the Himalaya. You'll see Tibetan traders and sadhus from as far away as South India. The shrines, in a grove of trees, include a Buddhist gompa, a Vishnu temple and the Jwalamai (Goddess of Fire) Temple, which shelters a spring and natural gas jets that provide Muktinath's famous eternal flame. It's the combination of earth, water and fire in such proximity that accounts for Muktinath's great religious significance. You can find more information on the shrines at www.muktinath.org.

Muktinath itself has no accommodation, for that you have to go to nearby **Ranipauwa** (where the 4WDs from Jomsom stop). This dusty town comprises a string of hotels set up for both Indian pilgrims and Annapurna Circuit trekkers. In the middle of the settlement is a police checkpost, where you'll need to register, and an ACAP visitor centre that doubles as a safe drinking water station.

🛏 Sleeping

Hotel Bob Marley   HOTEL **$**
(📞9857650097; Ranipauwa; r Rs 200) This funky hotel has 25 clean rooms, each floor has a solar-heated bathroom featuring a pebble-floor shower. Bob Marley receives raves for its delicious food, particularly pasta, cooked by an experienced chef who also grows his own herbs.

Hotel North Pole   HOTEL
(📞9847670336; Ranipauwa; r Rs 300; 📶) The North Pole is a good choice with comfortable rooms, a friendly hostess and very good food in the downstairs restaurant.

Kagbeni

One more excursion from Jomsom, which could easily be appended to a visit to Muktinath, is the beautiful village of Kagbeni (2840m). Kagbeni (or Kag) is found upstream on the Kali Gandaki, on the road/trail to Lo Manthang. You could walk along the river or catch a share 4WD the roughly 10km from Jomsom. You can't venture north of Kagbeni without an Upper Mustang permit, but you can explore the village and even trek back to Jomsom via the high west-bank route that takes you through the village of **Phalyak** (seven to eight hours).

Kagbeni retains its medieval feel with its narrow, covered flagstone alleys, antique chörtens, and large ochre monastery

perched above the town. As you wander through town, look for the clay effigies of the village protectors. 'Evi' (Grandmother) is a small figure attached to a wall, while 'Meme' (Grandfather) is a huge, knife-wieldling figure in a permanent state of arousal. Pay a visit to **Kagchode Thubten Sampheling Gompa** (Kagbeni; Rs 200; ⊙6am-6pm), a Sakyapa monastery founded in 1429. The main hall holds some fine festival masks and kangling (trumpets), as well as a 500-year-old text written in gold.

For a taste of forbidden Mustang, cross the Kali Gandaki on the bridge below the gompa and hike an hour north out to the village of **Tiri** on the west bank of the valley. No restricted-area permits are required on this side of the river as far as Tiri. Above Tiri is the **Sumdu Choeden Gompa**, the entrance of which is guarded by fine slate carvings of the Four Guardian Kings.

🛏 Sleeping

New Asia Trekkers Home   HOTEL **$**
(📞9847680504; r with/without bathroom Rs 300/150) This comfortable option has solar hot showers and great valley views from the upstairs rear rooms.

Hotel Shangri-La   HOTEL **$**
(📞9841163727; Kagbeni; r with/without bathroom Rs 400/200; 📶) The venerable Shangri-La has warm hosts, solar hot water and a heated dining table. If you can, join the porters and family in the cosy kitchen for a chat and a feed. The 'potatoes fried in sesame seeds with sauce and veg' is recommended.

Red House Lodge   HOTEL **$**
(📞993691011; Kagbeni; r Rs 300-500) With its private 350-year-old Tibetan-style chapel and Buddhist murals in the dining room, the rambling Red House Lodge is probably the most interesting option in town.

The Terai & Mahabharat Range

Best Places to Eat

➡ KC's Restaurant (p255)

➡ Nanglo West (p267)

➡ Candy's Place (p271)

➡ Chitwan Bar & Restaurant (p254)

Best Places to Stay

➡ Tiger Tops Tharu Lodge (p253)

➡ Sapana Village Lodge (p251)

➡ Forest Hideaway (p274)

➡ Lumbini Village Lodge (p262)

Why Go?

When you think of Nepal it's usually the Himalaya that comes to mind, not the flat, hot subtropical plains of the Terai. However, this narrow strip of land, wedged between the Indian border and the Himalaya and for the most part untouched by the 2015 earthquake, holds some of Nepal's most fascinating and varied attractions, including its famous national parks, Chitwan and Bardia – home to tigers, rhinos and elephants.

The Terai (sometimes spelt Tarai) is also home to over half Nepal's population, a vibrant mix of cultures showcased through the thatched mud-hut villages of the Tharu and the vibrant art of the Maithili people. There's also Lumbini, renowned as the birthplace of the Buddha and destination for pilgrims from around the world. Likewise, Janakpur, an important Hindu pilgrimage town, pulsates with religious fervour.

Rising from the Terai are the Chure Hills, followed by the Mahabharat Range, a region of dramatic gorges, awe-inspiring terracing and enduring mountain villages.

When to Go
Bhairawa

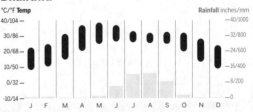

°C/°F **Temp**   **Rainfall** inches/mm

Oct–Mar Ideal climate to visit the Terai; the best wildlife-viewing is from January.

Nov–Dec Visit during Sita Bibaha Panchami, the festival celebrating Sita's marriage to Rama.

Late Dec Chitwan Festival is known for its elephant race; it also has food stalls.

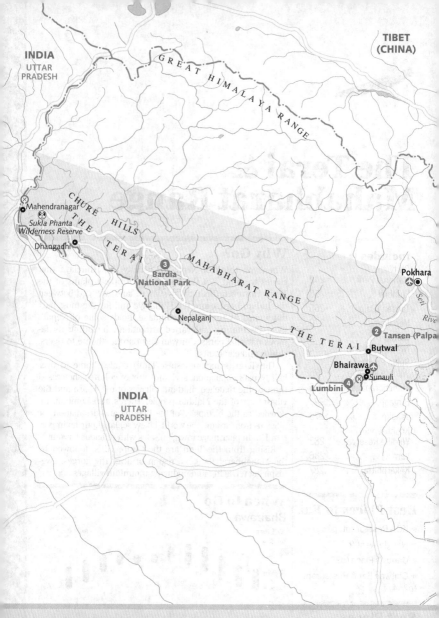

The Terai & Mahabharat Range Highlights

1 Take a rolling ride on an elephant to spot tigers, hornbills and rhinos in **Chitwan National Park** (p242).

2 Explore the narrow streets of medieval **Tansen (Palpa)** (p265) before hiking down to the abandoned palace of Ranighat.

3 Raft the mighty Geruwa River and follow it with a jungle walk in the wilds of **Bardia National Park** (p272).

4 Cycle among Buddhist temples through the peaceful

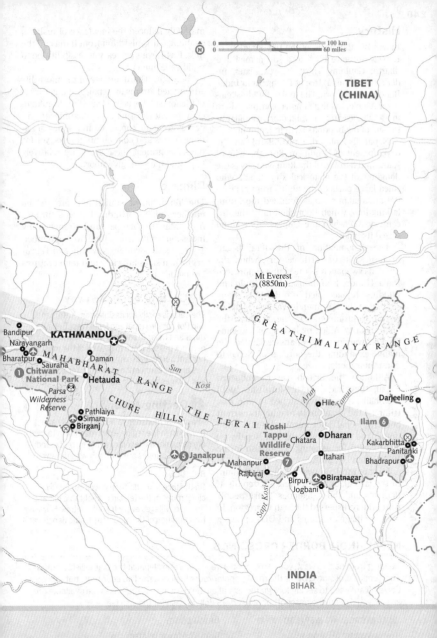

landscaped gardens of
Lumbini (p259).

5 Watch Maithili women
produce their signature naive
art in **Janakpur** (p281).

6 Wander through the
peaceful manicured tea
gardens of **Ilam** (p286).

7 Spot a rare Bengal florican
or Gangetic dolphin in **Koshi
Tappu Wildlife Reserve**
(p283).

History

In 563 BC, the queen of the tiny kingdom of Kapilavastu gave birth to a son named Siddhartha Gautama. Thirty-five years later, under a Bodhi (pipal) tree at Bodhgaya in India, Buddhism was born. The Indian Buddhist emperor Ashoka made a famous pilgrimage here in 249 BC, leaving a commemorative pillar at the site of the Buddha's birth in Lumbini.

Nepal also played a pivotal role in the development of Hinduism. Sita, the wife of Rama and heroine of the Ramayana, was the daughter of the historical king Janak, who ruled large parts of the plains from his capital at Janakpur. Janak founded the Mithila kingdom, which flourished until the 3rd century AD when the Guptas from Patna seized its lands.

The depopulation of the Terai began in earnest in the 14th century, when the Mughals swept across the plains of northern India. Hundreds of thousands of Hindu and Buddhist refugees fled into the hills, many settling in the Kathmandu Valley, which later rose to prominence as the capital of the Shah dynasty. Aided by legions of fearsome Gurkha warriors, the Shahs reclaimed the plains, expanding the borders of Nepal to twice their modern size.

Although the British never conquered Nepal, they had regular skirmishes with the Shahs. A treaty was signed in 1816 that trimmed the kingdom to roughly its current borders. Nepal later regained some additional land (including the city of Nepalganj) as a reward for assisting the British in the 1857 Indian Uprising.

Most of the Terai was heavily forested until the late 1950s. There were scattered settlements and the indigenous Tharu people were widely dispersed through the region. In 1954, drainage programs and DDT spraying markedly reduced the incidence of malaria, enabling mass migration from India and the hills. Fertile soils and easy accessibility led to rapid development.

Today, the Tharu are one of the most disadvantaged groups in Nepal, and huge areas of the forest have been cleared for farmland. Only patches of this once-magnificent wilderness remain, conserved in a series of national parks and community forests, yet for the subcontinent these areas are relatively large and increasingly important.

Climate

The Terai has a similar climate to the northern plains of India: hot as a furnace from May to October and drenched by monsoon rains from June to September. Try to visit in winter (November to February) when skies are clear and temperatures are moderate.

🛈 Getting There & Away

The Terai is easily accessible from Kathmandu and Pokhara in Nepal and from West Bengal, Bihar and Uttar Pradesh in India. The Indian rail network passes close to several of the most important border crossings and there are frequent bus and air connections from the Terai to towns and villages across Nepal.

🛈 Getting Around

The annual monsoon rains can severely affect transport in the region – dirt roads turn to mud, dry streambeds become raging torrents, and roads and bridges are routinely washed away.

BICYCLE

On the face of it, the Terai is well suited to cycling: much of the terrain is pool-table flat and there are villages every few kilometres. However, the condition of the roads, the traffic density and

NEPAL–INDIA BORDER CROSSINGS

Heading from east to west, you can cross between India and Nepal at the points listed below. The Sunauli crossing is by far the most popular route between the two countries, but immigration staff are used to seeing foreign tourists at all the crossings. Nepali visas are available on arrival: you'll need one passport photo and US dollars cash for the visa fee.

BORDER CROSSING (NEPAL TO INDIA)	ONWARDS TO:
Mahendranagar to Banbassa	Delhi & hill towns in Uttaranchal
Belahiya to Sunauli	Varanasi, Agra & Delhi
Nepalganj to Jamunaha/Rupaidha Bazaar	Lucknow
Dhangadhi to Gauriphanta	Lucknow, Delhi
Birganj to Raxaul Bazaar	Patna & Kolkata
Kakarbhitta to Panitanki	Darjeeling, Sikkim & Kolkata

unpredictable driver behaviour require riders to be super-alert and highly cautious. If you run out of steam or courage along the way, you can usually put your bike on the roof of a bus.

BUS

Buses and microbuses are the main form of transport around the Terai. However, road safety can be an issue, particularly for night travel. To maximise safety, travel in daylight hours and avoid the front seats.

Roof riding is prohibited in the Kathmandu Valley, but there is no such restriction in the Terai. Riding on the luggage rack with the wind in your hair can be an exhilarating experience, but in no sense of the word is it safe.

CENTRAL TERAI

The Central Terai is the most visited part of the plains. The highway from Mugling to Narayangarh is the principal route south from Kathmandu and Pokhara, and the border crossing at Sunauli is the most popular border crossing between Nepal and India. Its chief attractions include Chitwan National Park, which rightfully remains high on most visitors' to-do lists, and Lumbini, the revered birthplace of the Buddha. The 2015 earthquake caused damage to many villages but most places visited by tourists were unaffected, though landslides blocked stretches of the Mugling–Narayangarh highway, and locals remain vigilant for future slips.

Narayangarh & Bharatpur

📞 056

Narayangarh (also Narayangadh and Narayanghat) sits on the banks of the Narayani River, where the Narayangarh–Mugling Hwy (the major road into the hills to Kathmandu and Pokhara) meets the Mahendra Hwy, which runs the length of Nepal from Mahendranagar to Kakarbhitta. Along with its twin city Bharatpur, which has an airport, it's an important hub, with visitors on their way to or from Chitwan National Park, India and Kathmandu.

🛏 Sleeping & Eating

Hotel Satanchuli   HOTEL $
(Map p244; ☏056-531930; Narayangarh; s/d Rs 600/800, without bathroom Rs 500/600) This colourful hotel is the best option near the Pokhara bus stand. It's clean, has river views, and you can jump straight out of bed and onto the bus.

Hotel Gangotri   HOTEL $$
(Map p244; ☏056-525746; www.hotelgangotri. com; Pulchowk, Narayangarh; r from Rs 1150, with AC Rs 1700-2450; ❄🖥) About 50m along the Mugling Hwy, towards Mugling from the Pulchowk intersection, the Gangotri has boxy standard rooms, slightly better air-cooled rooms with TVs, and comfortable air-con rooms in the new wing. The attached multicuisine restaurant (mains Rs 150 to Rs 280) is best for its Indian dishes.

Hotel Global   HOTEL $$
(Map p244; ☏056-525513; www.hotel-global.com. np; Chaubiskoti Chowk, Bharatpur; s US$20-40, d US$25-50; ❄@🖥🏊) This business hotel boasts manicured gardens, a gym, a sauna, and a sparkling palm-fringed swimming pool – all this only a short walk from the airport. The standard rooms are a little undersized, while the 'deluxe' options offer more comfort and all amenities.

New Kitchen Cafe   INTERNATIONAL $
(Map p244; ☏056-520453; mains Rs 125-350, thali Rs 240-380; ◷8am-9.30pm; ❄) Just south of the bridge over the Narayani, this bustling restaurant serves the best food in town in either the air-con dining room or the small garden. The menu is extensive, though the set meals (Indian and Nepali *thalis*) are probably the best choice.

ℹ Information

Nabil Bank (◷10am-5pm Sun-Thu, to 3pm Fri) has both foreign exchange and an ATM accepting foreign cards.

ℹ Getting There & Away

AIR

Bharatpur Airport (2km south of Narayangarh) is the closest airport to Chitwan National Park. There are several daily flights to/from Kathmandu (US$106, 30 minutes) with **Buddha Air** (☏056-528790; www.buddhaair.com), **Yeti Airlines** (☏056-523136; www.yetiairlines.com) and **Nepal Airlines** (☏056-530470; www.nepal airlines.com.np).

BUS

The main bus stand in Narayangarh is called the **Pokhara bus stand**, and it is found at the east end of Narayangarh on the highway to Mugling. Buses/ microbuses run regularly to Pokhara (Rs 275/380, five hours) and Kathmandu (Rs 350/450, five hours). A few buses also run to Gorkha (Rs 155, three hours) and local buses head to Devghat (Rs 30, 20 minutes). Buses to Kathmandu can also be caught at the busy Pulchowk intersection.

Central Terai

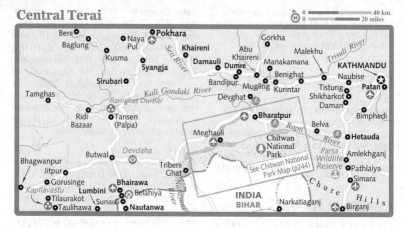

The **Bharatpur bus park** is about 1km south of the airport. From here there are buses to Butwal (Rs 200, three hours), Sunauli/Bhairawa (Rs 280, three hours), Birganj (Rs 200, three hours), Janakpur (Rs 450, six hours), Biratnagar (Rs 800, nine hours), Kathmandu (Rs 350, five hours), Nepalganj (Rs 700, 10 hours), Kakarbhitta (Rs 900, 12 hours) and Mahendranagar (Rs 1050, 12 hours).

For Sauraha, you can take a local bus from the side of the Mahendra Hwy south of Pulchowk (just before you reach the next intersection) to Tandi Bazaar/Sauraha Chowk (Rs 30, 20 minutes). From there you can take a share jeep (Rs 60) to **Bachhauli bus park** (Map p250), but it's much quicker to take a taxi (Rs 1800-2000) all the way from Pulchowk or Bharatpur airport.

Around Narayangarh

Devghat

Hidden away in the forest 6km northeast of Narayangarh, Devghat marks the sacred confluence of the Kali Gandaki and Trisuli rivers, two important tributaries of the River Ganges. Hindus regard the point where the rivers meet as especially sacred and many elderly high-caste Nepalis come here to live out their final years and eventually die on the banks of the holy river. Far from being gloomy, the calm, contemplative atmosphere is wonderfully soothing after the hectic pace of the plains.

The village is reached via a suspension footbridge high over the rushing waters of the Trisuli. The best way to experience Devghat is to wander the streets, which are lined with ashrams and temples that hum and ring with chants and clashing cymbals. On the first day of the Nepali month of Magh (mid-January), thousands of pilgrims flock to Devghat to immerse themselves in the river to celebrate the Hindu festival of Magh Sankranti.

Local buses to Devghat (Rs 30, 20 minutes) leave from the Pokhara bus stand in Narayangarh.

Chitwan National Park

♪ 056

Chitwan National Park is one of the premier drawcards in Nepal, and there was little damage in the 2015 earthquake to areas visited by tourists. The World Heritage–listed reserve protects over 932 sq km of forests, marshland and rippling grassland, and is home to sizeable wildlife populations. It's little wonder this place is so popular.

Meaning 'Heart of the Jungle', Chitwan is famous as one of the best wildlife-viewing national parks in Asia, and you'll have an excellent chance of spotting one-horned rhinos, deer, monkeys and up to 544 species of birds. If you're extremely lucky, you'll see leopards, wild elephants and sloth bears – though it's the once-in-a-lifetime chance to spot a majestic royal Bengal tiger that attracts people in their droves.

Sadly, Chitwan lost many animals during the decade-long Maoist insurgency, when the army was preoccupied with the conflict and unable to provide adequate protection from poachers. However, the good news is that recent census figures show rhino numbers are substantially recovering (503 individuals in 2011) and tiger numbers are steadily increasing (around 120 adults in 2013).

The best option for experiencing Chitwan National Park is to stay in one of the luxury lodges located on the edge of the park away from the crowds at Sauraha. The government stopped the luxury lodges from operating inside the park in 2012. Most of these lodges have developed alternative lodges just outside the national-park boundaries. Though this experience doesn't come cheaply, the sense of adventure, less crowding and access to more remote parts of the park make it very worthwhile.

That said, most budget travellers opt for the more affordable lodging in Sauraha, a tourist village on the northern bank of the Rapti River, a border of the park. Sauraha has a lively backpacker scene, and while many enjoy its social nature – it's a great place to have a beer watching the sunset over the river – others are let down by its insensitive and overly commercial development.

Two whole days in the park is really the minimum for wildlife-spotting. The nature of dense jungle, tall grass and the nocturnal hours kept by many animals are all factors that make spotting animals far from guaranteed. A good approach is to treat wildlife-viewing as one would the pastime of fishing: some days you'll get plenty of bites, others not a nibble. Irrespective, it's all about the thrill of the chase

CHITWAN'S BIG FIVE

Chitwan has some high-profile species that everyone wants to see, including the following.

One-Horned Indian Rhino
Chitwan is one of the last refuges of the rare one-horned Indian rhinoceros (*gaida* in Nepali), and they are one of the most commonly seen animals on elephant safaris in the park. Only about 3000 survive worldwide, most of them in Chitwan and Kaziranga National Park in Assam, India. Sadly, poaching significantly reduced Chitwan's rhino population during the Maoist insurgency, though the good news is that recent counts have confirmed the population is rebounding.

Asian Elephant
The Asian elephant (*hathi*) is the world's second-largest land mammal behind its African counterpart. The elephants you're most likely to see in Chitwan are domestic elephants that ferry visitors around on wildlife-spotting safaris, though there's a small population of approximately 25 to 30 wild elephants in the adjoining Parsa Wildlife Reserve plus wandering migrants from Bihar's Valmiki National Park.

Royal Bengal Tiger
The intelligence, size and power of the royal Bengal tiger (*bagh*) make it one of the most majestic and feared animals in the subcontinent. Both locals and foreigners have been attacked by tigers at Chitwan – a very rare occurrence but something to think about before joining a guided walk. There are currently around 120 tigers in Chitwan; sightings are rare as tigers lie low during daylight hours. It's said that tigers are a hundred times more likely to spot you, rather than vice versa.

Gharial
The gharial is a bizarre-looking crocodile, with a slender, elongated snout crammed with ill-fitting teeth and a bulbous protuberance at the end of its snout, resembling a *ghara* (local pot) from which it gets its name. Gharials are adept at catching fish, and 110-million-year-old fossils have been found with the same basic body plan, attesting to the effectiveness of the gharial design. Gharials are endangered but there are breeding programs, and young gharials have been released into many rivers in the Terai.

Sloth Bear
These shaggy black bears (*bhalu*), the size of a large dog, have a reputation as the most-feared animal (tiger included) among locals. They get their name from being confused with sloths in the 19th century, owing to their long claws and excellent tree-climbing abilities. The bears' diet consists mainly of termites and ants – they use their protruding muzzles to vacuum them up through a gap between their teeth, a sound that can be heard up to 100m away.

Chitwan National Park

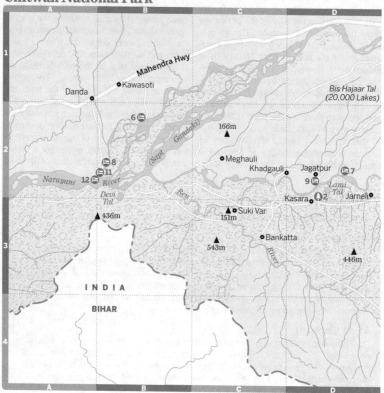

THE TERAI & MAHABHARAT RANGE CHITWAN NATIONAL PARK

Chitwan National Park

⊚ Sights
1	Elephant Breeding Centre	E2
2	National Park Headquarters	D2

⊟ Sleeping
3	Hotel Gangotri	E1
4	Hotel Global	E1
5	Hotel Satanchuli	E1
6	Island Jungle Resort	B2

7	Kasara Resort	D2
8	Machan Country Villa	B2
9	Machan Paradise View	D2
10	Sapana Village Lodge	E2
11	Temple Tiger Green Jungle Resort	B2
12	Tiger Tops Tharu Lodge	A2

⊗ Eating
13	New Kitchen Cafe	E1

and being out and about in tiger and rhino country. Be aware that the popular four-day, three-night packages out of Kathmandu and Pokhara include a day of travel at either end.

History

Chitwan National Park was created in 1973, but the area has been protected since at least the 19th century as a hunting reserve. Britain's King George V and his son, the young future Edward VIII, managed to slaughter a staggering 39 tigers and 18 rhinos during just one blood-soaked safari to Chitwan in 1911. Despite the occasional slaughter, Chitwan's status as a hunting reserve probably protected more animals than were killed.

Until the late 1950s, the only inhabitants of the Chitwan Valley were small communities of Tharu villagers, who were blessed with a degree of resistance to malaria. After a mas-

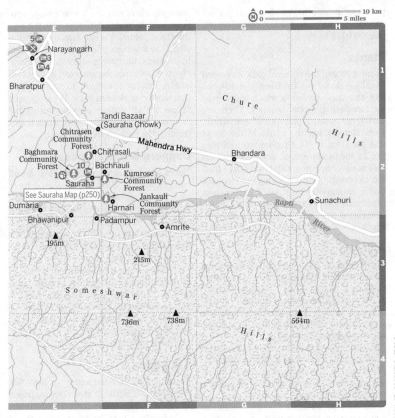

sive malaria-eradication program in 1954, land-hungry peasants from the hills swarmed into the region and huge tracts of the forest were cleared to make space for farmland.

As their habitat disappeared, so did the tigers and rhinos. By the mid-1960s there were fewer than 100 rhinos and 20 tigers. News of the dramatic decline reached the ears of King Mahendra and the area was declared a royal reserve, becoming a national park in 1973. Some 22,000 peasants were removed from within the park boundaries, but it was only when army patrols were introduced to stop poaching that animal numbers started to rebound. Chitwan was added to the Unesco World Heritage list in 1984.

While animal populations have increased markedly since then, there was an alarming drop in numbers during the Maoist rebellion. Poachers reduced rhino and tiger numbers by a quarter, selling animal parts on to middlemen in China and Tibet. With regular army patrols and several significant arrests of poachers, protection has been restored and wildlife numbers are once again on the rise.

Geography

Chitwan National Park covers an impressive 932 sq km. A further 499 sq km is set aside as the Parsa Wildlife Reserve and multiuse conservation areas have been created in the community forests of Baghmara, Chitrasen, Jankauli and Kumrose, which have been replanted with trees to provide villages with a source of firewood and fodder. Because of the topography, most tourist activities are restricted to the flood plain of the Rapti River.

As well as the river, there are numerous tal (small lakes) dotted around the forest. The most interesting of these, particularly for viewing birds, are **Devi Tal** near Tiger Tops Jungle Lodge and **Lami Tal** near Kasara. There's another group of lakes and pools just outside the park boundary, known collectively as **Bis Hajaar Tal** (literally '20,000 lakes').

Plants

Around 70% of the national park is covered in sal forest; sal is a large-leaved hardwood tree, the heavy timber of which is favoured for furniture and boat building. There are also large swaths of *phanta* (grassland), particularly along the banks of the Rapti and Narayani rivers. Growing up to 8m in height, the local elephant grass provides excellent cover for rhinos and tigers, and food for elephants. When walking or elephant riding through the forest, you'll see *shisham* (a valuable timber species), towering kapok (silk cotton tree), strangler figs and the pungent curry leaf tree, among many others.

Animals

Chitwan boasts 68 different species of mammals, including rhinos, tigers, deer, monkeys, elephants, leopards, sloth bears, wild boar and hyenas. Birdwatchers can tick off 544 different species of birds, while butterfly-spotters have identified at least 67 species, some as large as your hand.

The one-horned Indian rhinoceros is the most famous animal at Chitwan and you stand a good chance of seeing one on an elephant safari. Chitwan also has significant populations of gharial crocodiles.

As well as these high-profile animals, you may spot barking deer, spotted deer, hog deer, sambar and massive gaurs (Indian wild oxen). The most commonly seen monkey at Chitwan is the stocky rhesus macaque, but you also have a very good chance of spotting the larger and more elegant grey langur. Spotted deer are often seen following the langurs around, taking advantage of their profligate feeding habits. They also cooperate to alert each other when predators are in the area: the hoots of monkeys or deer serve as a good indicator to keep your eyes peeled for a lurking tiger.

Birds seen in Chitwan include bulbuls, mynahs, egrets, parakeets, jungle fowl, peacocks, kingfishers, orioles and various species of drongos. Keen birders should keep an eye out for rare species, such as ruby-cheeked sunbirds, emerald doves, jungle owlets and crested hornbills.

When to Visit

The most comfortable time to visit Chitwan is from October to March, when skies are relatively clear and the average daily temperature is a balmy 25°C. However, the best time to see animals is late January to March when the towering *phanta* grass is slashed by villagers, improving visibility considerably. At other times the grass can grow as tall as 8m, making it difficult to spot animals that may be as close as a few feet away. Jeep safaris are virtually impossible during the monsoon (June to September), when tracks through the park become impassable.

Dangers & Annoyances

Tigers, leopards, elephants and rhinos are all quite capable of killing humans, and there have been some serious attacks on tourists. Most people have a good experience on jungle walks, but you should be aware that there's a small but significant risk – being chased by a rhino seems a lot less funny when you consider the phrase 'trampled to death'.

Insects are another unwelcome aspect of life in the jungle. Mosquitoes in large numbers are inescapable year-round. Malaria may be present in some areas of the park, so remember to bring DEET-based insect repellent. During the monsoon the forest comes alive with *jukha* (leeches).

◉ Sights

National Park Headquarters   NATIONAL PARK
(Map p244; ☑ 056-521932; gharial breeding project admission Rs 100; ☺6am-6pm) The National Park Headquarters are inside the park at Kasara, about 13km west of Sauraha on the south bank of the Rapti River. Most people visit as part of an organised jungle safari and there's a small visitor centre with displays on wildlife, including orphaned and injured animals. At the **gharial breeding project** you can see both gharial and marsh mugger crocodiles up close; the program has been a great success in releasing both endangered species back into the wild.

Elephant Breeding Centre   ZOO
(Map p244; ☑ 056-580154; foreigner/SAARC Rs 50/25; ☺6am-6pm) This centre, about 3km west of Sauraha on the far side of the small Bhude Rapti River, provides many of the elephants for elephant safaris at Chitwan. It's fascinating watching the interaction between mother and baby elephants, as well as the multitask use of their trunk (which has a staggering 40,000 muscles), such as covering themselves in dust to ward off mosquitoes or scratching their backside with a bamboo stick.

The elephants spend much of the day grazing in the jungle, so you need to come before 10.30am or after 3.30pm if you want to see the baby elephants. The mother elephants are chained up when they are stabled, which does disappoint many tourists, but it is for their safety and yours. As adorable as the baby elephants may seem, treat them with caution as most have a playful streak and are surprisingly powerful.

Morning is a good time to visit. Not only are there fewer tourists, but you also get to watch the mahouts (elephant carers) prepare *kuchiis* – elephant sweets made from molasses, salt and rice wrapped in grass. The breeding centre is an easy walk or cycle along the road past Jungle Lagoon Safari Lodge.

Tharu Cultural Show   TRADITIONAL DANCE
(tickets Rs 100; ⊙ 7pm & 7.30pm) Most of the larger lodges put on shows of traditional Tharu songs and dances for guests, including the popular stick dance, where a great circle of running men whack sticks together in time. It's very much a tourist experience, but the shows are fun and they provide employment for local people. In Sauraha there are nightly performances at the **Sauraha Tharu Culture House** (Map p250; admission Rs 100; ⊙ show 7.30pm) and the **Tharu Culture Program** (Map p250; admission Rs 100; ⊙ show 7pm).

**Wildlife Display
& Information Centre**   MUSEUM
(Map p250; admission Rs 100; ⊙ 7am-5pm) Aimed more at school groups than tourists, this educational centre has displays on wildlife, including a rather macabre collection of animal foetuses and reproductive organs in jars, plus skulls, plaster-cast footprints and a collection of animal poo.

Activities

You'll need to add another Rs 1500 to prices: this is the cost of a daily park permit. Also, for some activities there is a minimum group size to achieve these per-person costs.

Elephant Safaris

For many visitors, lumbering through the jungle on the back of a five-tonne jumbo spotting wildlife is the defining Chitwan experience. It's the best way to see wildlife, offering a fantastic vantage point high above the tall grasses of the *phanta*. The wildlife are much more tolerant of elephants than of noisy jeeps or walkers, and they also effectively mask the scent of humans. Elephants also play an important role in the park on patrols, looking for poachers. Note that at the time of writing elephant safaris were restricted to the park buffer zones (or community forests). Nevertheless, these zones have abundant wildlife.

Riding an elephant is thrilling rather than comfortable. Elephants move with a heavy, rolling gait, and three or four passengers are crammed into each wooden howdah (riding platform). Each elephant is controlled by a mahout, who usually works with the same elephant throughout its life.

ELEPHANT WELLBEING

Many visitors to Chitwan are upset by the sight of shackled elephants at the breeding centre, as well as the treatment dished out by some mahouts, who occasionally whack their skulls with sticks and pull their ears with metal hooks to prevent them straying off course. It's one of the unfortunate drawbacks to transforming elephants into domestic animals. Most of the elephants are otherwise treated well and spend a good five hours each day grazing in the park.

The commercial use of elephants in Nepal's national parks remains controversial. Despite the breeding centres, elephants are still captured in India and smuggled into Nepal to satisfy tourist demand. Animal-welfare organisations have released very distressing reports about the traditional training/desensitising methods and ongoing treatment of 'domesticated' elephants. Subsequently, many tourists refrain from riding elephants based on these reports.

In a positive move, the WWF has launched an initiative to introduce less severe training methods that involve psychological techniques, compared to the more distressing traditional methods employed by mahouts. Also, Elephant Aid International (www.elephantaidinternational.org) is working with the government to introduce compassionate elephant care and chain-free corrals in Chitwan.

THE TERAI & MAHABHARAT RANGE CHITWAN NATIONAL PARK

DON'T MISS

ELEPHANT BATH TIME

Every day (excepting some cold winter days) from around 10am to noon, the elephants in Sauraha march down to the river near the Hotel River Side for their morning soak and scrub, and everyone turns out to watch the spectacle. If you bring your swimming costume and Rs 100, you can join in with elephant bath time; it's quite commercialised but the elephants seem to enjoy the process. The highlight for many is sitting on the back of a submerged elephant and shouting *chhop!* – if you get the accent right you'll be rewarded with a refreshing trunkful of cold water. Lodges with their own elephants offer similar elephant bathing experiences.

→ **Government-Owned Elephants**

The national park has its own herd of domesticated elephants, although at the time of writing most of these were not being used to provide tourist safaris. This situation is apt to change so check out the latest from the National Park Visitors Centre (p255). Three government elephants were, however, providing safaris at the **National Trust for Nature Conservation** (Map p250; foreigner/SAARC per person Rs 2500/1500) located behind the Wildlife Display & Information Centre (p247). The major benefit of taking one of these (more expensive) safaris (7.30am and 3pm) is that they go to Ichhani Island – still in the buffer zone, but a place little frequented by other safaris.

If reinstated, the majority of government **jungle safaris** (foreigner/SAARC per person Rs 2500/1000) will depart the National Park Visitors Centre at Sauraha at 8am and 4pm daily, and 7am and 5pm during summer. Children are half-price. There are no advance bookings so you will need to line up early in the morning to purchase a ticket from the Visitor Centre, or better yet organise it through your hotel (a service that helps with the employment of locals). Safaris last one to two hours and run through the community forest and dense *phanta* along the Rapti River, a favourite feeding ground for deer and rhinos.

→ **Privately Owned Elephants**

Most of the luxury lodges have their own elephants, and elephant safaris are included in their package tours. In Sauraha, elephants

are owned by various resorts and hotels and these elephants (currently there are 52) are 'pooled' into the **United Elephant Cooperative** (Map p250; ☑ 056-580080; per person Rs 1200), which coordinates the riding business as well as looking after the wear and tear on the elephants and the environment. The easiest and best way to arrange these elephant safaris is through your accommodation, although there is usually some small saving in going to the cooperative directly.

Morning and afternoon safaris last 1½ hours and are run in either the Baghmara or Kumrose community forests, which are buffer zones on the northern edge of the park with decent wildlife populations. Although not strictly 'inside' the park, you still need to purchase the Rs 1500 park permit. From Sept to Jan, spotting wildlife in the community forests is often better than inside the park, where long grass makes visibility difficult.

Jungle Walks

Exploring the park on foot when accompanied by a guide is a fantastic way to get close to the wildlife. Most walks start with a gentle canoe drift downstream followed by the walk. Be aware that you enter the park with the real risk of encountering bad-tempered mother rhinos, tigers or sloth bears protecting their young. Generally, the bigger the group, the safer the walk, but the experience of your guide counts for a lot. Levels of experience vary and some of the guides have a worryingly devil-may-care attitude to creeping up on rhinos. Therefore, jungle walks are not recommended for the faint-hearted. Rules stipulate two guides are required even if there is only one customer. Before you opt for a whole-day jungle walk, consider the very real risks associated with venturing deep into the park and being far from rescue and medical facilities, possibly without communication.

Jungle walks (cost per person based on 3 walkers for half-day Rs 1300) can be arranged through any of the lodges or travel agents in Sauraha. Independant guides hang around the National Park Visitors Centre. Don't worry, they'll find you! Although they can be irritating when they are spruiking for business, they are, as a rule, well-intentioned, licensed, informed and local Tharu. Another option is to use one of the cooperatives such as **United Jungle Guide Service** (Map p250; ☑ 580219; 1½ hour safaris Rs 800, plus park fees) and **Nepal Dynamic Eco Tours** (Map p250; ☑ 9845107720; half-day Rs 1300-1500 plus park fees), organised groups of local guides providing numerous options for jungle walks. Ask them about the more adventurous multiday jungle walks where you exit the park each night to stay in a Tharu village.

Canoeing

An altogether more relaxing way to explore the park is on a **canoeing trip** (per person from Rs 1500) on the Rapti or Narayani Rivers. You have an excellent chance of spotting water birds and crocodiles. The most typical canoe trips (for example if you have bought a package tour) start from Sauraha and include a one-hour trip downriver followed by a two-hour guided walk back to Sauraha, with a stop at the elephant breeding centre. Canoe trips can be easily arranged either through your hotel or a booking agency in Sauraha.

Longer excursions are ideal for those not on a package as they get you away from the crowds. One recommended option is a two-hour canoe ride followed by a 16km walk to Kasara (park HQ) and a jeep ride home. This will cost around Rs 4000 per person for a group of three or more (Rs 5000 per person for a couple).

4WD Safari

It may not have quite the same romance as riding through the jungle on the back of an elephant, but **4WD safaris** (half-/full-day per jeep up to 7 passengers Rs 11,000/13,000) are another popular way to explore the park. Animals are less concerned by the rumble of engines than you might suspect and you'll have the opportunity to go further into the jungle. Safaris can be booked either through your hotel or an agency in Sauraha.

Cycling

You can't cycle inside the park, but the surrounding countryside is ideal for bicycle touring, with dozens of small Tharu farming communities to visit. Another possible destination is **Bis Hajaar Tal**, bird-filled lakes and ponds about 1½ hours northwest of Sauraha, accessible via the Mahendra Hwy. Bicycles can be rented in Sauraha.

🛏 Sleeping

Most travellers, especially budget travellers, will stay at Sauraha on the north bank of the Rapti River. The alternatives include the upmarket lodges, which have resorts on the edge of the park, plus a few budget lodges and homestays in Tharu villages. The lodges and guest houses at Chitwan were not seriously affected by the 2015 earthquake.

Many people visit Chitwan on package tours arranged through travel agents in Kathmandu, Pokhara or overseas. This is by far the easiest approach if you plan to stay at one of the lodges outside of Sauraha, where transport to and from the lodge is not straightforward. However, if you're planning to stay in Sauraha, packages are unnecessary and expensive, and it's easy enough to arrange accommodation and activities independently. Discounts of 20% to 50% are available in the low season, particularly from May to September.

🛏 Sauraha

Most independent travellers to Chitwan stay in the village of Sauraha on the northern

---

THARU VILLAGES

Sauraha is surrounded by small Tharu villages, which you can explore by bike or on foot. Resist the urge to hand out sweets, pens and money; instead, if you want to help local people, shop in the village shops or eat in village bhojanalayas (restaurants). Farming is the main industry and many people still decorate their houses with Mithila paintings and adobe bas-reliefs of animals. The nearest Tharu village is **Bachhauli**, a pleasant cycle or 20-minute walk out through the rice or bright-yellow mustard fields. Here you will find the informative **Tharu Cultural Museum & Research Centre** (admission Rs 25; ⊙ 7am-5pm) with colourful murals and exhibits on artefacts and local dress.

Harnari is one of the best villages to get a taste of Tharu culture. Bordering the Kumrose Community Forest, it's less visited than Bachhauli and has a more authentic feel. There's a tiny **Tharu Cultural Museum** (admission by donation) here with displays of ornaments and a rakshi distillery pot. If it's closed, ask around and someone will open it up. It's a 20-minute bike ride from Sauraha.

Sapana Village Lodge (p251) runs excellent tours of Tharu villages and organises activities, from walking tours and planting rice in the fields with villagers to fishing trips and cooking and art classes.

Sauraha

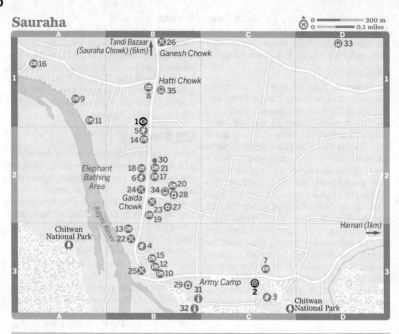

N 0 ———————— 200 m
   0 ———————— 0.1 miles

Tandi Bazaar
(Sauraha Chowk) (6km)
Ganesh Chowk

Hatti Chowk

Elephant
Bathing
Area

Rapti River

Gaida
Chowk

Chitwan
National Park

Harnari (1km)

Army Camp

Chitwan
National Park

Sauraha

fringes of the park. There are dozens of lodges and hotels here, from upmarket package accommodation to simple guesthouses run by local villagers. Almost all have room fans and mosquito nets or insect screening on the windows.

★Chitwan Gaida Lodge   LODGE $

(Map p250; ☑ 056-580083, in Kathmandu 01-4444527; www.chitwangaidalodge.com; r Rs 500-800, with AC Rs 1200-2000; 🛜) Run by one of Nepal's leading ornithologists, Tika Ram Giri, Gaida Lodge has a range of rooms including the original bungalows plus the new modern rooms in a four-floor building. The rooms on the 4th floor have treetop views and catch a cool breeze. The cool green garden has a bird pond and numerous hammocks to lounge in. This is *the* place for birdwatchers.

Travellers Jungle Camp   HOTEL $

(Map p250; ☑ 9855055845, 056-580013; www.nepaljunglecamp.com; r budget Rs 1000, deluxe Rs 1500-2000; ❋🛜) This is a long-standing family-owned hotel, where you'll receive a warm welcome, enjoy a relaxing garden and even meet the resident pachyderm, Chanchal Kali. All rooms are spick and span, while the spacious deluxe rooms have excellent mattresses – a noteworthy item when comparing Sauraha lodges. The owner is well attuned to travellers' needs and the website offers packages for independent travellers.

Chitwan Riverside Resort   HOTEL $

(Map p250; ☑ 056-580297, in Kathmandu 01-4256696; www.chitwanriverside.com; r Rs 1500-2000; ❋🛜) Here it's all about the idyllic riverside location away from bustling Sauraha bazaar. There's a choice between lovely cottages without views or rooms in the newer building with excellent river views. The shaded viewing platform atop the riverbank is a magnificent spot to sit back during sunset with a beer and, if you're lucky, you'll spot some thirsty wildlife.

Sauraha Resort   HOTEL $

(Map p250; ☑ 9855066114, 056-580114; www.sauraharesort.com; r Rs 1000-2000; ❋🛜) This low-key, family-run hotel is close to town but tucked back from the street. Rooms range from simple twins and larger doubles (with an extra single bed and TV) to air-con doubles. All feature mosquito nets and fans. Although low-key, all the jungle activities can be arranged here and the new front-of-house restaurant should be running by the time you read this.

Hotel River Side   HOTEL $

(Map p250; ☑ 056-580009, in Kathmandu 01-4441572; www.wildlifechitwan.com; r Rs 1500-4500; 🛜) Take your choice between delightful terracotta-tiled huts or the less atmospheric modern rooms with a balcony delivering unbeatable river views. The cheapest rooms on the bottom floor are unremarkable but decent. There's a riverside restaurant, helpful staff and a garden full of hammocks.

Hotel Shiva's Dream   HOTEL $

(Map p250; ☑ 056-580488; www.hotelshivasdream.com.np; r Rs 800, with AC Rs 1500-2000; ❋) This budget option is run by the same family as Bardia's Forest Hideaway (p274). They are familiar with package and independent tourists alike. The spacious rooms in the three-storey building are tidy enough, with mosquito nets and sizeable bathrooms, but the rooms and restaurant are in need of some updating. We were told that renovations were planned.

Hotel Nature Heritage   HOTEL $

(Map p250; ☑ 056-580432; www.hotelnatureheritage.com.np; r Rs 1800-2200; ❋🛜) This rather imposing cement tower has a range of clean and comfortable rooms, all appointed with TVs, air-con and running hot water. The mattresses are on the thin side, however. The room tariff increases as you climb the stairs and gain river views.

Jungle Lagoon Safari Lodge   LODGE $

(Map p250; ☑ 056-580126; www.lagoon.com.np; r Rs 1000; 🛜) On the road to the elephant breeding centre, Jungle Lagoon is a pleasant low-key 'resort' on a lovely spot by the river. Priding itself as a 'birdwatching paradise', it's a bit ramshackle, even run-down, but agreeable all the same considering the location and the tariff. Rooms are very basic and well worn, but there were renovations happening when we visited.

Jungle Adventure World   HOTEL $

(Map p250; ☑ 056-580301, in Kathmandu 9845065985; www.jungleadventureworld.com; r Rs 1500, with AC Rs 2000) This rustic lodge comprising bungalows scattered in a shady garden has a laidback tropical-island feel. The older bungalows are semidetached and well worn, while the newer ones are detached with lanterns on each private porch. The garden makes for a great place to escape the heat.

Chitwan Rest House   HOTEL $

(Map p250; ☑ 056-580261; ro.chaudhary@yahoo.com; r Rs 600) Located 500m north of Gaida Chowk, this is a friendly, uberbudget option with basic rooms (no piped hot water) set in neat adobe cottages with a small but verdant garden and a cheap restaurant.

★Sapana Village Lodge   LODGE $$

(Map p244; ☑ 056-580308; www.sapanalodge.com; s/d incl breakfast US$35/45-60; ❋🛜)

Situated 1.5km north of Sauraha, this serene lodge is an excellent option for those with an interest in Tharu culture. Set up with the aim of supporting the local Tharu community, rooms are decked out in charming village-style designs with vibrant paintings and rugs. The alfresco lounge and outstanding restaurant look over the Budhi Rapti River and rice paddies.

The lodge has its own elephants including a mother and young and all the wildlife activities can be organised here. Accommodation plus activity packages are detailed on its website.

Hotel Hermitage
HOTEL $$

(Map p250; ☑056-580090, in Kathmandu 01-4424390; www.nepalhotelhermitage.com; cottage Rs 2500, boathouse Rs 3500; ✸@✵) Although apparently geared towards travellers on a package, this lodge nonetheless boasts very experienced guides and commands one of the better elevated riverside positions, while still being an easy stroll from town. Rooms in the moat-surrounded 'boathouse' are spacious and cool while the restaurant and 'drinks' area are perfectly positioned on the river bank.

River View Jungle Camp
HOTEL $$

(Map p250; ☑056-580096, mobile 9851011483; www.rvjcnepal.com; B&B cottage US$15-35, B&B deluxe r US$30-65; ✸✵) This is a good central choice with expert staff. Its khaki brick cottages are set along a long garden leading all the way to the river. The rooms are tidy with fans and air-con, mosquito nets and relia-

ble hot water. The deluxe rooms in the new building overlooking the river have private balconies, modern bathrooms, flatscreen TVs and plush mattresses.

Royal Park Hotel
HOTEL $$

(Map p250; ☑056-580061, in Kathmandu 01-4412987; www.royalparkhotel.com.np; r incl breakfast US$30; ✸✵✵) Set in extensive park-like gardens, the attractive adobe-and-thatch bungalows boast huge rooms and gorgeous stone- or marble-tiled bathrooms. Upstairs rooms are best, with soaring ceilings and inviting balconies. There is a restaurant and regular cultural shows when a group is being hosted.

Jungle Safari Lodge
HOTEL $$

(Map p250; ☑056-580046; www.junglesafarilodge.com; r incl breakfast Rs 2500, ste Rs 5000; ✸@✵) A long-standing, central hotel that has experienced staff and a warm welcome. There have been some recent renovations, and so rooms vary depending on age. Try and book one of the newer rooms which have comfy beds and modern bathrooms. There is a nice terrace for outside dining

Chitwan Tiger Camp
HOTEL $$

(Map p250; ☑056-580060, in Kathmandu 01-4441572; www.chitwantigercamp.com; s/d US$25/40, deluxe US$40/60; ✵) The budget rooms are downstairs and fairly standard, while the upstairs rooms with tubs and bamboo decor are much better but perhaps a little overpriced at the rack rates. For a long time Tiger Camp had an excellent lo-

---

CHITWAN'S EMBEDDED SAFARI LODGES EXTINCT?

By far the most atmospheric way to visit Chitwan was to stay at one of the upmarket lodges *inside* the park. The resorts were expensive, but it's hard to put a price on the experience of staying deep in the jungle, surrounded by the sounds of wildlife.

The pioneer of these lodges was Tiger Tops Jungle Lodge, which was opened years before the national park was declared – indeed it was the owners of Tiger Tops that lobbied hard for the national-park designation. The concept was to provide a high-value safari experience rather than five-star luxury.

In recent times there were six lodges within the national park. All were forced to close and relocate outside the park's perimeter in July 2012 when their leases were not renewed by the Minister for Forests and Soil Conservation. Media reports suggest that the government's own Minister for Tourism lobbied his colleague to renew the lodge leases to no avail.

In some cases, such as with Tiger Tops' famous Jungle Lodge, the buildings are being maintained, providing a focus for day trips, while appeals continue for a reappraisal for the blanket closure. Among the arguments put forward by the lodges is that they provided a permanent presence of naturalists moving about within the park, effectively increasing the anti-poaching patrols. In the meantime, most of the lodges are operating pretty much as they were by taking safaris into the park from their lodges on the park perimeter.

JUNGLE SAFETY

Chitwan and Bardia national parks are among the few wildlife parks in the world that you can explore on foot (when accompanied by a guide). It's both an exhilarating and humbling experience being brought back to a level playing field within the animal hierarchy, where your only protection is the bamboo stick carried by your guide (which can be surprisingly effective in beating off advancing animals). The sound of a twig snapping in the forest or the warning cry of deer and monkeys, alerting each other of nearby predators, will make your heart race.

Jungle walks are a real risk. While dangerous run-ins are not overly common, you'll hear enough stories of tourists experiencing terrifying encounters with animals to make you want to devise a plan of retreat if an angry rhino charges at 40km/h in your direction. Nearly all incidents involve protective mothers in the company of their young. The most crucial piece of advice is to never venture into the park without a guide, nor outside the park visiting hours.

Rhinos

Being charged by rhinos is the most common dangerous encounter tourists have in the park. With poor eyesight, rhinos rely on a keen sense of smell that enables them to sniff out threats, which includes humans. If you are charged, the best evasive action according to Eak Krishna Shrestha, naturalist of over 25 years, is 'to climb the nearest big tree', which are usually easy enough to climb. Alternatively, hiding behind a tree can be effective, though be prepared for several repeated charges from the rhino. Failing trees, Eak suggests 'running zigzag before dropping an item of clothing or your camera as a decoy'.

Sloth Bears

Due to their unpredictable temperament, sloth bears have the reputation as one of the most feared animals in Chitwan. Their nocturnal hours make sightings rare, though mothers and cubs sometimes move about during the day. Eak, who bears the scars of a sloth bear attack, warns that 'males go for the face; however, females go for down there!' [pointing to his nether region]. 'If in danger, it's best not to run; rather, stay perfectly still and huddle in a group to make you look more threatening, while your guide bangs a stick on the ground to scare [the bear] away.'

Tigers

In the unlikely event you cross paths with a tiger, which are known to be extremely shy, the best advice according to Santa Chaudhari (p273), a naturalist from Bardia National Park, is 'not to run; maintain eye contact and back away slowly' – certainly easier said than done. In 2009 Santa had the opportunity to test this theory – successfully.

Elephants

Due to numerous deaths of villagers each year, locals rightfully fear wild elephants. If you are in a threatening situation, the most effective means of escape is to simply run for dear life!

cation on Sunset Point, but the prime beachfront position was lost when the river bank was reinforced. Still, it's not far to walk to find a beach lounge and a cold beer.

Elsewhere

Sauraha isn't the only place to base yourself in Chitwan. The luxury lodges that were once inside park have expanded or developed lodges on the park's boundaries away from the throng at Sauraha. At the other end of the scale, you can stay in a Tharu village homestay. There are 20 village houses in Amaltari (Baghkhor village), near Tiger Tops Tharu Lodge, best booked through a travel agent in Kathmandu.

★ Tiger Tops Tharu Lodge   LODGE $$$
(Map p244; ☑ in Kathmandu 01-4411225; www.tigertops.com; Amaltari; inclusive packages per person per night US$200; @🕤🕸) ✎ Chitwan's number-one lodge is situated near the Narayani River on the western edge of the park. Built with local material in the traditional Tharu style, rooms are arranged

in two long houses or you can opt for a safari-style tent. As well as wildlife activities with expert guides there are village tours and cultural shows.

The lodge has its own organic farm and proudly supports the local community with a medical clinic and school. The lodge is in Amaltari, Nawalparashi, 7km off the Mahendra Hwy at Danda, a small town just past Kawasoti. Guests are usually picked up and dropped off at Bharatpur airport.

Temple Tiger Green Jungle Resort
LODGE $$$

(Map p244; ☑ in Kathmandu 01-4263480; www. greenjungleresort.com; Amaltari Ghat; packages per person per night US$225; ✳@🖀) Another well-regarded, ecofriendly lodge that has relocated from inside the park. Temple Tiger Green Jungle Resort offers large, comfortable, modern villas with thatched roofs that overlook rural Tharu vistas. Wildlife lectures as well as meals are taken in the central restaurant which has a bar. Activities include elephant, jeep and canoe safaris, plus village tours.

Kasara Resort
LODGE $$$

(Map p244; ☑ in Kathmandu 01-443757; www. kasararesort.com; Patihani; packages per person per night US$180; ✳🖀🌊) The latest addition to the luxury lodge scene, Kasara Resort is near the Chitwan National Park headquarters and is more about creature comfort than rustic safari. Although all the wildlife-watching and safari activities are at your fingertips, it's the luxe resort that quickly impresses. Accommodation is in regular Deluxe villas or the more palatial Jungle View villas. Package prices include food and certain activities, including elephant safaris.

Machan Paradise View
LODGE $$$

(Map p244; ☑ in Kathmandu 01-4225001; www. machanwildliferesort.com; 1-/2-night package US$140/260, additional nights US$135; ✳🖀🌊) Machan Paradise View is west of Sauraha near the village of Jagatpur and close to the park headquarters at Kasara. Accommodation is in five bungalows, each containing four modern and spacious rooms. All the usual activities are catered for and include excursions to nearby lakes.

Machan Country Villa
LODGE $$$

(Map p244; ☑ in Kathmandu 01-4225001; www. machanwildliferesort.com; 1-/2-night package per person US$190/380, additional nights US$135; ✳@🖀) This new addition to Machan resort group is situated on the northern bank of the Narayani River in the village of Gauch-hada, towards the western end of the park. Rooms, either in the pretty, thatched bungalows or the more utilitarian longhouse are modern and spacious and tastefully decorated with Mithila paintings

Island Jungle Resort
LODGE $$$

(Map p244; ☑ in Kathmandu 01-4220162; www. islandjungleresort.com; 3-day/2-night package per person US$200, additional nights US$80; 🖀) This resort was formerly on a large island inside the park but moved across the Narayani River at the western end of the park. The cottages are simple but comfortable, and arranged to face the main dining hall. There are great riverside views and you can visit the former lodge within the park whilst on safari.

✗ Eating

Most lodges and hotels have restaurants though there are several independent places in the main bazaar at Sauraha for those not on all-inclusive packages. All serve beer, cocktails and a familiar menu of travellers' fare. Most open from 6am and close at around 10pm. For real bargain-basement meals, there are a few rustic bhojanalayas in the bazaar.

★ Chitwan Bar & Restaurant
INTERNATIONAL $

(Map p250; mains Rs 110-350; ⊙7am-10pm) This simple gathering of chairs and tables on the sandy riverbank prides itself on its Nepali *thalis* and local fish dishes, and it does seem to manage the coldest beer in these parts. It usually has an offer such as 'buy one cocktail get one free'. This also makes for a delightful spot for breakfast.

Sweet Memory Restaurant
NEPALI $

(Map p250; Hamro [Ganesh] Chowk; mains Rs 150-450; ⊙7am-9pm) A tiny family-run shack restaurant with plenty of flowers and pot plants, Sweet Memory prides itself on its home-style cooking. The momos and the chicken curry are recommended, and it also serves up good filtered coffee, coffee cocktails and sweet lime *(mausambi)* juice. It's tucked down the side of a tall, overshadowing building.

Sauraha Beach Restaurant
INTERNATIONAL $

(Map p250; mains Rs 100-300; ⊙6.30am-10.30pm) Right on Sunset Point with a scattering of low tables and reclined chairs, this is a good place for sunset drinks and alfresco dining. Choose from Nepali, Indian, Italian, Chinese and more. For a better view or perhaps to keep drinking while the flood waters rise, there is an elevated platform.

★ **KC's Restaurant** INTERNATIONAL **$$**
(Map p250; mains Rs 350-550; ⊘ 6.30am-10.30pm)
Rightfully the most popular choice in Sau-
raha, KC's is set in a cool, thatch-roofed
bungalow with an open terrace overlooking
the manicured garden, with a fire pit at the
back for winter dinners. The chefs here look
the part and the well-executed menu runs
from Nepali and Indian curries to pizzas and
pasta. We recommend the lassis, top-up-able
thalis and authentic tandoori dishes.

Jungle View Restaurant INTERNATIONAL **$$**
(Map p250; Gaida Chowk; mains Rs 270-550;
⊘ 6.30am-10pm; 🛜) A pleasant rooftop restaurant overlooking Gaida Chowk, Jungle
View has good curries and BBQ plus all your
cheesy traveller favourites including pizzas,
enchiladas and mousaka. Happy hour (4pm
to 10pm) brings popcorn with your beer.

🛍 Shopping

Souvenir shops in Sauraha sell the usual
range of Tibetan and Nepali arts and crafts.
Local specialities include tiger pug-mark
ashtrays, elephant-poo paper products, and
woodcarvings of elephants and rhinos, including dubious mating scenes.

Happy House HANDICRAFTS
(Map p250; ☎ 056-580026; Gaida Chowk; ⊘ 7am-
9pm) With a good selection of souvenirs this
small, family-run business produces its own
honey in various delectable flavours, and
sells colourful Mithila paintings on handmade paper produced by women's craft cooperatives near Janakpur.

Women's Community Shop HANDICRAFTS
(Map p250; ⊘ 8am-5pm) 🖉 This co-op outlet,
near the visitors centre, sells a small selection
of dusty souvenirs including the aforemen-
tioned poo paper, with all proceeds going to
developing local women's community groups.

ℹ Information

The **Chitwan National Park Office** (Map p250;
☎ 521932; foreigner/SAARC/child under 10yr
per day Rs 1500/750/free; ⊘ ticket office 6-9am
& noon-4pm) in Sauraha handles admission fees
to the park, although this is usually bundled into
the overall charge when booking a tour either
independently or as a package. Should the Government elephants be put back into service for
safaris, this will be the place to book.

The small **National Park Visitors Centre**
(Map p250; ⊘ 6am-4pm) has displays on
Tharu culture and wildlife, including dioramas on
the Chitwan food chain.

There are several ATMs in town, though not all
accept foreign cards. The following were accepting foreign cards at the time of research, though
they frequently run out of money and regular
power cuts play havoc. The **Prabhu Bank** has an
ATM near Travellers Jungle Camp and one south
of Gaida Chowk, where there is also a **Himalaya
Bank** ATM. The **Kumari Bank** ATM is directly north
of Hotel Shiva's Dream. There are also several private moneychangers accepting foreign currency
and travellers cheques. **Chitwan Money Changer**
(Map p250; ⊘ 7am-8pm) changes cash.

ℹ Getting There & Away

AIR
If you're bound for Chitwan, the best option is to
fly into Bharatpur and take a taxi (Rs 1800-2000
to Sauraha). Both Buddha Air and Yeti Airlines
offer daily flights to Bharatpur from Kathmandu
(US$106, 30 minutes). Travel agents and hotels
can make bookings.

BUS
By far the easiest way to reach Chitwan is by
tourist bus from Kathmandu (Rs 500, five to
seven hours). Buses leave the Thamel end of
Kantipath in Kathmandu at around 7am.

From Pokhara, tourist buses (Rs 400 to Rs
450, five to seven hours) depart from the tourist
bus stand at 7.30am. The final stop is Bachhauli
tourist bus park, a 15-minute walk from Sauraha. Jeeps, and the dreaded hotel touts, wait to
transfer new arrivals to hotels for Rs 50. There's
no obligation to commit to staying at any particular resort, regardless of what the touts say.

There is one tourist bus (Rs 600) that heads
for the Indian border at Sunauli/Belahiya. When
leaving Sauraha, all the tourist buses leave
Bachhauli at 9.30am. Any hotel or travel agent
can make bookings.

A more comfortable option is the daily air-
con bus operated by **Greenline** (Map p250;
☎ 560126; www.greenline.com.np), which runs
to/from Kathmandu or Pokhara for US$20 includ-
ing brunch. From Kathmandu or Pokhara it leaves
at 7.30am; from Greenline's office in Sauraha, it
leaves at 9.15am. **Rose Cosmetics** (Map p250;
☎ 9845024203; Hathi Chowk) in Sauraha runs a
daily microbus (Rs 500) to Kathmandu (Kalanki)
departing at 5am and arriving before noon. The
return journey departs Kathmandu at 1pm.

You can also pick up public buses at Tandi
Bazaar (also known as Sauraha Chowk) on the
Mahendra Hwy, about 6km north of Sauraha.
Destinations include Kathmandu, Pokhara and
Bhairawa/Sunauli (Rs 300, five to six hours). For
the airport in Bharatpur you can get a local bus
from Tandi Bazaar to Narayangarh (Rs 30).

CAR
Travel agents and hotels can arrange transfers
to Chitwan by private car. The going rate is

THE TERAI & MAHABHARAT RANGE CHITWAN NATIONAL PARK

around US$90 per person, with a minimum of two passengers, and the journey from Pokhara or Kathmandu takes about five hours.

RAFT

A more interesting way to arrive at Chitwan is by river raft. Most of the big Kathmandu rafting operators offer trips down the Trisuli and Narayani Rivers, culminating at the national park, usually as part of a package tour. The rafting experience is more of a leisurely drift – but there are some fine views and the sandy beaches along the riverside offer great camping spots.

Mugling is the main embarkation point on the Prithvi Hwy, about halfway between Kathmandu and Pokhara. It takes two or three days to raft down to Chitwan. Most people combine rafting with a safari package in the national park; expect to pay around US$90 per person for the rafting section of the trip. Rafting companies can usually make arrangements.

❶ Getting Around

BICYCLE

Several shops in Sauraha, particularly around Gaida Chowk, rent out bicycles for exploring the surrounding villages; the going rate is Rs 250–Rs 300 per day.

JEEP & PONY CART

From Sauraha, a reserved jeep (ie a nonshared vehicle) to the Bachauli bus stand costs Rs 300. By shared *tonga* (pony cart) it will cost Rs 100. A taxi to Tandi Bazaar on the Mahendra Hwy is Rs 700, while one to Bharatpur Airport costs Rs 1800–Rs 2000.

Sunauli & Bhairawa

✍ 071

Sunauli is the most popular tourist border crossing between Nepal and India, seeing scores of people on the way south to Varanasi or Delhi, or northwards to Lumbini, Pokhara and Kathmandu. There was little damage from the 2015 earthquake and the border crossing was one of the main channels for aid agencies bringing emergency relief to people in the hills. Most people refer to both sides of the border as Sunauli, though officially the Nepali border town is called Belahiya.

Typical of many border towns, it is dusty and chaotic and you won't want to hang around for any length of time. Most people just get their passports stamped and continue on their way. If you do need to spend a night here, there are hotels along the unattractive strip, but it makes more sense to stay in the more relaxed town of Bhaira-

wa 4km north. To further confuse things, Bhairawa is also known as Siddharthanagar, but you can get away with Bhairawa for the town and Sunauli for the border.

Buses run directly from the border to most major towns in Nepal, so unless you plan to stay overnight or are heading to Lumbini, there's no real need to go into Bhairawa.

🛏 Sleeping & Eating

All the hotels here have restaurants. The midrange hotels have quite good restaurants serving Nepali, Indian, Chinese and Continental dishes.

🛏 Sunauli

New Cottage Lodge HOTEL $

(✍ 071-418067; s Rs 300, r with bathroom Rs 600; 🛜) Travellers on a very tight budget may consider the very basic rooms here, a couple of hundred metres north of Nepal Immigration. Those on the 2nd floor offer Western toilets, hot showers and insect screens on the windows. Do check a few rooms before deciding on one and settling in.

Hotel Aakash HOTEL $

(✍ 071-418072; aakashshahi@hotmail.com; s/d Rs 800/1000, with AC Rs 1400/1600; ❄🛜) Although the lobby, air-con and room tariff suggest a quantum leap above Belahiya's typical dives, this hotel's rather gloomy and grubby rooms are really only a marginal step up. It's close to immigration, has a good travel desk out front for booking onward buses and there's a State Bank of India ATM.

Hotel Mamata HOTEL $

(✍ 071-520312; hotel_mamata@yahoo.com; r Rs 1200, with AC Rs 2000) Hotel Mamata is probably the best hotel close to the border, with decent rooms and professional management, but don't expect luxury. There is a good restaurant and two ATMs in front of the building that accept foreign cards.

🛏 Bhairawa

Hotel Nirvana HOTEL $$

(✍ 071-520515; www.nirvanathehotel.com; Paklihawa Rd; s/d incl breakfast US$50/60; ❄@🛜) This is easily the best hotel in town, boasting three-star amenities, deep mattresses, a multicuisine restaurant and professional staff. There's also airport pick-up (for a charge), a bar and (best of all) a quiet location, so sleep on those wonderful beds is guaranteed. Car travel to/from Lumbini can be arranged. Ask for a discount.

CROSSING THE BORDER: BELAHIYA TO SUNAULI

Border Hours

The immigration offices on both sides of the border are open 24 hours, but the Indian border post is closed to vehicles from 10pm to 6am. After 7pm and before 7am, you may need to go searching for the immigration officials on either side.

Foreign Exchange

There are no moneychangers on the Indian side of Sunauli. Several moneychangers on the Nepali side of the border exchange Nepali and Indian rupees, as well as cash and travellers cheques in US dollars, UK pounds and euros. Shops and hotels on both sides of the border accept Indian and Nepali rupees at a fixed rate of 1.6 Nepali rupees to one Indian rupee.

Onward to India

Regular buses run from Sunauli to Gorakhpur (₹94, three hours, every 15 minutes from 4am to 7pm) from where you can catch trains to Varanasi. A few morning (4.30am, 5.30am, 6.30am and 7.30am) and afternoon (4.30pm, 5.30pm and 6.30pm) buses run direct to Varanasi (₹271, 11 hours), but it's a long, bumpy ride. Faster collective cars and jeeps to Gorakhpur hang out alongside the road after Indian immigration and leave when full (₹150 to ₹300, two hours).

Be wary of buying 'through' tickets from Kathmandu or Pokhara to Varanasi. Some travellers report being intimidated into buying another ticket once over the border. Travelling in either direction, it's better to take a local bus to the border, walk across and take another onward bus (pay the conductor on board). Travellers have also complained about being pressured into paying extra luggage charges for buses out of Sunauli. You shouldn't have to, so politely decline.

Hotel Glasgow   HOTEL **$$**
(☎071-523737; www.theglasgowhotel; Bank Rd; s/d Rs 1200/1400, with AC Rs 1600/1800; ❀☎) The best-value place in the centre of town, Hotel Glasgow has comfortable if variable-sized rooms, piping-hot showers, attentive staff and a decent restaurant and bar. Plus there's a fast-food cafe downstairs. It suffers less from road noise than the similar Hotel Yeti.

Hotel Yeti   HOTEL **$$**
(☎071-520551; hotelyeti@ntc.net.np; cnr Bank Rd & Siddhartha Hwy; r US$40, with AC US$50-80; ❀☎) Yeti has a range of rooms, though the best are usually reserved for tour groups. Independent travellers should check the plumbing in their room before accepting it, and do ask for a discount. Unfortunately, all rooms face the noisy road.

ⓘ Information

The government of Nepal runs a small **tourist information office** (☎071-520304; ⊗10am-5pm Sun-Fri) on the Nepal side of the border. Bhairawa has several banks but it's usually easier to change money at the border. The State Bank of India ATM beside the Hotel Aakash, Balahiya, accepts only Visa credit cards, while the Nabil Bank and Siddhartha Bank ATMs at the Hotel Mamata accept most foreign cards.

In Bhairawa the Nabil and Standard Chartered bank ATMs accept most foreign cards.

ⓘ Getting There & Away

AIR

Buddha Air (☎071-526893; www.buddhaair. com), **Yeti Airlines** (☎071-527527; www. yetiairlines.com) and **Nepal Airlines** (www. nepalairlines.com.np) offer daily flights between Kathmandu and Bhairawa (US$135, 35 minutes). Bhairawa airport is about 1km west of town. A taxi to/from Bhairawa/Sunauli costs Rs 400/500. Airline offices and agents are found around the junction of Bank Rd and Siddhartha Hwy, Bhairawa, near Hotel Yeti.

BUS

Buses for Kathmandu and Pokhara leave from both Sunauli/Belahiya and Bhairawa. From Sunauli, Kathmandu-bound buses (Rs 550, eight hours) leave around 7am. Tourist-class air-con buses cost Rs 800–Rs 1200. Buses to Pokhara (Rs 600, eight hours) leave at 7am and 8am. After these times and for all other destinations, you will need to head to Bhairawa. Be suspicious of travel agents in India or Nepal who claim to offer 'through tickets' between the two countries: everyone has to change buses at the border.

The most comfortable option is the **Golden Travels** (☎071-520194) air-con bus (currently running under the name 'Taraknath' to Kathmandu; US$15, six to seven hours); it leaves Kathmandu's Kalanki junction by the southeastern ring road at 7.30am and Sunauli at 7am. Services run daily in conjunction with the Baba Bhairav Travels and Buddha Darshan travel companies, so don't be worried if you end up on a bus with one of these names.

From the bus stand in Bhairawa there are frequent microbuses to Kathmandu (Rs 600, eight hours) via Narayangarh (Rs 350, three hours). For Pokhara, there are buses (Rs 550, nine hours) via Tansen (Rs 250, five hours) along the Siddhartha Hwy, as well as via the Mugling Hwy (Rs 650, eight hours).

Also from Bhaiwara there are services every 15 minutes to Butwal (Rs 80, 45 minutes), from where you can connect with many more services heading west and up the Siddhartha Hwy. Heading east from Bhairawa, there is one bus to Janakpur (Rs 900, eight hours) leaving at 6.10am.

Local/micro buses for Lumbini (Rs 50/80, one hour) and Taulihawa (Rs 100, three hours) leave from the junction of the Siddhartha Hwy and the road to Lumbini, about 1km north of Bank Rd.

❶ Getting Around

Crowded share jeeps and local buses shuttle between the border and Bhairawa for Rs 20. A rickshaw will cost at least Rs 100–Rs 150.

Lumbini

▶ 071

It was in Lumbini, around the year 563 BC, that one of history's greatest and most revered figures, Siddhartha Gautama – better known as the Buddha – was born. It's no great surprise to learn that the World Heritage–listed Lumbini is of huge religious significance and attracts Buddhist pilgrims from around the world.

Located 22km west of Bhairawa, the spiritual heart of Lumbini is Maya Devi Temple, which marks the spot where Queen Maya Devi gave birth to Siddhartha Gautama. In the adjoining sacred garden you'll find the pillar of Ashoka, ancient ruins of stupas, and maroon- and saffron-robed monks congregating under a sprawling Bodhi (pipal) fig decorated with prayer flags.

Maya Devi Temple is set in the middle of the large 4km by 2.5km park grounds known as the Lumbini Development Zone. Designed by Japanese architect Kenzo Tange in 1978, it's still a work in progress that comprises landscaped lakes and numerous monasteries that have been or are being constructed by Buddhist communities from around the world.

Cited as evidence of good karma by some Buddhist devotees, none of the temples or monuments at Lumbini were seriously affected by the 2015 earthquake.

Most people rush through Lumbini, allowing only a few hours to look around. However, you could easily spend one or two days exploring the zone and its monasteries, and soaking up the peaceful atmosphere.

History

After many years of work at Lumbini, archaeologists are fairly certain that Siddhartha Gautama, the historical Buddha, was indeed born here. A huge complex of monasteries and stupas was erected on the site by his followers, and the Indian emperor Ashoka made a pilgrimage here in 249 BC, erecting one of his famous pillars.

Shortly after this, an unknown cataclysm affected Lumbini. When the Chinese pilgrim Fa Hsien (Fa Xian) visited in AD 403, he found the monasteries abandoned and the city of Kapilavastu in ruins. Two hundred years later, Hsuan Tang (Xuan Zang), another Chinese pilgrim, described 1000 derelict monasteries and Ashoka's pillar shattered by lightning and lying on the ground.

However, the site was not entirely forgotten. The Nepali king Ripu Malla made a pilgrimage here in 1312, possibly leaving the nativity statue that is still worshipped in the Maya Devi Temple.

Mughal invaders arrived in the region at the end of the 14th century and destroyed the remaining 'pagan' monuments at both Kapilavastu and Lumbini. The whole region then returned to wilderness and the sites were lost to humanity, until the governor of Palpa, Khadga Shumsher Rana, began the excavation of Ashoka's pillar in late 1896.

◉ Sights

Maya Devi Temple   BUDDHIST TEMPLE
(foreigner/SAARC Rs 200/100; ◷ 6am-6pm) This temple sits on the site of the the Buddha's birth, according to Buddhist scholars. You will need to buy your entrance ticket 50m north of the gate to the Sacred Garden. At the gate you must remove your shoes. (A spare pair of socks may be a useful item as there is a fair bit of walking round the garden to see everything.)

Excavations carried out in 1992 revealed a succession of ruins dating back at least 2200 years, including a commemorative stone on a brick plinth, matching the description of a

THE BIRTH OF THE BUDDHA

The historical Buddha, Siddhartha Gautama, was the son of Suddhodana, ruler of Kapilavastu, and Maya Devi, a princess from the neighbouring kingdom of Devdaha. According to legend, the pregnant Maya Devi was travelling between the two states when she came upon a tranquil pond surrounded by flowering sal trees. After bathing in the cool water, she suddenly went into labour, and just had enough time to walk 25 steps and grab the branch of a Bodhi (pipal) tree for support before the baby was born. The year was around 563 BC and the location has been positively identified as Lumbini.

After the birth, a seer predicted that the boy would become a great teacher or a great king. Eager to ensure the latter, King Suddhodana shielded him from all knowledge of the world outside the palace. At the age of 29, Siddhartha left the city for the first time and came face to face with an old man, a sick man, a hermit and a corpse. Shocked by this sudden exposure to human suffering, the prince abandoned his luxurious life to become a mendicant holy man, fasting and meditating on the nature of existence. After some severe austerities, the former prince realised that life as a starving pauper was no more conducive to wisdom than life as a pampered prince. Thus was born the 'Middle Way'.

Finally, after 49 days meditating under a Bodhi tree on the site of modern-day Bodhgaya in India, Siddhartha attained enlightenment – a fundamental grasp of the nature of human existence. He travelled to Sarnath, near Varanasi, to preach his first sermon and Buddhism was born. Renamed Buddha ('the enlightened one'), Siddhartha spent the next 46 years teaching the Middle Way – a path of moderation and self-knowledge through which human beings could escape the cycle of birth and rebirth and achieve nirvana, a state of eternal bliss.

The Buddha died at the age of 80 at Kushinagar, near Gorakhpur in India. Despite his rejection of divinity and materialism, all the sites associated with the Buddha's life have become centres for pilgrimage and he is worshipped as a deity across the Buddhist world. Devotees still cross continents to visit Lumbini, Bodhgaya, Sarnath and Kushinagar.

The ruins of Kapilavastu were unearthed close to Lumbini at Tilaurakot, and more recently, the site of Devdaha, the home of Maya Devi, was identified on the outskirts of the Nepali town of Butwal.

stone laid down by Emperor Ashoka in the 3rd century BC. There are plans to raise a grand monument on the site, but for now a sturdy brick pavilion protects the temple ruins.

You can walk around the ruins on a raised boardwalk. The focal point for pilgrims is a sandstone carving of the birth of the Buddha, reputedly left here by the Malla king, Ripu Malla, in the 14th century, when Maya Devi was worshipped as an incarnation of the Hindu mother goddess. The carving has been worn almost flat by centuries of veneration, but you can just discern the shape of Maya Devi grasping a tree branch and giving birth to the Buddha, with Indra and Brahma looking on. Directly beneath this is a marker stone encased within bulletproof glass, which pinpoints the spot where the Buddha was born.

The sacred pond beside the temple is believed to be where Maya Devi bathed before giving birth to the Buddha. Dotted around the grounds are the ruined foundations of a number of brick stupas and monasteries dating from the 2nd century BC to the 9th century AD.

Ashokan Pillar   MONUMENT

The Indian emperor Ashoka visited Lumbini in 249 BC, leaving behind an inscribed sandstone pillar to commemorate the occasion. After being lost for centuries, Ashoka's pillar was rediscovered by the governor of Palpa, Khadga Shumsher Rana, in 1896. The 6m-high pink sandstone pillar has now been returned to its original site in front of the Maya Devi Temple.

Lumbini Museum   MUSEUM

(071-580318; foreigner/SAARC Rs 70/20; 10am-4pm Wed-Mon) Tucked away at the northern end of the compound, this museum is devoted to the life of the Buddha, with artefacts and photos from Buddhist sites around the world.

World Peace Pagoda   BUDDHIST TEMPLE

(dawn-dusk) Located outside the main compound, but easily accessible by bike, the

Lumbini

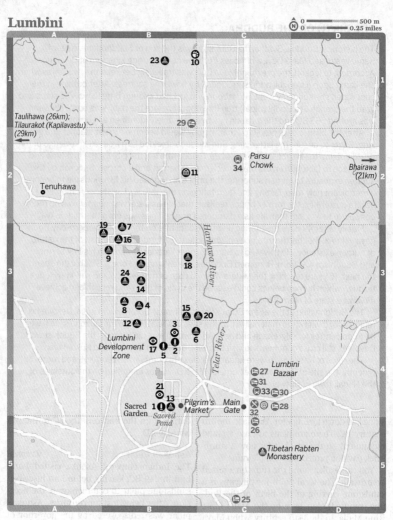

N 0 ——————— 500 m
0 ——————— 0.25 miles

Taulihawa (26km);
Tilaurakot (Kapilavastu)
(29km)

Tenuhawa

Parsu
Chowk

Bhairawa
(21km)

Harhawa River

Telar River

Lumbini
Development
Zone

Lumbini
Bazaar

Sacred
Garden

Pilgrim's
Market

Main
Gate

Sacred
Pond

Tibetan Rabten
Monastery

impressive gleaming white World Peace Pagoda was constructed by Japanese Buddhists at a cost of US$1 million. The shining golden statue depicts the Buddha in the posture he assumed when he was born. Near the base of the stupa is the grave of a Japanese monk murdered by anti-Buddhist extremists during the construction of the monument.

Lumbini Crane Sanctuary WILDLIFE RESERVE
The wetlands surrounding the World Peace Pagoda are protected as a crane sanctuary and you stand a good chance of seeing rare sarus cranes stalking through the fields. There's no formal entrance to the sanctuary and no admission fee – just stroll into the damp meadows behind the pagoda.

Buddhist Monasteries

Since the Lumbini Development Zone was founded in 1978, Buddhist nations from around the world have been constructing extravagant monasteries in a dedicated monastic zone. Separated by a long canal, the monastic zone is divided into Mahayana and Theravada sects. Each reflects the unique interpretation of Buddhism of its home nation and together the monasteries create a fascinating map of world Buddhist philosophy.

Lumbini

The site is spread out, so hire a bicycle in Lumbini Bazaar or rent a rickshaw. Unless otherwise stated, all the monasteries are open daily during daylight hours.

At the time of writing, a Lumbini Pilgrim & Visitor Centre was under construction, just east of the Eternal Flame. A helpful information centre could be just what this large and at times perplexing site needs to facilitate visitors – check for the latest developments when you arrive.

➡ West Monastic Zone

The West Monastic Zone is set aside for monasteries from the Mahayana school, which is distinguished by monks in maroon robes and a more clamorous style of prayer involving blowing horns and clashing cymbals.

Panditarama International
Vipassana Meditation Centre   MEDITATION
(☏ 071-580118; www.panditarama-lumbini.info) A meditation centre, where practitioners can study for a nominal donation. To reach it, start at the Eternal Flame (just north of the Maya Devi Temple), and follow the dirt road along the west bank of the pond.

Drubgyud Chöling Gompa   BUDDHIST MONASTERY
This classic Tibetan-style gompa was built in 2001 by Buddhists from Singapore and Nepal. The mural work inside is quite refined

and a gigantic stupa under construction next door appears almost finished.

Manang Samaj Stupa   BUDDHIST TEMPLE
This grand yet tasteful chörten (Tibetan reliquary stupa) was constructed by Buddhists from Manang in northern Nepal.

Zhong Hua Chinese
Buddhist Monastery   BUDDHIST MONASTERY
This elegant monastery is one of the most impressive structures at Lumbini. Reached through a gateway flanked by Confucian deities, the elegant pagoda-style monastery looks like something from the Forbidden City.

Korean Buddhist Temple   BUDDHIST TEMPLE
The government of South Korea is (slowly) building this massive temple. The temple interior is magnificent and well worth a look.

Vietnam Phat
Quoc Tu Temple   BUDDHIST TEMPLE
Vietnam's contribution to Lumbini is a charming pagoda-style temple featuring beautiful landscaping and a dragon-adorned roof.

Mother Temple of the
Graduated Path
to Enlightenment   BUDDHIST TEMPLE
The Austrian Geden International Foundation constructed this complex of stupas and

THE TERAI & MAHABHARAT RANGE LUMBINI

monastery buildings, the latter in classical Greek style.

Great Drigung
Kagyud Lotus Stupa   BUDDHIST TEMPLE
(⊙8am-noon & 1-5pm) This truly extravagant stupa is one of the most beautiful buildings here and was constructed by the German Tara Foundation. The domed ceiling of the main prayer room is covered in Buddhist murals.

Nepal Vajrayana
Mahavihara Temple   BUDDHIST TEMPLE
This tiered-roof temple representing Nepal is almost complete, but was still being constructed at the time of writing.

Sokyo Gompa   BUDDHIST MONASTERY
The Japanese Sokyo Foundation funded the construction of this traditional Tibetan-style gompa.

Linh Son Monastery   BUDDHIST MONASTERY
This elegant, pastel-hued monastery was constructed by the French World Linh Son Buddhists.

➡ East Monastic Zone
The East Monastic Zone is set aside for monasteries from the Theravada school, which is common throughout southeast Asia and Sri Lanka, and recognisable by the monks' saffron-coloured robes.

Royal Thai
Buddhist Monastery   BUDDHIST MONASTERY
(⊙8am-noon & 1-5pm) Close to the north end of the pond, this stunning and imposing *wat* (Thai-style monastery) is built from gleaming white marble.

Myanmar Golden Temple   BUDDHIST TEMPLE
The Myanmar Golden Temple is one of the oldest structures in the compound. There are three prayer halls – the most impressive is topped by a corncob-shaped shikhara (tower), styled after the temples of Bagan. Within the temple grounds is the nearby Lokamani Pula Pagoda, a huge gilded stupa in the southern Burmese style, inspired by the Shwedagon Paya in Yangon.

Gautami Nun's Temple   BUDDHIST TEMPLE
This modest building is the only monastery in the compound built for solely for female devotees.

Sri Lankan Monastery   BUDDHIST MONASTERY
The grand and moated Sri Lankan Monastery contains elaborate and colourful murals depicting the life of Buddha.

Dhama Janami Vipassana Centre   MEDITATION
This small meditation centre hosts followers of the Theravada school. A short walk south from here takes you to the Eternal Flame, passing the huge ceremonial bell inscribed with Tibetan characters.

☞ Tours

Hiring a guide to explain the various sights within the Development Zone is a good way to learn about the Buddhist sites in Lumbini. Otherwise, many hotels and travel agents rent out bicycles for Rs 150 per day.

Holiday Pilgrims
Care Tour & Travels   GUIDED TOUR
(✆580432) Attached to Lumbini Village Lodge, this company arranges tours that really get under the surface of life in the Terai. Village tours (Rs 500) are available by bicycle, and the company provides a free map so you can make your own way around by bike.

It also runs a birdwatching tour that includes visiting a 'vulture restaurant', where clean, diclofenac-free meat is served up to endangered vultures.

☆ Festivals & Events

Buddha Jayanti   BUDDHIST
The most important Buddhist celebration at Lumbini is this annual festival held in April or May, when busloads of Buddhists from India and Nepal come here to celebrate the birth of the Buddha. Pilgrims also come here to worship each *purnima* (the night of the full moon) and *astami* (the eighth night after the full moon).

Rupa Devi   HINDU
(⊙Apr–May) Many Hindus regard the Buddha as an incarnation of Vishnu and thousands of Hindu pilgrims come here on the full moon of the Nepali month of Baisakh (April to May) to worship Maya Devi as Rupa Devi, the mother goddess of Lumbini.

🛏 Sleeping & Eating

Most of the budget options are in Lumbini Bazaar (also known as Buddhanagar), the small village opposite the eastern entrance to the Lumbini Development Zone. The upmarket hotels are either in the Development Zone north of the Bhairawa–Taulihawa Rd or on the periphery road around the eastern side of the Development Zone. Most people eat in their hotels.

★ Lumbini Village Lodge   HOTEL $
(✆071-580432; lumbinivillagelodge@yahoo.com; dm Rs 250, s Rs 450-500, d Rs 650-750; 🛜) This

charming and welcoming budget lodge has a cool central courtyard shaded by a mango tree, and big, spotless rooms with fans and insect-screened windows. It's all kept bright with a fresh paint job every year. By the time you read this, the new terrace restaurant should be finished. The owners run tours of the surrounding villages.

Lumbini Guest House HOTEL $
(☑071-580142; www.lumbiniguesthouse.com; s/d Rs 500/600, deluxe r without/with AC Rs 1200/2000; ✳@☎) The Lumbini Guest House is a comfortable budget option in the bazaar, with a decent multicuisine restaurant. All rooms are spacious and clean, with attached bathrooms and LCD TVs, plus there are several air-con rooms to shelter from the heat.

Sunflower Travellers Lodge HOTEL $$
(☑580338; sunflower2099py@gmail.com; r Rs 2400, with AC Rs 2700, mains Rs 160-380; ✳☎) On the eastern periphery road, this bright guesthouse has cheerful rooms and efficient Chinese management. Rooms are spotless, with tubs and plenty of hot water, but there are no TVs. There's a small upstairs restaurant with excellent Chinese food, and a downstairs souvenir shop.

Hotel Peace Land HOTEL $$
(☑071-580286; www.hotel-peaceland.com; r incl breakfast US$40, set dinner US$10, mains Rs 250-350; ✳☎) This inviting hotel represents a business expansion for successful local restaurateurs. The deep yellow corridors lead to cool and comfortable rooms. However, the rack rate seems overly optimistic, especially considering the discount offered to locals, so do ask for a discount. The restaurant here is the best in town.

Hotel Lumbini Garden New Crystal HOTEL $$
(☑071-580145; www.newcrystalhotels.com; s/d US$62/70; ✳@☎) Aimed at well-heeled pilgrims, usually in tour groups, this is a comfortable three-star hotel and rooms boast all the amenities you could ask for. There's a multicuisine restaurant and bar, and plenty of religious paraphernalia available in the lobby. There are 72 mostly Western-style rooms, plus a handful in Japanese-style.

Buddha Maya Garden Hotel HOTEL $$$
(☑071-580220, in Kathmandu 01-4434705; www.ktmgh.com; s/d from US$120/140; ✳☎) Set in large grounds about 500m southeast of the site, this well-run resort offers comfortable accommodation in Lumbini with very spacious rooms in a tranquil village setting. There's an excellent restaurant (though avoid the buffet at dinner if you can), bicycles for hire and staff who are keen to help. Ask about discounts.

Lumbini Hokke Hotel HOTEL $$$
(☑580136; s/d US$90/105; ✳@☎) Built with real style, the Hokke looks a bit like a traditional Japanese village; rooms are Western-style (seven rooms) or Japanese-style (20 rooms), with tatami floors, paper partitions and Japanese furniture. The restaurant serves top-notch Japanese set meals as well as other cuisines. To top it off there are traditional Japanese bathhouses.

Lumbini Invitation 365 INTERNATIONAL $
(Fusian Garden; ☑071-580211; mains Rs 150-250; ☎) This popular little restaurant is better known by its former name 'Fusian Garden'. The new owners have kept the extensive menu ranging from burgers and pancakes to momos, though as usual the Nepali *thali* is probably the best-value meal. It's also a great place to quench a thirst.

❶ Information

There's a **tourist information centre** (☉6pm-6pm) at the ticket office that displays the master plan of the complex.

There are five ATMs in Lumbini Bazaar, with the Everest Bank being the most reliable for foreign cards. For cash moneychangers, try your hotel.

❶ Getting There & Away

Local buses run regularly between Lumbini and the local bus stand in Bhairawa (Rs 50, one hour). Taxis from Lumbini Bazaar charge Rs 1000 to the main Bhairawa bus stand and Rs 1100 to the border at Sunauli (Belahiya). Lumbini Village Lodge helps arrange share taxis so a group of travellers can share the cost.

To reach Taulihawa from Lumbini, take a local bus to the junction with the Bhairawa road (Rs 20) and change to a bus bound for Taulihawa (Rs 130, 1½ hours).

A public bus bound for Kathmandu (Rs 580, nine to 10 hours) departs Lumbini Bazaar at 7am. Sakura Travels runs a semi-tourist bus (ie no air-con) to Kathmandu's Kakani bus stand (Rs 750, nine hours). Buddha Darshan's air-con tourist bus to Kathmandu costs Rs 1050. Buy tickets at any travel agency or have your hotel organise it for a small fee.

❶ Getting Around

The best way to get around the compound is by bicycle – Lumbini Village Lodge in Lumbini Bazaar charges Rs 150 per day for reliable Hero-brand bikes.

Hiring a rickshaw is a good alternative. Rickshaw wallahs loiter near the entrance to the Development Zone, charging around Rs 200 per hour.

Around Lumbini

Tilaurakot

About 29km west of Lumbini, Tilaurakot has been identified as the historical site of Kapilavastu, where Siddhartha Gautama spent the first 29 years of his life. The site sits in a peaceful meadow on the banks of the Banganga River. Although you can still see the foundations of a large residential compound, it takes a certain amount of imagination to visualise the city of extravagant luxury that drove the Buddha to question the nature of existence. The showy shrine nearby with several carved pachyderms is dedicated to Maya Devi.

There's a small museum (admission Rs 70; ☉10am-4pm Wed-Mon) at the final turn-off to Tilaurakot that displays some of the artefacts found at the site.

The best way to get here is through Lumbini Village Lodge, which can organise a vehicle for Rs 700 with a day's notice. Another option is to catch a local bus from the Lumbini Bus Stand to the junction (Rs 15, 10 minutes) and change to a bus bound for Tilaurakot (Rs 60, 1½ hours), 3km north of Taulihawa. You can take a rickshaw to the site from Tilaurakot for Rs 100/175 one way/ return. Otherwise a taxi can make the return trip from Lumbini for around Rs 2500.

THE SIDDHARTHA HIGHWAY

Most travellers heading from Sunauli to Pokhara follow the Mahendra Hwy to Narayangarh, then the Prithvi Hwy from Mugling to Pokhara. A more interesting route is the dramatic Siddhartha Hwy, which weaves its way north through the dramatic Tinau Gorge towards Pokhara via the scenic mountain village of Tansen. It's a spectacular mountain road clinging to near-vertical canyon walls with views of peaks, valleys and impressive waterfalls, but it is vulnerable to landslides and the risk there has increased since the 2015 earthquake, so check the situation locally before you travel.

Buses run regularly on this route, and it is also regarded as one of the finest motorcycle journeys in Nepal. Landslides often block the highway during the monsoon.

Butwal

☑ 071

Crowded, dry and dusty, Butwal has all the hallmarks of a typical Terai town, its bustling streets dominated by bell-ringing rickshaws. Sitting on an ancient trade route from the Indian plains towards the Himalaya, Butwal remains an important trade and transport hub at the crossroads of the north–south Siddhartha Hwy and east–west Mahendra Hwy. Nevertheless, Butwal offers no sights of interest for visitors, and hence most people choose to pass right through. There was little damage here in the 2015 earthquake.

Archaeologists have identified a village 15km east of Butwal as the site of the kingdom of Devdaha, home to Maya Devi. There's a small memorial park on the site, signposted off the Mahendra Hwy towards Narayangarh.

🛏 Sleeping & Eating

Hotel Kandara   HOTEL $
(☑540175; Traffic Chowk; s/d Rs 670/900, r with AC Rs 1800; ❄️ 🛜) Situated on the busy highway near Traffic Chowk, Kandara is a reasonable budget choice where you can take your pick between simple rooms with attached bathrooms and deluxe rooms with bathtubs and air-con. There's a decent restaurant and safe off-street parking.

Nanglo West   NEPALI $
(☑071-544455; Siddhartha Hwy; mains Rs 155-290; ☉noon-9.30pm; 🛜) This branch of the successful chain is a bit of a poor relative and isn't as appealing as other Nanglo Wests. The menu features burgers, momos, pizza and Newari dishes, and there's pleasant garden seating, but if you're after a decent coffee after the drive through Tinau Gorge you may be disappointed. It's on the highway where it emerges from the gorge, about 1km north of Traffic Chowk.

ℹ Information

There are several ATMs around Traffic Chowk; the one opposite the Hotel Royal takes international cards.

ℹ Getting There & Away

All long-distance buses leave from the main bus park just south of Traffic Chowk. There are buses every half-hour or so to Kathmandu (Rs 510, seven hours) and Pokhara (Rs 490, eight hours) via Mugling and the Prithvi Hwy. There are also several daily buses on the scenic route to Pokhara (Rs 450, six hours) via Tansen (Rs 100, 2½ hours). Local buses leave for Sunauli/Bhairawa (Rs 80, 45 minutes) every 10 minutes.

Along the Mahendra Hwy, there are regular buses east to Narayangarh (Rs 250, three hours), and west to Dhangadhi (Rs 845, 10 hours) and Mahendranagar (Rs 955, 12 hours) for connections to Nepalganj (get off at Kohalpur) and Bardia National Park (alight at Ambassa – blink and you'll miss it).

Tansen (Palpa)

📞 075 / ELEV 1372M

Tansen, perched high above the Kali Gandaki River on the road between Butwal and Pokhara, is far enough off the radar to make it a rewarding detour for independent travellers. Tansen's main attraction is both its Newari charm and distinct medieval feel. Lining Tansen's steep cobblestone streets, which are too steep for cars, are wooden Newari houses with intricately carved windows, from where the clacking of looms can be heard. On winter mornings a blanket of mist is cast over the bowl-shaped Madi Valley, earning it the moniker 'White Lake'.

Chatting to locals, you'll find they're fiercely proud of their home town, which no doubt stems from its rich history during the glory years as the capital of the Magar kingdom of Tanahun. Until the rise of the Shahs, Tanahun was one of the most powerful kingdoms in Nepal. Troops from Palpa even came close to conquering Kathmandu in the 16th century under the leadership of King Mukunda Sen. The power of the Magars waned in the 18th century and Tansen was reinvented as a Newari trading post on the trade route between India and Tibet.

Today Tansen remains the administrative headquarters of Palpa district, and many Nepalis still refer to the town as Palpa. The town escaped serious damage in the 2015 earthquake.

🎯 Sights

Sitalpati   SQUARE

The main square in Tansen is dominated by (and named after) a curious octagonal pavilion, used for public functions in the days when Tansen was ruled by the governors of the Shah regime. Today it's a popular meeting spot for locals to have a chat. At the northwest corner of the square, the small, two-tiered **Bhimsen Mandir** is sacred to the Newari god of trade and commerce.

Several shops on the square sell dhaka, the fabric used for traditional Nepali jackets and *topis* (cloth hats), while to the west of the square, visit **Karuwa Factory** (admission free; ⏰ 10am-6pm) FREE to see Tansen's famed brass jugs being made.

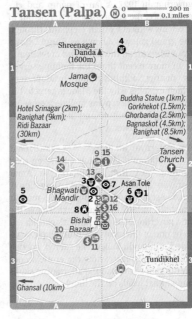

Tansen (Palpa)

Tansen Durbar   PALACE

At the southern end of Sitalpati is the striking Tansen Durbar, which has been restored after being razed during one of the Maoist insurgency's most violent battles. The original building was built for the provincial governor in 1927. A fan of pomp and circumstance, the governor used to ride out to greet his subjects, on an elephant, through the grand gateway known as **Baggi Dhoka (Mul Dhoka)**, on the south end of Sitalpati.

In more recent times the building served as district administration headquarters, which explains why the Maoists targeted it. The reconstruction plans include a museum featuring local culture and history, but this is yet to eventuate.

Amar Narayan Mandir HINDU TEMPLE

At the bottom of Asan Tole (the steep road running east from Sitalpati), the Amar Narayan Mandir is a classic three-tiered, pagoda-style wooden temple. The mandir was built in 1807 by Amar Singh Thapa, the first governor of Tansen, and it's considered to be one of the most beautiful temples outside Kathmandu Valley. The carved wooden deities are exquisite; note the erotic scenes on the roof struts and the alternating skulls and animal heads on the lintel.

Devotees come here every evening to light butter lamps in honour of the patron deity, Lord Vishnu.

At the start of the steps to the Amar Narayan Temple is the similar but smaller **Mahadev Mandir**, sacred to Shiva.

🛏 Sleeping & Eating

⭐**City View Homestay** HOMESTAY $
(☑ 075-520563, 9847028885; shrestha.manmohan@gmail.com; r Rs 500-600) Easily the best option in town is to stay in the spotless simple rooms within the home of Man Mohan Shrestha, the energetic man behind the volunteer tourist-information service known as GETUP. From the roof there are indeed great views of the city and beyond. If Mohan's rooms are full, he can find similar nearby homestays.

Hotel Gauri Shankar Guest House HOTEL $
(☑ 9847043540; Silkhan Tole; r Rs 800-1000, without bathroom Rs 400) This budget hotel is a just-bearable cheapie with adequately clean rooms with TVs and Western toilets. Go for rooms on the 2nd level away from the noisy street.

WALKS AROUND TANSEN

Tansen is surrounded by excellent walking country. The tourist office GETUP can recommend walks, provide maps and brochures at cost price, and help organise local guides.

One of the nicest short walks is the one-hour stroll up **Shreenagar Danda**, the 1600m-high hill directly north of town. The trail starts near the small **Ganesh Mandir** (temple) above Tansen and climbs steeply through open woodland to the crest of the hill. When you reach the ridge, turn right; a 20-minute stroll will take you to a modern **Buddha statue** and a viewpoint with fabulous views over the gorge of the Kali Gandaki River to the Himalaya.

Another short and easy walk is the two-hour stroll to the **Bhairab Sthan Temple**, 9km west of Tansen. The courtyard in front of the temple contains a gigantic brass trident and inside is a silver mask of Bhairab, allegedly plundered from Kathmandu by Mukunda Sen. The walk follows the road from Tansen to Ridi Bazaar.

If you fancy something more challenging, the three-hour walk to the village of **Ghansal** passes several hilltop viewpoints, emerging on the highway about 3km south of Tansen. The walk is mainly downhill and there are spectacular valley views from Bhut Dada, about halfway along the route.

Other possible destinations for walks include **Ghorbanda**, a potters' village northeast of Tansen on the way to Pokhara, and **Bagnaskot**, on the ridge east of **Gorkhekot**, which has a small Devi temple and a wonderfully exposed hilltop viewpoint. From Bagnaskot you can continue to **Aryabhanjyang** on the Siddhartha Hwy. To return you can hop on a southbound bus coming from Pokhara. A good option between December and March is to get dropped off at the Organic Coffee plantation near Bartung, the highway turn-off to Tansen.

All these walks can be completed in a day if you get an early start, or there's simple homestay lodging along the way if you're not in a hurry.

If you are keen to go on longer walks and experience Magar village homestays, there's an overnight walk to **Baugha Gumha** and a four-day trek to **Kaudelake** and **Remigha** (Rimgha). You can also follow the old trade route from Tansen to Butwal – GETUP has maps (Rs 30) with a detailed description of all these trails and can provide advice and local guides.

Hotel Srinagar
HOTEL $$

(☎ 075-520045; www.hotelsrinagar.com; s/d US$35/45; ☎) This upmarket option is about 2km from town on the ridge, a 20-minute walk west of the summit of Shreenagar Danda. Although rather isolated, the views of Dhauligiri and the Annapurna range are simply sensational. The wood-panelled rooms are comfortable with renovated bathrooms, and the restaurant terrace has views to the mountains on one side and the 'white lake' on the other.

Palpali Chhen
B&B $$

(☎ 075-521845; reservations@palpalichhen.com. np; Bank Rd; s/d inc breakfast Rs 2400/2800, deluxe Rs 3000/3400; ☎) This is a new enterprise by the folks from Nanglo West. It is a bright, spotless hotel with standard rooms that are rather pokey, and those we looked at lacked windows. Superior rooms, however, are much brighter with windows, bouncier mattresses and flat-screen TVs. It's only a short walk up to Nanglo West for lunches and dinners and anything in between.

Hotel the White Lake
HOTEL $$

(☎ 075-520291; Silkhan Tole; s/d S$15/18, deluxe r s/d US$25/30; ☎) The sprawling White Lake has a variety of rooms – the standard ones are pretty ordinary and overpriced, but the new wing boasts more comfortable deluxe rooms. The restaurant and terrace, as well as some of the rooms, have vertigo-inducing views of the 'white lake'.

★ Nanglo West
NEPALI $$

(☎ 075-520184; mains Rs 175-425, Newari set Rs 315-415; ⊙10am-7pm; ☎) You can't go without sampling the Nepali delights at this atmospheric oasis in the centre of Tansen. In addition to a great Newari set *thali* with veg, chicken or mutton, it serves local dishes like *choela* (dried buffalo or duck meat with chilli and ginger), served with *chiura* (flattened rice) and spiced potatoes in curd. There's also an international menu.

Out front you'll find Nanglo West's bakery (open from 7am to 7pm) with delicious buttery biscuits, cream cakes and pastries. Freshly baked goods arrive on the shelves around 10am.

Royal Inn
NEPALI $

(☎ 075-555780; mains Rs 170-350; ⊙10am-9pm; ☎) Housed in a delightfully restored Newari house (duck your head through the doorways!) is this atmospheric restaurant run by young, enterprising locals. In addition to the

recommended Nepali *thali*, there are pizzas, burgers, *thukpa* (Tibetan noodle soup) and superb momos.

ⓘ Information

Your first port of call should be **GETUP** (Group for Environmental & Tourism Upgrading Palpa; ☎ 075-520563, 9847028885; shrestha. manmohan@gmail.com; ⊙9am-5pm Sun-Fri), probably the most helpful tourist information centre in the country. Led by the irrepressible Man Mohan, this NGO was set up to promote Tansen as a tourist destination. Here you can obtain excellent trekking maps (Rs 30) for all the short treks around Tansen, including the classic loop to Ranighat. GETUP can also arrange guided trips to metalwork and fabric workshops as well as organic coffee plantations.

Prabhu and NBL banks have ATMs at the southern end of Bank Rd, and Himalayan Bank has an ATM near Hotel the White Lake; all accept foreign cards. For foreign exchange there are moneychangers and several banks on Bank Rd, including **Nepal Bank Limited** (⊙10am-3pm Sun-Fri).

ⓘ Getting There & Away

The bus station is at the bottom of town at the southern entrance to Tansen, and the ticket office is at the east end of the stand. Buses to Pokhara (Rs 315, five hours) leave at 6am and 10am; there are also buses/microbuses to Kathmandu (Rs 620/850, 11 hours).

There are regular services south to Butwal (Rs 100, 2½ hours) from 6.30am to 5pm. There're also buses to Bhaiwara (Rs 140) where you can change for Lumbini. One tourist bus from Pokhara heading to Lumbini (Rs 300) passes through Bartung (on the highway) around midday, but check timings. Local buses for Ridi Bazaar (Rs 120, two hours) leave fairly regularly during the same hours – get an early-morning start if you want to be back the same day.

If you get dropped off by any bus at Bartung on the highway, rather than the bus park, either take a taxi up to Tansen or ask directions for the foot-trail or shortcut up to Tundikhel. Walking to town along the winding road will take forever.

Around Tansen

As well as the popular walks around Tansen, there are a few other interesting places that you can reach on foot or by bus.

Ranighat Durbar

The most famous sight near Tansen is the eerie Ranighat Durbar on the east bank of the Kali Gandaki. Fancifully referred to as Nepal's Taj Mahal, this crumbling baroque palace

SALIGRAMS

Saligrams are black stones that, when broken open, reveal the fossilised remains of prehistoric ammonites (molluscs) that lived in the ancient Tethys Sea 140 million years ago. During the geological collision that gave birth to the Himalayas, the sea dried up and the fossils ascended with the growing mountains. Today the Himalaya continue to rise and the Kali Gandaki and her tributaries wash through the ancient sediments to reveal these fossils. Hindus venerate saligrams as manifestations of the god Vishnu, who was turned to stone by the beautiful and virtuous Vrinda after he tried to seduce her.

was built in 1896 by Khadga Shamsher Rana in memory of his beloved wife, Tej Kumari. Khadga was an ambitious politician who was exiled from Kathmandu for plotting against the prime minister. Khadga followed up with another abortive attempt to seize power in 1921 and was exiled again, this time to India. After his departure, the Durbar was stripped of its valuable fittings, but the building still stands, despite the 2015 earthquake, slowly fading on the banks of the Kali Gandaki.

You can walk to Ranighat in three to four hours (return trip eight hours) along an easy-to-follow trail, beginning in Gorkhekot at the east end of Shreenagar Danda. You should aim to leave before 8am and start your return before 1.30pm. Take a flashlight to look around the palace and in case you get caught on the trail after sunset.

The route down to the river is mainly downhill, through rice paddies and forest from which the ruined palace materialises. The return leg is fairly tough going, following a steeply ascending trail on the next ridge, emerging near Hotel Srinagar. It's not possible to walk here during the monsoon due to the slippery conditions. There's basic accommodation in Ranighat if you choose to stay the night, and renovations to help preserve the building have started.

GETUP in Tansen sells a guide and map (Rs 30). Rafting trips on the Kali Gandaki sometimes make it as far as the palace.

Ridi Bazaar

About 28km northwest of Tansen by road (or 13km on foot), the Newari village of Ridi Bazaar sits at the sacred confluence of the Kali Gandaki and Ridi Khola rivers. Ridi is a popular destination for pilgrimages, and the site is further sanctified by the presence of saligrams – the fossils of ammonites that are revered as symbols of Vishnu.

The principal religious monument in Ridi is the **Rishikesh Mandir**, which was founded by Mukunda Sen in the 16th century. According to legend, the Vishnu idol inside was discovered fully formed in the river and miraculously aged from boy to man. The temple is on the south bank of the Ridi Khola, near the bus stand.

To reach Ridi on foot, take the trail leading northwest from the Tansen–Tamghas road near Hotel Srinagar. Buses to Ridi (Rs 120, two hours) leave from the public bus stand in Tansen.

THE TRIBHUVAN HIGHWAY

From Birganj, the easiest and quickest route to Kathmandu or Pokhara is along the Mahendra Hwy to Narayangarh and then north to Mugling, but when were the best travel experiences ever easy? It's much more fun to take the winding and dramatic Tribhuvan Hwy, which leaves the Mahendra Hwy at Hetauda, east of Chitwan National Park. The route is prone to landslides in the monsoon and saw a fair bit of damage in the 2015 earthquake, but the scenery is breathtaking and you can stop on the way at Daman for some of the best Himalayan views in Nepal.

Hetauda

📋 057

The bustling town of Hetauda marks the junction between the flat Mahendra Hwy and the steep, spectacular Tribhuvan Hwy. The 2015 earthquake caused some damage but reconstruction is underway. There isn't any great reason to stop here except to change buses or prepare your bike and legs for the steep climb to Daman. Several banks with ATMs can be found at Buddha Chowk.

🛏 Sleeping & Eating

⭐ **Motel Avocado & Orchid Resort** HOTEL $
(📋 057-520429; www.orchidresort.com; Tribhuvan Hwy; Nissen huts s/d Rs 500/800, s/d from Rs 1200/1600, deluxe from Rs 1800/2000; 🅰) This delightful hotel rests among a garden of orchids, rhododendrons and avocado trees, and

is a great choice for travellers on all budgets. The budget rooms are in converted Nissen huts with attached bathrooms, cold showers and bucket hot water, while the 'motel' rooms are well appointed and comfortable. The multicuisine restaurant deserves a special mention for its curries, tandoori and garden BBQs.

Decades of passing cyclists and motorcyclists have contributed to the journals housed in the restaurant and make for good reading. Orchid and birding enthusiasts can arrange local tours here.

ⓘ Getting There & Around

The main bus stand is just west of Buddha Chowk. There are regular morning and afternoon buses to Pokhara (Rs 400, six hours) and Kathmandu (Rs 400, six hours) via Narayanghar (Rs 120, one hour). You can also pick up services to destinations east and west along the Mahendra Hwy. Local buses and minibuses run regularly to Birganj (Rs 80, two hours).

Buses along the Tribhuvan Hwy leave from a smaller bus stand, just north of Motel Avocado's gate. There are buses every hour or so to Kathmandu (Rs 400, eight hours) via Daman (Rs 150, four hours) until around 2pm. Microbuses destined for Palung cost Rs 240 to Daman. Rickshaws and autorickshaws can ferry you from town to the bus stand for Rs 100.

There is a more direct route to Kathmandu through Bimphedi and Pharping, but it was a rough, mostly gravel road at the time of writing, and only suitable for 4WDs (share jeeps to Kathmandu are Rs 400). The long-term plan for a tunnel to be built between Bimphedi and Kulekhani and to upgrade the road into Kathmandu–Terai 'fast track' may eventuate one day, but we are not holding our breath.

Daman
☑ 057

Perched 2322m above sea level, with clear views to the north, east and west, Daman boasts what is arguably *the* most spectacular outlook on the Himalaya in the whole of Nepal. There are unimpeded views of the entire range from Dhaulagiri to Mt Everest from the concrete viewing tower (Rs 30) inside the Daman Mountain Resort. Many buildings around Daman were damaged in the 2015 earthquake, but the resort hotels were not badly affected.

The Mountain Botanical Gardens (⊙10am-5pm) comprise over 78 hectares of forest. February to March is the best time to visit, when the rhododendrons (the national flower of Nepal) are in bloom.

About 1km south of the village, a trail leads west through the forest to the tiny Shree Rikheshwar Mahadev Mandir, sacred to Shiva. On the way, you can drop into a gorgeous little gompa in a glade of trees draped with thousands of prayer flags. From the highway, it's 1km to the gompa and 1.5km to the temple.

🛏 Sleeping & Eating

There are a couple of rustic guesthouses right on the highway in the middle of the village that have very basic rooms (from Rs 300) and daal bhaat. The rustic Sherpa House Daman (☑9845070584; r Rs 400) was damaged in the earthquake but the owners hope to reopen after repairs.

Daman Mountain Resort   HOTEL $
(☑9847175577; www.damanresort.com; s/d Rs 500/1000, deluxe r Rs 1500; 🛜) This ageing resort of concrete bungalows is a slightly more comfortable option than Sherpa House. It's certainly not the Savoy, but the rooms not suffering from damp are reasonable. For running hot water you need to take a deluxe room.

Everest Panorama Resort   HOTEL $$
(☑057-621482, in Kathmandu 01-4428500; s/d US$96/120; 🛜) Easily the most charming place to stay in Daman, this upmarket mountain resort features cute cottages scattered across a sunny hillside facing the Himalaya. All the rooms have heaters, TVs, hot showers and mountain views, while the restaurant (mains Rs 190 to Rs 520) provides the only Western food in Daman. Guided walks and mountain biking can be arranged. Reception is a 200m walk from the highway along a winding forest path.

ⓘ Getting There & Away

There are three daily buses to Kathmandu: a microbus (Rs 250, four hours) and three buses (Rs 220) departing at 7.30am, 9am, noon and 3pm. In addition, there are numerous buses to Palung (Rs 30), from where many buses leave for Kathmandu. There are also buses to Hetauda (Rs 250, four hours) leaving at 7am, 9am, 10.30am and 1pm. Alternatively, this is one of the most spectacular (and gruelling) mountain-bike routes in Nepal.

WESTERN TERAI

The Mahendra Hwy runs west from Butwal to meet the Indian border at Mahendranagar, passing through one of the least developed parts of Nepal. Few travellers pass through the area, though growing numbers are visiting the spectacular Bardia National Park.

Western Terai

Nepalganj

📞 081

Nepalganj is a gritty border town with a hectic Indian (in particular, Uttar Pradesh) flavour. You'll hear more Hindi spoken than Nepali. As Nepal's second city, Nepalganj is an important transport hub with mountain flights to remote airstrips in northwestern Nepal, a busy border with India and the closest airport to Bardia National Park. The town escaped serious damage in the 2015 earthquake.

With its oppressive heat and dust, many see it as a necessary evil on the way to somewhere else, though it is also culturally rich, and home to Nepal's largest Muslim community, as well as having a sizeable expat community of foreign-aid workers.

If you find yourself spending time in Nepalganj, take a stroll through the old bazaar where you'll find some attractive silver Tharu jewellery. There are half a dozen small temples strung out along the main road through the bazaar, with the garish **Bageshwari Mandir**, devoted to Kali, probably the most interesting.

Nepalganj is 16km south of the Mahendra Hwy and 6km north of the Indian border. It's about 1km from the Nepali border post at Jamunaha to the Indian border post at Rupaidha Bazaar – it's walkable, but easier by rickshaw.

🛏 Sleeping & Eating

Vinayak Guest House HOTEL $
(📞 081-522138; Surkhet Rd; r Rs 250-600, with AC Rs 1500; ❄) Vinayak caters to those on a tight budget, and the overall impression is of a drab and damp hotel with basic rooms

CROSSING THE BORDER: NEPALGANJ TO JAMUNAHA/ RUPAIDHA BAZAAR

Border Hours

Both sides of the border are open 24 hours, but you may have trouble finding officials in the wee hours. The immigration office is about 1km from the border.

Foreign Exchange

There are several moneychangers on the Nepali side of the border, but they only exchange Indian and Nepali rupees. The Nabil and Standard Chartered banks in Nepalganj may be able to exchange other currencies.

Onward to India

For Rs 200–Rs 300 you can take a rickshaw from the Nepalganj bus stand to the border at Jamunaha and on to the bus stand in Rupaidha Bazaar. From here, buses and share taxis run regularly to Lucknow (seven hours). The nearest point on the Indian rail network is Nanpara, 17km from the border.

that are just adequate for travellers stuck for the night.

Traveller's Village GUESTHOUSE $$
(☑ 081-550329; travil@wlink.com.np; Surkhet Rd; s/d US$25/35; ✳@☎) The hotel of choice for UN and NGO workers, it is located about 2km northeast of Birendra Chowk, almost opposite the UN compound. Traveller's Village is run by a welcoming American lady (Candy) who's lived here for more than 20 years. Rooms are cosy and spotless, with air-con, hot water and TV. Reservations are absolutely essential.

Kitchen Hut HOTEL $$
(☑ 081-551231; www.kitchenhut.com.np; Surkhet Rd; s/d Rs 2000/2500; ✳@☎) The odd name of this modern business hotel, situated about 3km northeast of Birendra Chowk, is explained by the fact that this venture started as one of Nepalganj's best restaurants. The spacious rooms are cool and tiled, and sport flat-screen TVs. Very good multi-cuisine dishes are served in the Tripti restaurant. Free pick-up from airport and bus station is on offer.

Hotel Sneha HOTEL $$
(☑ 081-520119; hotel@sneha.wlink.com.np; Surkhet Rd; s/d/ste US$40/50/60; ✳☎✳) This big, old-fashioned conference hotel is set in sprawling grounds, about 2km south of Birendra Chowk. The spacious rooms are set around a courtyard of royal palms and boast soft mattresses and modern amenities. The attached casino does nothing to improve the atmosphere, but the patrons usually don't interfere with the hotel guests.

JUMLA

Hidden away in the foothills of the Sisne Himalaya, the remote village of Jumla (2730m) is the gateway to the wild northwest – the least developed and most inaccessible region of Nepal. Apart from foreign-aid workers, the few visitors to Jumla are here for trekking in the remote Karnali region. Most popular is the nine-day trek to/from Rara National Park with its famous sky-blue lake, the largest in Nepal. You can also trek to Dolpo from here. For details of these treks, check out Lonely Planet's *Trekking in the Nepal Himalaya*. If you find yourself in Jumla, the best place to stay is **Kanjirowa Hotel** (☑ 9741111733; r Rs 1500-2000), a recently constructed stone hotel near the airport. It has comfortable, Tibetan-decorated rooms and an excellent restaurant.

★ Candy's Place INTERNATIONAL $
(☑ 081-550329; Surkhet Rd; mains Rs 280-420) Upstairs at Traveller's Village, Candy's Place is an unapologetic American comfort-food oasis in Nepalganj. If you've OD'd on daal bhaat, Candy serves up juicy cheese-and-bacon burgers, oven-roasted chicken with real stuffing, and tenderloin steak that can be washed down with South African red wine. For dessert there's banana cake, butterscotch ice cream or Candy's famous lemon meringue pie.

ℹ Information

Nabil Bank (🕙10am-4.30pm Sun-Thu, to 2.30pm Fri) has foreign-exchange services and a 24-hour ATM.

ℹ Getting There & Away

AIR
Nepalganj is the main air hub for western Nepal. There are several daily flights to Kathmandu (US$183, one hour) through **Yeti Airlines** (☑ 081-526556; www.yetiairlines.com) and **Buddha Air** (☑ 081-525745; www.buddhaair.com). Nepal Airlines (p382) and **Tara Air** (☑ 081-526556) have morning flights to Jumla (US$90, 45 minutes), Dolpo (US$110) and Simikot (US$140), though delays and cancellations are common due to poor weather. Tara Air also offers occasional flights to Rara for US$110.

BUS

The bus stand is about 1km northeast of Birendra Chowk. Buses to Kathmandu (Rs 1180–Rs 1230, 12 hours) and Pokhara (Rs 1100, 12 hours) leave early in the morning or early in the afternoon. Kathmandu buses run via Narayangarh (Rs 920, 10 hours). Buses for Mahendranagar (Rs 600, five hours) leave hourly from 5.30am until 1pm. Buses to Butwal (Rs 500, seven hours) leave hourly.

Local buses to Thakurdwara (for Bardia National Park) leave at 11.20am and 1.30pm (Rs 350, three hours).

❶ Getting Around

Shared tempos (three-wheelers) and *tongas* (horse carriages) run between the bus stand and the border for Rs 25. A cycle-rickshaw costs around Rs 200 to the airport and about the same to Rupaidha Bazaar in India. A taxi to the airport costs Rs 600.

Bardia National Park

♪ 084

Untouched by the 2015 earthquake, Bardia National Park is the largest national park and wilderness area in the Terai and has excellent wildlife-watching opportunities. Bardia is often described as what Chitwan was like 30 years ago, before being overrun by tourism. The park protects 968 sq km of sal forest and grassland, and together with the 550-sq-km Banke National Park (p365) it protects one of Asia's largest stretches of tiger habitat. The

TALKING TIGER

Though there a fewer tigers in Bardia than Chitwan you probably stand a much better chance of seeing one here if you put in the hours at one of the 'hotspots'. The hotspots for tiger sightings are **Tinkuni** (three corners), **Kingfisher**, and the **Balcony**. All the guides know these places well and you will certainly be taken to them on a safari. Don't be surprised to find a large troop of tiger-spotters already in position when you arrive. Some people spend the entire day sitting and waiting (and whispering) with a packed lunch for that elusive glimpse. The best time of the year to see tigers is February to May and the best tactic is to sit and wait at one of the hotspots. Don't forget to bring binoculas or a telephoto lens for your camera, and maybe a book to while away the hours.

tiger numbers are increasing after their demise during the Maoist insurgency.

As well as tigers, there are also healthy populations of wild elephants and one-horned rhinos among the 30 species of mammals living here. The rhinos were reintroduced from Chitwan starting in 1986 in a bid to extend their range to help conserve the species. Unfortunately the early progress was all but lost when poachers took advantage of the insurgency and the population was decimated. Today the population is slowly recovering, with 31 being counted in 2014.

Bardia also has more than 250 species of birds, including the endangered Bengal florican and sarus crane. Gharial and marsh mugger crocodiles and Gangetic dolphins are occasionally spotted on rafting and canoe trips along the Geruwa River, the eastern channel of the Karnali River

During the Maoist insurgency, tourism dried up, lodges were mothballed and the wildlife was hit hard by poaching owing to inadequate protection. The good news is that all this is now being reversed, and while it's a long, arduous journey out here, it's well worth the effort.

❍ Sights

Crocodile Breeding Centre
& Rhino Centre   ZOO

(adult Rs 125; ☉ dawn-dusk Sun-Fri) In the park headquarters there's a small breeding centre for marsh mugger and gharial crocodiles, as well as turtles, so you can get up close and personal with the reptiles. Nearby there is also an enclosure containing Shivaram, a rhino who was injured as a baby in Chitwan. Blind in one eye, he used to wander freely around the park headquarters until he killed a man. If you have your park permit (Rs 1000), the admission fee to visit the animal exhibits is waived.

Tharu Cultural Museum   MUSEUM

(adult Rs 50; ☉ noon-3pm Tue-Sat) Also located near the park headquarters is this small museum that explores the customs and rituals of the Tharu people. If you have paid for admission to the Crocodile Breeding Centre, the admission fee to the museum is waived. You can also arrange cultural tours of the villages through most hotels; otherwise you can rent a bike and explore by yourself.

Elephant Breeding Centre   ZOO

(adult Rs 50; ☉ dawn-dusk) South of the park headquarters, the Elephant Breeding

SANTA CHAUDHARI, WILDLIFE GUIDE

Santa was born in the village of Gobrella, near Tiger Tops Karnali Lodge, and has lived in Bardia all his life. He has been a wildlife guide in the national park for more than 18 years.

You spend a lot of time in the park. What is the best way to see wildlife? All ways are good. The wildlife may or may not be there. You can venture far into the forest on a 4WD safari, but the elephant can take you into the tall grass – where it is not a safe place to walk. Being on foot is also good.

How about that tiger encounter? You see the photos all over the place – a tigress and her four cubs by a river. It was 2009. I was escorting the photographer and his wife on a jungle walk when the tigress appeared across the river at Tinkuni. It was amazing. But then the tigress must have picked up our scent. The roar and the charge will be with me forever. There wasn't a lot of time. She had crossed the river and was directly below us. One more leap was all she needed. I raised my bamboo pole and made as much noise as I could. She backed away and so did we. It could have been so different.

So tigers are the most fearsome animals here? I am most afraid of wild elephants. They are clever and strong, and waving a bamboo pole is not likely to scare an angry elephant.

Centre is worth a visit in the morning and afternoon when the elephants have returned from grazing in the park (10am to 4pm). The mothers and calves are occasionally visited by free-ranging wild males – if this happens during your visit you should keep well clear of the male and exercise caution.

🏃 Activities

You'll need to add a further Rs 1000 for the cost of the park permit per day for most of the prices quoted here. For some activities there is a minimum group size to achieve these per-person costs.

Elephant Safari

An exciting way to explore the park, and the best way to spot wildlife, is on an **elephant safari** (foreigner/SAARC Rs 2500/1500). These are best done early in the morning or late afternoon. Rides on the park elephants should be booked in advance at the park headquarters – your lodge will help you arrange this. If you are on a package it will already be done for you.

Fishing

The Karnali and Babai rivers are famous for *mahaseer,* the giant South Asian river carp that can reach 80kg in weight. Anglers can obtain fishing permits (Rs 2000) at the park headquarters. To fish the Karnali you also need to pay for the daily park permit (Rs 1000), whereas to fish the Babai you need to pay the daily park permit plus a special 'Conservation Fee' (Rs 2000). Due to

their endangered status, any fish you catch will need to be released back into the water.

Guided Walks

A great way to spot wildlife in the park, and potentially the most thrilling, is on a **guided walk** (half-/full day Rs 300/1500, birdwatching 3hr/full day Rs 750/6500). Venturing into the park on foot with your guide, however, is obviously a risk you take into your own hands. (See box on p253.) Three-hour birdwatching tours venture into the buffer zone, full-day birding trips enter the park and come with a packed lunch.

4WD Safari

Jeep safaris (half-/full day per person, min four people Rs 5000/6000) can be arranged directly through the lodges. These include the park permit and a guide, as well as lunch on the full-day safari. An alternative half-day trip takes you to see the blackbuck that reside outside the park. A jeep will cost Rs 8000, and can be shared by up to five passengers. Alternatively, you and your guide can take the bus (three hours), which will cost Rs 350.

Rafting

The Geruwa River forms the western boundary of the park, and a downstream drift in an **inflatable raft** (per person, min 2/max 4 passengers Rs 5000-6000) is a relaxing way of experiencing the picturesque river and park, as well as giving you a chance of spotting a Gangetic dolphin, plus animals and birds along the riverbank. Stopping for lunch, you get to walk around the sandy bank where you can observe the heavy traffic of animal footprints. Crater marks of elephants and rhinos are criss-crossed with perfectly imprinted tiger pugmarks and delicate monkey and deer prints. This is not white-water rafting, although there are some gentle dips, and there are opportunities for a brief swim in the river.

🛏 Sleeping & Eating

Most of the lodges are in close vicinity to each other near the village of Thakurdwara, on the border of the park buffer zone, about 13km from the Mahendra Hwy.

★ Forest Hideaway   LODGE $
(☑ 084-402016, in Kathmandu 01-4225973; www.foresthideaway.com; safari tents Rs 400, dm Rs 600, r Rs 1000-1200, deluxe r incl breakfast Rs 1800; @🖂) This resort is run by the experienced Mohan Aryal and offers expert guides, a restaurant-bar and moneychanging. The mud-walled budget cottages feature fans and insect netting. The safari tents on raised platforms are atmospheric, while the deluxe rooms have mosquito nets and solar hot water. The leafy garden has hammocks and outdoor seating. Pick-up/drop-off transport can be arranged with Mohan.

If you stay here a minimum of two nights, pick-up and drop-off at Ambassa is free.

Bardia Jungle Cottage   LODGE $
(☑ 084-402014; www.bardiajunglecottage.com.np; r Rs 400-1000; 🖂) Right opposite the army camp entrance, this low-key, long-standing lodge offers a great range of rooms from simple mud-walled singles to cement cottages with tiled bathrooms. Cross a tiny bamboo bridge to the central dining hall to hear stories from the owner Premi, a former park warden, who offers numerous activities from fishing to volunteering.

Bardia Wildlife Resort   LODGE $
(☑ 084-402041; wildlifeparadiseresort.com; r Rs 500-1200) Situated in a peaceful spot along the riverbank, 1.5km south of park headquarters, this simple family-run lodge has a true safari feel. All rooms have attached bathrooms and solar hot water. There's a campfire and a lovely garden with papaya trees. The hostess is Bardia's first and only female safari guide.

Bardia Adventure Resort   LODGE $
(☑ 084-402023; www.bardia-adventure.com; r Rs 800-1500) With a prime location looking out to the jungle, this resort has simple Tharu-style, thatched mud-floor huts ranging up to comfortable carpeted cottages with

tiled bathrooms. The highlight here is the resort's own watchtower, where you can enjoy a cold beer while keeping your eyes peeled for a leopard lurking on the park's perimeter.

Racy Shade Resort   LODGE $
(☑ 9748021341; www.racyshaderesort.com; r Rs 1000-1500; 🖂) This lodge is a bit more polished than 'rustic', with neatly trimmed lawn paths leading from the open-sided restaurant-bar through leafy grounds to the thatched-roof rooms. The cheaper rooms are perfectly comfortable, while the deluxe rooms boast verandahs and big bathrooms, some with tubs.

Jungle Base Camp   LODGE $
(☑ 084-402007; www.junglehukum.blogspot.com; r Rs 300-1000) The budget rooms at Jungle Base Camp are rustic mud-and-thatch huts with dirt floors and lantern lighting that exude a certain jungle charm. More rupees bring a sturdy mock-Tharu cottage with attached bathroom and a private verandah with table and chairs. Showers are cold with hot water arriving in a bucket unless you pay for the comfortable deluxe rooms.

Mango Tree Lodge   LODGE $$
(☑ 084-402008; www.mangotreelodge.com; r Rs 1000-3000; 🖂) 🌿 With a biogas plant, organic garden and solar water heaters, Mango Tree Lodge leads the ecofriendly trend in Bardia. The open-sided communal dining and recreation room is one of the best we've seen. From the spacious suites down to the thatch-roofed traditional cottages, these Tharu-decorated rooms are a delight. There's even a wood-fired pizza oven.

Bardia Tiger Resort   LODGE $$
(☑ 084-402002; www.bardiatigerresort.com; r Rs 3200; 🌣🖂) Looking more like a typical Sauraha lodge than a Bardia mud hut, this lodge boasts air-conditioning and big comfy mattresses in every one of its modern, spacious rooms. There is a generator to keep the electric hot water and air-con operating around the clock, plus a large conference hall.

★ Tiger Tops Karnali Lodge   LODGE $$$
(☑ in Kathmandu 01-4361500; www.tigertops.com; inclusive packages per person per night US$250, signature room US$350; 🖂) 🌿 Run by the same pioneering team as Tiger Tops in Chitwan, this top-end lodge is set on the southern edge of the buffer zone near Thakurdwara and offers the most experienced wildlife guides in Bardia. Accommodation is in stylish

Tharu-style cottages; the signature rooms could be used for a safari fashion shoot. Package rates include all meals and activities (park fees and local transfers are extra).

ⓘ Information

Park fees should be paid at the **park headquarters** (📞429719; permits foreigner/SAARC/child under 10yr Rs 1000/500/free; ⊙ dawn-dusk Sun-Fri), located about 13km south of the Mahendra Hwy in the village of Thakurdwara. The bumpy access road leaves the highway at Ambassa, about 500m before the Amreni army checkpost.

The park headquarters has a small **visitor information centre** (⊙10am-4pm Sun-Fri), which features informative wildlife displays. However, the best source of such information is through your lodge.

Most of the lodges are close to Thakurdwara, but because of the poor condition of the roads, visitors usually arrange to be transferred to the lodges by 4WD. Note that much of the park is inaccessible from May to September because of high river levels.

ⓘ Getting There & Away

If you intend to make your own way to the park, call ahead to make sure your lodge is open and able to arrange a pick-up from Ambassa (Rs 1200 one way). The nearest airport is at Nepalganj and your lodge will charge about Rs 6000 (Rs 7000 for air-con) to pick you up or drop you off. If you're on a package, ensure this is all included.

To reach Bardia by public transport, buses leave Pokhara (Rs 1050, 14 hours) at 1pm and 1.30pm; from Kathmandu (Rs 1050, 14 hours) there are five buses departing between 1pm and 5pm. There's also a bus (Capital Express) from Kathmandu leaving at midday that includes dinner (Rs 1400, 14 hours). There are two buses leaving from Narayangarh heading to Bardia (Rs 750, nine hours) at midnight and 4pm.

In the other direction buses depart Ambassa for Pokhara at 3pm and 4.30pm. Several buses originating in Mahendranagar and Danghadi bound for Kathmandu pass through Ambassa and your lodge should be able to help you make a connection. These buses are usually better than the grand-sounding Capital Express (Rs 1400) which leaves Ambassa at 4pm.

Painfully slow local buses depart Thakurdwara at 7am, 8am and 9am bound for Nepalganj (Rs 350, five hours) via Ambassa (Rs 70). Change at Ambassa for buses to Mahendranagar (Rs 350, four hours).

GHODAGHODI TAL

This picturesque grouping of oxbow lakes is renowned for its birdwatching. Located about 40km west of Chisopani, the scene is straight out of an Impressionist painting, with lotus flowers, water lilies and dappled light. The lakes are home to 142 different species of birds, including the grey-headed fishing eagle. Through your hotel you can organise an air-con 4WD and guide for Rs 15,000 (for up to five people), or you can catch a bus (Rs 700 return) from Ambassa.

Sukla Phanta Wildlife Reserve

Tucked against the Indian border and far from the epicenter of the 2015 earthquake, Sukla Phanta Wildlife Reserve (📞099-521309; foreigner/SAARC per day Rs 1000/500) covers 305 sq km of sal forest and *phanta* (grassland) along the banks of the Bahini River. The terrain is similar to Bardia National Park, and the reserve has tigers, rhinos, crocodiles, wild elephants and Nepal's largest population of swamp deer, as well as large numbers of migratory birds.

The few visitors who make it to the park generally come on package tours with the accommodation providers listed here, or on day trips from Mahendranagar with a hired car and driver (Rs 5000 per jeep). Elephant rides (foreigner/SAARC Rs 1000/400) can be booked at the Park Headquarters, but it will be easier to allow your accommodation host to organise this for a small additional fee.

The best time to visit is from November to February; the main vehicle track within the park is impassable from June to September because of monsoonal flooding.

🛏 Sleeping & Eating

Shuklaphanta Jungle Cottage   LODGE $
(📞099-524693; shuklaphantajc@gmail.com; r Rs 1200, with AC Rs 2000; ※ 🛜) Located in the buffer zone close to the reserve's headquarters, this new lodge sports comfortable rooms in a garden similar to the lodges in Bardia. It grows its own organic vegetables for the restaurant and can organise jeep safaris, elephant rides, birdwatching and even excursions to Nainital in India.

CROSSING THE BORDER: DHANGADHI TO GAURIPHANTA

The little-used border crossing from Dhangadhi to Gauriphanta, Uttar Pradesh, is useful for moving on to Lucknow, New Delhi or visiting Dudhwa National Park. Nepali immigration is open from 8am to 5pm. From Dhangadhi there are daily flights to Kathmandu and buses to the Mahendra Hwy that continue west to Mahendranagar and east towards Ambassa, for Bardia National Park, and Nepalganj and beyond.

Suklaphanta Wildlife Camp LODGE $$
(2-night & 3-day packages from US$175) Located about 500m from the reserve's headquarters, this permanent camp of safari tents is run by the **Suklaphanta Nature Guides Association** (☏ 9741060150; www.suklaphantanature. webs.com). Rates include meals, accommodation, park fees and jeep transfer to/from Mahendranagar. Transfer to/from Dhanghadi Airport and New Delhi can be arranged.

Mahendranagar
☏ 099

Mahendranagar is the most westerly border crossing into India and offers an interesting back route to Delhi and the hill towns of Uttaranchal. While it's not somewhere you'll want to spend any length of time (ie only until your bus is ready to depart), it's somewhat less chaotic than other India–Nepal border crossings. If you have time here, Mahendranagar provides a useful base to visit Sukla Phanta Wildlife Reserve and surrounding Tharu villages.

Mahendranagar is just south of the Mahendra Hwy, about 5km east of the Indian border. From the Nepali border post at Gaddachauki, it's about 1km to the Indian border post at Banbassa.

🛏 Sleeping & Eating

Hotel Sweet Dream HOTEL $
(☏ 099-522313; Mahendra Hwy; r Rs 800, with AC Rs 1500; ❄️📶) This hotel is conveniently located about 100m east of the bus station. Rooms are reasonably maintained with carpet and attached bathrooms. The restaurant has an international menu, though the Indian food is the best option. The interior design is odd and seemingly ad hoc, but Mahendranagar is not a town to get too choosy.

Hotel New Anand HOTEL $
(☏ 099-521693; r Rs 1000, with AC Rs 1600; ❄️📶) The anything-but-new Anand is a typical concrete block with basic and tolerable rooms each with a hot-water geyser in the bathroom, a TV and a comfy chair to watch it from. Its best features are its central location opposite the Nabil Bank and its helpful management.

Hotel Opera HOTEL $$
(☏ 099-522101; www.hoteloperanepal.com; r Rs 1200, deluxe Rs 2000-3500; ❄️📶) This is the

CROSSING THE BORDER: MAHENDRANAGAR TO BANBASSA

Border Hours
The Nepali side of the border is open to tourists 24 hours, but before 5am and after 8.30pm you may need to go searching for immigration officials. The Indian side of the border (Gadda Chowki) is open 24 hours, but is only open to vehicles from 6am to 8am, noon to 2pm and 6pm to 8pm.

Foreign Exchange
There's a small bank counter near the Nepali customs post, but it only exchanges Indian and Nepali rupees. In Mahendranagar, Nabil Bank has foreign exchange and an ATM. An autorickshaw into town costs around Rs 100.

Onward to India
From the Indian border post, take a rickshaw to the bus station in Banbassa, where you can pick up long-distance buses to Delhi (₹275, 10 hours). Local buses and shared jeeps serve Almora, Nainital and other towns in Uttaranchal. There's also a slow metre-gauge train to Bareilly, where you can pick up trains to other destinations in India.

For further information, head to shop.lonelyplanet.com to purchase a downloadable PDF of the Delhi chapter from Lonely Planet's *India* guide.

FAR WESTERN NEPAL

Nepal's far west is a true frontier ripe for exploration and it was almost untouched by the 2015 earthquake. Currently it is still an off-the-beaten-track destination, but that is changing as tourism entrepreneurs move to promote and open up the destination for mainstream tourism. One such group is the **Tourism Development Society** (www.farwest nepal.org) based in Dhangadhi. As well as promoting local accommodation, this not-for-profit organisation can help arrange cultural tours to Hindu pilgrimage sites and to Tharu villages, where you can stay with a local family in traditional homestays. Also on offer are adventurous multiday treks into the hills. For more information contact the organisation.

    Khaptad National Park is one of the highlighted trekking destinations in far western Nepal. This park features oak and pine forests surrounding undulating grasslands and wildflower-carpeted meadows. Wildflower enthusiasts and birdwatchers are especially rewarded. It was declared a national park in 1984 and was named after a Hindu holy man, Khaptad Baba. **Khaptad Baba Ashram**, near the park headquarters, is a focal point of the park, attracting Shiva-worshipping pilgrims. Treks into Khaptad start from the town of Silghadi, an eight-hour drive from Dhangadhi airport.

'best' hotel in town. And while the rooms are certainly spacious, the plumbing leaves something to be desired – so check the shower before deciding on a room. It's in a reasonably quiet location but the associated casino is hardly an attraction. It probably boasts the best restaurant in town, serving hearty Nepali and Indian dishes.

ⓘ Information

The Nepal Tourism Board runs a small **tourist information centre** (☏ 099-523773; ⊙ 9.30am-5pm Sun-Fri) on the Nepal side of the border. If you need to check email, there are numerous places with access for Rs 20 per hour.

    A 15-minute autorickshaw ride (Rs 120) from the border, **Nabil Bank** (☏ 525450; ⊙ 10am-5pm Sun-Thu, to 3pm Fri) has a foreign exchange service and an ATM.

ⓘ Getting There & Away

There are no longer flights departing from Mahendranagar airport. The closest airport is at Dhangadhi, 60km east of Mahendranagar, which has daily **Buddha Air** (☏ 091-575288) and **Yeti Airlines** (☏ 091-520004) flights to Kathmandu (US$216, one hour). Buses to Dhangadhi (Rs 110) leave every 30 minutes from the main bus station. A taxi will cost Rs 3500.

    The bus station is about 1km from the centre on the Mahendra Hwy. Long-haul buses leave for Kathmandu (Rs 1400, 15 hours) at 5am, 5.30am, 11.50am, 2pm, 3pm, 3.30pm, 4pm and 4.30pm. There's a single Pokhara service (Rs 1080, 16 hours) at 2.20pm. Local buses run every 30 minutes to Nepalganj (Rs 600, five hours), passing the turn-off to Bardia National Park at Ambassa (Rs 350, four hours).

ⓘ Getting Around

Buses and tempos run regularly between the bus station and the border for Rs 100. From the border into the main town a rickshaw/taxi costs around Rs 100/400.

    Taxis can be hired for trips to Sukla Phanta Wildlife Reserve for around Rs 6000 to Rs 7000 per day.

EASTERN TERAI

Bound by the Indian states of Bihar, Sikkim and West Bengal, the eastern Terai is broadly a mirror image of the west. The rolling hills of the Mahabharat Range are squeezed between the dry eastern plains and the Himalaya. The Mahendra Hwy cuts east to meet the Indian border at Kakarbhitta, providing easy access to Sikkim and Darjeeling. Low-lying areas were largely untouched by the 2015 earthquake, but some towns in the hills sustained damage.

Birganj

There's very little in the hectic border town of Birganj to suggest that you're not in India. As the main transit point for freight between India and Nepal, the town is mobbed by trucks, deafened by car horns and jostled by rickshaws. The town saw little damage in the 2015 earthquake, but with its oppressive heat, clouds of dust and total chaos it's not a place you'll want to hang around too long, and it is most commonly visited by travellers crossing to/from Kolkata in India.

Eastern Terai

The clock tower on the main road serves as a useful landmark, leading south to the town centre and Indian border, while eastwards takes you to the bus station.

🛌 Sleeping & Eating

There are a number of noisy and very rough budget places near the main bus stand, and a handful of more comfortable choices in the centre.

Hotel Makalu   HOTEL $
(☑ 051-523054; hmakalu@gmail.com; cnr Campus & Main Rds; r with/without bath from Rs 1400/Rs 2000; ❉🛜) This faded hotel is calm and relaxed – just what you need in hectic Birganj. Rooms have TVs, carpets and 24-hour hot showers, and there's a good Indian restaurant. It's very popular so book ahead.

Hotel Vishuwa   HOTEL $$
(☑ 051-527777; www.vishuwa.com; Bypass Rd; s/d Rs 3800/4000; ❉🛜🏊) On the outskirts of town, the three-star Vishuwa is the best choice for those wanting true comfort. It also has the best restaurant in town.

ℹ️ Information

There are several banks in town with ATMs, while fast internet access (Rs 30 per hour) is available along the main road.

ℹ️ Getting There & Away

Buddha Air (☑ Kathmandu 01-5542494; Campus Rd) has up to five daily flights between Simara (the airport for Birganj) and Kathmandu (US$100, 20 minutes). The airport is 22km from Birganj, and a taxi costs around Rs 1000.

THE BUDDHA OF BARA

At the start of 2005, nobody had heard of Ram Bahadur Banjan. By the end of the year, thousands of Nepali Buddhists were hailing the long-haired 16-year-old Tamang boy as the second incarnation of the Buddha.

Followers of the teenage guru – who is known as Om Namo Guru Buddha Gyani or Dharma Sangha – claim that he had been meditating without food or water in the forest east of Birganj for nearly 10 months. Although that sounds unlikely, the Nepali government asked the Nepal Academy of Science and Technology to investigate the claim and, if necessary, declare a miracle. Before any conclusions could be reached, Banjan mysteriously disappeared.

After reappearing on three brief occasions, in late 2008 he re-emerged from the jungle in Ratanpuri, 150km southeast of Kathmandu, to worldwide media attention. Devotees came in their hundreds of thousands to see him, with many suspecting he had attained enlightenment in Bodhgaya, just like the historical Buddha did in 592 BC.

While Dharma Sanga himself denies he's the reincarnation of Buddha, this hasn't stopped an ever-growing legion of devotees flocking to hear his talks, including many foreigners.

Buses leave from the large, sprawling, ear-splittingly noisy bus stand at the end of Ghantaghar Rd (New Rd). There are plenty of buses to Kathmandu (ordinary/deluxe/air-con Rs 550/600/800, six to seven hours) from 5am until 8pm. However, the most comfortable and quickest option is to get a Tata Sumo '4WD' (Rs 550-800, four to five hours), which depart every 20 minutes, finishing up around 5pm. There are also morning buses to Pokhara (Rs 600, eight hours) via Narayangarh (Rs 250, four hours) at 5am, 6.30am and 7.30am. Regular buses head to Janakpur (Rs 250-350, five hours) every 20 minutes until 4pm.

ⓘ Getting Around

Rickshaws charge around Rs 300 to go from town to the Nepali border post and on to Raxaul Bazaar. Alternatively, you can take a tempo or *tonga* from the bus station to the Nepali border post for Rs 25 and then walk to the Indian side, but it's likely they'll charge more for your bag.

Janakpur

Like the other border towns in the Terai, Janakpur's way of life is unmistakably Indian, but there's a lot more going on here than rickshaws and bustling bazaars. What makes Janakpur (also referred to as Janakpurdham) one of the most fascinating towns in the Terai is its electrifying religious atmosphere mixed with a rich historical and cultural heritage. Even though there's no architecture predating 1880, it manages to evoke an aura of grandeur not found elsewhere in the Terai.

Janakpur is best known as an important pilgrimage site for Hindus all over Nepal and India, who come to pay homage to the city's connection with the Hindu epic the Ramayana. Legend has it that it's the site where Sita was born, and where she was married to Rama.

The other lure in Janakpur is its Maithili culture. Janakpur was once the capital of the ancient kingdom of Mithila, a territory now divided between Nepal and India: more than two million people in the area still

---

CROSSING TO INDIA: BIRGANJ TO RAXAUL BAZAAR

Border Hours

The Nepali side of the border is officially open from 5am to 9pm, but the staff sometimes clock off early and you'll need to find someone to stamp you in or out of Nepal. Similarly, the Indian side is staffed from 5am to 9pm, but you can find someone at other times. Nepali visas are available on arrival from the Nepal immigration office, but payment must be in US dollars.

Foreign Exchange

There are no facilities at the border, but there are banks and moneychangers in Birganj. The Indian rupee is widely accepted in Birganj.

Onward Transport

The border is 3km south of Birganj, from where it's a further 2km to the bus station in Raxaul Bazaar. Most people take a rickshaw straight through from Birganj (Rs 300).

From Raxaul, there are regular buses to Patna (non-air-con/air-con ₹180/230, six hours) or you can take the daily Mithila Express train to Kolkata's Howrah train station, departing Raxaul at 10am. Seats cost sleeper/3AC/2AC ₹365/990/1425 (note that sleeper and two-tier class prices include air-con) and the trip takes 18 hours. The Satyagrah Express runs daily to New Delhi (sleeper/3AC/2AC ₹455/1215/1765, 24 hours, departing at 9.05am).

Janakpur

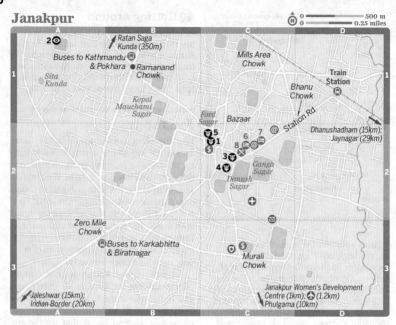

speak Maithili as their native tongue and the Maithili people are famous for their wildly colourful paintings.

Janakpur is actually the third city on this site. The city mythologised in the Ramayana existed around 700 BC, but it was later abandoned and sank back into the forest. Simaraungarh grew up in its place, but this city was also destroyed, this time by Muslim invaders in the 14th century. The 2015 earthquake caused some damage to historic buildings, though not the total destruction reported immediately after the disaster.

☉ Sights

★ Janaki Mandir   HINDU TEMPLE
At the heart of Janakpur lies the marble Janaki Mandir, one of the finest pieces of architecture in Nepal. Built in extravagant baroque Mughal style that leaves it looking like a palace made of sweets, the Janaki Mandir is Janakpur's most important temple and is dedicated to Sita, the wife of Rama and heroine of the Ramayana. It's believed to stand on the spot where King Janak found the infant Sita lying in the furrow of a ploughed field. Cracks appeared in the temple walls after the 2015 earthquake, but the structure has been stabilised and is once again mobbed by pilgrims.

A steady stream of pilgrims file in through the gatehouse to worship the Sita statue in the inner sanctum. The temple is particularly popular with women, who wear their best and most colourful saris for the occasion. Early evening is the most atmospheric time to visit, as the temple is draped with colourful lights and pilgrims arrive en masse.

The temple only dates from 1912, but with its white marble arches, domes, turrets and screens, it feels much older.

At the back of the complex is a small museum (admission Rs 15) with some amusingly naff moving statues telling the story of Rama and Sita.

Ram Sita Bibaha Mandir   HINDU TEMPLE
(admission Rs 5, camera/video Rs 5/21; ⊙5am-9pm) This rather bizarre temple, which sits right next door to the city's centrepiece, the Janaki Mandir, marks the spot where Rama and Sita were married. The temple is topped by a modernist interpretation of a tiered pagoda roof, and the walls are glass so you can peer in at the kitsch life-sized models of Sita and Rama.

Traditional Villages   VILLAGE
The sugar-cane fields and Maithili villages around Janakpur form a lush and magical mosaic. Many of the villages are built in the

Janakpur

⊙ **Top Sights**
   1 Janaki Mandir C2

⊙ **Sights**
   2 Bihar Kunda.. A1
   3 Janak Mandir & Danush Sagar............C2
   4 Ram Mandir & Danush Sagar..............C2
   5 Ram Sita Bibaha Mandir C2

⊜ **Sleeping**
   6 Hotel City Star.......................................C2
   7 Hotel Welcome......................................C2

⊗ **Eating**
   8 Rooftop Family Restaurant C2

traditional Mithila style, with mud walls decorated with colourful paintings and raised wall engravings of people and animals.

The easiest village to reach from Janakpur is **Kuwa**, about 1km south of Murali Chowk. People are very friendly, as long as you aren't too intrusive with your camera, and you can drop in on the Janakpur Women's Development Centre (p281).

If you feel like roaming further afield, **Dhanushadham**, 15km northeast of Janakpur, marks the spot where Rama allegedly drew Shiva's magic bow. Worshippers believe a fossilised fragment of the broken bow lies here.

Further rural adventures and wall art await in the village of **Phulgama**, a 30-minute bus ride (Rs 20) south of Janakpur.

Ram Mandir & Danush Sagar   HINDU TEMPLE
Hidden away in a stone courtyard southeast of the Janaki Mandir, the **Ram Mandir** is the oldest temple in Janakpur (constructed in 1882), built in the classic tiered pagoda style of the hills. The main temple is sacred to Rama but there are several smaller shrines to Shiva, Hanuman and Durga dotted around the compound. It's busiest in the early evening, when the courtyard is filled with incense smoke and music.

Opposite the entrance are a series of ghats (steps for ritual bathing) leading down into the **Danush Sagar**, the largest ceremonial tank at Janakpur. There are small shrines all around the perimeter and vendors in front sell flower garlands, *tika* powder, sacred threads and other ritual objects for pujas (prayers).

THE TERAI & MAHABHARAT RANGE JANAKPUR

MITHILA ART

The vibrant artwork produced by Maithili women can be traced back as far as the 7th century and is a tradition that has been passed from generation to generation. As the former capital of the kingdom of Mithila, it is appropriate that Janakpur has emerged as the centre for both preserving and promoting the ancient art of Mithila painting.

Mithila painting is part decoration, part social commentary, recording the lives of rural women in a society where reading and writing are reserved for high-caste men. Scenes in Mithila paintings colourfully record the female experience of life in the Terai – work, childbirth, marriage and the social network among village women. Today you will also see more modern subject matter, such as aeroplanes and buses, blended with traditional themes like Hindu mythology and village life.

Traditionally, Mithila paintings were used as a transient form of decoration during festivals when the mud walls of village huts were painted in white and ochre with abstract patterns or complex scenes of everyday village life. You can still see houses in the villages surrounding Janakpur with painted walls and raised patterns. More recently, Mithila painting has taken off as a more contemporary and collectable art form, with the women painting on canvases of rough handmade paper that is similar in texture to the mud hut walls. Not only are Mithila paintings now exhibited in galleries across the world, but more importantly the art has also opened up a whole new industry for women in impoverished rural communities.

One of the best-known social projects is the **Janakpur Women's Development Centre** (JWDC, Nare Bekas Kendra; ☑ 9808205576, 041-620932; www.jwdconline.com; ⊗ 10am-5pm Sun-Thu, to 4pm Fri Apr-Sep, 10am-4pm Sun-Fri Oct-Mar), just south of Janakpur in the village of Kuwa. Around 40 Maithili women are employed at the centre, producing paper paintings, papier-mâché boxes and mirrors, screen-printed fabrics and hand-thrown ceramics. Money raised goes directly towards improving the lives of rural women. A rickshaw from Janakpur to the centre will cost around Rs 150–Rs 200.

Nearby is the small **Janak Mandir**, sacred to the father of Sita.

If you head west from Ramanand Chowk, you'll reach two more ceremonial tanks – **Bihar Kunda** and **Ratan Saga Kunda.**

Festivals & Events

Maha Ganga Aarati   CULTURAL
(Ganga Sagar; ☉7pm Mar-Sep, 6pm Oct-Feb) Every evening at the large, central bathing tank of Ganga Sagar, a small puja ceremony involving a lot of crashing of cymbals, ringing of bells and waving of candles takes place. Anyone is welcome to join in.

Sita Bibaha Panchami   HINDU
By far the most interesting time to visit Janakpur is during the fifth day of the waxing moon in November/December, when tens of thousands of pilgrims descend on the town to celebrate the re-enactment of Sita's marriage to Rama (also known as Vivaha Panchami). There are processions and performances of scenes from the Ramayana in the streets.

Rama Navami   HINDU
Celebrations for Rama's birthday in March/April are accompanied by a huge procession, which attracts many sadhus (wandering Hindu holy men).

Holi   HINDU
In March, Janakpur gets boisterous during this riotously colourful affair, but be warned: foreigners are not exempt from a ritual splattering with coloured powder and water.

Tihar   HINDU
If you visit during in October/November, you'll see Mithila women repainting the murals on their houses.

Sleeping & Eating

Hotel City Star   HOTEL $
(☏041-530327; Shiv Chowk; r Rs 1000; ✳🛜) A solid budget choice in the centre of all the action. The City Star has small, luridly painted rooms that are kept spotless and have hot-water bathrooms. Interior rooms lack windows but on the plus side are much quieter.

⭐ **Hotel Welcome**   HOTEL $$
(☏9801620064, 041-520646; www.nepalhotel welcome.com; Station Rd; d with/without AC Rs 3200/2000, tr Rs 4000; ✳🛜) The hotel 'where welcome never ends' has spent the

past couple of years receiving a serious facelift (still ongoing at the time of writing), which is making its 60 or so rooms the easy standout choice in town. Other pluses, alongside the spacious rooms decorated with art and bright colours, are the helpful management and in-house restaurant.

Rooftop Family Restaurant   INDIAN $
(Station Rd; mains Rs 120-250; ☉9.30am-9.30pm) Facing the small Janak Mandir, this upstairs restaurant, which has more class than most other places to eat in the city centre, has an excellent selection of vegetarian curries, plus cold beer and outdoor tables.

❶ Information

Everest Bank has an ATM tucked away inside the eastern entry of Janaki Mandir.

There are several internet cafes in town for around Rs 30 per hour.

❶ Getting There & Around

Buddha Air (☏Kathmandu 01-5542494; www. buddhaair.com) and **Yeti Airlines** (☏Kathmandu 01-4465888; www.yetiairlines.com) both have three daily flights between them from Janakpur to Kathmandu (US$117, 20 minutes). The airport is a Rs 120 rickshaw ride south of the centre. If arriving at Janakpur airport, rickshaws are considerably cheaper if you make the short walk outside the airport.

Regular daily buses to Kathmandu (deluxe/ air-con Rs 700/1000, 10 hours) via Narayangarh (Rs 450–Rs 700, five hours) depart from the highway at Ramanand Chowk. The first bus is at 5.30am and last at 5pm. There are also buses to Pokhara (Rs 700, 12 hours) at 6.40am and 3pm. Local buses run hourly to Birganj (Rs 250–Rs340, four hours) until about 3pm.

Buses heading east to Kakarbhitta (Rs 525, seven hours) are at the dusty 'new' bus park near Zero Mile Chowk from 6am to 6.30pm. You'll also find several morning buses for Biratnagar (Rs 350, five hours) until 10.30am. Either of these buses can also be picked up at Ramamamd Chowk. The bus stand is a Rs 50 rickshaw ride from central Janakpur.

There was a very slow, metre-gauge railway line leading across the border to India and the dusty plains town of Jaynagar. However, at the time of writing it was closed while the line is upgraded. This work will mean no trains puff out of Janakpur until 2016 at the earliest. Train buffs might still enjoy the stroll down to the station to check out the couple of rusty old trains being slowly eaten away by the vegetation.

Koshi Tappu Wildlife Reserve

The smallest of the Terai's national parks, **Koshi Tappu Wildlife Reserve** (☑025-621327; per day foreigner/SAARC/child under 10yr Rs 1000/500/free; ☺6am-6pm) is a birdwatcher's paradise. Consisting of 175 sq km of wet and grassland habitat, Koshi Tappu (translating to 'river islands') is home to at least 493 species of birds, as well as being the last habitat of the endangered arna (long, pointy-horned wild water buffalo). It was founded in 1976 to protect a small triangle of *phanta* and *tappu* (small islands) in the flood plain of the Sapt Kosi River – one of the three main tributaries of the Ganges. There was no major damage from the 2015 earthquake.

It's a wonderfully serene spot and most travellers who visit are birdwatchers in search of rare species such as the swamp francolin, Bengal florican and sarus crane. Migratory species from Siberia and Tibet take up residence from November to February. While it lacks heavy hitters like tigers and rhinos, there's still plenty to see – including Gangetic dolphins, blue bulls, deer, golden jackals, marsh muggers, fishing cats, mongooses, civet cats and porcupines. Gangetic dolphin are best spotted from the bridge at Koshi Barrage.

⊙ Sights & Activities

★Birdwatching   BIRDWATCHING
Every lodge has a resident ornithologist who leads bird-spotting walks around the park (usually included in package rates). Early morning, when the air is cool and the mist is lifting, and late afternoon as the sun varnishes the waters pink, are the prime bird-watching times and, birder or not, it's hard not to enjoy the experience.

Some of the lodges also have bird hides that can be a good spot to tick a few species off your list.

River Trips   RAFTING
Exploring the park on the river via a gentle paddle in a rubber dinghy, canoe or *dunga* (wooden boat) is a great way to see larger wildlife, particularly arna, but isn't quite so good for birdwatching. Rates are usually included in the lodges' package rates; otherwise the going rate for a wooden boat and driver is Rs 1500 per hour or the lodges can supply a rubber dingy for US$50 per hour.

Elephant Safaris   SAFARI
(foreigner/SAARC Rs 2000/1000) A popular way to explore Koshi is by elephant; however, here it's more about the experience itself rather than for spotting wildlife. Rides are arranged at the park headquarters before 8am or after 4pm.

Jeep Safaris   WILDLIFE WATCHING
Many lodges offer morning or late-afternoon jeep safaris as part of their package. Although you're unlikely to see a huge amount of wildlife, it's a good way of getting a feel for the park and its habitat, and jeep safaris are normally combined with a birdwatching walk.

🛏 Sleeping

While rates initially appear exorbitant, keep in mind they include all meals and activities. Prebooking is essential. Lodges close during the monsoon (June to August).

★Koshi Camp   TENTED CAMP $$$
(☑9851003677; www.kosicamp.com; half board s/d US$95/135, package per person per night US$155) Located in the delightful village of Madhuban, 7km from the highway, Koshi Camp is a popular choice for birders. It has an attractive setting on the edge of the park with its own pond and bird hide. Lodging is in tents with comfy beds and spotless en suite bathrooms.

The bird guides here are first-rate and the restaurant has a safari feel, with plenty of ornithological reading material on hand.

Koshi Tappu Birdwatching Camp   TENTED CAMP $$$
(☑9842503673, 9807368484; www.koshitappu. net; full board excl activities s/d US$70/140, 3 day package incl activities s/d US$250/500) Right next to the park offices and information centre, this new camp has five small and immaculate tents with separate, shared bathrooms plus a couple of rooms in mud-walled houses (same price as tents). The grounds are still a little bare and lack character but this will surely change as the vegetation grows.

Koshi Tappu Wildlife Camp   TENTED CAMP $$$
(☑01-4226130; www.koshitappu.com; half-board s/d US$125/140, all-inclusive with activities s/d US$225/340) The longest established of the park's camps, this one has pleasingly mature and landscaped gardens, a ramshackle bird hide (the viewing slots are bit too low for

THE TERAI & MAHABHARAT RANGE KOSHI TAPPU WILDLIFE RESERVE

comfort) overlooking a swamp, and tents that don't quite justify the high prices. Bathrooms are in shared, separate blocks. It's in the village of Prakashpur.

❶ Information

The **information centre** (⊙ 6am-6pm) at the park headquarters in Kusaha has an interesting museum, with displays of elephant, deer and arna skulls, and a desiccated gharial. Here is where you arrange elephant safaris.

❶ Getting There & Away

Most visitors come on a package tour with a prearranged pick-up from Biratnagar airport, but it's easy enough to travel here as an independent traveller. The best way is to fly from Kathmandu to Biratnagar then take a taxi (Rs 3000, two hours) to Koshi Tappu.

By public transport, you can catch a bus along the Mahendra Hwy to Laukahi (Rs 150 from Biratnagar), 10km east of the Koshi Barrage. Get off at the police station, from where two daily buses (Rs 25) pass along the village road to the Koshi Camp and Koshi Tappu Wildlife Camp at noon and 4pm (returning in the morning). Otherwise, call ahead for one of the lodges to pick you up for around Rs 1000. For the park headquarters and Koshi Tappu Birdwatching Camp, get off at Jamuha, from where it's a further 2.5km walk.

Buses from Kathmandu (12 to 14 hours) are Rs 1000 for an ordinary bus and Rs 1200 for a deluxe bus (which let's be honest is only deluxe in name), while from the east, you can jump on any bus heading along the Mahendra Hwy.

Biratnagar

For what is Nepal's major industrial centre and second most-populous city (approximately 260,000 people), Biratnagar is surprisingly low-key. Sure, you'll have to dodge a rickshaw here or there in the town's centre, but it's neither as polluted nor swarming with bustling activity as you might expect. However, for visitors there's nothing much to do here and the city serves mainly as a transit hub. The town has experienced a surge in population following the 2015 disaster because of its reputation as a safe haven from earthquakes.

🛏 Sleeping & Eating

★**Hotel Eastern Star** HOTEL **$$**
(☑ 021-471626; easternstar_brt@wlink.com.np; Road Cess Chowk; s/d with fan Rs 1500/1900, s/d with AC from Rs 1850/2150; ❇ ☎) The best-value place in town, it has a wonderful location in a quiet area south of the bus park. Rooms, which have a certain faded charm, are massive and well furnished, and have comfortable beds, satellite TV and clean bathrooms. Staff are friendly, and there's a good Indian restaurant and well-stocked bar.

Hotel Panchali HOTEL **$$**
(☑ 021-472520; www.hotelpanchali.com.np; s/d with fan Rs 1200/1500, s/d with AC Rs 2200/2500; ❇ ☎ �) For business travellers, or those who aim to be, this garishly painted block is currently the newest, and best, option in a city without a lot of smart hotels. Rooms are fairly no-frills, but everything is kept ship-shape smart and the bathrooms are, for once, fairly pleasant. It's close to the bus park.

Unique Fast Food VEGETARIAN, INDIAN **$**
(Main Rd; mains Rs 100-160; ⊙ 9am-9pm) Fans of the *dosa* will want to head to this popular South Indian vegetarian eatery, with an impressive array of different types of *dosa* – including the 'Unique special *dosa*' with paneer.

Angan INDIAN, VEGETARIAN **$**
(Main Rd; mains Rs 230-310; ⊙ 8am-9pm) Part of an Indian chain, this place offers cool, air-conditioned comfort and cleanliness and an array of veg curries and tandoori dishes, but it's best known for its *thalis* and none come more impressive than the *thali* special (Rs 345).

❶ Information

There are several banks with ATMs along or just off Main Rd, as well as a whole load of internet cafes at Traffic Chowk.

❶ Getting There & Away

Buddha Air (Kathmandu ☑ 01-5542494; www.buddhaair.com) and **Yeti Airlines** (Kathmandu ☑ 01-4465888; www.yetiairlines.com) both have numerous daily flights between Biratnagar and Kathmandu (around US$150–US$190, 35 minutes). A rickshaw to the airport will cost around Rs 150.

The bus stand is a Rs 30 rickshaw ride southwest from Traffic Chowk in the city centre. There are regular buses to Kathmandu (normal/deluxe/air-con Rs 920/1120/1420, 14 hours) via Narayangarh from 4am to 4pm, and two buses to Pokhara (Rs 1100, 12 hours) at 4.30am and 3.30pm. Several buses leave every morning for Janakpur (Rs 400, six hours). There are also regular services to Kakarbhitta (Rs 218, three hours) from the Mahendra Hwy.

Local buses run to Dharan (Rs 80, 1½ hours) throughout the day. There are also early-morning buses to Dhankuta (Rs 250, three hours) and Hile (Rs 300, 3½ hours).

Dharan to Hile

About 17km north of the busy and uneventful roadside town of Itahari, Dharan marks the start of yet another dramatic route into the hills. From here, a decent tarmac road runs north into the foothills of the Himalaya, providing access to a series of attractive hill towns and trekking trailheads. The area was badly affected by an earthquake in 1988 but escaped serious damage in the 2015 earthquake.

Dharan

The sprawling town of Dharan has three distinct characters. On the far western perimeter you'll find an affluent, almost middle-class suburban park feel, with quiet streets lined with well-maintained bungalows, neatly paved pavements, rubbish bins and a country club with a golf course. Up until 1990 Dharan was the Gurkha recruiting area, and its wealth can be largely attributed to money brought in by these world-famous Nepali–British soldiers. The eastern side has steep streets and a relaxed village feel with banana plants, bamboo-forested hills and rustic shacks. Dividing the two areas is the lively Dharan Bazaar, which has a more typical Terai flavour, with its flat and dusty market.

Dharan is one of the *shakti peeths,* marking the spot where part of the body of Shiva's first wife, Sati, fell after she was consumed by flames. There are several important Shaivite temples northeast of the centre in the village of **Bijayapur**. A short walk from here is the **Budha Subba Mandir**, set among dense bamboo thickets down the path, with a curious collection of rocks covered in mud – said to represent the reclining body of Mahadev (Shiva). You're likely to encounter chickens being sacrificed. To reach Bijayapur, take a right at Chata Chowk (a 10-minute walk from Dharan Bazaar), which leads to steps at the bottom of the hill; from here it's a 20-minute walk. An autorickshaw costs Rs 300 return.

🛏 Sleeping & Eating

New Dreamland Hotel & Lodge   HOTEL $
(📞 021-525024; r with/without bathroom Rs 1200/700, with AC Rs 2300; ❀ 📶) If you can cope with the near-incessant traffic noise then Dreamland, with its large, carpeted rooms, exceptionally helpful staff and attractive garden restaurant, is an excellent choice. To get there from Bhanu Chowk (the clocktower square in the town centre), head west three blocks.

Hotel Nava Yug   GUESTHOUSE $
(📞 021-524797; r Rs 700-800, without bathroom Rs 400) A fair cheapie in the heart of the Dharan Bazaar, this place is a little decrepit, with simple rooms and hot water coming by the bucket, but considering its central bazaar location it's surprisingly quiet (note that we didn't say it was quiet – just quieter than you might imagine!).

★ Olive Cafe & Restaurant   PIZZERIA, INTERNATIONAL $
(Putali Line; pizzas Rs 295-330, mains Rs 300; ⊙ 10am-10pm) This place must have got lost on its way to Thamel, the tourist central of Kathmandu, but we're sure glad it did. It offers very acceptable wood-fired pizzas, as well as some local dishes and pasta creations all served up in a setting, adorned with wooden masks, that invites you to linger over dinner.

ⓘ Getting There & Around

Several buses a day leave from Bhanu Chowk for Kathmandu (normal/deluxe Rs 800/1000, 14 hours) with the first at 4.30am and the last at 5pm. There are also buses to Biratnagar (Rs 80, 1½ hours). Heading north, local buses run regularly from 4am to 4pm for Bhedetar (Rs 55, 45 minutes), Dhankuta (Rs 175, two hours) and Hile (Rs 215, three hours). There are also buses east to the Indian border at Kakarbhitta (Rs 295, four hours).

Bhedetar

Arriving from the hot dusty plains of the Terai, the cool climate of tiny, laid-back Bhedetar makes for a refreshing change. Perched at 1420m, Bhedetar's soaring views over Everest and Makalu are spectacular on a clear day and the village basically exisits just as a mountain viewpoint for tourists (most of whom are local tourists). The best views are from **Bhedetar Charles Point** (foreigner/SAARC Rs 100/23, camera foreigner/SAARC Rs 100/25; ⊙ dawn-dusk), named after Prince Charles, who visited in the 1980s.

🛏 Sleeping & Eating

Hotel Aruu Valley Hilltop Restaurant   GUESTHOUSE
(📞 9842055086; r Rs 1200-1600, without bathroom Rs 600; 📶) Hotel Aruu Valley Hilltop

Restaurant is a pleasant place to spend the night. Set among a garden of bright flowers, its rooms are delightfully decorated and have thick carpets, wicker furniture and comfortable beds with warm blankets.

Hile

Hile was once the starting point for the camping trek to Makalu and the end point for the lodge trek from Lukla, but the road has advanced along the valley, reaching almost as far as Tumlingtar and Khandbari. As a result, Hile is no longer the busy trekking hub it once was. Nevertheless, the village has a bustling bazaar feel, particularly during the weekly Thursday market, and there's a good mountain viewpoint about 30 minutes' walk above town (follow the Basantapur road to the army post, then turn north along the trail to Hattikharka). And if neither of those appeal then it's simply a fine place to get off the beaten track.

🛏 Sleeping & Eating

At the time of writing a huge new hotel complex was under construction on the hill above town.

Most hotels serve filling Tibetan food and warming wooden pots of *tongba* (hot millet beer).

Hotel Mountain   HOTEL $
(026-540403; r with/without bathroom Rs 600/500) Very close to the bus park, this lodge is a little (very little) more upmarket than the other town-centre options. There are valley views from the rear-facing balconies and a reasonable restaurant serving the basics (mains Rs 120–Rs 200).

Kanjirowa Makalu Hotel   HOTEL $
(☑026-540509; r from Rs 1200; ☎) A smart red-brick hotel on the outskirts of town, its large rooms are by far the most comfortable in Hile. It has a good international menu and a bar with an impressive cocktail list.

❶ Getting There & Away

Frequent local buses run from Dharan to Hile (Rs 215, two hours), with the last bus at 4.30pm. A few continue up the Arun Valley as far as Leguwa (Rs120, three hours). Some buses from Dharan continue to Basantapur (Rs 100 from Hile, 1½ hours).

Ilam

Like its neighbour Darjeeling across the border, Ilam (pronounced 'ee-lam') is synonymous with one thing – tea. The two share an almost identical climate and topography and, while Darjeeling is a household name, Ilam quietly sets about its business in making a name for itself internationally through its quality tea.

Situated in the far east of Nepal, 90km from the border at Kakarbhitta, Ilam is a pleasingly pretty town of timbered green buildings, and a walk through the small clusters of green tea plants that carpet the surrounding hills will take you to one of the most tranquil spots in the Terai. A concrete walkway leads through the tea fields up the hill to what locals quaintly call a 'viewing point' but what is actually a large mirrored tower block that from a distance looks like a bad hotel! Otherwise there are many other paths you can wander along.

🛏 Sleeping & Eating

Chiyabari Cottage Ilam   GUESTHOUSE $
(☑9842636512, 027-520149; r Rs 1500; ☎) Perched on the hill overlooking magical views of the tea plantations and surrounding hills, this cheery guesthouse has spacious rooms, each of which is enlivened by an aquarium full of colourful fish – seriously!

It's a top spot for a meal or drink at sunset. Call to arrange free transport pick-up to avoid the sweaty climb up here.

Green View Guest House   HOTEL $
(☑027-520616, 9842627063; r with/without bathroom Rs 900/1500; ☎) An old favourite, Green View has large rooms with something of a tack overload, but it's well run, friendly and has a prime location at the edge of a tea garden, and several rooms do indeed have a green view – of tea plantations. Cheaper rooms, which share bathrooms, are over the road in a separate building.

Friends Hotel & Restaurant   HOTEL $
(☑9842780400; r with/without bathroom Rs 800/600) Rooms at this town centre place are carpeted, brightly painted and come with TVs, and some have little balconies with views down the valley. It's the best of the cheapies in Ilam.

Shopping

Ilam Tea House TEA
(⊙7am-6pm) Those wanting to buy tea of varying qualities can fill up at the Ilam Tea House near the Green View Guest House.

ⓘ Information

There are several ATMs in the bazaar, while Bank of Asia up the road also has an ATM and can exchange foreign currency.

ⓘ Getting There & Away

The dusty bus/jeep stand is to the west of town, while the taxi stand is just off the main square.

The road to Ilam branches off at two points along the Mahendra Hwy. Buses and jeeps depart at either Charali (if arriving from Kakarbhitta) or Birtamod (if you're coming from Kathmandu). Jeeps do the journey in a little more than three hours (Rs 250) from either place. There are two daily buses direct to Kathmandu (Rs 1600, 18 hours) at 1pm and 1.30pm.

If you're heading high to conquer the Kanchenjunga trails, jeeps go fairly frequently throughout the morning to Taplejung (Rs 700, 6-7 hours).

Around Ilam

A pleasant half-day trip from Ilam is the attractive lake at **Mai Pokhari**. The 1½-hour jeep trip along a rocky track leads you to this peaceful spot, which was declared a Ramsar site in late 2008. An important pilgrimage site for Hindus and Buddhists, the lake is a striking emerald colour and is covered in water lilies and teeming with goldfish. Surrounded by cone trees and rhododendrons (which bloom in March), it makes for a beautiful stroll, and is home to 300 species of birds.

Your best bet to get here is to catch a jeep or taxi to Biblate, from where you can arrange onward transport to Mai Pokhari. Otherwise it makes for an excellent eight-hour round-trip walk from Ilam.

Some other trips possible from Ilam include the **Kanyam Tea Gardens**, located 46km from Ilam, where you can visit the tea factory. If you're getting the bus here, it's about a 15-minute walk down the hill to the factory. Here you'll also find a picnic spot popular with groups of merry Nepali teenagers.

Another excellent option is a visit to **Sandakpur**, on the border with India, where you can watch an incredible sunrise over four of the world's five highest peaks; it's also a habitat for red pandas. However, it's not the easiest place to get to: it involves getting a taxi from Ilam Bazaar to Biblate (Rs 25, 15 minutes), then another taxi for 2½ hours to Khorsanitar (Rs 250 if you're lucky enough to find a shared taxi). Otherwise a privately hired jeep from Ilam to Khorsanitar will cost around Rs 6000 for a special hire). Once you finally get to Khorsanitar it's a six-hour walk to Sandakpur. There are several basic lodges here, and you'll need to ensure you bring warm clothing.

Kakarbhitta

Kakarbhitta (Kakarvitta) is the easternmost crossing between India and Nepal, and is just a few hours' drive from Siliguri and Darjeeling in West Bengal and Gangtok in Sikkim. Like Nepal's other border towns, Kakarbhitta is hot, dusty and, on the border itself, rather stressful. Therefore, there isn't any great reason to linger here other than to break up your journey. However, 10 minutes' walk south (or a Rs 40 rickshaw ride) is the **Satighata tea plantation**, which can be a nice way to spend some time.

🛏 Sleeping & Eating

Most of the town's masses of hotels are crammed together in the narrow alleys leading west from the back of the bus stand. For meals, all the hotels have restaurants serving Indian, Nepali and Chinese fare.

Hotel Darbar HOTEL $
(☑09742619129, 023-562384; s/d Rs 1200/1400; ❄⑳) The best deal in town, the Darbar offers large, carpeted and well-furnished rooms with fans and air-con and hot-water bathrooms. There's a generator to keep you lit up during the town's frequent blackouts. The owner is exceptionally helpful and speaks superb English.

Hotel Rajat HOTEL $
(☑09851089479; tw Rs 800-1000; r with AC Rs 1600; ❄⑳) The welcome here is friendly and the rooms are simple but inviting. The pricier rooms in particular are well cared for. But cheap or expensive, all rooms are very pink. There's a bistrolike restaurant with gingham tablecloths downstairs. It's just behind the bus stand.

CROSSING TO INDIA: KAKARBHITTA TO PANITANKI

Border Hours

Both sides of the border are staffed from around 7am to 10pm; however, when it's cold/wet the border hours can be more flexible and it sometimes closes as early as 7pm. At such times you can often still cross but you'll need to go searching for immigration officials.

Foreign Exchange

Nepal Bank operates a **foreign exchange desk** (☉7am-5pm) close to the border. You can change cash and travellers cheques in US dollars, UK pounds and euros, as well as Indian and Nepali rupees. There are loads of other exchange places on either side of the border.

Onward Transport

It's about 100m from the Kakarbhitta bus stand to the border, and a little under 1km to the Indian border post at Panitanki (aka Raniganj); around Rs 100 by rickshaw from Kakarbhitta bus stand to the Indian border including waiting time at the Nepali immigration. Otherwise you can catch a shared taxi or jeep from outside the Nepali immigration office to Siliguri for ₹ 100 (or ₹ 1200 for a special hire). From Siliguri you can head to Darjeeling by shared jeep (₹ 150-200, three hours). You can also catch a train to Kolkata: the Kanchanjunga Express (sleeper/3A 320/860; 11 ½ hours), which departs at 7.50am, and the Darjeeling Mail (sleeper/3A 350/910; 10 hours), departing at 8pm.

ℹ Information

Sunrise has an ATM here, but it's closed in the evenings and unreliable at other times, so bring enough cash for onward travel. If you do need an ATM, go to Birtamod, 13km from Kakarbhitta. There are dozens of money-exchange offices.

Tourist Information Centre (☉10am-4pm Sun-Fri) The government of Nepal runs a small tourist information centre, but it's more countrywide than local information. It's just before the Nepali border.

ℹ Getting There & Away

AIR

The nearest airport is at Bhadrapur, 10km southeast of Birtamod, which in turn is 13km west of Kakarbhitta. A taxi from Kakarbhitta bus stand to the airport costs Rs 1000, or you can take a local bus to Birtamod, then a second bus to Bhadrapur followed by a rickshaw to the airport. **Yeti Airlines** (📱Kathmandu 01-4465888; www.yetiairlines.com) and **Buddha Air** (📱Kathman-

du 01-5542494; www.buddhaair.com) have daily flights to Kathmandu (around US$185, 50 minutes) – any of the travel agents around the bus stand can issue tickets.

BUS

Travel agents in Kathmandu and Pokhara offer 'through-tickets' to Darjeeling, but you must change buses at Kakarbhitta, then again change at Siliguri – it is just as easy, and cheaper, to do the trip in stages.

There are several daily services to Kathmandu (standard/deluxe Rs 1145/1375, 14 to 16 hours). Prices vary slightly between companies but these are the average prices. The first buses depart around 4.30am and the last around 5.15pm. There are also buses to Pokhara (Rs 1140, 15 hours).

To get to Ilam, there are plenty of buses to Birtamod (Rs 30, 25 minutes), from where you can take a bus or jeep. There are four or more daily buses to Janakpur (Rs 525, seven hours), Biratnagar (Rs 218, 3½ hours) and Birganj (Rs 720, 10 hours).

Trekking Routes

Best Everest Detours

➡ Gokyo Lakes (p299)

➡ Chhukung (p297)

➡ Kunde & Khumjung (p296)

Best Annapurna Detours

➡ Milarepa's Cave (p301)

➡ Upper Pisang (p301)

➡ Jhong & Purang (p305)

➡ Praken Gompa (p301)

Why Go?

Easily the best way to see Nepal is on foot, following a network of trails trodden for centries by porters, traders, pilgrims, mountaineers and locals travelling from village to village, plains to hills, Nepal to Tibet. Nothing beats strolling from teahouse to teahouse under crystal-clear Himalayan skies as 8000m peaks tower above you. Although trekking routes close to Kathmandu were badly damaged in the 2015 earthquake, most trails around the country escaped with only minor damage, including in the Annapurna and Everest regions.

The following treks are ideal for travellers who want to turn up and trek without too much forward planning – permits are easy to organise and trekking lodges line the trails every hour or so offering meals and accommodation. En route, you'll meet Sherpas, Gurungs, Rai and Thakali people and hike through villages, monasteries and sacred lakes. These cultural interactions are what give these treks much of their charm.

Our best advice is not to rush your walk. Adding on a few days to your itinerary allows you to take in side trips, detours and monasteries, or just take a day off every now and then. These just might end up being the highlights of your trip.

Trekking Safety Tips

➡ Never trek alone.

➡ Always carry an emergency supply of food, water purification, warm clothes, a whistle and a detailed map.

➡ Take care of altitude sickness and don't skip the acclimatisation days.

➡ Register with your embassy before setting off and make sure someone knows your itinerary.

➡ Tell your lodge if attempting a day trip detour.

➡ Make sure you have comprehensive health and evacuation insurance.

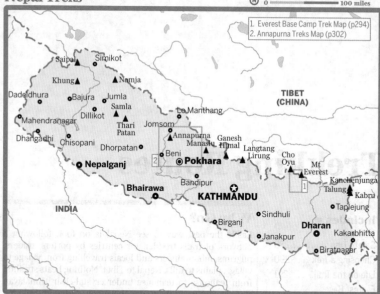

0 ———— 200 km
0 ———— 100 miles

1. Everest Base Camp Trek Map (p294)
2. Annapurna Treks Map (p302)

Saipal · Simikot

Khung▲ · ▲Namja

Dadeldhura · Bajura · Jumla

Mahendranagar · Dillikot · Samla

Dhangadhi · Chisopani · Thari Patan · Jomsom

Dhorpatan · Annapurna · Ganesh Himal

Nepalganj · Beni · **Pokhara** · Manaslu · Langtang Lirung · Cho Oyu · Mt Everest

Bhairawa · Bandipur · ☆ **KATHMANDU** · Kanchenjunga · Talung ▲ · Kabru

INDIA · Sindhuli · Taplejung

Birganj · **Dharan** · Kakarbhitta

Janakpur · Biratnagar

Lo Manthang

TIBET (CHINA)

CHOOSING A TREK

The popular teahouse treks described in this chapter account for the bulk of trekking trips in Nepal. Easily the most popular options are the Annapurna Circuit trek and Everest Base Camp (EBC) trek, which saw some damage in the 2015 earthquake but remains fully open to trekkers. Both treks offer spectacular scenery, cultural depth and plenty of scope for detours, as well as plenty of crowds.

Treks closer to Kathmandu, such as the Langtang Valley trek, Gosainkund trek and Tamang Heritage Trail, were a popular choice for travellers before the disaster, but the earthquake caused widespread destruction. Buildings were damaged in every village in the Langtang Valley and Langtang village itself was completely destroyed. Immediately north of the earthquake epicentre, the trekking regions of Manaslu and Tsum were also badly damaged, with sections of trail swept away and some lodges damaged. Until trails and infrastructure are rebuilt, most trails in these areas will remain off limits to trekkers.

Over the past few years Everest has become very busy in high season, while the Annapurna region has been affected by road construction. The Annapurna Circuit has the advantage of being a loop route, while

Everest is an out-and-back trek, returning to Lukla via the same route, unless you add on the excellent side trips to the Gokyo Lakes or over the Three Passes. Everest requires a flight (or week-long approach walk), which makes it a slightly more expensive option than Annapurna.

If that's not enough for you, it is also possible to combine treks. The Annapurna Sanctuary Trek is easily pinned onto the end of the Annapurna Circuit to create a full month of superb trekking.

For full information on these routes, as well as camping and teahouse treks in more remote regions, see Lonely Planet's *Trekking in the Nepal Himalaya*.

Shorter Treks

If you don't have time for a big trek, several shorter treks from Pokhara in the southern foothills of the Annapurnas can give you a delightful taste of life on Nepal's trails. The Ghandruk Loop (three days) and Ghorepani and Ghandruk loop (six days) both offer fine mountain views, villages and trekking lodges, while trips to Ghachok or Panchase offer quieter trails away from the main Annapurna routes. All are excellent low-altitude or winter choices.

EARTHQUAKE DAMAGE ON THE TRAILS

With most trekking lodges around Nepal built using traditional methods, it would have been impossible for trekking to not be affected by the 2015 earthquake. Across the country, thousands of rural homes collapsed and many trekking lodges suffered the same fate. However, there is some positive news. Damage was localised and the Annapurna region and eastern and western Nepal were mostly unaffected. The Everest region also escaped the worst, though many died in an avalanche at Everest Base Camp and houses and lodges were damaged around Namche Bazaar. News from central Nepal is less positive. Many trekkers and local people lost their lives in Langtang, Helambu and Manaslu and trekking in these regions is likely to be impossible until lodges and trails are restored. If you plan to trek in central areas of Nepal, seek local advice on the status of trails and lodges before you set off.

It's also possible to cobble together a mini-trek of several days around the rim of the Kathmandu Valley, linking medieval towns and viewpoints such as Nagarkot.

You can also throw in a couple of flights here and there to speed up the trekking process. As an example, fly in to Jomsom, overnight in Marpha (to aid acclimatisation) and take a few days to hike to the surrounding villages of Kagbeni and Muktinath before flying back to Pokhara for a four- or five-day trip.

A week-long Everest taster from Lukla could take you on a loop through Namche Bazaar, Thame, Khunde, Khumjung and Tengboche Monastery, avoiding high altitude. This is a particularly good option in winter (December to February).

LIFE ON THE TRAIL

Routes & Conditions

Most trails are clear and easy to follow, though they are often steep and taxing, with long stretches of switchbacks or stone staircases. A typical day's walk lasts from between five to seven hours and rarely spends much time on level ground. Distances on a map quickly become irrelevant with the many ups and downs and twists and turns of Nepal's trails.

A little rudimentary knowledge of the Nepali language will help to make your trek easier and more interesting, although finding your way is rarely difficult on the major trekking routes and English is fairly widely spoken.

Sleeping & Eating

On the Everest and Annapurna treks it's unlikely that you will walk more than an hour or two without coming across some kind of teahouse offering food and lodging, giving you great flexibility to walk as far as you wish and avoid the crowds. These lodges range from simple extensions of a traditional wooden family home to quite luxurious places with private rooms, multipage menus, attached toilets and even wi-fi. Most mattresses are foam (of varying thicknesses) and some bedding is always supplied. Nevertheless, it's still a good idea to carry a sleeping bag, especially at higher elevations and during peak season. Solar hot showers or a bucket of hot water are often available for between Rs 100 and Rs 300 and most places can recharge your batteries for around Rs 300.

Teahouse food centres on endless carb combinations of pasta, noodles, potato, rice and vegetables, plus momos (dumplings), rice and a half-dozen types of tea, by the cup or pot. Breakfast is normally eggs, porridge or muesli. The local staple of daal bhaat (rice, lentils and vegetables) is nutritious, available everywhere and requires minimum fuel for preparation. With most places offering a free refill of rice and daal, it's also the only meal that will truly fill you up after a day's trekking.

Lodges on the main trails stock expensive Snickers bars, toilet paper etc, but it's wise to carry your own emergency food supplies such as muesli bars, dried fruit or chocolate. You can save some money by bringing your own instant coffee, though most places charge a fee for a cup of boiling water.

The lodges around Jomsom and Namche Bazaar specialise in delicious apple pie, a trekkers' staple these days, along with local versions of pizza. It's surprising how many places even have cold beer available as well; before you complain about the price (up to Rs 550), consider that somebody had to carry that bottle of beer all the way up there and will probably have to carry the empty bottle back again!

Organised Treks

Organised camping treks generally camp each night and all you have to do is eat and crawl into your tent. Even erecting the tent is handled by the trekking crew, who put it up for you at the site selected by your *sirdar* (group leader). The porters carry virtually all of the ingredients with them and there will be a cook with well-drilled assistants who can turn out meals with impressive ingenuity.

For the treks in this chapter most organised small groups stay in lodges and the fee you pay covers your accommodation and food costs. It's also possible to just hire a guide and porter from an agency and then arrange and pay for all other costs yourself.

EVEREST BASE CAMP TREK

Duration 14 to 20 days

Maximum elevation 5545m

Best season October to December

Start Lukla

Finish Lukla

Permits TIMS card, Sagarmatha National Park ticket

Summary Spectacular high mountain scenery, Sherpa culture, excellent lodges and views of beautiful Mt Ama Dablam are the highlights of this busy and popular trek.

Everybody wants a glimpse of the world's highest mountain and that's the reason why the Everest Base Camp Trek is so popular. The trek has a number of stunning attractions, not least of these is being able to say you've visited the highest mountain in the world. The trek gets you right into the high-altitude heart of the high Himalaya, more so than any other teahouse trek. There

LUXURY TREKKING

If you demand a bit of luxury on your trek and don't want to rough it in a tent, several companies offer deluxe lodges in the Annapurna and Everest regions. You'll get the best rates on an organised trek (as opposed to turning up on your own).

Ker & Downey (www.keranddowneynepal.com) operates treks staying in its deluxe chain of lodges in Dhampus, Ghandruk, Majgaun and Birethanti on the approaches to the Annapurna Sanctuary. Jomsom boasts the luxury **Mustang Lodge** (www.mustangresorts.com).

There is a good selection of luxury lodges in the lower reaches of the Everest region, allowing you to make a week-long trek to Namche Bazaar and around. Priority is given to guests on these company's treks but independent trekkers can also make bookings. However, this region saw some earthquake damage and lodges may be closed for repairs or closed entirely if buildings have been deemed uninhabitable – contact the following lodges in advance if you plan to stay.

Nepal Luxury Treks (☎01-4371537; www.nepalluxurytreks.com; r US$150-225) Operates the luxury Everest Summit Lodges in Lukla, Monjo, Tashinga (near Photse; closed till 2016), Mende (near Thame) and Pangboche, as well as a lodge in Kagbeni on the Annapurna Circuit.

Yeti Mountain Home (☎01-4000711; www.yetimountainhome.com; r US$115-185) A chain of six attractive stone lodges in Lukla, Monjo, Phakding, Namche Bazaar, Thame, and Kongde, the latter on a particularly remote and spectacular ridge.

Everest Sherpa Resort (☎01-447884; www.everestresort.com; s/d US$127/150) On the ridge above Namche Bazaar, but damaged by the earthquake.

Hotel Everest View (☎038-540118, in Kathmandu 01-5011648; www.hoteleverestview.com; s/d US$115/180) Said to be the highest hotel in the world, but on the same ridge above Namche as Everest Sherpa Resort.

are some lovely villages and gompas (monasteries), and the friendly Sherpa people of the Solu Khumbu region make trekking through the area a joy. Most of the trek is through the Sagarmatha National Park, a Unesco World Heritage Site (Sagarmatha is the Nepali name for Everest) and a refuge for musk deer, snow leopard, Himalayan tahr, black bear and many spectacular types of irridescent pheasant.

This region was badly shaken by the 2015 earthquake, and most villages sustained some damage, though only a small number of lodges were completely destroyed. The villages of Khumjung, Pheriche and Thame were particularly badly affected, but repairs are underway and there are open lodges in all of the key overnight stops along the route.

A return trek to Everest Base Camp from the airstrip at Lukla takes at least 14 days but you are better off budgeting a further week to take in some of the stunning and less-visited side valleys. If you have the time, one way to beat the crowds and acclimitise slowly is to walk in from Shivalaya (six days). If you fly straight to Lukla, be sure to schedule acclimatisation days at Namche and Pheriche to avoid altitude sickness.

The trek reaches a high point of 5545m at Kala Pattar, a small peak offering views of Mt Everest and the Khumbu Icefall. Ironically, the Everest views from base camp are actually quite unimpressive (in the words of mountain writer Ed Douglas, 'Everest is like a grossly fat man in a room full of beautiful women'). Far more stirring are the graceful lines of surrounding peaks, such as Ama Dablam, Pumori and Nuptse. Perhaps the best scenery of the trek is found in the neighbouring Gokyo Valley, off the main trail.

In the last decade the tourist crowds in the Khumbu region have swollen to record numbers, with 36,000 attempting the trek each year. Trekker numbers will doubtless have dropped since the earthquake, but this is still one trek you might consider tackling outside of October or November, when you won't face such a scramble for bed space and aeroplane seats, and you won't have to share the trails with 10,000 or so other trekkers.

Facilities on the Everest trek are excellent. The upper reaches of the trek are through essentially uninhabited areas but lodges operate throughout the trekking season. These days trekking and mountaineering are the backbone of the Sherpa economy. More than half of the population in the region is now involved with tourism, and the bookstore, trek-gear shops, bakeries and internet cafes in Namche Bazaar make it look more like an alpine resort than a Sherpa village.

The walking on this trek is (surprisingly) not all that strenuous, mainly because new arrivals can only walk a few hours each day before they have to stop for the night to acclimatise. If trekkers fail to reach their goal, it is usually because they didn't devote enough time to acclimatisation. It may be tempting to keep walking at the end of a three-hour day, but it's essential to take it slowly on the first 10 days of this trek.

Emergency Facilities

There are small hospitals in Jiri, Phaplu and Khunde (just north of Namche Bazaar); the Himalayan Rescue Association (HRA) has a medical facility in Pheriche. In the Gokyo Valley the International Porters Protection Group runs clinics in Macchermo and Gokyo. All three have foreign doctors and offer a recommended free talk on acute mountain sickness (AMS) at 3pm.

Access

Flights from Kathmandu to Lukla

Most Everest trekkers opt to fly to Lukla (US$165) from Kathmandu to maximise their time in the high mountains, and up to 75 flights land here each day during the high season. Tara Air has the most flights and is the best option. Backlogs of hundreds of trekkers (7000 in October 2011!) can build up during spates of bad weather, so give yourself a buffer of a day or two to get back to Kathmandu.

Flight safety at Lukla is not good. In 2008 a Yeti Airlines plane crashed at Lukla due to bad visibility, killing all 18 passengers. In 2010 an Agni Air plane crashed between Lukla and Kathmandu, killing 14. In 2012 a Sita Air flight to Lukla crashed near Kathmandu, killing all on board.

Shivalaya Trek

While most people fly in and out of Lukla these days, it's possible to trek in or out from the trailhead at Shivalaya, just past Jiri. The trek from Shivalaya to Lukla is a hard slog

Everest Base Camp Trek

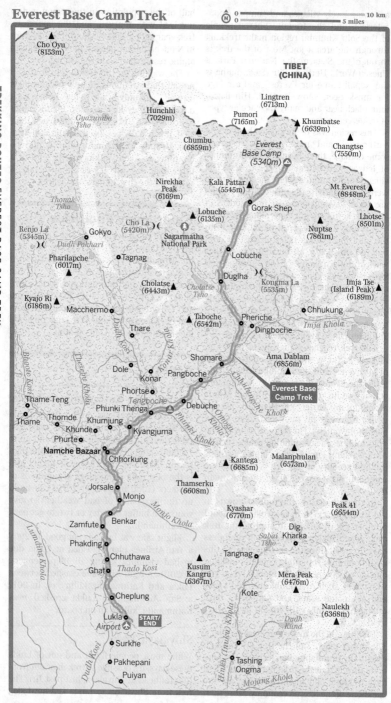

EVEREST NUTS

The world's highest peak has attracted many commendable achievements: the first ascent without oxygen (1978), first summit with an artificial leg (1998), the first ski descent (2000), the first blind ascent (2001), most ascents (21), youngest ascent (aged 13), oldest ascent (aged 78) and fastest ascent (eight hours). Sherpa Babu Chiru spent a particularly amazing 21 hours on top of Everest without oxygen in 1999.

But there have also been some admirably silly achievements. Perhaps most ambitious was the Briton Maurice Wilson, who planned to crash his Gypsy Moth airplane halfway up the mountain and then climb from there to the top, not letting his almost total lack of mountaineering or flying experience get in the way of an obviously flawed plan. He eventually froze to death at Camp III dressed in a light sweater (and, it is rumoured, women's clothing).

Maybe it's something in the national psyche (this is, after all, the nation that gave us Monty Python), for it was also a team of Brits who trekked all the way to Everest Base Camp to play the 'world's highest game of rugby' at 5140m. They lost.

Our personal Everest heroes are the British (!) pair who carried an ironing board up Everest to 5440m to do some extreme ironing ('part domestic chore, part extreme sport'). For anyone contemplating a repeat expedition, the duo have revealed that expedition preparation can be limited to three important factors: 'a few beers, a drunken bet and a stolen ironing board'.

and pretty sparse in the breathtaking-views department, but you will have the trails to yourself. The trek doesn't follow valleys, it cuts across them, so day after day it is a tiring process of dropping down one side of a steep valley and climbing up the other. By the time you reach the base camp your ascents will total almost 9000m – the full height of Everest from sea level!

Note that villages along this route were damaged in the 2015 earthquake, and many buildings were destroyed in Jiri and Shivalaya – check locally to make sure that trails are open and accommodation is available at all your planned stops before embarking on this route.

Assuming trails are open, Kathmandu's Ratna Park (City) bus station has buses at 8am to Shivalaya (Rs 745, eight hours), at 5.45am to Bhandar (Rs 960, 10 hours) and at 6am and 8am to Jiri (Rs 630, six hours). Buy tickets in the northwest corner of the bus station. Keep a close eye on your luggage.

Travellers have reported being asked to buy a Gauri Shankar Conservation Area permit (Rs 2000) in Shivalaya, even though the trek only passes through the conservation area for an hour or two.

Proposed road construction from Jiri to Surkhe (just before Lukla) will likely change this trek over the coming years. Dirt roads currently run to Bhandar and Kinja.

The trek stages generally work out as follows:

Day One	Shivalaya to Bhandar
Day Two	Bhandar to Sete
Day Three	Sete to Junbesi
Day Four	Junbesi to Nunthala
Day Five	Nunthala to Bupsa
Day Six	Bupsa to Lukla

The Trek

Day One: Lukla to Phakding

After flying to Lukla, which escaped serious earthquake damage, arranging your packs and maybe a porter, trek downhill to lodges at Cheplung (Chablung). From here the trail contours along the side of the Dudh Kosi Valley before ascending to Ghat (Lhawa; 2530m). The trail climbs again to Phakding, a boisterous collection of 25 lodges and several bars at 2610m. Some lodges were damaged but most remain open following the earthquake.

Alternatively, you could continue to Zamfute or Benkar, though the earthquake damaged lodges in both villages.

Day Two: Phakding to Namche Bazaar

The trail crosses the river on a long, swaying bridge and then leads you along the river to climb to Benkar (2700m), a decent alternative overnight stop. A short distance beyond Benkar the trail crosses the Dudh Kosi on a suspension bridge to its east bank, and then climbs to Chumoa. Teahouses were damaged along this section of the route so check locally to make sure accommodation is available if you plan to stop before Namche Bazaar.

From Chumoa, it's a short climb through forests to Monjo (2800m), where there are some good places to stay, despite a fair bit of earthquake damage. Show your entrance ticket or buy one for Rs 3000 at the Sagarmatha National Park entrance station and register your TIMS card, then descend to cross the Dudh Kosi. On the other side it's a short distance to Jorsale (Thumbug; 2830m), the last settlement before Namche Bazaar. This is a good lunch stop, though several places were damaged by the quake. The trail then crosses back to the east side of the river before climbing to the high suspension bridge over the Dudh Kosi.

It's a tough two-hour climb from here to Namche Bazaar (3420m). As this is the first climb to an altitude where AMS, also known as altitude sickness, may be a problem, take it easy and avoid rushing. Half way up is a public toilet marking the first views of Everest. There is another national park entrance station just below Namche where permits are again checked.

Day Three: Acclimatisation Day in Namche Bazaar

Namche Bazaar is the main trade and administrative centre for the entire Solu Khumbu region and has outdoor-gear shops, restaurants, bakeries, pharmacies, hotels with hot showers, bars, massage, a post office, a moneychanger, a bank, an ATM and wi-fi everywhere. Earthquake damage here was minor. Pay a visit to the **Sherpa Culture Museum** (☐038-540005; www. sherpa-culture.com.np; Chhorkhung; admission Rs 100; ☺6am-sunset), on the ridge east above town. The nearby **Sagarmatha National Park Visitor Centre** (Chhorkhung; ☺8am-4pm Sun-Fri) **FREE** was being used for relief effort at the time of writing but is expected to reopen for tourists in the near future. There is a colourful market each Saturday.

There is plenty to do around Namche Bazaar and you should spend a day here acclimatising. Remember that victims of AMS are often the fittest, healthiest people who foolishly overextend themselves. It's helpful to do a strenuous day walk to a higher altitude as part of your acclimatisation, coming back down to Namche to sleep. One popular day trip is the seven-hour return walk west to Thame, but most houses and the town monastery were destroyed in the earthquake; check locally that things are open before you set off from Namche. Alternatively try the strenuous but scenic six-hour loop hike north to Khunde and Khumjung villages.

Day Four: Namche Bazaar to Tengboche

The slightly longer route from Namche Bazaar to Tengboche via Khumjung and Khunde is more interesting than the direct one, though many buildings on this ridge were damaged in the earthquake. The route starts by climbing up to the Syangboche airstrip. Above the airstrip is the Hotel Everest View, listed in the Guinness Book of Records as the highest hotel on earth.

From the hotel or the airstrip you climb to Khunde (3840m), then Khumjung (3790m), which lost a number of houses in the disaster. From here you drop down to rejoin the direct trail to Tengboche. The trail descends to the Dudh Kosi (3250m) where there are several small lodges and a series of picturesque water-driven prayer wheels. A steep 400m ascent brings you to Tengboche (3870m). The famous gompa, which has a background of Ama Dablam, Everest and other peaks, burnt down in 1989 but rose phoenix-like from the ashes. Locals are hopeful that it will also bounce back from the 2015 earthquake, which damaged many buildings. There are several busy lodges, or you can carry on 30 minutes downhill to quieter Debuche.

During the October/November full moon the colourful Mani Rimdu festival is held here with masked dancing and Tibetan opera in the monastery courtyard – accommodation becomes extremely difficult to find. See www.tengboche.org for upcoming dates.

Day Five: Tengboche to Pheriche/Dingboche

Beyond Tengboche the altitude really starts to show. The trail drops down to Debuche, crosses the Imja Khola and climbs through rhododendron forest past superb mani stones (carved with the Tibetan Buddhist mantra *om mani padme hum*) to Pang-

TREKKING PEAKS

If you want to take the next step from trekking to mountaineering, consider a short mountaineering course that takes in one of Nepal's 'trekking peaks'. Several companies organise mountaineering courses and ascents in the Solu Khumbu region and can add these onto an organised trek through the region.

Most popular is a six-day course and ascent of **Island Peak**, properly known as Imja Tse (6189m), from a base in Chhukung. After acclimatisation, briefing, training and a half-day hike to base camp, the peak is generally climbed in a single eight-hour day, departing early in the morning. It's physically demanding but not technically difficult – only the last section is on ice and snow, though guides report that retreating glaciers mean some rock climbing is increasingly required. Trips run weekly in season (mid-October to mid-November, end March to May) and cost US$700 from Chhukung to Chhukung.

The second most popular option is to the false summit of **Lobuche East** (6119m), a more technically difficult ascent that requires two days' of training. The six-day round trip from Dzongla costs around US$700. Trips operate in November and from mid-April to mid-May.

Also in the Everest region, **Mera Peak** (6476m) involves more trekking than climbing, though it is the highest of the trekking peaks. It's a minimum 15-day trip from Lukla and involves trekking up to Mera La (5415m), from where the climbing begins. Camping trips from Kathmandu cost around US$2000, though you can now arrange a simpler teahouse-based trek for around $1500. Trips run in November, April and May.

For all of these trips you will need to hire your own plastic climbing boots and gaiters, available either from Kathmandu or Namche Bazaar. Prices include permits, equipment, guides, tent accommodation and food. Expect a group size of around six to eight climbers.

Other possible trekking peak ascents in the Everest region include Phari Lapche (6017m), Macchermo (6273m) and Kyozo/Kyajo Ri (6186m). In the Annapurna region, Pisang Peak (6091m) and Chulu East (6584m) are both five-day excursions from Manang.

Himalayan Ecstasy (Map p88; ☎01-4700001; www.himalayanecstasynepal.com) is one of the best options for well-run tuition and peak climbing. In addition to the main trekking peaks they also offer Island and Lobuche Peaks together in one trip for US$1350.

The following companies in Kathmandu also organise ascents.

Alternative Nepal (p83)

Climb High Himalaya (Map p88; ☎01-4701398; www.climbhighhimalaya.com; Mandala St)

Equator Expeditions (p49)

Mountain Monarch (☎01-4373881; www.mountainmonarch.com; Hattigauda)

---

boche (3860m). The gompa in the upper village above the main trail is the oldest in the Khumbu and houses the skull and hand of a yeti. Despite some earthquake damage, the village is a good place for a lunch stop.

The trail then climbs past Shomare and Orsho to Pheriche (4240m), where there is an HRA trekkers' aid post and possible medical assistance. Pheriche sustained some of the worst earthquake damage in the Everest region and many lodges collapsed; accommodation is available, but you may want to continue to Dingboche (4410m), 30 minutes over the hill, which escaped serious damage.

Day Six: Acclimatisation Day in Pheriche/Dingboche

Another acclimatisation day should be spent at Pheriche or Dingboche. As at Namche, a solid day walk to a higher altitude is better than just resting; the village of Chhukung (4730m, six hours return) is a possible destination and offers great views.

Nangkartshang Gompa, an hour's climb up the ridge above Dingboche, offers good views east to Makalu (8462m), the world's fifth-highest mountain. Chhukung is a six-hour return hike up the Imja Khola Valley, which

THE GREAT HIMALAYAN TRAIL

If you are up for a challenge, you might want to consider the Great Himalayan Trail, a 2500km walk across the entire spine of the Nepal Himalaya, from Kanchenjunga in the east to Humla in the west. There are several logistical hurdles to overcome, mainly with coordinating a whole fistful of timed trekking permits, but at least one trekking company (World Expeditions) offers the trail as a commercial trip, lasting for 157 days and costing a cool US$30,000. Several extreme athletes have already completed the route (self-supported) in as little as 47 days.

The trail is partly a pre-existing network of trekking routes and partly a slick marketing campaign aimed at getting trekkers into regions currently not benefiting economically from tourism. Perhaps the best way to attempt the trail is to do it in segments, biting off chunks such as the Annapurna–Manaslu route or Jiri–Everest section, and doing it over several years.

For more information see the excellent website for the **Great Himalaya Trail** (www.thegreathimalayatrail.org). And good luck.

offers stunning views. There is food and accommodation at Chhukung and some great full-day side trips to Chhukung Ri and Island Peak Base Camp, but don't overnight here before spending a night first at Dingboche.

Day Seven: Pheriche/Dingboche to Duglha

From Pheriche, the trail climbs to Phulang Kala (4340m) then Duglha (4620m). It's only a two-hour trek to Duglha, but the Himalayan Rescue Association (HRA) doctors at Pheriche urge everyone to stay a night here in order to aid acclimatisation. There are two lodges here.

Day Eight: Duglha to Lobuche

From Duglha the trail goes directly up the gravely terminal moraine of the Khumbu Glacier for about an hour, then bears left to a group of memorials to lost climbers and Sherpas, including Scott Fischer who died in the 1996 Everest disaster. It's a short climb past views of Pumori to the summer village of Lobuche (4930m). Only a few lodges were damaged here but the altitude, cold and crummy beds will combine to ensure a fitful night's sleep.

Day Nine: Lobuche to Gorak Shep

The return trip from Lobuche to Gorak Shep (5160m) takes just a couple of hours, leaving enough time to continue to the peak of Kala Pattar (three hours return) – or you can overnight in Gorak Shep and reach Kala

Pattar early the next morning for the best chance of good weather. At 5545m this small peak offers the best view you'll get of Everest on this trek.

Gorak Shep was the base camp for the 1952 Swiss expedition to Everest and it escaped serious damage in the earthquake. There is good accommodation here, but the altitude makes life uncomfortable. If the altitude is getting to you, descending to Lobuche or, better, Pheriche or Dingboche makes a real difference.

Day 10: Gorak Shep to Everest Base Camp & Lobuche

If you want to visit EBC (5360m), it's a six-hour round trip from Gorak Shep. EBC is dotted with tents in the April/May climbing season but the earthquake triggered an avalanche that killed 18 climbers and guides and activity here is somewhat subdued. Outside of climbing season, there's not a great deal to see except for views of the Khumbu Icefall; Everest itself is hidden from view by the surrounding peaks. If you only have the energy for one side trip, make it Kala Pattar.

The two-hour trek back down to Lobuche seems easy after all the climbing, and some trekkers continue for another three hours down to Dingboche or Pheriche the same day.

Day 11: Lobuche to Dingboche

Descend to spend the night at Pheriche or Dingboche, which boasts Nepal's highest internet cafe and fine views of Island Peak (Imja Tse; 6189m) and Lhotse (8516m).

Days 12 to 14: Dingboche to Lukla

The next three days retrace your steps down to Lukla via Tengboche and Namche Bazaar. If you are flying out of Lukla, get to the airline office between 3pm and 4pm the day before your flight to reconfirm your seat. Your lodge owner will often do this for you. If the weather has been bad, you might be vying for a flight with hundreds of other trekkers, but generally you shouldn't have a problem.

Alternative Routes & Side Trips

The side trips off the Everest Base Camp Trek rank as some of the region's highlights so it makes sense to add an extra week or so to your itinerary to explore the region more fully.

A particularly scenic side trip is the six-day detour from Namche Bazaar to the Gokyo Valley, culminating in the spectacular glacier and lake views from Gokyo Ri (5360m). It's important to ascend the valley slowly, overnighting in Phortse Thenga, Dole, Macchermo and Gokyo to aid acclimatisation. Note that some lodges were badly damaged in Macchermo and Dole. From Gokyo you can rejoin the main EBC trail near Khumjung or upper Pangboche.

You can combine both the Gokyo Valley and Everest Base Camp by crossing the Cho La (5420m) via Dzonglha, for a total duration of 17 days, but you need to take this route seriously and enquire about the conditions before setting out. Some months the pass is clear of snow; at other times you'll need crampons for this high crossing. You can hire a guide (Rs 2000) at most lodges to guide you across the glacier and pass.

Throw in the high crossings of the Renjo La (5345m), between Thame and Gokyo, and the Kongma La (5535m), between Lobuche and Chhukung, and you get the Three Passes Trek, a 20-day trek for experienced connoisseurs. Thame was very badly damaged in the earthquake so you should check that trails are open and accommodation is available before attempting this route.

Another recommended three-day side trip is up the Imja Khola Valley to Chhukung, for awesome mountain views. Chhukung is also the staging post for climbers heading to Island Peak and the valley is well worth exploring.

As an alternative to flying back to Kathmandu you can escape the crowds on the nine-day teahouse trek southeast from Lukla to Tumlingtar, from where you can fly or bus back to Kathmandu. For full details see Lonely Planet's *Trekking in the Nepal Himalaya* guide.

ANNAPURNA CIRCUIT TREK

Duration 12 to 19 days

Maximum elevation 5416m

Best season October to November

Start Besi Sahar or Bhulebule

Finish Jomsom or Naya Pul

Permits TIMS card, ACAP permit

Summary The sense of journey, the challenging crossing of a high pass, and the possibility of excellent day trips to monasteries and mountain lakes make this a Himalayan classic.

For scenery and cultural diversity this has long been considered the best trek in Nepal and one of the world's classic walks. It follows the Marsyangdi Khola (Marsyangdi Valley) to the north of the main Himalayan range and crosses a 5416m pass to descend into the dramatic desertlike, Tibetan-style scenery of the upper Kali Gandaki Valley. There was only minor damage to this route from the 2015 earthquake, and damaged buildings are being restored.

The walk passes picturesque villages home to Gurungs, Manangis and Thakalis, offers spectacular mountain views of the numerous 7000m-plus Annapurna peaks and boasts some of the best trekking lodges in Nepal. The circuit is usually walked counter-clockwise because the climb to Thorung La (5416m) from the western side is too strenuous and has too much elevation gain to consider in one day. Thorung La is often closed due to snow from mid-December to March, and bad weather can move in at any time. It's essential to take your time between Manang and the pass in order to acclimatise properly.

The useable road on the Marsyangdi side had reached as far as Chame at the time of research. A bridge was under construction here and there were a series of disconnected roads continuing beyond here all the way to Manang. On the Kali Gandaki

DAMS, ROADS & AUTOMOBILES

Road construction is having an effect on the Annapurna Circuit but it is certainly not the disaster made out by some. You are still guaranteed to cross raging torrents on giddying suspension bridges, meet friendly locals, lose your breath on ridiculously steep trails, and be gobsmacked by the mountain views.

The first half of the circuit on the Manang side is less affected by traffic than the Kali Gandaki Valley on the west side, but the construction activity (including roads) associated with hydro projects is certainly making a visual impact. While some trekkers now end their trek in Jomsom by driving or flying back to Pokhara, they are missing out on some excellent trekking.

From Bhulebule to Tatopani, a network of alternative trails with red-and-white markers takes you off the road and into the countryside. Furthermore, the trails with blue-and-white markers take you on some fabulous detours and side trips. The scenery on the new trails is equally if not more spectacular than the old route, and the lodges are excellent. The nature of the trail has changed, however, in reality this trek was never a 'wilderness' experience, and it can still be walked the entire way and augmented with numerous day hikes from overnight bases. Go see for yourself...

side, a seasonal road runs all the way to Jomsom and Muktinath. A fragile road also continues from Jomsom to Lo Manthang. Our best tip for this trek is to remember that the side trips and excursions from places like Manang, Muktinath and Jomsom rank as some of the highlights of the trek. It's worth adding a couple of days to your itinerary and exploring some of these trails. You'll be better acclimatised for the pass and you'll manage to shake some of the crowds. This is not scenery to rush through.

Access: Kathmandu or Pokhara to Besi Sahar

Buses run to Besi Sahar between 6.30am and 10am from Kathmandu (Rs 400, six hours), with tourist buses (Rs 450) at 7am, 8am and 10am. From Pokhara (Rs 450, five hours), there is a tourist bus leaving at 6.30am from the tourist bus park, or you can take any bus or microbus bound for Kathmandu and change at Dumre. Buses also run daily from the Gonabu bus stand in Kathmandu to Bhulebule (Rs 475) at 6.45am and 8.30am.

From Besi Sahar (800m) buses and jeeps run every hour or two to Bhulebule (Rs 200, 30 minutes to one hour). Drivers insist on charging foreigners three or four times the local price! Cramped jeeps run as far as Chame (Rs 1600), when the dirt road isn't blocked by monsoon landslides.

The Trek

Day One: Besi Sahar to Bhulebule

If you arrive in Besi Sahar at lunchtime, it's possible to take the bus or hike along the road to Bhulebule or even Ngadi that same day. If you did not get your ACAP permit in Kathmandu or Pokhara, you can purchase one (Rs 2000) in Besi Sahar at the ACAP Entry fee office, about 200m south of the TIMS office and opposite the Gateway Himalaya Resort. If you get all the way to the Dharapani ACAP checkpoint without a permit, you will have to pay Rs 4000 for one.

You can either follow the road all the way or cross to the eastern bank and follow the alternative trail marked by the red-and-white trail markers – although this too has been impacted by road building and the Upper Marsyangdi hydro project. You enter the Annapurna Conservation Area in Bhulebule, though the first checkpoint is in Dharapani.

Day Two: Bhulebule to Ghermu

Again the trail avoids the road at Bhulbule and crosses to the east bank of the Marsyangdi, continuing to Ngadi (an alternative night halt but visibly impacted by dam construction) before reaching Bahundanda (1270m), 'Hill of the Brahmins', on a ridge. Bahundanda has several lodges, shops and restaurants, and a police checkpost where you will be asked to register.

From Bahundanda the trail drops steeply to Lili Bhir and then follows an exposed trail to Kanigaon and Ghermu (1140m), with its views of the high waterfall on the other side of the Marsyangdi Khola.

Day Three: Ghermu to Tal

Descend to Syange (1080m) and cross to the west bank of the Marsyangdi on a suspension bridge. The trail/road then climbs steeply and crosses a cliff face to the stone village of Jagat, perched strategically in a steep-sided valley and looking for all the world like the toll station for the Tibetan salt trade that it was. The trail descends before leaving the road and climbing through forest to Chamje (1410m).

The rocky trail crosses the Marsyangdi Khola leaving the road on the other side of the valley, and follows the river steadily upstream to Tal (1700m), a former lakebed. Here the valley has been filled by ancient landslides and the river meanders through the fertile flat before disappearing under some huge boulders. Tal is the first village in the Manang district.

Day Four: Tal to Chame

This is a long day, so consider breaking your walk in Timang or Koto. The trail follows the valley then climbs a stone stairway before dropping down to cross the Marsyangdi to join the road. The road continues past Khotro and Karte to Dharapani (1960m), which is marked by a stone entrance chörten typical of the Tibetan-influenced villages from here northward. In upper (northern) Dharapani is an ACAP Checkpoint where you will need to register. Just beyond here at Thoche is the confluence with the Dudh Khola and Manaslu trail.

A landslide roared through the centre of Bagarchhap (2160m) in late 1995 and managed to wipe out much of it, including two lodges. There are more lodges at nearby Danaque.

The trail climbs steeply from Danaque, gaining 500m to Timang and then continues through a forest, past the traditional village of Thanchowk to Koto (2640m), at the junction of the Nar-Phu Valley. Nearby Chame (2710m) is the headquarters of the Manang district and it has lodges, internet cafes, trek-gear shops, a health post and a bank. At the entrance to the village you pass a large mani wall adorned with prayer wheels. There are fine views of Annapurna II (7937m) as you approach Chame.

Day Five: Chame to Upper Pisang

The trail runs through forest in a steep and narrow valley and recrosses to the south bank of the Marsyangdi Khola at 3080m. Views include the first sight of the soaring Paungda Danda rock face, an awesome testament to the power of glacial erosion. The trail/road continues to climb to the popular lunch spot at Dhukur Pokhari. After the village follow the red-and-white markers to leave the road and cross to the northern bank of the river. This trail leads up to Upper Pisang (3310m) where you'll get amazing views and decent accommodation.

Day Six: Upper Pisang to Manang

The walk is now through the drier upper part of Manang district, cut off from the full effect of the monsoon by the Annapurna Range. The people of the upper part of the Manang district herd yaks and raise crops for part of the year, but they also continue to enjoy special trading rights gained way back in 1784. Today they use these rights to buy goods in Bangkok and Hong Kong to resell in Nepal.

From Upper Pisang there are two trails, north and south of the Marsyangdi Khola, which meet up again at Mungji. The southern route via the road and airstrip at Hongde (3420m) involves dropping to Lower Pisang. It also involves much less climbing than the northern route, but the mountain views on the upper trail via Ghyaru and Ngawal (3660m) are infinitely better and this walk will aid your acclimatisation.

The trail continues from Mungji (3500m) past the picturesque village and gompa of Bragha (3470m) to nearby Manang (3540m), where there are numerous lodges, shops, a museum and an HRA post (it's worth attending the free daily lecture on altitude sickness). Bragha also has good lodges plus some excellent side trips, and is a quieter place to base yourself than Manang village.

Day Seven: Acclimatisation Day in Manang

It's important to spend a day acclimatising in Manang before pushing on to Thorung La (5416m). There are some fine day walks and magnificent views around Manang, and it's

Annapurna Treks

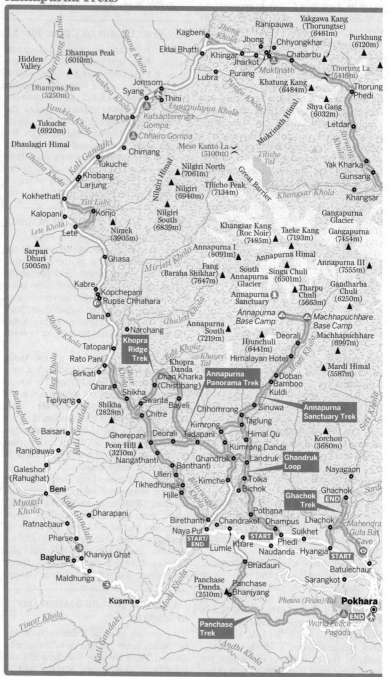

Hidden Valley

Barbung Khola

Dhampus Peak (6010m) ▲

Dhampus Pass (5250m)

Yamkim Khola

Tukuche (6920m) ▲

Dhaulagiri Himal

Ghatta Khola

Kali Gandaki

Suang Khola

Panbaja Khola

Kagbeni

Eklai Bhatti

Jhong Khola

Jomsom

Syang

Thini

Marpha

Katsapterenga Gompa

Chhairo Gompa

Chimang

Khobang

Larjung

Tukuche

Kokhethati

Kalopani

Konjo

Lete Khola

Lete

Nimek (3905m)

Sarpan Dhuri (5005m)

Ghasa

Kabre

Kopchepani

Rupse Chhahara

Dana

Narchang

Tatopani

Khopra Ridge Trek

Rato Pani

Birkati

Ghara

Tiplyang

Baisari

Shikha (2828m) ▲

Shikha

Swanta

Chitre

Ghorepani

Deorali

Tadapani

Poon Hill (3210m) ▲

Nangathanti

Banthanti

Ulleri

Tikhedhunga

Hille

Kimche

Ranipauwa

Galeshor (Rahughat)

Beni

Myagdi Khola

Ratnachaur

Pharse

Baglung

Khaniya Ghat

Maldhunga

Kusma

Titi Lake

Ranipauwa

Jhong

Khingar

Jharkot

Purang

Lubra

Chhyongkhar

Muktinath

Chabarbu

Yakgawa Kang (Thorungtse) (6481m) ▲

Purkhung (6120m) ▲

Thorung La (5416m)

Thorung Phedi

Khatung Kang (6484m) ▲

Shya Gang (6032m) ▲

Letdar

Yak Kharka

Gunsang

Khangsar

Nilgiri North (7061m) ▲

Nilgiri (6940m) ▲

Nilgiri Himal

Tilicho Peak (7134m) ▲

Nilgiri South (6839m) ▲

Great Barrier

Khangsar Khola

Meso Kanto La (5100m)

Tilicho Tal

Muktinath Himal

Marsyangdi Khola

Gangapurna Glacier

Khangsar Kang (Roc Noir) (7485m) ▲

Taeke Kang (7193m) ▲

Gangapurna (7454m) ▲

Annapurna I (8091m) ▲

Fang (Baraha Shikhar) (7647m) ▲

South Annapurna Glacier

Singu Chuli (6501m) ▲

Annapurna Himal

Annapurna III (7555m) ▲

Tharpu Chuli (5663m) ▲

Gandharba Chuli (6250m) ▲

Mirisiti Khola

Annapurna Sanctuary

Annapurna Base Camp

Machhapuchhare Base Camp

Machhapuchhare (6997m) ▲

Annapurna South (7219m) ▲

Hiunchuli (6441m) ▲

Deorali

Ghalet Khola

Khopra Danda

Dhan Kharka (Chistibang)

Annapurna Panorama Trek

Bayeli

Doban

Bamboo

Kuldi

Himalayan Hotel

Mardi Himal (5587m) ▲

Chhomrong

Sinuwa

Annapurna Sanctuary Trek

Taglung

Kimrong

Himal Qu

Korchon (3680m)

Kumrong Danda

Ghandruk

Landruk

Ghandruk Loop

Nayagaon

Kimche

Tolka

Bichok

Ghachok Trek

Ghachok END

Pothana

Dhampus

Lhachok

Mahendra Gufa Bat Cave

Birethanti

Chandrakot

Naya Pul

START/END

Lumle

Khare

START

Phedi

Naudanda

Suikhet

Hyangja

START

Batulechaur

Sarangkot

Bhadauri

Panchase Danda (2510m) ▲

Panchase Bhanjyang

Phewa (Fewa) Tal

Pokhara

END

Panchase Trek

World Peace Pagoda

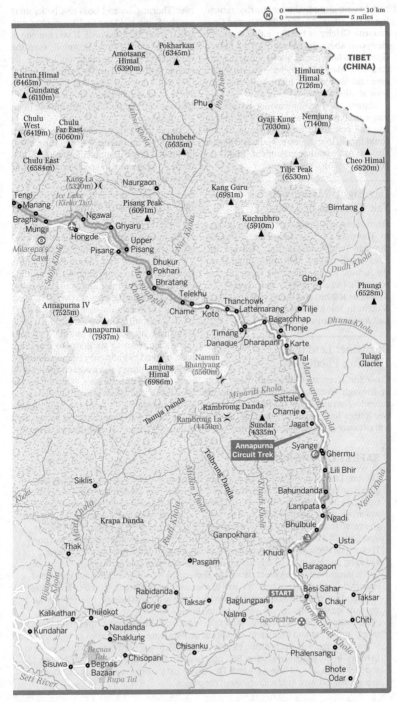

best to gain altitude during the day, returning to the village to sleep. The view of Gangapurna Glacier is terrific, either from the viewpoint above the lake or from the Praken Gompa, an hour's walk above Manang. More strenuous day hikes include to Milarepa's cave and the Ice Lake, high above the valley floor at 4600m.

Manang is a major trading centre and you can buy batteries, sunscreen, chocolate and just about anything else a trekker could break, lose or crave. Manang/Hongde airport has weather-dependent flights to Pokhara (US$110, weekly).

Day Eight: Manang to Yak Kharkha or Letdar

From Manang it's an ascent of nearly 2000m to Thorung La. The trail climbs steadily through Tengi and Gunsang, leaving the Marsyangdi Valley and continuing along the Jarsang Khola Valley. The vegetation becomes shorter and sparser as you reach Yak Kharkha (4020m) and then Letdar (4230m). A night in Yak Kharkha or Letdar is important for acclimatisation.

Day Nine: Letdar to Thorung Phedi

Cross the river at 4310m and then climb up through desolate scenery and avalanche zones to Thorung Phedi (4540m). There are two lodges here – at the height of the season as many as 200 trekkers a day may cross over Thorung La and beds can be in short supply. Some trekkers find themselves suffering from AMS at Phedi. If you are one of these, you must retreat downhill; even the descent to Letdar can make a difference. Be sure to boil or treat water here; the sanitation in Letdar and Thorung Phedi is poor. There is a satellite phone in Thorung Phedi that you can use for US$5 per minute in an emergency.

There is another lodge, Thorung High View Camp, an hour above Thorung Phedi at 4850m, but it is uncomfortable and potentially dangerous to spend a night at this altitude.

Day 10: Thorung Phedi to Muktinath

Phedi means 'foot of the hill' and that's exactly where it is, at the foot of the 5416m Thorung La. The trail climbs steeply but is well used and easy to follow. The altitude will have you gasping and snow can cause problems; when the pass is covered in fresh snow it is often impossible to cross – don't try it. Wait until it stops snowing and a mule team have been through cutting a trail. It takes about four to six hours to reach the pass, marked by chörtens (Tibetan Buddhist stupas) and prayer flags, and en route you'll pass a couple of teahouses, plus one on the pass itself. The effort is worthwhile as the view from the top – from the Annapurnas, along the Great Barrier to the barren Kali Gandaki Valley – is magnificent. From the

SAFETY ON THORUNG LA

Thorung La (5416m) is one of Nepal's highest passes and crossing it is potentially dangerous. In terms of altitude acclimatisation it is safest to cross it from east to west. The trek up to the pass from Manang is not difficult, but it is a long way at high elevation, which can cause problems. Be sure to read up on acute mountain sickness (AMS) before you go, so that you can be aware of the symptoms. Be prepared to return all the way to Besi Sahar if it is impossible or dangerous to cross Thorung La. Trekkers have died on Thorung La because of altitude sickness, exposure, cold and avalanches. All trekkers, including porters, must be adequately equipped for severe cold and snow.

It is impossible to give exact dates, but Thorung La is usually snowbound and closed from mid-December to March. The trail to the pass can be extremely hard to find in fresh snow and you should be prepared to turn back or stay put in a lodge in bad weather. At any time local storms or cyclones generated in the Arabian Sea or Bay of Bengal can close it with sudden and massive snow falls. In such conditions, and at these altitudes, simply sitting out bad weather in a lodge can be life saving.

Tragically this was made all too clear in October 2014 when almost 1.8m of snow fell in 12 hours. In the ensuing days over 500 people were rescued in the vicinity of Thorung La and Muktinath, and 43 lives were lost. Those who lost their lives were caught outdoors by avalanches, extreme cold and white-out conditions.

pass you have a knee-busting and sometimes slippery 1600m descent to Muktinath (3800m).

Some people start out for the pass at 3am, but this is not only unnecessary but also potentially dangerous due to the risk of frostbite and accidents in the darkness. A better starting time is 5am to 6am.

Muktinath, a pilgrimage site for Hindus and Buddhists, has no accommodation; for that you'll have to continue for 10 minutes to nearby Ranipauwa, where there is also an ACAP checkpoint.

Day 11: Muktinath to Kagbeni

From Ranipauwa the road descends through a desertlike trans-Himalayan landscape to the dramatic village of Jharkot (3500m), with its large chörten, gompa and atmospheric animist totems. The trail continues to Khingar (3400m) and then follows the road down steeply to the medieval-looking village of Kagbeni (2840m).

If you have half a day to spare, it's worth making the short detour across the valley to the traditional villages of Chhyongkhar, Jhong and Purang, all culturally part of Mustang but visitable without the need for extra permits.

There's an interesting alternative route (trail-marked in blue-and-white stripes) to Jomsom that bypasses the road and goes via the village of Lubra. Check first in Ranipauwa as the route is not passable when river levels are high.

Day 12: Kagbeni to Jomsom

The Tibetan-influenced settlement of Kagbeni has a number of good lodges and is as close as you can get to Lo Manthang, the capital of the legendary kingdom of Mustang further to the north; the permit fee is US$100.

From Kagbeni it is a dusty but mostly flat stroll along the road or river bed to Jomsom (2760m). Jomsom is the major centre in the region and it has facilities such as a hospital, an ACAP visitor centre and a police checkpost (where you must register and get your ACAP permit stamped). Some buildings here were damaged by the earthquake. Jomsom has regular morning flights to Pokhara (US$111) and bus and jeep services down to Ghasa, Beni and eventually Pokhara, so this is where some travellers end their trek.

If you have the time, it's worth continuing south to the traditional whitewashed stone village of Marpha (2680m), which has a gompa and several smaller shrines. The town boasts some of the best accommodation to be found along the trail, which makes it a good alternative to staying in Jomsom.

If walking, try to be on the trail early in the morning in the Kali Gandaki Valley, as strong winds tend to pick up after 11am.

Days 13 to 19: Jomsom to Naya Pul

The Annapurna Circuit south of Jomsom follows the new road south through the Kali Gandaki Valley to Naya Pul. This section of the trek has become less popular since the road was constructed but it's still a very rewarding walk if you take the detours on the east bank that avoid the road as much as possible. Furthermore, the trail leaves the road altogether at Tatopani to cross the ridge at Ghorepani and descend to Naya Pul. ACAP's progress in building trails and bridges on the east bank to enable trekkers to avoid the road is very successful. There are excellent lodges at Marpha, Tukuche, Larjung, Lete, Kalopani, Ghasa and Tatopani. Figure on three days to Tatopani or four to five days to Ghorepani.

South of Jomsom it's worth detouring down the east bank via Dhumba Lake to Katsapterenga Gompa, before returning to the road at Syang and continuing to Marpha.

Just south of Marpha another detour heads down the eastern bank from the Tibetan settlement around Chhairo Gompa to Chimang, which offers superb views of Dhaulagiri, the world's sixth largest mountain.

Back on the west bank, Tukuche (2580m) is one of the valley's most important Thakali villages and once was a depot and customs spot for salt traders from Tibet. Several grand houses and gompas hark back to a more prosperous past.

The road continues to Khobang and Larjung (2560m), past good views of Dhaulagiri (8167m) and Nilgiri North (7061m). Larjung is the base for a tough excursion up to the Dhaulagiri Icefall.

Another excursion branches off the road at Kokhethati, leading to Titi Lake (2670m) for views of the eastern flank of Dhaulagiri and then down to the villages of Konjo and Taglung, with their spectacular views of Nilgiri peak. The trails eventually rejoin the road just south of Lete (2480m).

The road continues south to Ghasa (2000m), the last Thakali village in the valley, and then a foot trail branches down the east side of the narrowing gorge, rejoining the road after a couple of hours at the waterfall of Rupse Chhahara (1560m). The road continues down to Dana and Tatopani (1190m), noted for its hot springs.

From Tatopani continue up the steep side valley from Ghar Khola, gaining an epic 1600m past Sikha and Chitre to Ghorepani in the Annapurna foothills. This is one of the hardest days on the circuit.

An hour's climb from the ridge at upper Ghorepani (also known as Deorali) will take you to Poon Hill (3210m), one of the best Himalayan viewpoints in the lower hills.

From Ghorepani you can descend the long, stone staircases to Nangathanti (2460m), Banthanti (2250m) and Ulleri, which is a large Magar village at 1960m, before continuing steeply to Tikhedhunga, Birethanti (1000m) and the nearby roadhead at Naya Pul.

A two-day trail also runs from Ghorepani to Ghandruk, where you can join up with the Annapurna Sanctuary Trek.

If you decide to take local transport between Jomsom and Pokhara, you'll have to change transport in Ghasa and Beni. You may have to stay overnight in Beni.

Naya Pul to Pokhara

Catch a bus or from Naya Pul (Rs 180, two hours), or a taxi from Birenthanti (Rs 2000) to Pokhara.

ANNAPURNA SANCTUARY TREK

Duration 10 to 14 days

Maximum elevation 4095m

Best season October to November

Start Phedi

Finish Naya Pul

Permits TIMS card, ACAP permit

Summary Classic walk through Gurung villages climbing to an amphitheatre surrounded by 7000m and 8000m peaks.

This trek leads right into the frozen heart of the Annapurna Range, a magnificent arena of rock and ice on a staggering scale. The trail starts in rice paddies and leads through a gorge of bamboo and forests to end among glaciers and soaring peaks – an unparalleled mountain experience. Other highlights include sublime views of fish-tailed Machhapuchhare (6997m) and one of Nepal's largest and prettiest Gurung villages at Ghandruk, which is a short detour off the main trail. This route was not affected by the 2015 earthquake.

The return trek can take as little as 10 days but 14 days will give you more time to soak up the scenery. You can add a walk to the sanctuary onto the Annapurna Circuit for an epic 25- to 30-day walk.

There are several possible routes to the sanctuary, all meeting at Chhomrong. One alternative is to start in Naya Pul and take a jeep as far as Kimche. The diversion from the Annapurna Circuit Trek branches off from Ghorepani to reach Chhomrong via Tadapani.

Access: Pokhara to Phedi

Buses leave every 40 minutes or so from Pokhara's Baglung bus stand to Phedi (Rs 70, 1½ hours), a cluster of shacks, from where the trail starts up a series of stone steps. Alternatively catch a bus to Naya Pul (Rs 180, two hours) and a jeep to Kimche (Rs 300) before walking to Ghandruk.

The Trek

Day One: Phedi to Tolka

From Phedi the trail climbs steeply to Dhampus (1750m), which stretches for several kilometres from 1580m to 1700m. The views are stupendous. Dhampus has a number of hotels strung along the ridge.

The trail climbs to pretty Pothana (1990m) and descends steeply through a forest towards Bichok. It emerges in the Modi Khola Valley and continues to drop to Tolka (1810m). If you have the energy, continue 45 minutes to the better accommodation at Landruk.

Day Two: Tolka to Chhomrong

From Tolka the trail descends a long stone staircase and then follows a ridge to the Gurung village of Landruk (1620m). Ten minutes from here the path splits – north takes you to Chhomrong and the sanctuary, or you can detour west downhill towards Ghandruk.

The sanctuary trail turns up the Modi Khola Valley to Himal Qu (also known as Naya Pul; 1340m). It then continues up to Jhinu Danda (1750m), and its nearby hot springs, before a steep climb to Taglung (2190m), where it joins the Ghandruk to Chhomrong trail.

Chhomrong (2210m) is the last permanent settlement in the valley. This large and sprawling Gurung village has excellent lodges, fine views and an ACAP office where you can enquire about trail conditions in the sanctuary.

Day Three: Chhomrong to Bamboo

The trail drops down a set of stone steps to the Chhomrong Khola, and then climbs to Sinuwa and on through rhododendron forests to Kuldi (2470m). The trek now enters the upper Modi Khola Valley, where ACAP controls the location and number of lodges and limits their size. This section of the trail is a bottleneck and you may find the lodges in Bamboo (2310m) are full during the high season, in which case you may have to continue for an hour to the next accommodation in Doban or sleep in the dining room. In winter it is common to find snow from this point on.

Day Four: Bamboo to Himalayan Hotel

The trail climbs through rhododendron forests to Doban (2540m) and on to the two lodges at Himalayan Hotel at 2840m. This stretch of the trail passes several avalanche chutes. If you arrive early, it's possible to continue on to Deorali to make the following day easier.

Day Five: Himalayan Hotel to Machhapuchhare Base Camp

From Himalayan Hotel it's on to Hinko (3100m) then to lodges at Deorali, at the gateway to the sanctuary. The next stretch of trail is the most subject to avalanches and you detour temporarily to the east side of the valley to avoid a dangerous chute.

At Machhapuchhare Base Camp (which isn't really a base camp since climbing the mountain is not permitted), at 3700m, there is decent accommodation available. Be alert to signs of altitude sickness before heading off to Annapurna Base Camp.

AVALANCHES ON THE SANCTUARY TRAIL

There is significant danger of avalanches along the route to the Annapurna Sanctuary between Doban and Machhapuchhare Base Camp. Trekkers have died and trekking parties have been stranded in the sanctuary for days, the trail blocked by tonnes of ice and snow. Always check with the ACAP office in Chhomrong and lodges in Deorali for a report on current trail conditions, and do not proceed into the sanctuary if there has been recent heavy rain or snow.

Day Six: Machhapuchhare Base Camp to Annapurna Base Camp

The climb to the Annapurna Base Camp at 4130m takes about two hours and is best done early in the day before clouds roll in. If there is snow, the trail may be difficult to follow. The lodges here can get very crowded at the height of the season. The frozen dawn is best observed from the glacial moraine a short stroll from your cosy lodge.

Days Seven to 14: Annapurna Base Camp to Naya Pul

On the return trip head south to Chhomrong (two days) and on to Ghandruk (one day) via the deep valley of the Khumnu Khola. From Ghandruk you can follow the valley directly down to Kimche, Birethanti and Naya Pul in a day. Transport is available from Kimche to Naya Pul (Rs 300). Alternatively, detour west to Ghorepani to visit Poon Hill, before descending to Birethanti (four days) and Naya Pul. Buses to Pokhara stop in Naya Pul (Rs 180, two hours).

OTHER ANNAPURNA TREKS

Ghachok Trek (Two Days)

This interesting two-day trek ascends the hills north of Pokhara to the traditional Gurung villages around Ghachok. It starts from Hyangja, near the Tashi Palkhel Tibetan settlement, and crosses the Mardi Khola to Lhachok before ascending to the stone-walled village of Ghachok, where you can stop overnight in a teahouse before turning south and returning to Pokhara via Batulechaur. With more time, you can extend this walk (beyond the reach of roads) to visit some even more remote villages in the valley leading north from Ghachok.

Ghandruk Loop (Three Days)

This is a short but steep trek offering mountain views and Gurung villages, with numerous quality lodges with excellent mountain views at Ghandruk. The trail starts at Phedi and follows day one of the Annapurna Sanctuary trail to overnight at Tolka (1810m). From Tolka trek 45 minutes to Landruk (an alternative first night halt) and then drop steeply down a stone staircase to the Modi Khola at 1315m. It's then a very steep climb up more stone stairs, thankfully via several refreshment stops, to Ghandruk (1970m). Next day descend to the road at Kimche where you can catch transport or continue walking back to Birenthanti and Naya Pul.

Panchase Trek (Three to Four Days)

Panchase is a region close to Pokhara, boasting scenic and cultural attributes with the added benefits that it is easily accessed from Lakeside and no ACAP or TIMS cards are required. There are several variations of the route featuring the high point of Panchase Danda (2500m) and it can be done in any direction. Simple homestay and teahouse accommodation is available at Panchase Bhanjyang and other nearby villages.

Trails to Panchase start west of Pokhara, either at Naudanda or Khare on the Baglung Highway or west of Phewa Tal at Ghatichhina. The trails climb through traditional villages to Panchase Bhanjyang (2030m), where you can stay overnight. Start early the next morning to trek up to the peak of Panchase Danda for a sunrise vista of the Himalaya. The trek can then conclude along any of the several routes back to Pokhara, including one where you visit the Peace Pagoda and return to Lakeside via a boat ride on the lake.

Annapurna Panorama (Six Days)

This loop walk features Gurung villages and marvellous views from the popular Poon Hill (3210m) viewpoint and is a good choice in winter. It can also be done in either direction. The overnight stops on this trek are shared with the Annapurna Circuit and Sanctuary treks and therefore teahouse accommodation is plentiful.

The trail starts at Naya Pul, on the road from Pokhara to Baglung, and follows the Annapurna Circuit trail in reverse for the first two days, with overnight stops in Tikhedhunga and Ghorepani. On day three, most people leave before dawn for the short 1.5km hike to Poon Hill and its fine vista of snowy peaks, including Annapurna South (7273m) and Machhapuchhare (6997m). Relax in Ghorepani for the rest of the day.

Day four involves a gentle descent to Tadapani, and day five continues downhill to Ghandruk, a scenic Gurung village of stone and slate houses with a colourful Buddhist monastery. The final day is an easy descent back to Kimche, Birethanti or Naya Pul, all of which offer jeeps or buses back to Pokhara. Alternatively, head east across the valley to Landruk and stop overnight at Tolka, before continuing to Phedi on the Baglung Hwy.

Khopra Ridge (Eight to Nine Days)

This trek detours from the more frequented Annapurna trails to take you closer to the mountains. It can be done in either direction, and via a number of different routes, and be appended to either the Annapurna Circuit or Annapurna Sanctuary treks. Formerly frequented only by camping groups, there are now community-owned lodges allowing teahouse trekking.

Start trekking from Naya Pul or Kimche (or Phedi) to take one or two days to reach Ghandruk. Day two takes you to Tadapani. On day three head towards Ghorepani but detour north to overnight in Bayeli (3450m). The next halt is in Chistibang (2990m) where there are two lodges, before reaching the high point of the trek at Khopra Danda (3660m). From here there is an ambitious optional side trek up to the sacred lake Khayer Tal (4830m). The return route is via the village of Swanta (day six) before the trail joins the Annapurna Circuit at Chitre. Head east to Ulleri (day seven) via Ghorepani, and then to Birenthanti or Naya Pul the following day.

RESTRICTED AREA & OTHER TREKS

The teahouse treks are the ones walked by the vast majority of trekkers in Nepal. If you want to head off the beaten track, it's possible to explore remote areas like Makalu and Kanchenjunga in the east or Humla and Dolpo in the west, but you must be very self-sufficient. In these relatively untouched areas there is little surplus food for sale and the practice of catering to trekkers has not yet developed. There are basic lodges during high season along the Manaslu, Tsum, Nar-Phu, Mustang and Makalu treks, but for other regions you will need to make camping arrangements through a trekking company. Note that the Manaslu region was hit badly by the 2015 earthquake and local guides recommend against attempting the Around Manaslu and Tsum Valley treks until infrastructure is restored. Most of these regions require a trekking permit that can only be arranged trough a trekking agency. Throw in flights for you and your porters and it's easy to see that the remoter the trek, the more expensive it becomes.

See Lonely Planet's *Trekking in the Nepal Himalaya* for the complete story on trekking in Nepal. It has comprehensive advice on equipment selection, a dedicated health and safety section, and comprehensive route descriptions for both the popular treks and interesting, less heavily used routes. The following are currently the most popular treks.

Nar-Phu A seven-day add-on to the Annapurna Circuit trail that takes you to the photogenic traditional villages of Nar and Phu near the Tibetan border.

Mustang The most popular of the restricted-area treks leads to this long-forbidden Tibetan kingdom in a remote and arid land of spectacular Tibetan monasteries, canyons and cave complexes that border Tibet. The new road from Jomsom to the Chinese border is changing the region quickly. Possible as an organised teahouse trek.

Tarap Valley Loop Popular 12-day loop in remote Dolpo that follows the Tarap Valley to the Tibetan-style villages and monasteries around Do Tarap, then crosses the breathtaking 5000m-plus passes of the Numa La and Baga La to arrive at the turquoise Phoksundo Lake, probably the most beautiful lake in Nepal. Camping only.

Beni to Dolpo Excellent 12-day traverse from Beni, northwest of Pokhara, to Tarakot in outer Dolpo, crossing six passes and a huge swathe of midwestern Nepal in the footsteps of the book *The Snow Leopard*. Camping only.

Kanchenjunga Least visited of all is the far east, where two long routes lead right to the base of the world's third-highest mountain. Camping only.

Makalu Base Camp Another trek that gets you right into the heart of the mountains, following the Barun Valley up to base camp at around 5000m, offering fine views of Everest and Lhotse. The 15-day trek involves a flight to Tumlingtar and then a drive to Num, or you can trek in from Lukla in 11 days. It's just about doable as a simple teahouse trek but only in high season.

ⓘ **MUSTANG & DOLPO PERMITS**

Following the 2015 earthquake, the Nepal government has cut the permit fee for Mustang and Dolpo to encourage trekking, making this an excellent time to explore these fascinating regions outside the earthquake damage zone.

Biking, Rafting & Kayaking

Best Places to be a Beginner

➜ Trisuli River (p316)

➜ Pokhara to Sarangkot & Naudanda (p316)

➜ Upper Sun Kosi (p317)

Best Places to be an Adrenaline Junkie

➜ Upper Mustang – Jomsom to Lo Manthang (p313)

➜ Marsyangdi (p318)

➜ Karnali (p319)

Why Go?

While Nepal may be synonymous with trekking, its world-class rapids and exhilarating mountain descents are made for white-water rafting and mountain biking. The bike trails suggested here are best suited to more experienced riders with a good level of fitness. And while most can be done on your own, you'll often need to rely on locals for directions, so hiring a guide or signing up for an organised tour will make life considerably easier. Meanwhile the rafting and kayaking routes are suitable for beginners and pros alike, and your choice is dependent on how much of a buzz you can handle.

With the nature of mountain biking and rafting, these physical pursuits were not adversely affected by the 2015 earthquakes, but check before you set off for a route to make sure the trails are clear and rivers are flowing freely.

When to Go

For cyclists October to November offers generally clear skies, warm day time temperatures and it's not too cold at night.

For rafting Mid- to late October through to the end of November offers the warmest waters and rapids that are exciting without being life threatening. March to May is good for families.

MOUNTAIN-BIKE ROUTES

Note that some features of these biking routes may have changed since the 2015 earthquake – seek local advice before you set off.

The Scar Road from Kathmandu

Distance 65km

Duration Seven hours, or two days with overnight in Kakani

Start/Finish Kathmandu

Summary Fine views and a challenging descent through a national park, after a tough initial climb of around 700m.

This trip northwest of Kathmandu can be a fairly demanding ride, and is suited to more experienced riders; a guide is recommended. You'll see some damage from the 2015 earthquake but trails are open for business.

Leaving Kathmandu (elevation 1337m), head towards Balaju on the Ring Rd 2km north of Thamel, and follow the sealed Trisuli Bazaar road towards Kakani, 23km away at an altitude of 2073m. You start to climb out of the valley as the track twists and turns past Nagarjun Hill, which provides the road with a leafy canopy. Once you're through the initial pass and out of the valley, the road continues northwest and offers a view of endless terraced fields to your left. (If you don't fancy the climb, you can avoid cycling on the road by putting your bike on the roof of the early-morning bus to Dhunche and getting off here.) On reaching the summit of the ridge, take a turn right (at a clearly marked T-junction), instead of continuing down to Trisuli Bazaar. (If you go too far, you reach a checkpoint just 100m beyond.) At this point magnificent views of the Ganesh Himal (*himal* means a range with permanent snow) provide the inspiration required to complete the remaining 4km of steep and deteriorating blacktop to the crown of the hill at **Kakani** for a well-deserved rest. It's an excellent idea to overnight here at the Tara Gaon, or another such guesthouse, and savour the dawn views over the Himalaya.

After admiring the view, descend for just 30m beyond the gate and take the first left onto a 4WD track. This track will take you through the popular picnic grounds frequented on Saturday by Kathmandu locals. Continue in an easterly direction towards Shivapuri. The track narrows after a few kilometres near a metal gate on your left. Through the gate, you are faced with some rough stone steps and then a 10-minute push/carry up and over the hilltop to an army checkpoint. Here it's necessary for foreigners to pay a Rs 500 entry fee to the Shivapuri National Park, plus a Rs 1000 fee for their bike. Exit the army camp, turning right where the Scar Rd is clearly visible in front of you. You are now positioned at the day's highest point – approximately 2200m.

Taking the right-hand track you will start to descend dramatically along an extremely steep, rutted single trail with several water crossings. The trail is literally cut into the side of the hill, with sharp drops on the right that challenge a rider's skill and nerve. As you hurtle along, take time to admire the view of the sprawling Kathmandu Valley below – it's one of the best. In recent years the trail has become quite overgrown so you may have to carry your bike for several stretches and seek out the correct path. A guide would be useful for this section.

The trail widens, after one long gnarly climb before the saddle, then it's relatively flat through the protected Shivapuri watershed area. This beautiful mountain-biking section lasts for nearly 25km before the trail descends into the valley down a 7km spiral on a gravel road. This joins a sealed road, to the relief of jarred wrists, at **Budhanilkantha**, where you can buy refreshments. Take a moment to see the Sleeping Vishnu just up on your left at the main intersection. From here the sealed road descends gently for the remaining 15km back into the bustle of Kathmandu, although this part of the ride is generally through busy city traffic and not much fun.

Kathmandu to Pokhara

Distance 263km

Duration Five days

Start Kathmandu

Finish Pokhara

Summary Fine views and challenging trails that take you off the beaten track and through historic Newari towns.

BIKING, RAFTING & KAYAKING

Biking, Rafting & Kayaking in Nepal

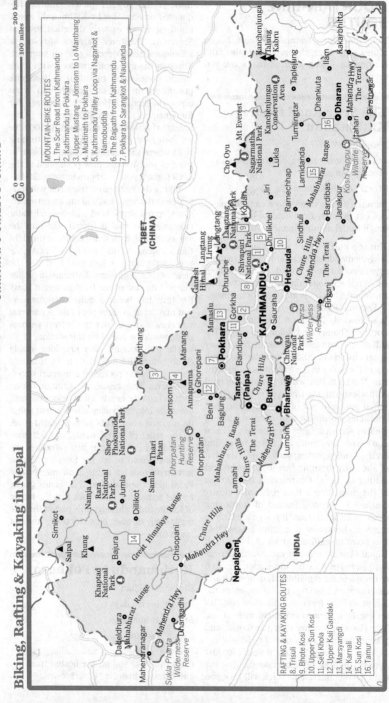

0 ——— 200 km
0 ——— 100 miles

MOUNTAIN-BIKE ROUTES
1. The Scar Road from Kathmandu
2. Kathmandu to Pokhara
3. Upper Mustang – Jomsom to Lo Manthang
4. Muktinath to Pokhara
5. Kathmandu Valley Loop via Nagarkot & Namobuddha
6. The Rajpath from Kathmandu
7. Pokhara to Sarangkot & Naudanda

RAFTING & KAYAKING ROUTES
8. Trisuli
9. Bhote Kosi
10. Upper Sun Kosi
11. Seti Khola
12. Upper Kali Gandaki
13. Marsyangdi
14. Karnali
15. Sun Kosi
16. Tamur

It's possible to ride from Kathmandu to Pokhara in 12 to 14 hours along the busy Prithvi Hwy, but unless you're in a hurry the back roads are much better suited to mountain biking. This route will take you along some fairly rural trails that see few foreigners, so a guide or an organised tour is a good idea. Otherwise you'll need to rely on villagers to point you in the right direction. Hotels and places to eat can be a little thin on the ground in places and many tour companies recommend doing this ride as a full camping trip. You'll see a fair bit of earthquake damage along the route, but the trails themselves are in good shape.

Day one sees you leaving Thamel in a northerly direction along the busy tarmac road, taking a left at the Kantipath exit. Continue along this road for 3km, past the American embassy and cross the Ring Rd at Maharajganj. From here it's a steady 6km uphill to **Budhanilkantha**, taking a break to see the Sleeping Vishnu. Continuing on, you leave the tarmac behind in a cloud of dust. The trail begins with a 3.5km climb to the army checkpoint where you pay the entry fee to Shivapuri Nagarjun National Park (p136). Follow the rocky trail through the forest for 4km until you reach a clearing. Ignore the first small road on your right, and instead take the next right after it, leading you downhill for 18km. Ignore the crossroads and head straight. If unsure, ask locals the way to Bidur, or better yet, get a guide.

After the descent you head along a mostly flat road with the Likhu Khola on your right. After 8km you'll cross the river and then go on to a paved road where the river will be on your left for about 5km before meeting the Trisuli River. Cross the bridge on your right and take a left through the village, riding through town before taking another left at the small paved road. On reaching the main road, head right and ride 3km to Bidur, from where you need to look out for a small turn on your right. Ask the locals for the way to Nuwakot Durbar, a steep 1.5-hour climb from Bidur.

Day two is an up-and-down affair that covers a distance of 65km, starting with a gradual climb along a tarmac road from Trisuli Bazaar 12km uphill to Samari. From here it's a rough trail that passes through Taksar, finishing up on a sealed road leading to Dhadhing Besi (via Ratmate), where you spend the night.

The next day starts along tarmac, taking you up to Muralibhanjyang, from where it's a dirt road past Nepal's second-largest *tar* (flatland river valley) at Tallo Rampur. Continue along the Budhi Gandaki River, which you cross, and then pass through Bunkghat. The last stretch is a gradual ascent to the Newari town of **Gorkha**, famous for its Shah palace at Gorkha Durbar.

Day four starts with a 10km descent, crossing Daraudi River at Chhepetar. From here it's a relatively easy 35km cross-country ride passing more *tar*s and jungle, finishing up the day at Sundarbazaar.

This brings you to the final day, saving the best views till last, as you whiz past towering Himalayan vistas. It's an undulating day of riding that covers around 63km, finishing up with a night out in Pokhara to celebrate the completion of your ride.

Upper Mustang – Jomsom to Lo Manthang

Distance 210km

Duration 12 days, including a rest day

Start/Finish Jomsom

Summary An epic journey through remote and stunning stretches of the country. It's a challenging and technical ride, suitable for experienced riders only.

The first obstacle is forking out the US$500 permit to visit the restricted region of Upper Mustang (applicable for 10 days). Furthermore, you'll need to be part of an organised tour – but this can be as simple as employing a guide, which in the long run is a good idea to make sure you're on the right path. With the amount of hills you're about to tackle, a porter is highly recommended too.

Flying into Jomsom (unless you're nuts and want to ride there from Pokhara, an increasingly popular uphill assault), the journey begins with a gentle two-hour ride that'll take you to the first night's stop at the Buddhist village of Kagbeni (2801m). Day two is a mostly uphill ride along the jeep track to Muktinath, taking things slowly to get acclimatised to the altitude, while allowing you to take in stunning mountain views. The next day takes you into the restricted region of Upper Mustang, starting with an uphill climb to Gyu La (4077m). This involves carrying your bike at times, but you are rewarded with a 1000m descent along a single track. The final stage is a slight climb and river crossing to reach Chele (3050m), where you spend the night.

The next day is shorter but no less taxing, as you head up into the hills taking on no less than four passes, all exceeding 3600m. You'll be following jeep and single tracks, with a mix of steep climbs and descents, and once again you'll have to lug your bike uphill at times. Stop for the night below Syangboche La (3800m) on the Syangboche River.

While day five begins with more climbing (sigh), once you've cleared Syangboche La and Nyi La (4010m), rest assured the remainder of the day has mostly flat tracks. It also has some of the best scenery you'll see on the trip, with great views of the Himalaya, valleys and bright-yellow mustard fields. Overnight in Charang (Tsarang), with its 400-year-old Gulpa Sect Monastery.

Day six sets out to the crowning jewel of the journey, the walled kingdom city of Lo Manthang. You'll catch your first glimpse of it as you cross the 'Windy Pass' of Lo La (3950m). Today is a bit of a climb, but riding is mostly easy along a jeep track, with a 25km total riding distance. Arrive in Lo Manthang at lunch time, and take a well-earned break. Spend a day or two here taking in the atmosphere of this amazing medieval kingdom. An option for your 'rest day' is a side trip up to Garphu following the Kali Gandaki River to Ghom cave.

After giving your legs a day off, it's time to leave Lo Manthang, starting with a challenging climb over Pangga (Samduling) at 4090m, a 75% rideable single track. From here it's a thrilling downhill road to Dhakmar, with dramatic landscapes. Head on to Ghami (Ghemi) for the night; it's your last stop in Mustang.

Heading back, on day nine you retrace the same trail with a single-track climb followed by a downhill to Syangboche, spending the night in Samar. Day 10 takes you over Dajori La (3735m) and Taklam La (3624m), passing sky burials en route. Next you cycle downhill to spend the night in Chhusang. From here you leave Upper Mustang and head back into the Annapurna region, a steady ride along the river taking you back to Kagbeni. You have the option to overnight or continue on down the valley to Jomsom, where you either fly to Pokhara or Kathmandu, or otherwise complete the ride through to Pokhara.

There are teahouses on this route.

Muktinath to Pokhara

Distance 164km

Duration Four days (two if you rush)

Start Kagbeni

Finish Pokhara

Summary Downhill journey that follows half the Annapurna Circuit, mostly along the jeep track from Jomsom.

While the construction of the road from Jomsom has trekkers mourning the death of the Annapurna trek, mountain-bikers are salivating at this new trail opening up to them. Most people start this increasingly popular route by flying into Jomsom.

From Jomsom enjoy a mostly flat two-hour ride to Kagbeni. Day one proper is a 1000m climb up to Muktinath. Day one proper is a 1000m climb up to Muktinath, with arid desert landscape and spectacular views to Dhaulagiri and other 8000m peaks. The next day is an undulating trail taking you to Marpha via Lupra, with 30% of the day involving pushing or carrying your bike. Day four sees another downhill leg heading to Tatopani, where you can soothe those aching leg muscles in natural hotwater springs. Getting back on the bike for the final day, a descent leads you along the Kali Gandaki River to Beni. From here it's a highway ride to Nau Danda and then a jeep track to Sarangkot. Hang around for the night to see spectacular sunrise views of the Himalaya, or finish the journey via the steep narrow trail to Pokhara.

Kathmandu Valley Loop via Nagarkot & Namobuddha

Distance 110km

Duration Three days

Start/Finish Kathmandu

Summary A circular route past a classic selection of the valley's cultural sights. There are varying routes on offer, so you can tailor your trip according to tastes. Another popular option goes via Bhaktapur and Changu Narayan.

This route passes through areas that were badly affected by the 2015 earthquake, but the biking trails themselves are mostly unaffected. From Thamel head east past the Royal Palace, follow the road straight through Naxal and cross over the Ring Rd to visit the Pashupatinath Temple. Continue along a hectic road to **Bodhnath**, stopping to explore this fascinating Tibetan Buddhist town. Pedal on to Jorpati, where you take a right, and traffic becomes light, passing along the edge of Gokarna Forest. Continue on to Sankhu, along the old trade route from Kathmandu to Lhasa, for another temple stop and refreshments. From here it's a jeep trail that heads mostly uphill past the Vajrayogini Temple and Lapsiphedi village en route to Jarsingpouwa. Trails from here are mostly flat until you reach Kattike, from where you'll need to suck it up for the 10km uphill to Nagarkot, where you'll spend the night.

Following the **trekking trail** (www.netifnepal.org/itineraries.htm) linking Nagarkot to Dhulikhel; the rough track is a one- to two-hour ride. To access it, you'll need to follow the tarmac road heading to the viewing tower, pass by the army camp and head down to the village of Rohini Bhanjyang. From here you choose the trail on the left side; look out for the signs. After 1km, take a right down a small trail that'll lead you through to the villages of Kankre and Tanchok. From here the trail continues to Opi, passing farmhouses, from where it's a further 5km to Dhulikhel. Stop here for lunch, refreshments and mesmerising mountain views. The final leg is a two-hour up-and-down journey through gorgeous scenery to **Namobuddha**, home to a monumental Tibetan Buddhist monastery up on a hill.

Get an early start to explore Namobuddha Monastery, before jumping on your bike for a downhill section followed by a cross-country trail to the Newari town of Panauti. Leave at least an hour to explore the old town before heading off. Don't let the heavenly first 4.5km of tarmac lull you into a false sense of security. The road soon deteriorates into 3km of dirt road to the village of Kushadevi, followed by 2.5km of bone-jarring stony track to Riyale. From here the valley starts to close in and gets increasingly remote – this is definitely not the place to blow a tyre! It's amazing how remote the route is, considering how close it is to Kathmandu. If you're not an experienced mountain biker, you're probably better off considering this as a motorbike route.

The next 8.5km is on a smooth dirt road that switchbacks up the hillsides to **Lakuri Bhanjyang** (1960m). You may find some basic food stalls but the actual summit is currently occupied by the army. In the past, travel companies have set up tented camp accommodation near here but this depends on tourism numbers and the level of army presence. Figure on spending two to three hours to get to here.

From this point on it's all downhill. The first section drops down the back side of the hill, blocking the views, but you soon get great views of the Annapurna and Ganesh Himal massifs – particularly spectacular in sunset's pink glow.

A further 5km of descent, rough at times, brings you to the turn-off left to Sisneri and the first village on this side of the pass. Soon the asphalt kicks in again, shortly followed by the pleasant village of **Lubbhu**, with its impressive central three-tiered Mahalakshmi Mahadev Temple. Traffic levels pick up for the final 5km to the Kathmandu ring road near Patan; be prepared for 'civilisation' to come as a bit of a shock after such a beautiful, peaceful ride.

The Rajpath from Kathmandu

Distance 150km

Duration Two days

Start Kathmandu

Finish Hetauda

Summary Classic but gruelling on-road ride over a 2488m pass, culminating in incomparable Himalayan views at Daman.

The ride begins on the Kathmandu–Pokhara (Prithvi) Hwy, which gives the only access to the valley, and passes through earthquake affected areas, but the road is fully operational. After leaving the valley, the highway descends to Naubise, at the base of the Mahesh Khola Valley, 27km from Kathmandu, where the Rajpath intersects with the Prithvi Hwy. Take the Rajpath, which forks to the left and is well signposted, for Hetauda. Start a 35km climb to Tistung (2030m) past terraced fields carved into steep hillsides.

On reaching the pass at Tistung you descend for 7km into the beautiful Palung Valley before the final steep 9km climb to **Daman**, at a height of 2322m.

This day's ride (almost all climbing) takes between six and nine hours in the saddle. With an early start it is possible to stay in Daman, which will give you the thrill of waking up to the broadest Himalayan panorama Nepal has to offer. The following day the road climbs a further 3km to the top of the pass, at 2488m. At this point you can savour the very real prospect of an exhilarating 2300m descent in 60km!

As you descend towards the Indian plains, laid out before you to the south, notice the contrast with the side you climbed, as the south side is lush and semitropical. With innumerable switchbacks and a bit of speed you should watch out for the occasional bus and truck looming around blind corners. The road eventually flattens out after the right turn to cross a newly constructed bridge and the first main river crossing. The rest of the journey is a gently undulating route alongside a river; a further 10km brings you to **Hetauda**. (Note that there are useful cyclists' notebooks in the Motel Avocado.) After a night's rest you can continue along the Rajpath towards India or turn right at the statue of the king in the centre of town and head towards Chitwan National Park.

Pokhara to Sarangkot & Naudanda

Distance 54km

Duration Seven hours, or an overnight trip

Start/Finish Pokhara

Summary Work up a sweat getting to two of Pokhara's best Himalayan viewpoints, followed by a great downhill coast.

Leave early and ride along Lakeside (towards the mountains) to the last main intersection and sealed road. Turn right; this is the road that returns to central Pokhara. After 2km you turn left and continue straight (north). This intersection is the zero kilometre road marker. After a further 2km there is a smaller sealed road to the left, signposted as the road to Sarangkot.

This winds its way along a ridge into Sarangkot, providing outstanding views of the Himalaya, which seems close enough to reach out and touch. After 6km a few teahouses make a welcome refreshment stop just where the stone steps mark the walking trail to the summit. From here your path is a 4WD track that closely hugs the edge of the mountain overlooking Phewa Tal. Continue until you join a Y-intersection that doubles back sharply to the right and marks the final climb to **Sarangkot**. You can turn this ride into a relaxed overnight trip by staying in lodges here.

From Sarangkot continue straight ahead, riding the narrower motorcycle trails leading to Kaski and Naudanda. After the Sarangkot turn-off the trail soon begins to climb to Kaski, towards the hill immediately in front of you. The section to Kaski takes around 30 to 60 minutes, and you may need to push your bicycle on the steeper section near the crown of the hill. Over the top you follow the trail through to **Naudanda**. You are now at around 1590m, having gained around 840m of altitude from Pokhara. The trail is rocky in parts and will test your equipment to the extreme, so do not consider riding this trail on a cheap hired bicycle.

From Naudanda it's a 32km downhill run to Pokhara along the smooth asphalt highway. The route starts with a twisting 6km descent into the Mardi Khola Valley then descends gently as it follows the river, allowing an enjoyable coast almost all the way to Pokhara.

RAFTING & KAYAKING ROUTES

Trisuli

Distance 40km

Duration One to two days

Start Baireni or Charaudi

Finish Multiple locations

Summary Popular introduction to rafting, and a wild ride during the monsoon.

With easy access just out of Kathmandu, the Trisuli is where many budget river trips operate, and is the obvious choice if you are looking for a short introduction to rafting at the cheapest possible price.

After diving into the valley west of Kathmandu, the Prithvi Hwy follows the Trisuli River. Most of the rapids along this route are class II to class III, but the water can build up to class IV in the monsoon.

The Trisuli has some good scenery, but with the main busy road to Kathmandu beside the river it is not wilderness rafting. Some operators have their own fixed campsites or lodges, ranging from safari-style resorts to wind-blown village beaches complete with begging kids and scavenging dogs.

When booking, ask where the put-in point is: anything starting at Kuringhat or Mugling will mainly be a relaxing float. During the mid-monsoon months (August to early October) the Trisuli changes character completely as huge runoffs make the river swell like an immense ribbon of churning ocean, especially after its confluence with the Bhodi Gandaki. At these flows it provides a classic big-volume Himalayan river so make sure you choose a reputable company to go with.

Multiday trips continue downriver towards Narayangarh and Chitwan National Park, but the rapids below Kurintar are much more gentle.

Bhote Kosi

Distance 18km

Duration Two days

Start 95km from Kathmandu, near the Tibetan border

Finish Lamosangu

Summary Just three hours from Kathmandu, the Bhote Kosi is one of the best short raft trips to be found anywhere in the world.

The Bhote Kosi is the steepest river rafted in Nepal – technical and totally committing. With that said, beginners can still give it a go. With a gradient of 16m per kilometre, it's a full eight times as steep as the Sun Kosi, which it feeds further downstream. The rapids are steep and continuous class IV, with a lot of continuous class III in between.

This river is one of the most fun things you can do right out of Kathmandu and a great way to get an adrenaline fix during the

EARTHQUAKE LANDSLIDES

The 2015 earthquake caused landslides in many areas, particularly in Sindhupalchowk, Dolakha and Gorhka districts, and many areas are thought to be at risk of further slips because of the destablising effects of the tremors. Nepal has a long history of deadly floods caused by landslides – in 2014, 156 people died when a landslide blocked the Sun Kosi river near Jure and thousands were evacuated when the Kali Gandaki river was blocked by a landslide near Beni just weeks after the 12 May tremor. There were no issues on main rafting rivers at the time of writing but it pays to check locally before booking a trip in case of further blockages.

low-water months, but it should only be attempted with a company that has a lot of experience on the Bhote Kosi, and is running the absolute best guides, safety equipment and safety kayakers.

Sadly, a huge landslide and the subsequent build up of a natural damn in mid-2014 has, for the moment at least, rather taken the shine of this river and currently few people are rafting it. Enquire with Kathmandu agencies for the latest news.

Upper Sun Kosi

Distance 20km

Duration One day

Start Khadichour

Finish Dolalghat

Summary A great place for a short family trip or learner kayak clinics.

The top section of the Upper Sun Kosi from below the dam to near Sukute Beach is a class III white-water run offering a good opportunity to get a feel for rafting.

The lower section is a mellow scenic float, with forest down to the river, and it is a popular river for kayak clinics. At high flows during and just after the monsoon rains the Upper Sun Kosi is a full-on class III to IV high-adrenaline day trip.

Seti Khola

Distance 32km

Duration Two days

Start Damauli

Finish Gaighat

Summary A quieter river that is perfect for beginners, birdwatchers, families and learner kayakers.

The Seti is an excellent two-day trip in an isolated area, with beautiful jungle, white sandy beaches and plenty of class II to III rapids. The warm water also makes it a popular place for winter trips and kayak clinics. During the monsoon the river changes radically as monsoon runoff creates class III to IV rapids.

The logical starting point is Damauli on the Prithvi Hwy between Mugling and Pokhara. This would give you 32km of rafting to the confluence with the Trisuli River. From the take-out at Gaighat it's just a one-hour drive to Chitwan National Park.

Upper Kali Gandaki

Distance 60km

Duration Three days (two days rafting)

Start Beni or Baglung

Finish Andhi Khola

Summary Diverse trip down the holy river, through deep gorges and past waterfalls.

The Upper Kali Gandaki is an excellent alternative to the Trisuli, as there is no road alongside, and the scenery, villages and temples all combine to make it a great trip.

The rapids on the Kali Gandaki are technical and continuous (at class III to IV, sometimes even class V depending on the flows), and in high water it's no place to be unless you are an accomplished kayaker experienced in avoiding big holes. At medium and lower flows it's a fun and challenging river with rapids that will keep you busy.

The Kali Gandaki is one of the holiest rivers in Nepal, and every river junction is dotted with cremation sites and burial mounds. If you're wondering what's under that pile of rocks, we recommend against exploring! Because of the recent construction of a dam at the confluence with the An-dhi Khola, what was once a four- to five-day trip has now become a three-day trip, starting at either Beni or Baglung (depending on the operator) and taking out at the dam site. At very high flows it will probably be possible to run the full five-day trip to Ramdhighat by just portaging the dam site. This option would add some great white water and you could visit the fantastic derelict palace at Ranighat.

If you can raft to Ramdhighat beside the Siddhartha Hwy between Pokhara and Sunauli, you could continue on to the confluence with the Trisuli at Devghat along the **Lower Kali Gandaki**. This adds another 130km and three or four more days. The lower section below Ramdhighat doesn't have much white water, but it is seldom rafted and offers a very isolated area with lots of wildlife.

Marsyangdi

Distance 27km

Duration Four days (two days rafting)

Start Ngadi

Finish Phaliya Sanghu (Phalesangu)

Summary A magnificent blue whitewater river with a spectacular mountain backdrop. Best suited to experienced rafters.

The Marsyangdi is steeper and offers more continuous white water than most other rivers in Nepal; it's not called the 'Raging River' for nothing! You can go by bus to Khudi or Bhulbule, from where it's a short walk up to the village of Ngadi, with great views of Manaslu ahead of you the whole time.

From Ngadi downstream to the dam side above Phaliya Sanghu, it's pretty much solid white water. Rapids are steep, technical and consecutive, making the Marsyangdi a serious undertaking. Successful navigation of the Marsyangdi requires companies to use previous experience on the river and to use the best guides and equipment. Rafts must be self-bailing, and should be running with a minimum of weight and gear on board. Professional safety kayakers should be considered a standard safety measure on this river.

A hydro project has severely affected this world-class rafting and kayaking river but it is still possible to have a two-day run on the rapids before reaching the dam. You could divert around the dam and continue on the lower section for another two days but at this stage it is hard to tell how much water will be released and whether it will be worth doing. Future dams are planned for the river so you might want to raft this one soon.

Karnali

Distance 180km

Duration 10 days (seven days rafting)

Start Dungeshwar

Finish Chisopani

Summary A classic trip in far western Nepal down its largest and longest river.

The Karnali is a gem, combining a short (two-hour) trek with some of the prettiest canyons and jungle scenery in Nepal. Most experienced river people who have paddled the Karnali find it one of the best all-round river trips they've ever done. In high water the Karnali is a serious commitment, combining huge, though fairly straightforward, rapids with a seriously remote location. The river flows through some steep and constricted canyons where the rapids are close together, giving little opportunity to correct for potential mistakes. Pick your company carefully.

At low water the Karnali is still a fantastic trip. The rapids become smaller when the river drops, but the steeper gradient and constricted channel keep it interesting.

The trip starts with a long, but interesting, two-day bus ride to the remote far west of Nepal. If you're allergic to bus rides, it's possible to fly to Nepalganj and cut the bus transport down to about four hours on the way over, and two hours on the way back. The new road now runs from Surkhet to Dungeshwar on the river. Once you start on the Karnali it's 180km to the next road access at Chisopani, on the northern border of the Bardia National Park.

The river section takes about seven days, giving plenty of time to explore some of the side canyons and waterfalls that come into the river valley. Better-run trips also include a layover day, where the expedition stays at the same campsite for two nights. The combination of long bus rides and trekking puts some people off, but anyone who has ever done the trip raves about it. Finish with a visit to the Bardia National Park for an unbeatable combination.

Adventurers can raft the even more remote **Seti Karnali**, a rarely run scenic stretch of river that starts at Gopghat and takes around seven days to get to Chisopani.

Sun Kosi

Distance 260km

Duration Eight to nine days (seven days rafting)

Start Dolalghat

Finish Chatara

Summary A self-sufficient expedition through central Nepal from the Himalaya to the Gangetic plain.

This is the longest river trip offered in Nepal, traversing 270km through the beautiful Mahabharat Range on its meandering way from the put-in at Dolalghat to the take-out at Chatara in the far east of the country. It's quite an experience to begin a river trip just three hours out of Kathmandu, barely 60km from the Tibetan border, and end the trip looking down the hot, dusty gun barrel of the north Indian plain just eight or nine days later. Because it's one of the easiest trips logistically, it's also one of the least expensive for the days you spend on a river.

The Sun Kosi (River of Gold) starts off fairly relaxed, with only class II and small class III rapids to warm up on during the first couple of days. Savvy guides will take this opportunity to get teams working together with precision.

The river volume increases with the air temperature as several major tributaries join the river, and from the third day the rapids become more powerful and frequent. During high-water trips you may well find yourselves astonished at just how big a river wave can get.

While the lower sections of large-volume rivers are usually rather flat, the Sun Kosi reserves some of its biggest and best rapids for the last days, and the last section is non-stop class IV before a final quiet float down the Sapt Kosi. Some companies add an extra day's rafting on the lower section of the Tamur, from Mulghat down.

BIKING, RAFTING & KAYAKING KARNALI

At the right flow it's an incredible combination of white water, scenery, villages, and quiet, introspective evenings.

Note that a new highway is being built alongside the top 40km of the Sun Kosi; once complete (and no one knows when this will be), it'll allow shorter six-day trips on the river and will also probably halve the return time from the take-out.

Tamur

Distance 131km

Duration 11 days

Start Dobhan

Finish Chatara

Summary Remote expedition in the foothills of Kanchenjunga in the far east of the country; includes a three-day trek.

Way out in the far east, this river combines one of the best short treks in Nepal with some really challenging white-water action. The logistics of this trip make it a real expedition, and while it is a little more complicated to run than many rivers in Nepal, the rewards are worth the effort.

First you have to get to Basantapur, a 16-hour drive from Kathmandu or a one-hour flight to Biratnagar and then a six-hour drive. Most expeditions begin with a stunning three- or four-day trek from Basantapur up over the Milke Danda Range, past the alpine lake of Gupha Pokhari to Dobhan. At Dobhan three tributaries of the Tamur join forces, combining the waters of the mountains to the north (including Kanchenjunga, the world's third-largest mountain). The first 16km of rapids is intense, with rapid after rapid, and the white water just keeps coming through towering canyons until the big finale. The best time to raft is at medium flows between mid-October and mid-November.

Understand
Nepal

Nepal Today

Over the last few decades, Nepal has endured economic hardship, a Maoist uprising that turned into a civil war, the collapse of a centuries-old monarchy, and the creation of a democratic federal republic. However, Nepal's greatest crisis of modern times was a result of geology rather than politics; the massive earthquakes that hit Nepal on 25 April and 12 May 2015 killed more than 8500 people, causing devastation across central parts of the country.

Best in Print

The Snow Leopard (Peter Matthiessen) Classic and profound account of a trek to Dolpo.

Arresting God in Kathmandu (Samrat Upadhyay) Nine short stories from the first Nepali writer to be published in English.

Snake Lake (Jeff Greenwald) Memoir of family loss set against Nepal's political revolution.

Little Princes (Conor Grennan) Moving and inspiring account of volunteering in a Nepali orphanage.

While the Gods Were Sleeping (Elizabeth Enslin) Part memoir, part-anthropological account of the author's time living as a wife in a Brahman family in western Nepal.

Kathmandu (Thomas Bell) Impressionistic historical portrait of Kathmandu from the British journalist, published in India and available in Kathmandu.

Best in Film

Himalaya (1999; Eric Valli) Stunningly shot in Dolpo; also released as *Caravan*.

Everest (1998; David Breashears) Imax film shot during the disastrous 1997 climbing season.

Destruction and Reconstruction

The tremors that shook the Kathmandu Valley in April and May 2015 saw destruction on a level that had not been seen for almost a century. Temples and palaces crumbled to dust, houses toppled, roads buckled and landslides and avalanches wiped whole villages off the map. The economic cost of the disaster has been estimated at US$10 billion, nearly half of Nepal's gross domestic product, but the human cost is even more tragic; thousands of families lost loved ones and hundreds of thousands were left homeless.

Nepal's greatest challenge over the coming years will be to rebuild lives and livelihoods. Across the country, thousands of homes and businesses need to be stabilised and repaired, and many more homes need to be built to accommodate the homeless. The tourist industry, which employs 4% of the population but indirectly supports millions more, was particularly badly hit following the disaster and bookings have collapsed in many areas. With tourism contributing nearly 10% of GDP, this is income that Nepal can ill afford to lose.

Money has flooded into Nepal from international donors since the disaster, but the country has a long way to go to raise the estimated US$6.7 billion needed for reconstruction. Nepal's recovery will depend on the resilience of its people through lean years to come, as well as the goodwill of foreign governments and the willingness of foreign travellers to look beyond the tragedy and return to Nepal's hotels, restaurants and trekking lodges.

Recovering From War

Against this backdrop, the ordinary struggles of day to day politics seem somehow less important, but Nepal is still struggling with the legacy of a decade of armed conflict. Inflation is rampant, and crumbling infrastructure, held back by years of under-investment, makes daily life a struggle for most Nepalis. Kathmandu's population, in particular, boomed during the civil war and the city is now close to breaking point, with daily electricity shortages a crippling fact of life.

Politically speaking, disappointingly little has been achieved since the end of the war. Years of deadlock and wrangling between Communist and Congress parties has resulted in the fall of six governments in six years. The political infighting has repeatedly delayed the writing of a new constitution, to the growing frustration of many Nepalis.

Since the end of the civil war the Maoists have seen a spectacular fall from grace, from winning the national election in 2008 to coming a dismal third in 2013. As former fighters start to lose political influence and contentious issues such as immunity from crimes committed during the civil war come to a head, there is always the danger that Nepali politics will return to the days of strikes and political violence.

The wounds of the People's War will doubtless take a long time to heal. Over 1000 Nepalis remain unaccounted for, victims of political 'disappearance' or simple murder, and finding justice for these crimes may prove elusive.

Economic Ups And Downs

Despite the political impasse there are signs of life in Nepal's economy. A recent spate of multibillion dollar contracts with both China and India should see some huge hydroelectric and road building projects over the coming years. India's role in developing Nepal's rivers and China's influence on Nepal's Tibetan refugee community remain hot topics as Nepal tries to juggle influences from its giant neighbours.

The Chinese presence in Nepal in particular is becoming pronounced. As road, air and eventually even train links bridge the Himalaya, Chinese tourists are becoming an essential part of the Nepali economy. Large swathes of Thamel are now devoted exclusively to Chinese tourists and Nepal's ever-adaptable guides and touts are rapidly learning the new language.

Tourism remains essential to Nepal's economy, employing around one million people directly or indirectly, and things are once again booming. Hotels and restaurants are crammed to capacity and funds are being poured into infrastructure and hotel construction.

Twin tragedies shook the tourism industry in 2014. In April 16 Sherpas were killed on the Khumbu icefall, shutting down Everest climbing for a season as Sherpa families sought compensation in a labour dispute with the government. Just six months later a blizzard in central Nepal killed 43 trekkers and guides in the Annapurna region, turning a spotlight on mountain safety and renewing calls for tighter controls on Nepal's trekking industry.

A long-term problem for Nepal is the large numbers of Nepalis heading abroad every year in the search for work and opportunities. Remittances remain the number one source of foreign currency for Nepal, dwarfing tourism, but halting the brain drain is essential to the country's future.

POPULATION: 31 MILLION (2014 ESTIMATE)

AREA: **147,181 SQ KM**

LIFE EXPECTANCY: **67 YEARS**

ADULT LITERACY RATE: **57%**

GROSS NATIONAL INCOME: **US$730 PER CAPITA**

AVERAGE AGE: **23 YEARS**

if Nepal were 100 people

16 would be Chhetri
13 would be Brahman-Hill
7 would be Magar
7 would be Tharu
57 Tamang, Newar & Other Groups

belief systems
(% of population)

81 Hindu · 9 Buddhist · 4 Muslim · 3 Kirant · 3 Other

population per sq km

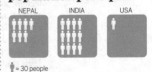

NEPAL · INDIA · USA

≈ 30 people

History

Squeezed between the Tibetan plateau and the plains of the subcontinent – the modern-day giants of China and India – Nepal has long prospered from its location as a resting place for mountain traders, travellers and pilgrims. An ethnic melting pot, it has bridged cultures and absorbed elements of its neighbours, yet has retained a unique character. Despite ancient roots, the modern state of Nepal emerged only in the 18th century and is still forging itself as a modern nation state.

The Kiratis & Buddhist Beginnings

Nepal's recorded history emerges from the fog of antiquity with the Hindu Kiratis. Arriving from the east around the 7th or 8th century BC, these Mongoloid people are the earliest known rulers of the Kathmandu Valley. King Yalambar, the first of their 29 kings, is mentioned in the Mahabharata, the Hindu epic, but little more is known about the Kiratis.

In the 6th century BC, Prince Siddhartha Gautama was born into the Sakya royal family of Kapilavastu, near Lumbini, later embarking on a path of meditation and thought that led him to enlightenment as the Buddha, or 'Enlightened One'. The religion that grew up around him continues to shape the face of Asia.

Around the 3rd century BC, the great Indian Buddhist emperor Ashoka visited Lumbini and erected a pillar at the birthplace of the Buddha. Popular legend recounts how he then visited the Kathmandu Valley and erected four stupas around Patan (these still exist), but there is no evidence that he actually made it there in person. Either way, his Mauryan empire (321–184 BC) played a major role in popularising Buddhism in the region, a role continued by the north Indian Buddhist Kushan empire, which spanned the 1st to 3rd centuries AD.

Over the centuries the resurgent faith of Hinduism came to eclipse Buddhism across the entire subcontinent. By the time the Chinese Buddhist pilgrims Fa Xian (Fa Hsien) and Xuan Zang (Hsuan Tsang) passed through the region in the 5th and 7th centuries the site of Lumbini was already in ruins.

References for most things in Nepal are notoriously inconsistent. Spellings, statistics, historical dates and temple names always have several variants. We use the most commonly agreed options, with alternative names in brackets.

TIMELINE	60 million BC	100,000 BC	c 563 BC
	The Himalaya rise as the Indo-Australian tectonic plate crashes into the Eurasian plate. The Tethys Sea is pushed up, resulting in sea shells atop Mt Everest and fossilised ammonites in the Kali Gandaki Valley.	Kathmandu Valley is created as a former lake bed dries. Legend relates how the Buddhist Bodhisattva Manjushri created the valley by cutting the Chobar Gorge and draining the lake's waters.	Siddhartha Gautama is born in Lumbini into royalty and lives as both prince and ascetic in Nepal before gaining enlightenment, as the Buddha, under a Bodhi (pipal) tree.

Licchavis, Thakuris, then Darkness

Hinduism reasserted itself in Nepal with the arrival from northern India of the Licchavis. In AD 300 they overthrew the Kiratis, who resettled in the east to become the ancestors of today's Rai and Limbu people.

Between the 4th and 9th centuries the Licchavis ushered in a golden age of cultural brilliance. Their strategic position allowed them to prosper from trade between India and China. The chaitya (a style of stupa) and monuments of this era can still be seen at the Changu Narayan Temple, north of Bhaktapur, and in the backstreets of Kathmandu's old town. It's believed that the original stupas at Chabahil, Bodhnath and Swayambhunath date from the Licchavi era.

Amsuvarman, the first Thakuri king, came to power in 602, succeeding his Licchavi father-in-law. He consolidated his power to the north and south by marrying his sister to an Indian prince and his daughter Bhrikuti to the great Tibetan king Songsten Gampo. Together with the Tibetan king's Chinese wife Wencheng, Bhrikuti managed to convert the Tibetan king to Buddhism around 640, profoundly changing the face of both Tibet and the Himalaya. As Buddhism lost ground in India, Buddhism's key texts and concepts would eventually return to Nepal from Tibet across the high Himalayan passes.

From the late 7th century until the 13th century, Nepal slipped into its 'dark ages', of which little is known. Tibet invaded in 705 and Kashmir invaded in 782. The Kathmandu Valley's strategic location and fertile soil, however, ensured the kingdom's growth and survival. King Gunakamadeva is credited with founding Kantipur, today's Kathmandu, around the 10th century.

The Golden Age of the Mallas

The first of the Malla (literally 'wrestlers' in Sanskrit) kings came to power in the Kathmandu Valley around 1200, after being exiled from India. This period was a golden one that stretched over 550 years, though it was peppered with fighting over the valuable trade routes to Tibet.

The first Malla rulers had to cope with several disasters. A huge earthquake in 1255 killed around one-third of Nepal's population. A devastating Muslim invasion by Sultan Shams-ud-din of Bengal less than a century later left hundreds of smouldering and plundered Hindu and Buddhist shrines in its wake, though the invasion did not leave a lasting cultural effect (unlike the invasion of the Kashmir Valley, which remains Muslim to this day). In India the damage was more widespread and many Hindus were driven into the hills and mountains of Nepal, where they established small Rajput principalities.

Travellers can visit the archaeological site of Kapilavastu, at Tilaurakot, where Siddhartha Gautama (the Buddha) lived for the first 29 years of his life.

In 2013 archaeologists unearthed a sixth-century BC shrine underneath Lumbini's Maya Devi shrine, making this the earliest Buddhist shrine ever uncovered. Within the shrine were the remains of a tree, possibly the tree that Maya held onto when giving birth to Siddhartha (the Buddha).

c 250 BC	57 BC	AD 464	629
Mauryan Emperor Ashoka (r 268–231 BC) visits Lumbini, embraces Buddhism and reputedly builds four stupas on the outskirts of Patan, ushering in a golden age for Buddhism.	Nepal's official Vikram (Bikram) Samwat calendar starts, in spring. Thus to Nepalis the year 2016 is 2073.	Nepal's earliest surviving inscription is carved into the beautiful Changu Narayan Temple in the Kathmandu Valley on the orders of King Manadeva.	The Chinese Buddhist pilgrim Xuan Zang (Hsuan Tsang) visits Lumbini and describes the Ashoka pillar marking the Buddha's birthplace. His text helps archaeologists relocate and excavate the lost site in 1895.

Apart from this, the earlier Malla years (1220–1482) were largely stable, reaching a high point under the third Malla dynasty of Jayasthithi Malla (r 1382–95), who united the valley and codified its laws, including the caste system.

After the death of Jayasthithi Malla's grandson Yaksha Malla in 1482, the Kathmandu Valley was divided up among his sons into the three kingdoms of Bhaktapur (Bhadgaon), Kathmandu (Kantipur) and Patan (Lalitpur). The rest of what we today call Nepal consisted of a fragmented patchwork of almost 50 independent states, stretching from Palpa and Jumla in the west to the semi-independent states of Banepa and Pharping, most of them minting their own coins and maintaining standing armies.

The rivalry between the three kingdoms of the Kathmandu Valley expressed itself not only through warfare but also through the patronage of architecture and culture, which flourished in the climate of jealous one-upmanship. The outstanding collections of exquisite temples and buildings in each city's Durbar Sq are testament to the fortunes spent by the kings in their attempts to outdo each other.

The building boom was financed by trade, in everything from musk and wool to salt and Chinese silk. The Kathmandu Valley stood at the departure point for two separate routes into Tibet, via Banepa to the northeast and via Rasuwa and the Kyirong Valley near Langtang to the northwest. Traders would cross the jungle-infested Terai during winter to avoid the virulent malaria and then wait in Kathmandu for the mountain passes to open later that summer. Kathmandu grew rich, and its rulers converted their wealth into gilded pagodas and ornately carved royal palaces. In the mid-17th century Nepal gained the right to mint Tibet's coins using Tibetan silver, further enriching the kingdom's coffers.

In Kathmandu, King Pratap Malla (1641–74) oversaw that city's cultural high point with the construction of the Hanuman Dhoka palace and the Rani Pokhari pond. He also built the first of several subsequent pillars that featured a statue of the king facing the protective temple of Taleju, who the Mallas had by that point adopted as their protective deity. The mid-17th century also saw a high point of building in Patan.

The Malla era shaped the religious as well as the artistic landscape, introducing the dramatic annual chariot festivals of Indra Jatra and Machhendranath. The Malla kings shored up their divine right to rule by claiming to be reincarnations of the Hindu god Vishnu and by establishing the cult of the Kumari, a living goddess whose role it was to bless the Malla's rule during an annual celebration.

The cosmopolitan Mallas also absorbed foreign influences. The Indian Mughal court influenced Malla dress and painting, introduced the Nep-

A History of Nepal by John Whelpton is one of the few available titles on the subject. It focuses on the last 250 years and explains not only political events but also the changes in people's lives. It's for sale in Nepal at a discounted local price.

The mid-14th century saw the de facto rule of Malla Queen Devaladevi, the most powerful woman in Nepal's history.

879	c 1260	1200–1500	1349
The Newari lunar calendar, the Nepal Samvat, is introduced as the national calendar and used officially until the late 18th century. It is still used for Newari festivals in the Kathmandu Valley.	Nepali architect Arniko travels to Lhasa and Kublai Khan's capital Dadu (Beijing), bringing with him the design of the pagoda and changing the face of religious temples across Asia.	The Khasa empire of the western Mallas reaches its peak in the far western Karnali basin around Jumla. Its lasting contribution is Nepali – the national language spoken today.	Muslim armies of Sultan Shams-ud-din plunder the Kathmandu Valley, destroying the stupa at Swayambhunath and carrying off cartloads of booty.

alis to firearms and exported the system of land grants in return for military service, a system that would have a profound effect in later years.

But change didn't only come from abroad. A storm was brewing inside Nepal, just 100km to the east of Kathmandu.

Unification under the Shahs

In 1768 Prithvi Narayan Shah, ruler of the tiny hilltop kingdom of Gorkha (halfway between Pokhara and Kathmandu), stood poised on the edge of the Kathmandu Valley, ready to realise his dream of a unified Nepal. It had taken more than a quarter of a century of conquest and consolidation to get here but Shah was about to redraw the political landscape of the Himalaya.

Shah had taken the strategic hilltop fort of Nuwakot in 1744, after fighting off reinforcements from the British East India Company, but it took him another 24 years to take Kathmandu, finally sneaking in while everyone was drunk during the Indra Jatra festival. A year later he eventually took Kirtipur, after three lengthy failed attempts. In terrible retribution his troops hacked over 50kg of noses and lips off Kirtipur's residents; unsurprisingly, resistance melted away in the wake of the atrocity. In 1769 he advanced on the three cowering Malla kings and ended the Malla rule, thus unifying Nepal.

Shah moved his capital from Gorkha to Kathmandu, establishing the Shah dynasty, whose line continued right up until 2008. Shah himself, however, did not live long after his conquest; he died in Nuwakot in 1775, just six years after unification, but is still revered as the founder of the nation.

Shah had built his empire on conquest, and his insatiable army needed ever more booty and land to keep it satisfied. Within six years the Gurkhas had conquered eastern Nepal and Sikkim. The expansion then turned westwards into Kumaon and Garhwal, only halted on the borders of the Punjab by the armies of the powerful one-eyed ruler Ranjit Singh.

The expanding boundaries of 'Greater Nepal' by this time stretched from Kashmir to Sikkim, eventually putting it on a collision course with the world's most powerful empire, the British Raj. Despite early treaties with the British, disputes over the Terai led to the first Anglo-Nepali War, which the British won after a two-year fight. The British were so impressed by their enemy that they decided to incorporate Gurkha mercenaries into their own army, a practice that continues to this day (Gurkha troops served recently in Iraq and Afghanistan).

The 1816 Sugauli treaty called a screeching halt to Nepal's expansion and laid down its modern boundaries. Nepal lost Sikkim, Kumaon, Garhwal and much of the Terai, though some of this land was restored to Nepal in 1858 in return for support given to the British during the Indian

> Nepal's flag is like no other, consisting of two overlapping red triangles, bearing a white moon and a white 12-pointed sun (the first mythological kings of Nepal are said to be descendants of the sun and moon).

> Nepal's founding father, Prithvi Narayan Shah, referred to Nepal as 'a yam between two boulders' – namely China and India – a metaphor that is as true geologically as it is historically.

1380	1428–82	1531–34	1641–74
Ame Pal founds the kingdom of Lo (Mustang). The present king of Mustang, Jigme Palbar Bista, traces his family back 25 generations to this king. Mustang remains an independent kingdom until 1951.	The rule of Yaksha Malla, the high point of the Malla reign, ends in the fracture of the Kathmandu Valley into the three rival kingdoms of Kathmandu, Patan and Bhaktapur.	Sherpas (literally 'easterners') settle in the Solu-Khumbu region near Mt Everest. The Nangpa La remains the most important Sherpa trade route with Tibet.	Rule of Malla king Pratap Malla, a dancer, poet and great supporter of arts, who shapes the face of Kathmandu, building large parts of Hanuman Dhoka palace.

Mutiny (Indian War of Independence). A British resident was sent to Kathmandu to keep an eye on things but the British knew that it would be too difficult to colonise the impossible hill terrain and were content to keep Nepal as a buffer state. Nepalis to this day are proud that their country was never colonised by the British, unlike the neighbouring hill states of India.

Following its humiliating defeat, Nepal cut itself off from all foreign contact from 1816 until 1951. The British residents in Kathmandu were the only Westerners to set eyes on Nepal for more than a century.

On the cultural front, temple construction continued apace, though perhaps of more import to ordinary people was the revolutionary introduction, via India, of chillies, potatoes, tobacco and other New World crops.

The Shah rulers, meanwhile, swung from ineffectual to sadistic. At one point the kingdom was governed by a 12-year-old female regent, in charge of a nine-year-old king, while Crown Prince Surendra (r 1847–81) expanded the horizons of human suffering by ordering subjects to jump down wells or ride off cliffs, just to see whether they would survive.

The Ranocracy

The death of Prithvi Narayan Shah in 1775 set in motion a string of succession struggles, infighting, assassinations, backstabbing and intrigue that culminated in the Kot Massacre in 1846. This blood-stained night was engineered by the young Chhetri noble Jung Bahadur and it catapulted his family into power, just as it sidelined the Shah dynasty.

Ambitious and ruthless, Jung Bahadur organised (with the queen's consent) for his soldiers to massacre 55 of the most important noblemen in the kingdom in one night, while they were assembled in the Kot courtyard adjoining Kathmandu's Durbar Sq. He then exiled 6000 members of their families to prevent revenge attacks.

Jung Bahadur took the title of prime minister and changed his family name to the more prestigious 'Rana'. He later extended his title to *maharajah* (king) and decreed it hereditary. The Ranas became a parallel 'royal family' within the kingdom and held the reins of power, as the Shah kings were relegated to listless, irrelevant figureheads, requiring permission even to leave their palace.

The family line of Rana prime ministers held power for more than a century, eventually intermarrying with the Shahs. Development in Nepal stagnated, although the country did at least manage to preserve its independence.

Jung Bahadur Rana travelled to Europe in 1850, attending the opera and the races at Epsom, and brought back a taste for neoclassical architecture that can be seen in Kathmandu today. Under the Ranas, *sati* (the

The first cars were transported to the Kathmandu Valley in parts, on the backs of porters, before there were even any roads or petrol in the kingdom. You can see one of these, an early Hudson, at Kathmandu's National Museum.

For a impressionistic historical portrait of Kathmandu check out journalist Thomas Bell's kaleidoscopic *Kathmandu*, published in India and available in Kathmandu.

18th century	1729	1750	1768–69
Capuchin missionaries pass through Nepal to Tibet, later supplying the West with its first descriptions of exotic Kathmandu.	The three kingdoms of the Kathmandu Valley send presents to the Qing court in Beijing, which from then on views Nepal as a tributary state.	King Jaya Prakash Malla builds Kathmandu's Kumari Temple, followed by the Nyatapola Temple in Bhaktapur, the literal high point of stupa-style architecture in Nepal.	Nepal is unified under Prithvi Narayan Shah (1723–75), known as the father of the Nepali nation, to form the Shah dynasty. Kathmandu becomes the capital.

Hindu practice of casting a widow on her husband's funeral pyre) was abolished, 60,000 slaves were released from bondage, and a school and college were established in the capital. Despite the advances, the peasants in the hills were locked in a medieval existence, while the Ranas and their relatives lived lives of opulent luxury.

Modernisation began to dawn on Kathmandu with the opening of the Bir Hospital, Nepal's first, in 1889. Over the next 15 years Kathmandu saw its first piped water system, the introduction of limited electricity and the construction of the Singh Durbar, considered at one time the largest palace in Asia. The 29-year reign (1901–29) of Prime Minister Chandra Shumsher in particular brought sweeping changes, including the introduction of electricity and the outlawing of slavery. In 1923 Britain formally acknowledged Nepal's independence and in 1930 the kingdom of Gorkha was renamed the kingdom of Nepal, reflecting a growing sense of national consciousness.

Elsewhere in the region dramatic changes were taking place. The Nepalis supplied logistical help during Britain's invasion of Tibet in 1903, and over 300,000 Nepalis fought in WWI and WWII, garnering a total of 13 Victoria Crosses – Britain's highest military honour – for their efforts.

After WWII, India gained its independence and the communist revolution took place in China. Tibetan refugees fled into Nepal in the first of several waves when the new People's Republic of China tightened its grip on Tibet, and Nepal became a buffer zone between the two rival Asian giants. Meanwhile King Tribhuvan, forgotten in his palace, was being primed to overthrow the Ranas.

> You can visit the birthplace and launching pad of Nepal's unifier, Prithvi Narayan Shah, at Gorkha, and see his second royal palace at Nuwakot.

Restoration of the Shahs

In late 1950 King Tribhuvan was driving himself to a hunting trip at Nagarjun when he suddenly swerved James Bond–style into the Indian embassy, where he then claimed political immunity and jumped into an Indian Air Force jet to Delhi. At the same time, the recently formed Nepali Congress Party, led by BP Koirala, managed to take most of the Terai by force from the Ranas and established a provisional government that ruled from the border town of Birganj. India exerted its considerable influence and negotiated a solution to Nepal's turmoil, and King Tribhuvan returned in glory to Nepal in 1951 to set up a new government composed of demoted Ranas and members of the Nepali Congress Party.

Although Nepal gradually reopened its long-closed doors and established relations with other nations, dreams of a new democratic system never quite got off the ground. Tribhuvan died in 1955 and was succeeded by his cautious son Mahendra. A new constitution provided for a parliamentary system of government, resulting in Nepal's first ever general election in 1959. The Nepali Congress Party won a clear victory and BP

1790–92	1814–16	1815	1846
Nepal invades Tibet and sacks Shigatse. Avenging Chinese troops advance down the Kyirong Valley as far as Nuwakot. As part of the ensuing treaty the Nepalis pay tribute to the Chinese emperor until 1912.	Anglo-Nepali War ends in victory for Britain. The ensuing Treaty of Sugauli establishes Nepal's boundaries and gives Britain the right to recruit Gurkha soldiers and maintain a residency in Kathmandu.	5000 Nepali soldiers begin serving as troops in the East India Company after impressing the British with their valour and loyalty.	The Kot Massacre ends in the killing of the cream of the court aristocracy, ushering in the Rana era (1846–1951) and sidelining the Shah kings to puppet status.

Koirala became the new prime minister. In late 1960, however, the king decided the government wasn't to his taste after all, had the cabinet arrested and swapped his ceremonial role for direct control (much as King Gyanendra would do 46 years later).

In 1962 Mahendra decided that a partyless, indirect *panchayat* (council) system of government was more appropriate to Nepal. The real power remained with the king, who chose 16 members out of the 35-member National Panchayat, and appointed both the prime minister and his cabinet. Political parties were banned.

Mahendra died in 1972 and was succeeded by his 27-year-old British-educated son Birendra. Nepal's hippie community was unceremoniously booted out of the country when visa laws were tightened in the run-up to Birendra's spectacular coronation in 1975. Simmering discontent with corruption, the slow rate of development and the rising cost of living erupted into violent riots in Kathmandu in 1979. King Birendra announced a referendum to choose between the *panchayat* system and one that would permit political parties to operate. The result was 55% to 45% in favour of the *panchayat* system; democracy had been outvoted.

Nepal's military and police apparatus were among the least publicly accountable in the world and strict censorship was enforced. Mass arrests, torture and beatings of suspected activists were well documented, and the leaders of the main opposition, the Nepali Congress, spent the years between 1960 and 1990 in and out of prison.

During this time over one million hill people moved to the Terai in search of land and several million crossed the border to seek work in India (Nepalis are able to cross the border and work freely in India), creating a major demographic shift in favour of the now malaria-free Terai.

People Power

In 1989, as communist states across Europe crumbled and pro-democracy demonstrations occupied China's Tiananmen Sq, Nepali opposition parties formed a coalition to fight for a multiparty democracy with the king as constitutional head; the upsurge of protest was called the Jana Andolan, or People's Movement.

In early 1990 the government responded to a nonviolent gathering of over 200,000 people with bullets, tear gas and thousands of arrests. After several months of intermittent rioting, curfews, a successful strike and pressure from various foreign-aid donors, the government was forced to back down. On 9 April King Birendra announced he was lifting the ban on political parties and was ready to accept the role of constitutional monarch. Nepal had become a democracy.

In May 1991 the Nepali Congress Party won the general election and two years later a midterm election resulted in a coalition government led

For some interesting historical snippets check out the blog www.historylessonsnepal.blogspot.co.uk.

1850	1854	1856	1911
Jung Bahadur Rana travels to Europe, becoming the first Nepali ruler to cross the *kalo pani* (black water, or ocean) and thus temporarily losing his caste.	The Muluki Ain legal code formalises the Nepali caste system, defining diet, legal and sexual codes and enshrining state discrimination against lower castes. The law is revised only in 1963.	Peak XV is declared the world's highest peak. It is later renamed Everest after the head of Trigonometric Survey, George Everest (who actually pronounced his name eve-rest).	King George V visits the Terai on a hunting trip as a guest of the maharajah of Nepal, bagging 39 tigers and 18 rhinos, travelling with a small army of beaters.

by the Communist Party. This was one of the few times in the world that a communist government had come to power by popular vote.

Political stability did not last long, and the late 1990s were littered with dozens of broken coalitions, dissolved governments and sacked politicians. After a decade of democracy it seemed an increasing number of people, particularly young Nepalis and those living in the countryside, were utterly disillusioned.

The People's War

In 1996 the Maoists, a Communist-party splinter group, angered by government corruption, the dissolution of the communist government and the failure of democracy to deliver improvements to the people, declared a 'people's war'. The Maoists presented the then prime minister with a 40-point charter of demands that ranged from preferential state policies towards backward communities to an assertive Nepali identity, an end to privately funded schools and better governance.

The insurgency began in the Rolpa district of midwestern Nepal and gathered momentum, but it was initially ignored by Kathmandu's politicians. The repercussions of this nonchalance finally came to a head in November 2001 when the Maoists broke their ceasefire and attacked an army barracks west of Kathmandu. The initial Maoist forces were armed with little more than ancient muskets and *khukuris* (Gurkha knives) but

For background on the Maoist rebellion read *Himalayan People's War: Nepal's Maoist Rebellion*, edited by Michael Hutt.

TRANS-HIMALAYAN TRADE

For centuries, hardy caravans of yaks and goats criss-crossed the high Himalaya, bringing salt harvested from Tibet's great inland lakes to exchange for rice and barley carried up from the Middle Hills of Nepal. Wool, livestock and butter from Tibet were exchanged for sugar, tea, spices, tobacco and Indian manufactured goods. Twelve major passes linked Nepal and Tibet, the easiest of which were in Mustang, ensuring that the Kali Gandaki Valley became the main entrepôt for transferring, storing and taxing the trade.

Over the last half-century much of the traditional border trade has dried up. The arrival of the Indian railway line at the Nepali border greatly aided the transportation of cheap Indian salt, sounding a death knell for the caravan trade. The real nail in the coffin came in the 1960s, when the Chinese closed the borders to local trade.

Ironically the Chinese are currently leading a resurgence of trade and road construction. Chinese truckers now drive over the passes to Lo Manthang in Mustang and in 2012 another road border crossing opened at Rasuwaghadi, linking the Tibetan Kyirong Valley with Nepal's Langtang region along a route long used for trade and invasion. You'll see the occasional yak caravan headed for the Tibetan border laden with timber and the medicinal root *yartse gumba,* as well as telltale cans of Lhasa Beer littering trekking routes in the Manaslu, Everest and Mustang regions.

1914–18	1934	1949	1951
Around 100,000 Nepalis fight and 10,000 lose their lives in WWI. Thirty years later 200,000 Gurkha and army forces serve in WWII, mostly in Myanmar (Burma).	A massive earthquake destroys much of the Kathmandu Valley, killing over 8000 people in under a minute, injuring 16,000 and destroying a quarter of all homes in Nepal.	Bill Tilman gets permission from King Tribhuvan to trek in Nepal, including around the Kali Gandaki, Helambu and Solu-Khumbu regions. He is the first foreigner to trek to Everest Base Camp.	King Tribhuvan and the Nepali Congress Party, with Indian support, overthrow the Rana regime and establish a new coalition government. Nepal opens its doors to the outside world.

they quickly obtained guns looted from police stations, homemade explosives and automatic weapons, all bankrolled by robbery and extortion (in September 2000 Maoists stole Rs 50 million from a bank in Dolpo) and aided by an open border with India.

Initial police heavy-handedness fuelled a cycle of violence and retribution that only succeeded in alienating the local people. Political disenfranchisement, rural poverty, resentment against the caste system, issues of land reform and a lack of faith in the squabbling, self-interested politicians of distant Kathmandu swelled the ranks of the Maoists, who at their peak numbered 15,000 fighters, with a further militia of 50,000. Attacks spread to almost every one of Nepal's 75 districts, including Kathmandu. At their peak Maoists effectively controlled around 40% of the country, including two protected areas in the far west and several of Nepal's main trekking routes (for years trekkers in the Annapurna region were forced to hand over 'donations' to Maoist gangs).

The political temperature reached boiling point when the king brought in the army and armed militias loyal to the government in 2001. The USA labelled Nepal's Maoists a terrorist group and handed over millions of dollars to help fight Nepal's own 'war on terror'. Although they were self-declared Maoists, the group owed more to Peru's Sendero Luminoso (Shining Path) than to any Chinese connection. Ironically the 'people's' armed struggle was led by two high-caste intellectuals: Pushpa Kamal Dahal (known by his *nom de guerre* Prachanda, which means 'the fierce') and Baburam Bhattarai, both of whom would later serve as Nepal's prime minister.

One early victim of the war was the freedom of the Nepali press. Between 2002 and 2005 more journalists were arrested in Nepal than in any other country and in 2005 Reporters Sans Frontiers described Nepal's media as the world's most censored.

Several Maoist truces, notably in 2003 and 2005, offered some respite, though these reflected as much a need to regroup and rearm as they did any move towards a lasting peace. By 2005 nearly 13,000 people, including many civilians, had been killed in the insurgency. Amnesty International accused both sides of horrific human-rights abuses, including summary executions, abductions, torture and child conscription. Dark days had come to Nepal.

Stalled Development & the Failure of Aid

During the second half of the 20th century Nepal saw impressive movements towards development, namely in education and road construction, with the number of schools increasing from 300 in 1950 to over 40,000 by 2000. Since then relentless population growth (Nepal's population grew from 8.4 million in 1954 to 26 million in 2004) has simply

Forget Kathmandu: An Elegy for Democracy, by Manjushree Thapa, starts with Nepal's royal massacre, moves to a political history of the last 200 years, then ends with a description of a trek through Maoist-held areas in 2003.

Nepal is said to get its name from Nepa, the name given to the Newari kingdom of the Kathmandu Valley; the word Nepa is derived from the name of a mythological Hindu sage, Ne, who once lived in the valley.

1953	1954	1955–72	1959
Everest is summited for the first time by New Zealander Edmund Hillary and Tibetan Sherpa Tenzing Norgay on 29 May, just in time for the coronation of Queen Elizabeth II.	Boris Lissanevitch establishes Nepal's first hotel, the Royal, in the Bahadur Bhawan palace. Its Yak and Yeti Bar becomes the expat hub for mountaineers and diplomats until its closure in 1971.	The rule of King Mahendra sees the introduction of elections, which are then voided as the king seizes direct power, introducing the *panchayat* system of government.	Nepal's first general election is held. The Dalai Lama flees Tibet and China closes the Tibet–Nepal border, seriously affecting the trade of salt for grain and creating great social change in the Himalaya.

cancelled out many of these advances, turning Nepal from a food exporter to a net importer within a generation.

The Maoist insurgency only worsened the plight of the rural poor by bombing bridges and telephone lines, halting road construction, diverting much-needed government funds away from development and causing aid programs to suspend activity due to security concerns. It is estimated that during the decade-long conflict the Maoists destroyed Rs 30 billion of government infrastructure, while the government blew US$108 billion on military spending. Caught in the middle, an entire generation of rural Nepali children missed out on their education.

After a half-century of outside assistance and more than US$4 billion in aid (60% of its development budget), Nepal remains one of the world's 10 poorest countries, with the highest income disparity in Asia and one of its lowest health-spending levels. Seven million Nepalis lack adequate food or basic health care and education.

Royal Troubles & Political Change

On 1 June 2001 the Nepali psyche was dealt a huge blow when Crown Prince Dipendra gunned down almost every member of the royal family during a get-together in Kathmandu. Ironically Dipendra did not die straight away and was pronounced the king of Nepal, despite being in a coma. His rule ended two days later, when he too was declared dead. King Birendra's brother Gyanendra was then crowned in what may for him have been a moment of déjà vu – he had already been crowned once before, aged three, and ruled as king for three months, after his grandfather Tribhuvan fled to India in 1950.

In the days that followed the massacre, a tide of emotions washed over the Nepali people – shock, grief, horror, disbelief and denial. A 13-day period of mourning was declared and in Kathmandu impromptu shrines were set up for people to pray for their king and queen. About 400 shaven-headed men roamed the streets around the palace on motorbikes, carrying pictures of the monarch. Half a million stunned Nepalis lined the streets during the funeral procession. When the shock of this loss subsided the uncertainty of what lay ahead hit home.

The beginning of the 21st century saw the political situation in the country turn from bad to worse. Prime ministers were sacked and replaced six times between 2000 and 2005, marking a total of nine governments in 10 years. The fragile position of Nepali politicians is well illustrated by Sher Bahadur Deuba, who was appointed prime minister for the second time in 2001, before being dismissed in 2002, reinstated in 2004, sacked again in 2005, thrown in jail on corruption charges and then released.

Confusingly, three Koirala brothers have all served as prime ministers of Nepal; BP Koirala in 1959, MP Koirala in 1951 and 1953 and GP Koirala, four times, most recently in 2006. Their cousin Sushil Koirala was prime minister in 2015.

Massacre at the Palace: The Doomed Royal Dynasty of Nepal, by Jonathan Gregson, takes a wider look at Nepal's royal family and reveals that assassination and murder have been part of royal life for centuries; it also examines the recent massacre. Also published as *Blood Against the Snows.*

1960	1965	1975	1990
Eradication of malaria opens the Terai to rapid population growth. Today the Terai contains around half of Nepal's population and most of its industry and agricultural land.	Colonel James 'Jimmy' Roberts founds Mountain Travel, Nepal's first trekking company, and leads a group of women up the Kali Gandaki Valley, laying the path for Nepal's trekking industry.	Birendra is crowned king in Kathmandu's Hanuman Dhoka, three years after the death of his father Mahendra. The king wears the traditional jewel-encrusted and feathered headdress of the Shah kings.	The mass demonstrations of the People's Movement force King Birendra to accept a new constitution, restoring democracy and relegating the king to the role of constitutional Hindu monarch.

Nepal's disappointing experiment with democracy faced a major setback in February 2005 when King Gyanendra dissolved the government amid a state of emergency, promising a return to democracy within three years. Freedom of the press was curtailed and telephone lines were cut periodically to prevent demonstrations. Tourism levels slumped and a mood of pessimism descended over the country.

Everything changed in April 2006, when days of mass demonstrations, curfews and the deaths of 16 protestors forced the king to restore parliamentary democracy. The following month the newly restored parliament voted to reduce the king to a figurehead, ending powers that the royal Shah lineage had enjoyed for over 200 years. The removal of the king was the price required to bring the Maoists to the negotiating table,

THE ROYAL MASSACRE

The night of 1 June 2001 has entered the annals of history as one of Nepal's greatest tragedies, a bloodbath that could have been lifted straight from the pages of Shakespeare.

That night, in a hail of bullets, 10 members of Nepal's royal family, including King Birendra and Queen Aishwarya, were gunned down during a gathering at the Narayanhiti Palace by a deranged, drunken Crown Prince Dipendra, who eventually turned a weapon on himself. The real motive behind the massacre will never be known, but many believe Dipendra's rage was prompted by his parents' disapproval of the woman he wanted to marry.

The initial disbelief and shock gave way to suspicion and a host of conspiracy theories, many concerning the new king, Gyanendra (who was in Pokhara at the time of the massacre), and his son Paras (who emerged unscathed from the attack). None of this was helped by an official inquiry that initially suggested the automatic weapon had been discharged by accident, or the fact that the victims were quickly cremated without full post-mortems and the palace building then razed to the ground. Other theories included that old chestnut – a CIA or Indian secret-service plot.

A surreal royal exorcism followed on the 11th day of mourning, as a high-caste priest, dressed in the gold suit, shoes and black-rimmed glasses of King Birendra and donning a paper crown, climbed onto an elephant and slowly lumbered out of the valley, taking with him the ghost of the dead king. The same scapegoat ritual (known as a *katto* ceremony) was performed for Dipendra, except that a pregnant woman dashed underneath his elephant en route, believing this would ensure she give birth to a boy. She was trampled by the elephant and died, adding a further twist to the tragedy.

Doubtless, the truth of what really happened that night will never be known. In the words of Nepali journalist Manjushree Thapa: 'We lost the truth; we lost our history. We are left to recount anecdotes and stories, to content ourselves with myth.'

1996–2006	May 1996	June 2001	Feb 2005
A decade-long Maoist insurgency brings the country to its knees and results in the death of 13,000 Nepalis. Development projects stall and tourism levels plummet.	Eight climbers die on a single day, May 11, on Everest, making this the single worst year for Everest fatalities. An Imax film and Jon Krakauer's book *Into Thin Air* chronicle the disaster.	Prince Dipendra massacres 10 members of the royal family in the Narayanhiti Palace, including his father, King Birendra, before shooting himself. The king's brother, Gyanendra, is crowned king of Nepal.	King Gyanendra dismisses the government and assumes direct control of the country in a state of emergency, citing the need to crush the Maoist rebels.

and a peace accord was signed later that year, drawing a close to the bloody decade-long insurgency.

The ensuing pace of political change in Nepal was head-spinning. One month after the Maoists achieved a majority in the April 2008 elections parliament abolished the monarchy completely by a margin of 560 votes to four, ending 240 years of royal rule. The new government saw former guerrilla leader Pushpa Kamal Dahal as prime minister and Dr Baburam Bhattarai as finance minister. In 2009 Pushpa Kamal Dahal resigned due to infighting, hinting at political turmoil to come.

Former Maoist 'terrorists' became cabinet ministers, members of the People's Liberation Army joined the national army and a new constitution was commissioned (though close to a decade later it has still to be written), all as part of a process to bind the former guerrillas into the political mainstream. After a decade of darkness, violence and social upheaval, a renewed optimism in the political process was palpable throughout Nepal. It remains to be seen whether this spirit of optimism can survive the ongoing political wrangles and the economic uncertainty that Nepal now faces after the worst earthquake in nearly a century (see p000).

Following the 2008 abolition of the monarchy, the king's face was removed from the Rs 10 note, the prefix 'Royal' disappeared from the name of the national airline as well as national parks, and the king's birthday was dumped as a national holiday.

2006	May 2008	2014	April 2015
After weeks of protests, King Gyanendra reinstates parliament, which votes to curtail his emergency powers. Maoists and government officials sign a peace agreement and the Maoist rebels enter an interim government.	Parliament abolishes the Nepali monarchy, ending 240 years of royal rule.	Twin disasters hit Nepal's mountains. On April 16 Sherpa guides are killed on the Khumbu icefall in Everest's single deadliest disaster. In October 43 trekkers and porters die after heavy snowfall in the Annapurna region.	A massive 7.8-magnitude earthquake strikes central Nepal, killing 8500 and causing devastation across the Kathmandu Valley.

People & Culture

Nepal's location between India and Tibet, the diversity of its 60 or more ethnic and caste groups, its isolating geography and myriad (up to 123) languages have resulted in a complex mosaic of customs and beliefs that make it hard to generalise about a 'Nepali people'. Yet visitors are unanimous in praising the gentle and hospitable nature of the hardy people that inhabit this spectacular and physically challenging country.

The National Psyche

Perhaps the dominant Nepali cultural concepts are those of caste and status, both of which contribute to a strictly defined system of social hierarchy and deference. Caste determines not only a person's status, but also their career and marriage partner, how that person interacts with other Nepalis and how others react back. This system of hierarchy extends even to the family, where everyone has a clearly defined rank. The Nepali language has half a dozen words for 'you', each of which conveys varying shades of respect.

When it comes to their religious beliefs, Nepalis are admirably flexible, pragmatic and, above all, tolerant – there is almost no religious or ethnic tension in Nepal. Nepalis are generally good humoured and patient, quick to smile and slow to anger, though they also have a reputation as fierce fighters.

The Nepali view of the world is dominated by prayer and ritual and a knowledge that the gods are not remote, abstract concepts but living, present beings who can influence human affairs in very direct ways. Nepalis perceive the divine everywhere, from the greeting *namaste,* which literally means 'I greet the divine inside of you', to the spirits and gods present in trees, passes, sacred river confluences and mountain peaks.

The notions of karma and caste, when combined with a tangled bureaucracy and deep-rooted corruption, tend to create an endemic sense of fatalism in Nepal. Confronted with problems, many Nepalis will simply respond with a shrug of the shoulders and the phrase *khe garne?,* or 'what is there to do?', which Westerners often find frustrating yet oddly addictive.

Traditional Lifestyle

The cornerstones of Nepali life are the demands (as well as the rewards) of one's family, ethnic group and caste. To break these time-honoured traditions is to risk being ostracised from family and community. While young Nepali people, especially in urban areas, are increasingly influenced by Western values and lifestyle, the majority of people still live by traditional customs and principles.

In most ethnic groups, joint and extended families live in the same house. In some smaller villages extended clans make up the entire community. Traditional family life has been dislocated by the large number of Nepali men forced to seek work away from home, whether in Kathmandu or the Terai, or abroad in India, Malaysia or the Gulf States.

Arranged marriages remain the norm in Nepali Hindu society and are generally between members of the same caste or ethnic group, although there is a growing number of 'love marriages'. Child marriages have been illegal since 1963 and today the average age of marriage for girls is just under 19. The family connections generated by a marriage are as much a social contract as a personal affair, and most families consult matchmakers and astrologers when making such an important decision.

To decide not to have children is almost unheard of and Nepali women will often pity you if you are childless. Having a son is important, especially for Hindu families, as some religious rites (such as lighting the funeral pyre to ensure a peaceful passage into the next life) can only be performed by the eldest son. Girls are regarded by many groups as a financial burden whose honour needs to be protected until she is married.

Changes in trading patterns and traditional culture among Nepal's Himalayan people are examined in *Himalayan Traders*, by Christoph von Fürer-Haimendorf.

Children stay at school for up to 12 years; 70% of children will begin school but only 15% will reach their 10th school year, when they sit their School Leaving Certificate (SLC) board examination. Many villages only have a primary school, which means children either have to walk long distances each day or board in a bigger town to attend secondary school. The ratio of boys to girls at secondary schools can be almost 2:1 in favour of boys.

Despite what you may see in Kathmandu and Pokhara, Nepal is overwhelmingly rural and poor; 83% of people live in the countryside. Farming is still the main occupation and debt is a factor in most people's lives. Large areas of land are still owned by *zamindars* (absent landlords) and up to 50% of a landless farmer's production will go to the landowner as rent. It remains to be seen how the Maoist government will be able to make a dent into this imbalance.

Most rural Nepali families are remarkably self-sufficient in their food supply, selling any excess in the nearest town, where they'll stock up on things such as sugar, soap, cigarettes, tea, salt, cloth and jewellery. Throughout Nepal this exchange of goods has created a dense network of trails trodden by everyone from traders and porters to mule caravans and trekking groups.

The rhythms of village life are determined by the seasons and marked by festivals – New Year, harvest and religious festivals being the most important. Dasain remains the biggest event of the calendar in the Middle Hills and is a time when most Nepali families get together.

Older people are respected members of the community and are cared for by their children. Old age is a time for relaxation, prayer and meditation. The dead are generally cremated and the deceased's sons will shave their heads and wear white for an entire year following the death.

Population

Nepal currently has a population of around 31 million (2014 estimate), a number that is increasing at the rate of 1.2% annually. Over 2.5 million people live in the Kathmandu Valley and perhaps one million in

MOVING TIGERS

Nepal's national board game is *bagh chal*, which literally means 'move the tigers'. The game is played on a lined board with 25 intersecting points. One player has four tigers, the other has 20 goats, and the aim is for the tiger player to 'eat' five goats by jumping over them before the goat player can encircle the tigers and prevent them moving. You can buy attractive brass *bagh chal* sets in Kathmandu and Patan, where they are made.

Nepal's other popular game is *carom*, which looks like finger snooker. Players use discs that glide over a chalked-up board to pot other discs into the corner pockets.

Kathmandu. Four million Nepalis reside in India. Around half of Nepal's population lives in the flat fertile lands of the Terai, which also acts as the nation's industrial base, and the population here is increasing rapidly.

People

Up to 2.1 million Nepalis work overseas, with over 40% in India and 38% in the Gulf States, and smaller numbers in Malaysia and other countries. In 2013 workers overseas sent home US$4 billion, or about 25% of Nepal's GDP, making this Nepal's largest single source of foreign currency.

The human geography of Nepal is a remarkable cultural mosaic of peoples who have not so much assimilated as learned to coexist. The ethnic divisions are complex and numerous; you'll have to do your homework to be able to differentiate between a Limbu, Lepcha, Lhopa and Lhomi – and that's just the Ls!

Nepal is the meeting place of the Indo-Aryan people of India and the Mongoloid peoples of the Himalaya. There are three main physical and cultural zones running east to west: the north, including the Himalaya; the Middle Hills; and the Terai. People living in these zones have adapted lifestyles and farming practices to suit their environment but, thanks largely to Nepal's tortured topography, each has retained its own traditions. Social taboos, especially among caste Hindus, have limited further assimilation between groups.

Nepal's diverse ethnic groups speak somewhere between 24 and 123 different languages and dialects, depending on how finely the distinctions are made. Nepali functions as the unifying language, though less than half of Nepal's people speak Nepali as their first language.

People of the Himalaya

The hardy Tibetan peoples who inhabit the high Himalaya are known in Nepal as Bhotias (Bhotiyas), a slightly derogatory term among caste Hindus. Each group remains distinct but their languages are all Tibetan-based and, with a few exceptions, they are Tibetan Buddhists.

The Bhotias' names combine the region they came from with the suffix 'pa' and include the Sherpas (literally 'easterners') of the Everest region, the Dolpopas of the west and the Lopas, or Lobas (literally 'southerners'), of the Mustang region.

The website www. mountainvoices. org/nepal.asp. html has an interesting collection of interviews with Nepali mountain folk on a wide variety of topics.

The withering of Trans-Himalayan trade routes and the difficulty of farming and herding at high altitude drive these people to lower elevations during winter, either to graze their animals or to trade in India and the Terai. Yak herding and the barley harvest remain the economic bedrocks of the high Himalaya.

Thakalis

Originating along the Kali Gandaki Valley in central Nepal, the Thakalis have emerged as the entrepreneurs of Nepal. They once played an important part in the salt trade between the subcontinent and Tibet, and travellers will meet them most frequently in their adopted roles as

NEPALI NAMES

You can tell a lot about a Nepali person from their name, including often their caste, profession, ethnic group and where they live. Gurung and Sherpa are ethnic groups as well as surnames. The surname Bista or Pant indicates that the person is a Brahman, originally from western Nepal; Devkota indicates an eastern origin. Thapa, Pande and Bhasnet are names related to the former Rana ruling family. Shrestha is a high-caste Newari name. The initials KC often stand for Khatri Chhetri, a mixed-caste name. The surname Kami is the Nepali equivalent of Smith.

Sherpa names even reveal which day of the week the person was born: Dawa (Monday), Mingmar (Tuesday), Lhakpa (Wednesday), Phurba (Thursday), Pasang (Friday), Pemba (Saturday) and Nyima (Sunday). The one thing you can't tell from a Sherpa name is their sex – Lhakpa Sherpa could be a man or a woman!

hoteliers and lodge owners, especially on the Annapurna Circuit. Originally Buddhist, many pragmatic Thakalis have now adopted Hinduism.

Tamangs

The Tamangs make up one of the largest groups in the country. They live mainly in the hills north of Kathmandu and have a noticeably strong Tibetan influence, from their monasteries, known as *ghyang*, to the mani walls that mark the entrance to their villages. You can stay in traditional Tamang villages along the Tamang Heritage Trail.

According to some accounts, ancestors of the Tamang were horse traders and cavalrymen from an invading Tibetan army who settled in Nepal. They are well known for their independence and suspicion of authority, probably caused by the fact that in the 19th century they were relegated to a low status, with much of their land distributed to Bahuns and Chhetris. As bonded labourers they were dependent upon menial work such as portering. Many of the 'Tibetan' souvenirs, carpets and thangkas (religious paintings) you see in Kathmandu are made by Tamangs.

Tibetans

About 13,500 of the 128,000 Tibetans in exile around the world live in Nepal. Although their numbers are small, Tibetans have a high profile, partly because of the important roles they play in tourism and the Tibetan carpet industry.

Tibetans are devout Buddhists and their arrival in the valley has rejuvenated a number of important religious sites, most notably the stupas at Swayambhunath and Bodhnath. These two places are constantly humming with Tibetans praying, spinning prayer wheels and slowly circumambulating the great stupas.

For decades Tibetan refugees in Nepal have marked the anniversary of the failed 1959 uprising against Chinese rule in Tibet with annual protests. However, in recent years, with the increasing influence of Chinese investment and political power, the Nepali authorities have started to clamp down on the protestors. Police now quickly silence protests in notable areas such as near the Chinese Embassy and Bodhnath, further straining the relationship between the Tibetan community and the Nepali government.

Sherpas

The Sherpas who live high in the mountains of eastern and central Nepal are probably the best-known Nepali ethnic group. These nomadic Tibetan herders moved to the Solu Khumbu region of Nepal 500 years ago from eastern Tibet, bringing with them their Tibetan Buddhist religion and building the beautiful gompas (monasteries) that dot the steep hillsides. Traditionally Sherpas would be recognised by their Tibetan clothing, but modern Sherpas have developed Western tastes in clothes matching their relatively strong earnings. They are associated with the Khumbu region around Mt Everest, although only a small percentage of Sherpas actually live in the Khumbu; the rest live in the lower valleys of the Solu region. Potatoes were introduced to the region in the late 19th century and are now the main Sherpa crop.

Tourism stepped in after the collapse of trade over the Nangpa La in 1959, when the Chinese sent thousands of troops to enforce their claim on Tibet. These days the Sherpa name is synonymous with mountaineering and trekking, and Sherpas can be found working as high-altitude mountain guides as well as owners of travel agencies and trekking lodges.

PEOPLE & CULTURE PEOPLE

Sherpas: Reflections on Change in Himalayan Nepal, by James F Fisher, offers an anthropological snapshot of how tourism and modernisation have affected Sherpa religious and cultural life. Fisher worked with Edmund Hillary in the Khumbu in the 1960s, bringing the first schools and airstrip to the region.

Despite associations in the West, Sherpas actually do very little portering, focusing mostly on high-altitude expedition work. Most of the porters you meet on the trails are Tamang or Rai, or from other groups.

People of the Middle Hills

The Middle Hills of Nepal are the best places to witness village life at its most traditional. In the east are the Kirati, who are divided into the Rai and Limbu groups. The Newari people dominate the central hills around the Kathmandu Valley, while the Magars and Gurungs inhabit the hills of the Kali Gandaki northwest of Pokhara.

Moving west, the Bahun and Chhetri are the dominant groups, although the lines between castes have become blurred over time.

Rais & Limbus

The Rais and Limbus are thought to have ruled the Kathmandu Valley in the 7th century BC until they were defeated around AD 300. They then moved into the steep hill country of eastern Nepal, from the Arun Valley to the Sikkim border, where many remain today. Others have moved to the Terai or India as economic migrants. Many Rai work as porters in the Middle Hills.

Describing themselves as Kirati, these tribes are easily distinguishable by their Mongolian features. They are of Tibeto-Burmese descent and their traditional religion is distinct from Buddhism and Hinduism, although the latter is exerting a growing influence. Himalayan hunter-warriors, they are still excellent soldiers and are well represented in the Gurkha regiments.

Many of the men still carry a large khukuri (traditional curved knife) tucked into their belt and wear a *topi* (traditional Nepali cap). Some communities in upper Arun live in bamboo houses.

Newars

The Newars of the Kathmandu Valley number about 1.3 million and make up 5% of the population. Their language, Newari, is distinct from Tibetan, Nepali or Hindi, and is reputed to be one of the world's most difficult languages to learn. The Newars are excellent farmers and merchants, as well as skilled artists, famed across Asia. The Kathmandu Valley is filled with spectacular examples of their artistic work, and their aesthetic influence was felt as far away as Lhasa.

Their origins are shrouded in mystery: most Newars have both Mongoloid and Caucasian physical characteristics. It's generally accepted that their ancestors were migrants of varied ethnicity who settled in the Kathmandu Valley over centuries – possibly originating with the Kiratis, or an even earlier group.

Newars lead a communal way of life and have developed several unique customs, including the worship of the Kumari, a girl believed to be a living god, and the annual chariot festivals that provide the high point of the valley's cultural life. Living so close to the centre of power has also meant there are many Newars in the bureaucracies of Kathmandu.

Traditionally, Newari men wear *surwal* (trousers with a baggy seat that are tighter around the calves, like jodhpurs), a *daura* (thigh-length double-breasted shirt), a vest or coat and the traditional *topi* hat. Newari castes include the Sakyas (priests), Tamrakar (metal casters) and the Jyapu (farmers). Jyapu women wear a black sari with a red border, while the men often wear the traditional trousers and shirt with a long piece of cotton wrapped around the waist.

Gurungs

The Gurungs, a Tibeto-Burmese people, live mainly in the central midlands, from Gorkha and Baglung up to Manang and the southern slopes of the Annapurnas, around Pokhara. One of the biggest Gurung settlements is Ghandruk, with its sweeping views of the Annapurnas and

Both Magars and Gurungs have made up large numbers of Gurkha regiments, and army incomes have contributed greatly to the economy of their regions.

WHO ARE THE GURKHAS?

Gurkhas are renowned soldiers associated with unrivalled bravery, tenacity and loyalty, and a very big, very sharp knife – the khukuri. Nepalis who joined the British East India army after the Anglo-Nepalese War and who later enlisted with the British and Indian armies became known as Gurkhas. The British coined the name, derived from the town of Gorkha between Kathmandu and Pokhara, which was the home of Prithvi Narayan Shah, the founder king of Nepal.

The UK still maintains Gurkha recruiting centres in Nepal, most notably in Pokhara, where there is a Gurkha Museum (p209). Most Gurkhas are Rais, Limbus, Gurungs and Magars in roughly equal number, although Gurkha regiments do accept recruits from other ethnic groups.

Machhapuchhare. Gurung women wear nose rings, known as *phuli*, and coral necklaces.

The Gurungs (who call themselves Tamu, or highlanders) originally migrated from western Tibet, bringing with them their animist Bön faith. One distinctive aspect of village life is the *rodi*, a cross between a town hall and a youth centre, where teenagers hang out and cooperative village tasks are planned. In the 1970s photographs portraying the alarmingly brave honey-collecting antics of Gurung men became world famous. The harvesting of hives continues, but increasing demands from tourists have led to questions about its sustainability.

Magars

The Magars, a large group (around 8% of the total population), are a Tibeto-Burmese people who live in many parts of the midlands zone of western and central Nepal. With such a large physical spread there are considerable regional variations.

The Magars are excellent soldiers and fought with Prithvi Narayan Shah to help unify Nepal. Their kingdom of Palpa (based at Tansen) was one of the last to be incorporated into a unified Nepal.

The Magars generally live in two-storey, rectangular or square thatched houses washed in red clay. They have been heavily influenced by Hinduism, and in terms of religion, farming practices, housing and dress, they are hard to distinguish from Chhetris.

Bahuns & Chhetris

The Hindu caste groups of Bahuns and Chhetris are dominant in the Middle Hills, making up 30% of the country's population.

Even though the caste system was formally abolished in 1963, these two groups remain the top cats of the caste hierarchy. Although there is no formal relationship in Hinduism between caste and ethnicity, Nepal's Bahuns and Chhetris (Brahmin priests and Kshatriya warriors, respectively) are considered ethnic groups as well as the two highest castes.

Bahuns and Chhetris played an important role in the court and armies of Prithvi Narayan Shah and after unification they were rewarded with tracts of land. Their language, Khas Kura, then became the national language of Nepal and their high-caste position was religiously, culturally and legally enforced. Ever since, Bahuns and Chhetris have dominated the government in Kathmandu, making up over 80% of the civil service.

A number of Bahuns and Chhetris had roles as tax collectors under the Shah and Rana regimes and to this day many are moneylenders with a great deal of power. Outside the Kathmandu Valley, the majority of these groups are simple farmers, indistinguishable in most respects from their neighbours.

Bahun and Chhetri men can be recognised by their sacred thread – the janai, worn over the left shoulder and under the right arm – which is changed once a year during the Janai Purnima festival.

HUMAN TRAFFICKING IN NEPAL

Trafficking of girls is a major problem in Nepal's most impoverished rural areas. Some 10,000 to 15,000 girls are tricked or sold every year into servitude, either as domestic, factory or sex workers. It is believed that over 100,000 Nepali women work in Indian brothels, often in conditions resembling slavery, and around half of these women are thought to be HIV positive. When obvious AIDS symptoms force these women out of work, some manage to return to Nepal. However, they are shunned by their families and there is virtually no assistance available for them or their children.

Particularly common in the Tharu areas of Dang and Bardia is the tradition of selling young daughters, aged seven to 10, to work as *kamlaris*, or indentured slaves, in the families of wealthy high-caste households. One organisation, the Nepal Youth Foundation (www.nepalyouthfoundation.org) has come up with an ingenious way of persuading families to hold on to their daughters: it gives them a piglet and kerosene stocks for every girl they keep at home and pays to send the child to school. Since 2000 the organisation has steered over 12,000 girls away from slavery.

The Bahuns tend to be more caste-conscious and orthodox than other Nepali Hindus, which sometimes leads to difficulties in relationships with 'untouchable' Westerners. Many are vegetarians and do not drink alcohol; marriages are arranged within the caste.

People of the Terai

Until the eradication of malaria in the 1950s, the only people to live in the valleys of the inner Terai and along much of the length of the Terai proper were Tharus and a few small associated groups, who enjoyed a natural immunity to the disease. After the Terai opened for development, large numbers of people from the midlands settled here – every group is represented and around 50% of Nepali people live in the region.

A number of large groups straddle the India–Nepal border. In the eastern Terai, Maithili people dominate; in the central Terai, there are many Bhojpuri-speaking people; and in the western Terai, Abadhi-speaking people are significant. All are basically cultures of the Gangetic plain and Hindu caste structure is strictly upheld.

Tharus

The lives and roles of Nepali women are examined in the insightful *The Violet Shyness of their Eyes: Notes from Nepal,* by Barbara J Scot, and *Nepali Aama,* by Broughton Coburn, which details the life of a remarkable Gurung woman.

One of the most visible groups is the Tharus, who are thought to be the earliest inhabitants of the Terai and descended from either Rajasthani Rajputs or the royal clan of Sakya, the Buddha's family. More than 1.5 million Tharu speakers inhabit the length of the Terai, including the inner Terai around Chitwan, although they mainly live in the west.

Tharu clans have traditionally lived in thatched huts with wattle and daub walls or in traditional long houses. Their beliefs are largely animistic, involving the worship of forest spirits and ancestral deities, but they are increasingly influenced by Hinduism.

Over generations many Tharus have been exploited by *zamindars* and fallen into debt or entered into bonded labour. In 2000 the *kamaiyas* (bonded labourers) were freed by government legislation, but little has been done to help these people who are now without land and work. Consequently, in most Terai towns in western Nepal you will see squatter settlements of former *kamaiyas*. Visitors to Chitwan or Bardia national parks can tour Tharu villages, stay in village homestays and be entertained by traditional dances. Many Tharus work as wildlife guides in the tourism industry.

Maithili

Mithila was an ancient kingdom, also known as Videha, that was centred on what is now the city of Janakpur in eastern Nepal. The inhabitants of the Mithila region, the Maithili, speak their own language and their erstwhile kingdom is now divided between India and Nepal. Maithili are orthodox Hindus worshipping chiefly Shiva, Shakti and Vishnu with some ancient animist influences. Today they are best known for the enigmatic naive art (p281) produced by the women of the community.

Women in Nepal

Women have a hard time of it in Nepal. Female mortality rates are higher than men's, literacy rates are lower and women generally work harder and longer than men, for less reward. Women only truly gain status in traditional society when they bear their husband a son. Bearing children is so important that a man can legally take a second wife if the first has not had a child after 10 years.

Nepal has a strongly patriarchal society, though this is less the case among Himalayan communities such as the Sherpa, where women often run the show (and the lodge). Boys are strongly favoured over girls, who are often the last to eat and the first to be pulled from school during financial difficulties. Nepal has a national literacy rate of 66%, with the rate among women at 57%.

The annual festival of Teej is the biggest festival for women, though ironically it honours their husbands. The activities include feasting, fasting, ritual bathing (in the red and gold saris they were married in) and ritual offerings.

Traditional prejudice against daughters is reflected in the bitter Nepali proverb: 'Raising a girl is like watering your neighbour's garden.'

PEOPLE & CULTURE WOMEN IN NEPAL

Religion

From the simple, early morning offerings of a Kathmandu housewife at a local Hindu temple, to the chanting of Buddhist monks in a village monastery, religion is a cornerstone of Nepali life. Merge the concepts of Hinduism and Buddhism, add some Indian and Tibetan influences and blend this with elements of animism, faith healing and a pinch of Tantric practice and you get a taste of Nepal's fabulous spiritual stew.

Hinduism

Hinduism is a polytheistic religion that has its origins in the Aryan tribes of central India dating back about 3500 years ago. Hindus believe in a cycle of life, death and rebirth with the aim being to achieve *moksha* (release) from this cycle. With each rebirth you can move closer to, or further from, eventual *moksha;* the deciding factor is karma, which is literally a law of cause and effect. Buddhism later adapted this concept into one of its core principles.

The life of a Nepali Hindu is defined by 16 major rites (*sanskar* or *samskara*), from a baby's first haircut or meal of rice all the way through marriage to death rites. The core concepts of ritual bathing, purification and sacrifice date from the religion's earliest roots.

Despite common misconceptions, it is possible to become a Hindu, although Hinduism itself is not a proselytising religion. Once you are a Hindu you cannot change your caste – you're born into it and are stuck with your lot in life for the rest of that lifetime.

Hinduism in Practice

The Hindu religion has three basic practices: *puja* (religious offering or prayer), the cremation of the dead, and the highly stratified rules and regulations of the caste system.

You'll see cremation ghats at many rivers in Nepal but none are holier than those at Pashupatinath. Before a cremation the dead body is washed, laid on a bier and covered with a shroud. Afterwards the ashes

---

SADHUS

Sadhus are Hindu ascetics who have left their homes, jobs and families and embarked upon a spiritual search. They're an easily recognised group, usually wandering around half-naked, smeared in dust with their hair matted, and carrying nothing except a *trisul* (trident) and a begging bowl.

Sadhus wander all over the subcontinent, occasionally coming together at great religious gatherings such as the Maha Shivaratri festival at Pashupatinath in Kathmandu and the Janai Purnima festival at the sacred Hindu lakes of Gosainkund. You may also see sadhus wandering around Thamel and posing for photos in Kathmandu's Durbar Sq.

A few sadhus are simply beggars using a more sophisticated approach to gathering donations, but most are genuine in their search. Remember that if you take a picture of a sadhu, or accept a *tika* blessing from him, you will be expected to pay some *baksheesh* (tip), so negotiate your photo fee in advance to avoid any unpleasantness.

LINGAM & YONI

Apart from being a potentially great name for a Nepali crime-fighting duo, the lingam and yoni are the most common religious symbols in Nepal and you'll see thousands of them across Nepal. The phallic lingam represents male energy and Shiva in particular, while the vaginal yoni symbolises female energy and Parvati. Together they symbolise light and dark, passive and active, the union of the male and female and the totality of existence.

are swept into the Bagmati River. Before the burning of the body the chief mourner (normally the eldest son) takes a ritual purification bath; 10 days later the entire family bathes and the house is ritually purified.

Hindu temples are where the spiritual and mundane worlds intersect. Nepalis visit a temple for many reasons – to show devotion, perform a puja, pray for a boon or to gain *darshan,* a word that means viewing a deity but also has the connotation of being viewed by it. The central image in a temple is treated like a royal guest; awakened, washed, dressed, fed and put back to bed by the priest. Devotees make offerings to the deity, from coconuts and garlands of marigolds to milk, vermillion powder and incense.

There are four main Hindu castes: Brahmin (Brahman ethnic group; priest caste); Kshatriya (Chhetri in Nepali; soldiers and governors); Vaisya (tradespeople and farmers); and Sudra (menial workers and craftspeople). These castes are then subdivided, although this is not taken to the same extreme in Nepal as it is in India. Beneath all the castes are the Harijans, or 'untouchables' – the lowest, casteless class for whom the most menial and degrading tasks are reserved.

> Both Hindus and Buddhists see the land in terms of a sacred landscape. River confluences and sources, mountain lakes and high passes and peaks are all considered particularly sacred, while water sources teem with holy *naga* (serpent deities).

Hindu Gods

Westerners often have trouble coming to grips with Hinduism, principally because of its vast pantheon of gods. The best way to look upon the dozens of different Hindu gods is simply as pictorial representations of the many attributes of the divine. The one omnipresent god usually has three physical representations: Shiva the destroyer and reproducer, Vishnu the preserver and Brahma the creator.

Most temples are dedicated to one of these gods, but most Hindus profess to be either Vaishnavites (followers of Vishnu) or Shaivites (followers of Shiva).

The oldest deities are the elemental Indo-European Vedic gods, such as Indra (the god of war, storms and rain), Suriya (the sun), Chandra (the moon) and Agni (fire). Added to this are a range of ancient local mountain spirits, which Hinduism quickly co-opted. The Annapurna and the Ganesh Himal massifs are named after Hindu deities, and Gauri Shankar and Mt Kailash in Tibet are said to be the residences of Shiva and his partner Parvati.

The definitions that follow include the most interesting and frequently encountered 'big names', plus associated consorts, manifestations, reincarnations, vehicles and religious terminology.

> Thanks to the tendency towards assimilation and synthesis there is little religious tension in Nepal and religion has long played little part in the country's politics. In Kathmandu Tibetan Buddhists and Nepali Hindus often worship at the same temples.

Shiva

As reproducer and destroyer, Shiva is probably the most important god in Nepal – so it's important to keep on his good side! You can spot Shiva through his *vahana* (vehicle) the bull Nandi, which you'll often see outside Shiva temples, and also by the trident in his hand.

Shiva also appears as Nataraja, whose dance shook the cosmos and created the world, and as the terrible manifestation Bhairab who can appear in 64 different forms, none of them pretty.

> It is joked that Nepal has three religions – Hinduism, Buddhism and Tourism.

TIKA

A visit to Nepal is not complete without being offered a *tika* by one of the country's many sadhus (wandering Hindu holy men) or *pujari* (Hindu priests). The ubiquitous *tika* is a symbol of blessing from the gods and is worn by both women and men. It can range from a small dot to a full-on mixture of yoghurt, rice and *sindur* (a red powder and mustard-oil mixture) smeared on the forehead. The *tika* represents the all-seeing, all-knowing third eye, placed on an important *chakra* (energy point), and receiving this blessing is a common part of most Hindu ceremonies. It is an acknowledgment of a divine presence at the occasion and a sign of protection for those receiving it. Shops these days carry a huge range of tiny plastic *tikas*, known as *bindi*, that Nepali women have turned into an iconic fashion statement.

Shiva's home is Mt Kailash in Tibet. In the Kathmandu Valley, Shiva is most popularly worshipped as Pashupati, the lord of the beasts. The temple of Pashupatinath, outside Kathmandu, is the most important Hindu temple in the country.

Outside of the Kathmandu Valley, Shiva is most commonly worshipped as Mahadeva (Great God), the supreme deity.

Vishnu

Vishnu is the preserver in Hindu belief. In Nepal he often appears as Narayan, asleep on the cosmic ocean, from whose navel appears Brahma, who creates the universe.

Unlike in neighbouring India, Nepal's Hindu and Muslim communities coexist peacefully.

Vishnu has four arms and can often be identified by the symbols he holds: the *sankha* (conch shell); the disc-like weapon known as a *chakra;* the stick-like weapon known as a *gada;* and a *padma* (lotus flower). Vishnu's vehicle is the faithful man-bird Garuda; a winged Garuda will often be seen kneeling reverently in front of a Vishnu temple. Garuda has an intense hatred of snakes and is often seen destroying them. Vishnu's *shakti* (female energy) is Lakshmi, the goddess of wealth and prosperity.

Vishnu has 10 incarnations, including Narsingha (half-man and half-lion), Rama, the hero of the Ramayana, and Krishna, the fun-loving, gentle and much-loved cowherd.

Brahma

Despite his supreme position, Brahma appears much less often than Shiva or Vishnu. Like those gods, Brahma has four arms, but he also has four heads, to represent his all-seeing presence. The four Vedas are supposed to have emanated from his mouths.

Parvati

The cow is the holy animal of Hinduism, and killing a cow in Nepal brings a jail term.

Shiva's shakti is Parvati the beautiful. Just as Shiva is also known as Mahadeva (the Great God), Parvati is Mahadevi (or just Devi), the Great Goddess. Their relationship is a sexual one and it is often Parvati who is the energetic and dominant partner.

Shiva's shakti has as many forms as Shiva himself. She may be peaceful Parvati, Uma or Gauri, but she may also be fearsome Kali, the black goddess, or Durga, the terrible. In these fearsome forms she holds a variety of weapons in her hands, struggles with demons and rides a lion or tiger. As skeletal Kali, she demands blood sacrifices and wears a garland of skulls.

Ganesh

Ganesh, with his elephant head, is probably the most easily recognised and popular of the gods. He is the god of prosperity and wisdom, and there are thousands of Ganesh shrines and temples across Nepal. His parents are

Shiva and Parvati and he has his father's temper to thank for his elephant head. Returning from a long trip, Shiva discovered Parvati in bed with a young man. Not pausing to think that their son might have grown up a little during his absence, Shiva lopped his head off. Parvati then forced Shiva to bring their son back to life, but he could only do so by giving him the head of the first living thing he saw – which happened to be an elephant.

Chubby Ganesh has a super-sweet tooth and is often depicted with his trunk in a mound of sweets and with one broken tusk; one story tells how he broke it off and threw it at the moon for making fun of his weight, another tale states that Ganesh used the tusk to write the Mahabharata.

The kings of Nepal long enjoyed added legitimacy because they were considered to be incarnations of Vishnu.

RELIGION HINDUISM

Hanuman

The monkey god Hanuman is an important character from the Ramayana. Hanuman's trustworthy and alert nature is commemorated by the many statues of the god that guard palace entrances, most famously the Hanuman Dhoka in Kathmandu's Durbar Sq.

Machhendranath

A strictly Nepali Hindu god, Machhendranath (also known as Bunga Dyo) has power over the rains and the monsoon and is regarded as protector of the Kathmandu Valley. Typical of the intermingling of Hindu and Buddhist beliefs in Nepal, in the Kathmandu Valley at least, Machhendranath has come to be thought of as an incarnation of Avalokiteshvara, the Buddhist's Bodhisattva of Compassion.

Tara

The goddess Tara appears in both the Hindu and Buddhist pantheons. There are 108 different Taras but the best known are Green Tara and White Tara. Tara is generally depicted sitting with her right leg hanging down and her left hand in a mudra (hand gesture).

Sita is believed to have been born in Janakpur, and a temple there marks the site where she and Rama married. A great festival takes place on the site in November/December.

Saraswati

The goddess of learning and the consort of Brahma, Saraswati rides upon a white swan and holds the stringed musical instrument known as a *veena*. Students, in particular, honour Saraswati during the spring festival of Basanta Panchami, when locals flock to her shrine at Swayambhunath, outside Kathmandu.

PUJA & SACRIFICE

Every morning, Hindu women all over Nepal can be seen walking through the streets carrying a plate, usually copper, filled with an assortment of goodies. These women are not delivering breakfast but are taking part in an important daily ritual called *puja*. The plate might contain flower petals, rice, yoghurt, fruit or sweets, and is an offering to the gods made at the local temple. Each of the items is sprinkled onto a temple deity in a set order and a bell is rung to let the gods know an offering is being made. Once an offering is made it is transformed into a sacred object and a small portion (referred to as *prasad*) is returned to the giver as a blessing from the deity. Upon returning home from her morning trip, the woman will give a small part of the blessed offerings to each member of the household.

Marigolds and sweets don't cut it with Nepal's more terrifying gods, notably Kali and Bhairab, who require a little extra appeasement in the form of bloody animal sacrifices. You might witness the gory executions, from chickens to water buffalo, at Dakshinkali in the Kathmandu Valley, Manakamana Temple and the Kalika Temple at Gorkha, or during the annual Dasain festival in October, when these temples are literally awash with blood offerings. Formerly, the mother of all sacrifices was the controversial five-yearly Gadhimai Festival, when several million devotees slaughtered 100,000 buffalo, goats, chickens and even rats over the course of a few hours, but in July 2015 it was announced that the practice would be abolished and that the 2019 festival will be free from bloodshed.

Buddhism

Strictly speaking, Buddhism is a philosophy rather than a religion, as it is centred not on a god but on a system of thought and a code of morality. Buddhism was founded in northern India in the 6th century BC when prince Siddhartha Gautama achieved enlightenment.

The Buddha ('awakened one') was born in Lumbini in Nepal over 25 centuries ago but the Buddhist religion first arrived in the country later, around 250 BC, thanks to the great Indian-Buddhist emperor Ashoka. Buddhism eventually lost ground to Hinduism, although the Tantric form of Tibetan Buddhism eventually made its way full circle back into Nepal in the 8th century AD. Today, Tibetan Buddhism is practised mainly by the people of the high Himalaya, such as the Sherpas, Tamangs and Manangi, and by Tibetan refugees who have revitalised religious practice in the region over the last 50 years.

The Buddha was born a prince but renounced his privileged life to search for enlightenment. His insight was that severe asceticism did not lead to enlightenment any more than material comfort, and that the best course of action was to follow the Middle Way (moderation in all things). The Buddha taught that all life is suffering, and that suffering comes from our desires and the illusion of their importance.

By following the 'eightfold path' these desires can be extinguished and a state of nirvana, where we are free from their delusions, can be attained. Buddhists believe that life entails a series of reincarnations until nirvana is reached and no more rebirths into the world of suffering are necessary. The path that takes you through this cycle of births is karma, but this is not simply fate. Karma is a law of cause and effect; your actions in one life determine what you will experience in your next life. Only you are the master of your own fate.

> Actress Uma Thurman gets her name from the beautiful Hindu goddess Uma, a manifestation of Parvati. Uma forms half of the Uma-Maheshwar image, a common representation of Shiva and Parvati.

> The pipal tree, under which the Buddha gained enlightenment, is also known by its highly appropriate Latin name, *ficus religious.*

Buddhist Deities

The first images of the Buddha date from the 5th century AD, 1000 years after his death (stupas were the main symbol of Buddhism before this). The Buddha didn't want idols made of himself but a pantheon of Buddhist gods grew up regardless, with strong iconographical influence from Hinduism. As in Hinduism, the many Buddhist deities reflect various aspects of the divine, or 'Buddha-nature'. Multiple heads convey multiple personalities, mudra (hand gestures) convey coded messages, and everything from eyebrows to stances indicate the nature of the deity.

There are many different types of Buddha images, though the most common are those of the past (Dipamkara), present (Sakyamuni) and future (Maitreya) Buddhas. The Buddha is recognised by 32 physical marks, including a bump on the top of his head, his third eye and images of the Wheel of Law on the soles of his feet. In his left hand he holds a begging bowl and his right hand touches the earth in the witness mudra. He is often flanked by his two disciples.

> Bön is Tibet's pre-Buddhist animist faith, now largely considered a fifth school of Tibetan Buddhism. Nepal has small pockets of Bön followers.

Bodhisattvas are beings who have achieved enlightenment but decide to help everyone else gain enlightenment before entering nirvana. The Bodhisattva of Wisdom Manjushri has strong connections to the Kathmandu Valley. The Dalai Lama is considered a reincarnation of Avalokiteshvara (Chenresig in Tibetan), the Bodhisattva of Compassion.

Tibetan Buddhism also has a host of fierce protector gods, called *dharmapala,* who on one level at least symbolise the demons of the ego. Typical of Tantric deities (and with roots deep in Hindu iconography), these bloodcurdling deities have multiple arms and weapons, dance on a corpse and wear a headdress of skulls.

TIBETAN BUDDHIST SYMBOLS

Prayer Flags These multicoloured squares of cloth are printed with Buddhist sutras and an image of the wind horse *(lungta)* which carries the prayers to the heavens. Rooted in pre-Buddhist beliefs, they are strung on passes and houses to sanctify the air and pacify the gods. The five colours represent the elements of fire, water, air, wood and earth (some say ether).

Mani Stones These stones are carved with Tibetan mantras and placed in walls several hundred metres long as an act of merit. The most common mantra is *om mani padme hum,* which roughly means 'Hail to the jewel in the lotus'.

Prayer Wheels Containing up to one million rolled up printed prayers, prayer wheels are turned as an act of devotion and to gain merit. The wheels vary from the size of a fist to that of a small building (known as a *mani lhakhang*).

Tibetan Buddhism

The Buddha never wrote down his dharma (teachings) and a schism that developed later means that today there are two major Buddhist schools: Hinayana and Mahayana. One offshoot of Mahayana is Vajrayana, or Tibetan Buddhism, and it is this that you will see mostly in Nepal.

There are four major schools of Tibetan (Vajrayana) Buddhism, all represented in the Kathmandu Valley: Nyingmapa, Kagyupa, Sakyapa and Gelugpa. The Nyingmapa order is the oldest and most dominant in the Nepal Himalaya. Its origins come from the Indian sage Padmasambhava (Guru Rinpoche), sometimes called the 'second Buddha' and who is credited with the establishment of Buddhism in Tibet and the Himalaya in the 8th century.

The Dalai Lama is the head of the Gelugpa school and the spiritual leader of Tibetan Buddhists. In some texts the Gelugpa are known as the Yellow Hats, while the other schools are sometimes collectively referred to as Red Hats.

Padmasambhava (Guru Rinpoche) is a common image in Nyingmapa monasteries and is recognisable by his *khatvanga* staff of human heads and his fabulously curly moustache.

Islam

Nepal's small population of Muslims (about 4% of the total population) is mainly found close to the border with India, with a large population in Nepalganj. The first Muslims, who were mostly Kashmiri traders, arrived in the Kathmandu Valley in the 15th century. A second group arrived in the 17th century from northern India and they primarily manufactured armaments for the small hill states. Nepal's Muslims have strong ties with Muslim communities in the Indian states of Bihar and Uttar Pradesh.

Shamanism

Shamanism is practised by many mountain peoples throughout the Himalaya and dates back some 50,000 years. Its ancient healing traditions are based on a cosmology that divides the world into three main levels: the Upper World where the sun, moon, stars, planets, deities and spirits important to the shaman's healing work abide; the Middle World of human life; and the Lower World, where more malevolent deities and spirits exist.

Faith healers protect against a wide range of spirits, including headless *mulkattas,* who have eyes in their chest and signify imminent death; *pret,* the ghosts of the recently deceased that loiter at crossroads; and *kichikinni,* the ghost of a beautiful and sexually insatiable siren who is recognisable by her sagging breasts and the fact that her feet are on backwards.

During ceremonies, the *dhami* or *jhankri* (shaman or faith healer) uses techniques of drumming, divination, trances and sacrifices to invoke deities and spirits that he or she wishes to assist in the ritual. The shaman essentially acts as a broker between the human and spirit worlds.

Arts & Architecture

Despite the devastating effects of the 2015 earthquakes, Nepal is still blessed with an astonishing array of ancient temples and palaces, and countless priceless wood carvings and stone sculptures are dotted around its brick-lined backstreets. Walking through the historic towns of the Kathmandu Valley, you will still discover magnificent medieval architecture at every turn, alongside the remains of those buildings that were tragically lost in the disaster. Now, as ever, Nepal's artistic masterpieces are not hidden away in dusty museums but are part of a living culture, to be touched, worshipped, feared – or simply accepted as a glorious part of the scenery.

Architecture & Sculpture

Architecture and the sculpting arts in Nepal are inextricably intermingled. The finest woodcarvings and stone sculptures are often part of a building. Indeed a temple is simply not a temple without its deity statue and finely carved adornments.

The earliest architecture in the Kathmandu Valley has faded with history. Grassy mounds are all that remain where Patan's four Ashoka stupas once stood, and the impressive stupas of Swayambhunath and Bodhnath have been rebuilt many times over the centuries.

The Licchavi period from the 4th to 9th centuries AD was a golden age for Nepal, and while the temples may have disappeared, magnificent stone sculptures have withstood the ravages of time and can still be found. Beautiful pieces lie scattered around temples of the Kathmandu Valley. The Licchavi sculptures at the temple of Changu Narayan near Bhaktapur are particularly good examples, as is the statue of Vishnu asleep on a bed of serpents at Budhanilkantha.

No wooden buildings and carvings are known to have survived in Nepal from that period, or indeed before the 12th century. However, within Lhasa's Jokhang Temple there are carved wooden beams and columns dating from before the 9th century that are clearly the work of Newari artisans.

It was in the Malla period that Nepali artistry with wood really came into its own, as the famed skills of the valley's Newari people reached their zenith, particularly between the 15th and 17th centuries. Squabbling and one-upmanship between the city states of Kathmandu, Patan and Bhaktapur fuelled a competitive building boom as each tried to outdo the other with even more magnificent palaces and temples.

The great age of Nepali architecture came to a dramatic end when Prithvi Narayan Shah invaded the valley in 1769. These days traditional building skills are still evidenced in the periodically ongoing restoration projects in Kathmandu, Patan and Bhaktapur. Moreover, today's architects will often incorporate traditional features into their buildings, particularly hotels.

Newari Pagoda Temples

The Nepali architect Arniko can be said to be the father of the Asian pagoda. He kick-started the introduction and reinterpretation of the pagoda in China and eastern Asia when he brought the multiroofed Nepali pagoda design to the court of Kublai Khan in the late 13th century.

Kathmandu Valley's Unesco World Heritage Sites

Durbar Sq (p63), Kathmandu

Durbar Sq (p137), Patan

Durbar Sq (p153), Bhaktapur

Swayambhunath Stupa (p117)

Bodhnath Stupa (p128)

Pashupatinath (p124)

Changu Narayan (p168)

A FATAL FLAW

Nepal's traditional brick and timber buildings bore the brunt of the damage during the 2015 earthquakes, prompting questions about the safety of such structures in a seismically active area such as the Himalaya. However, the evidence of history speaks for itself – Nepal's historic buildings have endured centuries of tremors, and it was the geology of the Kathmandu Valley, with its base layer of moveable clay, that was ultimately responsible for the devastation. In places such as Panauti, built on solid bedrock, the damage to traditional buildings was almost negligible.

Nevertheless, modern buildings generally fared better in the quake, spared largely by virtue of their concrete foundations. This was, however, a lucky escape; a quake of magnitude 8 or more would have damaged even buildings reinforced with steel and concrete. Those traditional buildings that survived with only minor damage now face a new threat – many are being demolished to build new concrete houses that are perceived as being 'earthquake proof', something that may ultimately cause as much damage to Nepal's architectural heritage as the earthquake.

The distinctive Newari pagoda temples are a major feature of the Kathmandu Valley skyline, echoing, and possibly inspired by, the horizon's pyramid-shaped mountain peaks. While strictly speaking they are neither wholly Newari nor pagodas, the term has been widely adopted to describe the temples of the valley.

The temples are generally square in design, and may be either Hindu or Buddhist (or both, as is the nature of Nepali religion). On occasion, temples are rectangular or octagonal; Krishna can occupy an octagonal temple, but Ganesh, Shiva and Vishnu can only inhabit square temples.

The major feature of the temples is the tiered roof, which may have one to five tiers, with two or three being the most common. In the Kathmandu Valley there are two temples with four roofs and the Nyatapola temple at Bhaktapur and the Kumbeshwar temple at Patan have five, though the latter saw severe damage to its upper tier in the 2015 quake. The sloping roofs are usually covered with distinctive *jhingati* (baked clay tiles), although richer temples will often have one roof of gilded copper. The bell-shaped *gajur* (pinnacle) is made of baked clay or gilded copper.

The temples are usually built on a stepped plinth, which may be as high as or even higher than the temple itself. In many cases the number of steps on the plinth corresponds with the number of roofs on the temple.

The temple building itself has a small sanctum, known as a *garbha-griha* (literally 'womb room'), housing the deity. Worshippers practise individually, with devotees standing outside the door to make their supplications. The only people permitted to actually enter the sanctum are pujari (temple priests).

Perhaps the most interesting feature of the temples is the detailed decoration, which is only evident close up. Under each roof there are often brass or other metal decorations, such as *kinkinimala* (rows of small bells) or embossed metal banners. The metal streamer that often hangs from above the uppermost roof to below the level of the lowest roof (such as on the Golden Temple in Patan) is called a *pataka*. Its function is to give the deity a way to descend to earth.

The other major decorative elements are the wooden *tunala* (struts) that support the roofs. The intricate carvings are usually of deities associated with the temple or of the *vahana* (deity's vehicle) but quite a few depict explicit sexual acts.

Nepal, by Michael Hutt, is an excellent guide to the art and architecture of the Kathmandu Valley. It outlines the main forms of art and architecture and describes specific sites within the valley, often with layout plans. It has great colour plates and black-and-white photos.

NEPAL'S STOLEN HERITAGE

In recent decades Nepal has had a staggering amount of its artistic heritage spirited out of the country by art thieves, and this problem is only likely to grow following the destruction of so many monuments in the 2015 earthquakes. Virtually all the Nepali antique art that has come on to the international market in the last three to four decades has been stolen. Much of the stolen art languishes in museums or private collections in Europe and in the US, while in Nepal remaining temple statues are increasingly kept under lock and key.

One of the reasons photography is banned in some temples is that thieves often put photos of temple artefacts in their underground 'shopping catalogues'. Pieces are then stolen to order, often with the aid of corrupt officials, to fetch high prices in the lucrative international art market. United Nations conventions against the trade exist but are weakly enforced.

Catalogues of stolen Nepali art have been produced in an attempt to locate these treasures, and several pieces have been given back to Kathmandu's National Museum, including a Buddha statue stolen from Patan that was returned after a dealer tried to sell it to a museum in Austria for a cool US$200,000.

Shikhara Temples

The second-most common temples are the shikhara temples, which have a heavy Indian influence. The temples are so named because their tapering towers resemble a shikhara (mountain peak, in Sanskrit). Although the style developed in India in the 6th century, it first appeared in Nepal in the late Licchavi period.

The tapering, pyramidal tower is the main feature, and is often surrounded by four similar but smaller towers. These may be located on porches over the shrine's entrances.

The spire of the Mahabouddha Temple in Patan and the Krishna Mandir and the octagonal Krishna Temple, both in Patan's Durbar Sq, are all excellent examples of this style. Sadly, the similar Vatsala Durga Temple in Bhaktapur was completely destroyed in the 2015 earthquakes.

The Buddhist Gompa

The monastery of Tibetan Buddhists is called a gompa, and across the mountains of Nepal there are gompas that hum with prayers and clash with cymbals. Most historic gompas are located on a hill with a fine view, demonstrating their strategic importance and reflecting the desires of the monks for peace and solitude. Newer, more lavish gompas, such as the one at Jomsom, reflect the increasing wealth of Tibetan Buddhists in Nepal, and are often sited close to town. Conspicuous on the roof of most gompas is the golden dharma wheel flanked by two deer. The wheel is a representation of Buddha's teachings and the deer symbolise the Buddha's first sermon at Sarnath after reaching enlightenment – in a deer park.

You enter a gompa through an entrance vestibule decorated with colourful paintings of *Bhavachakra,* the Wheel of Life clutched by the fearsome Yama, and the Four Guardian Kings, watching over the four cardinal points of the world. Most small gompas have only one room, the *dukhang,* or assembly hall, decorated with bright murals and thangkas (religious painting on cloth). The main altar will be dominated by a central statue flanked by two or more others – the statues could include Sakyamuni, the historical Buddha; Jampa, the future Buddha; or the lotus-born saint Guru Rinpoche. Another common figure is the 11th-century poet Milerapa, who is said to have travelled widely throughout the Himalaya, including to Shey Gompa and the Manang valley.

Get a great overview of Buddhist and Nepali art at the Patan Museum and at Kathmandu's National Museum, both of which explain the concepts behind Buddhist and Hindu art and iconography in an accessible way.

The altar will usually have photos of important lineage holders, such as the Dalai Lama, plus bowls of water, flickering butter lamps and colourful *torma,* constructions of flour-and-butter dough. Hanging off to the side are demonic festival masks and ceremonial trumpets.

The Art of God Making

Newari art and craft skills extend far beyond the woodwork for which they are so well known and include ceramics, brickwork, stone sculptures and intricate metalwork. The finest metalwork includes the stunning images of the two Tara goddesses at Swayambhunath and the Golden Gate (Sun Dhoka) in Bhaktapur.

Statues are created through two main techniques – the repoussé method of hammering thin sheets of metal and the 'lost wax' method. In the latter, the statue is carved in wax, which is then encased in clay and left to dry. The wax is then melted, metal is poured into the clay mould and the mould is then broken, revealing the statue. Finishing touches include grinding, polishing and painting before the statue is ready to be sanctified.

The website www.mountain-musicproject.com has links to radio and video clips of several Nepali musicians, including Rubin Gandharba – the 'Nepali Bob Dylan'.

Painting

Chinese, Tibetan, Indian and Mughal influences can all be seen in Nepali painting styles. The earliest Newari paintings were illuminated manuscripts dating from the 11th century. Newari *paubha* paintings are iconic religious paintings similar to Tibetan thangkas. Notable to both is a lack of perspective, symbolic use of colour and strict iconographic rules.

Modern Nepali artists struggle to make a living, although there are a few galleries in Kathmandu that feature local artists. Some artists are fortunate enough to get a sponsored overseas exhibition or a posting at an art college outside the country to teach their skills. Commissioning a painting by a local artist is a way to support the arts and take home a unique souvenir of your trip.

The eastern Terai has its own distinct form of colourful mural painting called Mithila art (p281).

Music & Dance

The last decade has seen a revival in Nepali music and songs, both folk and 'Nepali modern'. The ever-present Hindi film songs have been partly supplanted by a vibrant local music scene thanks to advances made in FM radio.

In the countryside most villagers supply their own entertainment. Dancing and traditional music enliven festivals and family celebrations, when villages erupt with the energetic sounds of *bansari* (flutes), *madal* (drums) and cymbals, or sway to the moving soulful sounds of devotional singing and the gentle twang of the four-stringed *sarang*. Singing is one important way that girls and boys in the hills can interact and flirt, showing their grace and wit through dances and improvised songs.

You can see 'for-tourist' versions of Nepal's major dances at Newari restaurants in Kathmandu and Pokhara.

REPOUSSÉ METALWORK

Many of the richly decorated objects used for religious rituals in Nepal make use of the ancient technique of repoussé – where a design is hammered into the metal from the back using hammers and punches. First the metal shape is set into a bed of *jhau* (a mixture of resin and brick dust), then the design is painstakingly applied and the resin is melted away, allowing finishing touches to be added from the front using engraving tools. This style of metalwork has been produced since at least the 2nd millennium BC and the technique is still practised today in alleyways across the Kathmandu Valley.

There are several musician castes, including the *gaine,* a dwindling caste of travelling minstrels, the *ghandarba,* whose music you can hear in Kathmandu, and the *damai,* who often perform in wedding bands. Women generally do not perform music in public.

Nepali dance styles are as numerous and varied as Nepal's ethnic groups. They range from the stick dances of the Tharu in the Terai, to the line-dancing style of the mountain Sherpas. Joining in with an enthusiastic group of porters at the end of a trek is a great way to learn some of the moves. Masked dances are also common, from the Cham dances performed by Tibetan Buddhist monks to the masked Hindu dances of Nava Durga in Bhaktapur.

Providing a good introduction to Nepali folk music is the group Sur Sudha (www.sursudha.com), Nepal's de facto musical ambassadors, whose evocative recordings will take you back to the region long after you've tasted your last daal bhaat. Try its *Festivals of Nepal* and *Images of Nepal* recordings.

One of Nepal's most famous singers is the Tibetan nun Choying Drolma (www.choyimg.com). Her CDs *Cho* and *Selwa,* recorded with guitarist Steve Tibbetts, are transcendentally beautiful and highly recommended.

The folk song that you hear everywhere in Nepal (you'll know which one we mean when you get there) is '*Resham Pheeree Ree*' (My Heart is Fluttering Like Silk in the Wind).

The cultural organisation Spiny Babbler (www.spiny babbler.org) has an online Nepali art museum and articles on Nepali art. It is named after Nepal's only endemic species of bird.

Film

The Nepali film industry has come a long way since the 1980s and early '90s, when only four or five films were produced annually. According to John Whelpton in his *History of Nepal,* the first film shown in Kathmandu depicted the wedding of the Hindu god Ram. The audience threw petals and offerings at the screen as they would do at a temple or if the god himself were present.

The Oscar-nominated Nepali-French film *Caravan,* directed by Eric Valli, is the most famous 'Nepali' film and played to packed houses in Kathmandu. It features magnificent footage of the Upper Dolpo district of western Nepal as it tells the tale of yak caravaners during a change of generations. It was renamed for distribution abroad as *Himalaya.* Perhaps the best-known film shot in Nepal is Bernado Bertolucci's Little Buddha, which was partly filmed at Bhaktapur's Durbar Sq and the Gokarna Forest.

The 2013 documentary *Manakamana* toured Nepal and film festivals in the West to mixed acclaim. It follows the journey through real-time conversations and reflections of pilgrims as they ride the cable car to the

The Kathmandu International Mountain Film Festival (www. kimff.org) screens over 60 Nepali and international films every December. Film South Asia (www. filmsouthasia. org) is a biennial (odd years) festival of South Asian documentaries.

TIBETAN CARPETS

One of the most amazing success stories of the last few decades is the local Tibetan carpet industry. Although carpet production has long been a cottage industry inside Tibet, in 1960 the Nepal International Tibetan Refugee Relief Committee, with the support of renowned Swiss geologist Toni Hagen and the Swiss government, began encouraging Tibetan refugees in Patan to make and sell carpets.

Tibetan and New Zealand wool is used to make the carpets. The exuberant colours and lively designs of traditional carpets have been toned down for the international market, but the old ways of producing carpets remain the same. The intricacies of the senna loop method are hard to pick out in the blur of hands that is usually seen at a carpet workshop; each thread is looped around a gauge rod that will determine the height of the carpet pile, then each row is hammered down and the loops of thread split to release the rod. To finish it off the pile is clipped to bring out the design.

sacred Manakamana Temple. The 2014 film *Jhola,* exploring the practice of *suttee* (when a Hindu widow immolates herself on her husband's funeral pyre), was entered, but subsequently not nominated, for the Best Foreign Language Film in the 87th Academy Awards.

Literature

Nepal's literary history is brief, dating back to just the 19th century. The written language was little used before then, although religious verse, folklore, songs and translations of Sanskrit and Urdu dating back to the 13th century have been found.

One of the first authors to establish Nepali as a literary language was Bhanubhakta Acharya (1814–68), who broke away from the influence of Indian literature and recorded the Ramayana in Nepali; this was not simply a translation but a Nepali-ised version of the Hindu epic. Motiram Bhatta (1866–96) also played a major role in 19th-century literature, as did Lakshmi Prasad Devkota (1909–59) in the 20th century.

In a country where literacy levels are low, Nepal's literary community has always struggled. However, today a vibrant and enthusiastic literary community exists, meeting in teashops and bookstalls in Kathmandu and other urban centres.

Himalayan Voices: an Introduction to Modern Nepali Literature, by Michael Hutt, includes work by contemporary poets and short-story writers.

Environment & Wildlife

Nepal is both blessed and burdened by its incredible environment. Its economy, history, resources and culture are all intrinsically tied to the string of magnificent mountains that represent a continental collision zone. This often-daunting landscape has played a role in setting back development because of the logistical problems of bringing roads, electricity, health care and education to remote communities in mountainous areas. However, as the human population continues to increase and technology aids development of once-remote ecosystems, the Himalaya and plains are faced with enormous environmental threats.

The Lay of the Land

Nepal is a small, landlocked strip of land, 800km long and 200km wide. However, it fits a lot of terrain into just 147,181 sq km. Heading north from the Indian border, the landscape rises from just 70m above sea level to 8848m at the tip of Mt Everest. This dramatic landscape provides an outstanding variety of habitats for an incredible array of plants and animals.

Colliding Continents

Imagine the space currently occupied by Nepal as an open expanse of water, and the Tibetan plateau as the coast. This was the situation until 60 million years ago when the Indo-Australian plate collided with the Eurasian continent, bucking the earth's crust up into mighty ridges and forming the mountains we now call the Himalaya.

The Sanskrit word Himalaya means abode (alaya) of the snows (himal). There is no such thing as the Himalayas. To pronounce it correctly, as they do in the corridors of the Royal Geographical Society, emphasise the second syllable – him-aaar-liya, old chap...

The upheaval of mountains caused the temporary obstruction of rivers that once flowed unimpeded from Eurasia to the sea. Simultaneously, new rivers arose on the southern slopes of these young mountains as moist winds from the tropical seas to the south rose and precipitated. For the next 60 million years, the mountains moved up, and rivers and glaciers cut downwards, creating the peaks and valleys seen across Nepal today.

The modern landscape of Nepal – a grid of four major mountain systems, incised by the north–south gorges of rivers – is not the final story. The Indo-Australian plate is still sliding under the Eurasian Himalaya at a rate of 37mm per year and pushing the Himalaya even higher. As fast as the mountains rise, they are being eroded by glaciers, rivers and landslides, and chipped away by earthquakes and the effects of cold and heat.

Nepal is still an active seismic zone, as demonstrated by the massive earthquakes that struck central Nepal in April and May 2015.

Valley Low & Mountain High

Nepal's concertina topography consists of several physiographic regions, or natural zones: the southern plains, the four mountain ranges, and the valleys and hills in between. Most people live in the fertile lowlands or on the sunny southern slopes of mountains. Above 4000m the only residents are yak herders, who retreat into the valleys with the onset of winter.

EARTHQUAKE-PRONE NEPAL

The massive tremors that ravaged central Nepal on 25 April and 12 May 2015 were not the first major earthquakes to hit the former Himalayan kingdom. The phenomenal pressure created by the collision of the Indo-Australian and Eurasian plates has caused a series of catastrophic earthquakes over the centuries.

The 1934 Bihar-Nepal earthquake, which occurred on the same fault line as the 2015 tremors, killed an estimated 10,000 people, while a third of the population of Kathmandu are thought to have died in the deadly quake that struck in 1255. In all these cases, the damage was amplified by the geology of the Kathmandu Valley – a deep base of soft clay makes the area highly vulnerable to soil liquefaction in earthquake conditions.

Scientists believe that the 2015 quakes have relieved a considerable amount of pressure along the fault line, but with the Indo-Australian plate still sliding under the Eurasian plate at a rate of 3.7 centimetres per year, further tremors cannot be ruled out over the coming decades.

The Terai & Chure Hills

The only truly flat land in Nepal is the Terai (or Tarai), a patchwork of paddy fields, sal and riverine forests, tiny thatched villages and sprawling industrial cities. The vast expanse of the Gangetic plain extends for 40km into Nepal before the land rises to create the Chure Hills. With an average height of 1000m, this minor ridge runs the length of the country, separating the Terai from a second low-lying area called the inner Terai, or the Dun.

The Terai makes up only 17% of Nepal's area but holds around 50% of its population and 70% of its agricultural land.

Mahabharat Range

North of the inner Terai, the land rises again to form the Mahabharat Range, or the 'Middle Hills'. These vary between 1500m and 2700m in height and form the heartland of the inhabited highlands of Nepal. Locals cultivate rice, barley, millet, wheat, maize and other crops on spectacular terraced fields set among patches of subtropical and temperate forest. These hills are cut by three major river systems: the Karnali, the Narayani and the Sapt Kosi.

The Kali Gandaki Valley between the Annapurna and Dhaulagiri massifs is considered the world's deepest gorge, with a vertical gain of 7km.

Pahar Zone

Between the Mahabharat Range and the Himalaya lies a broad, extensively cultivated belt called the Pahar zone. This includes the fertile valleys of Kathmandu, Banepa and Pokhara, which were once the beds of lakes, formed by trapped rivers. After the Terai this is the most inhabited part of Nepal, and the expanding human population is putting a massive strain on natural resources.

The Himalaya

One-third of the total length of the Himalaya lies inside Nepal's borders, and the country claims 10 of the world's 14 tallest mountains. Because of the southerly latitude (similar to that of Florida), along with the reliable rainfall, the mountains are cloaked in vegetation to a height of 3500m to 4000m. People mainly inhabit the areas below 2700m.

The Trans-Himalaya

North of the first ridge of the Himalaya is a high-altitude desert, similar to the Tibetan plateau. This area encompasses the arid valleys of Mustang, Manang and Dolpo. The moisture-laden clouds of the monsoon drop all their rain on the south side of the mountains, leaving the

Saligrams (fossilised ammonites) are found throughout the Himalaya and are regarded as symbols of Vishnu – they also provide proof that the Himalaya used to lie beneath the ancient Tethys Sea.

MT EVEREST

Everest has gone by a number of different names over the years. The Survey of India christened the mountain 'Peak XV,' but it was renamed Everest after Sir George Everest (pronounced '*Eve*-rest'), the surveyor general of India in 1865. It was later discovered that the mountain already had a name – Sherpas call the peak Chomolungma, after the female guardian deity of the mountain, who rides a red tiger and is one of the five sisters of long life. There was no Nepali name for the mountain until 1956 when the historian Babu Ram Acharya created the name Sagarmatha, meaning 'head of the sky'.

Using triangulation from the plains of India, the Survey of India established the elevation of the summit of Everest at 8839m. In 1954 this was revised to 8848m using data from 12 different survey stations around the mountain. In 1999, a team sponsored by National Geographic used GPS data to produce a new elevation of 8850m, but in 2002 a Chinese team made measurements from the summit using ice radar and GPS systems and produced a height of 8844.43m.

So is Everest shrinking? No; the Chinese calculated the height of the bedrock of the mountain, without the accumulated snow and ice. In fact, Everest is still growing at a rate of 6mm a year as plate tectonics drives the Indo-Australian subcontinent underneath Eurasia. In 2011 the Chinese agreed with the Nepalis that the official height is 8848m.

As a postscript, a Chinese study after the 2015 earthquake concluded that the entire bulk of Mt Everest shifted southwest by three centimetres but remained the same height!

Trans-Himalaya in permanent rain shadow. Surreal crags, spires and badlands eroded by the scouring action of the wind are characteristic of this starkly beautiful landscape.

Wildlife

Nepal is a region of exceptional biodiversity, with a rare concentration of varied landscapes and climatic conditions. If you're a nature buff, it's worth carrying a spotters' guide.

Mammals & Birds

The diverse environments of the Himalaya and the Middle Hills provide a home for a remarkable array of birds, reptiles, amphibians and mammals. However, poaching and hunting threaten many mammal and bird species. Your best chances for spotting wildlife are in national parks and conservation areas, or high in the mountains far away from human habitation.

Bis Hajaar Tal (literally '20,000 lakes') in Chitwan National Park and the Koshi Tappu Wildlife Reserve are both Ramsar sites (www.ramsar.org), designated as wetlands of international importance.

Signature Species

Nepal has a number of 'signature species' that every visitor wants to see. Unfortunately, these also tend to be the species most threatened by poaching and habitat loss. Opportunities to view the following animals are usually restricted to national parks, reserves and sparsely populated areas of western Nepal. Chitwan National Park is home to most of the signature species, including tigers, leopards, rhinos and sloth bears.

At the top of the jungle food chain is the royal Bengal tiger (*'bagh'* in Nepali), which is solitary and territorial. Chitwan, Bardia and Banke National Parks and Sukla Phanta Wildlife Reserve in the Terai protect sufficient habitat to sustain viable breeding populations. In addition to loss of habitat, a major threat to tigers is poaching to supply body parts for Tibetan and Chinese traditional medicine and clothing.

The spotted leopard (*chituwa*) is more common than the tiger and is a significant threat to livestock. Like the tiger, this nocturnal creature has been known to target humans when it is unable, through old age or illness, to hunt its usual prey. The endangered snow leopard *(heung chituwa)* is so rare and shy that it is seldom seen, but there are thought to be 350 to 500 snow leopards surviving in the high Himalaya, particularly around Dolpo. Snow leopards are so elusive that many locals believe the animals have the power to vanish at will.

Found in the grass plains *(phanta)* of the Terai region, the one-horned rhinoceros *(gaida)* is the largest of the three Asian rhino species. Rhino populations plummeted due to poaching during the Maoist insurgency but they have gradually recovered since 2005 – today there are around 500 rhinos in Chitwan and smaller populations in Bardia National Park and Sukla Phanta Wildlife Reserve.

The lumbering and shaggy-coated sloth bear *(bhalu)* boasts a formidable set of front claws for tearing into termite mounds. The bear's poor eyesight and its tendency to swipe away with those claws when startled has earned it a gnarly reputation.

The only wild Asian elephants *(hathi)* in Nepal are in the western part of the Terai and Chure Hills. However, herds of domesticated elephants are found at all the national parks in the Terai, where they are used for antipoaching patrols and carrying tourists on safaris.

Perhaps the rarest animal of all is the endangered Ganges River dolphin *(susu)*. This mammalian predator lacks lenses in its eyes and is almost blind. It hunts its way through the silty waters of lowland rivers using sonar. There are thought to be fewer than 100 dolphins left in Nepal, with most living in the Karnali River.

Smaller Mammals

Deer are abundant in the lowland national parks, providing a vital food source for tigers and leopards. Prominent species include the sambar and the spotted deer. In forests up to 2400m, you may hear the uncannily doglike call of the barking deer *(muntjac)*. At higher altitudes, look for the pocked-sized musk deer, which stands just 50cm high at the shoulder. Unfortunately these animals have been severely depleted by hunting to obtain the musk gland found in the abdomen of male deer.

At high altitudes, look out for the Himalayan tahr, a shaggy mountain goat, and the blue sheep ('*naur*' in Tibetan, '*bharal*' in Nepali), which is genetically positioned somewhere between goats and sheep. The boulder fields and stunted forests of the high Himalaya also provide shelter for several small rodents. The mouse-hare *(pika)* is commonly spotted scurrying nervously between rocks on trekking trails. You must climb even higher to the Trans-Himalayan zone in western Nepal to see the Himalayan marmot, related to the American groundhog.

Soul of the Rhino, by Hemanta R Mishra, is an intriguing peek into the world of the one-horned Indian rhinoceros and the humans who share its habitat.

Nepalis divide the year into six, not four, seasons: Basanta (spring), Grisma (pre-monsoon heat), Barkha (monsoon), Sharad (postmonsoon), Hemanta (autumn) and Sheet (winter).

ENVIRONMENT & WILDLIFE WILDLIFE

CROCODILES

Nepal is home to two species of crocodile. The endangered and striking-looking gharial inhabits rivers, hunting for fish with its elongated snout lined with sharp teeth. Fossils of similar crocodiles have been found that date back 100 million years, attesting to the effectiveness of its odd-looking design. The gharial was hunted to the brink of extinction, but populations have recovered since the establishment of hatcheries.

The stocky marsh mugger prefers stagnant water and is omnivorous, feeding on anything within reach, including people. In fact, the Western word 'mugger' comes from the Hindi/Nepali name for this skulking predator.

Birds

More than 850 bird species are known in Nepal and almost half of these can be spotted in the Kathmandu Valley. The main breeding season and the best time to spot birds is March to May. Resident bird numbers are augmented by migratory species, which arrive in the Terai from November to March from Tibet and Siberia. The best places in Nepal for birdwatching are Koshi Tappu Wildlife Reserve and Chitwan National Park. The best spots in the Kathmandu Valley are Pulchowki Mountain, Nagarjun Hill and Shivapuri Nagarjun National Park.

Eight species of stork have been identified along the watercourses of the Terai, and demoiselle cranes fly down the Kali Gandaki and Dudh Kosi for the winter, before returning in spring to their Tibetan nesting grounds. The endangered sarus crane can be spotted in Bardia National Park and the Lumbini Crane Sanctuary.

Raptors and birds of prey of all sizes are found in Nepal. In the Kathmandu Valley and Terai, keep an eye out for the sweeping silhouettes of vultures and fork-tailed pariah kites circling ominously in the haze. In the mountains, watch for golden eagles and the huge Himalayan griffon and lammergeier.

There are six species of pheasant in Nepal, including the national bird, the *danphe*, also known as the Himalayan monal or impeyan pheasant. Females are a dull brown, while males are an iridescent rainbow of colours. In areas frequented by trekkers, these birds are often quite tame, though they will launch themselves downhill in a falling, erratic flight if disturbed.

Nepal hosts 17 species of cuckoo, which arrive in March, heralding the coming of spring. The call of the Indian cuckoo is likened to the Nepali phrase *kaphal pakyo,* meaning 'the fruit of the box myrtle is ripe'. The call of the common hawk cuckoo sounds like the words 'brain fever' – or so it was described by British *sahibs* (gentlemen) as they lay sweating with malarial fevers.

While trekking through forests, keep an eye out for members of the timalid family. The spiny babbler is Nepal's only endemic species, and the black-capped sibia, with its constant prattle and ringing song, is frequently heard in wet temperate forests. In the Pokhara region, the Indian roller is conspicuous when it takes flight, flashing iridescent turquoise on its wings. Local superstition has it that if someone about to embark on a journey sees a roller going their way it is a good omen.

Another colourful character is the hoopoe, which has a retractable crest, a long curved bill, eye-catching orange plumage, and black-and-white stripes on its wings. Nepal is also home to 30 species of flycatcher and 60 species of warbler, as well as bee-eaters, drongos, minivets, parakeets and sunbirds.

Birds of Nepal, by Robert Fleming Sr, Robert Fleming Jr and Lain Singh Bangdel, is a field guide to Nepal's many hundreds of bird species. *Birds of Nepal,* by Richard Grimmett and Carol Inskipp, is a comprehensive paperback with line drawings.

Nepal covers only 0.1% of the world's surface area but is home to nearly 10% of the world's species of birds, including 72 critically endangered species.

MONKEY MAYHEM

Because of Hanuman, the monkey god from the Ramayana, monkeys are considered holy and are well protected, if not pampered, in Nepal. You will often see troops of muscular red-rumped rhesus macaques harassing tourists and pilgrims for food scraps at Kathmandu's monuments and temples. These monkeys can be openly aggressive and they carry rabies, so appreciate them from a distance (and if that doesn't work, carry a stick).

You may also spot the slender common langur, with its short grey fur and black face, in forested areas up to 3700m. This species is more gentle than the thuggish macaque but again, keep your bananas out of sight and out of reach.

DINNER AT THE ROTTING CARCASS

Three of Nepal's nine species of vulture are critically endangered with thousands of vultures dying every year after scavenging dead cows that have been treated with the anti-inflammatory drug diclofenac. When the problem was recognised the drug was soon banned (2006) and a replacement found. Unfortunately, however, there is still illegal use of similar drugs in Nepal and India.

Nevertheless, a scheme to feed vultures with uncontaminated meat has yielded remarkable results. Nicknamed the 'vulture restaurant', the project doubled the vulture population of Nawalparashi district (near Tiger Tops Tharu Lodge) in the western Terai in just two years. Old cattle, being sacred to Hindus, are not killed and can become a burden to farmers. Now they can be sold to the vulture restaurant where they are tested for contamination, allowed to live out their full life, and only fed to vultures after a natural death. Five other vulture restaurants have been established across Nepal, including one near Lumbini and one near Pokhara.

Around watercourses, look out for thrushes, such as the handsome white-capped river chat and the delightfully named plumbeous redstart. Scan the surrounding trees for the black-and-white pied kingfisher and the white-breasted kingfisher with its iridescent turquoise jacket.

Different species of crows have adapted to different altitudes. The yellow-billed blue magpie and Himalayan tree pie are commonly seen in the temperate zone. Above the treeline, red- and yellow-billed choughs gather in flocks, particularly in areas frequented by humans. In the Trans-Himalayan region you will also see the menacing black raven, which scours the valleys looking for scavenging opportunities.

Bird Conservation Nepal (www.birdlifenepal.org) is an excellent Nepali organisation based in Kathmandu that organises bird-watching trips and publishes books, birding checklists and a good quarterly newsletter.

Plants

There are about 6500 known species of tree, shrub and wildflower in Nepal, but perhaps the most famous is *Rhododendron arboreum* (*lali gurans* in Nepali), the national flower of Nepal. It might better be described as a tree, reaching heights of 18m and forming whole forests in the Himalaya region. More than 30 other species of rhododendrons are found in the foothills of the Himalaya. The rhododendron forests burst into flower in March and April, painting the landscape in swaths of white, pink and red.

The best time to see the other wildflowers of the Himalaya in bloom is during the monsoon. The mountain views may be often obscured but the ground underfoot will be a carpet of colour. Many of the alpine species found above the treeline bear flowers in autumn, including irises, gentians, anemones and the downy-petalled edelweiss.

In the foothills of the Himalaya, as well as in the plains, look for the magnificent mushrooming canopies of banyan and pipal trees, which often form the focal point of villages. The pipal tree has a special religious significance in Nepal – the Buddha gained enlightenment under a pipal tree and Hindus revere various species of pipal as symbols of Vishnu and Hanuman.

Sal, a broad-leaved, semideciduous hardwood, dominates the low-lying forests of the Terai. Sal leaves are used as disposable plates and the heavy wood is used for construction and boat building. On the flat plains, many areas are covered by *phanta* – this grass can grow to 2.5m high and is used by villagers for thatching and by elephants for a snack on the run.

Himalayan Flowers & Trees, by Dorothy Mierow and Tirtha Bahadur Shrestha, is the best available field guide to the plants of Nepal.

National Parks & Reserves

Nepal's first national park, Chitwan, was established in 1973 in the Terai. There are now 10 national parks, three wildlife reserves, three conservation areas and, somewhat incongruously, one hunting reserve, protecting 18% of the land in Nepal. Entry fees apply for all the national parks and reserves, including conserved areas on trekking routes in the mountains.

The main agency overseeing national parks and conservation areas is the **Department of National Parks & Wildlife Conservation** (www. dnpwc.gov.np). However, the last few years have seen a shift in the management to international nongovernmental organisations (NGOs) and not-for-profit organisations with a degree of autonomy from the government of Nepal. The **National Trust for Nature Conservation** (www. ntnc.org.np), formerly the King Mahendra Trust for Nature Conservation, runs the Annapurna Conservation Area Project and Manaslu Conservation Area. The **Mountain Institute** (www.mountain.org) runs a number of conservation projects in the Himalaya.

NATIONAL PARKS & CONSERVATION AREAS

CA = Conservation Area, HR = Hunting Reserve, NP = National Park, WR = Wildlife Reserve

NAME	LOCATION	FEATURES	BEST TIME TO VISIT	ENTRY FEE (RS)
Annapurna CA (p299)	north of Pokhara	most popular trekking area in Nepal, high peaks, diverse landscapes, varied culture	Oct–May	2000
Banke NP (p363)	far western Terai	sal forest, tigers, one-horned rhinoceros	Oct–early Apr	1000
Bardia NP (p272)	far western Terai	Geruwa River, tigers, rhinoceros, over 250 bird species	Oct–early Apr	1000
Chitwan NP (p242)	central Terai	sal forest, rhinoceros, tigers, gharials, 450 bird species, World Heritage Site	Oct-Feb	1500
Dhorpatan HR	west-central Nepal	Nepal's only hunting reserve (access is difficult), blue sheep	Mar-Apr	3000
Kanchenjunga CA (p309)	far eastern Nepal	third-highest mountain in the world, blue sheep, snow leopards	Mar-Apr, Oct-Nov	2000
Khaptad NP (p277)	far western Nepal	core area is important religious site	Mar-Apr	3000
Koshi Tappu WR (p283)	eastern Nepal	Sapt Kosi River, grasslands, 439 bird species	Mar-Apr, Oct-Nov	1000

BANKE NATIONAL PARK

With the creation of the 550-sq-km Banke National Park in 2010, Nepal gained its 10th national park and was able to boast one of the largest stretches of tiger habitat in Asia. Banke adjoins Suhelwa Wildlife Sanctuary in India and is connected to Bardia National Park through community forests and buffer zones. Along with India's Katerniaghat Wildlife Sanctuary, these reserves provide an important corridor for wild elephants and rhinos, and, it is hoped, a significant boost to tiger conservation. This increase in officially protected tiger habitat was part of Nepal's 2010 pledge to double the country's tiger population by 2022 (the next Chinese zodiac Year of the Tiger).

The government imposed the first protected areas with little partnership with locals and initially without their cooperation. Recent initiatives have concentrated on educating local people and accommodating their needs, rather than evicting them completely from the land.

Langtang NP	northeast of Kathmandu	varied topography, culture, migratory birds	Mar-Apr	3000
Makalu-Barun NP & CA (p309)	eastern Nepal	bordering Sagarmatha NP, protecting diverse mountain landscapes	Oct-May	3000
Manaslu CA (p309)	west-central Nepal	rugged terrain, 11 types of forest, bordering Annapurna CA	Mar-Apr, Oct-Nov	2000
Parsa WR	central Terai	bordering Chitwan NP, sal forests, wild elephants, 300 bird species	Oct-Apr	1000
Rara NP (p271)	northwestern Nepal	Nepal's biggest lake, little visited, migratory birds	Mar-May, Oct-Dec	3000
Sagarmatha NP (p293)	Everest region	highest mountains on the planet, World Heritage Site, monasteries, Sherpa culture	Oct-May	3000
Shey Phoksumdo NP	Dolpo, western Nepal	Trans-Himalayan ecosystem, alpine flowers, snow leopards, blue sheep	Jun-Sep	1000
Shivapuri Nagarjun NP (p136)	northeast of Kathmandu	close to Kathmandu, many bird & butterfly species, good hiking & cycling	Oct-May	250
Sukla Phanta WR (p275)	southwestern Nepal	riverine flood plain, grasslands, endangered swamp deer, wild elephants	Oct-Apr	1000

Environmental Challenges

The environment of Nepal is fragile and a rapidly growing population is constantly adding to environmental pressures. Much of the land between the Himalaya and the Terai has been vigorously modified to provide space for crops, animals and houses. Forests have been cleared and wildlife populations depleted, and roads have eaten into valleys that were previously accessible only on foot. As a result, Shangri La is not immune to the environmental challenges that confront a shrinking planet.

Population growth is the biggest issue facing the environment in Nepal. More people need more land for agriculture and more natural resources for building, heating and cooking. The population of Nepal is increasing at a rate of 1.2% every year (as of 2013), and food security and growth is providing the economic incentive for the settlement of previously uninhabited areas.

There have also been some environmental successes in Nepal. Foreign and Nepali NGOs have provided solar panels, biogas and kerosene-powered stoves, and parabolic solar cookers for thousands of farms, trekking lodges, schools and monasteries across Nepal.

A number of organisations can provide more information on environmental issues in Nepal.

Bird Conservation Nepal (www.birdlifenepal.org)
Himalayan Nature (www.himalayannature.org)
International Centre for Integrated Mountain Development (www.icimod.org)
International Union for Conservation of Nature (www.iucnnepal.org)
National Trust for Nature Conservation (www.ntnc.org.np)
Resources Himalaya (www.resourceshimalaya.org)
Wildlife Conservation Nepal (www.wcn.org.np)
World Wildlife Fund Nepal (www.wwfnepal.org)

> Nepal's Terai national parks are under threat from an alien invader – the South American creeper *Mikania micrantha*, which is dubbed 'mile a minute' owing to its prodigious growth rate.

Deforestation

Almost 80% of Nepali citizens rely on firewood for heating and cooking, particularly in the mountains, leading to massive problems with deforestation. Nepal has lost more than 70% of its forest cover in modern times and travellers are contributing to the problem by increasing the demand for firewood in mountain areas.

As well as robbing native species of their natural habitat, deforestation drives animals directly into conflict with human beings. The loss of tree cover is a major contributing factor to the landslides that scar the valleys of the Himalaya after every monsoon.

It's not all doom and gloom though – in recent years, a number of community forests have been established on the boundaries of national parks. The forests are communally owned and the sustainable harvest of timber and other natural resources provides an economic alternative to poaching and resource gathering inside the parks. See the website of the **Federation of Community Forest Users** (www.fecofun.org.np) for more information.

> Nature Treks (www.nature-treks.com) offers organised walks with expert naturalists at Shivapuri Nagarjun National Park, Chitwan National Park, Bardia National Park and in the Langtang area.

Wildlife Poaching

Nepal's 10-year Maoist insurgency did not only affect human beings. Soldiers were withdrawn from national-park checkpoints, leading to a massive upsurge in poaching. Nepal's rhino population fell by 30% between 2000 and 2005; elephants, tigers, leopards and other endangered species were also targeted.

CLIMATE CHANGE IN THE HIMALAYA

Every year, during the monsoon, the Terai faces severe flooding problems exacerbated by deforestation on the mountain slopes and the plains themselves.

In the mountains, the flood risk comes from a different source. Rising global temperatures are melting the glaciers that snake down from the Himalaya, swelling glacial lakes to dangerous levels.

In 1985 a natural dam collapsed in the Thame Valley, releasing the trapped waters of the Dig Tsho lake and sending devastating floods roaring along the Dudh Kosi Valley.

Scientists are now watching the Imja Tsho in the Chhukung Valley with alarm. Since 1960 the lake has grown by over 34 million cu metres – when it ruptures, experts are predicting a 'vertical tsunami' that will affect one of the most heavily populated and trekked parts of the Himalaya.

Although there is no such thing as a 'normal' monsoon, the recent devastating monsoons of 2013 and 2014 raise concerns about climate change. In both years massive rain events inundated large areas of Nepal's Terai, as well as India, and led to massive landslides and loss of life and property.

The main engines driving poaching are the trade in animal parts for Chinese and Tibetan traditional medicine and to a lesser extent the trade in animal pelts to Tibet for traditional costumes known as *chubas*. Travellers can avoid contributing to the problem by rejecting souvenirs made from animal products.

Hydroelectricity

On the face of things, harnessing the power of Nepal's rivers to create electricity sounds like a win-win situation, but the environmental impact of building new hydroelectric plants can be devastating. Entire valleys may be flooded to create reservoirs and most of the energy may be diverted to the overpopulated Kathmandu Valley or exported to China and India.

As well as displacing local people and damaging the local environment, large hydro schemes affect the flow of water downstream, disrupting the passage of nutrient-rich silt to agricultural land in the plains.

Currently there are large-scale hydroelectric power plants on the Babai, Bhote Kosi, Kali Gandaki, Marsyangdi, Rapti, Roshi, Trisuli and West Seti Rivers. In 2014, India and Nepal agreed to four new large-scale projects.

For information on alternative energy projects in Nepal, visit the websites of the Centre for Rural Technology (www.crtnepal.org), the Foundation for Sustainable Technologies (www.fost-nepal.org) and Drokpa (www.drokpa.org).

Tourism

Tourism has brought health care, education, electricity and wealth to some of the most remote, isolated communities on earth, but it has also had a massive impact on the local environment.

Forests are cleared to provide timber for the construction of new lodges and fuel for cooking and heating, and trekkers contribute massively to the build-up of litter and the erosion of mountain trails.

Even the apparent benefits of tourism can have environmental implications – the wealth that tourism has brought to villages in the Himalaya has allowed many farmers to increase the size of their herds of goats, cows and yaks, leading to yet more deforestation as woodland is cleared to provide temporary pastures.

Water Supplies

Despite the natural abundance of water, water shortages are another chronic problem in Nepal, particularly in the Kathmandu Valley. Where water is available, it is often contaminated with heavy metals, industrial chemicals, bacteria and human waste. In Kathmandu, the holy Bagmati River has become one of the most polluted rivers on earth, although there have been concerted efforts to clean the river of visible litter.

In the Terai, one of the biggest problems is arsenic poisoning from contaminated drinking water. Up to 1.4 million people are thought to be at risk from this deadly toxin, which is drawn into wells and reservoirs from contaminated aquifers.

Survival
Guide

Directory A–Z

Accommodation

In Kathmandu and Pokhara there is a wide variety of accommodation, from rock-bottom fleapits to five-star international hotels. Prices are rising, especially in Kathmandu, but it's still possible to find a place with pleasant gardens and decent rooms for less than Rs 1500 (US$15) a night, including private bathroom and hot water.

Some of Nepal's best deals are now to be found in its stylish midrange and top-end accommodation.

Most hotels have a wide range of rooms under one roof, including larger (often top-floor) deluxe rooms that are good for families and small groups. Budget rooms are often on the darker, lower floors and have solar-heated hot-water showers, which won't be hot in the mornings or on cloudy days. Midrange rooms have better mattresses, satellite TV and a tub. Almost all hotels offer wi-fi these days.

The main towns of the Terai have hotels of a reasonable standard, with rooms with fans and mosquito nets costing around Rs 500 (US$5); grimy, basic places catering to local demand start at around Rs 100 (less than US$1). Some of the cheap places have tattered mosquito nets, if any at all.

Elsewhere in the country the choice of hotels can be very limited, but you will find what are commonly called teahouses (but are generally simple guesthouses) along most of the major trekking trails, making Nepal one of the few places in the world where you can trek for three weeks without needing a tent. On lesser-trekked trails, places may be spartan – the accommodation may be dorm-style or simply an open room in which to unroll your sleeping bag, and electricity and hot, running water a dream – but the Annapurna and Everest treks have excellent lodges and guesthouses every couple of hours and Langtang isn't far behind.

Many teahouses can be very cold at night.

All midrange and top-end hotels charge a value added tax (VAT) of 13% and a service charge of 10%. Most midrange and top-end places quote their prices in US dollars (though you pay in rupees). Budget places quote prices in rupees and sometimes include or quietly forget about tax.

Most hotels have different rates for single and double occupancy, but the 'single room' may be much smaller than the double. The best deal for a solo traveller is to get a double room for a single price.

Discounts

Nepal's hotel prices are highly seasonal, with peak season running from October to November and March to April, but even beyond this room rates fluctuate according to tourist demand. You will find that rates drop even lower during the monsoon season (June to September).

The exact room rate you will be quoted depends on the season and current numbers of tourists. At many hotels the printed tariffs are pure fiction, published to fulfil government star-rating requirements and in the hope that you might be silly enough to pay them. Some midrange hotels offer discounts for booking online (and a free airport transfer), but you'll get at least this much on the spot, if not more.

PRICE RANGES

The following price indicators refer to a double room with bathroom in high season. Rates generally do not include taxes, unless otherwise noted.

$ less than US$25 (Rs 2500)

$$ US$25-50 (Rs 2500-8000)

$$$ more than US$80 (Rs 8000)

If business is slow you can often negotiate a deluxe room for a standard-room rate or inclusive of tax. When business picks up (as is currently the case), you may just have to take what's on offer.

You can also negotiate cheaper rates for longer stays. In the cool of autumn and spring you can get a further discount on rooms that are air-conditioned simply by agreeing to turn off the air-con.

Activities

Nepal is the world's greatest trekking destination, even (and perhaps especially) if the only camping you do at home is lip-syncing to Kylie Minogue and Queen songs, as it is possible to avoid sleeping under canvas entirely.

There are also plenty of great day hikes around Nepal, particularly in the Kathmandu Valley and around Bandipur, Tansen and Pokhara.

Many adventure travel companies offer combination activity trips that include some rafting, kayaking and canyoning using a fixed riverside camp. Nepal is a great place to spend three or four days learning the basics of kayaking, rock climbing or mountaineering.

See our Outdoor Activities chapter (p43) for more information.

Children

Increasing numbers of people are travelling with their children in Nepal, and with a bit of planning it can be remarkably hassle-free. While many people trek with older

children, heading out on the trail with smaller children for any length of time or on any higher routes with children of any age is generally not to be advised. Check out Lonely Planet's *Travel with Children* for handy hints and advice about the pros and cons of travelling with kids.

➡ In the main tourist centres (Kathmandu and Pokhara), most hotels have triple rooms and quite often a suite with four beds, which are ideal for families with young children. Finding a room with a bathtub can be a problem at the bottom end of the market.

➡ Many Kathmandu hotels have a garden or roof garden, which can be good play areas. Check them thoroughly, however, as some are definitely not safe for young children.

➡ Walking the crowded, narrow and pavement-less streets of Kathmandu and other towns can be a hassle with young kids unless you can get them up off the ground – a backpack or sling is ideal. A pusher or stroller is more trouble than it's worth unless you bring one with oversized wheels, suitable for rough pavements.

➡ Keep meal times stress-free by eating breakfast at your hotel, having lunch at a place with a garden (there are plenty of these) and going to restaurants armed with colouring books, stories and other distractions.

➡ Disposable nappies are available in Kathmandu and Pokhara, but for a price – better to bring them with you if possible.

➡ Cots are generally not available in budget or midrange hotels; similarly, nappy-changing facilities and high chairs are a rarity.

➡ Trekking *is* possible with children, but it pays to limit the altitude; consider hiring a porter to carry younger children in a doko basket.

Customs Regulations

All baggage is X-rayed on arrival and departure, though it's a pretty haphazard process. In addition to the import and export of drugs, customs is concerned with the illegal export of antiques.

➡ You may not import Nepali rupees, and only nationals of Nepal and India may import Indian currency.

➡ There are no other restrictions on bringing in either cash or travellers cheques, but the amount taken out at departure should not exceed the amount brought in.

➡ Officially you should declare cash or travellers cheques in excess of US$2000, or the equivalent, but no one seems to bother with this, and it is laxly enforced.

Antiques

Customs' main concern is preventing the export of antique works of art, and with good reason: Nepal has been a particular victim of international art theft over the last 20 years.

It is very unlikely that souvenirs sold to travellers will be antique (despite the claims of the vendors), but if there is any doubt, they should be cleared and a certificate obtained from the **Department of Archaeology** (Map p68; ☑01-4250683; Ramshah Path, Kathmandu; ☉10am-2pm Sat, to 3pm Sun-Thu) in central Kathmandu's National Archives building. If you visit the department between 10am and 1pm, you should be able to pick up a certificate by 5pm the same day. These controls also apply to the export of precious and semiprecious stones.

Electricity

Electricity is 220V/50 cycles; 120V appliances from the USA will need a transformer. Sockets usually take plugs with three round pins, sometimes the small variety, sometimes the large. Some sockets take plugs with two round pins. Local electrical shops sell cheap adapters.

Blackouts ('load shedding') are a fact of life across Nepal, especially in Kathmandu; these peak in the monsoon period of June to August with up to six hours a day of cuts. Power surges are also likely, so bring a voltage guard with spike suppressor (automatic cut-off switch) for your laptop. Note that power supplies to some rural areas may be disrupted because of earthquake damage.

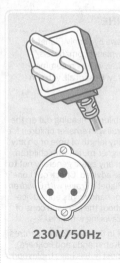

230V/50Hz

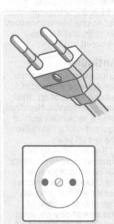

230V/50Hz

Embassies & Consulates

Travellers continuing beyond Nepal may need visas for Bangladesh, China, India, Myanmar (Burma) and Thailand.

The only visas available in Kathmandu for Tibet (actually there's no such thing as a 'visa for Tibet'; it's just a Chinese group visa and a travel permit for Tibet) are for organised groups. Individuals wishing to travel directly to China (not Tibet) will need to show an air ticket to Chengdu, Beijing, Shanghai or Guangzhou to prove that they aren't going to Tibet.

To find Nepali embassies and consulates in other countries, check out the websites of Nepal's **Ministry of Foreign Affairs** (www.mofa.gov.np) or **Department of Immigration** (www.nepal-immigration.gov.np).

Australian Embassy (☎01-4371678; www.nepal.embassy.gov.au; Bansbari, Kathmandu)

Bangladeshi Embassy (☎01-4390130; www.bangladoot.org.np; Basundhara, Chakrapath) Tourist visas are issued in a couple of days.

Canadian Consulate (Map p68; ☎01-4441976; canadaconsul@mail.com.np; 47 Lal Durbar Marg; ⊘9am-noon Mon-Fri) Canada only maintains a consulate offering limited assistance in Kathmandu.

Chinese Embassy (Map p68; ☎01-4440286; http://np.china-embassy.org/eng; Hattisar, Kathmandu) Visa applications are accepted on Monday to Friday from 9.45am to 11am; visas normally take three working days to be issued but can be done in just one day if you pay extra. The visa section is located in Hattisar; the main embassy is in Baluwatar.

French Embassy (Map p68; ☎01-4412332; www.ambafrance-np.org; Lazimpat, Kathmandu; ⊘9am-11.30am Mon, Thu & Fri) French embassy, but no consular section.

German Embassy (Map p68; ☎01-4217200; www.kathmandu.diplo.de; Gyaneshwar Marg 690, Kathmandu; ⊘9am-11.30am)

Indian Embassy (Map p68; ☎01-4410900; www.indianembassy.org.np; 336 Kapurdhara Marg, Lainchaur; ⊘9.30am-noon & 1.30-5pm Mon-Fri) Getting an Indian tourist visa in Nepal (or anywhere else) is a rather complicated and time-consuming process. Indian visa applications are only accepted after an online visa form (https://indianvisaonline.gov.in) has been completed. For full details on obtaining the visa see the embassy website. Tourist visas take between seven and 10 days to issue.

Israeli Embassy (Map p68; ☎01-4411811; http://kathmandu.mfa.gov.il; Lazimpat, Kathmandu; ⊘9am-5pm Mon-Thu, to 2pm Fri)

Japanese Embassy (☎01-4426680; www.np.emb-japan.go.jp; Pani Pokhari, Kathmandu; ⊘9am-1pm & 2-5pm Mon-Fri)

Myanmar Embassy (Burma; ☎01-5592811, 01-5592774; Nakkhu Height, Char Ghare, Sainbu Bhaisepati, Ward 4; ⊘visa applications 10am-noon) In an inconvenient location on the road to Bungamati, south of Patan.

Netherlands Embassy
(Map p138;✆01-5523444; www.netherlandsconsulate.org. np; Jawalakhel, Patan; ☺9am-4.30pm Mon-Thu, to 1pm Fri)

Pakistani Embassy (✆01-4374024; www.mofa.gov.pk/ nepal; Psuhpanjali, Narayan Gopal Chowk, Ring Rd, Maharajganj, Kathmandu)

Thai Embassy (✆01-4371410; www.thaiembnepal. org.np; Bansbari, Maharajganj, Kathmandu; ☺9.30am-noon & 2-4pm Mon-Fri) Most nationalities don't need a visa for stays of less than 15 days.

UK Embassy (Map p68; ✆01-4410583; www.ukinnepal. fco.gov.uk; Lainchhaur, Kathmandu; ☺8.15am-12.30pm & 1.30-5pm Mon-Thu, 8.15am-1.15pm Fri)

US Embassy (✆01-4234000; http://nepal. usembassy.gov; Maharajganj, Kathmandu; ☺8am-5pm Mon-Fri)

Food

You can eat like a king in Kathmandu and Pokhara, where restaurants offer a world map of cuisines, with dishes from Tibet, China, India, Japan, Thailand, Mexico, Italy, France and the Middle East. Take advantage of these offerings – once you start trekking it's rice and vegetables, all day, every day...

Interestingly, the Nepali word for eating is *khanu*, which is also used for the verbs 'to drink' and 'to smoke'.

Staples & Specialities

The staple meal of Nepal is *daal bhaat tarkari* – literally lentil soup, rice and curried vegetables. If you are lucky it will be spiced up with *achar* (pickles) and maybe some *chapati* (unleavened Indian bread), *dahi* (curd or yoghurt) or *papad* (pappadam – a crispy fried lentil-flour

pancake). To eat daal bhaat the local way, pour the soupy daal onto the rice, mix it into balls with your fingers, add a pinch of pickle and vegetables and shovel it into your mouth with your right hand. If you order daal bhaat, someone will come around offering free extra helpings of rice, daal or *tarkari*. Only very occasionally does it come with *masu* (meat).

Most Hindu Nepalis are vegetarians, some out of choice and some out of necessity. However, the Newars of the Kathmandu Valley are great meat eaters – *buff* (water buffalo) is the meat of choice, but goat is also common. Cows are sacred to Hindus and are never eaten. Some Kathmandu restaurants import real beef from India and you can also get yak steaks at some trekking lodges.

Spices feature heavily in Newari food, especially chilli, and Newari dishes are usually served with *chiura* (dry, beaten rice), which looks, and frankly tastes, like dry oatmeal porridge.

Many Newari dishes are only eaten at celebrations or family events, but several upmarket restaurants in Kathmandu now offer good Newari cuisine. Nepal is also one of the best places to try Tibetan cuisine, though most dishes are simple variations on momos (dumplings) or *thuk* noodle stews (*thukpa* are long noodles, whereas *thenthuk* is more like torn pasta).

One cheap and cheerful dish you'll find everywhere is

chow mein (thin noodles fried with vegetables or meat).

Many Nepalis round off a meal with a *digestif* of *pan* (betel nut and leaf mixture). Those little spots of red on the pavement that look like little pools of blood are (generally) *pan*.

Food Nepal (www. food-nepal.com) offers an excellent introduction to Nepali food and ingredients, with recipes from mango *lassi* to chicken chilli. *The Nepal Cookbook,* by the Association of Nepalis in the Americas, is a good collection of home recipes, or try the recently republished *Taste of Nepal,* by Jyoti Pathak.

Desserts

Like their Indian neighbours, Nepalis enjoy a huge range of sticky sweets, mostly based on milk curd, *jaggery* (palm sugar) and nuts. Top treats include *barfi* (milk fudge), *rasbari* (milk balls), *lal mohan* (deep-fried milky dough balls), *kheer* (rice pudding) and *julebi* (orange-coloured, syrupy, fried dough swirls).

Anyone who visits Bhaktapur should try the *juju dhau* (king of curds), wonderfully creamy thick yoghurt. *Sikarni* is a popular traditional dessert of whipped yoghurt with cinnamon, nuts and dried fruit. Because of the vagaries of refrigeration, avoid ice cream except in upmarket tourist restaurants.

Where to Eat & Drink

In 1955, Kathmandu had only one restaurant. These days, every other building in

PRICE RANGES

The following price indicators refer to a standard main course.

$ less than Rs 250

$$ Rs 250-500

$$$ more than Rs 500

Kathmandu is a restaurant, serving food from across the globe. However, travel outside Kathmandu and Pokhara and you'll find that menus quickly shrink to chow mein, fried rice, fried potatoes and daal bhaat.

At local restaurants, known as *bhojanalayas*, the custom is to eat with your right hand. Also look out for the vegetarian restaurants known as *misthan bhandar,* which serve Indian sweets and *dosas* (fried lentil-flour pancakes).

Nepali towns have a range of snack foods, from muffins in bakeries to grilled corn cobs on the street. A couple of *samsa* (samosas – potato curry, fried in a lentil-dough parcel) or *papad* make a great snack. Newari beer snacks are legendary – try a plate of *sekuwa* (spiced, barbecued meat) or 'masala peanuts' (with chilli and spices) when you have a beer.

Drinks
NONALCOHOLIC

The golden rule in Nepal is don't drink the water. Cheap bottled water is available everywhere but every bottle contributes to Nepal's mountain of waste plastic. You can purify your own water if you carry a water bottle and iodine drops or tablets.

Tea is almost always safe. Tourist restaurants often serve the world's weakest tea – typically an ineffectual Mechi tea bag dunked into a glass of sweet, hot milk. For proper Nepali *chiya* (sometimes called masala tea), the leaves are boiled with milk, sugar and spices. If you want Western-style tea, ask for

'milk separate'. Kathmandu and Pokhara now have dozens of places to get proper espresso coffee.

In Tibetan-influenced areas the drink of choice is black tea churned with salt and butter – providing useful metabolites for dealing with high altitude and cold weather. It's an acquired taste – locals often pour it over their *tsampa* (roasted barley flour).

In Indian-influenced areas, look out for *lassi* – a refreshing drink of curd (yoghurt) mixed with sugar and what may be untreated water (proceed with caution).

ALCOHOLIC

Nepali beer is pretty good, especially after a hard day's trek. Tuborg (Danish), Carlsberg (Danish) and San Miguel (Spanish) are brewed under licence in Nepal; local brands include Gorkha, Everest and Kathmandu Beer. Nepal Distilleries produces a variety of bottled spirits that claim to be rum, whisky, brandy and gin. Most are pretty grim, but Khukri Rum goes down well with mixers.

Officially, alcohol is not sold by retailers on the first two days (full-moon days) and the last two Saturdays of the Nepali month, but this rarely seems to affect tourist restaurants.

Gay & Lesbian Travellers

Nepal is the only country in South Asia that does not criminalise same-sex relations. A landmark Supreme Court hearing in December 2007 ordered the government to end discrimination against sexual minorities and to ensure equal rights. That said, there's not a big, open gay scene in Nepal and gay Nepalis are vulnerable to police harassment and blackmail. Gay couples holding hands in public will experience no difficulties, as this is socially acceptable, but public displays of intimacy by anyone are frowned upon.

Blue Diamond Society (☎01-4443350; www.bds.org.np) The first gay organisation in Kathmandu. It provides education, support and advice to Nepal's gay and transgender

THE LOCAL FIREWATER

On trekking routes, look out for the traditional home-brews of the hills. One drink you'll find everywhere is *chang,* a mildly alcoholic Tibetan concoction made from fermented barley or millet and water. It can be drunk hot or cold – local connoisseurs take it hot with a raw egg in it...

In eastern Nepal, look out for *tongba,* a Himalayan brew made by pouring boiling water into a wooden (or metal) pot full of fermented millet. The liquid is slurped through a bamboo straw and more hot water is added periodically to seep extra alcohol from the mash.

Harder spirits include *arak,* fermented from potatoes or grain, and *raksi,* a distilled rice wine that runs the gamut from smooth-sipping schnapps to headache-inducing paint stripper.

community, and runs the country's only AIDS/HIV prevention program. Its founder became the country's first openly gay member of parliament.

Insurance

A travel-insurance policy to cover theft, loss and medical problems is an excellent idea for travel in Nepal. There are a wide variety of policies available, so check the small print carefully. Some policies exclude 'dangerous activities', which may include riding a motorbike and trekking (and definitely bungee jumping and rafting).

Choose a policy that covers medical and emergency repatriation, including helicopter evacuation for trekkers and general medical evacuation to Bangkok or Delhi, which alone can cost a cool US$40,000.

You may prefer a policy that pays doctors or hospitals directly rather than you having to pay on the spot and claim later. In Nepal, most medical treatment must be paid for at the point of delivery. If your insurance company does not provide upfront payment, be sure to obtain a receipt so you can reclaim later. Some policies ask you to call back (reverse charges) to a centre in your home country where an immediate assessment of your problem is made.

Worldwide traveller insurance is available at http://www.lonelyplanet.com/travel-insurance. You can buy, extend and claim online anytime – even if you are already on the road.

Internet Access

Email and internet services are offered in dozens of places in Kathmandu and Pokhara and are generally around Rs 40 to 60 per hour. Internet access is available in pretty much every town. Internet is even becoming more available on the main trekking routes of Everest and Annapurna, though outside the bigger towns connections are often slow.

Most hotels aimed at tourists offer wi-fi and in Kathmandu and Pokhara many restaurants and cafes also have it.

Language Courses

Nepali is not a difficult language to learn, and you will see notices around Kathmandu advertising language courses. Most schools offer courses or individual tuition. Expect to pay about US$50 for a two-week course or around US$3 to US$5 per hour for private tuition.

There are often flyers around Bodhnath advertising Tibetan-language tuition as well as opportunities to volunteer teaching English to Tibetan refugees.

There are a number of language centres in Kathmandu and Pokhara.

Centre for Buddhist Studies (Map p129; ☑01-4483575; www.ryi.org; Kathmandu) Based at the Rangjung Yeshe Institute, this affiliate of Kathmandu University offers a variety of long-term courses on Buddhist studies and Tibetan languages. Some buildings were damaged in the 2015 earthquake and some classes have been moved to nearby locations.

Cosmic Brontosaurus Language School (Map p220; ☑9846069834; www.cosmicbrontosaurus.com; Pokhara; per hr Rs 450; ⊙noon-4pm) Offering individual or group lessons from beginner to advanced, the rather primitive classroom in a wooden shack along the lake is surrounded by banana plants and is the perfect spot to learn Nepali. Prem, who runs the school, is a lovely guy, and has several years' experience working with the UN as a translator.

Intercultural Training & Research Centre (ITC; Map p88; ☑01-4414490; http:// itcnepal.com; Kathmandu) This well-respected language centre works with many NGOs, including the UK's Voluntary Service Overseas (VSO). It offers crash courses (three hours), 60-hour beginner courses and six-week intermediate courses. Tuition is one-on-one and costs around Rs 350 to 400 per hour.

Kathmandu Environmental Education Project (KEEP; ☑01-4410952; www.keepnepal.org; Thamel, Kathmandu; ⊙10am-5pm Sun-Fri) Offers six-day Nepali-language classes over the last week of each month. Cost is US$40 per person.

Kathmandu Institute of Nepali Language (Map p88; ☑01-4437454; www.ktmnepalilanguage.com; Bhagwan Bahal, Kathmandu) Offers a week's beginner course (12 hours) and longer, more advanced courses all of which are tailored specifically to foreign tourists.

Legal Matters

Hashish has been illegal since 1973, but it's still readily available in Nepal. Thamel is full of shifty, whispering dealers. In practice, Nepali police aren't very interested in people with a small amount of marijuana on them (they're more focused on smuggling), but the technical penalty for drug possession is around five years in prison, so potential smokers should keep the less-than-salubrious condition of Nepali jails firmly in mind. Don't try taking any out of the country, either – travellers have been arrested at the airport on departure.

If you get caught smuggling something serious – drugs or gold – chances are you'll end up in jail, without trial, and will remain there until someone pays for you to get out. Jail conditions in Nepal are reportedly horrific. Bribery is sometimes used to avoid jail. This is illegal and can land the perpetrator in deeper strife. Denying that a bribe was offered – where the accused believed it was a legitimate fee – is the only defence.

Killing a cow is illegal in Nepal and carries a punishment of two years in prison.

Money

The Nepali rupee (Rs) is divided into 100 paisa. There are coins for denominations of one, two, five and 10 rupees, and banknotes in denominations of one, two, five, 10, 20, 50, 100, 500 and 1000 rupees. Since the abolition of the monarchy in 2008, images of Mt Everest have replaced the king on all banknotes.

Away from major centres, changing a Rs 1000 note can be difficult, so it is always a good idea to keep a stash of small-denomination notes. Even in Kathmandu, many small businesses – especially rickshaw and taxi drivers – simply don't have sufficient spare money to allow them the luxury of carrying a wad of change.

ATMs

Standard Chartered Bank has 24-hour ATMs in Kathmandu and Pokhara. Other banks, such as Himalaya Bank and Nabil Bank have ATMs and are present in most reasonably sized towns, but some don't accept foreign bank cards (despite Visa signs indicating that they do). Quite a lot of machines seem to have a per-transaction withdrawl limit of Rs 8000 but there doesn't appear to be any rhyme or reason as to which machines do and don't.

Frequent power outages can limit the machines' working hours, so use one when you see it's working. Using an ATM attached to a bank during business hours will minimise hassle in the rare event that the machine eats your card.

It's not a bad idea to inform your bank that you'll be using your card in Nepal, otherwise they might suspect fraud and freeze your card.

Changing Money

Official exchange rates are set by the government's Nepal Rastra Bank and listed in the daily newspapers. Rates at the private banks vary, but are generally not far from the official rate.

There are exchange counters at the international terminal at Kathmandu's Tribhuvan Airport and banks and/or moneychangers at the various border crossings. Pokhara and the major border towns also have official money-changing facilities, but changing travellers cheques can be time consuming elsewhere in the country, even in some quite large towns. If you are trekking, take enough cash in small-denomination rupees to last the whole trek.

The best private banks are Himalaya Bank, Nepal Bank and Standard Chartered Bank. Some hotels and resorts are licensed to change money but their rates are lower. Travellers cheques from the main companies can be exchanged in banks in Kathmandu and Pokhara for a 2% surcharge. Euro travellers cheques are also charged a flat US$10 fee per cheque. With each passing year it gets harder to change cheques.

When you change money officially, you are required to show your passport, and you are issued with a foreign exchange encashment receipt showing your identity and the amount of currency you have changed. Hang onto the receipts as you need them to change excess rupees back into foreign currency at banks. You can change rupees back into foreign currency at most moneychangers without a receipt.

Many upmarket hotels and businesses are obliged by the government to demand payment in hard currency (euros or US dollars); they will also accept rupees, but only if you can show a foreign exchange encashment receipt that covers the amount you owe them. In practice this regulation seems to be widely disregarded. Airlines are also required to charge tourists in hard currency, either in cash US dollars, travellers cheques or credit cards, and this rule is generally followed.

In addition to the banks, there are licensed moneychangers in Kathmandu, Pokhara, Birganj, Kakarbhitta and Sunauli/Bhairawa. The rates are often marginally lower than the banks, but there are no commissions, they have much longer opening hours (typically from 9am to 7pm daily) and they are also much quicker, the whole process often taking no more than a few minutes.

Most licensed moneychangers will provide an exchange receipt; if they don't, you may be able to negotiate better rates than those posted on their boards.

Credit Cards

Major credit cards are widely accepted at midrange and better hotels, restaurants and fancy shops in the Kath-

---

BARGAINING

Haggling is regarded as an integral part of most commercial transactions in Nepal, especially when dealing with souvenir shops, hotels and guides. Ideally, it should be an enjoyable social exchange, rather than a conflict of egos. A good deal is reached when both parties are happy, so keep things light; Nepalis do not appreciate aggressive behaviour. Remember that Rs 10 might make quite a difference to the seller, but to a foreign traveller it amounts to very little (less than US$0.10).

mandu Valley and Pokhara only. Most places levy a 3% to 4% surcharge to counter the credit card company's fees to the vendor.

Branches of Standard Chartered Bank and some other banks such as Nabil Bank and Himalaya Bank give cash advances against Visa and MasterCard in Nepali rupees only (no commission is charged), and will also sell you foreign-currency travellers cheques against the cards with a 2% commission.

International Transfers

In general, it's easiest to send money through companies such as **Western Union** (www.westernunion.com) or **Moneygram** (www.visitnepal.com/moneygram), which can arrange transfers within minutes. To pick up funds at a Western Union branch you'll need your passport and 10-digit transfer code.

Note that money can often only be received in Nepali rupees, rather than US dollars.

Tax & Tipping

It is possible for tourists to get the value added tax (VAT) refunded on consumer goods but it's an ordeal and is probably only relevant if you've made a major purchase. For more information, see the website of **Tribhuvan International Airport** (www.tiairport.com.np).

Round up the fare for taxi drivers. Trekking guides and porters expect a tip of 10% to 15% for a job well done.

TAXING TAXES

Most midrange and top-end hotels and restaurants add a 13% value added tax (VAT), as well as a 10% service charge. The service charge is craftily calculated from the total *after* VAT, resulting in a whopping 24.3% surcharge to your bill. You'll have to mentally figure in the taxes to avoid a nasty shock when your bill comes, though on the plus side it does away with the dilemma of how much to tip! Some budget places charge only VAT or service, especially restaurants. Where hotels quote their rates including tax we mention this in the review.

Opening Hours

Standard opening hours are listed in the following table.

BUSINESS	OPENING HOURS
Airline offices	9am-1pm & 2-6pm Sun-Fri, 9am-1pm Sat
Banks	9am-4pm Sun-Fri, 10am-noon Sat
Bars & clubs	generally close by 11pm or midnight, even in Kathmandu
Embassies	9am-1pm & 2-5pm Mon-Fri
Government offices	10am-1pm & 2-5pm (to 4pm in winter) Mon-Thu, 10am-1pm Fri (also 10am-5pm Sun outside the Kathmandu Valley)
Museums	generally 10.30am-4.30pm, often closed Tue
Restaurants	8am-10pm
Shops	10am-8pm (some shops closed on Sat)

Photography

Bringing a video camera to Nepal poses no real problem and there are no video fees to worry about. The exception to this is in the upper Mustang region, where there is technically an astonishing US$1000 fee to take video footage, though unless you're obviously a professional film crew it's highly unlikely anyone will ask you for this.

Memory Cards & Equipment

➡ Almost all flavours of memory stick, flash card etc and batteries are available in Kathmandu, but professional-level equipment involves a bit more of a hunt. Note that travellers have reported buying cheap cards in Kathmandu that do not have as much memory as the packet claims.

Photographing People

➡ Most Nepalis are content to have their photograph taken, but always ask permission first. Sherpa people are an exception and can be very camera-shy.

➡ Bear in mind that if a sadhu (holy man) poses for you, they will probably insist on being given *baksheesh* (a tip).

Restrictions

➡ It is not uncommon for temple guardians to not allow photos of their temple, and these wishes should be respected.

➡ Don't photograph army camps, checkpoints or bridges.

Post

The postal service to and from Nepal is, at best, erratic but can occasionally be amazingly efficient. Most articles do arrive at their destination...eventually.

Parcel Post

Having stocked up on gifts and souvenirs in Nepal, many people send them home from Kathmandu. Parcel post is not cheap or quick, but the service is reliable. Sea mail is much cheaper than airmail, but it is also much slower (packages take about 3½ months) and less reliable.

As an indication, a 2kg package to the UK/US costs Rs 1710/2010 via airmail, 25% less at 'book post' rate (a special rate for books only).

The contents of a parcel must be inspected by officials *before* it is wrapped. There are packers at the Kathmandu foreign post office who will wrap it for a small fee. The maximum weight for sea mail is 20kg; for airmail it's 10kg, or 5kg for book post.

If an object is shipped out to you in Nepal, you may find that customs' charges for clearance and collection at your end add up to more than the initial cost of sending it. Often it's worth paying extra to take it with you on the plane in the first place.

Postal Rates

Airmail rates for a 20g letter/postcard within Nepal are Rs 5/2; to India and surrounding countries Rs 25/20; to Europe and the UK Rs 40/30; and to the US and Australia Rs 50/35.

Public Holidays

A remarkable number of holidays and festivals affect the working hours of Nepal's government offices and banks, which seem to close every other day and certainly for public holidays and some or all festival days. Exact festival timings (and thus their public holiday dates) change annually according to Nepal's lunar calendar.

Prithvi Narayan Shah's Birthday 10 January

Basanta Panchami (start of Spring) January/February

Maha Shivaratri (Shiva's Birthday) February/March

Bisket Jatra (Nepali New Year) 14 April

Janai Purnima July/August

Teej (Festival of Women) August/September

Indra Jatra (Indra Festival) September

Dasain September/October

Tihar (Divali) October/November

Constitution Day 9 November

DASAIN STOPPAGES

Dasain (15 days in September or October) is the most important of all Nepali celebrations. Tens of thousands of Nepalis hit the road to return home to celebrate with their families. This means that while villages are full of life if you are trekking, buses and planes are fully booked and overflowing, porters may be hard to find (or more expensive than usual) and cars are difficult to hire. Many hotels and restaurants in regional towns close down completely, and doing business in Kathmandu (outside Thamel) becomes almost impossible.

The most important days, when everything comes to a total halt, are the ninth day (when thousands of animals are sacrificed) and the 10th day (when blessings are received from elder relatives and superiors). Banks and government offices are generally closed from the eighth day of the festival to the 12th day.

Safe Travel

In political terms, Nepal is more stable than it has been in years, and crime is not a major risk for travellers. However, the 2015 earthquakes have damaged infrastructure and placed millions of people in a very difficult economic position, so things could change. It makes sense to consult local and international news sources before you travel to Nepal so you are aware of any issues. Also be aware that damage from the earthquake has affected travel in many areas. Roads are damaged and some buildings are uninhabitable and Nepal faces an increased risk of landslides and avalanches following the disaster. As a general rule, it always pays to check that it is possible to travel to your chosen destination before starting any journey.

You should also heed the following general advice for travelling in Nepal:

➡ Register with your embassy in Kathmandu, especially if you plan to go trekking.

➡ Don't trek alone. Solo women should avoid travelling alone with a male guide.

➡ Be familiar with the symptoms of altitude sickness when trekking and follow the guidelines for safe acclimatisation.

➡ Avoid travelling on night buses as these are prone to accidents.

➡ Take photocopies of your passport, visa, air ticket, trekking permits and travellers cheques and keep these separate from the originals.

Demonstrations & Strikes

Nepal has a long history of demonstrations and strikes – some by politicians, some by students, some by Maoists, and some by all three! The

PRACTICALITIES

Newspapers

Nepal's main English-language papers are the daily *Kathmandu Post* (www.ekantipur.com/the-kathmandu-post), the *Himalayan* (www.thehimalayantimes.com) and *Republica* (www.myrepublica.com), which comes complete with a *New York Times* pull-out supplement. The *Nepali Times* (www.nepalitimes.com) comes out weekly.

Magazines

ECS (www.ecs.com.np; Rs 100) is a glossy, expat-oriented monthly magazine with interesting articles on travel and culture, plus apartment listings. *Himal* magazine (www.himalmag.com) is also good.

Discounts

There aren't any noticeable discounts for holders of student or senior cards. Those under 30 can sometimes get discounts on flights to India without a student card.

TV

Most hotel rooms offer satellite TV, which generally includes Star TV, BBC World and CNN.

Weights & Measures

Nepal has adopted the metric system of weights, alongside traditional measures used mainly in rural areas.

Radio

In the Kathmandu Valley you can tune in to the BBC World Service on FM radio at 103 MHz.

political situation has greatly improved but occasionally demonstrations still occur and they can turn violent.

A normal demonstration is a *julus*. If things escalate, there may be a *chakka jam* ('jam the wheels'), when all vehicles stay off the street, or a *bandh*, when all shops, schools and offices are closed. In the event of a strike the best thing to do is hole up in your hotel with a good book. In this case you'll likely have to dine at your hotel.

If political instability returns, it pays to heed the following points:

➡ Keep an eye on the local press and news websites to find out about impending strikes, demonstrations and curfews – follow websites such as www.ekantipur.com/the-kathmandu-post, www.thehimalayantimes.com and www.nepalitimes.com.np.

➡ Don't ever break curfews and avoid travelling by road during *bandhs* or blockades, particularly in a rented vehicle, as vehicles flouting travel bans are often vandalised. Be nervous if you notice that your car is the only one on the streets of Kathmandu!

➡ When roads are closed the government generally runs buses with armed police from the airport to major hotels, returning to the airport from Tridevi Marg at the east end of Thamel.

➡ The website www.nepalbandh.com warns of any upcoming strikes.

Electricity Supply

Power cuts are a fact of life in Nepal, especially in winter, when water and thus hydro power levels are at their lowest. Be prepared for some periods without electricity during your trip.

As well as conventional power failures, you will almost certainly encounter the problem of 'load-shedding', where areas are temporarily cut off from the mains power supply to avoid overloading the system. In Kathmandu, the electricity supply shifts from district to district every eight hours or so. Most hotels post a schedule of planned electricity cuts, which can last up to 16 hours a day in both Kathmandu and Pokhara. Try to choose a hotel with a generator and make sure your room is far away from it.

Scams

While the overwhelming majority of Nepalis couldn't be any nicer, there are some who are impressively inventive in their range of imaginative scams. Watch out for the following:

➡ Deals offered by gem dealers that involve you

GOVERNMENT TRAVEL ADVICE FOR NEPAL

Many foreign governments provide travel advice for their citizens, highlighting entry requirements, medical facilities, areas with health and safety risks, and civil unrest or other dangers. These official travel advisories should be your first port of call for up-to-date information on the travel situation in Nepal after the 2015 earthquakes. Some of this official travel advice can sound a little alarmist, but if your government issues a travel warning advising against 'all travel' or 'all but essential travel' to a specific area, then your travel insurance may be invalid if you ignore this advice. The following government websites provide travel advice for Nepal and other countries.

Australian Department of Foreign Affairs & Trade (www.smartraveller.gov.au)

Canadian Consular Affairs (www.voyage.gc.ca)

New Zealand Ministry of Foreign Affairs & Trade (www.safetravel.govt.nz)

UK Foreign & Commonwealth Office (www.gov.uk/foreign-travel-advice)

US Department of State (www.state.gov/travel)

buying stones to sell for a 'vast profit' at home. The dealers normally claim they are not able to export the stones without paying heavy taxes, so you take them and meet another dealer when you get home, who will sell them to a local contact and you both share the profit. Except they don't. And you don't.

➡ Children or young mothers asking for milk. You buy the milk at a designated store at an inflated price, the child then returns the milk and pockets some of the mark-up.

➡ Be wary of kids who seem to know the capital of any country you can think of; they are charming but a request for money will arrive at some point.

➡ 'Holy men' who do their best to plant a *tika* (a red paste denoting a blessing) on your forehead, only to then demand significant payment.

➡ Credit card scams are not unheard of; travellers have bought souvenirs and then found thousands of dollars worth of internet porn

subscriptions chalked up on their bill.

Theft

While petty theft is not on the scale that exists in many countries, reports of theft from hotel rooms in tourist areas (including along trekking routes) do occasionally reach us, and theft with violence is not unheard of. Never store valuables or money in your hotel room.

One of the most common forms of theft is when backpacks are rifled through when they're left on the roof of a bus. Try to make your pack as theft-proof as possible – small padlocks and cover bags are a good deterrent.

There's little chance of ever retrieving your gear if it is stolen, and even getting a police report for an insurance claim can be difficult. Try the tourist police, or, if there aren't any, the local police station. If you're not getting anywhere, go to **Interpol** (☎01-4420538; www.nepal-police.gov.np/interpol-section.html) at the Police Headquarters in Naxal, Kathmandu.

Telephone

The phone system in Nepal works pretty well and making local, STD and international calls is easy. Reverse-charge (collect) calls can only be made to the UK, USA, Canada and Japan.

Private call centres offer the cheapest and most convenient way to make a call. Look for signs advertising STD/ISD services. Many hotels offer international direct-dial facilities but always check their charges before making a call.

Private call centres charge around Rs 10 to 20 per minute to most countries.

Local phone calls cost around Rs 3 per minute, with long-distance domestic calls costing around Rs 5 per minute. Out in rural areas you may find yourself using someone's mobile phone at a public call centre.

Note that the phone network was affected by the 2015 earthquakes, with fixed lines and mobile signals affected in some areas. The Internet is often a more reliable communication tool than the telephone in rural areas.

Mobile Phones

Ncell (www.ncell.com.np) is the most popular and convenient provider for tourists, but in mountain areas Ncell reception is often non-existent. To get a SIM card take a copy of your passport and one photo to an Ncell office. Ncell offers a traveller package with which Rs 1000 gets you Rs 600 worth of calls, Rs 500 of international calls and 500MB of data, for 15 days. Otherwise, local calls cost around Rs 2 to 3 per minute and incoming calls are free. International calls cost around Rs 5 to 15 per minute depending on the destination. It's easy to buy a scratch card to top up your balance, in denominations from Rs 50 to 1000. You can normally get a SIM card on arrival at Tribhuvan Airport.

For 3G internet access, you can buy a USB data card and SIM card package for Rs 2300 to 2700, with which you can even get internet access on the Everest Base Camp Trek! (The first tweet from the summit of Everest was sent in May 2011…) Good-value data packages are available for short term visitors, but exact rates depend on the size of the data bundle you take.

Nepal Telecom (www.ntc. net.np) operates the Namaste Mobile network and has roaming agreements with companies such as Vodafone and Cingular, but signing up for a SIM card is a more laborious process than for Ncell. However, Namaste has a much wider reception in the mountains so is the one to go for if you're spending a lot of time hiking and contact with the world beyond is important to you.

You will need an unlocked GSM 900 compatible phone to use local networks.

Unlike using a landline, you need to dial the local area code when making a local call on a mobile.

Time

Nepal is five hours and 45 minutes ahead of GMT; this curious time differential is intended to make it very clear that Nepal is a separate place to India, where the time is five hours and 30 minutes ahead of GMT. There is no daylight-saving time in Nepal.

When it's noon in Nepal it's 1.15am in New York, 6.15am in London, 1.15pm in Bangkok, 2.15pm in Tibet, 4.15pm in Sydney and 10.15pm the previous day in Los Angeles, not allowing for daylight saving or other local variations.

Toilets

➡ Outside of Kathmandu and Pokhara, the 'squat toilet' is the norm, except in hotels and guesthouses geared towards tourists.

➡ Next to a squat toilet (*charpi* in Nepali) is a bucket and/or tap, which has a twofold function: flushing the toilet and cleaning the nether regions (with the left hand only) while still squatting over the toilet.

➡ In tourist areas you'll find Western toilets and probably toilet paper (depending on how classy the place is). In general, put used toilet paper in the separate bin; don't flush it down the toilet.

➡ Most rural places don't supply toilet paper, so always carry an emergency stash if you don't want to rely on the bucket/tap procedure.

➡ More rustic toilets in rural areas may consist of a few planks precariously positioned over a pit in the ground.

Tourist Information

The **Nepal Tourism Board** (☎01-4256909, 24hr tourism hotline 01-4225709; www. welcomenepal.com) operates an office in Kathmandu's Tribhuvan Airport and a more substantial office at the **Tourist Service Centre** (Map p68; ☎01-4256909 ext 223, 24hr tourism hotline 01-4225709; www.welcomenepal. com; Bhrikuti Mandap; ⊘10am-1pm & 2-5pm Sun-Fri, TIMS card 7am-7pm daily, national parks tickets 9am-2pm Sun-Fri) in central Kathmandu, both of which have simple brochures and maps.

The other tourist offices in Pokhara, Bhairawa, Birganj, Janakpur and Kakarbhitta are virtually useless unless you have a specific question.

Travellers with Disabilities

Wheelchair facilities, ramps and lifts (and even pavements!) are virtually nonexistent throughout Nepal and getting around the packed, twisting streets of traditional towns can be a real challenge if you are in a wheelchair. It is common for hotels to be multilevel, with most rooms on the upper floors. Many places – even midrange establishments – do not have lifts. Bathrooms equipped

---

NEPALI CALENDARS

Nepali holidays and festivals are principally dated by the lunar calendar, falling on days relating to new or full moons. The lunar calendar is divided into bright and dark fortnights. The bright fortnight is the two weeks of the waxing moon, as it grows to become *purnima* (the full moon). The dark fortnight is the two weeks of the waning moon, as the full moon shrinks to become *aunsi* (the new moon).

The Nepali New Year starts on 14 April with the month of Baisakh. The Nepali calendar is 57 years ahead of the Gregorian calendar used in the West, thus the year 2015 in the West is 2072 in Nepal. You can convert between Nepali and Gregorian dates at www.rajan.com/calendar.

The Newars of the Kathmandu Valley, on the other hand, start their New Year from the day after Deepawali (the third day of Tihar), which falls on the night of the new moon in late October or early November. Their calendar is 880 years behind the Gregorian calendar, so 2015 in the West is 1135 to the Newars.

with grips and railings are not found anywhere, except perhaps in some of the top-end hotels.

There is no reason why a visit and even a trek could not be customised through a reliable agent for those with reasonable mobility. As an inspiration, consider Erik Weihenmayer, who became the first blind climber to summit Everest in 2001 (and wrote a book called *Touch the Top of the World*), or Thomas Whittaker, who summited in 1998 with an artificial leg, at the age of 50.

Useful resources include the following:

Access-Able Travel Source (www.access-able. com) General accessible-travel information.

Accessible Journeys (☑800-846-4537; www.disa-bilitytravel.com) US company that has experience in arranging private tours for travellers with disabilities.

Navyo Nepal (☑01-4239436; www.navyonepal. com) In Nepal; has some experience running cultural tours and treks for people with disabilities.

Visas

All foreigners, except Indians, must have a visa. Nepali embassies and consulates overseas issue visas with no fuss. You can also get one on the spot when you arrive in Nepal, either at Kathmandu's Tribhuvan Airport or at road borders at Nepalganj, Birganj/Raxaul Bazaar, Sunauli, Kakarbhitta, Mahendranagar, Dhangadhi and even the funky Kodari checkpoint on the road to Tibet.

A Nepali visa is valid for entry for three to six months from the date of issue. Children under 10 require a visa but are not charged a visa fee. Your passport must have at least six months of validity. Citizens of South Asian countries (except India) and China need visas, but, if you're only entering once in a calender year, these are free.

You can download a visa application form from the websites of the Nepali embassy in Washington, DC (www.nepalembassyusa.org) or London (www.nep embassy.org.uk).

To obtain a visa upon arrival by air in Nepal you must fill in an application form and provide a passport photograph. Visa application forms are available on a table in the arrivals hall, though some airlines provide this form on the flight. For people with electronic passports there are now visa registration machines in the immigration hall, which, after inserting your passport, will automatically fill out the visa form for you. However you do it, getting through immigration can take up to an hour, depending on the numbers. A single-entry visa valid for 15/30/90 days costs US$25/40/100. At Kathmandu's Tribhuvan Airport the fee is payable in any major currency, but at land borders officials require payment in cash (US dollars); bring small bills. We haven't yet heard of it happening to anyone else but the last time we entered Nepal by air and asked for a 90-day visa we were also asked to show our driving license.

Multiple-entry visas are useful if you are planning

INDIAN VISAS & RE-ENTRY ENDORSEMENTS IN NEPAL

Many travellers get an Indian visa in Nepal but it's not a straightforward process. Visa applications must be made at the **India Visa Service Centre** (☑01-4001516; www.nepalsbi. com.np/indian_passport/; ☺9.30am–noon Mon-Fri), at the State Bank of India to the right of the embassy, not at the embassy itself. Applications are accepted only between 9.30am and midday but it pays to get there earlier than 9.30am so as to be one of the first people in line. You will need a printed copy of the completed online visa form (https://indian-visaonline.gov.in), your passport, a copy of your passport info pages and a copy of your Nepalese visa. You will also need two 51mm-by-51mm passport photos (this is larger than a standard passport photo but most passport photo places in Kathmandu know about Indian visa regulations), and the visa fee. Five working days later you will need to return to the embassy between 9.30am and 1pm with your passport and visa payment receipt. You will likely have to answer a few questions confirming your visa application details. At this point you will leave your passport with the embassy. The following working day you can collect your passport between 5pm and 5.30pm – hopefully with a shiny, new Indian tourist visa in it.

Visa fees for a six-month tourist visa vary depending on nationality but for most nationalities it's Rs 4350. However, for Japanese passport holders it's a mere Rs 1050, for US passport holders the fee is Rs 6450, and for UK passport holders it's a whooping Rs 13,600.

Transit visas (Rs 2300 for most nationalities) are issued the same day, but start from the date of issue and are non-extendable.

a side trip to Tibet, Bhutan or India. You can change your single-entry visa to a multiple-entry visa at Kathmandu's Central Immigration Office for US$20.

Don't overstay your visa. You can pay a fine of US$3 per day at the airport if you have overstayed less than 30 days (plus a US$2 per day visa extension fee), but it's far better to get it all sorted out in advance at Kathmandu's **Central Immigration Office** (Map p68; ☎01-4429659; www.nepalimmigration.gov.np; Kalikasthan, Dilli Bazaar; ⏰10am-4pm Sun-Thu, 10am-3pm Fri, 11am-1pm Sat), as a delay could cause you to miss your flight.

It's a good idea to keep a number of passport photos with your passport so they are immediately handy for trekking permits, visa applications and other official documents.

Visa Extensions

Visa extensions are available from immigration offices in Kathmandu and Pokhara only and cost a minimum US$30 (payable in rupees only) for a 15-day extension, plus US$2 per day after that. To extend for 30 days is US$50 and to extend a multiple-entry visa add on US$20. If you'll be in Nepal for more than 60 days you are better off getting a 90-day visa on arrival, rather than a 60-day visa plus an extension.

Every visa extension requires your passport, the fee, one photo and an application form, which must be completed online first. One of the questions on this online application form asks for your Nepalese street address with house/building number. As anyone who spends more than a few days in Kathmandu will know house numbers are very rarely used and just as rarely known. In fact most places don't have one. The computer system will throw a bit of a paddy if you don't fill this part in, but if you don't know the number, you can generally get away with just adding your favourite number. Nobody other than the computer system really seems to care if you do this. Collect all these documents together before you join the queue; plenty of photo shops in Kathmandu and Pokhara can make a set of eight digital passport photos for around Rs 250.

Visa extensions are available the same day, normally within two hours, though some travellers have paid an extra Rs 300 fee to get their extensions within 10 minutes. For a fee, trekking and travel agencies can assist with the visa-extension process and save you the time and tedium of queuing.

You can extend a tourist visa up to a total stay of 150 days within a calendar year, though as you get close to that maximum you'll have to provide an air ticket to show you're leaving the country.

You can get up-to-date visa information at the website of the **Department of Immigration** (www.nepalimmigration.gov.np).

Women Travellers

Generally speaking, Nepal is a safe country for women travellers. However, women should still be cautious. Some Nepali men may have peculiar ideas about the morality of Western women, given their exposure to Western films portraying women wearing 'immodest' clothing. Dress modestly, which means wearing clothes that cover the shoulders and thighs – take your cue from the locals to gauge what's acceptable in the area. Several women have written to say that a long skirt is very useful for impromptu toilet trips, especially when trekking.

Sexual harassment is low-key but does exist. Trekking guides have been known to take advantage of their position of trust and responsibility and some lone women trekkers who hire a guide have had to put up with repeated sexual pestering. The best advice is to never trek alone with a local male guide. **3 Sisters Adventure Trekking** (☎061-462066; www.3sistersadventure.com) in Pokhara is run by women and specialises in providing female staff for treks.

Transport

GETTING THERE & AWAY

Considering the enduring popularity of Nepal as a travel destination, there are surprisingly few direct international flight connections into Kathmandu and fares are normally much higher than they are to nearby Indian cities such as Delhi. If you are coming during the prime travel and trekking months of October and November, book your long-haul and domestic flights well in advance.

However, overland and air-travel connections to India are extensive, so it's easy to combine a dream trip to both Nepal and India, with possible add-ons to Bhutan and Tibet.

Following the April 2015 earthquake, some transport routes were disrupted, particularly in the border region between Nepal and Tibet, but at the time of publication, airports were operating as normal and travel was possible on most overland routes around and to and from Nepal.

Flights, tours and even treks can be booked online at lonelyplanet.com/bookings.

Entering the Country

Nepal makes things easy for foreign travellers. Visas are available on arrival at the international airport in Kathmandu and at all land border crossings that are open to foreigners, as long as you have passport photos to hand and can pay the visa fee in foreign currency (some crossings insist on payment in US dollars). Your passport must be valid for at least six months and you will need a whole free page for your visa.

Air

Airports

Nepal has one international airport, **Tribhuvan International Airport** (www.tiairport.com.np), just east of Kathmandu. There are few direct long-distance flights to Nepal – getting here from Europe, the Americas or Australasia will almost always involve a stop in the Middle East or Asia.

In 2014 Tribhuvan was voted the third worst airport in the world. This is actually more than a little unfair as there are lots of worse international airports but they're just not ones visited by many international tourists. A new international airport is under construction in Pokhara, but progress is very slow so don't expect to be able to use it anytime soon.

Facilities at the airport are limited – there are foreign exchange booths before and after immigration, and there is a dusty tourist information counter by the terminal exit. Fill out the forms for your visa on arrival before you go to the immigration counter, as queues can be long here. A small stand provides instant passport photos, but bring some from home to be safe.

On departure, all baggage must go through the X-ray machine as you enter the terminal. Make sure that customs officials stamp all the baggage labels for your carry-on luggage. There are a couple of cafes in departures once you pass through security.

There are plans to transform Bhairawa airport into an international airport by 2017.

Airlines

Because Nepal does not lie on any major transit routes, flights to Kathmandu are expensive, particularly during the peak trekking season (October to November). Budget travellers fly to India first, and then pick up a cheap transfer to Kathmandu, though this incurs its own visa hassles and the added expense often adds up to the same as the flight price difference. In May 2015 **British Airways** (www.ba.com) recommenced direct London–Kathmandu flights. These are the only direct flights between western Europe and Nepal.

Nepal's flagship carrier **Nepal Airlines** (☑081-520767; www.nepalairlines.com.np) is a shoestring operation. Delays and cancellations are common: Hong Kong–Kathmandu

CLIMATE CHANGE & TRAVEL

Every form of transport that relies on carbon-based fuel generates CO_2, the main cause of human-induced climate change. Modern travel is dependent on aeroplanes, which might use less fuel per kilometre per person than most cars but travel much greater distances. The altitude at which aircraft emit gases (including CO_2) and particles also contributes to their climate change impact. Many websites offer 'carbon calculators' that allow people to estimate the carbon emissions generated by their journey and, for those who wish to do so, to offset the impact of the greenhouse gases emitted with contributions to portfolios of climate-friendly initiatives throughout the world. Lonely Planet offsets the carbon footprint of all staff and author travel.

passengers were delayed for two full days in 2011 when a rogue mouse was spotted on board, and in 2007, after a fault with one of their planes, two goats were sacrificed in order to appease Akash Bhairav, the Hindu god of safety and protection. Goats or not, the airline has had a number of serious incidents and is, like all Nepalese airlines, banned from EU airspace. There are flights to Delhi, Dubai, Doha, Hong Kong, Bangkok and Kuala Lumpur.

Budget Indian airlines flying to Nepal include **Spice-Jet** (www.spicejet.com) and **IndiGo** (www.goindigo.in).

Regional airlines connecting Kathmandu to the Gulf States include **Air Arabia** (www.airarabia.com) and **Fly Dubai** (www.flydubai.com).

A number of other airlines serve Nepal (this list is not comprehensive and changes frequently).

Air China (☎01-4440650; www.airchina.com; Sundar Bhawan, Hattisar) Currently offers the only way of entering Tibet by air from Nepal.

Air India (Map p68; ☎01-4429468; www.airindia.in; Hattisar) Connects Kathmandu with several Indian cities including Delhi and Kolkata.

Bhutan Airlines (☎01-4001001; www.bhutanairlines.bt; Society Travel, Uttar Dhoka, Lazimpat) Taking you from one small Himalayan wonderland to another.

Biman Bangladesh Airlines (☎01-4434740; www.

biman-airlines.com; Nag Pokhari, Naxal) To Dhaka.

China Eastern (☎01-4411666; www.flychinaeastern.com; Hattisar) To and from the Chinese cities of Kunming and Shanghai.

China Southern Airlines (☎01-4427261; www.flychinasouthern.com; Marcopolo Business Hotel, Kamal Pokhari) To Guangzhou, China.

Dragonair (☎01-4444820; www.dragonair.com; Narayan Chaur, Naxal) Hong Kong to Nepal.

Druk Air (☎01-4239922; www.drukair.com.bt; Danfe Travel Centre, Durbar Marg) Taking very lucky people to Bhutan.

Etihad (☎01-4005000; www.etihadairways.com; Metro Park, Uttardhoka, Lazimpat) One of several high-quality airlines linking Nepal with the Middle East.

Jet Airways (www.jetairways.com) Good connections to Delhi.

Korean Airlines (☎01-4169192; www.koreanair.com; Heritage Plaza Block 1, Kamaladi) To and from Seoul.

Malindo Air (www.malindoair.com; ground fl, GR Complex, House No 531, Lazimpat) Malindo Air flies from Kuala Lumpur to Kathmandu.

Oman Air (☎01-4444381; www.omanair.com; Situ Plaza, Narayan Chaur, Naxal) Flies to and from Muscat, but connections to Europe and the USA aren't as impressive as some other local Middle Eastern carriers.

Qatar Airways (Map p68; ☎01-4440467; www.qatarairways.com; Sundar Bhawan, Hattisar) To Doha with excellent onward connections to Europe and the States.

Thai Airways (www.thaiairways.com; Annapurna Arcade, Palace Rd, Durbar Marg) Providing the most popular route between Southeast Asia and Nepal.

Turkish Airlines (☎01-4438363; www.turkishairlines.com; Zion House, Narayan Chaur, Naxal) Flights to Istanbul, but during the Nepalese winter (October to February) delays flying into and out of Kathmandu are commonplace.

Tickets

During the autumn trekking season, from October to November, every flight into and out of Kathmandu can be booked solid, and travellers sometimes have to resort to travelling overland to India to get a flight out of the region. To beat the rush, book well in advance and give yourself plenty of time between the end of your trek and your international flight home. If you are booking a flight in Kathmandu, book at the start of your trip, not at the end.

If you are connecting through Delhi on two separate tickets, you will likely need to collect your luggage and check in separately for the connecting flight, for which you will need to have arranged a transit or tourist visa in advance. Sometimes an airline representative can collect and check in the bags on your behalf but you should check this. Some airlines have refused to fly passengers to Delhi to connect with other flights if they don't have an Indian visa.

Asia

The most popular route between Southeast Asia and Kathmandu is the daily Thai Airways flight to/from Bangkok, though Nepal Airlines also covers this connection, as does Jet Airways on a much longer connection via Delhi or Mumbai.

There are also convenient flights to Hong Kong (Dragonair), Kuala Lumpur (Malaysia Airlines) and Seoul (Korean Airlines). There are no direct flights to Japan.

For China there are flights to Beijing, Chengdu and Lhasa (Air China), as well as Kunming (China Eastern) and Guangzhou (China Southern Airlines). Flights are insanely priced, costing around US$415 to US$450 to Lhasa, US$350 to US$450 to Chengdu (some flights via Lhasa!) and around US$380 to US$420 to Beijing.

You can only buy tickets to Lhasa as part of a tour-group package. You must also join an organised tour of Bhutan to fly to Paro.

Australia & New Zealand

There are easy connections from Australia and New Zealand through Bangkok, Seoul, Kuala Lumpur, Guangzhou and Hong Kong.

Canada

Flying from Canada, you can go east or west around the globe. Fares from Vancouver through Asia tend to be slightly cheaper than flights from Toronto via Europe or the Gulf. Jet Airways offers a convenient single-airline route from Toronto through Brussels to Delhi and on to Kathmandu.

Continental Europe

There are no direct flights between continental western

Europe and Kathmandu. The most direct option is via Istanbul with Turkish Airlines, but tight connections in Istanbul can cause problems if your inbound flight is delayed. Other than Turkish Airlines, most people fly via India or a Middle Eastern country.

India, Pakistan & Bangladesh

Seats between Kathmandu and Delhi can be found for less than US$140, especially if you book in advance online. Jet are the best carriers flying the Delhi–Kathmandu route, though budget Indian airlines like IndiGo and SpiceJet offer the cheapest fares. All fly daily. Fares are best booked online, though you may have trouble using a non-Indian credit card on some sites.

Indian Airlines flies from Kathmanda to Delhi, Kolkata and Varanasi. Buddha Air flies to Varanasi.

You can get to Dhaka with Biman Bangladesh Airlines, and to Karachi with Pakistan International Airways (PIA).

Good online Indian travel agencies include **Cleartrip** (www.cleartrip.com), **Make My Trip** (www.makemytrip.com) and **Yatra** (www.yatra.com).

UK & Ireland

With the reintroduction of British Airways flights in 2015 on the London to Kathmandu route you can now, finally, fly direct from western Europe to Kathmandu again. Other easy connections to Kathmandu from London and Dublin are with Etihad, Emirates and Qatar Airways, changing in the Gulf. All three airlines also fly from Manchester, Edinburgh and other regional UK airports. The fastest connection from London to Kathmandu is with Jet Airways or Indian Airlines, with one smooth change in Delhi. Cheaper Jet connections via Mumbai require an overnight stay.

USA

North America is halfway around the world from Nepal, so you can go east or west around the globe. Flying west involves a change in Asia – Korean Airlines offers good connections through Seoul, but you could also change in Bangkok, Hong Kong or Singapore. Flying east normally involves a stop in Europe and, quite often, again in the Gulf or in India. Jet Airways has a convenient route from New York with stops in Brussels and Delhi.

For reasonably priced fares to Nepal, start with specialist travel agencies like **Third Eye Travel** (☎1-800 456 3393; www.thirdeyetravel.com) and **USA Asia** (☎1-800 872 2742; www.usaasiatravel.com).

Land

You can enter Nepal overland at seven border crossings – six from India and one from Tibet.

Border Crossings
INDIA

All of the land borders between India and Nepal are in the Terai, and were unaffected by the earthquake. The most popular crossing point is Sunauli, near Bhairawa, which provides easy access to Delhi and Varanasi in India.

At the end of 2014 the first direct Delhi to Kathmandu bus service commenced operation. Buses are run by the Delhi Transport Corporation and leave Delhi at 10am and Kathmandu (Swayambhu) at 9am. Tickets cost ₹2300/1500 per adult/child. The journey takes around 30 hours.

Indian domestic train tickets can be booked in advance online at **Cleartrip** (www.cleartrip.com) or **IRCTC** (www.irctc.co.in). Get timetables and fares at **Indian Railways** (www.trainenquiry. com). **The Man in Seat 61** (www.seat61.com/India.htm) is a good general resource.

Belahiya/Sunauli

The crossing at Sunauli (p257) is by far the most popular route between India and Nepal. Regular buses run from Sunauli to Gorakhpur from where you can catch trains to Varanasi.

Once across the border, you can visit the Buddhist pilgrimage centre of Lumbini before you continue your journey. From Bhairawa buses run regularly to Kathmandu and Pokhara, usually passing through Narayangarh, where you can change for Chitwan National Park.

Mahendranagar/Banbasa

The western border crossing at Mahendranagar (p276) is also reasonably convenient for Delhi. There are daily buses from Delhi's Anand Vihar bus stand to Banbasa (10 hours), the nearest Indian village to the border. Banbasa is also connected by bus with most towns in Uttarakhand.

From Mahendranagar there are slow overnight bus services to Kathmandu (15 hours) but it's better to do the trip in daylight and break the journey at Bardia National Park, Nepalganj or Narayangarh. Check that the road is open because it sometimes gets blocked during the monsoon.

Kakarbhitta/Panitanki

The eastern border crossing at Kakarbhitta (p288) offers easy onward connections to Darjeeling, Sikkim, Kolkata and India's northeast states.

From Darjeeling, take a morning shared jeep to Siliguri (three hours), then another shared jeep or a taxi (one hour) to Panitanki on the Indian side of the border. Jeeps also run to the border from Kalimpong and Gangtok in Sikkim. Coming from Kolkata, you can take the overnight *Darjeeling Mail* or *Kanchanakaya Express* from Sealdah station to New Jalpaiguri (NJP) near Siliguri, then a bus to the border.

From Kakarbhitta there are both day and overnight buses to Kathmandu (14 to 16 hours) or Pokhara (15 hours), but it's more interesting to break the journey at Janakpur (five hours) or Chitwan National Park (accessible from Sauraha Chowk on the Mahendra Hwy).

Birganj/Raxaul Bazar

The border crossing from Birganj to Raxaul Bazar (p279) is handy for Patna and Kolkata. Buses run from the bus station in Patna straight to Raxaul Bazar (six hours). From Kolkata, take the daily *Mithila Express* train.

From Birganj, there are regular day/night buses to Kathmandu (six to seven hours) as well as faster Tata Sumo jeeps (four to five hours). There are also morning buses to Pokhara (eight hours), via Narayangarh (three hours).

Nepalganj/Jamunaha/Rupaidha Bazaar

Few people use the crossing at Nepalganj (p270) in western Nepal as it's not particu-

larly convenient for anywhere else. The nearest town in India is Lucknow, where you can pick up slow buses to Rupaidha Bazaar (seven hours), near the border post at Jamunaha. You might also consider taking a train to Nanpara, 17km from the border.

Over the border in Nepalganj, there are regular day/night buses to Kathmandu (12 hours) and buses to Pokhara (12 hours), passing through Narayangarh (eight hours). Yeti Airlines and Buddha Air have flights from Nepalganj to Kathmandu (US$187).

Dhangadhi/Gauriphanta

The little-used border crossing (p276) from Dhangadhi to Gauriphanta, Uttar Pradesh, is useful for moving on to Lucknow, New Delhi or visiting Dudhwa National Park. Nepal immigration is open from 8am to 5pm. From Dhangadhi there are daily flights to Kathmandu and buses to the Mahendra Hwy that continue west to Mahendranagar and east towards Ambassa (for Bardia National Park), Nepalganj and beyond.

TIBET

Officially only organised 'groups' are allowed into Tibet from Nepal. The good news is that travel agencies in Kathmandu are experts in assembling overland groups to get around this restriction. In general, travellers face fewer restrictions entering Tibet through China, so it makes more sense to visit Nepal after a trip through Tibet, not before.

Travelling overland to Tibet from Nepal is not an easy option. Altitude sickness is a real danger: the maximum altitude along the road is 5140m and tours do not always allow sufficient time to acclimatise safely. Adding to the problems, the road to the main border at Kodari was severely damaged by the 2015 earthquake, though it has since reopened. Landslides are highly likely on this route during the monsoon months (May to August) and

NEPAL–INDIA BORDER CROSSINGS

BORDER CROSSING (NEPAL TO INDIA)	NEAREST INDIAN TOWNS
Belahiya to Sunauli	Varanasi, Agra & Delhi
Mahendranagar to Banbasa	Delhi & hill towns in Uttarakhand
Dhangadhi to Gauriphanta	Lucknow & Delhi
Kakarbhitta to Panitanki	Darjeeling, Sikkim & Kolkata
Birganj to Raxaul Bazar	Patna & Kolkata
Nepalganj to Jamunaha/Rupaidha Bazaar	Lucknow

there are often additional restrictions on travel at times of political tension.

The vast majority of travellers enter Tibet at Kodari/Zhangmu on the Friendship Hwy, though organised groups can trek from Simikot through far-western Nepal to Mt Kailash. Other road connections, including the road from Tibet to Mustang and the new road between Kyirong and Langtang, are not open to foreigners.

Travel Restrictions

At the time of research, it was only possible to cross into Tibet with a Tibet Tourism Permit, which can only be arranged through a travel agency when you book a package tour to Lhasa. If you turn up at the border at Kodari with just a Chinese visa you'll be turned away, and Air China won't sell you an air ticket to Lhasa without this permit. Permits are valid for 21 days although it's sometimes possible to get a 28-day permit.

Prior to 2013, in order to get a group permit for Tibet it was mandatory to have a minimum of two people in a group and they had to be of the same nationality (bit of a nuisance if you were a mixed-nationality couple!). Today this is no longer the case and indeed permits can be issued for just one person.

In order to get a Tibet Tourism Permit, you must supply a ticket out of Tibet – either a flight ticket or train ticket to elsewhere in mainland China or a tour back to Nepal. Kathmandu-based tour companies can supply these. Getting a permit takes around 15 days, although it's possible to pay extra and get one in three days. Splitting from your group-visa members in Lhasa is almost impossible, but it is apparently possible (although a headache) to fly out of Tibet to Chengdu and then continue through China on a standard Chinese tourist visa.

Note that Tibet travel permits are not issued between late February and late March, and travel in Tibet is not allowed for foreign tourists during this period.

Tour Options

The easiest way to visit Tibet from Nepal is to join a drive-in, fly-out overland jeep tour from Kathmandu to Lhasa, overnighting in Nyalam, Dingri/Lhatse, Shigatse, Gyantse and Lhasa. Several agencies offer eight-day trips for as little as US$500, including permit fees, transport by cramped Land Cruiser or minibus, accommodation in dorms and shared twin rooms and sightseeing (but not meals). Trips normally leave on Tuesday and Saturday from April to October and weekly at other times. Don't expect too much from these budget tours. A private trip for four people in a Land Cruiser costs around US$800 to US$1000 per person.

Add on to this around US$30 (US$55 for US citizens) for a group visa and transport out of Tibet, which currently costs around US$415 to US$450 for a flight back to Kathmandu.

Some agencies also offer pricey trips that include a detour to Mt Everest Base Camp (on the Tibetan side). There are also very expensive trekking trips from Simikot in far-western Nepal to Purang in far-western Tibet, and then on to Mt Kailash. Land Cruiser trips to Mt Kailash are also possible. Rates increase from July to September, and there are fewer tours from December to February.

The agency will need one to two weeks to get your visa and permits. If you are continuing on to China, your agency will need to get you your own separate 'group' visa. For more details see Lonely Planet's *Tibet* and *China* guides.

Most of the companies advertising Tibet trips in Kathmandu are agencies for other companies. Explore Nepal Eco Tours & Travel, Royal Mount Trekking and Tashi Delek Nepal Treks & Expeditions run their own trips, so you can be confident that staff know what they're talking about.

Explore Nepal Eco Tours & Travel (Map p68; ☑01-4412508; http://explore-nepaltours.com; Tridevi Marg, Thamel)

Royal Mount Trekking (Map p68; ☑01-4241452; www.royaltibet.com; Durbar Marg)

Tashi Delek Nepal Treks & Expeditions (Map p88; ☑01-4410746; www.tibettour.travel; Thamel)

Dharma Adventures (Map p68; ☑01-4430499; www.dharmaadventures.com; 205 Tangal Marg)

Car & Motorcycle

A steady trickle of people drive their own motorbikes or vehicles overland from Europe, for which an international carnet is required. If you want to abandon your transport in Nepal, you must either pay a prohibitive import duty or surrender it to customs. It is not possible to import cars more than five years old. Make sure you bring an international driving permit.

GETTING AROUND

Getting around in Nepal can be a challenging business. Because of the terrain, the weather conditions and the condition of vehicles, few trips go exactly according to plan. Damage to roads from the 2015 earthquake has only exacerbated these problems. Nepali ingenuity will usually get you to your destination in the end, but build plenty of time into your itinerary and treat the delays and mishaps as part of the rich tapestry that is Nepal.

The wise traveller avoids going anywhere during major festivals, when buses, flights and hotels are booked solid.

Domestic Air Routes

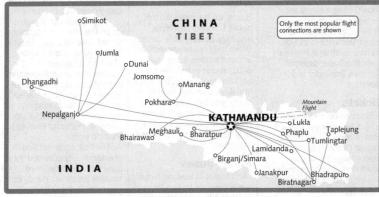

Only the most popular flight connections are shown

CHINA
TIBET

Simikot
Jumla
Dunai
Jomsom
Manang
Dhangadhi
Pokhara
Nepalganj
KATHMANDU
Lukla
Mountain Flight
Meghauli
Bharatpur
Bhairawa
Phaplu
Taplejung
Tumlingtar
Lamidanda
INDIA
Birganj/Simara
Janakpur
Bhadrapur
Biratnagar

Air

Considering the nature of the landscape, Nepal has an excellent network of domestic flights. Engineers have created runways deep in the jungle and high in the mountains, clinging to the sides of Himalayan peaks. However, pilots must still find their way to these airstrips using visual navigation and few planes pass without some kind of air disaster in the mountains. All of Nepal's domestic airports are functioning after the 2015 earthquake.

Because flights are dependent on clear weather, services rarely leave on time and many flights are cancelled at the last minute because of poor visibility. It is essential to build extra time into your itinerary. Even if you take off on time, you may not be able to land at your intended destination because of fog. It would be unwise to book a flight back to Kathmandu within three days of your international flight out of the country.

In the event of a cancellation, airlines will try to find you a seat on the next available flight (some airlines run extra flights to clear the backlog once the weather clears). If you decide not to wait, you should be able to cancel the ticket without penalty, though it can take a long time to arrange a refund.

Airlines in Nepal

The largest domestic airline is the notoriously unreliable **Nepal Airlines** (www.nepalairlines.com.np). All things considered, Nepal Airlines has a comparable safety record to other domestic airlines, but if your destination is served by a private airline, this will almost always be the better option. Nepal Airlines currently has services to Biratnagar, Pokhara, Lukla, Phaplu, Bhojpur, Lamidanda, Tumlingtar, Dolpo and Jumla among other airstrips.

Services are more reliable on Nepal's private airlines, though fares are slightly higher. Most flights operate out of Kathmandu, but there are minor air hubs at Pokhara, Nepalganj and Surkhet in the southwest and Biratnagar in the southeast. Most airlines also offer scenic 'mountain flights' in the morning – if you're flying from Kathmandu you will probably have to wait until the airline finishes its morning quota of mountain flights before domestic services begin.

A number of domestic airlines have offices in Kathmandu.

Buddha Air (☏01-5521015; www.buddhaair.com; Hattisar) One of the safer, and more reliable, airlines. Destinations include Pokhara, Bhadrapur, Janakpur, Bharatpur, Bhairawa, Biratnagar, Simara and Nepalganj.

Tara Air (☏01-4493426; www.taraair.com; Tilganga) Subsidiary of Yeti Airlines. Among other destinations it flies from Kathmandu to Lukla, Lamidanda, Phaplu, Meghauli and Dolpo, and from Pokhara to Jomsom and Kathmandu.

AIR SAFETY IN NEPAL

Nepal's domestic airlines have worrying safety records. There have been seven fatal accidents involving domestic airlines in Nepal since 2008. In the most recent incident in February 2014, a Nepal Airlines flight crashed into a hillside en route from Pokhara to Jumla, killing all 18 passengers and crew. In 2014 the website www.airlineratings.com listed Tara Air and Nepal Airlines as two of the world's four most dangerous airlines. No Nepalese airline is currently permitted to fly within EU airspace because of safety concerns.

Yeti Airlines (☎01-4465888; www.yetiairlines.com; Thamel Chowk) Sherpa-owned and the largest private airline with, for Nepal, a reasonable safety record. Destinations include Pokhara, Biratnagar, Nepalganj, Lukla, Bhadrapur, Janakpur, Bhairawa, Tumlingtar and Bharatpur.

Tickets

Airlines come and go and schedules change, so it's best to make reservations through a travel agent, a trekking agency or your hotel. Foreign visitors must pay for airfares in hard currency, typically US dollars. Residents and Nepali citizens pay approximately 40% of the tourist price, which helps if you are flying your guide or porter out to Lukla for the Everest trek.

All travellers are charged an insurance surcharge of US$2 per leg, as well as a fuel surcharge. Fares quoted generally include all these surcharges.

Note that domestic airlines have a 15kg allowance for hold baggage – and on some flights you cannot pay to carry excess baggage. Knives, cigarette lighters, gas cylinders and trekking poles are not permitted in carry-on luggage.

Bicycle

There are plenty of bicycle-rental shops in Kathmandu and Pokhara, and this is a cheap and convenient way of getting around. Generic Indian- and Chinese-made bicycles cost around Rs 350 to 450 per day to rent, but the clunky gears make even a downhill stretch seem like hard work. Several cycling agencies in Kathmandu rent out imported mountain bikes for around US$12 per day. Cycling around Kathmandu and much of the Kathmandu Valley was once a popular activity, but increased traffic and urban sprawl make this far less appealing today.

Bus

Buses are the main form of public transport in Nepal and they're incredibly cheap. Often they're also incredibly uncomfortable. Buses run pretty much everywhere and will stop for anyone, but you'll find it much easier to get a seat if you catch a bus at its source rather than mid-run. For longer-distance buses it's best to book a couple of days in advance.

Public Buses

Most towns in lowland Nepal are accessible by bus from Kathmandu or Pokhara, but Nepali buses are slow, noisy and uncomfortable, and breakdowns are almost guaranteed, even on the so-called 'deluxe' buses. Fortunately, services are frequent enough that you can always hop onto another bus if your first bus dies on a lonely stretch of highway.

On longer journeys, buses stop regularly for refreshments, but travel after dark is not recommended – drivers take advantage of the quiet roads to do some crazy speeding, and accidents and fatalities are depressingly common. In fact, you are 30 times more likely to die in a road accident in Nepal than in any developed country. Some night buses stop for a few hours' sleep, en route, but others keep blazing through the night with the music blaring at full volume. The single best thing you can do to stay safe is to avoid travelling by road at night.

Myriad private companies run 'ordinary buses' and faster, more expensive 'express buses' that offer seats with more padding and luxuries such as curtains to keep out the sun. Tickets can be purchased in advance at the relevant counter (ask locals where to go as signs are often in Nepali) or on board from the driver. 'Deluxe' buses often come with air-conditioning, and some

claim to offer nonstop services between two centres (but rarely does this happen).

Large pieces of baggage go on the roof – the conductor will take your bag up for a tip or you can do it yourself. Theft from luggage is not uncommon so padlock your bags shut and tie the straps to the railings. Always keep an eye on your belongings at rest stops – backpacks are extremely easy for thieves to walk off with.

The fast, frequent and phenomenally crowded 'local buses' that run between smaller towns are handy for day trips, but you'll have your work cut out getting on board with a backpack. Prices for foreigners are often bumped up by unscrupulous conductors on these buses.

Note that road travel in the far east and west of Nepal can be impossible after the monsoon. Every year the rains lead to floods that destroy stretches of road and wash away bridges.

Tourist Buses

Travel agencies run a number of useful bus services to popular tourist destinations, leaving from the Tourist Bus Park in Pokhara and the Thamel end of Kantipath in Kathmandu. These are more comfortable and less crowded than local buses but cost a little more.

Greenline (www.greenline. com.np; Tridevi Marg) has deluxe buses between Kathmandu, Pokhara and Sauraha (for Chitwan National Park).

Car & Motorcycle

Hire

There are no drive-yourself rental cars available in Nepal, but you can easily hire a car or jeep with a driver through a travel agency. Expect to pay between US$60 and US$100 per day, including fuel. Taxis are cheaper but less comfortable and you must negotiate a fare directly with the driver. Remember that you'll have to pay for the driver's return trip whether or not you return, as well as their food and accommodation for overnight trips.

Motorcycles can be rented in Kathmandu and Pokhara for around Rs 600 to 1500 per day depending on the type of bike. You'll need an international driving permit or a licence from your own country that shows you are licensed to ride a motorcycle – a car drivers' licence won't cut it. You must also leave your passport as a deposit. It's not a bad idea to take some digital photographs of the bike in case operators complain of damages that existed before you ever got on the bike.

Note that there are major fuel shortages in Nepal. Petrol stations can be dry for days at a time and the only option for motorists is to queue for hours at the few stations that have fuel or to buy fuel in reused bottles from local shops.

Insurance

If you are planning to drive a motorbike in Nepal, you should double-check to see if you are covered by your travel insurance. Rental companies rarely offer insurance and you will be fully liable for the vehicle and damage to other vehicles in the event of an accident.

Road Rules

If you do drive, be aware that you drive on the left-hand side of the road, left turns are allowed without stopping, and that traffic entering a roundabout has priority over traffic already on the roundabout. Locals rarely signal and other vehicles will pull out regardless of whether or not anyone is coming – drive defensively. Try to avoid any dealings with traffic police: locals are routinely stung for bribes and foreigners are increasingly being targeted.

Finally, our best advice is to trust nothing and nobody. Expect kids, chickens, ducks, women, old men, babies, cows, dogs and almost anything else that can move to jump in front of you at any moment, without any kind of warning. Good luck.

Tours

The winding roads of Nepal are glorious for mountain riding and several companies run fully supported motorcycle tours. Contact a recommended company for more information.

Asia-Bike-Tours (☑India 91-9312433859; www.asiabiketours.com) Motorbike tours of Nepal and surrounding countries.

Blazing Trails (☑UK 44 5603 666788; www.blazingtrailstours.com) UK-based motorbike tours to Nepal.

Wild Tracks Adventure (Map p68;☑01-4439590; www.wildtracksnepal.com; Baluwatar, Kathmandu) This Kathmandu-based agency organises motorbike trips around the country.

Hearts & Tears (☑9846020293; www.heartsandtears.com) Based in Pokhara, this agency offers good motorbike tours throughout Nepal.

Himalayan Enfielders (Map p68;☑01-4440462; www.himalayanenfielders.com; Lazimpat, Kathmandu) This Nepal-based operation runs motorbike tours, and can repair and service motorbikes.

Himalayan Offroad (Map p88;☑01-4700770; www.himalayanoffroad.com; Kathmandu) Motorbike tours of Nepal and Tibet; based in Kathmandu.

Himalayan Roadrunners (☑01-5570051; www.ridehigh.com) The longest established motorbike tour company.

Local Transport

Autorickshaw & Cycle-Rickshaw

Cycle-rickshaws are common in the old part of Kathmandu and in towns in the Terai, and they provide an atmospheric way to explore the crowded and narrow streets. Prices are highly negotiable.

Nepal's two-stroke, three-wheeled autorickshaws are being phased out everywhere, but a few are still hanging on in a couple of Terai towns.

Taxi

Metered taxis are found in larger towns such as Kathmandu and Pokhara, and these can be hired for both local and long-distance journeys. Metered taxis have black licence plates; private cars that operate as taxis for long-distance routes have red plates.

Taxis can be flagged down anywhere, and they loiter at official stops at tourist destinations such as Bhaktapur and Patan. On most routes, taxi drivers will refuse to use the meter – this is often an attempt to overcharge tourists, but it may also reflect rising fuel costs and traffic delays. If a driver refuses to use the meter, try another taxi. If no taxis are willing to use the meter, haggle down to reach a reasonable price. As a side note, we can't recall the last time a taxi driver volunteered to use the meter!

Tempo

Tempos are outsized autorickshaws that run on fixed routes in larger cities. Kathmandu's archaic, polluting diesel tempos have been replaced by electric and gas-powered *safa* (clean) tempos and petrol minibuses. Drivers pick up and drop off anywhere along the route; tap on the roof with a coin when you want to stop.

Health

Kathmandu has the best health facilities in the country, but standards at clinics and hospitals decline the further you get from the capital. In mountainous areas, there may be no health facilities at all. Trekkers who become unwell in the mountains are generally evacuated to Kathmandu, or overseas in the event of something really serious. Always take out travel insurance to cover the costs of hospital treatment and emergency evacuations.

Many of the most popular areas for visitors are remote and inaccessible, so you should read up on the possible health risks. While trekking, it makes sense to carry an emergency medical kit so that you can treat any symptoms until you reach medical care.

Before You Go

Insurance

Considering the terrain, potential health risks and high cost of medical evacuation, it is unwise to travel to Nepal without adequate health insurance.

Recommended Vaccinations

You do not officially require any immunisations to enter the country, unless you have come from an area where yellow fever is present – in which case, you must show proof of immunisation.

It is best to seek medical advice at least six weeks before travelling, since some vaccinations require multiple injections over a period of time.

Note that some vaccinations should not be given during pregnancy or to people with allergies.

Vaccinations you might consider:

Diphtheria and tetanus Vaccinations for these two diseases are usually combined and are recommended for everyone. After an initial course of three injections (usually given in childhood), boosters are necessary every 10 years.

Hepatitis A The vaccine for hepatitis A (eg Avaxim, Havrix 1440 or VAQTA) provides long-term immunity (possibly lifelong) after an initial injection and a booster at six to 12 months.

Hepatitis B Vaccination involves three injections, the quickest course being over three weeks with a booster at 12 months.

Influenza 'Flu' is considered by many to be the most common vaccine-preventable illness in travellers. This vaccine is annual.

Japanese encephalitis This is a mosquito-borne viral encephalitis that occurs in the Terai and occasionally in the Kathmandu Valley, particularly during the monsoon (August to early October). The vaccine is given as three injections over three to four weeks and is usually boosted at three years. Recommended only for prolonged stays to the Terai (especially the west) or Kathmandu Valley.

Meningococcal meningitis A single-dose vaccine boosted every three to five years is recommended only for individuals at high risk and for residents.

Polio This serious, easily transmitted disease is still found in Nepal. Everyone should keep up to date with this vaccination, which is normally given in childhood. A booster every 10 years maintains immunity.

Rabies Vaccination should be considered for long-term visitors, particularly if you plan to travel to remote areas. In Nepal the disease is carried by street dogs and monkeys. Vaccination is strongly recommended for children. Pretravel rabies vaccination involves having three injections over 21 to 28 days. If someone who has been vaccinated is bitten or scratched by

WARNING

Self-diagnosis and treatment can be risky, so you should seek medical help if you become ill. Although drug dosages appear in this text, they're for emergency treatment only. Correct diagnosis is vital.

an animal they will require two vaccine booster injections, while those not vaccinated will require more. The booster for rabies vaccination is usually given after three years.

Tuberculosis (TB) This disease is highly endemic in Nepal, though cases are extremely rare among travellers. Most people in the West are vaccinated during childhood.

Typhoid Drug-resistant typhoid fever is a growing problem in Nepal, particularly in the Terai, and vaccination is recommended. The vaccine is available as a single injection or oral capsules – ask your doctor for advice.

Yellow fever This disease is not endemic in Nepal and a vaccine for yellow fever is required only if you are coming from an infected area. The record of this vaccine should be provided in a World Health Organization (WHO) Yellow Vaccination Booklet and is valid for 10 years.

Medical Kit Checklist

Following is a list of items you should consider including in your medical kit – consult your pharmacist for brands available in your country.

☐ aspirin or paracetamol (acetaminophen in the USA) for pain or fever

☐ anti-inflammatory (ibuprofen) for muscle and joint pain, headache and fever

☐ antibiotics, particularly if travelling off the beaten track; in Nepal, antibiotics are sold without prescription, which has led to widespread resistance to some common antibiotics

☐ promethazine (Phenergan) for relief of severe nausea

☐ rehydration mixture to prevent dehydration during bouts of diarrhoea; particularly important when travelling with children

☐ antihistamine for allergies, eg hay fever; for skin conditions, carry hydrocortisone 1% cream

☐ cold and flu tablets, throat lozenges and nasal decongestant

☐ antifungal cream such as clotrimazole 1% for fungal skin infections and thrush

☐ antiseptic (such as povidone-iodine) for cuts and grazes

☐ bandages, crêpe wraps, Band-Aids (plasters) and other wound dressings

☐ water purification tablets

☐ scissors, tweezers and an electric thermometer (mercury thermometers are prohibited by airlines)

☐ sterile kit in case you need injections; discuss with your doctor

☐ motion-sickness tablets, such as Dramamine, for long bus rides

☐ Diamox (Acetazolomide) tablets if trekking above 3500m

Other Preparations

Visiting Nepal may take you to some very remote areas, so it makes sense to visit the doctor before you travel for a general check-up.

➡ If you have any pre-existing medical conditions, bring any medication you need from home.

➡ Ask your physician to give you a written description of your condition and your medications with their generic names in case you have to visit a doctor in Nepal.

➡ It pays to get a dental check-up well before embarking on a trek. One of our previous authors cracked a molar on a particularly tough piece of dried beef while on a research trek and had to walk for five days to reach a dentist who performed an emergency root canal operation without anaesthetic! Be warned.

➡ Contact-lens wearers should bring plenty of solution and take extra care with hygiene to avoid eye infections.

➡ Carry backup prescription glasses and sunglasses in case you can't wear your lenses at some point.

Websites

Medex (www.medex.org.uk) offers a free download of the useful booklet *Travel At High Altitude*, aimed at laypeople and full of good advice for staying healthy in the mountains. A Nepali translation of the booklet is also available on the website.

Centers for Disease Control and Prevention (www.cdc.gov)

Fit for Travel (www.fitfortravel.scot.nhs.uk)

International Society for Mountain Medicine (www.ismm.org)

Kathmandu CIWEC Clinic (www.ciwec-clinic.com)

MASTA (www.masta-travel-health.com)

Nepal International Clinic (www.nepalinternationalclinic.com)

Further Reading

Lonely Planet's *Healthy Travel Asia & India* is packed with information such as pre-trip planning, emergency first aid, immunisation and disease information, and what to do if you get sick on the road. *Travel with Children* from Lonely Planet includes advice on travel health for younger children. A useful health-care overview for travel in remote areas is David Werner's *Where There Is No Doctor*.

Specific titles covering trekking and health:

➡ *Medicine for Mountaineering & Other Wilderness Activities* (James A Wilkerson) covers many medical problems typically encountered in Nepal.

➡ *Mountain Medicine* (Michael Ward) has good background info on cold and high-altitude problems.

➡ *Altitude Illness: Prevention & Treatment* (Stephen Bezruchka) is essential reading for high-altitude trekking, written by an experienced Nepal trekker.

➡ *Wilderness First Aid & Wilderness Medicine* (Dr Jim Duff and Peter Gormly) is an excellent portable companion, available in Nepal at the Kathmandu Environmental Education Project (KEEP) or published abroad by Cicerone.

In Nepal

Availability & Cost of Health Care

Kathmandu has several excellent clinics, including the Nepal International Clinic and CIWEC Clinic (which has a branch in Pokhara).

While trekking, your only option may be small, local health posts, and even these are few and far between.

In remote areas, you should carry an appropriate medical kit and be prepared to treat yourself until you can reach a health professional.

Infectious Diseases
HEPATITIS

There are several different viruses that cause hepatitis (inflammation of the liver). The symptoms are similar in all forms of the illness and include fever, chills, headache,

fatigue, feelings of weakness as well as aches and pains, followed by loss of appetite, nausea, vomiting, abdominal pain, dark urine, light-coloured faeces, jaundiced (yellow) skin and yellowing of the whites of the eyes.

Hepatitis A and E are transmitted by contaminated drinking water and food. Hepatitis A is virtually 100% preventable by using any of the current hepatitis A vaccines. Hepatitis E causes an illness very similar to hepatitis A and there is at present no way to immunise against this virus.

Hepatitis B is only spread by blood (unsterilised needles and blood transfusions) or sexual contact. Risky situations include having a shave, tattoo or body piercing with contaminated equipment.

HIV & AIDS

HIV and AIDS are growing problems in Nepal, with an estimated 75,000 Nepalis infected with the virus, so insist on brand-new disposable needles and syringes for injections.

Blood used for transfusions is usually screened for HIV/AIDS but this cannot always be done in an emergency. Try to avoid a blood transfusion unless it seems certain you will die without it.

MALARIA

Antimalarial tablets are only recommended if you will be spending long periods in the Terai, particularly during the monsoon. There is no risk in Kathmandu or Pokhara, for short visits to Chitwan, or on typical Himalayan trekking routes.

It makes sense to take measures to avoid being bitten by mosquitoes, as dengue fever, another mosquito-borne illness, has been sporadically documented in the lowlands. Use insect repellent if travelling to the Terai, particularly if staying overnight in jungle areas or in cheap hotels.

Plug-in mosquito killers are more effective than combustible mosquito coils, which can cause respiratory problems.

RABIES

The rabies virus causes a severe brain infection that is almost always fatal. Feral dogs and monkeys are the main carriers of the disease in Nepal.

Rabies is different from other infectious diseases in that a person can be immunised after having been exposed. Human rabies immune globulin (HRIG) is stocked at the CIWEC clinic and the Nepal International Clinic in Kathmandu.

In addition to the HRIG, five injections of rabies vaccine are needed over a one-month period. Travellers who have taken a preimmunisation series only need two rabies shots, three days apart, if they are bitten by a possibly rabid animal.

If you receive a bite or a scratch from an animal in Nepal, wash the wound with soap and water, then a disinfectant, such as povidone-iodine, then seek rabies immunisations. Considering the risk, it makes sense to keep your distance from animals in Nepal, particularly street dogs and monkeys.

EMERGENCY TREATMENTS DURING TREKKING

While trekking it may be impossible to reach medical treatment, so consider carrying the following drugs for emergencies (the concentrations in which these drugs are sold in Nepal are noted next to the drug):

➡ azithromycin 250mg – a broad-spectrum antibiotic, useful for traveller's diarrhoea; take the equivalent of 500mg per day for three consecutive days

➡ norfloxacin 400mg or ciprofloxacin 500mg – for traveller's diarrhoea; the usual treatment is two tablets daily for one week

➡ tinidazole 500mg – the recommended treatment for giardiasis is four pills all at once for two days; for amoebiasis, take four pills at once for three days, then diloxanide furoate 500mg three times a day for 10 days.

RESPIRATORY INFECTIONS

Upper respiratory tract infections (such as the common cold) are common ailments in Nepal, especially in polluted Kathmandu. Respiratory infections are aggravated by high altitude, cold weather, pollution, smoking and overcrowded conditions, which increase the opportunities for infection.

Most upper respiratory tract infections go away without treatment, but any infection can lead to complications such as bronchitis, ear infections and pneumonia, which may need to be treated with antibiotics.

Fever

If you have a sustained fever (over 38°C) for more than two days while trekking and you cannot get to a doctor, an emergency treatment is a course of the broad-spectrum antibiotic azithromycin (500mg twice a day for seven days), but you should seek professional medical help as soon as possible.

Traveller's Diarrhoea

Even veteran travellers to South Asia seem to come down with the trots in Nepal. It's just one of those things. The main cause of infection is contaminated water and food, due to low standards of hygiene. However, diarrhoea is usually self-limiting and most people recover within a few days.

Dehydration is the main danger with diarrhoea, particularly in children, pregnant women or the elderly. Soda water, weak black tea with a little sugar, or soft drinks allowed to go flat and half-diluted with clean water will help you replace lost liquids.

In severe cases, take oral rehydration salts made up with boiled or purified water. In an emergency you can make up a solution of six teaspoons of sugar and half a teaspoon of salt to a litre of boiled or bottled water. Stick to a bland diet as you recover.

WATER

Don't drink the water in Nepal. Ice should be avoided except in upmarket tourist-oriented restaurants. While trekking, purify your own water rather than buying purified water in polluting plastic bottles.

Water Purification

The easiest way to purify water is to boil it thoroughly. Chlorine tablets (eg Puritabs or Steritabs) kill many pathogens but are not effective against giardia and amoebic cysts. Follow the directions carefully – filter water through a cloth before adding the chemicals and be sure to wet the thread on the lid to your water bottle. Once the water is purified, vitamin C or neutralising tablets can be added to remove the chemical taste.

Trekking filters take out all parasites, bacteria and viruses, and make water safe to drink. However, it is very important to read the specifications so that you know exactly what the filter removes from the water.

Another option is a UV light–based treatment such as a Steripen.

Loperamide (Imodium) or diphenoxylate (Lomotil) can be used to bring temporary relief from the symptoms, but they do not cure the problem.

In the case of diarrhoea with blood or mucus (dysentery), any diarrhoea with fever, profuse watery diarrhoea and persistent diarrhoea not improving after 48 hours, you should visit a doctor for a stool test. If you cannot reach a doctor, the recommended treatment is norfloxacin 400mg or ciprofloxacin 500mg twice daily for three days.

These drugs are not recommended for children or pregnant women. The preferred treatment for children is azithromycin in a dose of 10mg per kilogram of body weight per day (as a single dose each day for three days).

AMOEBIC DYSENTERY

Caused by the protozoan *Entamoeba histolytica,* amoebic dysentery is characterised by a gradual onset of low-grade diarrhoea, often with blood and mucus. Infection persists until treated.

If medical treatment is not available, tinidazole or metronidazole are the recommended drugs. Treatment is a 2g single dose of tinidazole daily or 250mg of metronidazole three times daily for five to 10 days. Alcohol should not be consumed while taking these medications.

CYCLOSPORA

This waterborne intestinal parasite infects the upper intestine, causing diarrhoea, fatigue and loss of appetite lasting up to 12 weeks. Fortunately, the illness is a risk in Nepal mainly during the monsoon, when few tourists visit. Iodine is not sufficient to kill the parasite but it can be removed by water filters and it is easily killed by boiling.

The treatment for *Cyclospora* diarrhoea is trimethoprim and sulfamethoxazole (sold commonly as Bactrim) twice a day for seven days. This drug cannot be taken by people who are allergic to sulphur.

GIARDIASIS

Also known as giardia, giardiasis accounts for around

12% of the diarrhoea among travellers in Nepal. The disease is caused by a parasite, *Giardia Lamblia,* found in water that has been contaminated by waste from animals.

Symptoms include stomach cramps, nausea, a bloated stomach, watery and foul-smelling diarrhoea, and frequent sulphurous burps and farts but no fever.

The best treatment is four 500mg tablets of tinidazole taken as a single dose each day for two consecutive days. Tinidazole cannot be taken with alcohol.

Acute Mountain Sickness (AMS)

Above 2500m, the concentration of oxygen in the air you breathe starts to drop off markedly, reducing the amount of oxygen that reaches your brain and other organs. Decreasing air pressure at altitude has the additional effect of causing liquid to leak from the capillaries into the lungs and brain, which can be fatal. The human body has the ability to adjust to the changes in pressure and oxygen concentration as you gain altitude, but this is a gradual process.

The health conditions caused by the effects of altitude are known collectively as altitude sickness or acute mountain sickness (AMS). If allowed to develop unchecked, AMS can lead to coma and death. However, you can avoid this potentially deadly condition by limiting your rate of ascent, which will allow your body to adjust to the altitude. There is also a 100% effective treatment if you do experience serious symptoms: descend immediately.

If you go trekking, it is important to read up on the causes, effects and treatment of altitude sickness before you start walking. Attend one of the free lectures on altitude sickness given by the Himalayan Rescue Association in Kathmandu.

The onset of symptoms of AMS is usually gradual, so there is time to adjust your trekking schedule or retreat off the mountain if you start to feel unwell. Most people who suffer severe effects of AMS have ignored obvious warning signs.

ACCLIMATISATION

The process of acclimatisation is still not fully understood, but it is known to involve modifications in breathing patterns and heart rate and an increase in the oxygen-carrying capacity of the blood. Some people have a faster rate of acclimatisation than others, but almost anyone can trek to high altitudes as long as the rate of ascent does not exceed the rate at which their body can adjust.

AMS is a notoriously fickle affliction and it can affect trekkers and walkers who are accustomed to walking at high altitudes as well as people who have never been to altitude before. AMS has been fatal at 3000m, although 3500m to 4500m is the usual range.

SYMPTOMS

On treks above 4000m, almost everyone experiences some symptoms of mild altitude sickness – breathlessness and fatigue linked to reduced oxygen in the blood being the most common.

Mild symptoms usually pass if you stop ascending and give your body time to 'catch up' with the increase in altitude. Once you have acclimatised at the altitude where you first developed symptoms, you should be able to slowly continue your ascent. Serious symptoms are a different matter – if you develop any of the symptoms described here, you should descend immediately.

MILD SYMPTOMS

Mild symptoms of AMS are experienced by many travellers above 2800m. Symp-

toms tend to be worse at night and include headache, dizziness, lethargy, loss of appetite, nausea, breathlessness, irritability and difficulty sleeping.

Never ignore mild symptoms of AMS – this is your body giving you an alarm call. You may develop more serious symptoms if you continue to ascend without giving your body time to adjust.

SERIOUS SYMPTOMS

AMS can become more serious without warning and it can be fatal. Serious symptoms are caused by the accumulation of fluid in the lungs and brain, and include breathlessness at rest, a dry, irritative cough (which may progress to the production of pink, frothy sputum), severe headache, lack of coordination (typically leading to a 'drunken walk'), confusion, irrational behaviour, vomiting and eventually unconsciousness and death.

PREVENTION

If you trek above 2500m, observe the following rules:

➡ **Ascend slowly** Where possible, do not sleep more than 300m higher than the elevation where you spent the previous night. If any stage on a trek exceeds this increase in elevation, take at least one rest day to acclimatise before you start the ascent. If you or anyone else in your party seems to be struggling, take a rest day as a precaution.

➡ **Climb high, sleep low** It is always wise to sleep at a lower altitude than the greatest height reached during the day. If you need to cross a high pass, take an extra acclimatisation day before you cross. Be aware that descending to the altitude where you slept the previous night may not be enough to compensate for a very large increase in altitude during the day.

➡ **Trek healthy** You are more likely to develop AMS if you are tired, dehydrated or malnourished. Drink extra fluids while trekking. Avoid sedatives or sleeping pills and don't smoke – this will further reduce the amount of oxygen reaching your lungs.

➡ **If you feel unwell, stop** If you start to display mild symptoms of AMS, stop climbing. Take an acclimatisation day and see if things improve. If your symptoms stay the same or get worse, descend immediately. If on an organised trip make sure your tour leader is aware of your conditions. Don't feel pressured to continue ascending just to keep up with your group.

➡ **If you show serious symptoms, descend** If you show any serious symptoms of AMS, descend immediately to a lower altitude. Ideally this should be below the altitude where you slept the night before you first developed symptoms. Most lodges can arrange an emergency porter to help you descend quickly to a safe altitude.

TREATMENT

Treat mild symptoms by resting at the same altitude until recovery. Take paracetamol or aspirin for headaches. Diamox (acetazolamide) can be used to reduce mild symptoms of AMS. However, it is not a cure and it will not stop you from developing serious symptoms. The usual dosage of Diamox is 125mg to 250mg twice daily. The medication is a diuretic so you should drink extra liquid to avoid dehydration. Diamox may also cause disturbances to vision and the sense of taste and it can cause a harmless tingling sensation in the fingers.

If symptoms persist or become worse, descend immediately – even 500m can help. If the victim cannot walk without support, they may need to be carried down. Any delay could be fatal; if you have to descend in the dark, seek local assistance.

In the event of severe symptoms, the victim may need to be flown to a lower altitude by helicopter. Getting the victim to a lower altitude is the priority – get someone else from the group to call for helicopter rescue and start the descent to the pick-up point. Note that a helicopter rescue can cost you US$2500 to US$10,000.

Emergency treatments for serious symptoms of AMS include supplementary oxygen, nifedipine, dexamethasone and repressurisation using a device known as a Gamow bag (this should only be administered by health professionals), but these only reduce the symptoms and they are not a 'cure'. They should never be used to avoid descent or to enable further ascent.

The only effective treatment for sufferers of severe AMS is to descend rapidly to a lower altitude.

Language

Nepali belongs to the Indo-European language family and has about 35 million speakers. It's closely related to Hindi and is written in the Devanagari script (also used for Hindi). Although Nepali is the national language and is used as a lingua franca between Nepal's ethnic groups, many other languages are also spoken in the country. The Newars of the Kathmandu Valley speak Newari. Other languages are spoken by the Tamangs, Sherpas, Rais, Limbus, Magars, Gurungs and other groups. In the Terai (bordering India), Hindi and Maithili are often spoken.

It's quite easy to get by with English in Nepal. Most people visitors have to deal with in the Kathmandu Valley and in Pokhara will speak some English. Along the main trekking trails, particularly the Annapurna Circuit, English is also widely understood.

Most Nepali consonant sounds are quite similar to their English counterparts. The exceptions are the so-called retroflex consonants and the aspirated consonants. Retroflex sounds are made by curling the tongue tip back to touch the roof of the mouth as you make the sound – they are indicated in this chapter by a dot below the letter, eg ṭ or ḍ as in *Kaṭhmanḍu*. Aspirated consonants are pronounced more forcefully than in English and are made with a short puff of air – they are indicated in this chapter by adding h after the consonant, eg ph is pronounced as the 'p' in 'pit', and th is pronounced as the 't' in 'time'.

As for the vowels, a is pronounced as the 'u' in 'hut', ā as the 'ar' in 'garden' (no 'r' sound), e as in 'best' but longer, i as in 'sister' but longer, o as in 'sold', u as in 'put', ai as in 'aisle' and au as the 'ow' in 'cow'. The stressed syllables are indicated with italics.

BASICS

Even if you learn no other Nepali, there is one word every visitor soon picks up – *namaste* (pronounced na·ma·ste). Strictly translated it means 'I salute the god in you', but it's used as an everyday greeting that encompasses everything from 'Hello' to 'How are you?' and even 'See you again soon'. It should be accompanied with the hands held in a prayer-like position, the Nepali gesture equivalent to Westerners shaking hands.

Hello./Goodbye.	na·ma·ste
How are you?	ta·pāi·lai kas·to chha
Excuse me.	ha·jur
Please (give me).	di·nu·hos
Please (you have).	khā·nu·hos
Thank you.	dhan·ya·bad

Unlike in many other countries, verbal expressions of thanks are not the cultural norm in Nepal. Although neglecting to say 'Thank you' may make you feel a little uncomfortable, it is rarely necessary in simple commercial transactions – foreigners saying *dhanyabad* all the time sound distinctly odd to Nepalis.

Yes. (I have)	chā
No. (I don't have)	chhai·na
I	ma
OK.	theek·cha
Wait a minute.	ek chhin par·kha·nos
good/pretty	ram·ro
I don't need it.	ma·lai cha·hi·na
I don't have it.	ma san·ga chhai·na

WANT MORE?

For in-depth language information and handy phrases, check out Lonely Planet's *Nepali Phrasebook*. You'll find it at **shop.lonelyplanet.com**, or you can buy Lonely Planet's iPhone phrasebooks at the Apple App Store.

LANGUAGES OF NEPAL

Language	Estimated % of the Population
Nepali	47.8
Maithili	12.1
Bhojpuri	7.4
Tharu	5.8
Tamang	5.1
Newari	3.6
Magar	3.3
Rai	2.7
Awadhi	2.4
Limbu	1.4
Gurung	1.2
Sherpa	0.7
Other	6.5

Do you speak English?	ta·*pāi* an·*gre*·ji *bol*·na *sak*·nu *hun*·chha
I only speak a little Nepali.	ma a·li a·li ne·*pā*·li *bol*·chhu
I understand.	ma *bujh*·chu
I don't understand.	*mai*·le bu·*jhi*·na
Please say it again.	*phe*·ri *bha*·ṇu·hos
Please speak more slowly.	ta·*pāi* bi·*stā*·rai *bol*·nu·hos

ACCOMMODATION

Where is a ...?	... *ka*·hā chha
campsite	*shi*·vir
guesthouse	*pā*·hu·na ghar
hotel	*ho*·ṭel
lodge	laj

Can I get a place to stay here?	ya·hā bās *paun*·chha
Can I look at the room?	ko·thā *her*·na *sak*·chhu
How much is it per night?	ek *rāt*·ko *ka*·ti *pai*·sā ho
Does it include breakfast?	bi·*hā*·na·ko *khā*·na *sa*·met ho

clean	sa·*fā*
dirty	*mai*·lo
fan	*pan*·khā
hot water	*tā*·to *pā*·ni
room	ko·thā

EATING & DRINKING

I'm a vegetarian.	ma sāh·kā·*ha*·ri hun
I don't eat spicy food.	ma *pi*·ro *khan*·di·na
Please bring me a spoon.	*ma*·lai *cham*·chah *lyau*·nu·hos
Can I have the bill?	bil *pau*·na *sak*·chhu

banana	*ke*·rah
bread	*ro*·ṭi
cauliflower	*go*·bi
chicken	*ku*·kha·ra/murgh
egg	phul
eggplant	*bhaṇ*·ṭa
fish	*mā*·chha
lentils	daal
meat	*ma*·su
mutton	*kha*·si
okra	ram·*to*·ri·ya
peanut	*ba*·dam
potato	a·lu
(cooked) rice	bhāt
spinach	sag

cold beer	*chi*·so *bi*·yar
boiled water	u·*māh*·le·ko *pa*·ni
hot lemon	*ta*·to *pa*·ni·mah *ka*·ga·ti
lemon soda	so·ḍa·mah *ka*·ga·ti
milk	dudh
sugar	*chi*·ni
tea	*chi*·ya
yoghurt	*da*·hi

EMERGENCIES

Help!	gu·*hār*
It's an emergency!	*ā*·paṭ par·yo
There's been an accident!	dur·*gha*·ṭa·nā *bha*·yo
Please call a doctor.	*dāk*·ṭar·lai bo·*lāu*·nu·hos
Where is the (public) toilet?	shau·*chā*·la·ya *ka*·hā chha
I'm lost.	ma ha·*rā*·ye

HEALTH

Where can I find a good doctor?	*rām*·ro *dāk*·ṭar *ka*·hā *pāin*·cha
Where is the nearest hospital?	ya·hā as·pa·tāl *ka*·hā chha
I don't feel well.	ma·*lāi san*·cho *chhai*·na

Signs

खुला	Open
बन्द	Closed
प्रवेश	Entrance
निकास	Exit
प्रवेश निषेध	No Entry
धूम्रपान मनाही छ	No Smoking
मनाही/निषेध	Prohibited
शाचालय	Toilets
तातो	Hot
चिसो	Cold
खतरा	Danger
रोक्नुहोस	Stop
बाटो बन्द	Road Closed

I'm having trouble breathing.	sās pher·na sak·di·na
I have altitude sickness.	lekh lāg·yo
I have a fever.	jo·ro ā·yo
I have diarrhoea.	di·shā lāg·yo
medicine	au·sa·dhi
pharmacy/chemist	au·sa·dhi pa·sal
I have ...	ma·lāi ... lāg·yo
asthma	dam·ko bya·thā
diabetes	ma·dhu·me·ha
epilepsy	chā·re rog

SHOPPING & SERVICES

Where's the market?	ba·zār ka·hā chha
What is it made of?	ke·le ba·ne·ko
How much?	ka·ti
That's enough.	pugyo
I like this.	ma·lai yo ram·ro lag·yo
I don't like this.	ma·lai yo ram·ro lag·en·a
cheap	sas·to
envelope	kham
expensive	ma·han·go
less	kam
little bit	a·li·ka·ti
money	pai·sa
more	ba·dhi
stamp	ti·ka
bank	baink

... embassy	... rāj·du·tā·vas
museum	sam·grā·ha·la·ya
police	pra·ha·ri
post office	post a·fis
tourist office	tu·rist a·fis
What time does it open/close?	ka·ti ba·je khol·chha/ ban·da gar·chha
I want to change some money.	pai·sā sāt·nu man·lāg·chha
Is there a local internet cafe?	ya·hā in·tar·net kyah·phe chha
I'd like to get internet access.	ma·lai in·tar·net cha·hi·yo
I'd like to check my email.	i·mel chek gar·nu·par·yo
I'd like to send an email.	i·mel pa·thau·nu·par·yo

TIME & DATES

What time is it?	ka·ti ba·jyo
It's one o'clock.	ek ba·jyo
minute	mi·nat
hour	ghan·tā
day	din
week	hap·tā
month	ma·hi·nā
yesterday	hi·jo
today	ā·ja
now	a·hi·le
tomorrow	bho·li
What day is it today?	ā·ja ke bār
Today is ...	ā·ja ... ho
Monday	som·bār
Tuesday	man·gal bār
Wednesday	budh·bār
Thursday	bi·hi·bār
Friday	su·kra·bār
Saturday	sa·ni·bār
Sunday	āi·ta·bār

TRANSPORT & DIRECTIONS

Where?	ka·hā
here	ya·hā

Numbers

0	*sun*·ya	शून्य
1	ek	एक
2	*du*·i	दुइ
3	tin	तीन
4	chār	चार
5	panch	पाँच
6	chha	छ
7	sāt	सात
8	āṭh	आठ
9	nau	नौ
10	das	दस
11	e·*ghār*·a	एघार
12	*bā*·hra	बाह्र
13	*te*·hra	तेह्र
14	*chau*·dha	चौध
15	*pan*·dhra	पन्ध्र
16	*so*·hra	सोह्र
17	*sa*·tra	सत्र
18	a·*ṭhā*·ra	अठार
19	un·*nais*	उन्नाईस
20	bis	बीस
21	ek kais	एककाईस
22	bais	बाईस
23	teis	तेईस
24	*chau*·bis	चौबीस
25	pach·*chis*	पच्चीस
26	chhab·bis	छब्बीस
27	sat·*tais*	सत्ताईस
28	aṭ·*ṭhais*	अट्ठाईस
29	u·*nan*·tis	उनन्तीस
30	tis	तीस
40	*chā*·lis	चालीस
50	pa·*chās*	पचास
60	*sā*·ṭhi	साठी
70	sat·*ta*·ri	सत्तरी
80	a·si	असी
90	*nab*·be	नब्बे
100	ek say	एक सय
1000	ek ha·*jār*	एक हजार
10,000	das ha·*jār*	दस हजार
100,000	ek lākh	एक लाख
200,000	*du*·i lākh	दुइ लाख
1,000,000	das lākh	दस लाख

there	*tya*·hã
What is the address?	the·*gā*·nā ke ho
Please write down the address.	the·*gā*·nā *lekh*·nu·hos
How can I get to ...?	... ko·*lā*·gi ka·ti pai·sā *lāg*·chha
Is it far from here?	ya·hã·ba·ta ke *tā*·dhā chha
Can I walk there?	hi·ḍe·ra jā·na sa·kin·chhu

boat	nāu
bus	bus
taxi	*tyakh*·si
ticket	*ti*·kaṭ

I want to go to ...	ma ...·mā jān·chhu
Where does this bus go?	yo bus ka·hã jān·chha
I want a one-way ticket.	*jā*·ne *ti*·kaṭ *di*·nu·hos
I want a return ticket.	*jā*·ne·*āu*·ne *ti*·kaṭ *di*·nu·hos
How much is it to go to ...?	... *jā*·na ka·ti par·chha
Does your taxi have a meter?	ta·*pāi* ko *tyakh*·si mã *me*·ter chha

TREKKING

Which way is ...?	... *jā*·ne ba·to ka·ta par·chha
Is there a village nearby?	na·ji·kai gaun par·chha
How many hours to ...?	... ka·ti ghan·ṭā
How many days to ...?	... ka·ti din
Where is the porter?	bha·ri·ya ka·ta ga·yo
I want to sleep.	ma·lai *sut*·na man lag·yo
I'm cold.	ma·lai jā·ḍo lag·yo
Please give me (water).	ma·lai (pa·ni) *di*·nu·hos

bridge	pul
cold	jā·ḍo
downhill	o·*rā*·lo
left	*bā*·yã
right	*dā*·yã
teahouse	*bhat*·ti
uphill	u·*kā*·lo
way/trail	*sā*·no *bā*·ṭo

GLOSSARY

Beware of the different methods of transliterating Nepali and the other languages spoken in Nepal. There are many and varied ways of spelling Nepali words. In particular, the letters 'b' and 'v' are often interchanged.

ACAP – Annapurna Conservation Area Project

Aditya – ancient *Vedic* sun god, also known as Suriya

Agni – ancient *Vedic* god of the hearth and fire

Agnipura – Buddhist symbol for fire

AMS – acute mountain sickness, also known as altitude sickness

Annapurna – the goddess of abundance and an incarnation of *Mahadevi*

Ashoka – Indian Buddhist emperor who spread Buddhism throughout the subcontinent

Ashta Matrikas – the eight multi-armed mother goddesses

Avalokiteshvara – Buddhist bodhisattva of compassion, known in Tibetan as Chenresig

bagh chal – traditional Nepali game

bahal – Buddhist monastery courtyard

ban – forest or jungle

bandh – strike; see also *julus* and *chakka jam*

Bhadrakali – Tantric goddess who is also a consort of *Bhairab*

Bhagwati – a form of *Durga*, and thus a form of the goddess *Parvati*

Bhairab – the 'terrific' or fearsome Tantric form of *Shiva* with 64 manifestations

bhanjyang – mountain pass

Bhimsen – one of the Pandava brothers, from the *Mahabharata*, seen as a god of tradesmen

bhojanalaya – basic Nepali restaurant or canteen

Bhote – Nepali term for a Tibetan, used in the names of rivers flowing from Tibet

Bodhi tree – a pipal tree under which the *Buddha* was sitting when he attained enlightenment; also known as 'bo tree'

bodhisattva – a near-*Buddha* who renounces the opportunity to attain *nirvana* in order to aid humankind

Bön – the pre-Buddhist animist religion of Tibet

Brahma – the creator god in the Hindu triad, which also includes *Vishnu* and *Shiva*

Brahmin – the highest Hindu caste, said to originate from *Brahma's* head

Buddha – the 'Awakened One'; the originator of Buddhism

chaitya – small *stupa*

chakka jam – literally 'jam the wheels', in which all vehicles stay off the street during a strike; see also *bandh* and *julus*

chakra – *Vishnu's* disc-like weapon; one of the four symbols he holds

Chandra – moon god

chautara – stone platforms around trees, which serve as shady places for porters to rest

Chhetri – the second caste of Nepali Hindus, said to originate from *Brahma's* arms

chörten – Tibetan Buddhist *stupa*

chowk – historically a courtyard or marketplace; these days used more to refer to an intersection or crossroads

daal – lentil soup; the main source of protein in the Nepali diet

Dalai Lama – spiritual leader of Tibetan Buddhist people

danda – hill

deval – temple

Devi – the short form of *Mahadevi*, the *shakti* to *Shiva*

dhaka – hand-woven cotton cloth

dharma – Buddhist teachings

dhoka – door or gate

Dhyani Buddha – the original Adi *Buddha* created five Dhyani Buddhas, who in turn create the universe of each human era

doko – basket carried by porters

dorje – Tibetan word for the 'thunderbolt' symbol of Buddhist power; *vajra* in Nepali

durbar – palace

Durga – fearsome manifestation of *Parvati*, *Shiva's* consort

gaida – rhinoceros

Ganesh – son of *Shiva* and *Parvati*, instantly recognisable by his elephant head

Ganga – goddess of the Ganges

Garuda – the man-bird *vehicle* of *Vishnu*

Gautama Buddha – the historical Buddha, founder of Buddhism

Gelugpa – one of the four major schools of Tibetan Buddhism

ghat – steps beside a river; a 'burning ghat' is used for cremations

gompa – Tibetan Buddhist monastery

gopi – milkmaids; companions of *Krishna*

gufa – cave

Gurkhas – Nepali soldiers who have long formed a part of the British army; the name comes from the region of Gorkha

Gurung – western hill people from around Gorkha and Pokhara

Hanuman – monkey god

harmika – square base on top of a *stupa's* dome, upon which the eyes of the *Buddha* are painted

hathi – elephant

himal – range or massif with permanent snow

hiti – water conduit or tank with waterspouts

hookah – water pipe for smoking

howdah – riding platform for passengers on an elephant

Indra – king of the *Vedic* gods; god of rain

Jagannath – *Krishna* as Lord of the Universe

janai – sacred thread, which high-caste Hindu men wear looped over their left shoulder

jatra – festival

jayanti – birthday

jhankri – faith healers who perform in a trance while beating drums

Jogini – mystical goddesses and counterparts to the 64 manifestations of *Bhairab*

julus – a procession or demonstration; see also *bandh* and *chakka jam*

Kali – the most terrifying manifestation of *Parvati*

Kalki – *Vishnu's* tenth and as yet unseen incarnation during which he will come riding a white horse and wielding a sword to destroy the world

Kam Dev – *Shiva's* companion

karma – Buddhist and Hindu law of cause and effect, which continues from one life to another

KEEP – Kathmandu Environmental Education Project

Khas – Hindu hill people

khat – see *palanquin*

khata – Tibetan prayer scarf, presented to an honoured guest or Buddhist *lama*

khola – stream or tributary

khukuri – traditional curved knife of the *Gurkhas*

kosi – river

kot – fort

Krishna – fun-loving eighth incarnation of *Vishnu*

Kumari – living goddess; a peaceful incarnation of *Kali*

kunda – water tank fed by springs

la – mountain pass

lama – Tibetan Buddhist monk or priest

lingam – phallic symbol signifying *Shiva's* creative powers

Machhendranath – patron god of the Kathmandu Valley and an incarnation of *Avalokiteshvara*

Mahabharata – one of the major Hindu epics

Mahadeva – literally 'Great God'; *Shiva*

Mahadevi – literally 'Great Goddess', sometimes known as *Devi*; the *shakti* to *Shiva*

Mahayana – the 'greater vehicle' of Buddhism; a later adaptation of the teaching, which lays emphasis on the *bodhisattva* ideal

makara – mythical crocodile-like beast

Malla – royal dynasty of the Kathmandu Valley responsible for most of the important temples and palaces of the valley towns

mandala – geometrical and astrological representation of the path to enlightenment

mandir – temple

mani – stone carved with the Tibetan Buddhist chant *om mani padme hum*

Manjushri – Buddhist *bodhisattva* of wisdom

mantra – prayer formula or chant

Mara – Buddhist god of death; has three eyes and holds the *wheel of life*

math – Hindu priest's house

mela – country fair

misthan bhandar – Indian-style sweet house and snack bar

naga – serpent deity

Nagpura – Buddhist symbol for water

namaste – traditional Hindu greeting (hello or goodbye), with the hands brought together at chest or head level, as a sign of respect

Nandi – *Shiva's vehicle*, the bull

Narayan – *Vishnu* as the sleeping figure on the cosmic ocean; from his navel *Brahma* appeared and went on to create the universe

Narsingha – man-lion incarnation of *Vishnu*

Newar – people of the Kathmandu Valley

nirvana – ultimate peace and cessation of rebirth (Buddhism)

om mani padme hum – sacred Buddhist *mantra*, which means 'hail to the jewel in the lotus'

padma – lotus flower

pagoda – multistoreyed Nepali temple, whose design was exported across Asia

palanquin – portable covered bed usually shouldered by four men; also called a *khat*

Parvati – *Shiva's* consort

pashmina – goat-wool blanket or shawl

Pashupati – *Shiva* as Lord of the Animals

path – small, raised platform to shelter pilgrims

phanta – grass plains

pipal tree – see *Bodhi tree*

pokhari – large water tank, or small lake

prasad – food offering

prayer flag – square of cloth printed with a *mantra* and hung in a string as a prayer offering

prayer wheel – cylindrical wheel inscribed with a Buddhist prayer or *mantra* that is 'said' when the wheel spins

Prithvi – *Vedic* earth goddess

puja – religious offering or prayer

pujari – priest

purnima – full moon

rajpath – road or highway, literally 'king's road'

Ramayana – Hindu epic

Rana – a hereditary line of prime ministers who ruled Nepal from 1846 to 1951

rath – temple chariot in which the idol is conveyed in processions

rudraksha – dried seeds worn in necklaces by *sadhu*s

SAARC – South Asian Association for Regional Cooperation; includes Bangladesh, Bhutan, India, Nepal, Pakistan and Sri Lanka

sadhu – wandering Hindu holy man

Sagarmatha – Nepali name for Mt Everest

sal – tree of the lower Himalayan foothills

saligram – a black ammonite fossil of a Jurassic-period sea creature that is also a symbol of *Shiva*

sankha – conch shell, one of *Vishnu's* four symbols

Saraswati – goddess of learning and creative arts, and consort of *Brahma;* carries a lute-like instrument

seto – white

Shaivite – follower of *Shiva*

shakti – dynamic female element in male/female relationships; also a goddess

Sherpa – Buddhist hill people of Tibetan ancestry famed for work with mountaineering expeditions; with a lower-case 's' it refers to a trek staffer or high-altitude porter

shikhara – Indian-style temple with a tall, corn-cob-like spire

Shiva – the most powerful Hindu god, the creator and destroyer; part of the Hindu triad with *Vishnu* and *Brahma*

sindur – red vermilion powder and mustard-oil mixture used for offerings

sirdar – leader/organiser of a trekking party

stupa – bell-shaped Buddhist religious structure, originally designed to hold the relics of the *Buddha*

Sudra – the lowest Nepali caste, said to originate from *Brahma's* feet

sundhara – fountain with golden spout

tabla – hand drum

tahr – wild mountain goat

tal – lake

Taleju Bhawani – Nepali goddess, an aspect of *Mahadevi* and the family deity of the *Malla* kings of the Kathmandu Valley

tappu – island

Tara – White Tara is the consort of the *Dhyani Buddha* Vairocana; Green Tara is associated with Amoghasiddhi

teahouse trek – independent trekking between village inns (ie no camping)

tempo – three-wheeled, automated minivan commonly used in Nepal

Thakali – people of the Kali Gandaki Valley who specialise in running hotels

thali – literally a plate with compartments for different dishes; an all-you-can-eat set meal

thangka – Tibetan religious painting

third eye – symbolic eye on *Buddha* figures, used to indicate the *Buddha's* all-seeing wisdom and perception

thukpa – noodle soup

tika – red sandalwood-paste spot marked on the forehead, particularly for religious occasions

tole – street or quarter of a town; sometimes used to refer to a square

tonga – horse carriage

topi – traditional Nepali cap

torana – carved pediment above temple doors

Tribhuvan – the king who in 1951 ended the *Rana* period and Nepal's long seclusion

trisul – trident weapon that is a symbol of *Shiva*

tunala – carved temple struts

tundikhel – parade ground

Uma Maheshwar – *Shiva* and *Parvati* in a pose where *Shiva* sits cross-legged and *Parvati* sits on his thigh and leans against him

Upanishads – ancient *Vedic* scripts; the last part of the *Vedas*

vahana – a god's animal mount or *vehicle*

Vaishnavite – follower of *Vishnu*

Vaisya – caste of merchants and farmers, said to originate from *Brahma's* thighs

vajra – the 'thunderbolt' symbol of Buddhist power in Nepal; *dorje* in Tibetan

Vedas – ancient orthodox Hindu scriptures

Vedic gods – ancient Hindu gods described in the *Vedas*

vehicle – the animal with which a Hindu god is associated

vihara – Buddhist religious buildings and pilgrim accommodation

Vishnu – the preserver; one of the three main Hindu gods, along with *Brahma* and *Shiva*

wheel of life – Buddhist representation of how humans are chained by desire to a life of suffering

yak – cow-like Nepali beast of burden (only pure-blood animals of the genus *Bos grunniens* can properly be called yaks; cross-breeds have other names)

yaksha – attendant deity or nymph

Yama – *Vedic* god of death; his messenger is the crow

Yellow Hats – name sometimes given to adherents of the *Gelugpa* school of Tibetan Buddhism

yeti – abominable snowman; mythical hairy mountain man of the Himalaya

yogi – yoga master

yoni – female sexual symbol, equivalent of a *lingam*

zamindar – absentee landlord and/or moneylender

Behind the Scenes

SEND US YOUR FEEDBACK

We love to hear from travellers – your comments keep us on our toes and help make our books better. Our well-travelled team reads every word on what you loved or loathed about this book. Although we cannot reply individually to your submissions, we always guarantee that your feedback goes straight to the appropriate authors, in time for the next edition. Each person who sends us information is thanked in the next edition – the most useful submissions are rewarded with a selection of digital PDF chapters.

Visit **lonelyplanet.com/contact** to submit your updates and suggestions or to ask for help. Our award-winning website also features inspirational travel stories, news and discussions.

Note: We may edit, reproduce and incorporate your comments in Lonely Planet products such as guidebooks, websites and digital products, so let us know if you don't want your comments reproduced or your name acknowledged. For a copy of our privacy policy visit lonelyplanet.com/privacy.

OUR READERS

Many thanks to the travellers who used the last edition and wrote to us with helpful hints, useful advice and interesting anecdotes:

A Jill Allegretti, Kate Allen, Karin Altherr, Harris Anderson, Suzanne Anderson, Anca Ansink, Ardit Arianna, Harriet Astley **B** Henner Becker, Alan Bigelow, Rinske Bloemendal, Helen Bonser, Anthony Branchini **C** John Caselli, Freya Chapman-Amey, Varvara Chinenova, Andreas Constandinos, Iara Cury **D** Katie Dominy, Edward Douglas, Daniel Ducai **E** Tobias Engel, Lars Eriksson **F** Martin Fluri **G** Anni Gaine, Jon Garrood, Marcie Gitlin, Raquel Gómez, Jon Gorroño, John Gros, Bernat Gual-Ricart **H** Bruno Haine, Matthew Harris, James Harrison, Kevin Hoang, Charlotte Hoei, Petricia Horshauge **J** Géraldine Jacquinot, Lies Jansen, Sarah Johns, Alex Jones, Nicholas Jordan **K** Saurav Kapur, Robert Keyes, Kay Kindig, Ico Kloppenburg, Tashi Klose, Nydia Köhne **L** Derek Larney, Amalie Larsen, Line Lauridsen, Kathrine Lausten, Ben Leeuwenburgh, Matilda Lundborg, Viktoria Lundborg, Lisa Lyons **M** Leslie Marshall, Luigi Martire, Margit McLaughlin, Marcos Mendonca, Aishling Middelburg, Gregory Mieden, Nigel Moss **P** Gary Parkinson, Noam Pasa, John Patterson, Nadia Persaud, Roger Phillips, Christopher Psomadellis **Q** Aston Quin **R** Michael Rosebaugh **S** Olof Säll, Henrik Simonsen, Barney Smith, Pat Smith, Floortje Snels, Morten Starostka, Jezz Sterling, Tom Stuart, Peter Svedberg & Caroline Svedberg-Wibling **T** Nathan Tift, Michael Turner, William Turner **V** Stefano Vallarino, Silke Van Damme, Dieuwke van der Hoeven, Cecile van Noppen, Bart Van Renterghem, Anne-Sophie Van Wesemael, Michele Volpi, Edwin Vossen, Dano Vukicevich **W** Sam Walton, Alice Wauchope, Pamela Willett **Y** Vincent Yu **Z** Sarah Zuniga

AUTHOR THANKS

Bradley Mayhew

Thanks to Niraj and Rajesh at Himalayan Encounters and to Mukhiya and Maya Gurung. Cheers to Steve Webster and thanks to Phurba Gyaljen Sherpa for helping me around the Khumbu. Thanks to my wife Kelli for joining me in Kathmandu. Thanks also to Wanda Vivequin for hotel and trekking recommendations and Kim for trekking help.

Lindsay Brown

I am very grateful for the guidance of Stan Armington, Nepal trekking pioneer and author.

I also thank Durga Bandari, Dawa Lama (Big), Dawa Lama (Small), Ram Roka, Narendra Lama (ACAP), Jack Baucher, DB Chaudhary, Ram Din, Mohan Aryal, Man Mohan Shrestha, fellow authors Bradley Mayhew and Stuart Butler, and life and travelling companion Jenny Fegent.

Stuart Butler

First and foremost I must, once again, thank my wife, Heather, and children Jake and Grace for their patience with this long project which involved so much time up in the mountains and out of touch. In Nepal huge thanks to Thiley Lama, Ghyalbu Tamang for a memorable ascent of Yala Peak, Dheeraj Chaudhary for finding me a couple of elephants at short notice, Prakash Neupane for his knowledge of Nepalese wildlife. Thank you also to Dinesh Chaudhary for rafting information and Kishor at Annapurna Mountain Bike Adventures. Thank you also to Rama for good driving in the Terai, all the staff at the Hotel Himal Ganesh in Kathmandu for hospitality and my co-author, Bradley Mayhew, for all his help. Finally, thanks to Ben Clift and John Gray for accompanying me on the mountain trails, but clearly Ben it would be you who would be eaten by a jaguar first....

POST-EARTHQUAKE UPDATE

Special thanks are due to the journalists and Nepal experts who helped to update our content following the 2015 earthquakes, specifically: Suraj Shakya, Ajay Narsingh Rana, Nabin Baral, Rabik Upadhayay, Abhi Shrestha, Niraj Shrestha, Robin from Rural Heritage, Tony Jones from Himalayan Encounters and Jennifer Berry from Kathmandu Inside Out.

ACKNOWLEDGMENTS

Climate map data adapted from Peel MC, Finlayson BL & McMahon TA (2007) 'Updated World Map of the Köppen-Geiger Climate Classification', *Hydrology and Earth System Sciences*, 11, 1633–44.

Cover photograph: Prayer wheel, Bodhnath Stupa, Bodhnath (Boudha), John Harper / Corbis ©.

THIS BOOK

This 10th edition of Lonely Planet's *Nepal* guidebook was researched and written by Bradley Mayhew, Lindsay Brown and Stuart Butler. The 9th edition was written by Bradley Mayhew, Lindsay Brown and Trent Holden, and the 8th was written by Bradley, Trent and Joe Bindloss. This guidebook was produced by the following:

Destination Editor
Joe Bindloss

Product Editors
Elizabeth Jones, Kate Mathews

Senior Cartographer
David Kemp

Book Designer
Wendy Wright

Assisting Editors
Michelle Bennett, Sarah Billington, Katie Connolly, Bruce Evans, Kate Evans, Samantha Forge, Victoria Harrison, Catherine Naghten, Charlotte Orr, Victoria Smith, Luna Soo

Assisting Cartographers
Gabriel Lindquist, Alison Lyall

Cover Researcher
Naomi Parker

Thanks to Shahara Ahmed, Sasha Baskett, Kate Chapman, Ryan Evans, James Hardy, Kate James, Chris Love, Virginia Moreno, Claire Naylor, Karyn Noble, Diana Saengkham, Ellie Simpson, Angela Tinson, Samantha Tyson, Tracy Whitmey, Juan Winata

Index

Map Legend

Sights

- Beach
- Bird Sanctuary
- Buddhist
- Castle/Palace
- Christian
- Confucian
- Hindu
- Islamic
- Jain
- Jewish
- Monument
- Museum/Gallery/Historic Building
- Ruin
- Shinto
- Sikh
- Taoist
- Winery/Vineyard
- Zoo/Wildlife Sanctuary
- Other Sight

Activities, Courses & Tours

- Bodysurfing
- Diving
- Canoeing/Kayaking
- Course/Tour
- Sento Hot Baths/Onsen
- Skiing
- Snorkelling
- Surfing
- Swimming/Pool
- Walking
- Windsurfing
- Other Activity

Sleeping

- Sleeping
- Camping

Eating

- Eating

Drinking & Nightlife

- Drinking & Nightlife
- Cafe

Entertainment

- Entertainment

Shopping

- Shopping

Information

- Bank
- Embassy/Consulate
- Hospital/Medical
- Internet
- Police
- Post Office
- Telephone
- Toilet
- Tourist Information
- Other Information

Geographic

- Beach
- Hut/Shelter
- Lighthouse
- Lookout
- Mountain/Volcano
- Oasis
- Park
- Pass
- Picnic Area
- Waterfall

Population

- Capital (National)
- Capital (State/Province)
- City/Large Town
- Town/Village

Transport

- Airport
- Border crossing
- Bus
- Cable car/Funicular
- Cycling
- Ferry
- Metro station
- Monorail
- Parking
- Petrol station
- Subway station
- Taxi
- Train station/Railway
- Tram
- Underground station
- Other Transport

Note: Not all symbols displayed above appear on the maps in this book

Routes

- Tollway
- Freeway
- Primary
- Secondary
- Tertiary
- Lane
- Unsealed road
- Road under construction
- Plaza/Mall
- Steps
- Tunnel
- Pedestrian overpass
- Walking Tour
- Walking Tour detour
- Path/Walking Trail

Boundaries

- International
- State/Province
- Disputed
- Regional/Suburb
- Marine Park
- Cliff
- Wall

Hydrography

- River, Creek
- Intermittent River
- Canal
- Water
- Dry/Salt/Intermittent Lake
- Reef

Areas

- Airport/Runway
- Beach/Desert
- Cemetery (Christian)
- Cemetery (Other)
- Glacier
- Mudflat
- Park/Forest
- Sight (Building)
- Sportsground
- Swamp/Mangrove

OUR STORY

A beat-up old car, a few dollars in the pocket and a sense of adventure. In 1972 that's all Tony and Maureen Wheeler needed for the trip of a lifetime – across Europe and Asia overland to Australia. It took several months, and at the end – broke but inspired – they sat at their kitchen table writing and stapling together their first travel guide, *Across Asia on the Cheap*. Within a week they'd sold 1500 copies. Lonely Planet was born.

Today, Lonely Planet has offices in Franklin, London, Melbourne, Oakland, Beijing and Delhi, with more than 600 staff and writers. We share Tony's belief that 'a great guidebook should do three things: inform, educate and amuse'.

OUR WRITERS

Bradley Mayhew

Coordinating Author, Itineraries, Planning Your Trek, Kathmandu, Kathmandu Valley & Around, Trekking Routes, Nepal Today, History, Religion, Health A self-professed mountain junkie, Bradley has been travelling to Nepal and the Himalaya for almost 20 years, including several months each in Pakistan, Ladakh, Tibet, Bhutan and Sikkim. Bradley has coordinated several editions of this guide and is also the coordinating author of Lonely Planet *Tibet, Bhutan, Central Asia* and *Trekking in the Nepal Himalaya* guidebooks. For this edition he focused on Kathmandu, the valley and the Everest region. He was most recently seen starring in a 10-part Arte TV documentary following Europe's most beautiful long-distance trails. See what he's up to at www.bradleymayhew.blogspot.com.

Read more about Bradley at:
lonelyplanet.com/members/nepalibrad

Lindsay Brown

Need to Know, If You Like..., Month by Month, Volunteering & Responsible Travel, Kathmandu to Pokhara, Pokhara, The Terai & Mahabharat Range, Trekking Routes, People & Culture, Arts & Architecture, Environment & Wildlife Nepal is a favourite destination for Lindsay, from the Terai's steamy jungles to the high-altitude mountain trails. A former conservation biologist and Publishing Manager at Lonely Planet, Lindsay first visited Nepal over 25 years ago and has spent the last decade or so regularly visiting the country. He has trekked, jeeped, ridden and stumbled across many a Himalayan mountain pass and contributed to Lonely Planet's *South India, India, Rajasthan, Delhi & Agra, Nepal* and *Pakistan & the Karakoram Highway* guides, among many others.

Stuart Butler

Outdoor Activities, Kathmandu Valley & Around, The Terai & Mahabharat Range, Trekking Routes, Biking, Rafting & Kayaking, Directory, Transport Stuart first travelled to Nepal over twenty years ago and has been a frequent visitor to both Nepal and the greater Himalaya region ever since. He has co-authored numerous Lonely Planet guides to South Asia but getting to spend weeks hiking the Nepalese Himalaya for this book made this project extra special. His travels for Lonely Planet, and for a wide variety of magazines and photo projects, have taken him beyond Nepal to the shores of the Arctic, the deserts of Asia and the forests of Africa. His website is www.stuartbutlerjournalist.com.

Read more about Stuart at:
lonelyplanet.com/members/stuartbutler

Published by Lonely Planet Publications Pty Ltd
ABN 36 005 607 983
10th edition – Dec 2015
ISBN 978 1 74321 007 9
© Lonely Planet 2015   Photographs © as indicated 2015
10 9 8 7 6 5 4 3 2 1
Printed in Singapore